BURT FRANKLIN RESEARCH & SOURCE WORKS SERIES 297

American Classics in History & Social Science 55

HISTORY OF
THE SUPREME COURT OF
THE UNITED STATES

HISTORY OF
THE SUPREME COURT OF
THE UNITED STATES

BY

GUSTAVUS MYERS

**BURT FRANKLIN
NEW YORK**

Published by BURT FRANKLIN
235 East 44th St., New York 10017
Originally Published: 1912
Reprinted: 1968
Printed in U.S.A.

Library of Congress Catalog Card No.: 68-56578

BURT FRANKLIN: **RESEARCH & SOURCE WORKS SERIES** 297

American Classics in History & Social Science 55

PREFACE

To a work such as this, avoiding as it does both theories and conclusions, and confining itself strictly to ascertainable facts, little or no prefatory note is required. Neither is any explanation necessary as to why the author chose to write the historical narrative of the Supreme Court of the United States. All departments of human activity are subject, or should be, to scrutiny and investigation, and the series of facts discovered become a definite part of knowledge to be explored, assembled and disseminated.

Quite true, while research has hitherto penetrated into all other branches of historical development, the courts have been singularly exempt. That they have been immune from searching inquiry; that around them has been created a myth, a fiction of supermundane superiority, is no reason why the case should continue so. On the contrary, the more their history and course have been shrouded in tradition and mystery, the more pressing is the necessity for learning and describing the actual facts. Only those who for sentimental or ulterior purposes would seek to disseminate fiction rather than facts can object to a serious inquiry into any institution and the collocation of verified facts. Such an objection at once discredits and disposes of itself in its obvious attack upon an attempt to bring out the truth, and in its aim to suppress the facts from becoming public information.

The long roll of facts herein set forth have not, it is needless to say, been created by the author. Good, bad or indifferent, they are all matters of record; there they lie in the archives awaiting the patient and sincere research of the

5

historical delver; and if nearly all of them are now presented for the first time that is not the fault of the facts but constitutes a standing exposure of the superficial, if not designedly partial character, of much of the extant work passed off as historical writing. Spurious as most of these writings are, destitute of the merit of even a disposition to plumb the truth, characterized by a desire to glorify the basest passions and gloze over the true causes and development of events, they have unfortunately had their influence in propagating confusion, falsehood, and, worst of all, popular submission to the ideas and conceptions demanded by the dominant class. But the day has even now dawned when such works are going to the rubbish heaps or perhaps being regarded as singular curiosities of "intellectual" vassalage.

For nearly a century and a quarter the Supreme Court of the United States has towered aloft in omnipotent sway over all other institutions. Absolute and final, its decrees have gone deep into the history of the nation, and have had their mighty effect upon those wars of classes and subdivisions of classes which it was once (and to some extent still is) the fashion to ignore in theory while asserting the fact in deed. During its whole existence the Supreme Court of the United States has been overwhelmed with laudation, although not at all times free from criticism.

But generalities do not concern us, nor do mere gilded words or fine assumptions have weight. What we do care about is to know the facts, so far as the annals can give them, of this all-powerful institution. We seek to learn its antecedents, its establishment, its development, its successive personnel, and its course, and what relation the whole bore to the great questions and interests of each associated era. This is the information supplied in the following pages; and if the facts presented are striking, original and voluminous, it should be remembered that they are only such as are in the records; without doubt many more underlying facts have never been introduced into the accessible archives, and these are lost to the authentic search of the historian.

As will be seen, this work is not one of a routine biographical or descriptive character, dependent upon injections of fanciful matter or dramatic coloring. It seeks to go to the basic depths, and in doing so it becomes far more than a narrative of a single institution. It carries with a comprehensive history of the development of capitalist resources, power and tactics, and of the great and continuing conflict of classes. It reveals the true sources of the primitive accumulation of wealth which necessarily beginning with the appropriation of land and the dispossession of the workers, have extended to the elaborate and conjointed forms of capitalist power subsisting to-day.

Palpably, a dominant class must have some supreme institution through which it can express its consecutive demands and enforce its will, whether that institution be a king, a Parliament, a Congress, a Court or an army. In the United States, the one all-potent institution automatically responding to these demands ·and enforcing them has been the Supreme Court of the United States. Vested with absolute and unappealable power, it has been able, with a marvelously adaptable flexibility, to transmute that will not merely into law but into action. Hence, the narrative of that court inevitably becomes a history of the origin and progress of capitalism and correspondingly of the forces in society antagonistic to the capitalist order.

Because, however, the Supreme Court as an institution has throughout its whole existence incarnated into final law the demands of the dominant and interconnected sections of the ruling class it should not be supposed that its members have necessarily been susceptible to the vulgar forms of venal corruption. That the rise and ever-expanding sway of the capitalist class have been accompanied by ceaseless fraud and bribery is overwhelmingly attested by the cumulative evidence. But no one can read the proofs herein presented without being impressed by the fact that the Supreme Court as a whole has been peculiarly free from venal corruption in an age when such corruption was common if not continuous. During the extended career of that Court, personal venality has not been the determining factor.

Instance after instance occurs where Justices, at the end of long service on that Bench, have died virtually penniless, or possessed of the most scantily moderate degree of means. Yet many of those very Justices were the same who by their decisions gave to capitalists vast resources, or powers translatable into immense wealth. The influences so consistently operating upon the minds and acts of the incumbents were not venal, but class, influences, and were all the more effective for the very reason that the Justices in question were not open to pecuniarily dishonest practices. From training, association, interest and prejudice, all absorbed in the radius of permeating class environment, a fixed state of mind results. Upon conditions that the ruling class finds profitable to its aims, and advantageous to its power, are built codes of morality as well as of law, which codes are but reflections and agencies of those all-potent class interests.

In the case of men whose minds are already permanently molded to such purposes, and whose character and station forbid the use of illicit means, immeasurable subservience can be obtained which crude and vulgar money bribery would hopelessly fail to accomplish. Under these circumstances a great succession of privileges and powers are given gratuitously, and class corruption appears as honest conviction because of the absence of personal temptations and benefits on the part of the Justices. In this deceptive and insidious guise supreme judicial acts go forth to claim the respect and submission of the working class against whom the decisions are applied.

Furthermore, in taking a large survey of historical events,

•the fact that nearly all of the men ascending to the Supreme Court of the United States had, as attorneys, served powerful individuals 'or corporations need occasion no undue comment. Understanding the development of modern society, and its evolutionary transitions, we can clearly perceive that certain men skilled in law had to do the indispensable legal work of capitalist interests, and whether this or that set of lawyers did it is immaterial historically. Able servitors of the ruling economic forces, it naturally followed that those forces, controlling Government, should select certain of those lawyers to go on the Supreme Court Bench; and how completely, consistently and accurately the personnel of the Supreme Court has represented the dominant class section or sections of each era is abundantly shown by the mass of facts in these chapters.

In conclusion I desire to express to my friends Frederick Sumner Boyd and Anne Sumner Boyd my deep appreciation of their kind services in connection with the final revision of the manuscript for publication, and to all those who have in substantial ways encouraged the preparation of this work, and placed means at my disposal, I wish to acknowledge my sincere appreciation.

New York, January, 1912.

CONTENTS

HISTORY OF THE SUPREME COURT OF THE UNITED STATES

CHAPTER I

CONDITIONS PRECEDING ITS ESTABLISHMENT: THE ACQUISITION OF THE LARGE LANDED ESTATES

Although founded as an original institution, apparently new in itself and dissociated from any prior experiment, the Supreme Court of the United States was, nevertheless, the legatee, from its inception, of an antique body of laws and a mass of customs, traditions, views and conditions growing out of long-standing conflicting interests.

Isolated from what has preceded them as some institutions may appear, because lacking a direct titular ancestor, they are no more so than any of the other manifold evidences of human activity. Their form may sometimes seem novel and unrelated, but their life principle and all of the display of instinct and conduct springing from it, have the most intimate connection with previous events, often reaching back to remote time. Neither are established institutions accidental, capricious or aimless. Their lineage is clearly traceable; and, imperfect as they may sometimes seem, they represent the definite expression at a particular time of a definite purpose to conserve certain ideas or conditions. This much is axiomatic. But at this point conventional historical inquiry stops without scrutinizing the growth and contests of antagonistic forces, and what special dominant section of those warring

13

forces institutions thus established were designed to represent. To ascertain these facts is a vital preliminary, essential to a clear knowledge of cause and effect springing from concrete economic conditions. When the Supreme Court of the United States was organized, there was, to be sure, a distinct environment, as there is in all times and ages. The environment then prevailing, however, was so fundamentally different from that related (or rather misrepresented) in the customary histories, that a narrative of it and the conditions leading up to it, is indispensable to a correct understanding of the history and career of the Supreme Court. Once this link is supplied, the nature of the personnel, and the current of the policy, of that Court become clear, and present a continuous and comprehensible account, leaving nothing to the imagination, and no enigmas over which to puzzle.

Steadily, through more than a century and a half, the process of forming on the soil of America a landed and trading aristocracy, on the one hand, and on the other, a menial and dependent laboring and slave class, went on uninterruptedly. Long before the outbreak of the Revolution, society was divided into various classes and these into grades, sharply defined from one another in law, as well as by extent of wealth or by tokens of rank or degradation. With the very settlement of the country, the European system of land and trade frauds had been transplanted — that system of land seizure by which the feudal barons had aggrandized themselves, and that system of fraud in trade by which European merchants had grown rich. Throughout New England, New York, Pennsylvania, Maryland, Virginia, the Carolinas and Georgia enormous estates were gradually acquired. Some were obtained by fraud upon the Indians, or by bribing royal officials, or both; still others by the officials clandestinely using their authority to secure vast estates for themselves.

Fraud in Ancient Massachusetts.

Orthodox Puritan piety went hand in hand with the commission of frauds, if the laws of the day shadow the conditions prevailing. In Massachusetts, then comprising also what is now the State of Maine and a portion of the present State of New York, the corruption of public officials became so general that an act was passed in the year 1645 imposing a penalty of £40 or whipping for corrupting any public official to deface the public records.[1] For forging land deeds, the offending person was to pay the aggrieved party double damages; if he could not or did not he was to be publicly whipped and a " Romaine F " was to be burned in his face.[2] The practices of the Puritan judiciary may be judged from Section ix, Act of 1635, which prohibited judges interested in civic causes, or related to the parties at action, from giving judgment.[3]

In Rhode Island the principal officials and elders were either seizing land, or by their official acts were awarding allotments to one another.[4]

The Connecticut Assembly was constantly passing laws directed at preventing land frauds; a supererogative attempt at virtuous conduct, inasmuch as many of the officials themselves were thus acquiring estates.

Conditions in Old Connecticut.

In May, 1667, the General Court of Connecticut, " being sensible of the great trouble and contention that doth and may arise in this colony by reason of great defects that are found in records," etc., found it necessary to pass an act aimed at

[1] " Plymouth Colony Laws ": 82.
[2] *Ibid.*
[3] " Ancient Charters and Laws of Massachusetts Bay, etc." Published By Order of the General Court, 1814.
[4] " Rhode Island Colonial Records, 1636–1663." Vols. I, II, etc., describe many instances.

forestalling frauds.[5] A statute passed by the Connecticut
General Court in May, 1717, sought to prevent frauds in
seizing lands from the Indians; it ordained that no Indian title
was good unless it had the approval of the Connecticut Assembly.[6]

The preamble of another law, enacted in October, 1718, declared its purpose to .be the preventing of unlawful entries
of vacant lands and the resulting alienations. The act recited the prevailing frauds, "whereby many persons have
been greatly defrauded, great disorders occasioned, divers
quarrels excited." The preamble went on to say that, because of these frauds, "the orderly settlement of plantations
[is] frustrated; which mischiefs are likely to continue, and
increase, unless sufficient remedy be provided." The land
in question, the act said, belonged to the government and
company of the Colony of Connecticut, by grant from the
crown of Great Britain; divers persons, under pretense of
having a right and property in the lands, and without obtaining any legal conveyance from the corporation, had presumed to enter upon the lands and improve or sell them. A
money penalty was provided in the case of unlawful entry,
and it was decreed that entry and possession did not make a
title.[7]

The preamble of a fourth act, passed in October, 1722,
reported that "some persons have pretended to purchase of
Indians their rights as natives of many considerable tracts
of land." All such deeds when secured without the consent
of the Assembly were, it was announced, *ipso facto,* void in
law. The lands, the act set forth, belonged to the colony;
"yet under color of such deeds, persons unacquainted with
the said laws may be imposed upon, deceived and greatly
wronged." A heavy specified money penalty was provided

  [5] "Connecticut Laws; Public Statute Laws" (Edition of 1808), Vol.
I: 434–435.
  [6] *Ibid.,* 436.
  [7] *Ibid.,* 436–437.

against those thus presuming to buy lands from the Indians, and the persons wronged could recover in court.[8]

Other acts, enacted in Connecticut in 1723 and 1729, brought joyous relief to many of the foremost men of the colony, who, before they had received any patent, had leisurely appropriated the common or undivided lands of the ancient towns, and had apportioned them among themselves. The acts recited that "many of the ancient proprietors have not only sold divisions so obtained, but also a considerable part of their interests and proportions in said common lands." The question had arisen whether these sales were valid — a question settled by the acts of 1723 and 1729 which confirmed them as legal.[9]

In May, 1727, another measure was passed by the General Court of Connecticut: "An Act To Prevent Frauds, Quarrels, and Disturbances in Bargains, Sales, Leases or other Alienations of Land in this Government." By this law any person attempting to give or receive any fraudulent deeds was to forfeit one-half the value.[10] Evidently, by the year 1723, the value of land in Connecticut had greatly increased; the preamble of an act passed in October of that year states that "whereas, in the first settlement of this colony land was of little value in comparison with what it is now," etc.[11]

These details as to how lands was appropriated in early settlement times, while apparently bearing no close relation to the establishment and functions of the Supreme Court of the United States, are of cognate importance, for it was from these conditions that the predominant class of that era and of later times — the owners of the landed estates — rose to

---

[8] *Ibid.*, 439.   [9] *Ibid.*, 439–441.   [10] *Ibid.*, 446.
[11] *Ibid.*, 444–445. It was an act forbidding the sales of the real estate of heiresses without their consent. Before that time, when heiresses married, their estates became the exclusive property of the husbands, and could be alienated or disposed of without the knowledge or consent of their wives. Heiresses must have been in slighter demand after the passage of this act.

great wealth and potency. Between the methods here described, the possessions obtained by means of them, and the precedents, laws and interests erected on them, on the one side, and the composition, character and policy of the Supreme Court of the United States, as it was first constituted, on the other, there was the most intimate association, as will be clearly seen.

The Whole of New Hampshire Appropriated.

When, after his appointment as Captain-General and Governor of Massachusetts Bay, New York and other provinces, the Earl of Bellomont arrived in New York, he quickly learned of widespread, popular discontent with the methods by which great areas of land were being seized by enterprising and unscrupulous individuals, or were being obtained by bribery. The proprietorship of what is now the State of New Hampshire was claimed by Colonel Samuel Allen, who had bought for £250 the claims of Captain John Mason, a director of the Plymouth Company. In surrendering their charter in 1635, the directors of that company had divided their territory among themselves individually; by lot, the ownership of New Hampshire went to Mason, who, some years previously, had obtained a patent to the same area from the company, the patent having been confirmed by King Charles I. Securing his appointment as Governor of New Hampshire in 1692, Allen declared the whole province his personal property.

Threatened with action for trespass, the settlers appealed to Bellomont, who investigated. Communicating to the Lords of Trade, June 22, 1700, Bellomont denounced Allen's title as unsound, and charged Allen with having attempted to get a confirmation of the claim by offering him, Bellomont, a bribe of £10,000 in money — an offer repeated three or four times.[12] Allen claimed eight or nine hundred thousand

[12] " Documents Relating to the Colonial History of the State of New York," Vol. IV: 673.

acres, valued by Bellomont at more than £3,000,000; Allen himself told Bellomont that he estimated the quit rents alone at £22,000 a year, not to mention the great value of the improved rents.

"And all this," added Bellomont, "besides the woods, which I believe he might very well value at half the worth of the lands. There never was, I believe, since the world began, so great a bargain as Allen had of Mason, if it be allowed to stand good, that all this vast estate I have been naming should be purchased for a poor £250, and that a desperate debt, too, as Col. Allen thought. . . . If Col. Allen shall at any time goe about to make a forcible entry on those lands he pretends to (for, to be sure, the people will never turn tenants to him willingly) the present occupants will resist him by any force he shall bring, and the Province will be put to a combustion, and what may be the course I dread to think. . . ." [13]

Mason, however, had left an heir who contested Allen's claim. In the long litigation ensuing, Allen was several times defeated, the last time in 1715. Allen's death was followed by that of his son; and after sixty years of turbulence and actions at law, the whole contention became outlawed, to the huge relief of New Hampshire settlers. [14]

Maine Claimed as a Private Estate.

The entire territory of what is now the State of Maine was claimed as his private property by Sir Fernando Gorges, who, for betraying the Earl of Essex to Queen Elizabeth, had received rich rewards. The claim descended to Gorges' grandson, Fernando Gorges, who, on March 13, 1677, sold it to John Usher, a Boston merchant, for £1,250. Usher soon learned that the British government had been contemplating

[13] *Ibid.*, 673–674.
[14] Lodge's "A Short History of the English Colonies in America," 402.

opening up the province to settlement; he, therefore, wisely turned over his deed to the governor and company of Massachusetts of which colony it remained a part until its creation as a State in 1820.[15]

The Practices in Pennsylvania.

Fraud in the acquisition of land was so notorious in the seventeenth century, that section 20 of the laws originally agreed upon and adopted by William Penn and his followers before they left England, in May 1682, stated that, to prevent frauds and vexations within the province of Pennsylvania, all conveyances were to be enrolled or registered within two months; else they were to be void. A man of extremely gentle character and unselfish in many respects, Penn did not, however, neglect to make ample provision for his personal fortune. Nor was it solely, as certain historical writers put it, the desire for religious freedom that urged Penn and his Quaker band to settle the wilds of Pennsylvania.

On July 11, 1681, Penn signed a contract — or, as it was termed, "certain conditions or concessions" — with a group of specified adventurers for their "mutual advantage." The ninth condition declared that "in every 100,000 acres, the governor and proprietary, [Penn] by lot, reserveth ten to himself, which shall lie but in one place." [16] By this condition an enormous private estate became vested in Penn and his descendants, and caused the greatest mischief. In addition, Penn's heirs, or proprietaries, set up a claim to the whole of the soil contained within the bounds of the original charter. Nearly a century later [17] the Legislature of Pennsylvania

[15] Donaldson's "The Public Domain: Its History," etc., 38.
[16] With the litigation growing out of this condition, the Supreme Court of the United States was called upon to do some extensive judicial construction a century and a half later. See case of Kirk vs. Smith, Wheaton's Reports, Supreme Court of the United States, Vol. IX: 257.
[17] November 27, 1779.

felt itself compelled to denounce the manner in which the Penn family had perverted and abused the terms of the charter granted to William Penn. The resolution declared that, although the charter was given and held " for the great ends of enlarging the bounds of human society, and the cultivation and promotion of religion and learning," and although " the rights of property, and powers of government, vested in William Penn and his heirs were stipulated to be used and enjoyed as well for the benefit of settlers, as for his own particular emolument," nevertheless the proprietaries had set up claims and had reserved quit rents and purchase money upon all grants of land — acts which " cannot longer consist with the safety, liberty and happiness of the good people of this commonwealth. . . ." [18]

The succession of laws passed under the governorship of William Penn indicate the prevalent practices, and show that, to some extent in Pennsylvania, the same method of getting land by fraud and other illicit acts obtaining in New England and elsewhere, were common. A law, decreed on February 7, 1700, dealt with " defacers of charters." It provided that whosoever should forge, deface, corrupt or embezzle any charters, gifts, grants, bonds, wills, conveyances or contracts, or who should deface or falsify any enrollment, registry or record, should forfeit double the value of the damage thereby sustained, one-half of the damages to go to the party wronged. The offender should be discarded from all places of trust, and be publicly disgraced as a false person, in the pillory or otherwise, at the discretion of the court.[19] That such a law was adopted indicates its necessity.

Another act, passed in the same year, tells of frequent overmeasure in the survey of land " through the negligence, ignorance or frauds of the surveyors or chain-carriers, and many

[18] Carey and Bioren's Pennsylvania Laws, 1700–1770, Vol. II: 230–231. This legislative resolution is further described later in this work.
[19] Ibid., Vol. I: 5.

surveys have thereby been made erroneous." [20] It would appear that, while the highest dignitaries in the province were themselves obtaining great estates by extra-legal means, they were, at the same time forbidding the common run of people from doing likewise.

The State of Affairs in Virginia.

In Maryland and Virginia, great estates were secured by the influential few by the most fraudulent methods; this was particularly so in Virginia, which then included an immense area. By the Virginia general land act of 1705, the right of extensive landholding was made dependent upon servant or slaveholding. No one was allowed to take up more than 5,000 acres unless he owned five or more titheable servants or slaves, in which case he was permitted to secure two hundred acres more for each servant or slave titheable. The same act aimed to prevent further land grabbing on a large scale by prohibiting grants of more than 4,000 acres, with a qualifying clause in favor of entries previously made for larger areas. If premises settled by inferiors and others were not seated and planted within three years from the date of the grant, the grant was void. Each free immigrant had an importation right to fifty acres, and another fifty acres were allowed for his wife and child. Payments for land could be made in tobacco. The provisions of this act were either ignored or evaded when it suited the interests of the influential class, or were altered by the further Acts of 1710, 1713, 1748, 1779 and those of other years.

"Although," says an old legal treatise on the subject, "it

[20] *Ibid.*, Vol. VI, Appendix: 54–55 and 61. The social state of Pennsylvania under Quaker rule may be gleaned from the laws. On February 7, 1700, thirteen acts were passed providing penalties for adultery, rape and various other sex crimes, bigamy, robbing and stealing, breaking into houses, the firing of houses, forcible entry, assault and battery, murder, spreading false news, defamation and other crimes. These acts were repealed in 1705, and stricter laws enacted in that year, and in succeeding years.

nowhere appears on the statute books, yet it is known that the Governor and Council, exercising the general powers of the crown, were in the practise of granting leave to individuals and companies to locate large tracts of land, by orders to that effect entered on their journal; and there were also some grants of lands, as compensation for military service by royal proclamations. The grants for military service are confirmed after the Revolution, and such entries in the council books as had been executed by actual surveys were also recognized, but all the rest are annulled." [21]

Vast Tracts Fraudulently Granted.

The methods by which great grants of the most valuable land in Virginia were obtained may be illustrated by the Vanmeter and other grants. On June 30, 1730, John Vanmeter of New York, was allowed to take up 10,000 acres on the Shenandoah River, for settlement by himself and his family of eleven children. As soon as he should bring in twenty families for settlement, he was to receive a grant of 20,000 additional acres (not previously located by Robert Carter, Mann Page or others) on the fork of the Shenandoah and Cohongaroota rivers.[22] He was allowed two years in which to complete this entry, and in the meantime all other persons were forbidden on the lands. By another order of the Council the grant was enlarged to 40,000 acres.

Without fulfilling the terms of the grant, the Vanmeters, in 1731 — a year after the grant — assigned their rights to Joist Hite and Robert M'Coy of Pennsylvania. On October 1, 1731, Hite and M'Coy petitioned the Council: That they and their families and a hundred other families were desirous of removing to Virginia, and prayed a separate grant of 100,000 acres of land. An " Order in Council " was graciously

[21] " The Revised Code of the Laws of Virginia," Vol. II, Appendix II (Land Laws, Edition of 1819) : p. 345.
[22] *Ibid.*

entered, granting their petition: thus Hite and M'Coy were allowed to enter the full 140,000 acres.[23]

But the whole of this area lay in the Northern Neck of Virginia, claimed by Lord Fairfax, who, in 1736, entered a caveat against the issuing of a patent to them. A litigation between the contestants and their heirs or lessees ensued which lasted for nearly half a century, Fairfax's opponents generally winning in court, and compelling Fairfax at one time — in 1771 — to appeal to King George III in Council.[24] The final settlement is not clear from the records.

Under pretext of colonizing the land, great stretches of the most accessible and valuable regions were thus acquired, and were soon formed into large estates, creating in their owners extensive powers of control of local government.

The Virginia court records attest that corruption and collusion were customary methods in obtaining land grants. One such case, for example, as stated in the court's statement of the case, disclosed these facts: That Wood Jones, in the year 1743, obtained an Order in Council for surveying 2,000 acres of land, and that, pending the dispute between Virginia and Governor Dinwiddie, he fraudulently paid the pistole fee demanded by the governor, and obtained a patent, notwithstanding that Jones' land patent covered lands patented to one Hatcher, in 1740. The Virginia High Court of Chancery stated that the grant to Jones was secured surreptitiously; that the officer who consummated the business either did not know that Jones' patent included another's land, or it was obtained by collusion between official and grantee.[25]

[23] "Revised Code, Laws of Va.," (Edition of 1819) Vol. II, 346.
[24] The circumstances of this contest bear the most pregnant and, perhaps, startling relation to the narrative of the Supreme Court of the United States, as will be completely seen later in this work.
[25] Case of White vs. Jones, Washington's. Virginia Reports (Court of Appeals), Vol. I: pp. 116–117. The decision in 1792, however, was in favor of the Jones grant, on the ground that so long a time had elapsed before the title was tested, and because fraud had not been definitely proved. The Chief Justice of this court was one of the greatest land jobbers and speculators of his time. See later.

A Group of Lords Become Feudal Proprietaries.

Much of the richest land in Virginia, especially that territory in what was called the Northern Neck, was originally granted by Charles II when he was a fugitive, and confirmed by James II after he (James) had ceased to reign; to such favorites as Lord Hopton, Lord John Culpeper, Lord John Berkeley (then Sir John Berkeley), Sir William Morton (one of the Justices of the King's bench), Dudley Wyatt and Thomas Culpeper. They surrendered the grant in order to have it renewed with extensions. The grant conferred on them the exclusive ownership of the Rappahannock and Potomac rivers in that section. It gave them all the islands, woods, underwoods, timber, fishings, royalty of hawking and hunting, mines of gold and silver, lead, tin and other metals, quarries of stone and coal, etc., to have, hold and enjoy forever, and transmit to their heirs.

Superadded to the grant were certain conferred powers of feudal baronial dominion, by which the grantees could create manors, hold baronial court, could be patrons of churches, nominate all ministers, receive all fees and emoluments, and possess themselves of goods of felons and fugitives, escheats and forfeitures.[26] They were empowered to give, grant or alienate all the granted land to anyone willing to buy, and were allowed a generous twenty-one years in which to settle their domain; otherwise a certain part of the grant was to be voided.[27] General jurisdiction of the vaguest kind only was reserved to the Governor, Council and Assembly of Virginia. For this absolute lordship, the grantees were, by the charter, required to pay to the crown in annual rent only a paltry six pounds, thirteen shillings and fourpence " in lieu of all services and demands whatsoever." A one-fifth part of all gold mined, and a one-tenth part of all silver, were also reserved to the Crown.

[26] " Revised Code, Laws of Va." (Edition of 1819), Vol. I: 343.
[27] Ibid.

Lord Fairfax Grants 300,000 Acres to Himself.

The intention of most of the members of the group of dissolute favorites to whom this rich present was given was to convert it into money to squander in England. His associates bought out Lord Hopton's interest; they in turn sold all their rights to Lord Thomas Culpeper, who became sole owner and proprietor in fee simple. Culpeper, in 1736, obtained a confirmation from the Virginia Assembly, and a release from the twenty-one year condition.[28] As the heir-at-law of Lord Culpeper, Lord Thomas Fairfax became the sole absolute proprietor, and his tenants were under " servile, feudal and precarious tenure." By the act of the Virginia Assembly, in 1748, all grants made by Fairfax were confirmed to the patentees, but they were to pay him rents, services and emoluments.[29]

So much, for the present, for these chronological facts; their great importance to the subject of this work will be dealt with later. At the time Fairfax inherited his domain, it was generally supposed that his power, in British and Colonial law, was merely a delegated power of sovereignty, to be exercised for the benefit of legitimate settlers. But Fairfax showed how this supposition could be evaded; it was quite simple, as he demonstrated, to vest a huge new estate in himself by a little circumlocution. On one occasion he made a grant of 300,000 acres to Bryant Martin, his nephew and agent. Martin promptly and fraudulently reconveyed it to Fairfax, who laid out the whole as a splendid manor.[30]

[28] " Revised Code, Laws of Va.," Vol. I: Chap. 3, p. 5.
[29] *Ibid.*, Chap. 4, p. 10.
[30] See statement of the court, in 1793, in the case of Jacob Westfall vs. John Singleton, Washington's Virginia Reports, Vol. I: 227. Fairfax did a thriving and dubious land-office business. He invited settlers in, promising them rights, and agreeing to convey land " for three lives, renewable forever," reserving to himself an annual rent. But although the rent was paid, Fairfax refused to convey, and much litigation resulted. (P. 228.)

Lavish Distribution by the Virginia Council.

It was by means of these "Orders in Council," given by members of the Virginia Council to themselves, or often fraudulently or corruptly granted to others, that nearly all the extensive Virginia estates were obtained. The manorial estate of Robert Carter, for instance, was thus secured, embracing 60,000 acres of land in Westmoreland County and in other counties; the seat of the estate was Nomini Hall, a great colonial mansion in Westmoreland County. Built between the years 1725 and 1732 of brick covered with strong white mortar, this manorial seat was seventy-six feet long and forty wide, and was of unusual magnificence for the time.

Carter's possessions were so large and valuable that he was called "King" Carter. His domain descended by entail to his grandson, Robert Carter, who, in addition to his landed estate, owned six hundred negro slaves, a flour mill near his mansion capable of milling 25,000 bushels of wheat a year, and was proprietor in part of an iron works in Baltimore.[31]

Another "Order in Council," June 12, 1749, gave to "a numerous company of adventurers," calling themselves the Loyal Company, license to take up and survey 800,000 acres of land, beginning at the North Carolina line and running westward to the Mississippi River;[32] and on October 29, 1751, another body of speculators, styling themselves the Greenbrier Company, were given a grant of 100,000 acres.[33]

Two of the leading members of the Loyal Company were Nicholas Lewis and Edmund Pendleton, both of whom by reason of the illicit profits from their speculations, became men of considerable wealth and great influence; Pendleton

[31] Phillip Vickars Fithian's "Journal and Letters, 1767–1774." Fithian was a tutor in Carter's family. Robert Carter, the grandson, was, like the other large landholders, of the governing class; as a member of the Provincial Council he was active in the making of laws.

[32] "Revised Code of the Laws of Virginia," Appendix II (Land Laws, Edition of 1819), p. 347.

[33] *Ibid.*

ascending after the Revolution, to the presidency of the Virginia Court of Appeals — a juridical post he long occupied,[34] and in which he was called upon to decide many important land disputes.

Although having anything but a clear title, and fully aware of conflicting claims to part of the land granted it, the Loyal Company hurried its surveys, and rushed ahead to sell many tracts to settlers at the rate of £3 per hundred acres. Caveats were filled by various persons claiming prior ownership. The greatest bitterness prevailed on the part of competing claimants and settlers, the one denouncing the company as an unprincipled band of speculative and corrupt usurpers, and the other asserting that they had bought nothing but bad titles, which they had to spend good money to defend.

The Operations of the Loyal Company.

The ensuing litigation delayed the completion of the Loyal Company's surveys within the term required by the condition of the grant. But this difficulty was easily solved by the Virginia Council, every member of which, it was suspected, was interested in the grant; an " Order in Council " was issued on June 14, 1753, granting the Loyal Company four more years in which to complete its surveys. The company then resumed its locations, and its sales to settlers, until the French and Indian war breaking out, an irruption of Indians drove the settlers away. That war over, both the Loyal Company and the Greenbrier Company petitioned Governor Dinwiddie and the Council to renew their grants with a further term of four years for the completion of surveys and the purchasing of rights.

[34] See Washington's Virginia Reports (Court of Appeals), Vol. I, Preface. Pendleton and his associates assigned their rights to other speculators. Evidently the full sums due them were not paid; in March, 1799, Pendleton and Lewis brought suit to enforce payment of the sums due them from their assignees. See, Rev. Code, Laws of Va., etc., Vol. II, Appendix II: 343.

In the meantime, under Governor Dinwiddie's proclamation of February 19, 1754, George Washington, on behalf of himself and other officers, secured a grant of 200,000 acres of land, for military services. This tract covered part of the area supposed to have been forfeited by the Loyal Company and the Greenbrier Company for non-performance of conditions. The two companies sought by every possible method to have their term extended.

But although some of their members were among the foremost politicians and men of wealth in Virginia, the royal officials dared not grant it, in view of a stern proclamation issued by George III, at the Court of St. James, on October 7, 1763. This proclamation, the result of many Indian outbreaks and wars and massacres, declared it to be essential to the security of the colonies that the Indian tribes should not be molested or disturbed in their hunting grounds. Whereas, "great frauds and abuses have been committed in the purchasing lands of the Indians, to the great prejudice of our interests, and to the great dissatisfaction of said Indians," the purchasing of lands reserved to the Indians was strictly prohibited.[35] In the face of this decree the Governor and Council decided, on May 25, 1763, that they could not grant the petition of the two companies.[36]

But the Loyal and the Greenbrier companies claimed an inalienable vested right in their grant. Was it their fault, they argued, that Indian hostilities had disturbed their operations? Could they be held accountable for non-performance of conditions because of the irruptions of Indians?

They did not, of course, mention that it was the long continuing abuses to which the Indians had been subjected that had driven the tribes to warfare; and if such a plea had been put forth in counter argument, it would not have been listened to in any court of law, for, by the old laws of Virginia, In-

[35] American State Papers: Public Lands, Vol. I: 37.
[36] "Rev. Code, Laws of Va.," Appendix II (Land Laws, Edition of 1819), p. 347.

dian captives had long been held legitimate objects of slavery. The Virginia act of 1672 speaks of Indian slaves or servants for life; the act of 1679 declared that Indian prisoners taken in war should be free purchase to the captor; the act of 1685 decreed that all Indians whose parents were not Christians at the time of their purchase, and all Indians, which (this was the pronoun used, not who; Indian slaves were held to be property, not persons) were sold by neighboring Indians to the whites as slaves, " are deemed as slaves to all intents and purposes." And although the Virginia act of 1705, according to a decision of the Virginia Court of Appeals, in 1793, had completely repealed all former laws, and had released all American Indians from a state of slavery, yet the servitude of Indians long prevailed.[37]

Washington's Grant Conflicts with the Loyal Company's.

When, in 1773, George Washington and the other officers and soldiers claiming to be entitled to their grant under Dinwiddie's proclamation, sought to have it confirmed, the Loyal Company and the Greenbrier Company came forward with a claim of prior vested rights, and objected to surveys on the land claimed by them. Finally, on December 16, 1773, an " Order in Council " was issued, recognizing the claims of the companies *as valid* and giving the soldiers land elsewhere.[38] The promoters of the company were extremely influential in both the Legislature and in the courts; and an act was secured without difficulty from the Legislature in May, 1779, apparently confirming only the lands actually surveyed, upon which, we are told, the Loyal Company " handed in very numerous surveys." [39] At the same time various other

[37] See, Case of Coleman vs. Dick and Pat, Washington's Virginia Reports, Vol. I: 239.
[38] " Revised Code, Laws of Va." (Edition of 1819), p. 347, etc. Washington and his fellow officers received their patents in 1772; the act of 1779 confirmed them.
[39] *Ibid.*

grants were confirmed, among them one of 28,627 acres to John Savage and others.

The precedent thus set in the case of these companies, and the arguments then used, proved to be, as we shall see, of the most stupendous importance in the decisions of the Supreme Court of the United States in the nineteenth century — decisions by which tens of millions of some of the most valuable public agricultural, coal, iron, timber and grazing lands, and gold, silver, copper and other mineral lands were alienated into large private holdings.

Enormous Feudal Estates Established in New York.

In New York and New Jersey far more extensive estates were granted by official favoritism or were obtained by bribing royal officials.

During the period under Dutch rule, when the province of New York and adjacent territory was called New Netherlands, the directors of the Dutch West India Company, all of them Amsterdam merchants, secured great domains.   For a few " duffels, axes, knives, and wampum," paid as purchase price to the Indians, the agents of Kiliaen van Rensselaer, an Amsterdam pearl merchant, bought, in 1630, a tract of land twenty-four miles long and forty wide, on the west bank of the Hudson.   The estate comprised, it was reckoned, seven hundred thousand acres, and included what are now the counties of Albany and Rensselaer, a part of Columbia County, and a strip of the present State of Massachusetts.[40]   Two other directors, Godyn and Bloemart, obtained great feudal estates in what is now New Jersey; one of these estates extended sixteen miles both in length and breadth, forming a square of sixty-four miles.[41]   These estates to the Patroons carried with them absolute feudal rights; the unquestionable sovereign rights of proprietorship, the right to decree laws, and the

[40] O'Callaghan's " History of New Netherlands," Vol. I: 124.
[41] *Ibid.,* 125.

exercise of "high, low and middle jurisdiction," and the appointment of all officials. The Patroon was also given the power of policing his domain with his own armed forces. All of these powers he could exercise "according to his will and pleasure."[42] From such conditions originated in America the great wealth and power of the Van Rennselaer family, which was so potent before, during, and after the Revolution, and which, as we shall have occasion to note, had great influence upon the bench of the Supreme Court of the United States.

Great Manorial Estates Secured by Bribery.

After the capture of New Netherlands by the British, and its transformation in name to New York and New Jersey, vast estates were obtained by the outright bribery of the royal Governor Fletcher. Lord Bellomont, Fletcher's successor, in a communication dated November 28, 1700, to the Lords of Trade in London, specified how it was that many of these estates had been granted.

For a bribe of £100, according to common report, as stated by Bellomont,[43] Captain John R. N. Evans, of the royal warship Richmond, secured a grant forty miles one way and thirty another, on the west bank of the Hudson River from the present town of Haverstraw to the town of New Paltz in Ulster County. Nicholas Bayard, the founder of an influential and aristocratic family, received from Fletcher a grant forty miles long and thirty wide, on both sides of Schoharie Creek.[44] To Colonel William Smith was granted an estate fifty miles long on Nassau — now Long Island. In one year

[42] "Documents Relating to the Colonial History of the State of New York," Vol. I: 89–100. Fuller details of the conditions at this time are given in the "History of the Great American Fortunes," Vol. I: 12–22.

[43] "Documents Relating to the Colonial History of the State of New York," Vol. IV: 463.

[44] Bayard was reputed to be the go-between in arranging with the sea pirates the price to be paid by them in return for Fletcher's protection.

Smith cleared £500, the proceeds of whales captured there, as he admitted to Bellomont.[45]

From Fletcher, Henry Beekman received the grant of one estate sixteen miles long in Dutchess County, and of another estate twenty miles in length along the Hudson River, and running eight miles inland, which particular estate was valued at £5,000.[46] By Fletcher's grant Peter Schuyler, Godfrey Delius and associates conjointly secured a grant fifty miles long in the Mohawk Valley, valued by them at £25,000. It was a grant, wrote Bellomont, which " the Mohawk Indians have often complained of."

Here was the origin of the wealth of the Schuyler family, which later, directly and indirectly, was such an important factor in influencing the course of the Federal Constitutional Convention, and the of the Supreme Court of the United States. Bellomont wrote to the Lords of Trade that it was charged that Fletcher had got at least £4,000 in bribes by his " intolerable corrupt selling away the lands of this province." [47]

The Origin of the Livingston Estate.

It was during this time, also, that another powerful family and fortune were being founded which later exercised a vast influence on American politics, and had its representatives on the Supreme Court bench.

The younger son of a poor exiled clergyman, Robert Livingston curried favor with one official after another, changing his politics whenever his self-interest demanded it, and held lucrative official posts for half a century, generally filling several offices at the same time.[48] In fact, offices were created by Governor Dongan apparently for his sole benefit. He also by the same favoritism became an army contractor,

---

[45] " Documents Relating to the Colonial History," etc., Vol. IV: 535.
[46] *Ibid.*, 39.
[47] *Ibid.*, 528.
[48] George W. Schuyler's " Colonial New York," Vol. I: 285–286.

and the saying was current of him that he made a fortune " by pinching the bellies of the soldiers."

In his " Albany Chronicles," Reynolds says that Livingston was in collusion with Captain Kidd, the sea pirate, and that Livingston loaned money at ten per cent. By grace of the royal governors, and by means of his own practices, Livingston, before his death at the age of seventy-four years in about the year 1728, had managed to become the lord of a manorial estate sixteen miles long, and twenty-four miles wide. On this estate he built flour and saw mills, a bakery and a brewery, and exercised feudal jurisdiction.

Futile Attempts at Confiscation.

Lord Bellomont made determined efforts to have these great estates confiscated. But he found, as he wrote November 28, 1700, to the Lords of Trade, that the Assembly of New York was largely composed of the very landed magnates whom he sought to overthrow. He set forth the grievances of the actual settlers, that they could get no land, and their objection to becoming " a base tenant to Mr. Delius, Colonel Schuyler, Mr. Livingston, and the others of the whole role of our mighty landgraves." Bellomont applied for a peremptory order of the King or an act of Parliament for the confiscation of these extravagant and corrupt grants given by Fletcher and other governors. Unless, Bellomont added, " the power of our Palatines, Smith, Livingston, the Phillipses, father and son . . . and six or seven more were reduced . . . the country is ruined." [49]

The Phillipses referred to were Frederick and his son Adolphus, who had received an immense grant of land in what is now Putnam County, new York. Fredrick Phillips was the employer of the sea-pirate, Captain Samuel Burgess, of New York, who, at first, was sent out by Phillips to Madagascar to

[49] " Documents Relating to the Colonial History of the State of New York," Vol. IV: 533–534.

trade with the pirates, and then soon turned pirate himself. The first voyage yielded Phillips and Burgess £5,000, the proceeds of trade and slave-snatching; from the second voyage they cleared £10,000 and three hundred slaves.

Marrying a relative of Phillips, Burgess continued piracy. Caught and imprisoned in Newgate, Phillips spent large sums of money to save him from death and finally succeeded. Burgess, however, resumed piracy, and met death from being poisoned in Africa while carrying off slaves.[50]

We shall have need of recurring to the Phillips' estate in a later chapter dealing with the means by which John Jacob Astor, in virtue of a noted Supreme Court decision, obtained part of it.

As a concession to Bellomont's urgent and repeated remonstrances to England, the New York Assembly annulled at least two of Fletcher's corrupt grants, but most of the extensive grants remained intact, causing popular uprisings in later generations. The corrupt, interested, intrenched forces against Bellomont were many and too powerful. The justices of the courts were either men of the large landholding class, or their servitors. Lewis Morris, Chief Justice of the Province of New York, was removed from office by Governor William Cosby for (among other accusations) sitting in his own cause in land and other cases. Morris denied these charges in a pamphlet published in 1735.[51] Doubtless his defense was not altogether without its extenuating features, inasmuch as Cosby himself was one of the large landholders and very active in presenting grants of estates. Perhaps the interests of competing landholders collided, and Morris serving

[50] " The Lives and Bloody Exploits of the Most Noted Pirates," 177-183. This work, published a century since, was a serious study of the various sea-pirates.

[51] " The Case of Lewis Morris, Esq., Late Chief Justice of the Province of New York, etc.: To Be Heard Before The Lords of Committee on Plantation Affairs." This document was published as a broadside.

one side, was made to suffer. Morris was later appointed
Governor-General of New Jersey.

Continuing Corruption of Royal Officials.

To put a stop to .the " extravagant grants " of land by
royal governors to favorites, accessories or bribers, Bellomont
had proposed to the Lords of Trade that no grant of more
than a thousand acres be made to any man, except, in the
case of larger grants, by special leave of the king. He also
recommended placing a quit rent of half a crown on every
hundred acres, this sum to go into the royal treasury. It was
not until subsequently that, in order to avert abuses and consequent popular dissatisfaction, a royal order was issued limiting to two thousand acres the amount of land to be granted
to any one occupant or settler. But this law was easily
evaded; the royal officials continued to pervert their authority
by fraudulently securing for themselves by indirection great
estates of the most valuable land, or corruptly gave them to
others, as is evidenced by the following examples, recited in
the court records:

In 1737, George Clarke was Lieutenant-Governor of the
Province of New York, in which official capacity he was member and vice-president of the Colonial Council of the province.
To this council the king intrusted the power of granting lands
for occupation and settlement, subject to the two-thousand-
acre limitation. At a meeting of the Colonial Council at Fort
George, on August 2, 1737, at which were present Clarke, Chief
Justice Kennedy of the Provincial Courts, Courtlandt, Kane
and Horsmander, all members of the Council, Clarke presented
a petition of William Corry, who had recently emigrated from
Ireland. The petition set forth that there was a large tract of
crown land in Mohawk County; that he, Corry, had engaged
to bring a number of families from Ireland, and he, therefore,
applied for a grant of 100,000 acres for himself and for such

other persons as *he should name,* the names to be inserted by him in the grant.

How Lieutenant-Governor Clarke Secured a Large Estate.

When this petition was presented, Clarke left the room. During the time that he was absent, the other members of the Council agreed that Clarke should grant the petition for 100,-000 acres. An order was accordingly made to that effect by the Council, and a survey ordered. Cadwallader Colden, then the surveyor-general of the province, with Clarke and Receiver-General Archibald Kennedy, were the King's regular commissioners for setting out all lands granted. They were instructed to make out the grant to Samuel Heath, William Crosby (Sheriff of New York), Francis Sylvester and nine others named by Corry as trustees, to, and for, his use; in the grant Corry had 26,000 acres specifically made out for himself.

Nearly a century later, Levi S. Chatfield, then Attorney-General of New York State, in bringing suit against George Clarke, a rich and powerful descendent of Lieutenant-Governor Clarke, for the annulment of that ancient grant and for the recovery of the lands to the State, recounted the preceding facts, and further set forth: That after the patent was issued, it was discovered that all the names of the grantees, except Corry, were used in joint trust for Corry and Lieutenant-Governor Clarke; that there was an agreement between Clarke and Corry by which Clarke " should pay half the charges and expenses of surveying the said land, and of procuring the patents, and should be interested in one-half the grant of 100,000 acres of land; and that one equal moiety of the 25,400 acres granted by the aforesaid letters patent to the said William Corry and his associates, were so granted in trust for the said Lieutenant-Governor George Clarke; and that, in compliance with the agreement and trust, the said William Corry, by deed of release to the said Lieutenant-Gov-

ernor George Clarke, dated February 18, 1738, released to
the said George Clarke, his heirs and assigns forever, 12,700
acres in, and the moiety of the said premises granted in, and
by, the said grant or letters patent." [52]

Attorney-General Chatfield further averred that Corry's petition was false and fraudulent; that none of the grantees had
ever removed from Ireland; that the names of everyone, except his own, had been fraudulently used by Corry; that Clarke
had concealed from the members of the Council and from the
Crown his own interest in the transaction; that 'the whole proceedings were a fraudulent device to evade the two-thousand-
acre restriction; and that no settlers were ever brought on the
land.[53]

Sir William Johnson's Methods.

Another such example of royal officials fraudulently getting
or giving large estates by exercise of their authority was
that of Governor Sir Henry Moore, of the Province of New
York. Herman Le Roy, William Bayard and other powerful,
rich men claimed that they were the owners of a certain 25,-
000 acres in the present Montgomery County, New York.
This land had been claimed and improved by settlers. But
Le Roy and Bayard could produce no title papers of any kind;
the records, according to their assertions, had disappeared.
Not being able to bring forward written proofs, they filed a

---

[52] Case of People of the State of New York vs. George Clarke,
Barbour's Supreme Court Reports (New York), Vol. X: 125.

[53] *Ibid.*, 120–156. This case, and other similar actions, were brought
at a time following the outbreak of the "Anti-Renters' War" in New
York, when the tenants of the great estates revolted against the feudal
customs, laws and exactions still prevailing. In deciding the case,
November 25, 1850, Judge Cady (who had been put on the bench by
the landholding class) did not attempt to controvert the charges of
fraud. He decided against the State on this ground: "It would be
an alarming doctrine to hold that every man in the State who holds
any land under a grant before the Revolution, may be turned out of
possession by the plaintiffs, if a king was cheated, who, one or two
hundred years since, made the grant" (page 152). Judge Cady held
further that the action was outlawed by the statute of limitations.

bill in court, in 1798, making this remarkable confession of facts as justifying their claims, and disproving those of the settlers:

That, on February 2, 1768, Governor Moore officially bought 25,000 acres in what is now Montgomery County for the alleged use of twenty-five specified settlers. But their names were really used to evade the one-thousand-acre law;[54] the so-called settlers were, the bill charged, actually used as dummies for Sir William Johnson, and had an agreement with him by which he paid all expenses, and by which they were to turn over the 25,000 acres to him. Sir William Johnson paid upwards of £600 in fees, and the whole tract was conveyed to him in fee simple.[55] On June 11, 1772, Johnson, for £375, conveyed 10,000 acres to Lord A. Gordon; another 2,000 acres to John Kelly; and by his will, dated 1774, Johnson bequeathed the remaining 13,000 acres to his two brothers and four sisters. Lord A. Gordon, on December 5, 1792, conveyed the 10,000 acres to R. and J. Watts who, on the same day conveyed the tract to Herman Le Roy and William Bayard. The particular explanation of the lack of title papers, in this case, as in similar cases, was that at the outbreak of the Revolution, Johnson's son buried the title papers; that they became lost or illegible; and that nine of the defendants, knowing this, tried to get the whole property and title.

In deciding this case in favor of Le Roy, Bayard and the other appellants, at Albany, in February, 1798, Judge Benson not only made no attempt to refute the plea made by the claimants, Le Roy and Bayard, of the original fraud, but he made light of it. The supposed illegality, said he, of the agreement between the original patentees and Sir William Johnson consisted in its being in contravention of the instruc-

[54] The law, at this time, seems to have limited the amount to be granted to any one settler at not more than 1,000 acres.

[55] Johnson's Cases (Court for the Trial of Impeachments and Correction of Errors) [N. Y.], Vol. I: 417–429.

tions from the king to the governor, restraining the patents
for land to a stated quantity. "The futility of this regulation," added Judge Benson, "was soon discovered, and the
instruction was for nearly half a century before the patent
mentioned in the bill issued considered altogether as a *dead
letter,* and a compliance with it a *mere matter of form.
. . .*"[56] Le Roy, Bayard and the other personages in whose
favor Judge Benson decided were men of the greatest wealth
and highest station in the society and politics of the day.
They were intimate personal friends and close business associates of John Jay, the first Chief Justice of the Supreme Court
of the United States, and as we shall see in Chapter V, Jay,
when special envoy of the United States to Great Britain,
asked his friend Nicholas Cruger to let Le Roy and Bayard
share in a certain "golden plan" for making "millions
sterling."

If Judge Benson's premises were correct that the law had
remained a dead letter, why had the beneficiaries taken such
pains to circumvent it? By the people at large, Benson's decision was regarded as another skillful theory of justification
in behalf of the great landowners then everywhere seeking
(and successfully so) to secure that which had been obtained
by fraud, and to aggrandize themselves still further. Judge
Benson's vote in connection with another notorious transaction is described later in this work.

John Jacob Astor Secures Land Obtained by Fraud.

A third instance of the fraudulent activities of royal governors in New York in the eighteenth century was that of
two grants in fee, one grant of 18,000 acres in what was then
Albany County, on March 25, 1768, ostensibly to Michael
Byrn and eighteen others, and a second grant of 25,000 acres.

[56] *Ibid.* It may be observed here that Chancellor Kent, that pre-
'eminent expounder of the all-pervading rights of property, studied law
under Judge Benson.

on May 8, 1770, to Sir William Johnson and twenty-five other persons. A quarter of a century later John Jacob Astor and two associates contended in court that not the occupying settlers but they were the real owners of these tracts of 43,000 acres. Astor and his associates could not show a single title paper. In support of their claim they put forward these " facts," evidently not apprehensive in the least that such a defense would militate against them.

That, when the two grants were made, Johnson paid all the fees; that the alleged settlers were simply his tools, and their names were inserted for his benefit, with the express intention of releasing to him the whole of the tract, which, in fact, was later turned over to him in fee. The appellants in this case — John Jacob Astor, William Laight and Peter Smith — declared, through their attorney, Aaron Burr,[57] that they had a regular title to the two tracts, one of 18,000, the other

---

[57] Aaron Burr, at this time, was one of the leading and most adroit Republican politicians in New York State. (The Republican Party of that day was the predecessor of the Democratic Party of later times.) Edward Livingston, Spencer (later Chief Justice of New York) and other noted lawyers appeared in these cases for the respondents. Evidently, there was some conflict of great interests not altogether stated in the court records.

Burr lived next door to Astor at No. 221 Broadway. It was Burr who consummated an adroit piece of business by which Astor became possessed of a lease of 465 lots of land, of later immense value, in New York City. In the year 1767 Trinity Church had leased these lots for 99 years to Abraham Mortier at a total annual rental of $269 a year; the lots were in the district now bounded by Greenwich, Spring and Hudson Streets. Upon the initiative of Burr, the Legislature, in 1797, determined upon an investigation as to how Trinity Church was expending its income. Of all things Trinity Church wanted no investigation of its affairs. It succeeded in suppressing any actual inquiry. Presently Burr turned up with a transfer of the Mortier lease to himself, and pledging it as security he obtained a $38,000 loan from the Manhattan Bank. When after his duel with Hamilton, Burr was forced to flee, Astor obligingly took this extraordinarily valuable lease off Burr's hands. The lease covered land in the business and residential district, and as the city rapidly grew and land values tremendously increased, it was a source of great revenue to Astor and his descendants.— For the full account with citations from official records see " History of the Great American Fortunes," Vol. I: 167–168.

of 25,000 acres, from Sir William Johnson's executors, who, it was set forth, had power to sell.

The lower courts had decided in favor of John Morgan, Jonathan Danforth and thirty-three other settlers. As their principal defense, when the case came up on appeal, Astor and his partners in the transaction made the explanation that early during the Revolution, Johnson's papers were put in an iron box and buried in the earth; that there they moldered, spoiled and became unrecognizable; and that the settlers, knowing this, sought to get title and property. The decision in the Court for the Trial of Impeachments and the Correction of Errors, at Albany, in February, 1799, was in favor of Astor and his fellow appellants, on virtually the same grounds as in the preceding case.[58]   The settlers were promptly dispossessed.

Also Plead Fraud in Justification.

Further facts disclosing official fraud and collusion in the granting of large estates came out in the similar case of Herman Le Roy, William Bayard and others against Peter Servis and other settlers in the same court, in 1801, on an appeal from a decision in favor of Servis. The bill of Le Roy and Bayard filed in court asserted in justification of their claim that, in 1768, Peter Servis and twenty-four other persons had petitioned Governor Sir Henry Moore to buy, for their use, 25,000 acres of land from the Oneida Indians in Albany, now Herkimer, County. The bill went on to state that for money or other valuable considerations, the petitioners agreed with Sir William Johnson that, on their getting the 25,000 acres, they would hold the same in trust for him, and duly convey the whole tract to him, provided he paid all costs, etc. This plan was carried out in 1769, and Johnson got the land.

Le Roy and Bayard interjected their customary defense,

[58] Johnson's Cases, etc., Vol. I: 429–435.

namely, that after Johnson's death, his son, Sir John Johnson, buried the papers so that they " were wholly lost or rendered illegible," and that Servis and his fellow settlers, aware of the fact, claimed the title, and attempted to get the property for themselves. The higher court's decision, in February, 1801, was in favor of Le Roy and Bayard,[59] and the settlers were ousted. These decisions, as will appear, have a deep bearing on later parts of this narrative. Sir William Johnson obtained 93,000 acres, all told, by these particular fraudulent operations. At one time Sir William Johnson's total estate was so vast that he had a domain " which made him, next to William Penn, the owner of the most extensive estate on the continent." [60] Considerable of this area, as has just been described, came into the possession of the Astor and other large landholding families of later times.

Landowners Become Lawmakers and Judges.

The great area of land thus obtained by fraud enabled the land magnates to set themselves up as the exclusive lawmaking and juridical class; this fact furnishes the explanation of why it was that, while the officials and their accessories were seizing land, they were at the same time passing laws providing the severest punishments for fraud and other offenses on the part of the generality of people. In a communication, dated September 20, 1764, to the Lords of Trade, at London, Lieutenant-Governor Cadwallader Colden, of New York, described how the land magnates had managed to usurp the lawmaking power by putting provisions in three of the large land grants guaranteeing to each Proprietor the privilege of sending a representative to the General Assembly. Hence, these landed proprietors became hereditary legislators. " The owners of other great patents," Colden further complained, " be-

[59] Caine's Cases (Court for the Trial of Impeachments and Correction of Errors) [New York], Vols. I–II: pp. 3–7.
[60] Roberts' " New York," Vol. II: 623.

ing men of the greatest opulence in the several American
counties where these Tracts are, have sufficient influence to
be perpetually elected for those counties. The General Assembly, then, of this Province consists of the owners of these
extravagant grants; the merchants of New York, the principal of them strongly connected with the owners of those
great Tracts by Family interest, and of Common Farmers,
which last are men easily deluded and led away with popular
arguments of Liberty and Privileges. The Proprietors of the
great tracts are not only freed from the quit rents which
the other land-holders in the Province pay, but by their influence in the Assembly are freed from every other public Tax
on their lands." [61]

Lords Proprietors of New Jersey.

Virtually the same condition prevailed in all the colonies.
The whole of East New Jersey and other parts at one time
belonged to a syndicate of twenty-four men, styling themselves " The Lords Proprietors of New Jersey." They professed to derive their title from a sale made to them in 1681
and 1682 by the widow of Phillip Carteret, the first Proprietary Governor. Their claims were recognized in law; they
made large sums of money in disposing of much of the land;
and before and at the time of the Revolution they were a
mighty financial, political and social influence in New Jersey,[62] a fact which, as we shall have reason to note, had a
close relation to the early composition of the Supreme Court
of the United States.

These details give an insight into the methods of possessing

[61] " Documents Relating to the Colonial History of the State of
New York," Vol. VII : 654-655.

[62] As late as 1884 the descendants of these Proprietors held a reunion
meeting in New Jersey, claiming (but it is not to be supposed seriously)
that their inherited rights as Proprietors were still valid. They published their proceedings in a pamphlet.

estates in the northern colonies and the accompanying establishment of a landed aristocracy.

Extensive Seizures in Carolina and Georgia.

In Carolina and Georgia — then covering a vast extent of territory included in a number of the present Southern States — great estates were likewise being acquired by fraud.

Writing from Savannah to the Lords of Trade, at London, April 20, 1763, Governor James Wright referred heatedly to the " very extraordinary procedure of the Governor [Boone] of South Carolina," in allowing the monopolization by a few of the most valuable areas of land. " I say, my lords," Wright continued, " this procedure has struck a general damp, and dispirited the whole province. I have called this, my lords, the death or destruction of the province; for an extension of limits to the southward, if the lands were properly parcelled out to people who would really cultivate and improve them, would draw some thousand inhabitants here; whereas, by this step taken in Carolina, great part of the lands, my lords, are ordered in large tracts to some wealthy settlers in Carolina, who probably will never see it themselves, and some of whom, it is said, have already more lands in that province than they can cultivate or improve.

" This, my lords, is pretty well known on this side of the water; and who, having a great number of slaves, claim what they call their family right, that is, fifty acres of land for each slave, although it is highly probable that their ancestors had land for those very slaves, and it is well understood here that many of those persons, especially those who have the largest tracts, have no intention to remove there or settle them; but probably some years hence, when it begins to get valuable, will sell it, and in the meantime those vast tracts of land are to lie waste and unimproved, as very great bodies yet do in Carolina, and if they should do anything at all

with those lands, it is expected that it will only be by sending an overseer and a few negroes just to make a trifling settlement, seemingly to comply with the terms of the grant or
by way of taking possession." [63]

Governor Wright estimated that Governor Boone had
granted 343,000 acres to less than two hundred persons —
many of them British lords or other speculators —" strangers
who have never contributed one farthing or one hour's fatigue
or hardship toward the support of the province." [64]   The 343,-
000 acres held by a few recipients " would accommodate a
thousand very good families and settlers "; hundreds of families were ready to come from North Carolina but could not
get land.   Frauds and abuses in the survey of land were very
numerous.

Governor Boone's Plea and Explanation.

When called upon by the Lords of Trade to explain, Governor Boone of South Carolina wrote, on August 17, 1763,
a long, abjectly apologetic letter, expressing his regrets at having committed and allowed abuses.   " I hope, my lords," he
wrote in part, " after what I have said, that your lordships
will rather look upon it as my misfortune than my fault that
I have incurred your displeasure."   Claiming that he was actuated by honest motives, he went on to make this invidious,
significant and self-protecting comparison, " I have been Governor of this province above two years, with as many, if not
more opportunities of benefiting myself than any of my predecessors ever had, had I chose to be remiss in my duty, as
I have been strenuous in the practice of it." [65]   The Lords of
Trade directed that no extravagant warrants for land should
be issued, and tried to break the large grants already made.
But their instructions came too late ; the grants remained valid.

---

[63] " American State Papers: Public Lands," Vol. I: 55.
[64] *Ibid.*
[65] *Ibid.*, 53–54.

With this resumé of some of the conditions under which the landholding class — the dominant class of the Revolutionary period — obtained its immense holdings, we shall now proceed to consider the conditions formulated for the laboring, servant and slave classes, and the methods by which another class — the trading class — acquired its wealth, and its corresponding political and social sway.

At first the trading class was largely identical with the Patroons, and with the companies and the manorial lords of the other colonies who by virtue of their charters, powers and privileges held a monopoly of trading. Even when the trading class began to reveal an independence of the landed class, the two were, nevertheless, often closely affiliated, and frequently comprised the same identity of interests.

All the conditions, the varied demands and contests, and the laws and traditions put in force by the governing classes, as well as the traditional subjugation of the working classes, were later reflected in the personnel of the Supreme Court of the United States selected to enforce and augment the powers by which the ruling classes benefited.

CHAPTER II

THE LABORING, SERVANT AND SLAVE CLASSES, AND THE GROWTH OF THE TRADING CLASS

While an extremely powerful and dictatorial landed aristocracy was thus being created by royal grants and official favoritism, or by illegal or fraudulent methods, severe statutes were enacted in all the colonies, the effect of which was to create and perpetuate a dependent and servile class of workers whom the laws differentiated into various menial classes.

Punitive Puritan Laws.

The extraordinarily profound piety ascribed to the Puritan fathers was accompanied with a series of drastic laws passed by them prescribing the sharpest limitations for the many of both sexes compelled to work for wages, or for those whom misfortune, in one way or another, branded as defenseless objects of legal and religious persecutions.

The act of the Massachusetts authorities in 1630, passed in response to the self-interested demands of those who had already acquired property and who needed a constant supply of subservient workers, was the first measure in that colony the purpose of which was to form a permanent class of practically hereditary working people. This act, "Respecting Masters, Servants and Laborers," opened by decreeing that no servant should give, or sell, any truck during time of service without the consent of masters. All workmen, it declared, should work the whole day — that is, as long as they should be ordered — allowing "convenient time for food and rest." Compulsory adherence to their tasks was decreed by Section

48

III. This provided that if any servants ran away from their
masters, the magistrate and two chief inhabitants were " to
press men and boats or pinnaces at the public charge, to pursue such persons by sea and land, and bring them back by
force of arms." [1] The next section placed the question of
the rate of wages exclusively in the power of the masters. It
decreed that the freemen of the towns should " agree amongst
themselves about the prices and rates of all workmen's labor,
and servant's wages." To this decision, workman, laborer
and servant were to bind themselves. Any master paying
wages exceeding the prescribed rates was to be punished at
the discretion of the court.[2] Section V provided that wages
for servants and workmen were to be paid in corn, the value
of which was to be adjudged by two disinterested freemen,
one to be chosen by the master, the other by the workman or
servant. If they could not agree a third arbiter was to be selected by the magistrate.[3]

Strict as this act was, it yet was not without its gleams of
prudent humanity — a remnant of feudal times when the lot
of the laborer had some necessary alleviating phases. Servants flying from the cruelty of the master, the act declared,
could be harbored by other persons without being held accountable to the law. But the servant had to prove the fact
of cruelty before the magistrate, who invariably was a landowner and employer himself.

And what if any servant should be maltreated? This con-
soling redress was decreed in Section VIII: That, " If any
man smite out the eye or tooth of his man servant or maid

[1] "Ancient Charters and Laws of Massachusetts Bay, etc., Published By Order Of The General Court, 1814": p. 155. The word
"servant" as used throughout the colonies in the seventeenth and
eighteenth centuries is by no means to be understood as being confined
to the narrower conception of the domestic servant of to-day. A servant then was not only one who gave personal household service, but
was bonded to perform many agricultural and other occupations for
manorial lords, merchants, shippers and plantation owners.
[2] *Ibid.*, 156.
[3] *Ibid.*

servant, or otherwise maim or disfigure them (unless it be by mere casualty) he shall let them go free from his serv- ice, and shall allow such further recompense as the courts may adjudge him." [4]   Appearing, however, before prejudiced courts, it was anything but easy for the maltreated servant to prove that the maiming was not done " by mere casualty "— an elastic qualification under which brutal masters took refuge.

By the next and last section of the act, faithful servants, after seven years' bonded service, were not to be sent away empty.   But (and this clause allowed the greatest abuses and impositions) servants unfaithful or unprofitable to masters were not to be freed until they had made satisfaction, accord- ing to the judgment of authority.[5]

An act adopted in Massachusetts in 1631 forbade hiring any person for less time of service than a year, unless he be a " settled housekeeper." [6]   The act of September, 1634, pro- hibited the allotting of any lot of land in any plantation to any servant " till he hath approved his faithfulness to his mas- ter during his time of service." [7]   In December, 1636, an act was passed in the same colony decreeing that no servant should be set free until he had served out the covenanted time; the penalty for infraction was to be set by the quarter courts.[8] This act also declared that no servant was eligible to any of- fice.[9]   The Massachusetts act of 1642 decreed that all unruly poor children were to be bound out for service, and the act of the Massachusetts General Court, in 1720, provided that all children of the poor, whether their parents received alms or not, and whose parents were unable to maintain them, were to be set to work or bound out by the selectmen or overseers — the male children until they were twenty-one, and the fe- males until eighteen, years old.

[4] *Ibid.*
[5] *Ibid.*
[6] *Ibid.,* Appendix, p. 711.
[7] *Ibid.*
[8] *Ibid.,* 429.
[9] *Ibid.*

Feudal Conditions Transplanted.

The Connecticut laws were similar to those of Massachusetts. The Rhode Island code of 1647 provided that the ar-
tificer or laborer must finish any work agreed upon and not
depart unless it were that his wages had not been paid. If
he quitted work he forfeited £5 to his employer, who could
recover in court by an action for debt.[10] In the province of
New Netherlands — later New York and New Jersey — distinctly feudal conditions copied from those in the monarchies
of Europe prevailed. Under the act of 1629, elaborated by
that of 1653, of the States General of Holland, any adventurer
who shipped over a certain number of adults received extensive grants of land, with feudal rights of proprietorship.
These exported peasants became his vassals. The power of
the Patroons — as the manorial lords under Dutch control
were styled — over their tenants or serfs was almost unlimited. The law ordained that no man or woman, son or daughter, man servant or maid servant could leave a Patroon's service during the time that they had agreed to yield service;
and no infraction of this law was permitted, no matter how
gross the abuses or breaches of contract the Patroon committed.

These laws were variously ratified and increased under British rule. By an act passed in New York, October 22, 1684,
against " Fugitive Servants And Their Entertainers," it was
provided that if any servant depart or absent himself from
his master's service, he or she should be adjudged to pay
the penalty of being forced to serve double their time in future service to the master.[11] The bonding of impoverished
boys, girls and adults in England and in America for long-
term services to the American manorial lords and merchants
was a fixed condition.

[10] " Rhode Island Colonial Records, 1636–1663." Vol. I: 183–184.
[11] " Laws of The Colony of New York ": 147.

The grandiose feudal lord of the manor was not only the proprietor of the soil, but for a long time he was the dominant manufacturer and trader, and the mass of people were his retainers or tenants. He owned and exported the furs gathered on his extensive domain, as also the timber for which (that being entirely a sailing-ship era) there was an immense demand both in Europe and America. He, too, had control over the inland river fisheries, and all other natural resources. He had his stores, his bakery, his flour mills, saw mills and brewery. Tenants were forced by him to sign covenants that they would trade nowhere else but at his stores and mills.[12]

His dominion, therefore, was one of arbitrary control over his dependents and he exacted their produce at will.

The perpetuation of a completely subordinated laboring class in Pennsylvania under Quaker rule was likewise insured by strict laws. An act passed by the General Assembly in Pennsylvania, in 1700, " for the better regulation of servants in this province and territories " declared that " for the just encouragement of servants in the discharge of their duties, and for the prevention of their deserting their masters," no servant, bound to serve time, should be sold, or disposed of, without the consent of the said servant. Violation of this law was to entail a penalty of £10, to be forfeited by the seller. Nor was any servant to be assigned by one master to another, under the same penalty.[13] Every servant faithfully serving four years or more, was to have a discharge " at the expiration of their servitude," and — the act generously read on —" shall be duly clothed with two compleat suits of apparel, whereof one shall be new, and shall also be furnished with one axe, one grubbing-hoe, and one weeding-hoe, at the charge of their master or mistress." [14]

[12] For a fuller description see " The History of the Great American Fortunes," Vol. I., Chaps. 1, 2 and 3.
[13] Carey and Bioren's " Pennsylvania Laws, 1700-1770," Vol. I : 14-16.
[14] Ibid.

Quaker Methods of Disciplining the Workers.

The quitting by servants of their master's service was prohibited by Section IV of the same act, which enacted that if any servant absented himself or herself from service for one day or more without consent, he should be obliged to serve five additional days to his or her indentured term of service for each day of absence, and that after the expiration of the term of servitude the courts were to give the master damages.[15] Inasmuch as few servants had any money after their long term of services, this meant that in lieu of damages they had to yield extra servitude.

The regulations for keeping servants in submission were so onerous, and their enforcement so tyrannous, that the practice of servants running away had become general. Section V made provision for this. Whoever apprehended any fugitive servant within ten miles of the master's abode and delivered the runaway to the Sheriff, was to receive a reward of ten shillings; within twenty miles, twenty shillings, and thus on with a graduated list of rewards.[16] The section following forbade the clandestine employing of other men's servants. Section VII was designed " for the more effectual discouragement of servants embezzling their masters' goods." Servants who were not paid, or were ill treated, frequently ran away, taking such necessary articles of apparel or other goods as they needed. The master made a charge of embezzlement. By the provision of Section VII the buyer of the goods was to pay back double value to the master, and the servant was required to make satisfaction by servitude after the expiration of his or her time, to double the value of the goods. If he were a black servant, he was to be severely whipped.[17]

[15] *Ibid.* The word servitude is the exact word used in the colonial laws.
[16] *Ibid.*
[17] *Ibid.*

Maryland Statutes of Bondage.

Equally strong, although in different respects, were the laws of Roman Catholic Maryland. Chapter XIX, of the Maryland law of April, 1715, prohibited, under heavy penalties, masters of ships or vessels, or any other person, from conveying away runaway servants who were under bond or bail. Any person enticing away a servant, apprentice or slave was, for each offense, to forfeit to the owner treble damages and costs for the time the servant, apprentice or slave was missing.[18] The Act of May, 1748, repeated and amplified the provisions of the act of 1715; it decreed a penalty of one hundred pounds of tobacco for every hour of harboring fugitive slaves or servants; the offender was to be lashed on the bare back not more than thirty-nine stripes for each offense, and servants harboring other servants were to receive the same number of lashings.

No servant, whether working for wages or indenture, should, according to the provisions of Chapter XLIV, Act of April, 1715, travel more than ten miles from the master's house without a note from the master, mistress, dame or overseer, or else be liable to penalties as a runaway.[19] For being unlawfully absent from the master's service, the servant or laborer was to give ten days additional service for each day's absence, and to pay costs. Anyone apprehending a runaway servant or slave was to get a reward of two hundred pounds of tobacco from the owner. No person was allowed to trade or barter with a servant under penalty of two thousand pounds of tobacco; goods thus bartered were to be recovered, and the offender was punishable by a lashing of thirty stripes upon the bare back.[20] A provision especially satisfactory to the rich planters was that all servants imported

---

[18] " Laws of Maryland," etc. (Edition of 1799), Vol. I. This volume is not paged.
[19] Ibid.
[20] Ibid.

without articles of indenture were to serve these terms of servitude (service) :

Servants more than twenty-two years old to serve five years; those between eighteen and twenty-two years old to serve six years; those between fifteen and eighteen years old to serve seven years; and all under fifteen years old were to serve until they were twenty-two years old.[21]   Inasmuch as, with the connivance of the authorities, a regular traffic was carried on by procurers in kidnaping men, women and children under various pretenses from Europe to the colonies, the significance of this statute can be seen at a glance.   A white woman having a child by a negro was, if a free woman, to serve seven years in servitude; and if she were a servant an additional seven years.   Any white man doing likewise with a negress was to undergo the same penalties.[22]   Free persons and servants (white laborers) could not be married without the express approval of master or mistress; the laws long kept the sharpest distinction between free whites, on the one hand, and bonded whites and whites of compulsory servitude, on the other.   During the very period of the Revolution — seven months after the adoption of the Declaration of Independence asserting that all men were born free and equal — the General Assembly of Maryland, in February, 1777, passed an act Chapter XII of which prohibited ministers, under penalty of £50 from marrying a free person and a servant without the consent of master or mistress.[23]

The drafters of the Maryland act of 1715, strained themselves, we may assume, to the utmost in inserting provisions placing the following restrictions upon the masters:

If they did not feed or take sufficient care of servants by allowing needed rest, or if they taxed any servant beyond his strength, they were to pay a penalty for each offense not exceeding one thousand pounds of tobacco.   For any one offense the master could give the servant ten lashes; this was

[21] *Ibid.*   [22] *Ibid.*   [23] *Ibid.*

legal; but if he gave more, he was subject to the same penalty.[24]

The same law provided most munificently what the servant
should receive after his long period of servitude. At discharge the master was to give each servant a new hat, a good
suit, a new pair of shoes, two hoes and one ax, and one gun of
twenty shillings price. Failing to do this, the master was to
pay a penalty of five hundred pounds of tobacco.[25]

Lords and Vassals in Virginia.

Extensive baronial domains and large estates in Virginia
were procured by British nobles, adventurers, companies,
planters and military officers with such facility that the most
pressing necessity there, as elsewhere, was a permanent supply of workers to hew the forests, cultivate the arable soil,
man the ships and otherwise develop and distribute the resources. The exportation from England of poor whites, convicted of one or another of the trivial offenses then punished
so severely in British law, supplied a portion of this demand
and kidnaping another part. The enslavement of Indians
and negroes furnished the remainder.

The Virginia act of 1670 declared that all servants, not
Christians, imported into Virginia by shipping, should be
slaves for life, but that those coming by land should serve for
a limited time. This statute seems to have applied to negroes, to Indians from other provinces, and even to white convicts.[26] The acts of 1672, 1679 and 1685, distinctly, as we
have seen, validated the enslavement of Indian captives. The
long continuing enslavement is evidenced by the fact that as

[24] "Laws of Maryland," etc. (Edit. of 1799), Vol. I.
[25] *Ibid.*
[26] We have seen how the Virginia general land laws of 1705 allowed
planters to acquire free lands in proportion to the number of servants
or slaves owned. The more slaves or servants, the greater the area of
land granted.

late as 1793 the case (Footnote 37, Chap. I), of Coleman vs.
Dick and Pat was before the Virginia Court of Appeals for
the determination of the question whether Indians could be
held as slaves. On that occasion the court held, as we have
stated, that a statute passed in 1705 was a complete repeal of
the acts of 1672, 1679 and 1685, " and since that period no
American Indian can be reduced to a state of slavery." But,
added the court, " foreign Indians coming within the description
of that act, might be made slaves." [27] The president of
the Virginia Court of Appeals at this time was the same Edmund Pendleton who was one of the promoters of the Loyal
Company which had obtained a grant of 800,000 acres of land
and which had ehriched itself by a succession of 'fraudulent
operations.

The conditions under which bonded white laborers, and
Indian and negro slaves toiled were not invariably hard;
here and there a humane and generous master was to be found,
but he was a very rare exception. So oppressive was the lot
of the servant, laborer and slave, on the whole, that at the
first opportunity a desperate flight for freedom was made.
To prevent this, severe laws were passed in Virginia exceeding in harshness those in other colonies.

The Virginia act of 1748 (22 George II, Cap. 17) offered
rewards in specified sums to those catching fugitive seamen.[28]
Any person harboring a servant who lacked the necessary
certificate attesting that his time of servitude had expired,
was required to pay the owner thirty pounds of tobacco, with
costs, for every day the runaway was sheltered.[29] The same
act decreed that if a runaway servant used a forged certificate
he was to stand for two hours in a public pillory; as for the
forger he was to forfeit £10 with costs, failing to pay which
he was to receive thirty-nine lashes on the bare back, " well

[27] Washington's Virginia Reports (Court of Appeals), Vol. I: 239.
[28] " Virginia Laws " (Edition of 1759), p. 314.
[29] *Ibid.*

laid on " at the common whipping post.[30]   If, after the arrest
of runaway servants, white or negro, no owner appeared at
the gaol after·a stated time, an iron collar was to be put by
the keeper of the gaol on the servant's neck, marked with the
letters " P. G." at the time the servant was delivered to the
person hiring him.[31]

Slaves Dismembered with Impunity.

Section XXXV of the same act was extremely ferocious.
It decreed that in the case of any slave notoriously guilty of
going abroad at night, or running away and lying out and
" who cannot be reclaimed from such disorderly courses by
common methods of punishment " (whipping and imprisonment), the court could order such a reprobate " to be punished
by dismembering, or any other way not touching life, as they
shall think fit; and if such slave shall die by means of such
dismembering, no forfeiture or punishment shall be thereby
incurred." [32]

The Virginia act of 1753 (22 George II, Cap. 7) altered
and extended some of the previous laws. By this act, all
servants (except convicts), who had been imported without
articles of indenture, were to serve a period of servitude of
not more than five years. Every owner was obliged to care
for sick or lame servants during the whole period of service.
If servants did not obey their owners' " just and lawful commands, and resist or offer violence to master, mistress or
overseer," a year more of servitude was to be added for each
offense. In cases of violations of penal laws in which free
persons were punishable by fine, servants were to be punished by whipping, " after the rate of twenty lashes for every
five hundred pounds of tobacco or fifty shillings current

[30] " Virginia Laws " (Edition of 1759), p. 314.
[31] Ibid., 316. The meaning of the letters " P. G." is not stated in the
statute.
[32] Ibid., 319.

money." But no servant was to get more than forty lashes
at one time.[33]

After having served their years of laborious servitude,
the servants, men and women, were cold-bloodedly turned out
in an impoverished condition, with nothing more than a few
articles allowed by law, and perhaps a few bits of money; but
money was scarce, tobacco largely being used in Maryland
and Virginia as currency. Frequently during their terms of
service, servants were forced to undergo a change of masters,
at least in Virginia; when planters fell in debt it was common
for them to sell their land and servants.[34] The most vigorous
part of the laborer's life was given in compulsory service to
the master; and usually after the expiration of his term of
servitude, his vitality was impaired, and he had no means of
securing subsistence. In custom and law he occupied a de-
graded position, from which in the South, at least, is derived
the old contemptuous sneer at " white trash." The best and
most valuable lands in the accessible portion of the country
had already been preëmpted by adventurous individuals,
manorial lords or planters who had acquired them by the
means described in the foregoing chapter. The poor white
owned nothing to speak of, and was virtually allowed to own
nothing; his situation was a dire one.

Houses of Correction and Workhouses.

The inevitable consequence was a quick and direct creation
of a destitute class. Many, incapable of working longer, or
filled with great repulsion because of their hard labor under
servitude, wandered pathetically about and became what were
called vagabonds; others took to theft or drink; still others
to begging; and the prostitution of women was early in evidence. How did the lawmakers meet these conditions?

They began to establish houses of correction and work-

[33] *Ibid.,* pp. 326–329.
[34] So stated in a broadside published at the time.

houses. By the Massachusetts act of 1646, houses of correction were ordered, and magistrates were required to commit to those institutions runaway servants, "idle persons, common drunkards and common night walkers," and to provide materials of work.[35] The act of 1699 of the same colony made more effective provision for houses of correction and workhouses, and the putting to work in those institutions of "rogues, vagabonds, common beggars and other lewd, idle and disorderly persons." For such as were stubborn and declined to work, ten lashes or a starvation diet were prescribed.[36]

The Massachusetts act of 1720, as we have seen, compelled the setting to work, or the bonding out, of all children of the poor. The New Hampshire act of 13 Anne decreed that any Indian, negro or mulatto servant found abroad, without satisfactory excuse, after nine o'clock at night was to be locked up in the house of correction, and returned to the master next morning. If the arrest happened to be in a place where there was no house of correction, then a lashing of ten stripes was to be given by the constable in place of imprisonment.[37] The Connecticut laws approximated those of Massachusetts and New Hampshire. The Rhode Island code of 1647 ordered each town to provide for the relief of the poor, maintain the impotent, and employ the able under an overseer.[38] But an order followed three years later — in 1650 — requiring that any man not having more than £5 could be adjudged a pauper, and treated legally as a pauper.[39]

The acts of Pennsylvania of May 31, 1718, August 19, 1749, and those of other years dealt with the establishment of measures for the relief of the poor. Beginning with a pre-

---

[35] "Ancient Charters and Laws of Massachusetts Bay," etc., 178.
[36] *Ibid.*, 334–338.
[37] "New Hampshire Acts And Laws" (Fowler's Edition of 1761), p. 41.
[38] "Rhode Island Colonial Records, 1636–1663," Vol. I: 184–185.
[39] *Ibid.*, 227.

amble that the poor within the city of Philadelphia and adjacent parts " are becoming very burthensome and expensive to the inhabitants," the Pennsylvania act of February 8, 1766, incorporated a society to be called, " Contributors to the Relief and Employment of the Poor in the City of Philadelphia." [40] The same act tells that whereas " great numbers of rogues, vagabonds and other idle and dissolute persons frequently come from the neighboring provinces to the said city, without following any labor, trade or business, or having any visible means of subsistence, and are not only dangerous members of society, but in the end become burthensome to the Publick "— therefore, they are to be committed to the House of Employment to be kept at hard labor for three months.[41]

Early in the settlement of New York, the idle and beggars became so numerous, that acts were passed on November 1, 1683, and on May 13, 1691, providing poorhouses for the maintenance of the poor and for the preventing of " vagabonds, beggars, idle persons, and those without manual crafts "; these laws made a special provision for beggars, requiring their deportation to towns from which they came.[42]

Badges of Degradation for the Poor.

But of all the colonies, the poor laws of Virginia, as in the case of servants and slaves, were the harshest. The poor were forced to wear the most humiliating and visible tokens of their degrading poverty. The act of 1748 (22 George II, Cap. 1, sect. 5) turned the poor over to the supervisor of the church parishes which were required to build houses for their

[40] Carey and Bioren's " Pa. Laws, 1700–1770," Vol. I : 417–419.
[41] *Ibid.*, 423–424. The succeeding law of March 9, 1771, said that the laws theretofore enacted had not answered " the good purposes expected."— *Ibid.*, Vol. II : 1.
[42] " Laws of The Colony of New York," pp. 131 and 237. The presence of beggars entailed expense and annoyance; accordingly each town sought to rid itself of them by driving them from its limits.

lodging and employment. The parishes were to provide cotton, hemp, flax and other materials for the setting of the poor at work. If inmates did not behave according to the rules, or were refractory, corporal punishment was to be administered, not exceeding ten lashes at a time for each offense. The vestries were allowed to dispose of the profits of the poor's work, and were to be held accountable.

By this law every such poor person was compelled " in an open and visible manner " to wear on the right sleeve of his or her upper garment a badge with the name of the parish (to which he or she belonged) cut in blue, red or green cloth. If the poor under supervision neglected or refused to obey, the church warden could punish by abridging the allowance of the offender to the slimmest possible diet, and apply not more than five lashes at one time for each offense. This act was to.be enforced in all of the courts.[43]

Violations of laws prohibiting the acquiring or conveying of land by fraud entailed, as we have seen, only a nominal money penalty. Not often, of course, were these laws enforced; the officials who made, interpreted and enforced them were mainly themselves involved in the grossest land frauds, or their influential friends were. Before the Revolution, judges in some of the colonies received no fee or reward; they were composed exclusively of manorial lords and other men of fortune and estates. When destitute workers resorted to theft they were punished under a code of the most barbaric laws designed to protect the property of the possessing class.

Barbaric Punishment for Offenses.

For burglary or robbing from any house or from any person on the highways, the Massachusetts act of 1642 imposed these penalties:

---

[43] " Virginia Laws " (Edition of 1759), pp. 282–286.

For the first offense the letter B was to be branded on the offender's forehead; he was to be again branded and severely whipped for the second offense; and for the third he was to be put to death. If the crime were committed on the Sabbath he was, in addition to branding, to suffer one ear to be cut off for the first offense; the second offense was to entail the cutting off of the other ear; and death was to be the penalty for the third offense.[44] The act of 1692 provided branding for the first offense; for the second, the culprit was to be set upon the gallows, neck in rope for an hour, and thirty-nine lashes were to be given. The third offense brought death.[45] Theft increased in Massachusetts, and the act of 1715, entailing the death penalty, was intended to decrease crime.[46] But it had no such effect. In 1770 an act was passed imposing death without benefit of clergy for entering a dwelling house at night with intent to steal.[47] The Rhode Island code of 1647 decreed death for burglary committed by all more than fourteen years of age. But the qualification was added that this clause did not extend to "poor persons that steale for Hunger, nor to fooles, nor to madd men." In the cases of such persons as, also, in the cases of those under fourteen years old, the crime was held to be larceny.[48]

What was the punishment for larceny? For the petty larceny of goods not exceeding twelve pence, the offender was to be "well whipt" for the first offense; for the second he was to serve two months in the House of Correction and be twice whipped.

Grand larceny included the theft of anything more than twelve pence in value. The first offense brought a severe whipping, and a term in the house of correction. The sec-

[44] "Ancient Charters and Laws of Massachusetts Bay," etc., p. 56.
[45] *Ibid.*, 239.
[46] *Ibid.*, 407.
[47] *Ibid.*, 669.
[48] "Rhode Island Colonial Records, 1636–1663," Vol. I: 167. This act was an explicit admission that many of the poor were compelled to steal, driven to it by hunger. Begging and other such crimes were generally prompted by the same incentive of self-preservation.

ond resulted in branding in the hand, and a sentence of imprisonment until the convicted person paid twice the amount to the party wronged, and four times the sum to the Colony [49] — which, assuredly, he never could.

The Quaker punishment for larceny in Pennsylvania was very much the same as that of the New England Puritans. Section XXIX of the Pennsylvania act of 1718, " for the advancement of justice," enacted that for larceny, first offense, the offender must restore goods or chattels, pay the costs of the prosecution, go to jail, and be publicly whipped on the bare back with stripes "well laid on, not exceeding twenty-one." The second offense brought the same penalties, with a public whipping of from twenty-five to forty stripes.[50]

Imprisonment of Debtors.

Such are some examples of the laws in the various colonies. But other laws in force bore heavily on the wage working laborer. In all the colonies laws were passed and enforced for the imprisonment of debtors. These laws were not in so many words specifically directed at the poor, but it was exclusively upon the laborers that their application fell. Falling in debt because of misfortune, or because of the extortions of landlord and tradesman,[51] the worker was summarily despatched to jail, and remained there under rigorous and wretched circumstances, unless he chose to avail himself of the alternative the law presented. This alternative was that the imprisoned worker could make satisfaction for his debts by pledging himself in servitude to his creditors.

[49] " Rhode Island Colonial Records, 1636–1663," Vol. I: 174.
[50] Carey and Bioren's " Pa. Laws, 1700–1770," Vol. I: 143.
[51] As has been noted, the tenants of the manorial lords and masters were covenanted to trade and buy exclusively at his stores. The owner was able to exact such prices as he pleased, with the result that tenants invariably were in debt. When it suited the particular interest or other motive of the owner to put the tenant in jail, he did so. See also Chapter III of this work showing the enormous prices exacted by merchants.

That those having property not only escaped the enforcement of these laws, but tried to pervert them fraudulently to
their own purposes is clearly shown, for example, in a Pennsylvania act, passed in the year 1730. Reciting that the prior
law contained no provision compelling the debtor to render
any account of his or her estate, the act went on to say that
" great abuses had been committed by persons claiming the
benefit of the law, in concealing their estates and making
them over in trust " [52]— thus revealing that Quaker professions of " brotherly love " went sadly astray when in conflict
with economic interest. This act declared that debtors should
render accounts; and, among other provisions, it gave landlords the right to recover up to one year's rent, by seizure of
imprisoned debtors' goods and chattels. The jailor, also, was
to rank as a creditor for his fees, but jailors, bailiffs and
others guilty of extortion were to be punished.[53]

But the abuses heaped upon the workers continued, as is
evident from the preamble of a Pennsylvania act adopted in
the year 1745. This act, " for the easy and speedy recovery
of small debts " began by saying that " it is found by experience that a great number of the lawsuits which are commenced in this province, are brought against the poorer sort
of people for small sums of money, who are unable to bear
the expenses arising by the common method of prosecution."
Although reducing the costs of actions two-thirds, this law
really made it easier for landlords and traders to collect from
small debtors; if the debts were not paid, the law decreed
imprisonment.[54]

The Existing Contrasts.

In all the colonies, but more markedly so in the South, there
were thus, broadly speaking, two classes, each the extreme and
the antithesis of the other.

[52] *Ibid.*, 232-247.   [53] *Ibid.*   [54] *Ibid.*, 278.

The various strata of the workers, as defined by law and usage, comprised one class. Hemmed in by harsh statutes, and oppressed by the power of a class invested with the full force of law and wealth, and construing those laws to their uttermost limits, the workers found themselves in a situation from which it seemed impossible to extricate themselves. In dress and living, as in other ways, the most obviously striking distinction was compelled between worker and master.

Attired in clothes of the coarsest materials, betokening plainly his occupation, lowliness and menial condition, the worker moved about in an environment surcharged with the suspicion and undisguised scorn of those who owned his labor, and often his life. Such little consideration as was afforded by law to prevent too brutal treatment of him was not because he was esteemed human. It arose, not always, but on the whole, from the aim of the more far-seeing of the master class to preserve his efficiency at the highest level possible.

Resplendent in gold and silver lace and buttons, delicate laces and fine apparel, his sword pendant on his embroidered belt always conspicuous, the master was a very different appearing person from the bent, clodded worker whom he looked down upon and treated with a haughty distrust and arrogance that awoke the bitterest but inarticulate resentment. The rude little tenant cottages or huts in which the slave, servant or laborer existed, grouped, as those mean habitations often were, about the manorial or plantation mansion, formed the sharpest contrast with the elegant style in which the master luxuriated. This environment in Virginia is described by Jefferson in his " Memoirs ":

" At the time of the first settlement of the English in Virginia, when land was had for little or nothing, some provident persons having obtained large grants of it, and being desirous of maintaining the splendor of their families, entailed their property upon their descendants. The transmission of these estates from generation to generation, to men who bore the same name, had the effect of raising up a distinct class of families, who, possessing by law the privilege of perpetuating their wealth, formed by these means a sort of patrician order, distinguished by the grandeur and luxury of their establishments. From this order it was that the king usually chose his counsellor of state."

It was then, much more than now, the fashionable mark of a gentleman not to " degrade " himself by labor of any kind; and the leisure of his rank in the South was considered to be well and truly signified by spending his time in hunting, athletic sports, carousing, dissipating, gambling,[55] and in social festivities — or, in the case of many of the " gentlemen " past youth by making a foible of reading, music and study and a science of debauchery. Some few there were who applied themselves seriously to such mental development as their environment and interests allowed; and these became the most astute representatives of their class.

In New England, it was the fashionable part of a gentleman to affect church patronization, which religious ardor, however, did not prevent his gratifying his appetite for some very unorthodox practices. The barriers separating classes and grades of classes in New York and New England almost approached the rigid precision in the South. At the base were the slaves, during the period in which Indian or negro slavery was in existence there. Then came the indentured servants; then the free laborers; after them the mechanics; then the yeomen or small farmers, above whom were the small merchants or traders. The next stratum was the professional class. Above these towered the gentlemen mer-

[55] A gentleman in the South lost caste if he did not gamble profusely and for high stakes. In Virginia and Maryland the stakes were usually tobacco. Thus, for example, one Beverly, during minorship, lost 25,000 pounds of tobacco to one Smith, and Smith sued to recover. See case on appeal of Buckner and other trustees of Beverly vs. Smith *et al.* Washington's Virginia Reports, Vol. I: 296.

chants or shippers, comprising those of wealth and large commercial operations. At the apex stood the lords of great estates, or royal officials, both often in one category.

Between these classes — or " orders " as they were termed — sharp lines of recognized caste were drawn. Whether at pious ceremonies in church or at public meetings, people were ranged in order of precedence according to their station. Up to the time of the Revolution students in Harvard College, according to Thwaites, were catalogued and regarded purely in the order of their social rank; and even after the actual custom was dropped the spirit long persisted. Each " order " was expected to look up to that above it, and all of the " lower orders " were called upon to yield the most reverential respect and obedience to the upper class.

The fashions, views and prejudices of the master class were absorbed, and in application even exceeded, by the professional men of whom the rich were clients. Some of the lawyers themselves sprang from the ruling class. With but the fewest and most creditable exceptions, all others of that profession sought to ingratiate themselves into the favor of the rich by flattering, pleasing and serving them with an excess of zeal in stamping down the worker still further by statutes ingeniously borrowed from mediæval law, or by harrowing the worker in the courts with lawsuits in which these attorneys by every subtle argument appealed to the prejudices of the judge, already antagonistic to the worker and prejudiced against him. Even if the judge, perchance, were impartially and leniently disposed, the laws, as they were, left him no choice. Reading the suits and speeches of the times, one sees clearly that the lawyers of the masters outdid even their clients in asserting the masters' lordly, paramount rights and powers, and in denying that any rights attached to the under class. This lickspittle subservience to their clients was subsequently, as we shall have abundant occasion to observe, transferred to the bench of the Supreme Court of the United States with the most far-reaching results.

Development of Native Manufacturing.

While the landlords and traders were thus enacting law after law causing or affirming the servitude and practical vilenage of the working people of every kind, they were themselves making profits in the exercise of the most fraudulent operations in trade. The very debts for which the worker was imprisoned were often claimed for bills for adulterated or otherwise spurious merchandise.

Landlord and trader were often the one and the same person; not so much the petty landlord, who owned a lot or two in the cities, but the lords of the great plantations and manorial estates.[56]   They, or their agents, traded with the Indians for furs, which were exported to Europe; they sold and exported the timber and lumber from their domains; from the estates along the seashore and rivers were exported great quantities of fish, especially to Roman Catholic countries; they had their grist mills, breweries and other industries. And out of the planter class developed a manufacturing class — not manufacturing in the modern factory sense, but an industry in which commodities were made by hand by bonded servants, slaves and wage workers.   A broadside published at the time [57] said that the wars in Europe had hurt the tobacco trade so much and had so reduced the planters " that for several years past the whole product of their tobacco would hardly clothe the servants that made it.   Some of the Planters," the broadside went on, " in hopes of better Success, have continued planting, till they have run themselves so far in debt,

[56] They were then called plantations in New England, as well as in the South.

[57] " The Present State of the Tobacco Plantations In America."   The exact date of this broadside is uncertain.

that they have been forced to sell part of their Land and Servants, to secure the rest.   Others, out of meer Necessity, have fallen into the manufacturing of Woolen, Cotton, Flax, Leather," and various other enumerated classes of goods, which, said the broadside, they had brought to great perfection.   Here we see the beginning of that manufacturing which later was to be so important a factor.

Debauching of Indians and Other Traders' Frauds.

So firmly established and so widespread early in the seventeenth century was the practice on the part of white traders of debauching and cheating the Indians, that in the " Certain Conditions or Concessions," agreed upon by William Penn in connection with his charter, in July, 1681, before he left England, this provision was inserted:

" Twelfthly.   And forasmuch as it is usual with the planters to over-reach the poor natives of the country in trade, by goods not being good of the kind, or debased with mixtures, upon which they are sensibly aggrieved, it is agreed, whatever is sold to the Indians, in consideration of their furs, shall be sold in the market place, and there suffer the test, whether good or bad; if good, to pass; if not good, not to be sold for good, that the natives may not be abused nor provoked." [58]

However sincere Penn may have been in seeking to prevent in Pennsylvania the debauching and swindling of Indians going on shamelessly in other colonies, the agreement was of absolutely no effect.   Quaker traders, not less than Puritan and Southern traders elsewhere, profited from the practice, and pushed it to such an extent that on May 22, 1722, a law was enacted in Pennsylvania prohibiting the selling of rum and other strong liquors to the Indians and " to prevent abuses that may happen thereby." [59]   Later acts for the pre-

[58] Carey and Bioren's " Pa. Laws," Vol. VI, Appendix, p. 10.
[59] Ibid., Vol. I: 87.

vention of these widespread abuses were passed on April 8, 1758, April 17, 1759, and April 2, 1763.[60]

The very liquor sold to the Indians and whites was adulterated. To prevent "fraud in mixing and adulterating rum, brandy, or such like spirits," a law was enacted in Pennsylvania in the year 1705.[61] An act passed in 1722 prohibited the use of unwholesome materials in making beer;[62] and these acts were reënforced by another act passed in 1723. Such fraudulent practices extended to other lines of trade in Pennsylvania; a fact that is of no little significance, seeing that that colony,— later State — became one of the foremost in manufacturing in the United States.

An act, passed in 1759, was designed " to prevent the exportation of bad or unmerchantable staves, beading boards and timber "; many abuses and frauds, the act said, went on in the exportation of stuffs to the foreign markets.[63] The decline in the export trade of shad and herring led to the passage of an act, in 1774, to prevent frauds in the packing and preserving of those goods for exportation.[64] The export of fish from the New England fisheries — comparatively large at the time, gradually fell off for the same reason, as official reports later showed.

Large fortunes were accumulated by ship owners from the export of fish, timber, tobacco, furs, corn, rice, manufactured products and other commodities and in the return importation of negro slaves and merchandise. These fortunes, and the men who acquired or inherited them, had the greatest influence in determining both the declaration and the course of the Revolution, the fashioning of the Constitution of the United States, the drafting of the State Constitutions, and the laws of

[60] *Ibid.,* p. 343, etc.
[61] *Ibid.,* 60. Evidently the Quaker lawmakers were much concerned for themselves in demanding strong drink; there was much mixing of water with rum, brandy, etc., the act complained.
[62] *Ibid.,* 166.
[63] *Ibid.,* 347–352.
[64] *Ibid.,* Vol. II : 122.

Congress; and some of them, as we shall see later, had their direct influence and their representatives upon the bench of the Supreme Court of the United States.   These wealthy shippers had a positive and keen personal interest in seeking to continue the actual substance — even if the form of government were .changed — of the conditions from which they profited.   But it was the conditions as a whole so conducive to the benefit of the predominating landed interests, with the allied but subordinate trading class, that prepared the way for later events to be now described.

CHAPTER III

THE REAL FORCES OF THE REVOLUTION AND THE DRAFTERS OF THE CONSTITUTION

The American Revolution of 1776 did not proceed from any intrinsic popular impetus for national independence. On the part of the intelligent elements of the working class, conscious of the oppression to which they were subjected, there had long been a smoldering sense of revolt; but it was a revolt against the tyranny of the manorial lords and other masters. At times it had broken out into spasmodic and abortive uprisings, which, necessarily local in their scope, had been speedily put down, and the leaders imprisoned or executed.

These outbreaks were not against British laws and exactions; they arose from conditions in Dutch, as well as in British, colonies. The laws weighing so intensely upon the various grades of the working population were, in general principle, imitated from the European codes, chiefly the British. In special character and adaptation, however, they were of native make. They were demanded, drafted and enlarged by the manorial lords and merchants in the colonial councils and legislatures, and enforced by officials of the same class. The remonstrances of the settlers to Lord Bellomont and Governor Wright revealed how, when a favorable occasion came, appeals for relief were made over the heads of the legislatures direct to the British Government.

The Revolution was declared by a combination of powerful men of the day — even then styled in official proclamations as capitalists — controlling much of the valuable natural resources and their products. Some of these dissatisfied mili-

73

tant personages were owners of vast estates; others were disgruntled shippers or merchants united, and with very good reason, by a common economic interest in seeking to secure control of a political state by means of which they could assist the development of trade and manufacture unshackled by the paralyzing laws ordained by the British trading class. These various groups were more or less interrelated by property interest and often by marriage; and all were agreed upon the distinct aim of vesting in themselves the power to acquire unlimited areas of the public domain unhampered by restrictive British laws and regulations.

Attached to the Revolutionary movement because of its supposed potentialities for bringing about an alteration of laws promising political freedom and social equality, were sincere, pecuniarily disinterested radicals. Making allowance for what proved to be alluring and empty phrases conceded by the men of large property to appease and move the multitude, the purposes of these radicals were entirely subverted, and their plans circumvented.

It is not the intention here to enter into a detailed narrative of the Revolution, nor to present any other facts than those strictly necessary to elucidating the subject of this work. To get a right understanding of subsequent events, a clear, logical summary of the genuine acts of the Revolution and of its sponsors and directors, is a necessary prelude. A chain of hitherto unpublished and illuminating facts herein set forth — facts significantly omitted from approved conventional histories — will serve to explain the real outcome of the Revolution and will show which class it was intended exclusively to benefit. These facts will also reveal the actual nature of the forces drafting the Constitution of the United States, and so vigorously pushing its adoption. Furthermore — what, at present, is more important — the facts in question will open a hitherto unsuspected vista through which may be seen in all their significance some of the real motives and

interests underlying and actuating the Supreme Court of the
United States from its very foundation.

Unlimited Areas of Land Sought.

American land proprietors, and adventurers seeking large
grants, had long been impatient with acts of king or Parliament placing limitations upon the area of land to be granted.

The bitter conflict that Lord Bellomont had with some of
them, his relentless exposure of their briberies, and the altered laws resulting, left lasting memories of resentment.
Most of the royal viceregents could be reached by bribery or
other insidious influences, but there was always imminent danger of the advent of an honest official like Bellomont.   The
successive kings and queens found the granting of immense
estates in America an inexpensive method of rewarding favorites.

Parliament and the Boards of Trade and of Plantations,
however, were more concerned with the general broad principle of colonization, and with developing a trade calculated
to increase the wealth of the aristocracy and traders of England, and with conserving the interests of both classes, who
regarded America as a prime field for exploitation.   The interests of the American landowners and shippers profited by
the shipping of supplies of timber, fish, tobacco and other
commodities, often fraudulent in some respect or other.   The
British traders complained of this widespread fraud; and thus
it is we find the records of Parliament in the seventeenth century numerously sprinkled with acts prohibiting fraud in the
exportation from America of this or that merchandise.

Pursuing their projects for wealth three thousand miles
across the Atlantic, at a time when news from Britain three
months old was fresh news, in a country being newly opened,
the land proprietors, for the most part, did not see why they
should respect this interference.   Between them and the trad-

ers of England the seeds of an economic conflict early developed. This conflict gathered new and important auxiliaries in the shippers and manufacturers. Timber was abundant in America, and with bonded labor, slaves and low-paid mechanics, ships could be built cheaply and rapidly. A great number of ships were constructed, and profitable cargoes were at hand. Hard by the iron deposits that were discovered, furnaces and foundries were erected; part of the abundance of furs was used for the manufacture of hats, and another part exported in the raw state. Planters, as we have seen, began to utilize their bonded and slave labor in the manufacture of linen and cotton cloth from the cotton and flax cheaply raised on new and fertile soil by the same labor. The wool of the flocks of sheep was turned into woolen cloth, and the hides of the cattle into leather goods. The trade of the colonies became world-wide.

These products made lucrative cargoes for the shippers, and supplied an expanding market for the manufacturing planters. But so fast were ships built, that the need for ever-increasing cargoes arose. The American shippers more and more resented the monopoly of the importation of tea granted by the British Government to the East India Company — tea then being in wide use. Conveying their cargoes to Europe, the American ships brought back cargoes of negro slaves from Africa, but the owners also wanted a share in the return transportation of tea and other commodities.

British Traders Strike at American.

During the same period England was becoming a more extensive manufacturing country; in its insular situation, with a fairly dense population dependent upon its industries and foreign trade, its trading class was compelled to bend every effort toward suppressing the threatening American competition. Consequently, Parliament, representing those interests, passed act after act designed to crush the American manufacturer, and cripple the American shipping trade.

Various laws prohibited the exportation of hats, and the sale in one colony of hats made in another; iron mills were forbidden; in fact everything that could be made from natural resources was legislated against. A heavy duty was put upon the importation of molasses, then extensively employed in making rum, and also used by fishermen; onerous duties were also put upon tea, nails, glass and paints. The shippers, some of whom individually owned three score ships, attempted to evade these regulations by smuggling, but they were confronted by another set of British laws, enforced by vigilant British officials.

From this conflict of trading interests between the trading class of Great Britain, and that of the American colonies, the American Revolution was born. It was estimated that probably nine-tenths of all the tea, wine, fruit, sugar and molasses consumed in the colonies were smuggled. The tea used in the colonies reached alone an item of $2,500,000 annually. Thomas Hancock, the greater part of whose fortune of £70,000 John Hancock inherited, gathered the larger part of it illicitly in the Dutch tea trade; and in the " Historical Essay," prefaced to his voluminous mass of biographical details in his " Loyalists of the American Revolution," Sabine says that immediately before the Revolution was declared, John Hancock was respondent in the Admiralty Court, in suits of the crown, to recover nearly half a million dollars as penalties for smuggling.

The greatest offending port in the practice of smuggling was Boston; there the British Government stationed twelve warships. At least a fourth of the signers of the Declaration of Independence were traders, or both shippers and landholders; more than one of them, Sabine says, was branded with the epithet of smuggler. Among the signers of the Declaration of Independence these were some of those having large shipping interests: John Hancock, John Langdon, Samuel Adams, William Whipple, George Clymer, Stephen Hopkins, Francis Lewis, Philip Livingston, Elbridge Gerry, Joseph Hewes, George Taylor, Roger Sherman, Henry Laurens and Robert Morris.

Americans Agitate for Native Factories.

In 1774, many of the conventions of deputies of the various colonies, composed, as those assemblies were, of landowners, merchants and lawyers, passed resolutions denouncing the monopoly of tea granted to, and exercised by, the East India Company, and demanding the establishment of native manufactories.

The Maryland convention of deputies, meeting at Annapolis, December 8 to 12, 1774, adopted a series of resolutions. To increase flocks of sheep and to promote the manufacture of wool in Maryland, the killing of lambs ought to be restricted. For the increasing of the manufacture of linen and cotton, every planter was advised to raise as much flax, hemp and cotton as he conveniently could. Then, referring to the general boycott placed on certain British goods, followed this illuminating resolution, which in itself supplies the clearest index as to why it was so great a number of workers were constantly being imprisoned for debt:

"One general rule, allowing a reasonable profit to the trader and preventing him from taking advantage of the scarcity of goods which may be occasioned by the non-importation would give great satisfaction to the merchants and people of this province, Resolved unanimously:

"That no merchant ought to sell his goods at wholesale for more than one hundred and twelve and a half per cent.; — at retail, for cash, for more than thirteen per cent.; — on credit, for more than one hundred and fifty per cent. on the prime cost; and that no merchant, or other person, ought to

engross [monopolize] any goods, wares, or merchandise whatsoever. . . ."[1]

If these rates of profit were considered "reasonable," what
was to be said of the previous prices exacted from the workers, the condition of most of whom forced them to buy on
credit?

In providing for military companies with the not far-dis-
tant plan of resisting England, this convention, as was to be
expected, ignored the common man because it feared him
under arms, and declared:

"Resolved, unanimously, That a well regulated militia, composed of the gentlemen, freeholders and other freemen is the
natural strength and only stable security of a free government,"— therefore, it was recommended to that class of inhabitants, between the ages of sixteen and fifty, that they
should form themselves into military companies.[2]

At the same time the other colonies were passing similar
resolutions. Those adopted by the Massachusetts Convention
of Deputies at Boston, on December 8, 1774, were the most
extensive and ambitious. In addition to calling for the establishment of woolen and cotton mills, it also recommended
measures for the creation of manufactories for making steel,
tinplates, fire-arms, saltpeter, paper, buttons, stockings and
other enumerated commodities.[3]

Run the Factories with Woman and Child Labor.

The purpose of these nascent capitalists[4] are to be seen

[1] Niles' "Principles and Acts of the Revolution in America; A
Collection of Speeches, Orations and Proceedings. . . . And Other
Fugitive or Neglected Pieces" (Edition of 1822), p. 131. It is a ques-
tion whether the "thirteen per cent." quoted above is correctly given by
Niles.

[2] Ibid., 182. A freeholder was one who owned a prescribed amount
of property.

[3] Ibid.

[4] Those who may think that the word capitalist is a fairly modern
coined word, are advised to consult the old British and Spanish royal
colonial proclamations, in which the word was frequently used.

clearly in the report of the proceedings of a company formed in Philadelphia for the establishment of woolen, cotton and linen manufactories. An elaborate account of a speech delivered at a meeting of this company at Carpenters' Hall, Philadelphia, on March 16, 1775, is to be found in Niles' "Principles and Acts of the Revolution in America." It does not specify the name of the company, nor does it give the name of the promoter who made the long speech, but it says that the account given was published at the time by request of the company.

Obscurely published, that speech is invested to-day with an historic importance because of the conditions it foretold.

The speaker dwelt at considerable length upon the great riches to be derived from the establishment of manufactories, and he described the factories of Great Britain as "the foundation of her riches and power. They have made her merchants nobles, and her nobles princes." He then proceeded to consider in turn each of the objections advanced against the foundation of factories.

The plan of the company, he said, was to employ the poor, "and the principal part of the business was to be carried on in their houses." Here, evidently, was the origin of the sweatshop system, at least in conjunction with the factory system. A certain portion of the work could be done in the homes of the poor, but the age of machinery had arrived, and factory buildings were quite necessary. The colonies were largely of an agricultural character; there was much apprehension that factories would absorb men who were wanted as tillers of the soil. The speaker went on to dissipate these fears of the large landholders. As to where the labor was to come from he said that in England the greater number of factory "hands" had been taken from the plow. But there would be little nead of such a drain in America. "Besides," he went on, "if these manufactories are conducted as they ought to be, *two-thirds of the labor of them will be carried on by those members of society who cannot be employed in agriculture, namely, by women and children."* [5]

Continuing, the speaker considered other objections. " A second objection," he said, " is, that we cannot manufacture cloths so cheap here, as they can be imported from Britain. It has been the misfortune of most of the manufactories which have been set up in this country, to afford labor to journeymen, only for six or nine months in the year, by which means their wages have necessarily been so high as to support them in the intervals of their labor. It will be found, upon inquiry, that those manufactories which occupy journeymen the whole year, are carried on at as cheap a rate as they are in Britain. The expense of manufacturing cloth will be lessened from *the great share women and children will have in them;* and I have the pleasure of informing you that the machine lately brought into this city for lessening the expense of time and hands in spinning is likely to meet with encouragement from the Legislature of our province. In a word the experiments which have already been made among us convince us that woolens and linens of all kinds may be made and bought as cheap as those imported from Britain, and I believe everyone who has tried the former will acknowledge that they wear twice as well as the latter.

" A third objection to manufactories is that they destroy health and are hurtful to population. The same may be said of navigation, and many other arts which are essential to the happiness and glory of a State. I believe that many of the diseases to which the manufacturers [factory workers] in Britain are subject, are brought on, not so much by the nature of their employment, but by their unwholesome diet, damp houses and other bad accommodations, each of which may be prevented in America." [6]

[5] Niles' " Principles and Acts of the Revolution In America," etc., p. 205. The italics are mine.— G. M.
[6] *Ibid.*

This meeting was held, and this project expounded, more than a year before the drafting and adoption of the principles embodied in the Declaration of Independence. Here we perceive the industrial capitalist class at work at its very birth calmly setting out to promote its wealth and power on the bodies of women and children. We see, also, that the plan was no vague, dimly defined one, but an alert, already matured, determined one of competing with England, and operating the machines, with the very cheapest labor obtainable — that of women and children. If former agricultural laborers did the factory work cheap in England, women and children would do it cheaper here, thus outdoing the capitalist class of England in cheapness of labor.

This was the plan resolved upon before the overt beginning of the Revolution, which pretended to act upon the principle that all men were born free and equal. And these facts must give a shock even to radical writers who, without tracing the origin of woman and child labor to its iniquitous source, have maintained that it was originally somewhat of an accidental development. This plan decided upon, it was easy to conscript women and children from the workhouses and houses of correction or arrange accommodations with the overseers of the poor into whose absolute jurisdiction the poor laws then placed the children of the poor.

Masses of men, having no interest in trade, and, in fact, cherishing well-founded grievances against those who by controlling the courses of trade control the destinies of men, will not fight simply to extend trade. A far stronger incentive than sordid gain is necessary to arouse popular imagination, daring and enthusiasm. So the landed, shipping and trading groups soon discovered. The more perspicacious of them saw that to stir the required ardor and to enroll volunteers, it was essential to make the mass believe that they were to fight for undying progressive principles for their own advancement and welfare, and that all should have a share in property. The associations, called patriotic societies, supplied a small number of volunteers of their own rank, but composed as they were, of certain landowners, traders, and large or small merchants, the greater part of their members remained at home to put through great land acquisitions under cover of the Revolution, or to profit from financial or trade operations at the expense and sacrifice of the Continental army and of the nation. The famous "Sons of Liberty" of New York were composed of middle-class merchants, one of whom, William Mooney, later founded the Society of "St." Tammany — the Tammany Hall of the future.

Inspiring Slogans for the Mass.

As a means of inciting popular temper and winning faith, the associated governing classes now professed to take up some of the very doctrines for the advocacy of which, previously, they or their ancestors had punished men with prison sentences or summary execution.

Clause I of the Bill of Rights of Pennsylvania asserted: "That all men are born equally free and independent, and have certain natural, inherent and inalienable rights, amongst which are the enjoying and defending life and liberty, *acquiring, possessing and protecting property,* and pursuing and obtaining happiness and safety." [7] In various forms other colonies asserted the same.

But the landowners, shippers, traders and lawyers, composing the majority who adopted the Declaration of Independence, apparently decided not to allow so momentous a declaration to receive the stamp of their authority. Giving the people the form, and smothering the substance, they omitted the all-important doctrine that every man was entitled to acquire and own property, and they left in the Declaration the meaningless phrase that every man was entitled to

---

[7] Carey and Bioren's "Pa. Laws," Vol. VI, Appendix, p. 30.

life, liberty and the pursuit of happiness. They were not ignorant of the fact that to live and enjoy life, the means of subsistence must first be assured; the prospect, however, of a surrender of their own caste, powers and privileges, a curtailment of the projects many of them had in mind and soon carried out, and the entrance of democracy into the affairs of government, affrighted them.

That the Revolution was essentially and definitely a traders' rebellion for liberty of trade to get what they wanted, make what they willed, and sell where they could, no small proportion of the workers were fully sensible. To get recruits, desperate action was found necessary. At the instigation of the merchants, small guerrilla mobs were repeatedly organized to terrorize and coerce the passive, unwilling or antagonistic. Bounties, then considered enormous, were held out as inducements for enlistment; the price (in paper) for a single recruit was, according to Sabine, as high sometimes as $750 and $1,000 on enlistment for the war, and the donation, in addition, of land bounties and emoluments by Congress. It was these inducements that brought into the Revolutionary army so large a number of foreigners.

On the other hand, although many of the great landholders from varying motives of self-interest, pushed forward the Revolution, there were other great landowners, who, having no interest in trade, and having benefited well under British rule, by the corrupt use of which they, as officials, had got their estates, did not desire a revolution. These pro-British landholders organized whole battalions, and even regiments, of Americans to fight in the royal army, and personally paid their expenses throughout the war.

Once the Revolution was satisfactorily under way, and a sufficiency of the people were deluded by the phrases handed out, or coerced into action, and absorbed by the war, the real promoters of the Revolution, backed by all the power of the governing class, proceeded on two special lines of policy. These were carried on at the same time, and both with the most immediate success.

Propertyless Disqualified from Voting.

The first of these operations was to counteract and annul in every possible way the dangerous agitation to confer equal rights on all. At the very height of the Revolution, State constitutions were adopted, depriving the propertyless of any voice in the government. Realizing what a popular impression the promise of equal rights made, Article I of the Massachusetts Convention of 1780 began with the clause that among the rights of all men was "that of acquiring, possessing and protecting their property." [8]

This was a palpable catchword and counterfeit. In the text of the Constitution itself, a strict property qualification for voters was established. No person was allowed to become a State Senator who did not have a freehold in the Commonwealth of £300 at least, or a minimum personal estate of £600.[9] Only men having a freehold estate in Massachusetts of an annual income of £3, or any estate of the value of £60, could vote for a State senator.[10] To be eligible for election to the Massachusetts House of Representatives, the candidate had to possess a freehold of the value of £100 in his town, or any rateable estate of the value of £200.[11] No man could be seated as governor unless he had a freehold in the Commonwealth of the value of £1,000, and declared himself of the Christian religion.[12]

The two most prominent advocates of this constitution in the Massachusetts convention were Elbridge Gerry and Nathaniel Gorham, both conspicuous members of the subsequent Federal Convention which framed the Constitution of the

[8] "Journal of The Massachusetts Convention, 1779-1780." p. 193.
[9] Ibid., 232.   [10] Ibid., 231.   [11] Ibid., 234.   [12] Ibid., 235.

United States, and one of whom, Gorham (as will be described), manipulated the Massachusetts legislature to grant him and Oliver Phelps an enormous area of land comprising many millions of acres (over which Massachusetts had jurisdiction) in New York State.[13]

These are significant examples of qualifying constitutional enactments adopted in some of the States during the period of the Revolution. In other colonies, particularly the slave-holding regions where the populace was less active than in the North, the demands of the upper class could be formulated more openly. The Maryland Bill of Rights, adopted November 3, 1776, stated that " the elections ought to be free and frequent," and that every man having property in, a common interest with, and an attachment to, the community, ought to have the right of suffrage." [14]

The Constitution of Maryland, adopted five days later, restricted the right to vote for members of the House of Delegates to only *free men,* having a freehold of fifty acres of land in their county, and to all free men having property above £30 current money.[15]   Candidates for the House of Delegates were required to have in the State real or personal property of more than £500 current money.[16] Fifteen State Senators were to be elected every five years by a body of electors — " men of wisdom, experience and virtue." [17]   To be elected a State Senator, the possession in the State of real and personal property more than the value of £1,000 current money was required.[18]   The Council to the Governor, it was further provided, was to be elected by the Legislature, and was to be

---

[13] See details later in this chapter.

[14] " The Laws of Maryland From The End of The Year 1799," etc., Vol. III: p. v.

[15] *Ibid.,* xi.

[16] *Ibid.*

[17] *Ibid.,* xiv. Here we see a precedent later followed by the " Fathers " in providing for indirect election of President and Vice-President.

[18] *Ibid.*

composed of only such selections as had a freehold of lands and tenements of more than £1,000 current money.[19] No man could be chosen for the Continental Congress unless he possessed the same extent of estate; and all candidates for governor were excluded except those having, in the State real and personal property of more than £5,000 value, current money, of which estate at least £1,000 was required to be in freehold.[20] These qualifications held fast for thirty-three years after the Declaration of Independence.

On July 2, 1776, two days before the adoption of the Declaration of Independence (or, according to some authorities, on the very day of its adoption), the Provincial Congress of New Jersey enacted, among other requirements, that no man could vote unless he was "worth £50 proclamation money, clear estate within the colony." [21] This law continued in force for more than half a century after the adoption of the Declaration of Independence. The old Rhode Island act of 1762, making necessary the possession of £40 to become a qualified voter, remained in force for more than eighty years. The New York Constitution of 1777 also hedged in the right to vote with strong property qualifications which were not abolished until fifty-six years after the Declaration of Independence. The Constitution of all the other colonies contained similar provisions. In South Carolina the elector had to possess fifty acres of land; in Connecticut he had to have a certain income, and in Massachusetts an income of £3 sterling, or a capital of £60.

As late as 1792, the drafters of the New Hampshire Constitution, well cognizant of its value for popular effect, inserted in the Constitution of that State adopted in that year the appealing philosophic generality:

"Section II. All men have certain natural, essential and

19 *Ibid.*, xv.
20 *Ibid.*, xvi.
21 1 Laws of New Jersey, p. 4.

inherent rights, among which are the enjoyment and defending life and liberty, acquiring, possessing and protecting property; in a word, of seeking and obtaining happiness." [22]   This
was an abstraction, and was intended to be.   In the succeeding clauses, property qualifications were embodied, debarring
from the electorate all who lacked property.   A member of
the New Hampshire lower house had to have an estate within
his district of the value of £100, one-half of which was to be
a freehold in his own right, and he had to be of the Protestant
religion; a State Senator was required to own an estate of
£200 in the State, and to be a Protestant; no man could be
governor unless he possessed an estate of £500.   He, too, had
to be of the Protestant faith.[23]

Old Conditions Maintained.

The Revolution gradually brought about certain reforms,
such as the abolition of entail and primogeniture by which
estates could no longer be bequeathed exclusively to the eldest
son, and it compelled the recognition of certain principles of
democracy.   But these reforms did not alter the condition of
the workers; what they really did was to allow the widest
latitude to the matured or embryo native capitalists, giving
them a free hand for the unfettered development of their
plans.   The iron laws designed to shackle the working class
continued, or were supplemented by others equally rigid.   Imprisonment for debt continued inexorably in some States for
half a century more, and other like or worse conditions obtained.

In the very city in which the Declaration of Independence
was drawn up, convicts were long regularly imported, and
sold like slaves.   Of this, the first Congress of the United

[22] "Constitution and Laws of the State of New Hampshire," etc.
(Edition of 1805), p. 1.
[23] Ibid., pp. 8-10.

States was forced to complain; and on March 27, 1789, the Pennsylvania Legislature passed an act declaring:

"Whereas, it has been represented to the House by the U. S. in Congress assembled, that a practice prevails of importing felons convict into this State under various pretences, which said felons convict so imported, have been sold and dispersed among the people of this State, whereby much injury has arisen to the morals of some, and others have been greatly endangered in their lives and property; for remedy thereof,"— and the act went on to decree a penalty of three months' imprisonment and £50 fine, in addition to costs of prosecution for any captain or master who violated the act by importing convicts.[24]

In the following year, on April 5, 1790, the Pennsylvania Legislature passed an act to "reform" the Penal Laws of that State. The preamble beneficently stated that "it is hoped that the addition of unremitted solitude to laborious employment, as far as it can be effected, will contribute as much to reform as to deter."[25] For robbery, burglary, sodomy and certain other crimes, all of the lands, tenements, goods and chattels of the criminal were to be forfeited, and he was to serve ten years in prison at hard labor. This was a grimly humorous statute; virtually none of those convicted had any lands, tenements, etc. Anyone convicted of stealing goods to the value of twenty shillings or more, was subject to a sentence of not more than three years at hard labor, and for the theft of goods under twenty shillings one year at hard labor.

Section XIII prescribed in detail how the convicts were to be treated. They were to be clothed in uniforms of the coarsest material; the males were to have their heads and beards close shaven at least once a week, and to be sustained upon bread,

[24] Carey and Bioren's "Pa. Laws," Vol. III: 344-347.
[25] *Ibid.* 441. The solitary cell, it should be noted, was, as a general institution, exclusively an American invention.

Indian meal, "or other inferior food." The labor was to be "of the hardest and most servile kind." An allowance of five per cent. to the keeper of the prison on articles made by the convicts was permitted. But this gratuity clause was repealed by act of April 18, 1795. If the convict, according to the act of 1790, committed any infraction of the rules, he was to get repeated whippings, not exceeding thirteen lashes at a time, or he was to be disciplined by a six days' close confinement in cell or dungeon, on bread and water.[26]

In addition to the great estates of Tories,— manorial lords, sinecurists and others who had remained loyal to King George — confiscated by States during the Revolution, there were vested in the United States Government at about the time of its organization, a vast area of public lands estimated at 513,-200,000 acres, some ceded by States, other areas acquired by treaty. What became of the best portions of these, and who got them, and how, we shall presently narrate. Ample land for all there certainly was; but no provision was made for distribution to the poor. The influential politicians, comprising many of the esteemed "Fathers of the Country," vied with one another, or banded together, to secure enormous domains for their personal profit; how well they succeeded the records reveal.

The particular provisions that were made for the poor may be seen, for instance, in an act passed by the New Hampshire legislature, February 15, 1791 (and it was but a type of the acts passed in other States), "for the punishment of idle and disorderly persons, for the support and maintainance of the poor," etc. It established more houses of correction "for the keeping and correcting of rogues, vagabonds, common beggars, lewd, idle and disorderly persons, and in which to employ the poor." If no such institutions existed in any

[26] Carey and Bioren's "Pa. Laws," Vol. III: 440-454. The administering of lashings was repealed by the act of 1795, but the close confinement in dungeons on bread and water was continued.— *Ibid.*, Vol. V: 121.

community, prisons could be used. Punishment was not to exceed hard labor, or wearing fetters and shackles during confinement, or whipping to the number of thirty-nine stripes. Among others specified, rogues, vagabonds, stubborn servants or children, persons using "subtle craft," and common night walkers could be incarcerated.

Overseers were also empowered to bind out by contract for a year's term the poor and the idle; the wages were to be paid to the overseers, who were to apply them to the maintenance of the person, family or children concerned. But poor children could be bound out till of age — males until they were twenty-one years old, and girls, until eighteen.[27] It was by means of such acts that the factory capitalists obtained their constant and cheap supply of woman and child labor.

Inquiry Into Reasons and Causes.

Meanwhile, during the Revolution and the drafting of the Constitution, what were the actual acts of the majority of the signers of the Declaration of Independence, and of those who drew up the Constitution? These were the functionaries who were among the most active and influential in the different colonies. They were, many of them, officials of the Continental Government, and later held the highest posts in the State or Federal Governments. While acts were being passed disqualifying, dispossessing and imprisoning the poor, what were the interests and motives animating those great dignitaries of the Revolution? Were they the heroic, incorruptible patriots it has been the fashion to represent them? Some, like Jefferson, no doubt were actuated by the highest, and for the age, most democratic, principles. But what of the majority?

In these painful questions lie most vital answers which

[27] "Constitution and Laws Of The State of New Hampshire," etc. (Edition of 1805), pp. 299-301.

will show the economic interests behind the successive actions of most of the men who made the Constitution of the United States, and will throw the most vivid light upon the future construction and career of the Supreme Court of the United States. This exposition will reveal the special reasons why it was that certain clauses, of the most tremendous importance, were inserted in the Constitution. No longer does it satisfy authentic historical inquiry to assert grandiloquently that acts and instruments have resulted from disinterested altruism. Men and women are the products of environment, and are, when grouped into classes, swayed by the varying interests from which they benefit, or the aims from which benefit is expected. What were the particular material interests of most of the leaders of the Revolution, and those of the drafters of the Constitution of the United States?

Whatever pretensions they assumed in public, for the awe and wonderment of the populace, and for the better molding of the mass to their ends, they, it must be said to their credit, made no pretense in the candor of their private circle. None would be more astonished than they, if, by some miracle, they could wake from the dead and read the effusive eulogies since published of their careers, attributing to them nothing but excess of virtue and motives superior to those impelling ordinary mortals.

They were human, all of them, and proved it so to their own gratification. Nor did they profess to pose as humanitarians, engrossed in promoting the good of the whole human race. Their acts revealed that the special interests they were furthering were those of a particular class, and that class their own. Many of them left the fullest evidences in the real annals that they were not so inactive as to allow splendid opportunities for self-enrichment to pass ignored. During the Revolution and afterwards, they and other notabilities took instant advantage of their power, their inside knowledge of affairs, and the stress of the times to accomplish schemes involving the most extensive land jobbing, and the procurement of other self-beneficial legislative acts. The Revolution was as excellent a cover for the successful carrying out of these enterprises, as was the Civil War, nearly a century later, when the most colossal frauds and thefts were consummated. Among those participating in this jobbery during, and after, the Revolution were several who became distinguished Justices of the Supreme Court of the United States. But even more:

Between the large and ambitious projects and schemes then accomplished or imitated, and the subsequent character and decisions of the Supreme Court of the United States, there lay a connection and sequence of the very gravest significance.

Absentee Landlords Covertly Retain Control.

One of the long-standing grievances of bona-fide settlers or those of that intention, was not only a grievance arising from the excessive and highly-centralized monopolization of accessible land. The blighting evils of absentee landlord ownership had also implanted deep popular hatreds and bitterness. Immense tracts of land in New York, Pennsylvania, Virginia, the Carolinas and other sections were held wholly or partly by British lords, or by companies composed of titled nobles and native personages. One of these powerful British companies for instance, was the Principio Company, embracing a number of British lords and Maryland and Virginia manorial lords. In this company " a certain Mr. Washington, a subject of the State of Virginia," had an undivided one-twelfth interest [28]— but whether it was the original and immortal George, the Maryland act of 1781 does not say. There were also many other companies, with some of which we shall have to deal anon. The property of the British and native

[28] " Laws of Maryland, 1682-1784," Vol. I, Chap. 23.

Tories was confiscated by general legislative acts during the Revolution, the acts, however, reserving to patriotic shareholders their rights.

But the confiscatory laws were often fraudulently evaded, and their force was later stealthily diminished by legislative enactment. "By our laws," wrote Jefferson, in 1781-1782, referring to Virginia,[29] "the same as the English in this respect, no alien can hold lands,[30] nor alien enemy maintain an action for money or other moveable things. Lands acquired or held by aliens become forfeited to the State; and, on an action by an alien enemy to recover money or other moveable property, the defendant may plead that he is an alien enemy. . . . By our separation from Great Britain, British subjects became aliens, and, being at war, they were alien enemies. Their lands were, of course, forfeited, and their debts irrecoverable. The assembly, however, passed laws at various times, for saving their property. They first sequestered their lands, slaves and other property on their farms in the hands of commissioners, who were mostly the confidential friends or agents of the owners, and directed their clear profits to be paid into the treasury." Jefferson further says that monies so turned were declared to be the property of the British subject, and if used by the State were to be repaid.

Of the great manorial estates, however, on which the native landgraves lived, many continued intact. The Livingstons, the Schuylers, the Van Cortlandts, the Van Rensselaers and others in New York, the Carrolls in Maryland and land magnates elsewhere not only discreetly espoused the Revolutionary cause, but were signers of the Declaration of Independence, members of the Federal Constitutional Convention and of the various State Constitutional Conventions. In this

[29] Jefferson's "Notes on The State of Virginia" (Edition of 1803), pp. 211-212.

[30] The astonishing connection between this fact and the operations of a certain Chief Justice of the Supreme Court of the United States is explained fully later in this work.

group were to be found the leading spirits of a party planning surreptitiously, and sometimes almost openly, for the establishment of a monarchy. In the " Secret Debates," the
speech of Luther Martin, a delegate from Maryland to the
Federal Constitutional Convention, is given in full, in which
speech he told of a powerful secret party favoring the establishment of a monarchical form of government. Beginning in 1776, a change was introduced in the laws by which
the old aristocratic power of entailing the estate to the eldest
son was gradually abolished. In that year, on motion of Jefferson, it was effaced in Virginia, and was suppressed in New
York in 1786.[31] Subsequently, in the next five decades the
practice was abolished in Georgia and North Carolina, and in
the newer States, Kentucky, Tennessee and Missouri. In the
original States of Vermont and South Carolina, and in Louisiana and other States later formed, the principal of entail was
never in statute. The reason for the abolition of the entail,
according to Chancellor Kent, was that it tended " to favor
the free circulation of property."

It was the abolition of the entail that introduced an element of disintegration in the individual holdings of great estates; where formerly the dimensions of the estates were preserved and usually enlarged from generation to generation,
the paternal property now was to be equally divided among
his children, but only so in case the will did not specifically
declare otherwise. The father still was endowed by law
with a large power of disposing of his property by testament
as he pleased.

But the manorial lords were not immediately dislodged.
For half a century many of the old seignorial landed families
remained potent political and social factors by reason of their
ancient wealth, and by stimulation from the new acquisitions
of land and the added wealth that they obtained from various
projects during, and after, the Revolution. Added to them

[31] Revised Statutes, Vol. III: Appendix, p. 48.

there came forward a new self-created division of the landed class, often cohering in schemes with them, and sometimes' separate. This new class was composed of certain leaders of the Revolution and other powerful politicians and rich merchants or adventurers who contrived to get vast areas of the public domain, and valuable banking, canal, turnpike and other privileges. These two sections formed the newer landed class which was the paramount class at the time of the organization of the Supreme Court of the United States, and for fifty years thereafter.

Creation of the Newer Landed Class.

The creation by law of a new division of the all-powerful landed class went on steadily during the critical years of the Revolution. These newer landholders became vested with large areas of what had been public land; and the time came when they and their successors in practice shared, and then outranked, in importance the manorial lords.

Although apparently disconnected, some of the facts given here are chronologically detailed for the important bearing that they have. They show the methods employed by the newer section of the landed class, and exhibit the plans and interests of many of the men who, in 1787, drafted the Constitution of the United States and those of the class represented by those delegates. Furthermore, in order to reveal what the drafters of the Constitution were meditating and what they were secretly preparing for at the very time they were creating that document, it has seemed advisable here to describe the ultimate result of some of the land-grasping schemes, even although in point of time, some of them overlap the date of the adoption of the Constitution. Finally, these facts in detail and in mass have their relation to the subsequent course of the United States Supreme Court. It may be said that only a few instructive examples of the widespread appropriation of the soil by a few, are given here.

The Revolution proved to be an auspicious time for the consummation of the boldest plans in acquiring property and power. Richard Henderson, a Virginian, had professed to buy, in Kentucky, a tract from the Cherokee Indians. With Henderson was associated some of the most noted politicians in Virginia. The pretended purchase was declared void on the ground of forgery. In October, 1778, an act was rolled through the Virginia Legislature, reciting that Richard Henderson and Company had " at great expense " made a purchase from the Cherokee Indians, and, " although the same has been declared void, yet this Commonwealth is likely to gain great advantages therefrom by increasing its inhabitants and establishing a barrier against the Indians." It was, therefore, enacted that Richard Henderson and Company should be vested with a grant of 100,000 acres in fee on the Ohio and Green rivers.[32]

When the United States Government, many years later, was making the treaty of Hopewell with the Cherokees, that tribe claimed a considerable area of Kentucky. To the astonishment of the Cherokees, the United States Commissioners produced what purported to be the original Indian deed conveying the land in that district to Henderson. Tassell, one of the Indian delegates, asserted that the signature of Oconestoto to the deed was a forgery; that Henderson had asked for only a small tract of land on the Kentucky River on which to feed his horses. Informed that all parties to the deed were dead, that the land had been sold by the company to settlers, and that the deed must stand, Tassell replied that they would let Kentucky go, but that he was sorry Henderson was dead; he " would like to have told him that he was a liar." [33]

The Virginia act of May, 1779, confirmed, as we have seen, the extensive grant of 200,000 acres to George Washington

[32] " Revised Code, Laws of Va." (Edition of 1819), Appendix II : 353–354. At one time Kentucky, Ohio and other present States were part of Virginia.
[33] " American State Papers : Indian Affairs," Vol. I : 42.

and other military officers, Savage's grant of 28,627 acres, and other large grants; revealing that Washington knew both the art of war and that of convincing legislatures, and that he could manage both at the same time. Large grants, by official legislative favor, abounded in Virginia, and especially in Kentucky and what were at that time other parts of Virginia, then being newly opened to settlement. Speculators and companies of speculators rushed forward to appropriate the best areas of land, and to anticipate the settlers, who were then put under necessity of buying from them. Benjamin Borden had one tract of 92,000 acres in one body, on the waters of the James River, and he also owned large tracts on the Catawba River, and in other States.[34] On December 15, 1772, the Virginia Legislature granted to George Muse, Adam Stephen and five other persons, 51,302 acres on the Ohio River; the next year these men divided it among themselves.[35] George Clymer, of Pennsylvania, one of the delegates to the Federal Constitutional Convention, in 1787, secured, with two associates, on May 30, 1784, a survey for a tract of 11,000 acres in Jefferson County, Kentucky. He waited twenty-two years, until Kentucky was filling with settlers, and then secured a patent from Governor Greenup,[36] thus avoiding all payment of taxes in the meantime. Clymer's share of the land was one-third; he never saw Kentucky; as a non-resident he was an example of the large absentee landlord element then appropriating the public domain.

Judges Make Grants to Themselves.

The judges of Virginia Courts usurped power in granting lands, and granted great tracts to themselves. Winthrop

[34] See case of Harvey and wife vs. Borden, Washington's Va. Reports, Vol. II: 156 (1795).

[35] Case of Hepburn vs. Auld, Cranch's Reports, Supreme Court of the United States, Vol. V: 264.

[36] Case of Lessee of George Clymer *et al.* vs. Dawkins, Howard's Reports, Supreme Court of the U. S., Vol. III: 675.

Sargent, Governor of the Northwest Territory, wrote from Vincennes, July 31, 1790, to President Washington detailing the gross frauds in seizing land, and the long continuing forgery of deeds.

"A court of civil and criminal jurisdiction," he continued, "established at this place by J. Todd, Esq., under the authority of Virginia, in June 1779, and who eked out their existence to the summer of 1787, have, during that long period, contrived to make large grants of land, *even* by their own acknowledgements, and without more authority for doing so than is set forth in No. 9 [a document submitted]. Many of these concessions which have been exhibited to me, they deny to have any knowledge of; and indeed, there are some reasons to conclude they may have been forged in the office of Mr. LeGrand, before mentioned, who was a servant of the court, and in whose handwriting the deeds have all been made out." [37]

Considering Governor Winthrop Sargent's activities at that time in the fraudulent operations of the Ohio Company of which he was one of the principal promoters and owners (see later in this chapter), the question fairly arises as to whether Sargent and his associates had designs themselves upon that portion of the Northwest Territory. But so far as his charges against the judges were concerned, they were fully borne out by the statement of a successor. In a communication from Vincennes, dated January 19, 1802, addressed to James Madison, Secretary of State, and laid before Congress by President Jefferson in a message, on February 18, 1802, General William Henry Harrison, as Governor of the North-

---

[37] "American State Papers: Public Lands," Vol. I: 10. (Doc. No. 4.) Were Sargent's exposures intended to divert attention from what his own appointees were doing? Thus, Judge Vanderburgh, appointed a United States Commissioner for the disposition of lands, by Gov. Sargent, held the conveyances to him of thirty-four distinct claims, embracing a large area of land, which he had got while occupying that post. Later, Vanderburgh surreptitiously obtained a confirmation of these claims from General John Gibson, Secretary of Indiana Territory. *Ibid.*, Vol. VII: 698. (Doc. No. 1333.)

west Territory, confirmed these charges of judicial land frauds.

"The circumstances," he reported, "mentioned in this letter I have considered of sufficient importance to be communicated to the President. The court established at this place under the authority of the state of Virginia in the year 1780 (as I have before done myself the honor to inform you) assumed to themselves the right of granting lands to every applicant. Having exercised this power for some time without opposition, they began to conclude that their right over the land was supreme.

"Accordingly, an arrangement was made by which the whole country to which the Indian title was supposed to be extinguished was divided among the members of the court, and orders to that effect entered upon their journals, each member absenting himself from the court on the day that the order was to be made in his favor, so that it might appear to be an act of his fellows only. The tract thus disposed of extends on the Wabash 24 leagues from La Pointe Coupee to the mouth of the White river, and forty leagues into the country west and 30 east from the Wabash, excluding only the land immediately around the town, which had before been granted to the amount of 20,000 or 30,000 acres."[38] Hundreds of thousands of acres were thus seized by the judges, sold to the speculators, and resold to settlers.

Important as are the details of these fraudulent methods, even more important is the fact here brought out, of the usurpation of power by the courts, and the additional fact that because the other courts and the officials passively acquiesced, therefore, it was held as ceasing to be usurped and becoming a recognized power of the court. These practices, as will be seen in the following chapters, had momentous

[38] "American State Papers: Public Lands," Vol. I: 123. The Northwest Territory was formed by ordinance of Congress in 1787. It comprised the present States of Ohio, Indiana, Illinois, Michigan, Wisconsin and Minnesota east of the Mississippi. Slavery was prohibited in it.

results both in the Constitutional Convention and in the claims later made by the Supreme Court of having the inherent power to set aside laws as unconstitutional. And what was subsequently accomplished under that doctrine of acquiescence will be clearly seen as we proceed.

In the light of these frauds, the Virginia act of 1799 directed at fraudulent obtaining of land warrants, was too evidently farcical except in its application to the uninfluential. It declared that he or she be adjudged a felon, without benefit of clergy, who should steal or otherwise purloin any land warrant, or who should alter and erase any warrant, or forge or counterfeit any official seal.[39] The practice was probably fairly widespread to call forth this act; but many of the very judges expected to enforce it were fraudulently acquiring great bodies of land. It was customary for grantees to assume a far larger area than their grants allowed — a practice later validated, as we shall see, by a notable decision of Chief Justice Marshall.[40]

On December 10, 1785, the Virginia Legislature granted to Martin Pickett one grant for 55,390 acres, and another for 44,470 acres of land in Kentucky; altogether, Pickett received a gift of 99,860 acres in Scott County, Kentucky. Eight years later Pickett deeded the patents to William and John Bryant, who conveyed them to James B. Clarke of New York City.[41] Charles Willing of the Willing family of Philadelphia, who were associated in trade with Robert Morris, obtained 32,000 acres of land in Kentucky, on treasury warrants issued in 1784, but claimants under him later unsuccessfully had to contest title to a portion of the grant with United States Senator Humphrey Marshall, a cousin of Chief Justice John Marshall.[42] On December 27, 1786, the Virginian author-

[39] "Rev. Code of Va." (Edition of 1819), Appendix II: 375.
[40] See later, Case of Taylor vs. Brown, Cranch's Reports, Supreme Court of the U. S., Vol. V: 235.
[41] Case of Lessee of Clark et al. vs. Courtney et al., Peters' Reports, Supreme Court of the United States, Vol. V: 319-357.
[42] Case of Lewis et al. vs. Marshall et al., V Peters, 470. See later.

ities gave a present to Phillip Barbour of 50,000 acres in Kentucky; Barbour sold some and deeded the remainder to Joshua Barney, who, in 1812, conveyed the land to John Oliver.[43] It was in evidence that neither Barney nor Oliver had ever been within the limits of Kentucky until many years after, some three months before an ejectment suit was brought, when Barney visited Kentucky. The papers in all these actions, and others, abound in charges of fraud, some of which were rejected, many more sustained.

In Georgia, likewise, large areas were presented to a few individuals. In 1786, one Webb, with others formed a land company, and agreed to buy not more than 200,000 acres of land on joint account from the State of Georgia. The company received grants from the State of 165,000 acres in all. Webb, for £400, thereupon transferred his interest to John McQueen, who assigned it to Pendleton, apparently at about the very time Pendleton was elected a delegate from Georgia to the Federal Constitutional Convention. He never took his seat, however. Of Pendleton's connection with the great Georgia land grants, approximating 35,000,000 acres, obtained by bribery in 1795, details are given in Chapter IV of this work. Wambursie, as the agent for Webb's (later Pendleton's) land company of 1786, sold 60,000 acres for $51,000 cash, to Holland capitalists. Out of this transaction extended litigation developed. The final ruling by the Supreme Court of the United States, in the case of Pendleton and Webb against Wambursie et al., in 1807, was in favor of Pendleton and Webb. (IV Cranch's Reports, 73.)

The Way Prepared for Huge Land Seizures.

Under the guise of its being a measure for the benefit of settlers, the Pennsylvania Legislature, on November 27, 1779,

---

[43] Case of Hawkins et al. vs. Barney's Lessee, V Peters, 457–469. Hawkins' lessee claimed some of the same land under a Virginia patent also.

passed an act for the purchase by the State of the lands and rights of the Penn family. The act referred to the rapid progress of neighboring States in locating and settling lands and how "multitudes of inhabitants are daily locating from this State." This monopolization of land, the act said, no longer was consistent with "the safety, liberty and happiness of the good people of this commonwealth, who, at the expense of much blood and treasure, have rescued themselves." The Legislature declared, therewith, that the soil of the whole grant was vested in the Commonwealth. Quit rents were abolished, and the former powers of the Proprietors were repealed. As compensation to the heirs of Thomas and Richard Penn, the late Proprietaries, an appropriation of £130,000 was allowed.[44] This large payment to the Penns was popularly considered as no better than rank jobbery.

Further laws followed. The act of April 10, 1781, ordered the selling of certain State property, " for the better support of the public credit." The act of March 12, 1783, decreed the sale of lands in the vicinity of Pittsburg, and along the Ohio and Allegheny rivers " for the purpose of redeeming, and paying off certificates of depreciation given to the officers and soldiers of the Pennsylvania line," and also to apportion lands among officers and soldiers.[45]

By the act of April 1, 1784, the powers of the Land Office, established by act of 1781, were extended, and all lands bought from the Indians were to be sold at the rate of £10 for every 100 acres, with the usual granting, surveying and patenting fees, and the rate of all lands west of the Alleghanies was fixed at three pounds, ten shillings for every 100 acres.[46] No one person was allowed to receive a grant of more than 400 acres. Another act followed in 1788 which lowered the price

[44] Carey and Bioren's " Pa. Laws," Vol. II : 230–231. Expressed in American currency, the amount was about $580,000.
[45] Ibid., 398.
[46] Ibid., 490–494. The purchase price for lands was reduced by act of April 3, 1792.

of lands in Northumberland and Luzerne counties to £20 per hundred acres.[47]

These laws, ostensibly enacted to conciliate the popular clamor for land, seemed most excellently conceived. But they were really designed, as we shall note at length, for the benefit of a powerful clique of land speculators among whom were some of the notable " Fathers " of the country, as also some of the distinguished patriots who drafted the Constitution of the United States, and at least one future Justice of the Supreme Court of the United States.

At the head of this clique were Robert Morris and Gouverneur Morris, both exceedingly influential in the Continental Government, in the Pennsylvania Legislature and in the Federal Constitutional Convention. These two Morrises were in no way related by blood. Gouverneur Morris belonged to the landed aristocracy of New York; his family owned a large estate, and ranked socially with the Livingstons, the Van Rensselaers, the Schuylers and other conspicuous landed families. The estate inherited by Gouverneur Morris lay principally in the district later called Morrisania, now a part of New York City, and was acquired by his ancestors. His grandfather was that Chief Justice Lewis Morris who, as we have noted in Chapter I, was tried for sitting in his own cause. His father was, for many years, Chief Justice of the Admirality Court. From 1781 to 1785 Gouverneur Morris was Assistant Minister of Finance under Robert Morris; and during that time, at the close of the Revolution, the two Morrises formed a commercial partnership in the East India and China trade.

The Comptroller-General of Pennsylvania was John Nicholson who shortly afterward became one of Robert Morris' partners in gigantic land transactions, and against whom impeachment proceedings were brought in 1794.[48] Another

[47] Carey and Bioren's " Pa. Laws," Vol. III : 285.
[48] See Chapter IV of this work for the full facts.

powerful politician concerned was James Wilson, one of the most active men in the Federal Constitutional Convention, and one of the first Justices of the United States Supreme Court to be appointed by Washington. The full operations of these and other notables are hereafter described in detail: how they and other politicians fraudulently bought up, at ten per cent. of their value, the military land certificates given as pay or bounties to the Revolutionary soldiers; and how by means of these, or by grants which they themselves, as members of Congress or legislatures, put through, or by bribery, secured enormous areas of public domain.

Robert Morris, Patriot and Financier.

Robert Morris, " the distinguished Financier of the Revolution," had begun his career in the counting room of Charles Willing, then the leading merchant of Philadelphia and engaged in the West India trade. Subsequently, Morris became a member of the firm of Willing and Morris, and, says a chronicler, they " employed an incredible number of ships." [49] This is an example of Morris' trading operations:

In 1783 William Alexander (later Lord Sterling) and Jonathan Williams made a certain contract with the Farmers General of France — a group of monopolists by royal favor oppressing the people of France to an intense degree, it may be explained, and thus helping to precipitate the French Revolution. By this contract Alexander and Williams were to supply the Farmers General with shipments of tobacco. The next year, in 1784, Robert Morris was taken in as a partner; he made a new contract with the Farmers General, calling for the delivery of 60,000 hogsheads of tobacco for the years 1785, 1786, and 1787. Litigation, arising from disagreements over the profits, later developed between the partners. [50]

[49] Frost's " Lives of American Merchants," 59.
[50] Case of Alexander vs. Morris and others, Call's Reports (Va. Court of Appeals), Vol. III: 87.

At about the same time Robert Morris became the owner of an extensive tract of land in what is now West Virginia. This tract had been granted by Virginia on an order of survey, June 12, 1770, to Albert Gallatin (later United States Secretary of Treasury). The survey, however, must have been assigned to Robert Morris, for whom Gallatin might have been acting; the patent was made out to Morris on February 10, 1786. The land covered by the patent seems to have been several hundred thousand acres. Nine years later, Morris assigned it to his partner, Thomas Willing. This Willing was the first president of the Bank of the United States, in the establishment of which monopoly Robert Morris and Alexander Hamilton were the prime movers. The tract was then turned over to the North American Land Company — one of Morris' land corporations - - and during the succeeding decades part of it was the subject of litigation.[51]

Hamilton's Business and Family Relations.

Between Alexander Hamilton, John Jay and Robert Morris, were the closest business relations, and even more intimate connections between Jay and Hamilton. These two — Hamilton and Jay — were among the strongest factors in bringing about the adoption of the Constitution; Hamilton in the Federal Constitutional Convention and Jay in New York. Jay was the son-in-law of William Livingston, a grandson of that Robert Livingston, the origin of whose fortune we have described in Chapter I. William Livingston was a member of the Federal Constitutional Convention. Hamilton was married to Elizabeth Schuyler, daughter of General Phillip Schuyler. In addition to the great estates that the original Schuyler had secured by bribing Governor Fletcher, two of his descendants, David and his son Peter, had in May, 1754, bought of the Mohawk Indians a tract of 43,000 acres of

[51] See Case of Armstrong vs. Morrill, Wallace's Reports, Supreme Court of the United States, Vol. XIV: 121.

land on the west side of Lake Canjadarage.[52] Inasmuch as
the law expressly prohibited grants of more than a thousand
acres to any individual, this large grant must have been obtained by the same fraudulent methods (narrated in Chapter I) by which Lieutenant-Governor Clarke and Sir William
Johnson got their grants. David and Peter Schuyler also
owned lands in Canajoharie, in Albany, in New York City
and in the colonies of Rensselaerwyck and Surinam, New
York.[53] General Phillip Schuyler continued to add to his estate. On July 20, 1772, he bought Cosby's manor, at Albany,
sold by the sheriff of Albany for arrears of quit rent.[54]

A few years before the Revolution, John B. Church, favored by a rich uncle, came to America, and during the Revolution became an army contractor in commissary supplies in
partnership with Jeremiah Wadsworth, and got rich. At the
same time General Phillip Schuyler was in charge of the
commissary department of the Continental army in the north.
" Their business relations," we are told, " led to a close acquaintance; " Church married one of Schuyler's daughters,
thus becoming Hamilton's brother-in-law.[55] Subsequently,

[52] Schuyler's " Colonial New York," Vol. I: 470.
[53] *Ibid.*
[54] See Case of Bradstreet vs. Huntington, Peters' Reports, Supreme
Court of the United States, Vol. V: 403.
[55] Monroe's " Pioneer History of the Phelps and Gorham Purchase "
(Edition of 1851), p. 496.— Sabine says that avarice and rapacity were
common during the Revolution. " Indeed," he goes on, " the stockjobbing, the extortion, the low arts and devices to amass wealth that
were practiced during the struggle are almost incredible. . . . Soldiers were stripped of their miserable pittance, that contractors for
the army might become rich in a single campaign. Many of the sellers
of merchandise monopolized articles of the first necessity, and would
not part with them to their suffering countrymen, and to the wives and
children of those who were absent in the field, unless at enormous
profits." At the same time these contractors also carried on traffic
with the royal troops. This traffic, Sabine relates, " was immense.
Men of all descriptions finally engaged in it, and those who at the
beginning of the war would have shuddered at the idea of any connection with the enemy, pursued it with avidity. . . ." " Loyalists of
the American Revolution," Vol. I: 141-142. Sabine's prefatory historical essay to his work is searching, but by no means unfriendly to the
American Revolution.

John B. Church, disgusted with the republican form of government adopted, went to England, ran for Parliament, and lived there until 1797. Hamilton was his permanent agent. Church's son, Philip, studied law with his uncle, Alexander Hamilton, and also in the office of Edmund Pendleton, and became Hamilton's private secretary.[56]

Hamilton Advances Money to Morris.

So close was the business association between Robert Morris, John Jay (first Chief Justice of the Supreme Court of the United States) and Alexander Hamilton, that according to Whitelock, in a laudatory biography of Jay: "At a private meeting, Hamilton and Robert Morris recommended buying new lands; Jay, on the other hand, advocated suburban property. By their respective purchases, the first lost money, the second was ruined, while the third realized a profit." [57]

This scant outline comes very far from doing justice to the extraordinarily large land ownership and speculations of the trio, particularly of Morris. Was there a secret compact or understanding between them? Whitelock intimates it, but does not say so. As a matter of fact, Morris extended his land operations to such an inordinate degree that at one time, at the close of the eighteenth century, he held the ownership of not less than 6,000,000 acres of land in the State of New York, Pennsylvania, the City of Washington and other parts of the country.

"General Hamilton," says Monroe, "as the agent of John B. Church, had in his absence, loaned to Robert Morris $80,000, and taken a mortgage on Morris Square, Philadelphia; the lien being afterwards transferred to 100,000 acres of land on Morris' reserve in the present county of Alleghany. In 1800 this mortgage was foreclosed, the land was sold at Can-

[56] "Pioneer History of the Phelps and Gorham Purchase," 496.
[57] Whitelock's "Life and Times of John Jay," p. 338.

andaigua . . . and bid in by Phillip Church for his father." [58]
This statement of Monroe's regarding Morris's conveyances of
land to John B. Church and others is consistent with Justice
Washington's statement of the case in 1812 in one of the
many suits arising later from Morris' land transactions.[59]
Robert Morris also, as will be related later, had the closest
business associations with Daniel Carroll (another delegate
to the Constitutional Convention) in vast speculations in City
of Washington real estate when the site of the National Capitol was selected. Robert Morris likewise was bound in business affairs with Oliver Phelps and Nathaniel Gorham of
Massachusetts, the latter of whom was an active delegate in
the Federal Constitutional Convention, and who (to repeat)
was, with Elbridge Gerry and a few others, the most aggressive and potent influence in securing the adoption by Massachusetts of the Constitution of the United States.

Livingston Cheats the Indians.

What was called the Phelps and Gorham purchase formed
one of the great scandals of the time, and was one of the
factors creating the popular unrest and agitation, then styled
insurrection.

To evade the provisions of the New York State Constitution forbidding the purchase in fee by individuals of the lands
of the Indians, a corporation called the New York Genesee
Land Company was formed. It was composed of eighty or
ninety men, "many of whom were wealthy and influential;"
one of the most prominent managers and directors was John
Livingston, of Livingston Manor.[60] In 1787 the company obtained leases, to endure for the full period of 999 years, of
nearly all of the lands of the Six Nations of the Indians, in

[58] " Pioneer History of the Phelps and Gorham Purchase," 447.
[59] See Fitzsimmons and others vs. Ogden and others, Cranch's Reports, Supreme Court of the United States, Vol. VII: 2.
[60] Monroe's " Pioneer History of the Phelps and Gorham Purchase,"
106.

New York, for an annual rent of two thousand Spanish milled dollars, and a definitely stated promise of a bonus of $20,-000.[61] To put the Indian chiefs in the desired happy state of mind to induce them to sign, Livingston had sent out fourteen sleighs loaded with goods, particularly with rum, into the Indian country.

When the circumstances of this transaction became known to the white public, and its provisions clear to the Indians themselves, a tremendous uproar resulted. The Six Nations accused Livingston of having cheated them.[62] Governor Clinton sent runners to all of the Six Nations warning them of the fraud practiced upon them; and under a special act that popular agitation forced through the Legislature, he called out the militia to expel the Lessees — as the members of the Company were called. Clinton, in behalf of the State, then opened negotiations with the Indians for the purchase of the land, to be set aside as a " Military Tract "— that is, land to be reserved and to be exchanged for the military certificates allotted to the Continental soldiers.

At the negotiations at Fort Schuyler Clinton was personally present; and when it appeared that the agents of the Lessees had corrupted or deceived Kirkland, the gospel minister among the Indians, and had debauched the Indians with " firewater," Governor Clinton ordered John Livingston, in writing, to leave within three hours and retire to a distance of forty miles.[63] At this council, Monroe says, Clinton made an exhaustive investigation. " It exposed a connected scheme of bribery, threats, intimidation, and deception practised upon

[61] Monroe's " Pioneer History," etc., 106.
[62] *Ibid.*
[63] *Ibid.*, 110–111. But Clinton was by no means the high-minded public official he professed. See details in Chapter IV of a scandalous transaction of great magnitude for which he, Aaron Burr and other officials were responsible. And Clinton's nephew and political protégé and successor, De Witt Clinton (as we shall later note), drew up and pushed through the Legislature the charter of the American Fur Company under cover of which John Jacob Astor debauched and swindled the Indians on a great scale.

the Indians." [64]   Treaties were concluded by Clinton with the
various tribes by which for a small money consideration and
slight annuities — one thousand dollars in land, and five hundred dollars annuity forever, in the case of Onondagas — the
State of New York obtained the principal area of territory at
present included in the counties of Cayuga, Onondaga, Seneca, Tompkins, Courtland, and parts of Oswego and Wayne.

The Phelps and Gorham Purchase.

At this point the Phelps and Gorham purchase developed.
During the Revolution, Oliver Phelps had been in constant
touch through business transactions with Robert Morris. All
of that area in New York State, now embraced in the counties of Chautauqua, Cattaraugus, Erie and Niagara, and a
large portion of the present counties of Allegany, Genesee
and Orleans, were claimed by Massachusetts as within its
jurisdiction under the old Plymouth Charter. By a treaty
adopted in 1786 between New York and Massachusetts, the
jurisdiction of the territory in question was ceded to New
York, which, in turn, ceded to Massachusetts the right of
buying the preëmption rights to the soil from the Indians.

Phelps and Gorham organized a company; and, on April 1,
1788, secured the passage of an act by the Massachusetts Legislature granting them all rights of purchase to certain of the
lands the preëmption rights of which had been ceded by New
York.[65] The stipulated price to be paid was one hundred
thousand dollars payable in the public paper of Massachusetts; the value of this currency was then only fifty cents on
the dollar. But Phelps and Gorham immediately encountered
a most serious obstacle in the New York Genesee Land Company and its nine hundred and ninety-nine year leases. True,
both Massachusetts and New York had declared these leases
null and void. But the Lessees, headed by the Livingstons,

---

[64] *Ibid.*, 112.
[65] " Massachusetts Special Laws, 1780–1805," Vol. I: 204.

and backed by John Jay and other powerful relatives and associates, were men of the greatest political and social influence; they had their members in the Legislature, on the Bench, and in other high positions; they were not to be trifled with, or set aside, which fact they soon and most energetically made known. The two companies came to an understanding; Phelps held a meeting with some of the principal Lessees, and made them stockholders in the Phelps and Gorham Company.

They Get 2,600,000 Acres.

This amiable compact arranged, the next step was a treaty with the Seneca Indians at Kandesega — now the city of Geneva. The Lessees were represented by John Livingston; Phelps acted for his company. By this treaty the Indians ceded in one deed alone a tract of at least 2,600,000 acres in return for a promised payment of $10,000, and the pact of an annuity of $500 forever. Evidently, Livingston and his fellow Lessees were still making threats against the Phelps and Gorham company, and demands upon it; Monroe tells that another compromise was made with the Lessees, stipulating the conveyance to them of four townships, "besides as may be well inferred, paying their immediate agents well for a forbearance in the work of mischief in which they were so persevering." [66]

In 1789, however, Phelps and Gorham found themselves under the painful prospect of having to hand over the $100,-000 (which they had agreed to pay Massachusetts) in currency the value of which had greatly increased. When they had signed the contract with Massachusetts, the paper of that State, as we have said, was rated at only one half of its face value. They had confidently expected to pay their obligations in this depreciated currency. But after the adoption of the Constitution of the United States, the value of that paper

[66] "History of the Phelps and Gorham Purchase," 140.

went up to nearly par. What was to be done? A very facile
way out of the difficulty was found; the Legislature generously released them from all obligations except what was included in the particular Seneca Indian treaty which had given
them 2,600,000 acres of land.

At an Indian Council, held at Tioga, in November, 1790,
Red Jacket and Farmer's Brother, two Seneca Chiefs, made
pathetic speeches, saying that they had been confused and
cheated by Livingston, Phelps and their partners; that they
had received only $5,000 instead of $10,000 from Phelps.
" When we discovered the fraud," said Red Jacket, " we had
a mind to apply to Congress to see if the fraud could not be
rectified. For when we took the money and shared it, every
one knows that we had but one dollar apiece. All our lands
came to was the worth of a few hogsheads of tobacco . . .
so that when we returned home there was not a bright spot of
silver about us." [67]

Monroe narrates that in these Indian treaties the use of bribery and spirituous liquors was common, and the consequent
frauds on them often impelled the Indians " to the fields of
blood and slaughter or to the stealthy assault with the tom-
ahawk and scalping. knife." Further, Monroe describes how
the Indians were pauperized to such an extent that they had
to eat their own horses.

But what of Phelps and Gorham? In 1795, Phelps " regarded himself as worth a million of dollars " and Gorham
was likewise a man of great wealth. These were not their
only land transactions; they even, in 1789, made a claim to
certain parts of the northwest corner of Pennsylvania, as
coming within the lines of their purchase, or conflicting with
them.[68] Phelps was, at the same time, a conspicuous political
leader in Congress. His land speculations became so vast,

[67] *Ibid.,* pp. 143–144.
[68] See "American State Papers: Public Lands," Vol. I: 7–8. Petition of Phelps and Gorham, and Report of House Committee on Public
Lands recommending that the boundaries of the cession be ascertained.

that he had to execute mortgages on his New York lands to
the State of Connecticut from which, in his reverses, he was
easily able to borrow money.

Morris Gets Four Million Acres in New York.

Of the preëmption rights ceded by New York to Massachusetts there still remained several million acres which had not
been included in the sale to Phelps and Gorham.   On March
5 and 8, 1791, the Massachusetts Legislature accommodatingly
sold the rights of preëmption to these lands to Samuel Ogden,
who, two months later, on May 11, 1791, assigned his contract to Robert Morris.[69]   Shortly afterward, Morris, then a
United States Senator from Pennsylvania, made a fraudulent
treaty with the Seneca Indians, similar to the treaties of Livingston and Phelps, but accompanied by an agreement more
favorable to the Senecas — an agreement by which they were
to receive the payment of $100,000.[70]   By this treaty Morris
acquired more than 4,000,000 acres in New York west of the
Phelps and Gorham purchase.

Even, says Monroe, before he had extinguished, that is to
say bought, the rights from the Indians, Morris sold to a company called the Holland Company, more than a million acres
in what are now the counties of Niagara, Erie, Chatauqua,
and all of the present counties of Allegany, Wyoming, Genesee and Orleans.   To himself Morris reserved a tract of about
five hundred thousand acres, these lands being between those
of Phelps and Gorham, and those conveyed to the Holland
Company.[71]   But, according to Justice Bushrod Washington's

---

[69] History of The Holland Company, N. Y. Assembly Doc. No. 224,
Assembly Documents, Vol. III.   (1837.)

[70] But was this $100,000 paid?   It was not.   By order of President
Washington, it was invested in the Bank of the United States, in the
name of the President, as trustee for the Indians.   Of this bank, promoted by Morris and largely founded by Hamilton, Morris' partner,
Thomas Willing, as we have noted, was the first president.

[71] " Pioneer History of the Phelps and Gorham Purchase," 442.

statement in deciding the case of Fitzsimmons and others vs. Ogden and others, in the Supreme Court of the United States, February 4, 1812, Morris' purchases from the State of Massachusetts in Ontario County (comprising a number of present New York counties) " amounted to upwards of four million acres "; of this area, said Justice Washington, Morris, by different deeds, conveyed to the Holland Company more than three million acres.[72] It was part of his reserved tract that Morris, through Alexander Hamilton, subsequently conveyed to John B. Church and to Samuel Ogden, Sir William Pulteney and others.

John Jay's intimate friend, Herman Le Roy, presently came into the transaction.

In the operations of the Holland Company there was to be seen a typical example of the full effects of absentee landlordism, for which some of the most eminent members of the Federal Constitutional Convention were responsible. The more than three million acres that Morris deeded were conveyed on July 20, 1793, ostensibly to Herman Le Roy (the same who obtained large areas that had been procured by fraud as described in Chapter I), John Linclaen and Gerrit Boon. But this conveyance was made to divert the attention of the mass of American people; the transfer was actually made in trust for the use of Wilhelm Willinck and eleven other Holland capitalists, who paid the purchase money.[73] The firm of Willinck and Van Strapporst were big bankers at Amsterdam; as the " bankers for the United States " in Holland they did a lucrative business making profits out of the Revolution, and later from the United States, by grace of Robert Morris, and by that of Alexander Hamilton, as Secretary of the Treasury. The Willincks later used these profits in taking mortgages on many American transportation

[72] VII Cranch, 2–22. Thomas Fitzsimmons, one of the plaintiffs in this suit, was one of the Pennsylvania delegates in the Federal Constitutional Convention.
[73] N. Y. Assembly Doc. No. 224, 1837: 13.

lines.[74]   Because of its being a company of Holland capitalists, it called itself the Holland Company.

In order to give a clear idea of the interconnected interests of Le Roy, Jay, Hamilton, Morris, the Willincks and other politicians and capitalists of the time, we shall at this point again call attention to certain facts brought out in a letter written by Jay from which communication extracts are given in Chapter V of this work.   When he wrote that letter Jay had not yet formally resigned as Chief Justice of the Supreme Court of the United States.   In that particular letter sent by Jay from London, in 1794, to Nicholas Cruger, Hamilton's patron, Jay informed Cruger that " a gentleman in Holland " had sent him (Jay) a plan for making his fortune. Jay sent the " golden " plan to Cruger, suggesting that Le Roy and Bayard participate in it.   This plan, it would appear, did not deal with land, but with mercantile, operations; Le Roy and Bayard were among the largest shipping merchants in New York; Hamilton was their attorney.

Here, for the present, we shall leave the Holland Company, to recur later in this work to its operations: the manner in which it secured fraudulent legislation, and in which it became possessed of vast areas of land in Pennsylvania; how it swayed the courts and cheated States and settlers; how its fraudulent pretensions were validated by a remarkable decision of the Supreme Court of the United States; and finally how, for half a century, it bled a hundred thousand settlers causing great agitation, uprising and riots.

The purpose of this particular chapter is to give a sufficient insight into the economic interests of the principal men who drafted the Constitution of the United States, and those of their associates and connections.   Abundant as the facts here related may seem, they are supplemented by as great and as

[74] See, for example, the case, in 1843, of William Willinck, Jr., vs. the Morris Canal and Banking Company, involving litigation growing out of a loan of $750,000 — N. J. Chancery Reports, Vol. III: 377.

indispensable an array in the following pages, in which their importance to the narrative of the Supreme Court of the United States will be more evident. There it will be further seen how Washington, Hamilton, James Wilson, Robert Morris, Gouverneur Morris, the Carrolls, Samuel Chase, John Jay, Thomas Fitzsimmons, Thomas Mifflin and other notables who either directly or indirectly caused the adoption of the Constitution, and some of whom formed the first bench of the Supreme Court, were abetting or putting through great fraudulent undertakings.

A succinct account, however, of one or two more notable transactions begun during the very time that the Constitution was being formulated, will be appropriate at this point.

Revolutionary Veterans Defrauded.

At the beginning of the Revolution, the old Roman plan used by Governor Dinwiddie in the French and Indian war of giving land for military services, was taken up by the colonies as a means of inducing recruits, and paying them for their services. According to rank and service, each soldier was entitled to a specified area of land.

Knowing the collective value of large assignments of these military certificates, the speculators sent out their agents to trade upon the pressing need of the soldiers for money, and buy up these land warrants issued by the various colonies. Congress, at the instance of Morris, Hamilton and others passed an act providing for the assumption of State debts.

Of this fact the people at large were in ignorance for some considerable time; there was only one post road extending along the seacoast, and communication was slow. " But the rich speculator, who was on the spot," explained Representative Bacon, in the debate on the judiciary system, in the House of Representatives, on February 19, 1802, " by going into the country where the people had been ignorant of what had been done, purchased up their certificates — the only reward they had received for their toil and wounds — at about one-tenth of their value. And it is possible that many of these purchases may have been done with public money." [75]

Jefferson says the same. " The accounts," he wrote, " of the soldiers of Virginia and North Carolina, having been examined by the proper officers of government, the balances due each individual ascertained, and a list of the balances made out, this list became known to certain persons before the soldiers themselves had information of it, and these persons, by unfair means, as is said, and for very inadequate considerations, obtained assignments from many of the soldiers of whatever sum should be due to them from the public, without specifying the amount." [76]   A law was enacted to protect the soldiers but it was of no effect.

Jefferson's statements are borne out by the actual records. Great numbers of military land warrants were bought by speculators for paltry sums. To instance one example of thousand of cases:

Waller, a veteran of the Revolution, had obtained warrants for about 5,000 acres " which had been unfairly purchased from him . . . for the trifling consideration of £20, at a time when the testator was intoxicated with liquor, and incapable of contracting." The Chancellor of Virginia decided that the fraud had been proved to his satisfaction, and gave judgment for Waller's heir. The Virginia Court of Appeals in sustaining the Chancellor's decision said that " a more palpable imposition was never practised, or better established than in this case." [77]   Redress was awarded in this particular case, but in large numbers of other cases the soldiers were absolutely defrauded. In other instances — and by no means a small number — assignments of military land warrants purporting to have been conveyed by soldiers were forged. Petition after petition went into Congress, for more than thirty

[75] " Abridgement of the Debates of Congress," Vol. II: 629.
[76] " The Writings of Thomas Jefferson," Vol. V: 175.
[77] Washington's Virginia Reports, Vol. I: 164.

years after the Revolution, from veterans who asserted that
they had been defrauded or their names forged.[78]

It was, to a very great extent, by means of these military
land certificates, thus obtained, that many of the most eminent
politicians secured large tracts of land. The raids began in
1787 when the Continental Congress and the Executive Departments were wholly under the control of the Livingstons,
the Carrolls, John Jay, Robert Morris and other Revolutionary eminences. Begun in the very year in which the Constitution was drafted, these schemes were projected and carried out either by members of the Federal Constitutional Convention, or by their associates.

Symmes, Dayton, Etc., Get a Slice of Ohio.

On October 15, 1788, by virtue of resolutions adopted in
July and October, 1787, the Board of Treasury contracted
with Judge John Cleves Symmes and Jonathan Dayton, of
New Jersey, and other associates, to grant them a tract of
1,000,000 acres in Ohio, the Government reserving five lots
out of each township. Dayton was a delegate to the Federal
Constitutional Convention from New Jersey, and was not
only a partner of Symmes, but also his agent; the city of
Dayton, Ohio, derives its name from him. Who the other
associates were the documents do not state. For this tract
Symmes and company agreed to pay the Government at the
rate of 66 2-3 cents an acre.

Of this specified amount they paid into the Treasury, before the ensealing of the contract, the sum of $82,198. This
was not paid in coin. One-seventh was paid in military land
warrants, and the remainder in Government securities [79]
which had been bought speculatively at a heavy discount be-

[78] See, "American State Papers: Public Lands," Vol. I: 17–18, 110–
111, 127, 597 and 911; Vol. II: 140–156, etc., etc.
[79] "American State Papers: Public Lands," Vol. I: 104–106. (Doc.
No. 55.)

cause of their low price. The remainder of the sums due the Government were to be paid as follows: The amount of $82,198 within a month after the delivery of patents, and the residue in six equal payments, with interest, payments extending through three years. It was agreed that one-seventh of those payments could be made in military certificates, acre for acre;[80] to this extent Symmes and Dayton were accordingly relieved from the necessity of having to pay in gold or silver. The tract covenanted for embraced all that rich section in the southern part of Ohio, now occupied by Cincinnati, Dayton, Hamilton and other cities and towns.

Sold the Site of Cincinnati Before They Had a Patent.

It appears that, extraordinarily favorable to them as was this contract, Symmes and Dayton at once commenced fraudulent operations. They were in collusion with Daniel Ludlow, the Government Surveyor,[81] Governor St. Clair and other officials. Although they received no patent from the Government until 1794, they began selling land in 1788. In the case of The City of Cincinnati vs. The Lessee of White,[82] before the United States Supreme Court, in January, 1832, Justice Thompson, in delivering the Court's opinion, stated these facts:

"Before the issuing of the patent, however, and, as the witnesses say, in the year 1788, Matthias Denman (of New Jersey) purchased of Symmes a part of the tract included

---

[80] *Ibid.* But Hamilton, as Secretary of the Treasury, made a settlement with Symmes, Dayton, etc., by which they obtained an *acre and a half* for every *acre* of military land warrants that they turned in.

[81] *Ibid.,* 128–130. Dayton, Ludlow, St. Clair and others, separately and together, made extensive purchases of land in what is now the town of Dayton and elsewhere. Ludlow became a rich landholder. See case of Ludlow vs. Carpenter, Ohio Reports, Vol. XIII: 580; Chief Justice Lane's statement of facts. For the facts revealing other great land frauds accomplished under Governor St. Clair and with his connivance, see later in this work.

[82] Peters' Reports, Supreme Court of the U. S., Vol. VI: 431–434.

in the patent, and embracing the land whereon Cincinnati now stands. That, in the same year, Denman sold one-third of his purchase to Israel Ludlow, and one-third to Robert Patterson. These three persons, being equitable owners of the land (no legal title having been granted) proceeded in January, 1789, to lay out the town. A plan was made and approved of all the proprietors," etc.[83]

Justice Thompson's statement went on to say that in March, 1795, Denman conveyed his interest, which was only an equitable interest, to Joel Williams, and that, on February 14, 1800, Symmes conveyed in fee to Williams certain lands described in the deed, some of which lands Williams conveyed to John Daily. Williams was a tavern-keeper; and, it may be parenthetically remarked, it was from him, in exchange for some secondhand copper stills, that Nicholas Longworth obtained thirty-three acres now in the heart of Cincinnati, thus laying the foundation of the immense Longworth fortune of to-day, a fortune in which Alice Roosevelt Longworth, a daughter of Theodore Roosevelt, shares by marriage with the present Nicholas Longworth.

The Government Cheated.

To return to Symmes: On April 11, 1792, he, Dayton and his associates petitioned Congress that the advanced price of public securities rendered impossible the strict fulfillment of the contract, and asked for a modification and more favorable terms.

Congress was compliant; many of its members held interest in the Symmes grant. In fact, Dayton, as a member of the House of Representatives, not only presented the petition, but he, Treadwell, and Nicholas Gilman (the last-named was one of the four delegates to the Federal Constitutional Convention of 1787 from New Hampshire) were appointed on April

[83] *Ibid.*, 433.

23, 1792, a House Committee to prepare and bring in a bill granting certain lands to Symmes, which bill was reported as passed.[84]   This law, enacted on May 5, 1792, authorized Presi-dent Washington to grant to the company in fee simple:

1. As much lands as had been paid for (under the Symmes contract of October 15, 1788) at the rate of 66 2-3 cents an acre.   2. Another tract of 106,850 acres, provided it was paid for in six months in military bounty certificates.   3. A town-ship of six miles square to contain 23,040 acres and to be held in trust for the use of an academy.   In conformity with this act, Washington, on September 30, 1794, gave Symmes and company a patent for 311,682 acres of land along the Ohio, and the Great Miami and Little Miami rivers, reserving five lots in each township, and one complete township of six miles square (to be located in about the center of the tract) for use of an academy.[85]   But Symmes and Dayton fraudu-lently sold part of this reserved township to various individ-uals, causing a prolonged scandal.[86]

Land Companies Swindle Settlers.

At the same time, in 1787, when Symmes, Dayton and as-sociates had made their first move, other land companies ob-tained great grants of land.   On October 29, 1787, Manasseh Cutler, Winthrop Sargent, and associates, composing the Ohio Company, made an agreement with William Duer and asso-ciates, by which in return for a tract of 100,000 acres of

[84] " History of Congress, March 4, 1789, to March 7, 1793," etc., p. 425.   See details in Chapter IV of this present work as to the bribery of members of Congress in another land-grasping scheme.

[85] " American State Papers: Public Lands," Vol. I: 104–106.   Later reports say 248,540 acres.

[86] *Ibid.*, 105.   See also Report of House Committee on Public Lands, March 21, 1836, reciting the full circumstances, and reporting in part: " Symmes failed to execute the trust thus reposed in him, and the object of the conveyance of said township [was] entirely defeated." The report was called forth by the application of the Woodward High School, of Cincinnati, for a grant of land.— *Ibid.*, Vol. VIII: 561.   (Doc. No. 1478.)

land, Duer and company were to allow Cutler, Sargent and company to have a share in the profit from the sales to European capitalists and immigrants of their lands; and, for the purpose of aiding the sale, a company called the Scioto was formed, to which the lands were conveyed.

By the act of April 21, 1792, the President was authorized to issue to the Ohio Company of Associates patents for 750,-000 acres of land; in addition, several other tracts within certain described boundaries in Ohio, were included. The same act also authorized the President to issue to the Ohio Company patents for an additional area of 214,285 acres, for which the company was required to pay in six months in " warrants issued for army bounty rights "; and a further quantity of 100,000 acres was to be patented to the Ohio Company in certain prescribed conditions.

It appears conclusive that Symmes, Dayton, Cutler, Sargent, Duer and associates in the various companies carried on the most extensive swindles. Notwithstanding the fact that the Symmes-Dayton company had paid for only a part of the lands in the contract, and although Congress had modified the contract in their favor, they insisted that they were entitled to the original quantity of a million acres and were not bound to make any further payment until they received it. Acting upon this pretense they sold large areas, not included in their patent, to settlers.[87] When the Government later offered this same land to the settlers at $2 per acre, the settlers protested that they had already paid Symmes. And it also seems that when Symmes sold them the lands, he deliberately so altered the contracts that he left their lands out of the area patented to him.[88] The settlers were thus left with bad titles, and found themselves in conflict with the Government which had come to their rescue.

The Scioto Company sold considerable of their Ohio land

[87] " American State Papers: Public Lands," Vol. I: 106.
[88] *Ibid.*, 112.   (Doc. No. 62.)

to companies and individuals in France. The Ohio Company
and the Scioto fell to quarreling over the question as to which
held the title to the land sold to French settlers, at Galliopolis,
Ohio. The consequence of this fight for the spoils was that
the settlers found themselves with bad titles; after paying
for their lands they discovered that there was no legal bar
to their dispossession. In a pathetic petition to Congress, they
expressed their regret at not being able to prosecute the
" authors of their misery," and solicited a grant of land elsewhere. Reporting on the whole transaction, on March 27,
1794, U. S. Attorney-General William Bradford concluded
by saying that if the settlers sued, each had to bring a separate
suit, and he spoke of the French settlers as " almost ex-
hausted by the many disappointments and difficulties which
they have had to struggle with for the space of three years." [89]

Gallatin, Secretary of the Treasury, reported to Congress,
in 1812, that the amount of land actually sold to the Ohio
Company, in 1792, was 964,285 acres and the extent actually
patented to Symmes was 248,540 acres.[90] Altogether, 11,046
military land warrants had been issued, covering a total of
1,562,250 acres; and of these 11,046 warrants, reported
George Graham, Commissioner of the General Land Office,
" the number of warrants located and not patented, and those
surrendered by the Ohio Company and J. C. Symmes amounted
to 10,928 warrants for 1,528,950 acres of land." [91] It is thus
established that a large proportion of the military land warrants issued to the soldiers of the Revolution, came into the
possession of two cliques of politician speculators who, on
the strength of them, obtained nearly a million and a quarter
acres of some of the finest lands in Ohio, including the sites
of many present large cities.

The reader may be astonished that such enormities as these
were committed at the very beginning of the Government, but

[89] " American State Papers: Public Lands, Vol. I, 29-30.
[90] *Ibid.*, Vol. II : 442.   [91] *Ibid.*, Vol. IV : 471.

we are simply giving the facts as they appear in the records.

Jonathan Dayton and His Speculations.

Even while officiating as Speaker of the House of Representatives, Jonathan Dayton was industriously buying in, through brokers, batches of military certificates.

Getting into a quarrel with his partners, the mercantile firm of Lawrence, Dayton and Company of New York City, over the profits of land warrants transactions, Dayton, joined by Lawrence, sued Childs, another member of the firm. The suit came up before Chancellor Livingston, in New York, in 1800. Childs alleged that the speculation in land warrants was a project and contrivance of Dayton while he was Speaker of the House, and produced sixteen letters Dayton had written to him.[92]

In one letter Dayton wrote to Childs that " a large company s forming itself here, for the purchase of the United tates lands, and part of their capital is to be 2,000 military ...nd warrants. . . ." On January 27, 1796, Dayton wrote, asking for the employment of some broker to inquire as to the terms for the purchase of two hundred land warrants, which, he had directly heard, were selling at $75 per hundred acres. " Don't mention my name to the broker," Dayton warned Childs. The committee in Congress, Dayton added, had reported a bill for the sale of lands, at $2 an acre, in the Northwest Territory, and it had agreed to accept military warrants. From time to time Dayton kept Childs fully informed as to the legislation being brewed in Congress, and he arranged with Childs for the purchase of army land warrants. Dayton concluded his letter of April 17, 1796, " The contents of this letter are of such a nature as to render it improper to be seen by any except yourself; burn it, therefore, when you have perused it." There were many other such

[92] These letters are to be found in full in John Wood's " Suppressed History of the Administration of John Adams (From 1797 to 1801). As Printed and Suppressed in 1802, And Republished in 1846."

letters.[93]   Dayton later withdrew his suit against Childs, paying full costs.

In a single month, March, 1800, Dayton secured in his own name 15,553 acres of land in exchange for five military land warrants, and Nicholas Gilman was likewise getting land for military certificates.[94]

Evidently John Wood did not exaggerate when he wrote, in 1802, that Dayton, the late speaker of Congress " is notorious from Boston to Georgia.   The deeds of other members of Congress were scarcely known beyond the circle of their respective States, but the speculations of this man have rung through the western world." [95]

But Dayton's actions were far from being exceptional; that he was chosen speaker is a sufficient commentary upon the character of the majority electing him.   The Senate also was ruled by such men as Robert Morris, Charles Carroll, Oliver Ellsworth, James Gunn, Gallatin, Sedgwick, Hillhouse and others who had voted for Hamilton's refunding plan after some had themselves made considerable purchases in the certificates of the Revolutionary army.

Nearly all of these men were at the same time manipulating State Legislatures to grant them great areas of land, bank charters, and charters for canal, bridge and turnpike companies.   Thus, Charles Carroll was one of the incorporators of the " Proprietors of the Susequehanna Canal " chartered with a capital of £18,500 (current money of Maryland), in 1784, by the Maryland Legislature.[96]   Gallatin had got a large area of land in Virginia; Morris was becoming a colossal landholder, and of the corrupt land transactions of Gunn and others we shall have more to say hereafter.

[93] " Suppressed History of the Administration of John Adams," 152–158.
[94] " American State Papers: Public Lands," Vol. I: 118.   (Report of Joseph Nourse, Register of the Treasury Department.)
[95] " Suppressed History of the Administration of John Adams," etc., 145.
[96] " Laws of Maryland, 1682–1784," Vol. I, Chap. 23.

Protests Against Land Grabbing.

The origin of the huge grants made to Symmes, Dayton, and the·Ohio Company and all of their associates, both open and in the background, dated, as, we have said, from 1787. The protest against giving millions of acres of the public domain to an unprincipled band of speculators soon, but impotently, made itself heard in Congress. The spoliation going on could not be deterred by mere protests.

In the debates in May, 1789, on Western lands, and the establishment of a Land Office, Representative Scott advanced the principle that the land ought to be sold in small quantities. " There are at this moment," he said, on May 28, 1789, " a great number of people on the ground who are willing to acquire by purchase a right to the land they are seated on." In Kentucky, hundreds of thousands of acres had been already granted to a few absentee landlords. Kentucky was full, said Scott; at least there were no more valuable lands to be got there with a clear title, and, therefore, no more settlers could be received. " They hope," went on Scott, referring to the settlers, " to get them [the lands] upon as good terms as they can procure them of the speculators. What will these men think who have placed themselves upon a vacant spot anxiously awaiting its disposition by the Government, to find their preëmption rights engrossed by the purchaser of a million acres? Will they expose themselves to be preyed·upon by these men?" Seven thousand souls, Representative Scott continued, were there waiting for lands; troops sent under General Harmer had driven out these squatting settlers, had burnt their cabins and had torn up their potato patches; but three hours after the troops had gone, the people returned, repaired the damage, and settled upon the land in defiance of the Government.[97] On July 13, 1789, Scott pointed out that the western territory (meaning east of Mississippi) could con-

[97] " Abridgement of the Debates of Congress," Vol. I: 99–100.

tain 2,000,000 farms, or at least 1,000,000, and that 6,000,000 people could live in comfort there.[98]

Hamilton Plans Further Big Land Seizures.

Popular protests, however, counted for nothing. The very next year, on July 20, 1790, Alexander Hamilton, as Secretary of the Treasury, submitted to Congress a plan for disposing of the public lands. These lands were the enormous area owned by the National Government. Part of the large areas originally owned by certain of the original States were still under the complete jurisdiction of those States. Hamilton's plan fully revealed the nature of further schemes under way on the part of leading capitalist politicians to appropriate the public domain, both that owned by the Federal Government and that by the States.

" Purchasers," reported Hamilton, " may be contemplated in three classes: moneyed individuals and companies, who will buy to sell again; associations of persons who intend to make settlements themselves; single persons, or families now resident in the Western country, or who may be emigrants thither thereafter. The two first will be frequently blended, and will always want considerable tracts. The last, will generally purchase in small quantities. Hence, a plan for the sale of the Western lands, while it may have due regard to the last, should be calculated to obtain all of the advantages which may be derived from the first two classes. For this reason, it seems requisite that the General Land Office should be established at the seat of Government. It is there that the principal purchasers, whether citizens or foreigners, can most easily find proper agents, and that contracts for large purchases can be best adjusted. . . ."

No actual settler, Hamilton recommended, should get more than one hundred acres, and the price of land should be thirty

98 " Abridgement of the Debates of Congress," Vol. I: 113.

cents an acre to be paid either in gold, silver or public securities. No credit should be allowed for any purchase of
less quantity than a township of ten miles square, nor more
than two years' credit for any greater quantity, and one quarter of the consideration was to be paid down.[99]   Although the
points of this plan were not immediately and formally adopted,
yet its recommendations were practically, as we have seen, put
into speedy effect by Washington and his cabinet by force of
executive authority.

Constitutional Convention Held in Secrecy.

With an understanding of the facts, both retrospective and
anticipatory, herein presented, no explanation is needed as to
why it was that the Federal Constitutional Convention held
its deliberations and proceedings behind locked doors, as
Luther Martin, Attorney-General of Maryland and a delegate
to the Convention, indignantly reported to the Maryland Legislature. No delegate, Martin wrote, was allowed to correspond with his constituents; taking of notes was permitted
only by special consent; the utmost precautions were exercised to prevent the debates and acts from reaching the public.

" So solicitous," wrote Martin, " were they that their proceedings should not transpire, that the members were prohibited even from taking copies of resolutions, on which the
Convention was deliberating, or extracts from any of the
journals, without formally moving for, and obtaining permission, by a vote of the convention for that purpose." [100]

Here was the epochal spectacle of a Constitutional Convention delegated in solemn meeting apparently to establish
a Republican democracy, yet not daring to trust the very
people for whom the Republic was theoretically founded with

[99] "American State Papers: Public Lands," Vol. I: 8–9. (Doc.
No. 3.)
[100] " Elliott's Debates," etc., Vol. I: 345.

any knowledge of its proceedings. Not until long after were the debates published. It was not that the delegates lacked trust in the intelligence of the people; they feared the results if their betrayal of the popular demands should become known.

When they did become known, after the Federal Convention had adopted the Constitution, and before the different States had taken action, there was a blaze of popular anger. The various eminent delegates whose handiwork it was hastened to exert every possible influence to bring about its adoption by the State Conventions: Gorham and Gerry in Massachusetts; Wilson, Robert Morris and McKean in Pennsylvania; Washington in Virginia; Daniel Carroll and Samuel Chase in Maryland; William Livingston and Jonathan Dayton in New Jersey; and Livingston's son-in-law, John Jay, and Alexander Hamilton in New York. In Delaware and Pennsylvania John Dickinson, a member of the Federal Constitutional Convention, was energetic for the adoption of that instrument; Dickinson had inherited the vast estate of " Crosia — dore," granted to Walter Dickinson in 1659; he had represented the Penn Proprietors and had obtained for them $580,-000 during the Revolution when their land was declared forfeited; and he had been President of the Supreme Council of Pennsylvania. In Connecticut Oliver Ellsworth argued stoutly for the Constitution; the presiding officer of the Connecticut Convention which ratified the Constitution was Matthew Griswold, who had inherited a baronial estate in that colony, and was a man of great wealth. But it is quite needless to enumerate other examples.

In the Pennsylvania Convention Wilson appeared as the principal defender of the Constitution; he admitted that the popular view of that instrument was that it was designed to perpetuate the powers of the aristocracy, and he devoted his arguments to attempting to counteract that belief. What Wilson's share in the drafting of the Constitution of the United states was, and the story of his performances leading up to the insertion of a particular clause advocated by him, is told in the next chapter.

These men held constant secret conclaves, or corresponded regularly; they issued essays and publications filled with alluring arguments to influence the public mind. During the publication of the " Federalist," the work so largely of Hamilton and Jay, the workingmen of New York City showed their feelings by a street demonstration. In trying with Hamilton to quell it, Jay so exasperated his auditors that a stone was hurled at him striking him on the head; he was left for dead but recovered.

All the great power of the land magnates was used to avert the threatened danger of the Constitution being rejected. The Livingstons, Van Rennselaers and Schuylers in New York; the Carrolls — the largest landowners in Maryland, and estimated one of the very richest families in the country — these, and all the rest of the-landed class combined to beat into line such antagonistic dependents as there were of every stripe — lawyers, clergy, college professors, tradesmen, workers and newspaper editors.

The banks controlled by Hamilton, Wilson, Robert Morris, Gouverneur Morris and other delegates [101] exercised the most effective influence upon tradesmen by the threat of withdrawing credit or by harassing them should they fail to support the adoption of the Constitution.[102]

Whom the Constitution Pleased.

These methods succeeded throughout the colonies. Writing from New York to Livingston, January 14, 1788, as to the

[101] The history of these banks is given in Chap. IV.

[102] It should not be imagined that elections then were " pure and undefiled." Far from it. The buying of votes in New York was an old story. And as far back as March 11, 1752, the Legislature of Pennsylvania had passed an act " for the prevention of bribery and corruption in the election of Sheriffs and Coroners within this province." Carey and Bioren's " Pa. Laws," Vol. I: 328.

pending question of whether the Constitution was likely to be adopted in Massachusetts, General Henry Knox wrote that "the commercial part of the State, to which are added all the men of considerable property, the clergy, the lawyers, including all of the officers of the late army, and also all the neighborhood of all the great towns" favored its adoption. "Perhaps," added Knox, "many of them would have been still more pleased with the new Constitution, had it been more analogous to the British Constitution." [103]

On the other hand, there were not lacking exponents of the popular hostility; one of these, writing under the name of "Brutus," expressed the opposing view. Pointing out that "the farmer, merchant, mechanic and other various orders of the people ought to be represented [in Congress] according to their respective weight and numbers," he went on:

"According to the common course of human affairs, the natural aristocracy of the country will be elected. Wealth always creates influence, and this is generally increased in large family connections; this class in society will forever have a great number of dependents; besides they will always favor each other. It is to their interest to combine — they will therefore constantly unite their efforts to procure men of their own rank to be elected. . . . It is probable that few of the merchants, and those of the most opulent and ambitious, will have a representation from their body. . . . The great body of the yeomen [the small farmers] of the country cannot expect any of their order in this assembly. . . . The mechanics of every branch must expect to be excluded from a seat in this body; . . . so that in reality there will be no part of the people represented but the rich, even in that branch of the Legislature called democratic. The well-born, and highest orders in life, as they term themselves, will be

[103] "Debates and Proceedings In The Convention of Massachusetts, 1788," etc., p. 399. Gen. Knox's wife, it may be said, had inherited a large share of the great Waldo estate, in what is now the State of Maine.

ignorant of the sentiments of the middling class," etc., etc. The representation, continued the paper, " is merely nominal — a mere burlesque, and that no security is provided against corruption and undue influence." [104]

Of the whole Constitution the people at large were suspicious to a degree little comprehended now. They saw that it was the product of a convention composed mostly of manorial lords or their attorneys and mouthpieces. They feared that the so-called democratic representation in Congress would resolve itself into a continuation of the old rule by the great land owners and traders; and that they were right events quickly proved.

But what especially aroused fears was the judiciary. During the Revolution only one of the royal judges in Massachusetts, for example, had espoused the popular cause, and this particular one — Cushing — did not do so until he was virtually compelled to give an expression of opinion; he then became one of the most stalwart and time-serving of the band of reactionaries. During more than a century the judges had acted arrogantly and often corruptly; they had usurped powers never granted to them, and had assumed the right to void laws as much as they pleased. In the Revolutionary period some judges were attacked by armed bodies of indignant patriots outraged by the actions of those judicial reactionaries. The people had long seen the landholders or their retainers put on the bench; and then, by the expedient of irresponsible judicial construction, those judges had validated titles obtained by fraud and corruption.

The greatest popular bitterness manifested itself against the courts. This feeling, grounded on the experience of centuries of oppression, was not to be allayed by smooth explanations on the part of the advocates of the Constitution. Of this popular sentiment the makers of the Constitution were fully aware. By adroitly dwelling upon the principle of representation in Congress, and by arguing and counter-arguing about it, and

[104] Essay III of " Brutus," *Ibid.,* 389–391.

emphasizing it, those advocates succeeded, to a considerable extent, in diverting the popular mind from the tremendous potential power that the Constitution had lodged in a small, omnipotent body, appointed for life. This handful of judicial rulers was the Supreme Court of the United States.

CHAPTER IV

THE SUPREME COURT UNDER CHIEF-JUSTICE JOHN JAY

If the various elements dissatisfied with the Constitution were led into attaching too much importance to the question of representation in Congress, and too little to the immense potential consequence of the Federal judiciary, the powerful landed class fully understood the supreme might of the courts.

As the superlative court of courts, the newly created Supreme Court of the United States was rightly anticipated by the manorial lords as the chief instrument by which their interests would be conserved and enlarged. Holding an inherited and expanding power, the accretion of centuries, and owning vast estates, the land grandees did not purpose to surrender either wealth or power. Their one guiding aim was to hold and extend, both. The import of such concessions as during those threatening times had to be made to the populace was cunningly magnified, but a considerable body of the artisans, laborers and small farmers were by no means deceived. Gloss and fine phrases aside, they saw with alarm that not only had the essentials of the old conditions been retained, but that the landholding families and traders were now exercising limitless license in securing great new accumulations of property, and securing the passage of whatever laws their interests and designs required.

Danger to the Manorial Lords.

The Revolution had established the principle of resorting to force to accomplish changes. With this " perilous " idea permeating the " lower orders," there was a considerable degree of probability that it might be repeatedly and formidably applied to strip the manorial landholders of their privileges and possessions, and to abolish all the superstructure of prestige, exclusiveness and caste. The workers were demanding the abolition of barbaric laws, and the small farmers, located as well as intending settlers, were uniting with artisans and laborers in denouncing the great and continual land jobbing by which powerful individuals, lauded as " statesmen," were appropriating millions of acres of the best soil and the most valuable resources. The tenants of the great manorial estates were in a restless state, on the verge of resorting to force to throw off the yoke riveted upon them by ancient laws. Above all, subversive doctrines had been agitated ; no longer was there a semblance of reverence felt for the aristocrats ; they were looked upon as enemies, to be divested of power at the first opportunity. Permeating what were stigmatized as the " lower orders " of society, there was a revolutionary aspiration for equality of opportunity and standing : that much the Revolution had implanted.

It has been said that the great value of revolutions is that at a blow they overcome all established conditions without having to wait for the slow, cumbrous processes of a dragging course of legislation, too often tricky and useless. But the American Revolution was not a Revolution in the sense of the transfer of power from one class to another. The class seizing hold of the reins after the American Revolution had been won well knew that however that Revolution abolished certain forms and details, it did not touch something of far more enduring and incisive effect.

The pillar left untouched was the long line of privileges and precedents established by a powerful feudal aristocracy and maintained by the courts since the reign of Richard II of England, and even before. These precedents had been established for the twofold purpose of justifying the maraudings, thefts and summary frauds by which the dukes, lords and barons had appropriated the British soil, and with the object of holding the working class in complete subjection. They were principles of law enunciated by judges put on the bench by those self-same pillagers; very often those judges were avowedly corrupt, like Lord Bacon, who admitted taking bribes. Or, if not purchasable by money, they were biased instruments — a fact well assured in advance of their appointment, in fact they would not have been elevated to the high bench by the all-powerful nobility whose purposes they served had their abject compliancy not been well attested. The decisions of these judges were followed by the American colonial judges; and presently we find the Supreme Court of the United States, when in need of precedents, going back to Lord Coke, Lord Bacon and such jurists.

John Jay Chooses to be Chief Justice.

The landed class, being by virtue of its wealth, its cohesiveness and its long hold on government, the dominant class, had no difficulty in getting President Washington, himself an extensive landholder, to fill the Supreme Court bench with men of its own class. When Washington gave John Jay his choice of Federal offices, Jay selected for himself, in 1789, the post of Chief Justice of the Supreme Court.

Why did Jay choose this position? It could hardly have been entirely from ambition or taste, inasmuch as six years later he resigned from the Chief Justiceship in order to undergo a long and tedious trip to Europe to execute a treaty by which, among other provisions, alien landholders and their American connections or purchasers were eventually able to recover large and highly valuable areas of confiscated estates. By making this treaty Jay performed a service of inestimable value to the landholding class; and it can be reasonably inferred that when he picked the seat of Chief Justiceship he realized the immeasurable importance of that commanding office. His appointment was hailed with unconcealed delight and gratification by the powerful landholders; among the mass of people a corresponding sense of deep dismay was not slow in expressing itself.

By hereditary ties and family and personal connections, Jay was allied by birth, marriage and interest with a number of the mightiest manorial lords in the United States.

His father, Peter, a rich merchant trading with the West Indies, was the only son of Augustus Jay, who, in 1685, had married Anna Bayard. The methods by which Nicholas Bayard, her father, obtained from Fletcher a grant of land forty miles long and thirty wide, have been related in Chapter I. John Jay's mother was Mary, a daughter of Jacobus Van Courtlandt, a very rich New York landholder and merchant, and long a politician and office holder of great influence, serving in the Assembly and as Mayor of New York City.

The Van Courtlandt family was one of the largest landholders in the State, having acquired its estate during the corrupt regimes of Governors Slaughter and Fletcher. Stephanus, the elder brother of Jacobus Van Courtlandt, was the right-hand lieutenant of both Slaughter and Fletcher. Of Lord Bellomont's full exposure of Fletcher's bribes and corrupt grants, sufficient details have been given in Chapter I. In 1683, Stephanus Van Courtlandt fraudulently secured a great tract of 83,000 acres, extending on the east side of the Hudson River, by an ostensible purchase from the Indians. This was one of the "extravagant grants" that Lord Bellomont did not succeed in confiscating.

In 1697, this estate was erected into the lordship and manor of Courtlandt; and Stephanus built a splendid manor house on the northern shore of Croton Bay. He had married, in 1671, Gertrude, a daughter of Schuyler, who had obtained his estate, too, by bribery and fraud, and whose descendants, as told in Chapter I, enlarged the estate by similar fraudulent means by favor of Courtlandt and other functionaries of the Provincial Council. Stephanus Van Courtlandt also secured great holdings of land on the west bank of the Hudson River, on Long Island, and in Sussex County.   Jacobus Van Courtlandt married Eva de Vries, stepdaughter of that Frederick Phillips (or Philipse, as it was often spelled), whose career as backer of the pirate, Captain Burgess, and whose methods as land appropriator have also been described in Chapter I.   Jacobus had an estate in Yonkers which was uninterruptedly owned by his descendants until 1889, when it was bought by the City of New York and converted into what is now Van Courtlandt Park. He also owned a large estate at Bedford, Westchester County, of which estate a portion descended to John Jay.

Jay's Further Powerful Connections.

Descended from an intermingled line of landed families, John Jay married into another mighty landed family, which, despite its support of the Revolutionary movement for political independence, had its alliance of family and interests with powerful British nobles.

This was the Livingston family.   Jay's wife, to whom he was married in April, 1773, was a daughter of William Livingston, fifth child of Philip, second Lord of Livingston Manor. This manorial seat comprised a tract of about 160,240 acres in the northern part of the present Dutchess County, New York. It had been confirmed to the time-server, political turncoat, sinecurist and army contractor, Robert Livingston, by Governor Hunter in 1715, with the feudal rights of court leet, court baron and advowson.[1]

This property, however, was only one of the far-reaching possessions of the Livingston family.   William Livingston who lived in New Jersey, was a delegate to the Federal Constitutional Convention, and Governor of New Jersey from 1776 to 1790.   He was very closely associated with the Lords Pro-

[1] Court leet was an ancient English feudal right investing the holder with the right to hold court.   Advowson was the right to nominate ministers, and otherwise control churches.

prietors of New Jersey. We have seen how, during that time, John Livingston, another member of the same family, and acting for it, was defrauding the Indians of vast tracts of land, and compelling Phelps and Gorham to admit him and other lessees into a partnership in the spoils.

Peter Van Brugh Livingston, a younger son of Philip, second lord of Livingston'Manor (and thus by marriage an uncle of Jay), had become a rich merchant in partnership with his brother-in-law William Alexander, subsequently raised to the peerage under the title of Lord Stirling. We have noted how William Alexander and Robert Morris were partners in that contract to supply the Farmers General of France with 60,000 hogsheads of tobacco. Peter Van Brugh Livingston was an intimate friend of Washington; he was president of the Provincial Congress; and after the adoption of the New York State Constitution of 1777, he was elected to the Legislature, and easily managed to have himself chosen president of the Assembly.

Other members of the Livingston family held high Federal, State and New York City offices. They were extraordinarily alert and self-assertive — those Livingstons.

At the outset of the Revolution John Jay and Robert R. Livingston were associated as partners in the practice of law. This Robert was a son of the first Robert R. Livingston who had married Margaret, the daughter of Colonel Henry Beekman. How Henry Beekman obtained two land grants from Fletcher, one of sixteen miles of land in Dutchess County, and the other running twenty miles along the Hudson, and eight miles inland, has been related in Chapter I. By combining his possessions with the Beekman estate, Robert R. Livingston (the first) became reputed to be, without exception, the richest landholder in New York.[2]

---

[2] The foregoing genealogical details are cited from " Prominent Families of New York," " National Cyclopedia Of American Biography," and other genealogical and biographical works.

The Livingston Family's Sway.

The political motto of the Livingston family was direct and concise: the family should always derive benefit, and nothing of any degree of value was to escape it. Robert Livingston, the founder of their fortune, had got hold of it primarily through being a politician. Assiduously emulating his example, his descendants set out to thrust themselves into every possible office and financial undertaking.

Robert R. Livingston the second was a member of the Continental Congress; he was on the committee drafting the New York State Constitution of 1777. Upon the adoption of that instrument, he became the first Chancellor of New York State, in which position he was promoter of a certain remarkable transaction which we shall be under pressing need of describing later. While serving as Chancellor he held a Federal office, that of Secretary of Foreign Affairs, a post created by Congress in 1781. In 1783 Livingston resigned this office, Jay succeeding him. Livingston was president of the New York Convention of 1788, called to take action on the Federal Constitution. The whole Livingston family used its influence for the ratification of that document.

For a century, the Livingston family, beginning with nothing, and becoming one of the richest in the colonies, had assiduously pushed themselves, their ties and connections into every office and scheme promising profit and assuring power. Like Robert Livingston, their progenitor, they had been sagacious in discerning the winning side in political contests, and were without compunction in changing front. Now the Livingstons again proved their political skill and great power by having Jay installed as Chief Justice of the Supreme Court of the United States.

Of an intensely aristocratic mind, haughty and arrogant, Jay, filled with the views of his class, both feared and despised the people. The laws so signally and disproportionately favoring the class of wealth, and burdening the workers, were the laws he had studied and absorbed; he considered them the proper laws and strove at every opportunity to perpetuate them. During the Revolution, he, Hamilton, the Livingstons, the Schuylers and other relatives or personal friends of their class had their private political club, in the arcana of which they discussed the turn of affairs and plotted conservative measures. Previous to the Federal Constitutional Convention, Jay wrote to Washington that he favored a Congress to be composed of two houses — the upper chamber to be elected for life.

Many of Jay's relatives and associates, as we have already seen, and as we shall perceive yet more clearly, were thoroughly unscrupulous in design, and corrupt in execution. We have remarked how Hamilton, Robert Morris and Jay held a private meeting to discuss land speculations, and how Morris, Livingston and their associates successfully manipulated the legislatures, and defrauded the Indians out of a huge domain; how Hamilton, as the confidential agent of John B. Church, who had grown extra rich out of the commissary department of the Revolutionary army, advanced money to Morris for his land speculations — this, too, has been narrated. Frequently Hamilton was charged with peculations,— an accusation against which his partisan and personal friends stoutly defended him.[3]

Open charges of corruption were also made against Jay. In his celebrated pamphlet [4]— one of the effects of which was the battering down of the Federalist Party — John Thompson Callender boldly asserted Jay's corruption. "If Washington," wrote Callender, "wanted to corrupt the American judges, he could not have taken a more decisive step than by the appointment of Jay."

This statement is merely a general one, made in a partisan

[3] See Henry Adams' "New England Federalism, 1800-1815": 63.
[4] "The Prospect Before Us," p. 34.

spirit, and unsupported by proof. Yet it is invested with a certain weight by reason of the fact that its author was willing to risk indictment and trial by publishing his strictures in the face of the Alien and Sedition Act. This law, passed in desperation by the Federalists to stifle criticism, was rigorously enforced and interpreted.[5] Callender's statement came at a time when, as we shall see, Jay's relatives and friends were undisguisedly, by force of legislative enactment and by the use of their official positions and the courts, consummating great schemes of spoliation in different directions.

Through Jay, the Landholders Control.

The charges of personal corruption were, however, comparatively immaterial. Not so much in a statutory sense but in a far more subtle, efficacious and dangerous degree Jay's mind was corrupted. His acts, generally speaking, were the product of that species of corruption. Against the " lower orders " his mind was filled with a mass of inflexible prejudices; he distrusted and dreaded them, and he held it laudable to curb their menacing aspirations. But in the rich and " well-born," Jay saw nothing but " intelligence, wisdom, virtue and stability "— one of the cant political phrases of the day, manifesting, however, what the aristocracy really thought of itself.

This was the class to whom the directing of government was to be intrusted and vigilantly restricted. In this class, according to Jay's creed, lay the right to rule with a strong hand; it was justifiable to strain every point to advance the political and pecuniary interests of the rich, and assure their supremacy. But nothing should be done to better the status of the workers, by increasing whose power that of the landholders and other capitalists would be correspondingly diminished.

It is idle to inquire into the honesty or dishonesty of these

[5] It was partly for the methods used in procuring Callender's conviction that impeachment proceedings were brought against Justice Samuel Chase, in 1805. See later.

beliefs. Springing from the personal interests of those holding them, they were not individual, but class, beliefs. Those
who declaimed against Jay's appointment did not clearly see
that it was a very natural result. With the landholding class
guiding the currents of the Revolution, and controlling the
conventions, it was an inevitable conclusion that great landholders should occupy, personally or through agents, the offices
of government, especially what they then completely realized
was the most puissant branch — the judiciary.

The insurrections in various States and the threatening
movements of tenants on some of the manorial estates, were
among the evidences of deep popular ferment. Laws aimed at
the landholders were always a possibility to be reckoned with
and provided against. If such laws were passed, the final resource of the landholders would be the courts. The courts
would be the bulwark against popular encroachments; the
courts would know how to find means of taking the stings
out of laws hostile to their class. All these tactics were not
only clearly thought out; they were discussed in aristocratic
clubs, and affirmed in the private circles of the judges themselves. Having himself large landed possessions, and connected by family ties, associations or other connections of interest, with many of the most powerful landholding families in
the country, Jay, from that class point of view, was an ideal
man for the Chief Justiceship. His associates (the Supreme
Court was then composed of five members in all) were likewise of the landholders or attached to them in interest.

The Associate Justices.

The first Associate Justice appointed by Washington, John
Rutledge, represented a different division of landholders. He
had inherited wealth from his father, who had married Sarah
Hext, an heiress of famed beauty. Studying law in England,
Rutledge had returned to his home in South Carolina, and

there was attorney for plantation owners. In the Federal Constitutional Convention he had been the chief mouthpiece of the Southern slave holders, who, possessing great rice, cotton and other plantations, found negro slavery profitable. He, perhaps more than any other delegate, was instrumental in defeating in that Convention the proposition to prevent the importation of slaves. Rutledge remained on the Supreme Court bench for a short time only, resigning in 1791 to become Chief Justice of the Supreme Court of South Carolina.

Judge William Cushing, of Massachusetts, was the third in order of Washington's appointments. He was the scion of two generations of royal judges. His grandfather long held the position of a judge of the Supreme Court of Massachusetts, and his father succeeded, remaining a judge of that court for a period of twenty-five years. His father resigning from the Massachusetts Supreme Court bench in 1771, William Cushing became his successor.

At the age of fifteen, William Cushing had entered Harvard, where, as we have noted, it was the custom to tabulate and range students according to their social rank; as the son of a royal judge William Cushing occupied the first order. During the four plastic years that he studied at Harvard, he could not help absorbing the caste spirit pervading that institution, which experience, added to that derived from his home environment and the atmosphere of rich associates, determined completely the bent of his mind and prejudices. The decisions of his grandfather, father and his own were always favorable to the governing class. Down to the critical years preceding the actual outbreak of the Revolution he so carefully refrained from expressing his views on that event that they were not known until he was directly challenged to reply whether he would receive his salary from the province or the crown. He finally decided to support the colonies — an exceptional step, inasmuch as he was the only one of the royal judges in the whole of Massachusetts to turn rebel.

On the reorganization of the Massachusetts judiciary, he became one of the judges of its Supreme Court, and on the resignation of John Adams, Cushing was elevated to be the Chief Justice, which office he held for twelve years.[6]

Here he made himself extremely obnoxious to the laboring and yeoman classes by his decisions and attitude. In 1785 and 1786 an uprising, or insurrection as it was called, took place in New England. It was a movement caused partially by the continued appropriation of land by a few, and the resulting evils, and more largely by the spurious currency issued by the financiers and other prominent leaders of the Revolution.

Suffering from debts, with no adequate means of paying them, numbers of the people rose in armed revolt. They complained, and with the fullest justice, that while the landholders and shippers were enriching themselves by all manner of schemes and practices, and making laws as they willed, the debtors' laws were enforced against the poor with pitiless rigor. The jails were crowded with poor debtors. For this condition the courts were especially blamed; they were denounced as " rich men's courts," and their discrimination in applying law aroused the most intense bitterness. The popular orators pointed out how, while " rich knaves and powerful plunderers " were allowed to keep their loot, the law was applied mercilessly to those having no property. On one occasion, Cushing's court was surrounded by an armed body of insurrectionists; and although he and other judges declared that " mob rule " would not influence them, the force of popular feeling was so great and threatening that the Massachusetts Legislature passed a law delaying the collection of debts.

Cushing sided wholly with the conservatives,— as the land-

[6] Prior to the Revolution, judges of the high courts in Massachusetts dressed impressively in scarlet robes, with deep facings and cuffs of black velvet. They wore wigs adorned with black silk bags, and were privileged to wear swords while on the bench. In the summer, however, black silk gowns were substituted for the robes. The object was, of course, to invest themselves with an atmosphere of awe.

holders and merchants were termed.   He was not only a member of the Massachusetts Convention of 1788, but he presided over the debates during the greater part of the session, during the absence of John Hancock; and it was by the influence of such men as Elbridge Gerry, Nathaniel Gorham, John Adams and others, joined with his own, that the Federal Constitutional Convention was ratified.   As an Associate Justice of the Supreme Court of the United States he presided over that court in the absence of John Jay; he remained on the bench until his seventy-eighth year, in 1810.

The career of Washington's next appointee, James Wilson, chosen as an Associate Justice in 1789, necessitates so extended a narrative, that the description will be deferred until a few words have been said about Washington's other appointees.

John Blair, appointed an Associate Justice in 1790, was a personal friend of Washington; he came from Williamsburg, Virginia, had studied law in London, England, had been a member of the Virginia Council, a judge, Chief Justice, and Chancellor in that province, and, as a member of the Federal Constitutional Convention, had voted for the adoption of the Constitution.   After a few years' service in the Supreme Court of the United States, he resigned.

James Iredell, appointed in the same year, was the leader of the Federalist Party in North Carolina.   He was the son of a merchant in Bristol, England, who, when James was seventeen years old, had sent him to North Carolina.   He became a deputy collector, supported the movement for political independence,[7] was appointed a judge of the Superior Court of North Carolina, in 1777, and then Attorney-General of that State.   In the North Carolina Convention of 1788, called to decide on the question of the Federal Constitution, he strenuously tried to secure its adoption, but failed.

---

[7] It was said of Iredell that by taking this step he alienated the favor of a rich uncle whose fortune he would have inherited.

Iredell's chief occupation during that period was in acting as the attorney for large North Carolina landholders, especially those whose estates had been confiscated. He was, for instance, the representative of the McCullohs, as well as their kinsman. Henry McCulloh had, under British rule, held various offices, including that of Commissioner of Crown Lands. He obtained a patent for 1,200,000 acres for himself and associates, but because of his failure to induce immigration to his huge domain, his affairs became somewhat embarrassed. However, he held onto a vast area of land; and in 1761, he caused his son, Henry Eustace McCulloh, an English lawyer, to come to North Carolina and act as his agent. There the younger McCulloh became a member of the Provincial Council, Collector of the Port of Roanoke, and later Representative in England of the Colony of North Carolina. As a member of the North Carolina Council, Henry Eustace McCulloh "sold his vote," says Sabine, "in favor of the Tuscarora grant of lands to Williams, Pugh and Jones for a thousand acres of land. The fact that he was thus bribed seems to have been notorious. . . ." Sabine goes on to tell that such was McCulloh's "tact and address," that when he adjusted his father's accounts with the Crown, he got "64,000 acres, without the payment of a single dollar." How he managed to do this, Sabine, unfortunately, does not tell.

The elder McCulloh's estate was apparently confiscated, but he had previously conveyed it to his son. In 1779, when Henry Eustace McCulloh's estate was confiscated, he went to England as agent for the North Carolina loyalists in prosecuting their claims for indemnity from the British Government. "He himself," Sabine relates, "was a claimant; and though he received a considerable sum, he was dissatisfied." Sabine further relates that when McCulloh was in England, Judge Iredell "rendered him much valuable service" in North Carolina for which, in return, Iredell considered himself badly treated; the particular nature of the service Sabine does not disclose.[8]   Iredell served on the bench of the Supreme Court of the United States until 1799.

Thomas Johnson, appointed by Washington in 1791, and serving until 1793, came from Maryland, was an ardent Federalist, and also belonged to the landholding group.   The arbitrary tone of the judiciary at that time may be seen from the fact that when the Grand Jury, at Baltimore, handed in a presentment against him for holding a place in two courts at the same time, Johnson haughtily told them to confine themselves to their proper sphere.

The next Associate Justice, appointed in 1793 by Washington, was William Paterson, of New Jersey.   Paterson was directly connected with the Van Rensselaer family, with the Lords Proprietors of New Jersey, and was the right-hand auxiliary of Governor William Livingston.   By family ties of various kinds Paterson was also connected with many other large landholding families.   Stephen Van Rensselaer Paterson, a twin brother of William Paterson, was long a Surveyor-General of the Lords Proprietors of New Jersey.   The mother of Stephen Van Rensselaer (the elder Stephen — there were father and son of that name) was a daughter of Philip Livingston, lord of Livingston Manor.   After his graduation from Harvard, in 1782, Stephen Van Rensselaer had been married to a daughter of General Philip Schuyler; hence by marriage, becoming a brother-in-law of Alexander Hamilton.   Stephen Van Rensselaer's second wife was a daughter of Justice William Paterson.   The immensity of Stephen Van Rensselaer's estate may be judged from the fact that in Rensselaer and Albany counties, New York, he owned 3,000 farms or about 436,-000 acres.[9]   The quasi-feudal conditions prevailing on the

[8] " Loyalists of the American Revolution," Vol. II : 54.
[9] Each of the various members of this family were large landholders. In 1782 John Van Rensselaer held about 32,000 acres in New York, part of which land he had leased on permanent ground rents, part for life, and the residue in fee simple.   Out of the entailing of his estate grew protracted litigation.   (See case of Van Rensselaer vs. Kearney et. al., Howard's Reports, Supreme Court of the United States, Vol. II : 259.)

Livingston, Van Rensselaer and other New York estates survived to the year 1846,[10] and were the prime cause of various
uprisings of the eighteenth century, and of the Anti-Renters'
movement of 1847–49. William Paterson had long been one
of the most active politicians in New Jersey; as a member of
the Federal Constitutional Convention he was, of course,
aligned with the landholding class. After serving as a United
States senator, he had succeeded William Livingston as Governor of New Jersey.

Samuel Chase, appointed an Associate Justice by Washington, in 1796, was a landholder and promoter of various enterprises. Born in Maryland, in 1741, the son of a Protestant
Episcopalian clergyman, he became a lawyer representing large
landholders and shippers. An indefatigable politician, he invariably got what he sought when he wanted a private act for
his special benefit from the Maryland Legislature. He was a
signer of the Declaration of Independence, and was authorized
by the Maryland act of 1783 to go to England and obtain from
two fugitive loyalists a transfer of Bank of England stock belonging to the State of Maryland, for which mission Chase
was praised by the Maryland Assembly for his " great zeal,
fidelity and ability." [11]

Becoming heavily involved in two land companies, Chase petitioned the Legislature for relief. In his memorial he set
forth that, in association with several others in these companies, he had become very largely indebted to the State and to
private creditors; that he personally owed considerable sums
of money, and also his partnership debts; and that his property was greatly insufficient to pay his debts. He further
stated that he had proposed to Thomas Dorsey, the only solvent
partner in the two companies, to convey to Dorsey all his

[10] " New York Constitution; Debates In Convention, 1846 ": 1052–1056.
Mr. Jordan, a delegate to the Convention of 1846, denounced the feudal
conditions. It was, he said, from such things relief was asked; " which
although the moral sense of the community will not admit to be enforced, are still actually in existence."
[11] " Laws of Maryland, 1682–1784," Vol. I, Chap. 76.

claims to all property in the two companies, and also his claim
to an undivided eighth part of certain confiscated British coal
and iron lands called the Nottingham Forges and White Marsh
Furnace.   These two properties comprised several thousand
acres, and carried with them sixty negro slaves, some teams,
coal wagons, houses and household furniture, and also three
hundred and forty-eight acres of a tract called Darnall's Camp,
bought by Chase and his partners from the State.

Why he fell into debt Chase did not explain.   But the Legislature was accommodating.   It passed a special act that if
Chase conveyed the property to Dorsey, he should be discharged from all debts, and that if any process was issued
against Chase it should be quashed.[12]   It need scarcely be said
that, at the same time, the iron laws against poor debtors were
being ruthlessly enforced in all of the courts with steadfast
rigor; prisons were crowded with debtors whose only crime
was that they owed a few dollars.[13]   Justice Chase's extreme
arrogance, and his abuse of the functions of the Supreme Court
of the United States for partisan purposes, later caused impeachment proceedings to be brought against him.[14]

Career of Justice James Wilson.

John Jay and the sundry Associate Justices were able men,
but in certain respects, the most energetic, dominating member
of the Supreme Court from 1789 to 1798 was James Wilson.
He, perhaps, more than any other incumbent left the stamp of
his particular subtle legal astuteness and his individuality upon
the proceedings and annals of that court.   Washington valued

[12] *Ibid.*, Vol. II, Chap. 10.
[13] This condition long continued.   A report for the year ending November 26, 1831, revealed that nearly one thousand citizens had been
imprisoned for debt in Baltimore.   More than half of this number owed
less than ten dollars, and of the entire number, only thirty-four were
individually under debts exceeding one hundred dollars.— Reports of
Committees, First Session, Twenty-Fourth Congress, Vol. II, Report
No. 732: 2.
[14] See Chapter V.

his learning so highly, that he placed his favorite nephew, Bushrod Washington (later an Associate Justice of the Supreme Court) in Wilson's office to study law, personally paying Wilson for his nephew's tuition. Wilson was deeply grounded in all of the subtleties of Roman and mediæval law, and very resourceful in never being at a loss for impressive authorities and precedents.

A Scotch lawyer, Wilson had emigrated to America. Here he made good headway; his clients were rich, and he was successful in their suits. Although he supported the movement for independence, he brought upon himself popular hatred by his sneers at the "lower orders," and his utterances and acts in support of rich Tories whom he defended during the Revolution. Pamphlets and other writings of the time abound in ridicule of his "lofty strut," and in denunciations of his attitude.

More serious was an attack upon him, on October 4, 1779, during his stay in Annapolis. Enraged at his conduct, a group of patriots rushed up to his house, and opened fire with a cannon. Anticipating this, Wilson had gathered his friends and had turned his house into a miniature fortress. The city troop were hurriedly summoned, the attackers was fired on, and several were killed and wounded.

Whatever were Wilson's acts and crimes, he, at least, was audaciously open and honest in his truckling to the rich and in his advocacy of their class interests; at a time when most politicians were secretly betraying the Revolution, while in words prating of democracy, this candid quality of Wilson's was certainly a virtue. Had he been lost, the whole capitalist class of to-day would have had good reason to mourn him. In the Federal Constitutional Convention, in which he was a delegate from Pennsylvania, he did some extraordinary skillful work; to him is due the farsightedness of inserting in the Constitution of the United States a modest-looking little clause which, however, has had the most far-reaching consequences.

And the fact that it was the personal experience of himself, Robert and Gouverneur Morris, Thomas Fitzsimmons and other Constitutional molders, in the notorious Bank of North America transaction, that led to the drafting and adoption of that clause, tends to prove that the men who drafted the Constitution knew fully the secret and ultimate purport of every clause.

The Bank of North America Transaction.

Under the patriotic pretence that the charter for which they asked was for a union of citizens to supply the army, a group of politicians, on April 1, 1782, pushed an act through the Pennsylvania Legislature, incorporating the Bank of North America. This bank had been chartered by the Continental Congress in 1781, but under the then loose Confederated government, that charter was not believed to be of any comprehensive account. The principal promoter of that charter in the Continental Congress was George Clymer, of Philadelphia; he and John Nixon were appointed by Congress to receive subscriptions for the Bank of North America. Clymer, in 1765, had married Elizabeth, a daughter of Reese Meredith, one of the leading Philadelphia merchants and shippers. With his father-in-law, and later with his brother-in-law, Samuel Meredith, Clymer engaged in an extensive mercantile business. He subsequently became the first president of the Philadelphia Bank.

By the provisions of the Pennsylvania Legislative act, the capital of the Bank of North America was placed at ten million " Spanish milled dollars and no more." [15] The directors of the bank, as specified by name in the act, comprised some of the foremost merchants and lawyers in Pennsylvania. Thomas Willing, partner of Robert Morris, was designated as president. The directors named were James Wilson, Thomas Fitz-

---

[15] " Statutes At Large of Pa., 1779–1781," Vol X: 406–408. The actual amount of its capital in American currency was about $400,000.

simmons, Cadwallader Morris, Samuel Osgood, William Bingham (one of the richest Pennsylvania merchants), Samuel Inglis, Samuel Meredith and others.[16] Wilson was also attorney for the bank, and in that representation Gouverneur Morris was associated with him. Of these men, four became delegates to the Federal Constitutional Convention held five years later — James Wilson, Thomas Fitzsimmons, George Clymer, and Gouverneur Morris. Robert Morris, who was deeply interested in the bank through his partner Gouverneur Morris, was also a member of the Federal Constitutional Convention.

In his work, published in 1833,[17] Gouge says that in nowise did the bank aid the Government; that the stockholders acted fraudulently in paying in only $70,000, or seven-fortieths of its capital. Robert Morris, then controlling the financial department of the Revolution, deposited $254,000 in the Bank of North America, and credited the Government with that amount of stock in the bank. Thus, by this ambidexterous operation, the individual stockholders acquired the power to circulate $400,000 in the bank's notes. The Government's own money was loaned back to it, and to other borrowers, as also the $400,000 additional money which the Government's deposits and sanction soon made current at par value. From these fraudulent methods the bank's stockholders reaped from twelve to sixteen per cent. dividends. "In 1785," says Gouge, of the Bank of North America, "the effects of its operation began to be apparent. . . . A temporary plentifulness of money, followed by great scarcity, usury, ruin to the many, riches to the few."

The Origin of a Famous Constitutional Clause.

Public outcry compelled the Pennsylvania Legislature to act. On September 13, 1785, an act repealing the Bank of North

[16] "Statutes at Large of Pa., 1779–1781," Vol. X: 406–408.
[17] "History of Paper Money and Banking In The United States."

America's charter was passed, the preamble of which act read:
" Whereas the bank established in the city of Philadelphia hath been found to be injurious to the welfare of this State, and in its tendency appears to be incompatible with the public safety, Therefore," etc., etc.[18]   The profits, however, were so rich that the directors had no intention of allowing the repealing act to stand.   James Wilson and Gouverneur Morris, as the bank's attorneys, argued vigorously in the Legislature: Was not the passage of the original act a grant of a vested right?   Could the charter be repealed without impairing vested rights, and the rights of innocent parties?   Whether it was influenced by these or more tangible arguments, the Legislature yielded.   On March 17, 1787, it reincorporated the Bank of North America for a term of fourteen years and allowed it an increased capital of $2,000,000 all told.[19]   Thomas Willing still remained president, and Fitzsimmons, Nesbit and some of the other original directors were renamed in the new act.   Among the stockholders, then or later, were some of the most eminent judges; Justice Yeates, of the Supreme Court of Pennsylvania, did not sit in a subsequent action because of his being a stockholder.[20]

In the very year that the Bank of North America was rechartered, the Federal Constitutional Convention adopted the well-known clause forbidding any State to pass legislation impairing the obligation of a contract.   Seven years later, Wilson and other noted politicians bribed an act through the Georgia Legislature, giving four companies a grant of about

[18] " Statutes at Large of Pa., 1785–1787," Vol. XII : 57.

[19] *Ibid.*, 415–416.

[20] Bank of North America vs. Fitzsimmons, Binney's Reports, Supreme Court of Pa., Vol. III : 360.   This bank is still in existence.   By a special act of Congress it is the only national bank in the United States not compelled to use the word national.   In view of the facts given in these chapters pertaining to the origin of the Bank of North America, it is extremely interesting to find that bank advertising in a recent number of the *Financier:*   " A Record of Progress — For 130 years this institution has upheld the principles of sound banking and its efficient service to financial institutions throughout the country has contributed largely to its success."

thirty-five million acres of public land, which transaction is fully described later in this chapter. When Georgia passed an act rescinding the grant, the Supreme Court of the United States later took refuge in that Constitutional clause forbidding the impairment of the obligation of a contract, and declared the rescinding act void. Under that decision, and later decisions, every privilege or franchise obtained by bribery or other fraud, since then, has been perpetual and indefeasible in law, and could not be repealed.

Commenting upon the origin of the Constitutional clause in question, Hunter, one of the most learned attorneys of his time, argued in the noted case of Sturges vs. Crowninshield: " The judges of the State Courts and of this Court have confessed that there is in these words ' impairing the obligation of contracts ' an inherent obscurity. . . . They are not taken from the English common law, or used as a classical or technical term of our jurisprudence in any book of authority. No one will pretend that these words are drawn from any English statute, or from the States ' statutes before the adoption of the Constitution. Were they, then, furnished from that great treasury and reservoir of rational jurisprudence, the Roman law? We are inclined to believe this. The tradition is that Mr. Justice Wilson, who was a member of the Convention, and a Scottish lawyer, and learned in the civil law, was the author of the phrase." [21]

And, according to a letter written by Gouverneur Morris to Timothy Pickering, in 1814, he (Gouverneur Morris) stated that the Constitution " was written by the fingers which write this letter." Morris went on to say in that letter: " Having rejected redundant and equivocal terms, I believed it to be as clear as our language would permit, excepting, nevertheless, a part of what related to the judiciary. On that subject it became necessary to select phrases, which, expressing my own

[21] Wheaton's Reports, Supreme Court of the United States, Vol. IV: 151.

notions, would not alarm others." Gouverneur Morris was so active in drawing up the final document, that Madison wrote of him that "the finish given to the style of the Constitution fairly belongs to Mr. Morris." Considering that Wilson and Gouverneur Morris, as the attorneys for the Bank of North America, had jointly made that noted argument before the Pennsylvania Legislature, those statements are of high importance.

The Sequel of Wilson's Bank Scandal.

But who was to determine the question of whether legislation impaired the obligation of contract, and was therefore unconstitutional? Self-evidently, the courts. Quite true, the majority of the Federal Constitutional Convention, in the face of the popular resentment against the courts, discreetly refrained from voting affirmatively on any proposition to endow the courts with power to set aside laws as unconstitutional. But the charge of the impairment of an obligation of contract presupposed, and carried with it, an action at law; such a contest would come exclusively within the jurisdiction of the courts. It would be the courts, and not the executive or Congress that would pass upon the controversy, and have the final decision as to whether legislation was unconstitutional or not. To this extent the adroit leaders in the convention, who understood perfectly at what they were aiming, succeeded in deceiving, not only many of the delegates, but the great body of the people.

With this clause accepted, no explicit provision was needed vesting power in the courts to declare laws unconstitutional. And that Wilson and his class colleagues had the foresight to discern the great and wide latitude allowed the courts by the acceptance of that seemingly harmless clause, is shown by the large number of laws which, under it, the Supreme Court of the United States has declared unconstitutional.

To understand fully the serene confidence that the landholders and traders of the Revolutionary period had in the courts as the final and unchangeable bulwark of their interests, and what they expected from the judiciary, it is only necessary to point out that the courts during the Revolution put themselves above law. They usurped power when they willed, and construed law as they pleased. Wilson knew that many of their acts were sheer usurpations, for, in a pamphlet, he defended usurpation. When he caused that memorable clause of his to be inserted in the Constitution, he knew, also, that the usurpations already put in practice would serve as precedents to invite and justify further usurpations.

In Chapter III we have already described how the Virginia court, established at Vincennes from 1779 to 1787, usurped the power of granting lands, and then, after its judges had usurped that power, clandestinely granted large areas of land to themselves.

So audaciously did they make a grand division of the plunder among themselves that they took only the most superficial precautions to conceal their malfeasances, nor do they seem to have been proceeded against in any actions, civil or criminal.

"Without dwelling," reported John Bandolet and Nathaniel Ewing, Government Land Commissioners for the district of Vincennes, to Gallatin, in 1812, "on the extraordinary circumstances of the above recited supposed grants, wherein the members of a court of justice have made to each other such unusual donations, and appropriated to themselves such a large and valuable part of the country, the Commissioners will observe that the State of Virginia never authorized the courts to grant lands. . . ."

In the same document (No. 1333, Vol. VII, American State Papers: Public Lands) the full details of that usurpation are further reproduced in a report of Secretary of the Treasury Levi Woodbury, on February 16, 1835. But the usurpations of the judiciary extended to the more serious and sinister length of annulling legislative acts.

Court Usurpation Already Established.

This usurpation Shirley seeks to explain thus: " In the dark days which preceded the Revolution," he says,[22] " the people of the Colonies had been thoroughly indoctrinated with the idea that the acts of Parliament of which they complained were unconstitutional, and therefore void, and that, in consequence, they were justified in resisting their enforcement. Judge Wilson, in a great pamphlet, had urged with great ingenuity and force that it was the right and the duty of the courts to set aside those acts. This view was supported by many of the most eminent politicians, statesmen and jurists of that day. This doctrine had sunk deep into the popular mind."

But it was not against acts of Parliament that the courts presumed to usurp this power. The unpopularity of the laws passed by Parliament supplied a very good pretext and justification for the assumption of a power directed, not against Parliament, but against the mass of the people. The fact that all the judges were royal officials, and that, when the Revolution broke out, only a few of those judges supported the movement for political independence (and they only under virtual compulsion) shows Shirley to have been in complete error on this point. Certainly judges drawing pay from the crown, were not likely to forfeit their positions and salary by declaring the laws of the crown null and void.

The usurped power of declaring laws void was a power first exercised by the courts at precisely that time during the Revolution when the insurrectionary movements of the people were manifesting themselves. These movements had for their object an armed protest against the old mediæval laws still in force and being reënacted, against the extortions of the landholders and merchants, and against the schemes and political and financial lootings so shamelessly carried on by the members of the governing class. The uprisings, or rather threatening

---

[22] " Dartmouth College Causes " (Edition of 1879) : p. 390.

upheavals, forced legislatures, in some instances, to pass laws of varying remedial qualities. The courts, representing the interests of the landlords, and composed of landowners or their retainers, came quickly to the rescue of their class.

That this usurpation of power was exercised against the legislatures is admitted by Shirley in his next paragraph. "The judges in Rhode Island," he wrote, "had set aside an act of the Legislature as unconstitutional. The same is true of New Jersey. In 1788 and 1793, the Court of Appeals in Virginia had done the same thing. The power of the highest court to set aside such acts was recognized in New Hampshire soon after the adoption of the written Constitution of 1784. From 1790 to 1799, they were repeatedly declared void by the highest court, and sometimes by inferior tribunals." [23]

The additional fact that James Wilson, the author of the clause in the Constitution prohibiting any State legislation impairing the obligation of a contract, had written a pamphlet urging the right of the courts to declare laws invalid, is of the greatest significance.

Hamilton's Banking Interests.

Undoubtedly Wilson with his Bank of North America experience fresh in mind, had a valuable coadjutor in Alexander Hamilton, whose speeches and writings prove that he fully grasped the overshadowing importance of lodging the real power in the judiciary. Hamilton had his own banking and other interests, not to speak of the vast interests of his relatives, connections and associates, and those of the whole class which he so brilliantly represented, to protect against the possibility of hostile legislation, then so imminent because of the bitter popular demonstrations.

The profits of the Bank of North America were so great that Hamilton and his associates decided to start a bank in

[23] "Dartmouth College Causes": 390.

New York City. In 1784, they organized the first banking company in New York State with a capital of $500,000; Hamilton personally drew up the articles of copartnership.

But the people had been so badly cheated in depreciated paper currency, that the Legislature was afraid to charter banks. "A memorial," says John C. Hamilton, "to incorporate the bank of which the constitution had been framed by Hamilton, was presented to the Legislature early in 1784, but so prevalent was the jealousy of moneyed influence that it was compelled to conduct it affairs during six years without corporate immunities." [24] So anxious was Hamilton to start his bank, that he opened it even before he had obtained lawful authority, and without waiting for those legislative favors by which directors were individually exempted from being sued. From 1784 to 1788 he, personally, was a director; [25] and up to the very day of his death he controlled that institution. It held a monopoly of banking powers in New York, and, like the Bank of North America, it was of the greatest service in facilitating great land speculations, and exercising pressure upon merchants in elections.

Not until March 21, 1791, was Hamilton able to secure a charter from the New York Legislature. How, it may be fairly asked, in view of later developments, did he get it? Was it given as a partisan present by his Federalist associates? Or was some stronger and more metallic inducement necessary to influence the legislators to defy public opposition — inducements such as Aaron Burr, it was revealed, gave in 1799 when he obtained the charter for the Manhattan Bank, and inducements such as others gave later in getting charters for the Mercantile Bank, the Bank of America and other banks? This

[24] Hammond's "Political History of the State of New York," Vol. I: 323.
[25] "A History of the Bank of New York, 1784–1884": 122. Hamilton, as Secretary of the Treasury, dealt extensively with the Dutch bankers, Willinck, the same to whom Robert Morris sold 3,000,000 acres of New York land.

we may suspect, but do not know. But we do learn that in 1790, a year after his becoming Secretary of the Treasury, Hamilton made the Bank of New York the agent for the sale of 200,000 guilders,[26] and that when he and Morris established the Bank of the United States, it was evidently Hamilton's plan to make the Bank of New York a branch factor of that institution; between the two banks, however, " a friendly arrangement was made." [27]   This matter of the chartering of banks deserves to be kept constantly in mind; in its proper place we shall have to make a further exposition of bank charters, and the close connection existing between the particular interests that certain other renowned Justices of the Supreme Court of the United States had in them, and some notable decisions following.

James Wilson's Bank of North America enterprise, his success in getting it rechartered in the teeth of the most violent popular antagonism, and the great service he rendered the propertied class both in the Federal Constitutional Convention and in the Pennsylvania Convention made him a man of mark. But, notable as were Wilson's banking activities, his land operations were far more extensive, and were considered more scandalous. Before, however, describing these, it is advisable to give an additional series of facts as to the continued and widespread seizure of land, under color of law, then in unmitigated process. Plundering of the public domain was the recognized order of the day.

The associated politicians and capitalists were exercising the freest hand in appropriating as much of the public domain as they wanted. The continued alienation of the State lands, and the despoilment of the National lands were carried on at the same time, and by politicians and capitalists of both political parties. Nearly all of Chief Justice Jay's relatives, intimate friends and business connections were deep in these legalized seizures; Associate Justice James Wilson was particularly con-

[26] " A History of the Bank of New York," etc., 39.   [27] *Ibid.*, 42.

spicuous, as were Robert Morris, Hamilton, Fitzsimmons, Jonathan Dayton, Aaron Burr and a large number of other leading lights, not omitting Washington himself.

The " Sufferers " Get a Donation of 500,000 Acres.

First the appropriation of the lands owned by the various States will be considered. The State of Connecticut held a large area, called the Western Reserve, in Ohio. In May, 1792, the Connecticut Legislature passed an act, under the pretence of making indemnity for losses caused by the incursions of the British army into various Connecticut towns. By this act, and another act passed in May, 1795, a tract of 500,000 acres of land in Trumbull County, Ohio, fronting Lake Erie, were conveyed to Thaddeus Burr and others.[28]

Another act was passed in October, 1796. It was entitled, " An Act for Incorporating the Proprietors of the Half Million Acres of Land lying south of Lake Erie." This act created the recipients as a corporation, and provided that they and their heirs should have succession. The next clause made provision that the Proprietors should have agents in meetings to represent them; the regulations prescribed show clearly that the act was designed to benefit men of wealth, and not the poor who had suffered. Proprietors in those towns whose allowed losses were £10,000 or less, could send one agent; those whose losses ranged from £10,000 to £20,000 could send two agents; those with a loss from £20,000 to £30,000 could send three; and so on in the same proportion. The voting in the meetings for the selection of agents was thus arranged by this law: Those whose losses were less than £100 should have one vote; those having lost £100 to £200, two votes; those with losses from £200 to £300, three votes, and so on up the list. But no single loss was to give more than ten votes.[29]   Another

---

[28] " Connecticut Laws: Public Statute Laws " (Edition of 1808), Vol. I: 456–457.
[29] Ibid., 451–455.

act, along the same lines, passed in May, 1797, allowed deeds of conveyance, for which no provision was made in the original act.[30] It became necessary, also, to get an act of incorporation from the Ohio Legislature; and this was obtained in 1803. This act incorporated "the owners and proprietors of half million acres of land lying south of Lake Erie, in the county of Trumbull."[31] The act pathetically called the land "Sufferers Land," although the company was composed very largely of capitalists and politicians who had bought up claims of losses on speculation, and had often fraudulently magnified them. The Ohio lands donated comprised all that valuable section of which the city of Cleveland is now the seat and center.

A Few Capitalists Get 5,542,000 Acres in New York.

After the Revolution, the State of New York owned, within its limits, more than seven million acres of what were then called "wild and unappropriated lands." In 1791, the New York Legislature enacted a law, authorizing the State Commissioners of the Land Office to dispose of these lands in *such parcels* and on *such terms* and in such a manner as they should judge *most conducive to the interest of the public.* The law thus virtually allowed the Commissioners to do as they pleased; Hammond says that the act was passed by consent of both political parties.[32] The Commissioners of the Land Office consisted of the Governor (then George Clinton), the Secretary of State, and the Attorney-General (then Aaron Burr), and the State Treasurer and the State Auditor.

These officials at once proceeded to do business. In the same year — 1791 — they sold the enormous area of 5,542,173 acres of land for the trifling sum of $1,030,432. This fact of itself

---

[30] "Connecticut Laws," etc., 456–457.

[31] "Ohio Laws, 1803," Chap. XXIX: pp. 106–114.

[32] Hammond's "Political History of the State of New York," Vol. I: 326.

caused a considerable public scandal; but the one circumstance looked upon as particularly and inexplicably flagrant was that to one individual — Alexander McComb — they disposed of a vast tract of 3,635,200 acres for the ridiculous price of eight pence an acre. Nor was this slight sum to be paid down; McComb was allowed to pay it in five installments, *without interest* and subject to a discount of six per cent., on payment in advance, which still further reduced the actual price.[33]

At the same time other large tracts were sold to other capitalists, among whom were the Roosevelts, James Caldwell, McGregor and others. These sales, however, were made at a higher rate than the sale to McComb; some of the lands were sold at about three shillings an acre, others for two shillings six pence, and some for one shilling an acre. Hammond relates that these sales were widely criticised as building up a land monopoly, and that it was urged as a suspicious matter that three and a half million acres of land were sold to McComb at eight pence an acre, while, on the other hand, five hundred thousand acres were sold by the same Commissioners, and at about the same time, to John and Nicholas Roosevelt for three shillings and a penny an acre. In the debate in the Legislature it was insinuated that Clinton, Burr and their friends were secretly interested in the McComb purchase, which accusation McComb denied.[34] Great profits were made by these speculators in disposing of the land at high prices to actual settlers.

The Holland Company.

It is necessary now to revert to the operations of the Holland Company, in the background of which we have seen Hamilton advancing John B. Church's money to Robert Morris. Presently Associate Justice James Wilson will enter.

Morris, as will be recalled, sold more than 3,000,000 acres of his 4,000,000 acres in New York State to eleven

[33] Davis' "Memoirs of Burr," Vol. I: 326.
[34] Hammond, Vol. I: 58.

Dutch bankers and other capitalists incorporating themselves
as the Holland Company. It will also be remembered that
Jay's relatives, the Livingstons, were among the group of capitalists interested in the fraudulent Phelps and Gorham purchase of 2,600,000 acres in New York State. When Morris'
project of conveying 3,000,000 acres of land to a coterie
of foreign capitalists became known, the wildest popular excitement resulted. The argument was advanced (and sound
law it was, too), that property could not be conveyed to aliens
or held by them. Morris, Wilson, the Livingstons and others,
and particularly Jay, as we shall see, had long had the best of
interested reasons for desiring the effacement of any such
prohibitive law. Pressure was brought to bear upon the Legislature, and on April 11, 1796, an act was passed authorizing
the Dutch bankers, Willinck, and other aliens and their descendants to hold property.

Both Burr and Hamilton were engaged in extensive land
grabbing, Hamilton in many different directions. Both of
these eminent patriots were, according to Turner,[35] " contractors for lands west of the Genesee River; the former [Burr]
for a tract upon the Holland Purchase." Burr, says Turner,
had made a contract for the purchase of the tract, at twelve
shillings per acre, at an early period of the Holland company's
ownership. Turner quotes in full a letter written to The-
ophilus Cazenove, first General Agent of the Holland Company,
in which Burr says that " it appears that the Tonawanta Bay
falls within my tract " on Lake Ontario. Burr's transaction
with the Holland Company, Turner continues, " was blended
with other transactions, and eventually abandoned. But out of
it had originated a bond for $20,000 which was given up.
The surrendering of the bond gave rise to reports that Col.
Burr had been bribed by agents of the Holland Company to
favor the passage of the bill allowing aliens to hold lands.
Burr held John B. Church responsible for the report," and

[35] " History of the Holland Purchase " (Edition of 1850) : 418.

challenged him to a duel, the result of which was ineffectual. Turner concludes by saying that Church apologized.[36] Perhaps Church was too hasty in accusing without being able to get the legal proof. Certainly, direct accusations of bribery were not wanting against Burr when he persuaded the Legislature to pass his artful Manhattan Bank bill, in 1799; at least ten legislators, it appeared,[37] knew of the real character of the bill which was ostensibly passed to provide New York City with pure water, but which contained a covert clause conferring banking powers on the Manhattan Company.

In the Pennsylvania activities of the Holland Company, James Wilson was openly and conspicuously interested. So, indirectly, was Hamilton, working through John B. Church and Tench Coxe. As Assistant Secretary of the Treasury under Hamilton, [38] Coxe seems to have been very close to Hamilton.

Justice Wilson's Participation.

In 1792, the State of Pennsylvania received a formal grant from the United States of what was called the Erie Triangle, comprising 202,187 acres in the northwestern corner of Pennsylvania, bordering on Lake Erie. Under the Pennsylvania act of 1786, opening all lands to settlers, the State officials began to sell it.

But they made no pretence of disposing of it to actual settlers, despite the law requiring that it be sold to actual settlers, and that it be settled within two years. Through dummies, and with the full connivance of the State officials, principally Comptroller-General John Nicholson, the Holland Company, in 1792–1793, bought eleven hundred and sixty-two tracts of

[36] *Ibid.,* 419. Hamilton and Burr were rivals in more than the political respect. Was it Hamilton's aim to discredit Burr through Church?

[37] See statement of facts in Spencer vs. Southwick, Johnson's Reports (N. Y.), Vol. IX: 314.

[38] " American State Papers: Miscellaneous," Vol. I: 57.

four hundred acres each, paying at the rate of £10, ten shillings per hundred acres; from those 1,162 tracts, 386 tracts were later deducted by reason of prior settlements, bounties and on other grounds.[39] The headquarters of the Holland Company was at what is now Meadville. Of about $380,000 that the Holland Company professed to have expended for improvements, settlements, etc., Judge James Wilson was credited with contributing the sum of $222,071.10 in all;[40] he must have been an uncommonly rich man to have been able personally to put in so large an amount; no doubt his Bank of North America supplied him with part of the funds.

Had it not been for the courts, however, especially the Supreme Court of the United States, this great fraudulent operation, and similar seizures in Pennsylvania, would never have succeeded. In a case that came up before Judge Huston, in the Supreme Court of Pennsylvania, thirty-eight years later, involving land in western Pennsylvania, Huston gave a very comprehensive survey of the land frauds of the time here dealt with.

"At one period of our history," wrote Judge Huston, in delivering the court's opinion, " from 1784 till December, 1786, our then Supreme Court made some decisions which alarmed everybody; and an act of Assembly was passed, declaring all warrants issuing for lands on which a settlement had been made, except to the settler or his legal representative, should be null and void. And soon after, the courts decided that all such warrants which *had* issued for land occupied by a settler were void. The same thing had been decided, and was the settled law, before the Revolution." [41] Judge Huston then cited from a decision of Judge Yeates [42] in which Yeates wrote that for some years after the Revolution the sentiments of

[39] See, Case of Commonwealth of Pa. vs. Tench Coxe, Dallas' Reports (Supreme Court of Pa.), Vol. IV: 175.
[40] *Ibid.* This is the exact amount stated in the court record in a suit brought by Pennsylvania in 1800, two years after Wilson's death.
[41] Case of Campbell vs. Galbreath, Watts' Reports, Vol. I: 70, etc.
[42] Lessee of Bonnet vs. Devebaugh, III Binney's Reports.

some of the judges of the Supreme Court of Pennsylvania
" were unfriendly to settlers and improvers," but that a change
of opinion took place about the year 1793.   The precise nature
of this change Judge Huston did not state.

Then, going on to describe at length the fraudulent processes
by which, through fictitious settlers, large speculators obtained
the land, and the prolonged scenes of riot and bloodshed ensuing in conflicts between pretended and actual settlers up
to the year 1802, Judge Huston continued, " The lands west
of the Alleghany were taken upon warrants paid for by Judge
Wilson, John Nicholson, Robert Morris, and many others,
none of whom were ever in or near that country, but they had
agents who procured the surveys, and paid for them money
furnished by the owner. . . ." [43]   Further facts concerning
the Holland Company we shall be under the necessity of nar-
rating later in their appropriate place in relation to a certain
decision of Chief Justice Marshall.

Wilson's land operations were by no means confined to any
particular section of Pennsylvania.   His gathering in of land
extended throughout that State; many of the most valuable
coal tracts in Pennsylvania derive title from his ownership.
He owned large areas of coal land in Huntington and Northampton Counties, Pennsylvania.   We find from the court records that, in consideration of debts that he owed to Benjamin
R. Morgan of Philadelphia, and General Henry Lee of Virginia, Justice Wilson, on August 20, 1796, made a deed to them
of all his real estate in those counties, which deed was followed
by a trail of litigation lasting for more than three-quarters
of a century.[44]   At the same time, Tench Coxe and John B.
Church were jointly acquiring extensive tracts of timber and
coal lands in Luzerne County and in other counties; in 1795
they made a division of their holdings, part going to Coxe, and

[43] *Ibid.,* 105.
[44] See, Case of Alleghany Railroad and Coal Company vs. Casey,
Pennsylvania State Reports, Vol. 79: 84–85.

part to Church; [45] Hamilton must have been acting for Church, who was not in the United States at that time.

The scandalous methods by which these valuable lands had been obtained, the accompanying violence and trickery and. the public bitterness induced the Legislature to pass an act, on April 11, 1795, "to prevent intrusions on lands within the counties of Northampton, Northumberland and Luzerne." Section II of this act provided that every person who combined or conspired to convey, possess or settle any lands under half-share rights or pretended titles, should, for each offense, pay $500 to $1,000 fine, and should be subject to imprisonment at hard labor for a term not exceeding eighteen months. If any State officer were resisted in ejectment proceedings, he was empowered to call out the militia.[46]

But the very courts expected to enforce this act, civilly and criminally, were then composed of judges who were either interested or subservient; and the act was almost entirely diverted, it is quite clear, and used as a weapon against actual settlers. The land speculators had seen to it that their law yers were put on the State benches equally as well as upon the bench of the Supreme Court of the United States.[47] This fact was well known; and at a time when the Pennsylvania Legislature was kept busy with impeachment proceedings against judges and officials, the State judges who had been counsel for the Holland Company preferred frankly to state the fact, and not sit in cases affecting it, rather than inflame public excitement, already great, and risk impeachment. The fact, however, that various kinds of actions, brought long after in the courts, were against the heirs, legatees or the as-

[45] See, Case of Steiner and Newbold vs. Coxe, IV Pa. State Reports, 14.

[46] Carey and Bioren's Pa. Laws, Vol. V: 72.

[47] Thus, Judge Breckenridge of the Pa. Supreme Court had been, as an attorney, counsel for the Holland Company (IV Dallas' Reports, 196). In the case of the Commonwealth of Pa. vs. Coxe he was disqualified from sitting, having, as he inserted in the records, been counsel for the Holland Company.

signees of Wilson, Coxe, Nicholson and others shows that these original appropriators were eventually successful in getting original title, by reason, as will be seen, of decisions of the Supreme Court of the United States.

Wilson's Illinois and Wabash Company.

The land transactions, individually or jointly, of Robert Morris, James Wilson, John Nicholson and their associates or connections were, indeed, phenomenally extensive and ubiquitous. One of Wilson's enterprises, however, met with failure; its character was so very shady that Congress, many of the conspicuous members of which were promoting that scheme and other great land grabs, dared not finally sanction it. This particular project of Wilson's was the Illinois and Wabash Land Company; the nature of this company was thus particularly described by President Jefferson: [48]

"During the regal government two companies, called the Loyal and the Ohio Company, had obtained grants from the Crown for 800,000 or 1,000,000 acres of land each on the Ohio, on condition of settling them in a given number of years. They surveyed some and settled them; but the war of 1755 came on and broke up the settlements. After it was over they petitioned for a renewal. Four other large companies then formed themselves, called the Mississippi, the Illinois, the Wabash and the Indiana Companies, each praying for immense quantities of land, some amounting to 200 miles square; so that they proposed to cover the whole country north between the Ohio and the Mississippi and a great portion of what is south.

"All of these petitions were depending, without any answer whatever from the Crown, when the Revolutionary War broke out. The petitioners had associated to themselves some of the nobility of England and most of the characters in America

[48] In a letter dated Washington, March 26, 1801, to M. de Reyneval.

of great influence.   When Congress assumed the Government, they took some of their body in as partners to obtain their influence; and I remember to have heard at the time that one of them took Mr. Girard as a partner, expecting by that to obtain the influence of the French court to obtain grants of those lands which they had not been able to obtain from the British government.   All these lands were within the limits of Virginia."

This, however, is only a general, incomplete description; the other necessary details will be here supplied.   Both the British and the Continental Governments had refused to recognize the claims of the Illinois and Wabash companies.   After the organization of the National Government, the Illinois and the Wabash companies were fused into one corporation, and James Wilson became its president.[49]   On December 17, 1791, Justice Wilson, William Smith and John Shee submitted an elaborate petition to the United States Senate, praying confirmation of their claims.   They represented that during the years 1773 and 1775 William Murray, an Illinois merchant, and specified others composing the Illinois Company, and Lord Dunmore and various British and American lawyers and merchants comprising the Wabash Company, had bought from the Indian tribes the great stretch of territory claimed on the Illinois and Wabash rivers.[50]   In the petition neither the exact extent of the tract was mentioned, nor specifically what the Indians had been paid.

Despite the fact that this claim obviously could not hold in law because, even if an actual purchase had been made (which was doubtful), it was in contravention of King George's procla-

[49] "American State Papers: Public Lands," Vol. I: 27.   (Docs. Nos. 11 and 12.)

[50] *Ibid.*   As nearly as can be made out from the records, one tract extended about forty by thirty leagues, and the other of the same dimensions, between the mouth of the White River and the mouth of the Wabash.   The promoters claimed to have given the Indians large quantities of strouds, blankets, guns, flour, beads, etc.   They had tried in 1781 to get the Continental Congress to confirm their claim, but were unsuccessful.—" American State Papers: Public Lands," Vol. II: 253.

mation of 1763, forbidding purchases from the Indians, Justice Wilson, acting for the company, made this proposition to the Senate: " That, however clear the claim of the company to the whole of their purchase may be, they hesitate not to express their willingness and desire that a reasonable compromise upon the subject may take place between the United States and them." The company modestly agreed to surrender to the United States all the lands claimed, on condition that the Government reconvey to the company one-fourth of the lands.[51]

That an offer of this character should have been urged was suggestive of the crass effrontery of its proposers.

The Senate Committee on Public Lands balked at this extraordinary proposal; it reported that the petitioners held no legal title to the lands, and it declined the proposition in toto.[52] On the other hand, the fullest encouragement was met with in the House in which the notorious Jonathan Dayton, himself putting through great land jobbery, was, with others of his kind, all powerful. The House Committee on Public Lands reported that the company's Indian deeds were good and valid, and it was recommended that the United States should agree to the proposal.[53]

As casting a piercing ray of light upon the methods used in Congress during this time, the great scandal arising from the bribery of members by Robert Randall to grant a twenty-two million acre claim, may be briefly referred to.

Three members of the House, Smith of South Carolina, Murray of Maryland and Giles of Virginia, testified, in December, 1795, that Randall had made overtures to get their support for a bill granting for a nominal sum a huge tract of land containing from eighteen to twenty million acres bordering on Lakes Erie, Huron and Michigan. Other members of the House corroborated the charges against Randall. It was brought out that Randall told members of the House that he already had thirty or forty members pledged in support of

[51] *Ibid.*   [52] *Ibid.*   [53] *Ibid.*

his bill; that shares in the grant were to be divided among members of Congress so as to get a majority; and that those who did not want shares, could get cash.[54]   In view of these revelations, the House virtuously had to take some action in its own defense; by a vote of 78 to 17 it found Randall guilty of "attempting to corrupt 'the integrity of its members." [55]

Congress Refuses to Admit Wilson's Claim.

During this time Justice Wilson was actively pushing his Illinois and Wabash bill in Congress.   In 1796, acting upon the favorable report of the House Committee on Public lands, he sought to get a confirmation from the Senate, claiming that the original cost and interest, exclusive of the consideration money paid to the Indians, amounted to £40,000 at least.

No doubt, the pushers of this fraudulent claim expected that by the application of perseverance and possibly of other means, they would be able to obtain some compromise or indemnity.

But with Randall's bribery scandal fresh in the public mind, both Senate and House were disposed to be exceedingly circumspect.   That the House of Representatives was by no means to be accused, as a whole, of having during those years an immoderate degree of integrity, was conclusively demonstrated by the fact that Jonathan Dayton (some of whose transactions have been described) was elevated to be its Speaker.   Wilson's memorial was referred to a committee consisting of Ross, Livermore, Tracy, Tazewell and Stockton, which committee, on February 3, 1797, reported, adopting the Senate Committee's adverse report of March 26, 1792.   The Senate, as a body, adopted the committee's adverse report on February 16, 1797.[56]   This action of the Senate thwarted Jus-

[54] Journal of the House of Representatives, First Session, Fourth Congress, 1795, pp. 58, 68, 72–80, etc.
[55] "American State Papers: Miscellaneous," Vol. I: 131. (Doc. No 66.)
[56] "American State Papers: Public Lands," Vol. I: 72–73. (Doc. No. 30.)

tice Wilson's large project, the only one of his enterprises that he did not succeed in consummating.[57]

In order to give a further clear account of the numerous other land undertakings and their ramifications, of Morris, Nicholson and their associated or abetting group of other politicians, it is necessary from here on to interweave the narrative of various other land transactions.

Robert Morris & Co. Get Nine Thousand Lots in Washington.

It need hardly be said that when the site of the present city of Washington was chosen as the location for the national capital, the politicians in touch with Washington's administration had the fullest advance knowledge. It is a circumstance further worthy of note that the Carrolls, especially Daniel Carroll of Maryland, owned a large part of the then waste lands now embraced within the District of Columbia. In the suit of Van Ness vs. the City of Washington, which came up before the Supreme Court of the United States, in January, 1830, the Government stated in its plea that, when the city was first laid out, David Burns (the father of Marcia Van Ness) had sold a considerable area of land to the Government for £25 (or a fraction more than $66.66) an acre,[58] " which price was more than threefold the market price or real value, independently of the adventitious and speculative valuation,

---

[57] But, twelve years after his death, the persistent promoters succeeding him again petitioned Congress. The House Committee on Public Lands refused to consider the claim. " Your committee submit," was its report in part on January 30, 1811, " as the result of their inquiries on this point, that although a few solitary instances may be found in the early settlements of the country of Indian deeds of land being recognized as valid, yet such were the consequences resulting from frauds practised on the simple natives, such the collision of claims and controversies . . . that Government, at a pretty early day, interfered and assumed a kind of guardianship over the rights of the natives " [requiring the consent of the Government to make a conveyance of lands valid].—" American State Papers: Public Lands," Vol. II: 253.

[58] In 1790 £1 equaled about $2.66 U. S. money.

superinduced by making this the permanent seat of government." [59]

The District of Columbia was ceded by Maryland and Virginia in 1789. In 1791, the greater part of the individual owners conveyed the land to Thomas Beall and John M. Gantt, in trust to be laid out as a city; Beall and Gantt, by order of President Washington, transferred their trust to Gustavus Scott, William Thornton and Alexander White, the Commissioners for laying out the City of Washington. All these men, it may be remarked, soon after branched out as extensive capitalists, having possessed themselves of funds to start various enterprises; Scott, for example, became one of the incorporators of the Washington and Baltimore Turnpike Company, chartered by the Maryland Legislature, in 1796. The Beall family was represented in the same company.

On September 29, 1792, President Washington directed that Washington city lots be sold, at public or private sale by the Commissioners. On December 10, 1793, Robert Morris, John Nicholson and James Greenleaf formed the North American Land Company, and signed articles of copartnership of the purchase and sale of large tracts of land in Pennsylvania and elsewhere in the United States. This partnership was to last five years certain, or for a longer time if the parties should consent. The purchases were to be made by Morris and Nicholson for the account of the company. Not only the lands so purchased but other great tracts then owned by Morris and Nicholson were to become the joint stock of the company. Greenleaf was to pay cash to the other partners for one-third of the said lands. No partner was permitted to buy lands on his own account, so as to interfere with the objects of the company. The clear profits were to be equally divided.[60]

Greenleaf had been speculatively buying up large tracts of

[59] Peters' Reports, etc., Vol. IV: 240.
[60] See statement of facts in the case of Gilmore vs. North American Land Company et. al., Peters' Reports, Vol. I: 460–465.

Washington city real estate, about as early as 1791, from Stoddert.[61]   On December 24, 1793, two weeks after the copartnership articles between Morris, Nicholson and Greenleaf were signed, an act was lobbied through the Maryland Legislature (which still had jurisdiction) providing that certificates granted by the Commissioners of the City of Washington should be sufficient to vest the legal estate in the purchasers.   But a clause reserved the Commissioners the right to resell any lots not paid for.   On that identical day, immediately after the passage of the act, Greenleaf, specifically as Morris' agent, made a contract with the Commissioners for the sale to them of nine thousand city lots.   Of these, the purchase of three thousand lots had already been contracted to Greenleaf as Morris' agent at £35 each, current money (which was at the rate of about $2.66 U. S. money, per £1), payable yearly in seven equal payments *without interest;* the other six thousand lots were sold at £30 each, to be paid annually in seven installments *without interest.*[62]

The negotiating attorney for Greenleaf was Judge William Cranch, a nephew of John Adams, and therefore a cousin of John Quincy Adams.   Cranch had married a sister of James Greenleaf.   It is chronicled that so heavily involved was Cranch by his own indorsements of notes in this transaction, that he had to seek the protection of the insolvency laws.[63]

Now was publicly seen the full and real import of the special law passed by the Maryland Legislature.   If a poor person had bought goods payable in installments, the legal ownership would have remained in the seller until the last penny of the debt had been paid.   But Morris and Greenleaf secured title as soon as they received a certificate from the Commissioners,

[61] See, Case of James Greenleaf's Lessee vs. James Birth, V Peters, 132–140.

[62] The full copy of Morris and Greenleaf's contract is to be found in Doc. No. 141, " American State Papers: Miscellaneous," Vol. I : 223–224.

[63] In 1802 Cranch was appointed Reporter for the Supreme Court of the United States, succeeding A. J. Dallas.

and could sell at once, paying the Government from the proceeds of their gradual sales. Thornton, Forrest, Scott and other Commissioners, and President Washington himself, were buying Washington city lots.[64]

When, sixteen years later, an action growing out of this contract was decided by Chief Justice Marshall, that jurist, who customarily made light of charges of bribing legislatures, and even after the charges had been proved, treated them as fiction, made (for him) this unusual comment as to the special act passed by the Maryland Legislature and the Morris and Greenleaf contract:

" A contract for 6,000 lots was concluded on the day that this act passed, immediately after its passage. In this contract was merged a former contract for 3,000 lots made with one of the purchasers in this second contract. It is impossible to reflect upon this fact without being persuaded that the law was agreed upon by the parties to the contract, and was specially adapted to it. The immensity of property disposed of by this sale, furnished motives of legislative aid by giving a speedy remedy to the commissioners which might not exist on the sale of particular lots occasioned by any partial default in the purchasers." [65]

Greenleaf as Morris' agent also contracted for the purchase of 220 lots owned by Daniel Carroll; about 428½ lots from Notley Young; and, on July 15, 1794, he made a contract with Uriah Forrest and Benjamin Stoddert for the sale to him of 239¼ lots owned by them. He, moreover, bought much additional Washington real estate.[66]

But, although Greenleaf, in these purchases, acted as Morris' agent, and by agreement was to buy all lands for joint account of Morris, Nicholson and himself, he nevertheless re-

---

[64] " American State Papers: Miscellaneous," Vol. I : 226–228.

[65] Case of Oneale vs. Thornton, VI Cranch, 69.

[66] Case of Gilmore vs. North American Land Company *et al.*, I Peters, 460–465. The " Duddington " estate of Daniel Carroll was taken over within the limits of the City of Washington.

served certain large lots in Washington to himself, by agreement with Morris and Nicholson.

The speculative holdings of the trio now were enlarged. On January 13, 1794, they entered into an agreement with Thomas Stokely and John Hoge by which Morris and Nicholson bound themselves to buy from the State of Pennsylvania, warrants for 120,000 acres of land located between the Ohio and the Alleghany rivers. Morris and Nicholson were to supply the funds; and for their work in locating and surveying the lands, Stokely and Hoge were to get one equal third part of the whole property.[67] In order to carry on his vast commercial and land speculations Morris already had been forced to borrow immense sums of money. From whence were the funds for the purchase of these 120,000 acres to come? How was Nicholson to raise his share of the money? As Comptroller-General of Pennsylvania, Nicholson received only a moderate salary.

Impeachment Proceedings Against Nicholson.

The means by which Nicholson obtained his capital were revealed, in 1794, when the Legislature of Pennsylvania was called upon to institute impeachment proceedings against him.

For twelve years Nicholson had been Comptroller-General; he was a powerful politician; and it was largely through him, William Bingham and Governor Thomas Mifflin (another member of the Federal Constitutional Convention of 1787) that Robert Morris and Justice James Wilson and their associates had been able to get a charter and a recharter for the Bank of North America. It was due to their connivance that Morris, Wilson, Coxe and others had been able to grasp enor-

---

[67] *Ibid.* An act passed April 3, 1792, by the Pennsylvania Legislature recited that as the most valuable lands in Pennsylvania, included in the purchase made from the Indians in 1758, had been appropriated to purchasers, those remaining lands which were "inferior" should be sold at a reduced price. The price was accordingly reduced.— Carey and Bioren's " Pa. Laws," Vol. IV : 133.

mous areas of the most valuable land in Pennsylvania. Nicholson and Morris, Bingham and others were associates in more than one corporation. While converting themselves into great landholders, they were rushing bills through the various legislatures, granting themselves valuable charters and rights for canal and other corporations. Thus, in 1792–1793, the Pennsylvania Legislature, under Governor Mifflin, passed an act incorporating the Conewago Canal Company, and naming Robert Morris, John Nicholson, William Bingham, David Rittenhouse,[68] Alexander J. Dallas and other politicians as proprietors and directors.[69] Dallas, as we have noted, was the first Reporter of the Supreme Court of the United States. Robert Morris was also president of the Schuylkill and Susquehanna Navigation Company,[70] and Rittenhouse one of the incorporators of the Delaware and Schuylkill Navigation Company, chartered in 1791.[71]

Nicholson Resigns.

One particular charge on which impeachment proceedings were brought against Nicholson was made by Christian Febriger, the State Treasurer. He accused Nicholson of having, as Comptroller-General, made a personal profit of at least twenty-five per cent. in illegally redeeming certain State certificates, called New Loan certificates.

[68] The Rittenhouse family of Philadelphia became well known to later generations by reason of its wealth and aristocratic airs. It shared in the profits of the great land jobbing of the times. A House Committee (of Congress) reported, on March 3, 1797, that when the Government brought suit for moneys due, David Rittenhouse fraudulently " transferred all his estate to his father; and after having made a fallacious return of outstanding debts, to assignees, he obtained a discharge, under the insolvent laws of Pennsylvania, from his private creditors."— See, " American State Papers: Miscellaneous," Vol. I: 157. (Doc. No. 96.)

[69] Carey and Bioren's " Pa. Laws," Vol. IV: 252, and " American State Papers: Miscellaneous," Vol. I: 851.— Nicholson was also a director of a company chartered to build a bridge over the Delaware. Dozens of charters for canal, turnpike, insurance and other companies were being rushed through the Legislature at this time.

[70] " American State Papers: Miscellaneous," Vol. I: 853.

[71] *Ibid.*, 847.

These were an outgrowth of the Revolutionary debt. According to this charge, Comptroller-General Nicholson had declared them redeemable, and certified them to Governor Mifflin, despite the fact that the law neither recognized them as a part of the State indebtedness, nor provided funds for their redemption. Of their total value of $63,075.37 it was charged that $60,220.41 of the certificates were subscribed for by Nicholson personally, were owned by him, and were in his name. Ten out of fourteen members of the whole Pennsylvania Senate pronounced Nicholson guilty of two of the most serious charges, but the vote failed of being the constitutional two-thirds required for impeachment. The question of removing him was then taken up; but Nicholson anticipated further action by resigning the office of Comptroller-General.[72]

Had not the most powerful political and social influences been used effectively in Nicholson's behalf, it is certain that he would not have been allowed to escape impeachment.

Did Nicholson now retire to private life a ruined man? By no means. He already owned millions of acres of land; and his associates had by then put through a gigantic land transaction in Georgia which eclipsed any land jobbery hitherto accomplished. It caused a national scandal of the widest and most lasting proportions, not only then deeply implicating Justice James Wilson, as it did, but seventeen years later, as we shall see, it figured importantly in the case of a decision of a noted Chief Justice of the Supreme Court and in the activities of a certain distinguished Associate Justice.

A Thirty-Five-Million-Acre Grant, and Wilson's Part.

Robert Morris, Nicholson, Zachariah Cox and Greenleaf were already interested in 12,500 acres of valuable land in Georgia which had been obtained in 1787, and came to them

[72] "Impeachment Trial of Judges Hopkinson and Nicholson" (Published in 1795), Vol. I, etc.: 69, 87, 762, 764, etc. This volume gives the official account of the testimony and proceedings.

by route of a fraudulent sheriff's sale.[73]   On January 7, 1795, an act was passed by the Georgia Legislature, over the Governor's protest, granting to four companies, more or less associated, a colossal total area of land, then owned by the State of Georgia.   The entire tract covered, it was variously estimated, from thirty to forty million acres.   The four companies were supposed (reckoning by the total purchase price of $500,000) to pay the State 2⅓ cents an acre for their grants; this sum, at $500,000, would seem to have made their total area in the grants 21,500,000 acres.   But according to the terms and boundaries of the grant, the area really amounted to 35,000,000 acres; the grantees themselves estimated the area at nearly 40,000,000 acres.[74]

This act was passed under the patriotic guise of being a law " for appropriating a part of the unlocated territory of this State for the payment of the late State troops, and for other purposes " etc.[75]   What the act did was to dispose of Georgia's vacant lands west to the Mississippi River.   Hence the grants were called the Yazoo grants, from the river of that name.   The four companies were:

I. The Georgia Mississippi Company.   The beneficiaries of the grant of nearly twelve million acres obtained by this company were New England capitalists of whom we shall have pressing need of saying more hereafter in the proper place.

II. The Upper Mississippi Company.

III. The Tennessee Company, of which Zachariah Cox was the head.

IV. The Georgia Company.   James Greenleaf held 2,500,-000 acres in this company.   The other incorporators and pro-

---

[73] See, Case of Field and others vs. Holland and others (VI Cranch, 8).   The record in this case includes a letter written by Holland, in 1795, stating that Morris, Nicholson, Greenleaf and Zachariah Cox were concerned in the property, and saying that he expected them to send a draft to lift an execution which he (Holland) held upon it.

[74] " American State Papers: Public Lands," Vol. I: 134.   (Doc. No. 74.)

[75] *Ibid.*, 152.

moters of the company were a crowd of the most conspicuous Southern politicians and aristocrats. The company had been incorporated on January 1, 1795 — only a little more than a month before it received its grant. Among its incorporators and promoters were Zachariah Cox, General and United States Senator James Gunn, Matthew McAllister, George Walker, William Longstreet and others, acting in trust for Wade Hampton.[76] John Randolph was credited with 28,000 acres, J. P. Carnes and Mrs. Elizabeth Carnes received an allotment of 162,000 acres; Robert Walton, an ancestor of the present enormously rich Goelet family, obtained as his share 74,000 acres.

The company's chief financial backer was Associate Justice James Wilson, of the Supreme Court of the United States; he advanced £25,000, which he got by selling land at exorbitant prices to settlers in Pennsylvania. For this £25,000 Wilson received ten shares entitling him to an allotment of 750,-000 acres.[77] Others advanced sundry sums, varying from a few hundred pounds to £2,000, £3,000 and £5,000. The purposes to which a large part of this money were put will presently be seen. In view of a decision handed down by Wilson in the Supreme Court in a case against Georgia — the Chief Justice and two Associate Justices concurring — that the States were not sovereign, this connection of Wilson's with the Georgia Land Company has its added significance when considered in connection with a subsequent decision of the Supreme Court of the United States.

In payment for their grants, the four companies tendered payment to Georgia in depreciated currency, which the State officials refused to accept. But claiming that it was legal

---

[76] *Ibid.*, 139–140.

[77] *Ibid.*, 141. Wilson's schemes and projects were numerous. On December 24, 1795, he secured the passage of an act by the Maryland Legislature by which he and others were authorized to raise $50,000 by means of a lottery for the capital of a company to improve the navigation of the Susquehanna River.—"Laws of Maryland, 1785," etc., Vol. II, Chap. 62.

payment, the companies, for ulterior reasons, which we shall describe later on, went rapidly ahead selling or distributing the lands. The Upper Mississippi Company sold more than 11,000,000 acres, for ten cents an acre, to Thomas L. Winthrop, Ebenezer Oliver, Benjamin Jay, George Blake, John Peck, Joseph Sewell, and other New England (chiefly Boston) capitalists; the Upper Mississippi and the Tennessee Companies appropriated their grants, and the Georgia Company distributed a total of 6,728,000 acres among its members and to others, and, in addition, reserved 1,000,000 acres to sell to settlers.[78]

Within, therefore, a brief time after these vast areas had been corruptly obtained, the allotments had been hastily made on a grand scale among a small clique of beneficiaries.

The North American Land Company.

Thirteen days after the Georgia Legislature passed the act making these grants, Robert Morris, John Nicholson and James Greenleaf, on February 20, 1795, entered into an agreement by which they formed the North American Land Company. By this agreement, 647,046 acres of the lands in Pennsylvania belonging to the copartnership of Morris, Nicholson and Company, "as well as other large quantities of land belonging to those partners, amounting in the whole to about six million acres, were to constitute the capital of the said land company." These lands were valued by the men making this contract at fifty cents an acre, and were to be divided into thirty thousand shares at $100 a share, at which price they were to be sold. The company was to exist fifteen years, and dividends were to be paid annually.[79]

In that same year a tract of five hundred thousand acres, in what is now West Virginia, were patented to Robert Morris

[78] "American State Papers: Public Lands," Vol. I: 141.
[79] Case of Gilmore vs. North American Land Company *et al.*, I Peters, 460–465.

by the State of Virginia,[80] but this tract does not seem to have been included in the North American Company's holdings. If Justice James Wilson was a member of this company, the court records do not state it; his heirs or assignees may have been included in "the others" sued. As we have seen, James Greenleaf held two million five hundred thousand acres in the Georgia Company, in which Justice James Wilson had put £25,000, constituting, by far, the largest investment made by any one of the interested individuals.

At this identical time, according to the bill in the action, twenty-two years later, of Gilmore vs. North American Land Company and others, Morris, Nicholson and Greenleaf were insolvent or greatly indebted, and they entered into the agreement of February 20, 1795, with intent to defraud their creditors. The answers of Greenleaf and the directors of the North American Land Company denied that they were insolvent at the time, but admitted that they were indebted to a large amount. Furthermore, those answers asserted positively that the purchase money for the particular lands bought by Gilmore under execution had been paid by Nicholson and not by Morris.

Justice Bushrod Washington, in delivering the decision of the Supreme Court of the United States, in October, 1817, held that, inasmuch as Morris had not paid in any money, his title was only an equitable one, arising from his partnership with Greenleaf and Nicholson. Hence, the agreement of 1795 could not, in law, be set aside. But an accounting was decreed, under Section 13, Statutes of Queen Elizabeth, by which a conveyance was deemed fraudulent if voluntarily made by the grantor at a time when he was indebted; such a

[80] See, Case of Henry C .King vs. Mullins (171 U. S. Reports, 404–437). King, in 1898, claimed to have derived title to certain of this land from Morris through various conveyances. King lost, the Supreme Court deciding that the lands had been forfeited by reason of non-payment of taxes from 1884 to 1888. See also case of King vs. Panther Lumber Company, same volume and same result.

conveyance, held Justice Washington, must have been made with intent to defraud creditors and others.[81]

The Great Disclosures of Bribery.

To resume the story of the Georgia Land grant: The news of the passage of the law giving the enormous grant of approximately thirty-five million acres to a few speculators was read with amazement throughout the entire Union. In Georgia, the mass of the people were roused to fury.

The real circumstances of the grant, however, might never have been revealed, had it not been that another group of capitalists had vainly tried to get the grant for themselves, after offering the State of Georgia a definite payment of $800,000. Defeated in their aim, and smarting for revenge, they at once got busy, and soon the entire State was ringing with charges that the associated four companies had used bribery to get their grant. That this was no idle rumor, but a serious enough fact, was soon proved by the results of Grand Jury investigations.

Clem Lanier, a Georgia State Senator, testified that he was offered two shares for twenty-five thousand acres to vote for the grant, although Longstreet had previously told him that a legislator's share was seventy-five thousand acres. The certificates of shares were signed by Judge Nathaniel Pendleton.[82] This was the same Pendleton who had been elected to the Federal Constitutional Convention, but had never taken his seat. Of Pendleton's earlier land grabbing we have already given facts in Chapter III.

State Senator Philip Clayton testified as to State Senator Robert Thomas: ". . . After the passing of the act, he [Thomas] brought a considerable sum of money to my house

---

[81] I Peters, 460–465.
[82] "American State Papers: Public Lands," Vol. I: 145. (Doc. No. 74.) Judge Pendleton, it may be remarked, was a close personal friend of Alexander Hamilton. He removed to New York City, and was one of Hamilton's seconds in the duel with Burr.

and asked me to take care of it; I believe it was two thousand dollars; on which I asked him how he got it, or if he got his proportion of the lands, or words to that effect; he said it is nothing to you, take care of it, and smiled. . . ."[83]

Another legislator, R. Flournoy, swore that Judge Pendleton offered him a share " provided the business succeeded "; that the meetings of the Georgia Mississippi Company were held in his [Flournoy's] quarters; and that General Gunn had tried to get him to bribe Senator Mitchell with shares for seventy-five thousand acres, but that Mitchell had refused the offer.[84]

State Representative James Sims testified that Gunn had said to him: " Sims, I suppose from what I have heard, you are a poor man, and now you have an opportunity of making something handsome for yourself and family; if you will prevail on Mann to vote for the bill, I will give fifty thousand acres of land." [85]

State Senator Thomas Wylly told Representative Gindrat that he [Gindrat] could have " ten likely negroes " for his share.[86] Many other legislators testified similarly.[87]

The Rescinding Act.

The people of Georgia were thoroughly exasperated by these revelations. They elected an entire body of new representatives, pledged to rescind the act. This annulling act was passed on February 13, 1796, and was so remarkable a document that it is well worth giving at length.

The preamble described the corrupt act of 1795,

" By which an enormous tract of unascertained millions of acres of the vacant territory of this State was attempted to be disposed of to a few individuals, in fee simple, and the

---

[83] *Ibid.,* 141.   [84] *Ibid.,* 145.   [85] *Ibid.,* 147.   [86] *Ibid.,* 145.
[87] For full testimony see *Ibid.,* 144–149. Chided for having sold his vote for $600 when others were getting $1,000, Representative Thomas Roburn replied, according to the testimony, " that it showed he was easily satisfied, and was not greedy " (p. 144).

same is not only unfounded, as being without express constitutional authority, as well as to principles and form of government, the good citizens of this State have chosen for their rule, which is democratical, or a government founded on equality of rights and which is totally opposed to all proprietary grants or monopolies in favor of a few, which tend to build up that destructive aristocracy in the new, which is tumbling in the old, world; and which, if permitted must end in the annihilation of democracy and equal rights — those rights and principles of government which our virtuous forefathers fought for and established with their blood."

The preamble then went on to say that such extravagant grants tended to establish a republican aristocracy, and that the " said usurped act " was not for the public good:

"1. Because self preservation, or the protecting itself, is the greatest good and first duty of every government; and, as has been shown, immense monopolies of land, by a few individuals, under the sanction of the Government are opposed to the principles of democracy or the fundamental laws the citizens of the State have chosen for their rule which, so far from being for the good or self preservation of democratical or equal government, is most manifestly for its destruction and injury.

" 2. Because the expression ' good of the State ' embraces . . . the enjoyment of all rights, natural or acquired, not expressly delegated for the purposes of government; and the sale of such an enormous tract to a few speculators which was, and is, the common right of all the good citizens of this State, is contrary to those rights, and therefore, to their manifest injury, and, of course, to the injury of the State."

The fourth reason given in the preamble for the repeal of the act said that " there was no necessity or pressing urgency for the sale of such an immense tract of territory, equal to some European kingdoms "; that the passage of the " said usurped act" had been accomplished by subterfuge; that the State needed only $30,000 for the alleged purpose for which the land was sold to the speculators, and that more than that sum was in the treasury unappropriated; and that no State or nation "is justified in wantonly dissipating its property or revenues, and a legal alienation can only take place from the most pressing necessity; and the territory attempted to be disposed of (was the said usurped act valid) was wantonly dissipated, it being disposed of for the trifling sum of five hundred thousand dollars, a sum not adequate to the annual quit rents such lands were charged with previously to the Revolution, by the British king; which wanton dissipation cannot be for the good of the State."

The fifth reason for the repeal declared: "Because, exclusive of the immense loss of revenue to which the State is exposed, from the relinquishment of taxation, the sum of five hundred thousand dollars was accepted as the consideration money for the sale, and the sum of eight hundred thousand dollars, offered by persons of as large a capital, and as much respectability and credit, and on terms more advantageous to the State, was refused; which, as it was (should the said usurped act have been declared valid) a clear loss of three hundred thousand dollars to the revenues of the State, it is evident that the law authorizing the sale was not deemed by the Legislature 'for the good of the State,' which must have consisted in obtaining the highest price and the most advantageous terms."

The preamble continued:

". . . And whereas, it does appear from sundry affidavits and proofs satisfactory to this Legislature, as well as from the presentments of the grand juries, on oath, of a considerable majority of the counties of this State . . . as also from the self evident proof of fraud, arising from the rejection of eight hundred thousand dollars, and the acceptance of five hundred thousand dollars for which the said territory was sold; that fraud and corruption were practiced to obtain the said act and grants, and that a majority of the members of the Legislature who voted in favor of the aforesaid act were engaged in the purchase, and a majority of one vote only appeared in favor of this usurped act in the Senate, and on which majority in that branch the same was passed, and corruption appears against more than one member of that body; which, exclusive of the many deceptions used, and the inadequacy of price for such an immense and valuable tract of country, and supposing it to be constitutional, which this Legislature declares it is not," etc., etc.[88]

The annulling act ordered that the act giving the grant be expunged from the records, and the deed be publicly burnt. This was done; the Legislature marched in solemn order to the front of the Capitol, and put the deed to the flames.

And the Remarkable Sequel.

Did this repealing act hold? Was it the finality of the transaction? Did the grant become thereby forfeited to the State of Georgia, and had the distinguished bribers spent their money for nothing?

At this point it would seem so. But there is a sequel still to be told in its appointed position later in this work — a sequel of the most impressive importance, in many respects, in the narrative of the Supreme Court of the United States. In due place further along in these chapters the termination is described and its immense significance to the generation of that time and to all generations since is pointed out. There the connecting links are all appropriately brought together: how the capitalists obtaining the claim of these grants refused to accept the repealing act as valid; how they fell back upon that very Constitutional clause which James Wilson, the

---

[88] This document is given in full in "American State Papers: Public Lands," Vol. I: 156–158.

principal backer of the briberies, had proposed in the Federal Constitutional Convention after his Bank of North America experience, that no State had the right to pass legislation impairing the obligation of contracts; how a certain illustrious lawyer, fifteen years later, acted as the chief attorney for the claimants and obtained from the Chief Justice then presiding a decision in their favor under which they received from the Government a total indemnity of nearly five million dollars; and how the very next year that attorney was put upon the bench of the Supreme Court of the United States, where he presently handed down a decision in favor of the Chief Justice, in a case involving that particular Chief Justice's personal interests.

Robert Morris Thrown Into Jail.

Some final facts remain to be given concerning the outcome of those great land transactions, in other parts of the United States, of Robert Morris, James Greenleaf, Justice James Wilson, John Nicholson and their train of associates.

On May 28, 1796, an agreement was made between Greenleaf, on the one part, and Robert Morris and Nicholson, on the other, by which Greenleaf agreed to sell to Morris and Nicholson his interest in the North American Land Company for a large sum of money. Morris' share in the property was not to be transferred until the money was paid; this sum, according to the answer in the suit of Gilmore, in 1817, was not paid.[89] The arrangement, as the court found, was a fraudulent one, intended to defraud creditors, which creditors were mainly the Government and various States; already, in 1795, Morris, Nicholson and Greenleaf were so deeply in debt as to be virtually insolvent. Their object was to retain

---

[89] Gilmore vs. North American Land Company, et al., I Peters, 460. The company's affairs were in such a queer and confused state that the court's decision in this case stated: "It appears that many shares in the company were disposed of; but it is quite uncertain what the real condition of the company's affairs is."

as much of the land as they could; anticipating judgments against them, they were resorting to various circumventing devices.

On June 8, 1797, a judgment was obtained in New York against Morris; his commercial and land operations had been so enormous, and to carry them he had had to borrow such volumes of money, that, when pressed by private creditors, he could not pay. The court judgment resulted in his being put in jail[90] in Philadelphia, where he remained imprisoned for some years. He persuaded Gouverneur Morris to advance the money for the payment of the judgment, which was then assigned to Adam Hoops, a personal friend of Robert Morris, and agent for the various parties concerned. One of the purposes of this assignment was to preserve to Morris the right to redemption in 1,500,000 acres which he had conveyed to the Holland Company, in the nature of a mortgage, as he supposed. Hoops later assigned the judgment to Gouverneur Morris, and on September 16, 1799, Robert Morris confirmed the trust deed. To an arrangement entered into by Robert Morris that Hoops, acting for the trustees, should buy in such lands as were sold under execution, Gouverneur Morris consented.

Certain of Morris' lands in New York were sold under judgment on February 6, 1800. Hoops made his bid at the sale, but being outbid and not having sufficient funds on hand, persuaded the sheriff to adjourn the sale until May 13, following, Gouverneur Morris supplying Hoops with the poundage for the sheriff's fees.

But on April 2, 1800, Gouverneur Morris, without letting Robert Morris, or the trustees, know anything about his plan, and without notice, assigned the judgment in question to the Holland Company, for a full consideration in money. Gouverneur Morris, after this act of duplicity toward his partner,

[90] Washington, who was a very intimate friend of Morris, wrote Mrs. Morris an autograph letter inviting her, during her husband's incarceration, to stay indefinitely in his mansion at Mount Vernon.

made an agreement, on the same day, with Thomas L. Ogden, agent of the Holland Company, that the sale of the lands should take place under the judgment, and should be bought in by Ogden for the Holland Company. Ogden did, indeed, buy in the lands at the sheriff's sale, but it seems that he, too, did some profitable fraud on his own account; he turned over to the Holland Company only 58,570 acres,— not half the extent of land claimed by that company.[91]

This transaction caused an extended litigation between the various personages concerned, three of whom — the two Morrises and Fitzsimmons — had been, as we have seen, members of the Federal Constitutional Convention. In fact, a long series of litigation for thirty-five years followed Morris' land jobbing transactions in New York, Pennsylvania, Washington and in other places. The docket of the Supreme Court of the United States was full of these involved cases.[92] Morris had also owned land in New Jersey, some of which, near what is now Belvidere, he had given, in 1793, to his son-in-law, Charles Croxall, who built a mansion there. Those who really benefited from Morris' misfortunes were a crowd of politicians and capitalists mostly in the background.

Nicholson's Enormous Estate.

Greenleaf held on to much of his property or passed it over to lessees. Nicholson left, at his death in December, 1800, an enormous estate in land in Pennsylvania, Virginia, Kentucky, North Carolina, South Carolina, Georgia and other States. Some of the Pennsylvania legislative documents es-

[91] The foregoing details are set forth in the case of Fitzsimmons and others vs. Ogden and others, VII Cranch, 2–22. (February 4, 1812.) Slow in his physical movements, Gouverneur Morris was exceedingly nimble mentally. He had lost a leg, and thereafter contented himself with a wooden leg, scorning to buy " one of those fancy legs."

[92] See, for example, the case of Van Ness vs. the City of Washington and the U. S., IV Peters, 232–286 (January, 1830), and other cases growing out of his Washington real estate speculations.

timated the area at from three to four million acres; other reports, notably a report in 1842, by the judiciary committee of the Pennsylvania House of Representatives, stated that it was five million acres.

The bulk of this estate was in Pennsylvania, and included extensive tracts of the very richest coal deposits. Nicholson was deeply in debt for taxes to the State of Pennsylvania, but by various legal devices he had, while Comptroller General, transferred large areas to various land companies in which he was a leading figure. One of these was the " Asylum Company "— a speculative land company organized for the purpose of selling land to settlers. The State of Pennsylvania held a lien upon Nicholson's estate for unpaid taxes amounting to $300,000. In 1805 the Legislature passed an act for the " more effectual and speedy recovery of debt due from the late John Nicholson," [93] and on March 19, 1807, it enacted a law to force the " Asylum Company " to give information which it had refused, and compelling it to file a schedule of the lands claimed by it.[94]   Considerable of the

[93] Carey and Bioren's " Pa. Laws," Vol. VII: 528.
[94] *Ibid.,* Vol. VIII: 210–211. Despite the State's lien, different individuals and corporations contrived to get hold of most of this valuable estate during the next forty years; the frauds and thefts by which they did so are set forth in many legislative documents, and formed a continuous scandal. To quote one of these documents: Writing on January 24, 1842, to William Elwell, chairman of the Judiciary Committee of the Pennsylvania House of Representatives, Judge J. B. Anthony of the Nicholson Court (a court especially established to pass upon questions arising from the disposition of the estate) said:
" On the 11th of April, 1825, an act passed the Governor to appoint agents to discover and sell the Nicholson lands at auction for which they were allowed *twenty-five per cent.* A Special Board of Property was also formed to compromise and settle with claimants. From what has come to my knowledge in relation to this act, I am satisfied that the commonwealth was seriously injured by the manner in which it was carried out by some of the agents. It was made use of principally for the benefit of land speculators; and the very small sums received by the State treasurer for large and valuable tracts sold and compromised, show that the cunning and astute land jobbers could easily overreach the Board of Property at Harrisburg. . . . Many instances of gross fraud might be enumerated, but it would serve no useful purpose." Judge Anthony further said that " very many of the most influential,

coal lands and iron deposit holdings of some of the largest present corporations in the United States, such as the Steel Trust and the Coal Trust, can be traced back to their acquisition by Nicholson and his partners.

Wilson Evades Warrants for His Arrest.

As for Justice James Wilson, signer of the Declaration of Independence, author of a memorable Constitutional clause pushed by him in the Federal Constitutional Convention, outclassing Jay on the high tribunal of the Supreme Court of the United States in point of legal skill, fertility and vigorous, dominant individuality — he presented a sorry figure in his last years.

That he had long been a notorious land speculator; that he had supplied the principal part of the funds to wrest the public lands from the Commonwealth of Pennsylvania, and to bribe the Legislature of Georgia — these and other acts in nowise lessened his standing in the great court. No impeachment proceedings were brought against him; nearly all the members of the Senate, and other high officials or personages, had been associated with him in his jobberies, or were concerned in similar ones.

But with the collapse of the Morris-Greenleaf-Nicholson fabric of colossal land ownership, difficulties poured fast on Wilson. Writs of arrest were issued against him, but to the last he was agile and resourceful. He evaded arrest in Pennsylvania, by exchanging circuits with his colleague, Justice Iredell of North Carolina.[95] Still in intense fear of being

astute and intelligent inhabitants and gentlemen of high standing" were participants in the frauds. (Pa. House Journal, 1842, Vol. II, Doc. No. 127: 700–704.) Much of the coal and iron lands now owned by the Coal Trust and the Steel Trust were thus obtained at the time by various individuals and corporations.

[95] At that time and for more than eighty years afterwards, it was the assigned practice of each Supreme Court justice to preside over the circuit court in the district from which he came.

pursued, arrested and prosecuted, he died at Edenton, N. C. on August 28, 1798. He left two children who were his heirs; and the cases which we have hitherto cited reveal that before writs of arrest were issued against him, he had made disposition of much of his property.

CHAPTER V

FROM JAY'S RESIGNATION TO MARSHALL'S ACCESSION

To the puzzled astonishment of the general public, Chief Justice Jay, after presiding over the Supreme Court of the United States for five years, stepped down from that office to go to England, as the plenipotentiary of the United States, and execute a new treaty.

This happened in April, 1794. ". . . No appointment," wrote Jay on April 17 of that year to his wife, referring to his selection as special envoy, " ever operated more unpleasantly upon me; but the public considerations which were urged, and the manner in which it was pressed, strongly impressed me with a conviction that to refuse it would be to desert my duty for the sake of domestic concerns and comforts." [1]

Jay Quits the Chief Justiceship.

As the sequel proved, Jay's quitting the Chief Justiceship amounted to a *de facto* resignation, although he did not formally resign until June 29, 1795, after his return from England. Jay did not again sit on the Supreme Court; and indeed it would seem that President Washington did not expect his return to that office, for in a secret and confidential letter, Washington, on April 29, 1794, asked Jay whether he would not consent to become the resident Minister of the United States at London after his mission as envoy was concluded.[2] Washington's intermediary on this occasion was Jay's former

---

[1] " Correspondence and Public Papers of John Jay," Vol. IV: 5.
[2] *Ibid.*, 9–10.

law partner, Robert R. Livingston, to whom the post was also offered. Both Jay and Livingston declined it. Washington's aim was to get rid of Gouverneur Morris, as United States Minister to Paris. Morris, as Justin McCarthy tells in his "French Revolution," was scandalously promoting the sale in Paris of his American lands. Morris removed, it was Washington's intention to transfer Pinckney from London to Paris, and put Jay in Pinckney's place.

That Washington should have taken Jay away from the Chief Justiceship argued powerful motives behind the mission to England. Of all the Governmental departments Washington fully recognized the supreme importance of the judicial department, of which, of course, the Supreme Court of the United States was the cardinal and head factor. When, on October 17, 1789, Washington had originally appointed Jay Chief Justice, he had, in enclosing Jay's commission, strongly urged him to accept. Washington in that letter had expressed the hope that Jay would not " hesitate a moment to bring into action the talents, knowledge, and integrity which are necessary to be exercised at the head of that department which must be considered as the keystone of our political fabric." [3] Washington, then, considered the judiciary as the chief bulwark of the political state, and at the apex of this judiciary was John Jay. Important as was the Chief Justiceship, it is evident that Washington in selecting Jay regarded the mission to England as of more importance at that juncture.

Already Jay had expressed his desire to retire to his estate and live in leisure with his family and his books. The life of a Supreme Court Justice was nomadic enough; it was the practice of the Supreme Court members, often two together, to preside over the Circuit Courts in different cities a great part of the year. They traveled over the country extensively, and it need hardly be explained that travel was then slow,

[3] " Correspondence and Public Papers of John Jay," Vol. III : 378.

rough, primitive and arduous.[4] Few leisure-loving lawyers cared for this onerous duty, and the only reason Jay had accepted was, in his own words, " to place the judiciary on a proper footing." In accepting the mission to London, Jay was further away than ever from his contemplated life of retirement. What were the deep actuating reasons?

Except the small, exclusive group cognizant of the secret reasons, no one could fathom why it was that Jay, after having himself selected the post of Chief Justice, should voluntarily quit it in order to draw up a treaty which any able, unattached politician could, it was supposed, do as well. Intelligent observers of events knew that, in addition to the nominal purposes, there must be at bottom potent aims prompting this extraordinary move, but precisely what were those aims was, for a time, a matter of some mystification.

As a landholder himself, and allied by descent, marriage and interest with many of the old manorial families of New York, Jay had chosen the highest judicial position in the land as one in which he could be of the most vital service to his class, as well, perhaps, as securing the memorable honor

[4] The Supreme Court of the United States was not then a distinct institution or entity, as it is now, separate from the Circuit Courts. It was, to a large extent, the whole Federal judicial system of the country, and its members decided criminal, as well as civil, cases. The supereminence of the Supreme Court was recognized by Washington. On July 18, 1793, Washington, through Thomas Jefferson, then Secretary of State, asked the Supreme Court for an opinion on the lines of separation between the different departments as drawn by the Constitution. This the Supreme Court declined to give, excusing itself on the ground of its being a court of last resort, and hence the impropriety of extrajudicially deciding questions.

Those who may be inclined to think that the Supreme Court was of no great importance because of the comparatively few civil cases decided may also consider this explanation in Dallas' Reports referring to the proceedings in 1793, of the Supreme Court of the United States then holding its session in Philadelphia: " The Malignant Fever which, during this year raged in Philadelphia, dispersed the great body of its inhabitants, and proved fatal to thousands, interrupted, likewise, the business of the Courts; and I cannot trace that any important cause was agitated during the present Term."— II Dallas : 480.

of being the first to fill that exalted seat.[5]   Was there a still
stronger and more pressing service that he could render to
the great landowners by his departing to frame a new treaty
with the British Government?   If so, what was the nature of
that service?

Its nature was not at all political, as conventional writers
would have it; the motive actuating Jay was one involving a
twofold purpose, springing from the most acute sense of self-
preservation on the part of the landed class and its adjuncts.

The French Revolution Terrifies the Landed Class.

As the French Revolution progressed, battering to ruin
the old feudal conditions, and, amid portentous upheavals of
the French artisans and peasants, overthrowing the aristocracy, the American landowning aristocracy was filled with
terror.   Great estates in France were confiscated, divided
and sold; the governing monarchy and aristocracy of ages
were supplanted by revolutionary committees; and the very
suspicion of being an aristocrat was a sufficient warrant for
the guillotine.   The frightful conditions long prevailing in
France by which the laborer was, in law and in fact, treated
worse than a beast of burden were swept away, at least for
the time.   The march of the French Revolution was hailed
with joy by the workers of America, and hardly less so by the
small merchants, who instinctively grasped its real purport in
assuring the advent of bourgeois power and rule over the
grave of the feudal regime.

But the American aristocracy, like the aristocracies of all
other countries, shuddered at the news of the successive con-
vulsions, and well realized that the French Revolution was

---

[5] The manner in which the office of Chief Justice was held is shown
by the deference in the address of the Lansingburgh (Federalist) Committee to Jay on June 30, 1792, in which it spoke of "Our respect for
your character, in the dignified office of Chief Justice of the United
States," etc.   "Correspondence and Public Letters of John Jay," Vol.
III: 436.

not one of mere phrases but was striking down to the depths. The feudal conditions, somewhat analogous to those in Europe, long prevailing in America, were the very conditions which the American landowners were bent upon maintaining, and had maintained. Some of the most powerful leaders of the American Revolution, such as John Adams, Hamilton, Jay and others had preferred a monarchical form of government, or, if not that, at any rate a mode as nearly as possible imitative. The American Revolution, as contemplated and molded by these men, was a rebellion for liberty of trade and colonial autonomy; had that right been granted at the outset, they would have remained steadfast monarchist loyalists.[6] They so admired the British form of government that they patterned the American form of government as closely after it as they dared.

These astute leaders of the American aristocracy closely followed the developments of the French Revolution, and knew that the portentous character of those events not merely affected France but were destined to have a world-wide influence on the thought and condition of peoples.

Jay had bitterly assailed the progress of the French Revolution. Even when acting as envoy in London he continued this denunciation. In a private letter to Washington written from London, March 6, 1795, he said that, "The French Jacobins have greatly injured the cause of rational liberty," and then proceeded to rejoice over their recent suppression, meaning the execution of Robespierre, St. Just and the Jacobin group.[7] In a letter from New York, January 19, 1796, Jay wrote to Robert Goodloe Harper that he had favored the overthrow of despotism and the establishment of a limited monarchy, but was terrified by the later revolutionary move-

[6] Thus, profiting from her experience with the American colonies, Great Britain gave the traders of Canada the full right to make whatever goods they wanted, and sell them where they pleased. The Canadian ruling classes have remained stanch monarchists.

[7] "Correspondence and Public Papers of John Jay," Vol. IV: 166.

ment which executed Louis XVI.[8] The counter-revolution
planned by the royalists with its inevitable train of butcheries,
had it been successful; the carefully-planned slaughter of the
people by the Swiss mercenaries on August 10; the immense
loss of life caused by the wars of the allies upon the French,—
these did not impress Jay with the slightest feelings of horror.
His class instincts and interests were entirely with the counter-
revolution.

With England leading the reactionary nations of Europe
against the France of the French Revolution, the American
aristocracy saw that the self-interest of all aristocracies demanded that every possible help be given to the British Government. This assistance could not be proffered in the form
of regiments and warships. Had the Federalists, the "party
of property," then in power, attempted a serious prosecution
of the war against France, a national insurrection would have
resulted.

But help could be extended in another way of so indirect
and subtle, yet withal so fundamental a kind, as not to seem
suspicious on its face. Better, perhaps, at this juncture than
armaments was an economic assistance to England, the fore-

[8] *Ibid.,* 201. As illustrative of the opinions of Jay's intimate set, the
instance can be cited of General Phillip Schuyler (Hamilton's father-
in-law) writing to Jay, May 17, 1800, deploring recent anti-Federalist
successes, and calling for measures to save the nation from "the mis-
rule of a Man [Jefferson] who . . . is in fact pervaded with the
mad French philosophy."— *Ibid., 273.*
The French Revolution, as led by Robespierre and his group, really
represented not the proletariat, but the aims of nascent capitalist class
to overthrow feudal rule and develop capitalism. This is admirably
explained in Kropotkin's recent " Great French Revolution." While
Jay was denouncing the French Revolution, his political opponents at
home recognized what the Revolution was actually accomplishing.
Thus, the Society of St. Tammany, of New York, largely a middle-class
organization, gave this toast at its dinner on May 12, 1793: " Success
to the armies of France, and Wisdom, Concord and Firmness to the
Convention." " The first sentence was hardly articulated," said the
New York " Journal and Patriotic Register," May 15, 1793, " when as
one the whole company arose and gave three cheers, continued by roars
of applause for several minutes; the toast was then given in whole and
the applause reiterated."   The Philadelphia Society likewise proclaimed
its support of the French Revolution, as did other societies.

most of manufacturing countries. With the gold from British trade, the English government was busy subsidizing other European nations in the coalition against France in a colossal effort to crush the French Revolution, and to restore the ancient régime. A tariff favorable to England, it was thought, could be arranged without having to run the gauntlet of effective opposition in the Senate; not until twenty years later did the manufacturers of cotton, woolen and other goods begin to acquire power sufficient to command legislation. In the United States of 1795 the large landholding class occupied and swayed virtually every branch of government.

This was one of the impelling reasons for Jay's mission; this was partly why he, who was secure for life in the lofty office of Chief Justice of the Supreme Court of the United States, voluntarily relinquished it for the brief and rather arduous business of arranging a new pact with Great Britain. As the most conspicuous representative of the American landed class, he could be trusted, every fiber and instinct of him. But there was another reason, which, added to the first, decided Jay to undertake the mission — a reason (considering popular feeling) of so delicate and dangerous a nature that none, at that critical period, had such strong motives as he for transforming the plan into a fact accomplished.

Manipulation of Confiscated Estates.

We have seen how, before the Revolution, vast areas of land in the colonies were owned by absentee British nobles, merchants and lawyers, and how prominent colonial personages were associated with them in companies, or as agents. These estates, as well as those of native Tories, were confiscated by general acts during the Revolution.

But such measures of confiscation, while seemingly effective, were, in many instances, only nominally so. To evade the confiscatory acts, estates were fraudulently conveyed to safe parties, while act after act was slid through legislatures during the Revolution, altering or emasculating the provisions of former acts, each successive law being more in favor of the absentee or expatriated landowners. The claims to a number of these confiscated estates, also, were bought by astute lawyers, or by capitalists for whom the lawyers were acting. These attorneys would never have purchased the claims had they not known of certain technical deficiencies in the laws by reason of which they had good hopes of recovering the estates, or their equivalent, in the courts.

As for the courts, they were filled with judges who had been attorneys for, or who were relatives of, families whose estates had been confiscated. The large estates, too, of a number of Jay's relatives or personal friends, such as William Bayard, the Van Schaak family and others, had been confiscated; and what was true of Jay's circle was true of that of almost all other judges and high Government officials.

Finally, British lords and merchants held claims for large sums due them from settlers or from other purchasers of lands, or from merchants. These claims had been outlawed by statutes passed during the Revolution, and had been bought up for almost nothing by speculators.

The plan under way contemplated nothing less than a series of stealthy articles and acts by which the courts would be able to find specious grounds for gradually restoring certain confiscated estates, or for validating the purchases of claims by American politicians. This plan was certain to provoke the wildest outburst of popular resentment and anger. But Jay affected, and really felt, a contempt for the people whom he despised as much as they hated him.

A number of important cases involving the recovery of confiscated British debts or British or Tory estates had come before the Supreme Court of the United States when Jay was Chief Justice. Chief Justice Jay and Justice Iredell and Judge Griffin had held that the debts were obligatory. But on one point they disagreed: the question whether specific payments of such debts already made to the various States by American debtors were barred from recovery or not. Chief Justice Jay had held in favor of the British creditors, and his associates for the American debtors.[9]

The noted and much discussed case of Ware, Administrator vs. Hylton and others,[10] was one of such cases. This suit had originally been instituted in 1791. The reason why it commanded so much public attention and aroused such acrimony was because it embodied the question of the rights of British creditors to recover debts contracted before the Revolution and sequestered by act of the Legislature.

The United States Circuit Court in Virginia decided in favor of the American debtors, Hylton and others. But when the case came up on appeal before the full Supreme Court of the United States in 1795–1796, that decision was reversed, and it was held that British creditors had the right to recover debts. Justices Chase, Paterson, Wilson, and Cushing each wrote opinions to this effect, and Justice Iredell's opinion was a qualified one, partly favoring both sides on different points. As one of the attorneys for the American debtors in this case, John Marshall had the opportunity of learning at first hand what the settled court law on the subject was — a knowledge which, as we shall see, he was not slow in applying to his own personal benefit.

The mass of the people were intensely stirred over the pertinacious efforts of British or Tory claimants to recover possession of confiscated estates. The historic case of Chisholm vs. Georgia arose over the efforts of two executors in South Carolina to regain certain confiscated property in Georgia. The question at issue was whether, under the Constitution, the citizens of another State could sue a State. Chief Justice Jay and Justices Cushing, Wilson and Blair held that they could; Iredell dissented.[11] Great opposition was excited by

[9] "Correspondence," etc., " of John Jay," Vol. III: 486.
[10] Dallas' Reports, Vol. III: 195–285.
[11] *Ibid.,* Vol. II: 419–480.

this decision not only in Georgia (where the Grand Jury presented it as a grievance) but in Massachusetts, Pennsylvania
and other States where the resentment over the efforts to recover confiscated estates was acute. Considerable popular
disturbances followed this decision, which was reversed in
1798 by the adoption of the Eleventh Amendment to the Constitution of the United States.

Jay's solicitude for the interests of his close friends, particularly Nicholas Cruger and Herman Le Roy and William
Bayard, may be learned from a significant letter written by
him from London, on September 11, 1794, to Cruger.   This
last-named personage was Alexander Hamilton's foremost
rich patron. LeRoy and Bayard were among the leading
men of wealth in New York City.   As we have seen in Chapter I, they were associated in getting fraudulent titles for
large areas of land validated.[12]   The judge confirming those
titles was Judge Benson, another intimate friend of Jay.[13]
The Bayard estates were confiscated during the Revolution
but were later regained under the provisions of Jay's treaty.

A " Golden Plan " for Millions Sterling.

" A gentleman in Holland," wrote Jay to Cruger, " has
been so obliging as to send me a plan to make my fortune,

[12] William Bayard, born in 1729, entered mercantile life, and became
one of the richest merchants of New York. He was the owner of all
the land on which the present city of Hoboken is built. During the
Revolution he went to England, and his estates were confiscated and
sold. Two of his sons, John and Samuel, entered the British army
and attained high rank. His third son, William (born in 1764), remained in New York, succeeded to his father's business, became one of
the largest ship owners in New York, was President of the Chamber
of Commerce from 1810 to 1827, and a director of the Bank of America,
and other banks. His daughter, Elizabeth, married Stephen Van Rensselaer (the younger). It was to William Bayard's country seat on
Greenwich Street that Hamilton was taken after his duel with Burr.
The Livingstons, Van Rensselaers, Bayards, Schuylers, Patersons and
other powerful landed families were, as we have said, closely related by
marriage.
[13] See, " Correspondence and Public Papers of John Jay," Vol. IV.

even to the extent of many millions sterling." Pleading with many expressions of regret that he unfortunately had no mercantile knowledge necessary for the execution of the plan, Jay then went on. " You will find this golden plan enclosed. If the extensive concerns in which you are already engaged should render its magnitude inconvenient, it might be well to let our friends LeRoy and Bayard share in it. . ." [14]

The nature of this " golden plan " is not stated in the published letter, but we note that it was of a mercantile character, which is to say one pertaining to international commerce in which LeRoy and Bayard were engaged. Those who may hold to the theory that Jay when in London was still Chief Justice of the Supreme Court of the United States, may well give this letter consideration. While acting as special envoy in England negotiating a treaty dealing extensively with questions of commerce, Jay receives and forwards to his friends a plan for reaping millions of sterling profit. That it was not an airy, conjectural proposal is seen by his use of the words " golden plan "; Jay was habituated to great restraint in talking and writing.

One other fact is certain, which fact bears the greatest relevance and importance to decisions of the Supreme Court under Chief Justice Marshall, and, as will be seen, to Marshall's own covert interests.

When Jay was arranging the treaty in London, the matter of confiscated estates was one of the questions considered by him. On September 13, 1794, Jay wrote in a private letter to Washington that ". . . I learn that Virginia is escheating British property and I hear of other occurrences which I regret. . ." [15] Three days later Jay wrote to Hamilton similarly.[16] In a private letter, dated December 18, 1794, Washington wrote to Jay: " The Virginia escheats of British

---

[14] *Ibid.*, Vol. IV: 57.
[15] " Correspondence and Public Papers of John Jay," Vol. IV: 59.
[16] *Ibid.*, 115. Jay's treaty was concluded on Nov. 19, 1794, and ratified by the United States on Aug. 18, 1795.

property do not, I am informed, stand upon the ground as related to you; but as I am not accurately enough read in the law respecting these escheats to be precise in my recital of it, I will request the Secretary of State to give you the principles thereof." [17]

Jay's Treaty Denounced.

Jay carried on his negotiations in England with Lord Grenville, Secretary of Foreign Affairs, a personal friend. It is not necessary here to dwell upon all the various phases of the treaty of 1794 agreed upon by Jay and Grenville; only one part of that treaty is of vital consequence to this work, and to the results of this part we shall have occasion to revert in Chapters VI and VII. By the provisions of Jay's treaty, British creditors were to be compensated for losses caused by laws of any of the States obstructing the collection of debts contracted prior to the Revolutionary war; the citizens of each country were to enjoy the right to hold and convey land in the territories of the other; and debts contracted, or engagements made, by the citizens of the one, with the other, country, were not to be impaired in case of national differences.

The ultimate purport of these clauses the generality of the American people did not clearly perceive. They could not foresee the remarkable extent to which the Supreme Court of the United States would go in using those clauses as a lever for a construction by which confiscated estates could be recovered.

But they did see enough to infuriate them. Even the commercial class and the Southern plantation owners were exasperated; in return for a few paltry, insignificant concessions granted by England for a period of twelve years, the United States, under Jay's treaty, agreed not to export molasses, sugar, coffee, cocoa or cotton to any part of the world. An-

[17] " Correspondence and Public Papers of John Jay," Vol. IV: 151.

other grievance of the Southern slaveholders was that the treaty contained no provision for indemnification for negroes carried away by the British during the Revolutionary war. The West India trade, for which merchants of Boston, Salem and other parts were so desirous, was granted only on condition that it should be carried on in vessels of less than seventy tons burden. No promise was exacted from England to desist from searching American merchantmen, or to refrain from the seizure of British-born sailors. In Philadelphia and elsewhere Jay was burned in effigy; in more than one instance an effigy of Jay was labeled in this wise or similar language; " Come up to my price and I will sell you my country." A copy of the obnoxious treaty was consigned to the flames by a crowd in front of Jay's own house.

The opposition of the planters and commercial interests finally had its effect in the Senate which rejected the West Indies' and the export clauses, but the popular opposition to the treaty, as a whole, was ignored. With the exception of those clauses, the treaty was ratified. No doubt the charge that Jay had sold out for a price was a calumny, although it revealed what the people were ready to believe of him, and the repute in which he was held. A much more dominating incentive than a venal one influenced Jay, mercenary as he was; every instinct, interest, prejudice and creed of his class was concentrated in him; his conduct, as a whole, proceeded from class motives, and was uniformly determined by them. Instances were not lacking, however, in which his acts seemed to justify grave suspicions that he was personally profiting.

Livingstons Change Policies Overnight.

Meanwhile a great change affecting the status of both political parties had happened in New York State. Most of the immensely powerful Livingston family had abruptly shifted from the Federalist to the Republican party.

According to Hammond, this transference had taken place as early as the year 1790, when Chancellor Robert R. Livingston, carrying with him his immediate connections, known as the " Livingston family," went over to the Republican camp, in opposition to Hamilton. The real cause, as ascribed by Hamilton's friends, was (Hammond wrote) Chancellor Livingston's disappointment at not being appointed Chief Justice of the Supreme Court of the United States. Hammond relates that he was informed " that *the family* one evening had a meeting for the purpose of deliberating on the subject, and that the result of their deliberations was such, that the next morning every member of it took a position in the ranks of the Republican party," except some Livingstons in Columbia County.[18]

If this explanation is correct it again reveals the inordinate appetite of the Livingstons for self-advantageous positions of power, since they had already had two representatives on the Supreme Court bench (composed of five members in all), in the persons of John Jay and William Paterson. Perhaps what Hammond means is that the Livingstons expected Chancellor Robert R. Livingston to be appointed Chief Justice when Jay resigned; it was about that time that distinct political party alignments began to form, developing in Washington's second administration into the Federalist and the Republican parties. Although there might have been some rankling feeling of disgruntlement over Chancellor Livingston's non-appointment, yet the extreme political sagacity of the Livingstons argued a much broader and keener outlook as a cause for their change of front. As events moved on, shrewd observers could descry signs that, while the Federalists might still hold some years more of power, defeat was foreshadowed. Exercising their traditional political shrewdness, the Livingstons always took care to array themselves on the vic-

[18] Hammond's " Political History of the State of New York," Vol. I: 106–107.

torious side. What was still more to their purpose, they did not neglect to have their able representatives and connections on both sides, so that, whichever party won, the family would be in a position to draw benefit.

Between the large landholders and politico-capitalists of both political parties there was, in action, only a fine exoteric difference of purpose. In words they might take violent issue with each other, but in deed they stood stanchly together. Both indiscriminately joined in granting the other great tracts of public land, and bank, canal, turnpike, insurance and other charters. In political creed, as affecting their own economic interests, or those of their particular or sectional constituencies, they often had cause to differ, out of which differences grew what seemed to be overshadowing issues involving the very fate of mankind. But while such of the working class as were enfranchised were duped into supporting one side or the other, the leaders of both political parties obstinately refused to pass any laws ameliorating the condition of the workers, at the same time using legislation to manufacture laws vesting in themselves enormous and perpetual powers and privileges.[19]

Jay and the Livingston Steamboat Monopoly.

Whatever might have been Chancellor Livingston's sense of disappointment from failure to appoint him Chief Justice, he and Jay, Hamilton's close friend, not only kept on very good terms, but Jay, when Governor of New York State, largely helped to put through an extraordinary act for the benefit of Chancellor Livingston, his former law partner.

To describe adequately this fact and other pertinent facts dealing with the further career of Jay and various other per-

[19] The rush to get charters of all descriptions from the various Legislatures was indescribable. Already, in 1791, the Legislature of Pennsylvania, for example, was driven into complaining that most of its time was consumed in enacting laws to incorporate private associations. — Carey and Bioren's " Pa. Laws," Vol. IV: 28.

sonages, a digression is necessary here from the consecutive narrative of the Supreme Court of the United States. It is an integral part of this work to portray individualities only in so far as they represent forces. To illumine the nature of those forces, and the enlarging or changing classes embodied in them, it is also necessary to describe the measures by which those ruling forces acquired more power, and the means by which successive divisions of the capitalist class became dominant.

Jay was nominated for Governor of New York State, and Stephen Van Rensselaer for Lieutenant-Governor, in 1795; thus two of the most powerful landed families in the State, and, in fact, in the whole country, composed the heads of the Federalist ticket. Hammond says that Jay did not want to be a candidate, but that probably Hamilton, Schuyler and others persuaded him to change his resolution.[20] Defeated in the year 1792, Jay was elected Governor in the next election, in 1795.[21] As Governor, Jay was the President, ex-officio, of a body called the Council of Revision, which had the power of approving or vetoing all laws.

Now it happened that on March 19, 1787, the New York Legislature had passed an act granting to John Fitch the sole and exclusive right of navigating craft, propelled by steam, in the waters of New York. Ten years later, Chancellor Robert R. Livingston came forward with the claim that he was the possessor of a mode of propelling boats by steam. Starting with the remarkable assumption that Fitch was dead, although there was no legal proof to that effect, the New York Legislature, on March 27, 1798, passed an act repealing the exclusive powers given to Fitch, and conferring similar privileges, for a term of twenty years, on Robert R. Livingston. The act was subject to final action by the Council of Revision, which, at the time, was composed of Governor Jay, Chief Jus-

[20] "Political History of the State of New York," Vol. I: 55.
[21] It was after being elected Governor that Jay formally resigned as Chief Justice.

tice Lansing of the State Supreme Court, Judge Lewis and Judge Benson [22] of the same court, and Chancellor Robert R. Livingston himself.

When the bill came before the Council of Revision, Livingston, not caring to hazard the chance of impeachment for taking part in voting for a bill benefiting himself exclusively, kept away. But his associates attended satisfactorily to the business. After making a show of objection to the bill because the facts as to the grounds from which Fitch's forfeiture was to arise, had not been found by some due process of law, the Council of Revision then sustained both the act itself and its constitutionality.[23] This finding was made the basis for further laws in favor of Livingston, after Jay ceased to be Governor. We shall proceed to tell what those laws were.

More Remarkable Laws for Livingston.

Robert R. Livingston was not an inventor; he had never been anything but a rich man and politician. Did he cause this bill to be passed so as to have a means of compelling Robert Fulton to come to terms? This does not appear. At any rate, on April 5, 1803, the Legislature of New York passed another act by which it was declared that the rights and privileges granted to Robert R. Livingston, by the act of 1798, should be extended to him and Robert Fulton for a period of twenty years from the passage of the act of 1803. Five years later,— on April 11, 1808,— an even more decisive law was enacted. It extended the Livingston and Fulton monopoly still further, and it forbade all persons to navigate any steamboat or vessel without securing a special license from

[22] In Chapter I we have given a remarkable decision made by Judge Benson at about this time in a noted case by which he justified title to land avowedly obtained by fraud. As for Judge Lewis, he had studied law with John Jay, and was related to the Livingston family by marriage.

[23] For the full history, see Wheaton's Reports, Supreme Court of the United States, Vol. IX: 1–240.

the firm of Livingston and Fulton.[24]   If such a license was not obtained, the offending boat or vessel was to be forfeited.[25]

These provisions were extraordinary enough, but even more extraordinary were those of the succeeding act of April 9, 1811.   This act provided that if the provisions of the former act were violated, Livingston and Fulton, in case any other steamboat navigated their territory, should have an action at law for such boat as if they themselves had been dispossessed by force.   The act further declared that they could immediately get an injunction.[26]

These cumulative acts raised an immense commotion in the mercantile world.   Everywhere the great landowners, with the revenues from land obtained by fraud, were breaking out of the bounds of being mainly landowners, and were becoming transformed into owners of banks, turnpikes, bridges, navigation companies and insurance companies.   Just as in the old days their sphere was one of part landowner, part seignorial trader, so now they hastened to avail themselves of each freshly discovered resource, each new invention, each newly-developed economic institution.[27]   But Livingston and Fulton, in getting the steamboat monopoly in New York waters (which meant the profitable Hudson River, Long Island Sound and other navigable water trade), came gradually into

[24] In 1806 Robert Fulton married Harriet Livingston, a niece of Chancellor Livingston.   By her he had four children.— Houghton's "Kings of Fortune," 284.   Their descendants are among the richest families of New York.

[25] Wheaton's Reports, Supreme Court of the United States, Vol. IX: 1–240.

[26] Ibid.

[27] Thus, to give one example of a large number of instances, Nicholas Cruger was one of the richest landholders in New York.   His will, made in February, 1791, revealed that his estate amounted to $644,814.15.   Of this amount, $122,905.62 was in real estate — exclusive of the land bought by Cruger after making his will.   The dower estate was valued at $71,713.   Cruger held $141,779.69 in stocks, including shares in the United Insurance Company, the Bank of the United States, Hamilton's Bank of New York, the Bank of Albany and Aaron Burr's Manhattan Company.   Various other properties made up the total inventory.— Johnson's Reports, Court of Errors [N. Y.], Vol. VII: 568.

conflict with nascent capitalists, not nearly as rich as they, but equally determined and aggressive. The whole mercantile class looked with alarm upon acts by which this great new method of transportation was monopolized by two men, with probably influential others covertly sharing the profits.

Prevailing Legislative Corruption.

The legislative acts were denounced as unconstitutional. The owners of the monopoly fell back in triumph upon that famous constitutional clause inserted by Justice James Wilson that no legislature could pass laws impairing the obligation of a contract. But if this claim was true of Livingston and Fulton's monopoly, why did it not apply with equal force to Fitch's? Livingston and Fulton also pointed out, as though the argument were invincible, that no less a jurist than John Jay, the first Chief Justice of the Supreme Court of the United States, had in the Council of Revision pronounced the original act constitutional, and that those great authorities, Judges Lansing, Lewis and Benson, had agreed with him.

To give an insight into the real methods by which legislatures were induced to pass such acts, a few facts will be given as to certain other charters granted by the New York Legislature during that period.

The bill chartering the Manhattan Bank, in which Aaron Burr and De Witt Clinton [28] were prominently interested, was passed in 1799 under the philanthropic guise of being a measure to incorporate a company to supply pure water to New York City with the plausible pretext of diminishing future

[28] It was De Witt Clinton who, some years afterward, drew the charter of John Jacob Astor's American Fur Company, and it was through De Witt Clinton's exertions that it became a law. For an extended description of the long-continued debauching, swindling and murdering of Indians, done upon the strength of this charter, see Vol. I, "History of the Great American Fortunes." De Witt Clinton was a nephew of Governor, later United States Senator, George Clinton. After serving as Mayor of New York City, De Witt Clinton repeatedly became Governor of New York State.

ravages by yellow fever. As we have seen, members of the legislature, including Senator (later Judge) Spencer, were openly charged with taking bribes. Jay, as president of the Council of Revision, signed that bill, probably, we may conjecture, in return for the help of Burr and Clinton in passing the act granting the steamboat monopoly to Livingston. Reciprocal exchanges were usual among politicians.

Six years after the passage of the Manhattan Company act, the Mercantile Bank received a thirteen years' charter. It was publicly charged by various members of the Assembly that this charter was secured by bribery — charges substantially proved before the legislative investigating committee.[29] And who, it may be asked, was the organizer and the president of the Merchants' Bank, founded and chartered under similar circumstances at this time? No less a personage than Oliver Wolcott, friend and admirer of Hamilton; the successor of Hamilton as United States Secretary of the Treasury, in 1795; and the intimate friend of Oliver Ellsworth, who followed Jay as Chief Justice of the Supreme Court of the United States.

In 1811, the New York Legislature chartered the Mechanics' Bank, with a time limit, under peculiar circumstances indicating bribery. Charges of corruption were so continuous that the Legislature, in 1812, in a fine outburst of ostentatious virtue, passed a resolution compelling each member to pledge himself that he had neither taken nor would take, "any reward or profit, direct or indirect, for any vote or any measure."[30] After this rhetorical effusion, intended to salve the public, the Legislature proceeded, in that very year, to charter the Bank of America. Flagrant charges of corruption were made, and an investigation was held. One Assemblyman testified that he had been offered the sum of $500 "besides a

---

[29] Journal of the (New York) Senate and Assembly, 1805: 351 and 399.
[30] Ibid., 1812: 134.

handsome present for his vote." [31]   Oliver Wolcott was the
chief organizer of this bank also, and remained its president
for two years.[32]   The chartering of the Chemical Bank, in
1824, was accomplished by bribery, according to the testimony
before a legislative investigating committee; the promoters of
the Chemical Bank set aside a considerable sum of money,
and $50,000 in stock for the bribery fund.[33]   The charter of
the notorious Seventh Ward Bank was later likewise obtained
by bribery.

These parallel circumstances of the securing of other charters may tend to explain why Livingston and Fulton were able
to get such amazing laws.   The final outcome of the long
litigation growing out of the Livingston and Fulton steamboat monopoly is described later in this work, comprehending,
as it does, one of the most noted of Chief Justice Marshall's
decisions.

Suffice to say here that it was generally believed that high
jurists and politicians were indirect beneficiaries of that
monopoly; for politicians to be stockholders in companies to
which they, as legislators, had granted charters, was not uncommon, nor was it unusual for judges to hold stock.

At Jay's death in 1829, Daniel Webster said of him, in the
customary high-flown rhetoric of the day: " When the spotless ermine of the judicial robe fell on John Jay, it touched
nothing less spotless than itself."   The facts, however, tell
otherwise.   Webster would have liked that generation and
future generations to believe his encomium of Jay.   The decisions of Jay were useful as precedents to Webster, the most
active corporation lawyer of his day, the attorney for schemes
and projects some of which Jay himself had helped to put

[31] Ibid., 259–260.
[32] The Wolcott family was one of the large landed interests in Connecticut and elsewhere.   It was one of the oligarchy that had almost
hereditarily ruled Connecticut politically for decades.   Oliver Wolcott
returned to Connecticut, and engaged in the manufacture of woolens in
Litchfield.   He became Governor of Connecticut, 1818–1827.
[33] Journal of the [N. Y.] Senate, 1824: 1317–1350.

through, and the ally by marriage and interest, of Jay's class.[34]

The Senate Rejects Rutledge.

When Jay resigned the Chief Justiceship of the Supreme Court, John Rutledge of South Carolina was appointed to succeed him. Rutledge's appointment was what might be termed an untimely anticipation of a period not yet arrived. So stanchly did Rutledge represent the interests of the large Southern slaveholders that in the Federal Constitutional Convention, he had — to quote the words of a eulogist —" stood firm and unyielding to what he esteemed the substantial interests of his section of the country." [35]   He had been one of the delegates refusing to concede to the proposal for the immediate prohibition of the importation of negro slaves.   " The people of North Carolina, South Carolina and Georgia," he had then declared, " will never agree to the proposed Constitution, unless their right to import slaves be untouched."   He had finally acceded in the Convention, however, to the proposal that the importation of slaves should not be prohibited prior to the year 1808.[36]

But although representing the great slave-owning landed proprietors of the South, Rutledge was not, at this juncture, viewed with approval by the great landowners of the North.

[34] After the death of his first wife, Webster married Catherine, daughter of Herman Le Roy. This was the same Le Roy who, as described in Chapter I, was one of those dispossessing settlers by securing, in virtue of court decisions, great tracts of New York land obtained by fraud and corruption before the Revolution. Le Roy was the founder of the great commercial firm of Le Roy, Bayard and Company, trading with many parts of North and South America. He was one of fifteen men in New York City who, in 1815, could boast of owning a carriage. As we have seen, Le Roy and Bayard were Jay's intimate business associates as well as his friends, and we have quoted previously from Jay's letter asking Cruger to let them share in a certain " golden plan " for making " millions sterling " profits.
[35] Van Santvoord's " Chief Justices," 194.
[36] Madison Papers, Vol. III: 1536.

who by force of more numerical representation in the Senate, dominated the Government.

Already, the great economic struggle between the two conflicting capitalist systems — that of so-called free white labor in the North, and that in the South of negro slavery — had begun. While the Southern capitalists were demanding that the right to import slaves be continued, the Northern capitalists were, as we have seen, as early as 1775, deliberately and with the most careful calculation, setting out to utilize woman and child labor in factories, as a system, knowing it to be cheaper than slave labor.

The conflict between these divergent systems had not, at the time of Rutledge's appointment, widened into the threatening stage that it did later, when it became so acute that the Southern slaveholders exerted every influence to dominate the Government, especially the Supreme Court of the United States. Rutledge, moreover, had made himself obnoxious to the majority of the United States Senate by denouncing the Jay treaty. This he opposed because it contained no provision indemnifying slaveholders for negroes appropriated by the British, and because that treaty would stop the exportation of cotton.

The Senate rejected Rutledge's appointment.[37] For some years his mind had showed symptoms of impairment; when the news of his rejection reached Rutledge, it totally gave way, and he soon died.

Ellsworth Succeeds Jay as Chief Justice

The appointment of Oliver Ellsworth, of Connecticut, as Chief Justice of the Supreme Court of the United States, was

[37] The appointment of Rutledge was a recess appointment. The note in III Dallas' Reports, 121, reads: "A commission bearing date the 1st July, 1795, was read by which, during the recess of Congress, John Rutledge, Esq., was appointed Chief Justice, till the end of the next session of the Senate." Before the rejection of his nomination, Rutledge presided as Chief Justice in the determination of at least one case — that of Talbot vs. Jackson.

wholly satisfactory to both the landowning class, and to its
auxiliary outgrowth, the banking interest. The same Senate rejecting Rutledge's appointment hastened to confirm Ellsworth's. He was commissioned Chief Justice on March 4,
1796.

Beginning as a rather obscure lawyer, Ellsworth had in-
gratiated himself into the favor of the Wolcotts, the Trum-
bulls and other powerful Connecticut families. Constituting
the coterie owning great landed estates in Connecticut, these
families had governed that Colony and State for generations
as though it were their private preserve. Like the Livingstons
in New York, they knew how to appropriate the highest official
positions for themselves, and retain them in the family circle.
As for Ellsworth, he had married into the Wolcott family, and
became a man of notable fortune.

As a member of the Continental Congress, Ellsworth had
been one of the group promoting the chartering of Morris'
Bank of Pennsylvania. Serving as the chairman of the committee of the Continental Congress reporting in the matter,
Ellsworth was, according to his eulogist Van Santvoord, one
of Morris' "most ardent and efficient coadjutors." Conspicuous in the Continental Congress in pushing the original charter
of the Bank of North America, Ellsworth was not unaware
of the quick-following frauds; and when James Wilson
proposed that ingenious constitutional clause of his, Ellsworth
knew to an accuracy what it really meant and how it would
be applied, not less so than Wilson, Clymer, Fitzsimmons,
Gouverneur Morris and his partner Robert Morris, four of
whom, as we have seen, were openly associated with that bank,
and one indirectly. In that convention Ellsworth, be it said to
his credit, made no effort to disguise his real attitude; he was
one of the boldest in implying his contempt for the people, and
in urging the policy of deluding the people with a sop. He
favored a yearly election for members of the House of Representatives; the people, he said, were fond of frequent elec-

tions, and might safely be indulged in one branch of Congress.[38]

In the Connecticut Convention, called to decide upon the Constitution, Ellsworth argued strenuously for its adoption. He and Oliver Wolcott (whose later Merchants' Bank and Bank of America charters were obtained by bribery, as already noted) served together on the Commission to settle the claims of Connecticut against the Federal Government. Both were concerned, too, in that fraudulent disposition by Connecticut of its great area of land in Ohio.

Ellsworth had long been one of the most powerful politicians in Connecticut, as well at the same time as in the National Government. He had been an Attorney-General of Connecticut. From 1780 to 1784 he had been a member of the Governor's Council, and from 1784 to 1789 one of the judges of the Supreme Court of Connecticut. As a United States Senator he was a member of the select committee to which Hamilton's refunding plan was referred, and was one of the most active supporters of that scandalous scheme. He, also, was on the select committee which reported favorably on Hamilton and Morris' plan for the incorporation of the Bank of the United States. When the question came up in Congress as to the proper title for the President of the United States, Ellsworth was a member of a committee of three of the Senate reporting that the President ought to be addressed as, "His Highness, the President of the United States and Protector of Their Liberties," [39] This proposed title, so strongly smacking of monarchism, was rejected by the House of Representatives. It is written of Ellsworth that he acquired a degree of wealth "at that time rare in Connecticut."

Ellsworth remained Chief Justice for a few years only; and were it not that he handed down opinions deciding that debts due to British subjects were recoverable, hardly any-

[38] Madison Papers, Vol. II: 846 and 929. .
[39] Van Santvoord, p. 226.

thing that he otherwise did was considered worthy of citation. In the annals of legal lore he occupies an obscure position, possibly, for one strong reason, because of the overshadowing vital contrast afforded by his successor's masterful ability, performances and long reign.

Bushrod Washington's Appointment.

Of the two appointments as Associate Justices made by President John Adams — those of Bushrod Washington and Alfred Moore — one is deserving of particular note.

Adams was an extremely rich man; his private income was reputed to be $25,000 a year, which, at that time, was regarded as something enormous. In his reverence for wealth, and his class distrust of the " lower orders," Adams was outspoken to a point approaching what his enemies viewed as the very extreme of bigotry.

But this charge was not well founded. Adams simply voiced with honest belief the views held by his whole class, and demanded by their interests; where Hamilton in Adams' position would have cautiously and unctuously cajoled the public, Adams threw calculating tact aside. Appointing corrupt men to office, conniving at the most colossal frauds and thefts when committed by members of his class, Adams was an ideal head for a government run by capitalists for capitalists. In the dull chronicles of the usual historical weaving, Adams has had to bear the odium of the disgraceful Alien and Sedition law, the real purpose of which was to stifle liberty of speech and of press. But the actual authors of this law were the landholders and other associated politico-capitalists obtaining huge areas of public land by fraud, and scheming either to have confiscated estates vested in themselves or in their immediate connections.

These men naturally objected to the caustic diatribes against their meditated alliance with the British governing class with the object of putting down the French Revolution. They were savagely upset by the biting exposure of their great frauds, either accomplished or projected. In these frauds nearly every member of the Cabinet and Senate had a hand as also many members of the House of Representatives. The claim for more than 11,000,000 acres of the 35,000,000 acres obtained by that grant bribed through the Georgia Legislature in 1795, was held by Adams' Massachusetts friends; and, as we shall see, Adams' son, John Quincy Adams, was one of the attorneys who later successfully argued that claim to a validation through the Supreme Court of the United States. This validation (to repeat) was based upon the plea that the Georgia rescinding act was in violation of the Constitutional clause forbidding any State to pass laws impairing the obligation of a contract.

As we have seen in Chapter IV, Wilson supplied by far the greater part of the funds for the securing of the bribed grant of 35,000,000 acres of land. At Justice Wilson's death, President Adams appointed Bushrod Washington, an Associate Justice of the Supreme Court. Bushrod Washington, as we have told, had been placed by his uncle, George Washington, in Wilson's office to study law, and had been associated in that capacity with Wilson during the very period when Wilson was engineering his Bank of North America transaction. He had inherited George Washington's Mount Vernon estate. All of the other Justices of the Supreme Court of the United States were well advanced in years, but Bushrod Washington was only thirty-six years old at the time of his being commissioned Associate Justice.[40] The Supreme Court's obituary on his life, published in 1830 as a preface to the third volume of Peters' Reports, narrates

[40] By reason of excessive study, Bushrod Washington became blind in one eye. In stature he was insignificant, and he was negligent in dress. He was immoderately addicted to snuff taking. Withal, he was the most punctilious stickler for forms and etiquette. He was said to have remained, on one occasion, sixteen hours at a stretch on the Supreme Court Bench.

the fact that Bushrod Washington had been placed by General Washington in the office of James Wilson to study law, and it further relates that Bushrod Washington was a great friend of John Marshall and had "commenced his intimacy and friendship with Mr. Chief Justice Marshall" when he (Bushrod Washington) was a student at William and Mary College. What exact and intimate connection these facts had in view of subsequent memorable decisions of the Supreme Court of the United States, we do not profess to judge; but these are the facts, and their significance is self-evident.

The Federalists Go Out of Power.

With the election of Jefferson, in 1800, the Federalists seemed swept out of power. Many causes conspired to bring about this great political change. The small merchants and petty shopkeepers, aiming at an unrestricted field for their own economic advancement, revolted against government by the large landholding families. Instead of the old hereditary aristocracy, based upon large possessions of land, the time was ripening for a newer aristocracy of money derived from industrial establishments and transportation as well as from land. On the other hand, the time was not propitious for the carrying out of the Federalist doctrine of concentration of powers in the National Government; the country was vast, communication was difficult and slow, and the two great conflicting economic systems of North and South were silently but more intensely clashing.

Such portions of the working class as had the right to vote enthusiastically supported the Republicans or Anti-Federalists, believing that the defeat of the Federalists meant a death blow to aristocracy. They did not see that a vastly more powerful industrial and transportation aristocracy would take the place of the old feudal aristocracy. Lastly there were dissensions within the ranks of the Federalists themselves.

The great landholders, bent upon annihilating both the influence and results of the French Revolution, were determined upon a bitter war with France, and an alliance with England. But President John Adams, whose interests and traditions lay more with the shippers than with the landholders, wanted no war; this attitude caused a wide breach between the Adams and the Hamilton factions.

Pack the Courts Before Going.

The Republicans [41] believed they now had a clear field of power. The Federalists, however, proceeded to execute into law a piece of strategy by which they were able to outgeneral their opponents, and retain practical power. The Republicans had the administrative offices, and a majority of the Legislators, but the crucial question was as to which side would control the judiciary.

This fact both parties thoroughly appreciated. They knew that the courts before, and during, the Revolution had gone to lawless lengths in doing as they willed. They knew that the courts had already, unquestioned, set aside acts of legislatures as null and void, and that they would and could do so again with acts of both legislatures and Congress. They knew that the courts were the prime instruments for sanctioning the acts of the ruling class, and that with judicial precedents already built up, and more that could be added, theories of law could be devised to suit any exigency. Theoretically, the three departments of governments each held coördinate jurisdiction, but this was merely a pleasant fiction. The courts were the real masters of destinies.

In the last days of their power, the Federalists passed a

[41] Again it should be pointed out that the Republican Party of that time is not the Republican Party of the present. The Republican Party of Jefferson's day developed into the Democratic Party. Thus, Tammany Hall still flaunts its campaign inscription: "Democratic-Republican Candidates." The Republican Party of these times is the descendant of the Federalist Party.

new judiciary act, creating a series of new courts, and nearly
three-score new judges. The most important post in the
whole government, however, was that of Chief Justice of
the Supreme Court of the United States. The President
lasted for four, perhaps eight, years in office; the Chief Justice held office for life. The President could recommend
laws; the Chief Justice could arrogate the sovereign power
(two members of the Supreme Court agreeing with him) of
abolishing laws with a stroke of the pen, or virtually making
laws far more binding than legislative law.

But the straining of both political parties for the control
of the judiciary was, judging by fundamentals, merely a
shallow conflict. This was later lucidly proved when Justices of both political stripes stood together in validating
immense land frauds and the fraudulent recovery of confiscated estates, and in the twisting and kneading of the Constitution to accord with particular or general interests of
each succeeding dominant division of the capitalist class, in
the declaration of perpetual vested private and corporate
rights, and in the continuation of chattel slavery. Quite true,
differences were revealed among various Justices over the
question of State's rights versus consolidation of power in
the National Government. But those differences exactly reflected the contentions prevailing at the particular time between capitalists of different sections.

All of the Justices, to whichever political parties they belonged, to whatever source they owed their appointment, believed in the domination of government by property for property, although while most of them believed that this rule
should be of the large propertied interests, a few there came
who held that the middle-class property element should hold
the power. But all were agreed upon the main point of
straining every interpretation and construction for the benefit
of property, even though there came times when a minority
Justice, or perhaps others with him, refused to concur in some

notorious decision handed forth by the majority. All, by their consistent actions, evinced irrefutable bias in favor of established conditions, so far as they applied to the general repression of the workers, and all were class prejudiced against any attempt of the working class to improve its conditions, and shake off the yoke of the oppression of numberless centuries.

A little while before leaving office, President Adams, on January 31, 1801, appointed John Marshall to be Chief Justice of the Supreme Court of the United States. Jefferson, who came from the same State as Marshall, and who was thoroughly conversant with his career and mentality, deplored the appointment as a public calamity. Toward Adams and others, Jefferson entertained a bitter enough hatred, but when Jefferson was extremely old and after he had forgiven all of his other foes, Marshall was the one man whom he could not bring himself to forgive.

All of Jefferson's political ideas, ideals and plans were upset and uprooted by Marshall's decisions, which forced into practice the very opposite of Jefferson's doctrines. We who have the advantage of retrospection may look back and, understanding the course of industrial progress, may see that in that particular respect, Jefferson was in error. For the next thirty-four years, Marshall was, in point of actual sovereignty, the ruler of the United States, and by force of decisions handed down by him, has, it may be safely said, ruled the courts (which rule the United States) ever since. Marshall's appointment signified the unrestricted development of private corporate institutions and power, which was an inevitable stage in the progress of society.

CHAPTER VI

THE AUTHENTIC JOHN MARSHALL

Of all of the Chief Justices of the Supreme Court of the United States, John Marshall, in reputation, biographical lore, and tradition has stood out fixedly as the most illustrious. Certain fervent writers have even classed him as of the three greatest men that America has produced, ranking with Washington and Lincoln. A multitude of eulogists have acclaimed him as one of the very foremost jurists of all ages, the quintessence and apogee of exalted judicial wisdom and virtue.

Long since, it became the settled fashion in particular quarters to reverence Marshall's very memory. But it has been remarked that this continuous laudation has singularly failed to touch and move the popular mind. Of other heroes, warrior and political, the people at large know, but they seem to lack all due appreciation of judicial heroes, and go their way caring nothing.

If to the unerudite run of people the name of John Marshall carries little, and means less, it signifies much to the aristocracy, or let us say, the oligarchy of wealth. Justly so to that highly conscious class, which always well rewards and honors its apostles and servers, the deeds and services of John Marshall stand out with a halo of dazzling greatness. To them, Marshall is the greatest of the great among judges.

In appearance he did violence to the prescribed fastidious apparel of awe with which a judge was expected to invest himself. He was careless, even sloven in his dress, looking more like a countryman than a jurist, often taking his seat on the Supreme Court bench with burrs sticking to his clothes —

yet these were but trivial peccadillos of no disparaging consequence.[1] True, in his own day, this absence of gowned dignity and stiff decorousness was animadverted upon by the devotees of aristocratic elegancy, who would have preferred to disseminate the idea of an awesomely-raimented Chief Justice. That, too, he frolicsomely pitched quoits, read novels ceaselessly and even went to market with a basket on his arm — this did not seem to comport with the stern, lofty dignity of his unapproachable office. But these minor things have all receded into the obscurity of time, although (what his critics overlooked) they well served their purpose of imparting an air of democratic simplicity to Marshall while, in works, he was laying the bulwarked foundations of an era of unrestricted capitalist development. And it is because of those works that the men of capital to-day so readily pronounce his incomparable excellence of greatness.

His Early Life.

Born in Fauquier County, Virginia, in the year 1755, John Marshall was the oldest of a family of fifteen children. His father, Thomas Marshall, was a planter of some slight fortune, and for a long time was surveyor and superintendent for that considerable part of Lord Fairfax's estate in the Northern Neck of Virginia. At one time the extent of this estate comprised twenty-one counties, or more than five million acres. In Chapter I we have related the facts as to the

---

[1] Of his personal appearance, William Wirt wrote:
"He is tall, meager, emaciated; his muscles relaxed, and his joints so loosely connected as not only to disqualify him apparently for any vigorous exertion of body, but to destroy everything like harmony in his air or movements. Indeed, in his whole appearance and demeanor — dress, attitudes, gesture, sitting, standing or walking — he is as far removed from the idolized graces of Lord Chesterfield as any other gentleman on earth." When holding his circuit court in Virginia, it was Marshall's habit to travel in an antiquated and rather disreputable gig. To those who did not know him as the famous Chief Justice, his shabby dress and idiosyncracies of personality frequently led to queer misunderstandings.

origin of the great Fairfax estate, and described how on one occasion Lord Fairfax fraudulently conveyed a tract of 300,000 acres to his nephew and agent, Thomas Bryant Martin,[2] who at once reconveyed them to Fairfax. Of the laws then prevailing in Virginia, we have given ample details in Chapter II. To recapitulate, they were laws made by the manorial lords and planters exclusively for their own purposes and benefit, and drafted with great severity for the chattel enslavement of the negro, and for the practical enslavement of the white laborer. There was hardly a vestige of a middle class during that time, so that John Marshall's father and the whole Marshall family belonged by interest and attachment to the landed aristocracy.

This was the environment in which John Marshall was born, and which he imbibed during his most sensitive years. One has only to read the various addresses and petitions to the proprietary manorial lords to know the immense humility and obsequiousness with which those eminences were treated. Towards Lord Fairfax, his employer, Thomas Marshall assumed and felt an unvarying deference, not by any means like the abject servility expected from the " lower orders," but still of a servile character customary from servitor and employé. Of all of Thomas Marshall's sons, John, being the oldest, was most imbued with the pervading caste ideas. He took off his hat humbly to Lord Fairfax and regarded his title, position and power with vast respect. For slave and laborer, his feeling was that of the prevailing aristocratic contempt. He looked upon them as the natural drudges for the aristocracy, to be held in their places and bonds by the strictest laws.

Unlike many other youths of their class, John Marshall and his brothers were not sent to private schools in their incipiency. Their father engaged a tutor to take their edu-

[2] In Washington's Va. Reports, Vol. I: 227, the name is given as Bryant Martin; in all other court reports it is given in full as Thomas Bryant Martin.

cation in hand at home. The consequence was that in their most impressionable years they remained cloistered in a narrow, caste atmosphere which sank deep. But, on the other hand, this personal, concentrated paternal supervision had the effect of developing certain mental qualities and marked individual characteristics so often suffering when children are educated in mass in the undiscriminating pedantry of classrooms. It was not until John was past fourteen years of age, that he was put in Rev. Mr. Campbell's school in Westmoreland County. When eighteen years old, he began his legal studies, and at the outbreak of the Revolution he enlisted in the Continental army. In 1780 he was admitted to practice at the bar.

His career from thence was partly that of engaging in politics, for which he had a precocious natural capacity, and in part that of a practising lawyer. When twenty-seven years old he was elected to the Virginia House of Delegates, and at the same time was appointed a member of the Virginia Council of State. Marrying a daughter of Ambler, the Virginia State Treasurer, in 1783, he removed to Richmond, but still was reëlected to the Legislature from Fauquier County, and then Henrico County. He continued in the Legislature until 1789. Hamilton's influence upon Marshall was very considerable; and, as a member of the Virginia Convention called to ratify or reject the Constitution, Marshall was conspicuously zealous in pushing its adoption.

Attorney for the Fairfax Estate.

As a lawyer, Marshall's specialty was landed estates; he represented the Fairfax interests,[3] and was attorney for other

---

[3] For example: Lord Fairfax, in 1741, sold 243 acres to James Crap. Claiming that Crap did not pay the office fees, Fairfax declared the land forfeited. In 1780, Fairfax, through his agent, sold the same land to Martin Pickett. Crap's assignee and Pickett contested for title to the land. John Marshall, as Pickett's attorney, won the case. Chief Justice Edmund Pendleton delivered the court's opinion.

British claimants in other cases.   More than this; he was extremely ambitious to possess the Fairfax estate for himself, but there were many obstacles to be encountered.   What they were, how he gradually and persistently overcame them by a series of adroit tactics, and how his securing of the Fairfax estate was the actual and predominating motive underlying, when he was Chief Justice, one of the most important decisions affecting constitutional law ever handed down by the Supreme Court of the United States — all of these facts are herewith duly narrated in consecutive order.

Lord Fairfax's entire estate had been confiscated during the Revolution by the Virginia General Act of October, 1777, which sequestered all of the property and estates of British subjects.   But the legal ingenuity of which Jefferson writes, was silently at work.

In May, 1779, an act was passed by the Virginia Legislature for the apparent purpose of establishing a land office, and ascertaining the terms and manner of granting waste and unappropriated lands.   In the act, unnoticed except by those interested, was this clause: " And that the proprietors of land within this commonwealth, may no longer be subject to any servile, feudal or precarious tenure; and to prevent the danger to a free state from perpetual revenue; Be it enacted, That the royal mines, quit rents, and all other reservations and conditions in the patents or grants from the crown of England, under the former government, shall be, and are hereby declared null and void; and that all lands, thereby respectively granted, shall be held in absolute and unconditional property, and to all intents and purposes whatsoever, in the same manner with the lands hereafter to be granted by the commonwealth, by virtue of this act." [4]   What this clause really did was to relieve the proprietors of all rents and other conditions, and at the same time admit of a construction by which title to their lands was absolutely confirmed.   The se-

[4] See, " Virginia Revised Statutes of 1783," Chap. 13, Sec. 6, p. 98.

cret agents of the royalist proprietors had done a fine stroke in getting that act passed.

Evidently, Lord Fairfax knew precisely the meaning of the act; before his death in December, 1781, he left the whole of his estate to his nephew, Denny Martin or Fairfax. This nephew had been born in England about the year 1750, lived there, and remained a British subject. The younger brother of Denny Fairfax was Thomas Bryant Martin, who was a citizen of the State of Virginia, and was, as we have seen, Lord Fairfax's agent and instrument.

The Doctrine of Acquiescence.

For many years the title to certain of Fairfax's estate had been contested by Hite and M'Coy under a grant to them which we have described in Chapter I. The suit of Hite and others against Fairfax and others came up before the Virginia Court of Appeals, in May, 1786. John Marshall appeared as the attorney for the Fairfax claim. For Hite and others, John Taylor, their attorney, began with the point that Fairfax's title was deficient and fraudulent; that the original proprietary grant to Fairfax had been made by Charles II while a fugitive, and that James II, in the fourth year of his reign, but after he (James) had been driven off the throne by a Revolution, had confirmed it.[5]

In reply, John Marshall made his principal point a doctrine which, when he was only thirty-three years old, we thus see him advancing, and which same redoubtable doctrine of acquiescence he later, as Chief Justice of the United States, made the foundation for perpetuating chattel slavery and all manner of oppressions. It was a doctrine that, for like purposes, has been used by the courts ever since, so that as law is now construed, it remains a fundamental and elastic method of confirming the property, power and tyranny of one class, and the helplessness of another.

[5] Call's Reports (Court of Appeals of Va.), Vol. IV: 66.

"The long and quiet possession of himself and his predecessors" (argued Marshall as to Fairfax); "the acquiescence of the country; the several grants of the crown, together with the various acts of the Assembly recognizing, and, in the most explicit terms, admitting his right, seemed to have fixed it on a foundation, not only not to be shaken, but not even to be attempted to be shaken. . . ."[6] This seemed an ingenious argument, but the statements were not true. Fairfax's claim had never been acquiesced in by Hite and M'Coy, nor by the officials who gave them their contravening grant. Marshall knew, too, that the Assembly acts were the products largely of Fairfax himself who, with a few other proprietaries, controlled that body.

It would seem self-evident that Governor Randolph of Virginia, in 1789, did not concede the claim of either Fairfax or Hite, for on April 30 of that year Governor Randolph gave to David Hunter, and his heirs forever, a grant of a part of that very land, in exchange for a land office treasury warrant dated January 23, 1788.

The Contest for the Fairfax Estate.

A hot contest now set in for the possession of the Fairfax estate. Because of its arable soil valuable for tobacco growing, its timber and other resources, its accessibility, lying as it did, on the Potomac River and other rivers, and its close proximity to the newly-established site of the National Capital, the prize was a rich one. In April, 1791, a declaration in ejectment was served on the tenants in possession. This action was brought in behalf of Hunter's grant. The Winchester district court admitted Denny Martin (otherwise Denny Fairfax) to defend the suit. It was action specifically for 788 acres of land in Shenandoah County.[7]

[6] Call's Reports, Vol. IV: 69.
[7] See, Munford's Reports (Supreme Court of Appeals of Va.), Vol. I: 218.

But the claim, as set up by the heir of Fairfax, covered about three hundred thousand acres of land in the Northern Neck of Virginia, and the real contention revolved around the point of whether Denny Fairfax, as Lord Fairfax's heir, had any claim whatever on an estate supposed to have been confiscated. The State of Virginia denied first, that Lord Fairfax had ever got this estate lawfully, or by legitimate methods; second, it asserted that the estate had been confiscated; third, it claimed that as an alien, Denny Fairfax could not hold lands. In opposition to these arguments, Marshall used much the same arguments that he had employed in the case of Hite vs. Fairfax. The court, in this case, decided in favor of Fairfax; as to the special circumstances leading to this decision, there are many obscurities in the available records, and the explanation cannot be extracted.

But the next step in the proceedings is incontestably clear. Presently it turned out that Marshall himself and his brother James had bought out Denny Fairfax's claims to the Fairfax estate in Virginia. This was considered news of the first importance in that State. That the purchase took place so soon after the drafting of Jay's Treaty was looked upon as signifying that if fresh assaults were made upon Fairfax's title, the claimants could fall back upon the provisions of that treaty as an additional ground for validation of their title. This coincidence of John Marshall's buying the Fairfax claim with the signing of Jay's Treaty was a matter of invidious comment. John Marshall's agent was his brother James Markham Marshall, also a lawyer, who personally negotiated in England with Denny Fairfax for the purchase of the Fairfax claim, for his brother John and himself. And, as showing the interconnection of landed interests, it may here be remarked that, in 1795, James Markham Marshall married Hester, daughter of Robert Morris, who at this time was engaged, as we have seen, in such enormous land transactions with Justice James Wilson and others.

Marshall Defends Jay's Treaty.

While James Markham Marshall was transacting this business in England, John Marshall was industriously advocating Jay's Treaty in Virginia. Its adoption meant much to him. He was the attorney for British claimants. His getting possession of the Fairfax estate, he astutely knew, hung much upon the ratification of that treaty. Both Hunter and the State of Virginia were pressing new litigation against any validation of the confiscated Fairfax estate. As an acute lawyer, Marshall was well aware of the full import of the provisions of Jay's Treaty, and to what extent they could be used in the courts for the restoration of confiscated estates. The Fairfax claim up to date had been at best, he knew, a shaky one, extremely unpopular, and kept alive by legal ingenuity and sophistry.

" The great question of the day," says a eulogist of Marshall, " was the adoption of Jay's Treaty with Great Britain. In Virginia, a bitter opposition assailed the treaty, and the entire State rang with denunciations of it. Even the influence of Washington was powerless to stay the tide of popular passion excited against the treaty, and those who upheld it. Meetings were held in Richmond, and the treaty was fiercely denounced. Marshall now came to the rescue, and before a meeting of the citizens of that place made such an unanswerable argument in favor of the treaty, that the men who had been foremost in assailing it now united in the adoption of resolutions indorsing the policy of the Administration. In the Legislature his efforts were equally successful, and the opponents of the Administration were forced to abandon their constitutional objections to the treaty, and to content themselves with a simple denial of the expediency of the measure at that time." [8]

Houghton goes on to say that " President Washington at-

[8] Houghton's " Lives," etc., 443-444.

tached so much importance to these services that he offered to his old friend and comrade the position of Attorney-General of the United States, but Marshall declined the offer, as he wished to devote himself to his practice, which had now become very lucrative. He continued to sit in the Legislature, which did not interfere with his private business, and remained the constant and vigilant friend of Washington's Administration. In 1796, he was offered the post of Minister to France, as Mr. Monroe's successor, but declined it for the same reason which made him refuse the Attorney-Generalship." [9]

The real reason why John Marshall wanted to remain in Virginia was certain pressing business concerning the Fairfax estate that he was consummating in the Virginia Legislature. To that body he was again elected in 1795. The action on the part of Marshall and other claimants for " Leeds Manor," was being sedulously pressed in the courts.

Had the outlook been good or even passable, Marshall was the very last who would have listened to compromise. It was tolerably clear that Denny Fairfax, as an alien, could neither hold nor convey escheated land. Aside from the purely legal aspects, popular sentiment was greatly stirred at the sight of aliens who had become enemies of the American Revolution obstinately asserting their rights to land which, according to common understanding, had been definitely confiscated. If Marshall could get a Legislative act specifically expunging the escheat or forfeiture, that would go far toward establishing his project of recovery. That is what he now did.

We shall relate the successive steps as they appear on the records. The action of Hunter vs. Fairfax's Devisee was in some form before the Supreme Court of the United States in 1796. It would seem that this was an appeal from the decision of the Virginia court in favor of Fairfax, for Hun-

[9] *Ibid.*

ter was now the plaintiff in error. On July 29, 1796, the Clerk of the Supreme Court of the United States received a letter from Hunter saying that Campbell, his attorney to argue the case, had died in Richmond on July 18, 1796, and praying for a postponement of the cause until the next term. This request was opposed by Lee and Ingersoll, attorneys for Fairfax's Devisee. But the Supreme Court granted the application,[10] and the case did not again come up before it until fourteen years later. The reasons why will duly appear.

Announces His Purchase of the Fairfax Claim.

Petitions were concocted, and the Virginia Legislature was manipulated to pass a resolution to the effect that if the devisees of Lord Fairfax, or their claimants, would relinquish all claims to lands supposed to lie within the Northern Neck, which lands were waste and unappropriated at the time of the death of Lord Fairfax, then the State of Virginia would relinquish all claims to any lands specifically appropriated by Lord Fairfax to his own use either by deed or actual survey.[11] This resolution was put forward as a measure designed to compromise the controversy.

Having lobbied the resolution of compromise through the Legislature, John Marshall then formally accepted the proposition in this letter:

"Richmond, November 24th, 1796, Sir, being one of the purchasers of the lands of Mr. Fairfax, and authorized to act for them all, I have considered the resolution of the General Assembly on the petitions of sundry inhabitants of the counties of Hampshire, Hardy and Shenandoah and have determined to accede to the proposition it contains. So soon as the conveyance shall be transmitted to me from Mr. Fair-

[10] Dallas' Reports, Vol. III: 305. In a footnote, Justice Chase said that the matter was "of great moment; and ought to be deliberately and finally settled."

[11] "Revised Code of the Laws of Virginia" (Edition of 1819), Vol. I: 352.

fax, deeds extinguishing his title to the waste and unappropriated lands in the Northern Neck shall be executed, provided an act passes during this session, confirming on the execution of such deeds, the title of those claiming under Mr. Fairfax, to lands specifically appropriated and reserved by the late Thomas Fairfax, or his ancestors, for his or their own use. I remain, Sir, with much respect and esteem, your obedient servant, John Marshall. The Honorable, the Speaker of the House of Delegates." [12]

Accordingly, on December 10, 1796, the Virginia Legislature passed an accommodating act. In the face of the intense public opposition to resurrecting the titles (and fraudulent titles at that), of aliens to confiscated estates, the Legislature dared not specifically say that aliens could hold and convey lands.

But the act circumvented that delicate point by removing the disabilities of the forfeiture. It innocently began asserting the right of the Commonwealth of Virginia to the lands of the alien, Denny Fairfax. Then it recited the terms of the previous compromise resolution, and gave the full text of Marshall's letter of acceptance. The enacting clauses following declared that if those conditions were carried out by a specific agreement, then Denny Fairfax, or those claiming under him, and their heirs, should hold the land in question "as if he, the said Denny, had been a native citizen of this Commonwealth, and as if no escheat or forfeiture had ever taken place." The act, however, contained a final clause reserving to all persons, other than the Commonwealth, any right or equity they might have in the Northern Neck lands.[13]

The law raised a considerable popular commotion, coming, as it did, at a time when great numbers of the Revolutionary

[12] *Ibid.*, 353. This letter is given precisely as it appears in the records. See, also, "The Statutes At Large of Virginia, etc., 1792 to 1806," Vol. II: 22–23.

[13] "Revised Code of the Laws of Va." (Edition of 1819), Vol. I: 353, and "The Statutes At Large of Va., etc., 1792 to 1806," Vol. II: 23.

veterans had been defrauded of their land warrants by cliques
of powerful politicians, and when settlers everywhere were
intensely aroused over the appropriation and monopolization
by the politico-capitalists of tens of millions of acres of the
best and most accessible land.   In the severe criticisms made,
it was pointed out that the patriots who had fought the Revolution could not obtain land, while aliens, enemies and trait-
ors like Fairfax could get a special law abolishing all penalties
of forfeiture.   But, after all, the law was not directly for
Fairfax's benefit; it was for John Marshall's, although the
one received the benefit of the purchase price, and the other
the estate.   Influenced by hostile public sentiment, the State
officials balked at enforcing the act, whereupon, on December
22 and 23, 1797, the Legislature formally requested the Governor of Virginia to carry the law into effect.

A Competitor Brings Legal Action.

Instead of this law compromising the controversy, still
fiercer litigation resulted.   Hunter was determined to keep
his grant, and Marshall to gain the estate — an estate not only
valuable commercially, but sentimentally endeared to Marshall by the memories of the youthful days spent on it, when
his father had been its superintendent.

Actions and counter suits kept the courts busy.   It has not
been possible to ascertain all of the intermediate circumstances between the time the compromise act was passed,
and the time, in 1810, when the case of Hunter vs. Fairfax's
Devisee came up on appeal before the Supreme Court of
Appeals of Virginia.   Frequently, the formal court records
of those days lack a statement of the case, and simply make
fleeting references in decisions to prior proceedings.   Thus
we learn from Judge Roane's decision, in the Supreme Court
of Appeals, in 1810, that Marshall, as one of the purchasers
of the Fairfax claim, had availed himself of the compromise
law by " reversing two judgments in favor of the Commor

wealth of Virginia, on the 10th of October, 1798, a record of which is before me." [14]   But what those judgments were, was not explained.   Judge Roane also strongly denounced the " said purchasers," for having availed themselves, on the one hand, of the benefits of the compromise act, while on the other, refusing to submit to such of its provisions as conflicted with their purposes.[15]

It would plainly appear from Judge Roane's decision that in violation of the explicit terms of the compromise law, Marshall set up claims to lands which he had expressly renounced in agreeing to the compromise. And apparently this move was taken under the provisions of Jay's Treaty, doubtless upon the grounds advanced by Marshall later that Fairfax's estate had never been specifically confiscated; that the whole of it was therefore vested in his heir, Denny Fairfax; and that inasmuch as Jay's Treaty provided for the payment of debts due to British subjects, Fairfax was entitled to recover the purchase price, and his claim was indirectly confirmed. This is probably Judge Roane's meaning in saying in his decision that the cause was revived under Jay's Treaty of 1794 providing for the payment of British debts.

The course, however, of the long litigation over the Fairfax estate and the peculiar circumstances attending its final determination, are so intimately interwoven, in many respects, with the narrative of the Supreme Court of the United States, that in order to present the successive steps taken, a considerable chain of other highly-important and closely-connected events must be related.

Marshall's Dominating Personality.

When Marshall was appointed Chief Justice of the Supreme Court, he had absolutely no reputation as a jurist. He had never had any judicial experience; his reputation was

[14] Munford's Reports, etc., Vol. I: 232.
[15] *Ibid.*

wholly that of a politician and land lawyer. In 1797 President Adams had appointed him, with Pinckney and Gerry, as Envoy Extraordinary to France, and for a brief time, in 1800, he had been in Congress, and had served as Adams' Secretary of State.

But a more forceful, dominating man than Marshall, Adams could not have appointed Chief Justice; in audacity of judicial construction, and arrogance and tenacity of purpose, Marshall soon revealed that he had the qualities necessary for executing the purposes under way.[16] These purposes were various. One aim was to retain and extend in the courts the autocratic and all-pervading power of judicial authority. Intimately woven with that aim, was the less general and more personal design of having the Supreme Court validate great fraudulent transactions of one kind or another, by the bold and simple process of declaring hostile legislative acts unconstitutional, or of asserting that the Supreme Court had original appellate powers of jurisdiction.

Already plans had been concerted by which the question of the unconstitutionality of the Georgia act rescinding the Yazoo land grant law was to be passed upon by the Supreme Court; we need hardly say again that John Quincy Adams was one of the attorneys later appearing in the open for the Yazoo claimants. In the litigation over the Fairfax estate, Marshall's own interests were involved; and, as we shall see, the final decision hung upon the point of whether the Supreme Court had the Constitutional power of deciding a case over the heads of a State Court. These cases were but two of a large number affecting fraudulent claims of immense value, and doctrines of immeasurable importance to the ruling class.

For the particular work in hand, Marshall, it must be admitted, was the very best choice that could have been made.

---

[16] The physical characteristic of Marshall most forcibly impressing spectators was his extremely small head, which was all the more noticeable in contrast with his tall, gaunt frame. His eyes were black and brilliant, and his face expressed obduracy and tenaciousness.

In selecting his premises in his decisions, Marshall was transparently sophistical and unscrupulous, but once he had chosen those premises he pursued them to a logical finish the temerity of which must excite admiration. Any doctrine or any subtle theory of law necessary to the justification of the aim in mind, ministered to his purpose, yet once started on his particular line of reasoning, he expounded it in the particular decision with an acuteness, lucidity and a conciseness of diction never as yet surpassed. But when his different decisions are compared, they abound in evident subterfuges and the grossest contradictions.

Almost immediately after he became Chief Justice the opportunity was presented of establishing an enduring precedent that the Supreme Court held the power of declaring laws of Congress unconstitutional, and that there were vested rights which no law could abolish.

The Case of Marbury vs. Madison.

Under the act rushed through by the Federalists creating additional judicial offices, William Marbury and three others were appointed justices of the peace in the District of Columbia. Jefferson, coming into office, instructed Madison, as Secretary of State, to refuse to issue their commissions. Marbury and his associates, moved by their counsel, in December, 1801, in the Supreme Court of the United States for a mandamus. But it was not until two years later that Marshall handed down his decision. He did not dare, at that time, openly to defy the administration by mandamusing the Government. This, if set as a precedent, would be a double-edged weapon. But by the following serpentine line of reasoning Marshall accomplished the adroit twofold purpose of seating the justices, and of asserting the right of the Supreme Court to declare laws unconstitutional:

He decided that Marbury's appointment was not revokable;

that when made it "vested in the officer, legal rights, which
are protected by the laws of his country." To withhold the
commission was an act not warranted by law, but was vio-
lative of a vested legal right. Now the case was brought
under an act of Congress authorizing the Supreme Court to
issue writs of mandamus to any person holding office under
the authority of the United States. To mandamus to deliver
a paper, Marshall held, was the same as to institute an original
action for that paper. The authority thus given to the Supreme Court, Marshall decided, was not warranted by the
Constitution; it was repugnant to the Constitution, and therefore void. It was emphatically, he said, the duty of the judicial department to say what the law was.[17] Thus, while
ostentatiously setting out to placate his opponents, the Republicans, by declaring a Federalist law invalid, he cleverly
made that the cover for seating Federal judges, and for arrogating the right of the Supreme Court to void laws of
Congress.

The Process of Restoring Confiscated Estates.

This done, the next undertaking was to make judicial constructions under which confiscated estates of Tories would
be restored by court order. It was a move, however, which
had to be done very slowly and discreetly; public feeling was
still intensely irritable. One case after another was taken
up, the decision in each of which was so devised, as inevitably

---

[17] Cranch's Reports, Supreme Court of the United States, Vol. I: 176.
In the very act of arrogating to themselves the supreme and final say
in government, the politicians on the Supreme Court bench had the
assurance to advance the pretension that they were safeguarding popular
liberties. "That the people," read an extract in Marshall's decision,
"have an original right to establish, for their future government, such
principles, as, in their opinion, shall most conduce to their own happiness, is the basis on which the American fabric has been erected."
This was a supererogative bit of claptrap. The effect of Marshall's
decision was to make *three* men (in a body of five) the sole and irresponsible dictators of what laws should stand, and what should not.

to supply cumulative precedents for the validation of Marshall's own claim to the Fairfax estate.

The first case was that of M'Ilvane vs. Daniel Coxe's Lessee, argued before the Supreme Court, in February, 1804. The action involved the leading question as to whether those who had gone over to the British in the American Revolution and who had become British subjects, or were aliens, could inherit lands in the United States. This was a question of great importance; it had never been decided either by the Supreme Court of the United States, or by the New Jersey courts.

Daniel Coxe had been born in New Jersey while it was a British colony, and had joined the British at an early stage of the Revolutionary war. In 1778 or 1779 he had been attainted in Pennsylvania for treason, and his estate confiscated by specific proceedings. At the conclusion of the war he had emigrated to England. There he had become an acknowledged British subject, and had received a pension from George III for his loyalty. And there, too, he had, as a British subject, carried on trade and commerce. In 1802, a relative of his died in New York, leaving an estate in New Jersey. Daniel Coxe, as next of blood, claimed right of inheritance. Another relative next of blood after Coxe excepted to Coxe as an alien, and falling back upon the fact that she was an American citizen, claimed the estate in her own right.

In his report of the argument in this case Cranch's footnote reads: " Present, *Cushing, Paterson, Washington* and *Johnson,* Justices. The Chief Justice did not sit in this case, having formed a decided opinion on the principal question, while his interests were concerned." [18]

A peculiar circumstance of this case was that although it was very elaborately argued before the Supreme Court in 1804,[19] there was no decision until four years later. Why

[18] II Cranch, 280.
[19] The argument is reported in full in II Cranch, 280–336.

this long delay of four years? The Supreme Court, then, was not clogged with excess of cases. Were the Justices apprehensive of public feeling?

Impeachment Action Against Associate Justice Chase.

Perhaps, also, the fact that the House of Representatives, in 1804, had irreverently brought impeachment proceedings against Associate Justice Samuel Chase had its sobering weight.

The accusations of " high crimes and misdemeanors " with which Chase was charged were sundry. One charge was that he had acted in a manner "highly arbitrary, oppressive and unjust " in the case, in 1800, of John Fries, accused of treason under the Alien and Sedition laws; that he had sought to prejudice the jury against Fries; and that in consequence of Chase's "irregular conduct," Fries was unjustly sentenced to death. Another charge was that Chase had acted likewise with " manifest injustice, partiality and intemperance " in procuring the conviction of John Thompson Callender, who had severely criticized Jay and other judges and officials.[20] These, and other charges, it was widely recognized, were so well founded that the Adams administration had not dared to carry out the court's sentence, but extended pardons. The number of votes in the Senate favoring Chase's impeachment lacked the constitutional two-thirds majority required, and he was let off by a strict partisan vote. This is the only instance of impeachment proceedings against a Supreme Court Judge in the entire history of that Court.

With deciding upon the right of British subjects to hold and inherit estates, the Supreme Court of the United States still kept up a policy of cautious evasion. This was again

[20] " Report of the Trial of the Hon. Samuel Chase, One Of The Associate Justices of the Supreme Court of the U. S., Before The High Court of Impeachment Composed of The United States Senate," etc. Published at Baltimore, 1805, pp. 9–11.

shown by the case of Lambert's Lessee against Paine, coming up before the Supreme Court, in February, 1805. This suit involved the question of whether a British subject, born in England in the year 1750, and who had always resided in England, could, in the year 1786, take and hold lands in Virginia by descent or by devise. This note appears on the official record:

> " Feb. 18.
>
> This cause was again argued at this term by the same counsel before *Cushing, Paterson, Washington* and *Johnson. Marshall,* Ch. J., having formerly been counsel for one of the · parties, did not sit, and *Chase, J.* was absent." [21]

The action concerned a Virginia estate of about six thousand acres of land, devised to George Gilmer, a British subject. Each of the four justices sitting [22] handed down separate opinions. The majority of the court said that by the will, Gilmer derived a fee in the land. But every one of the Justices evaded the crucial question as to whether an alien could hold land. " As the majority of the court," read Justice Washington's opinion, " is in favor of the defendant upon the construction of the will, I do not think it necessary to say anything upon the doctrine of alienage, as [he significantly added] that question may possibly come on in some other case, in which it must be decided." [23]

The Holland Company's Frauds Validated.

But if the Supreme Court was careful to dodge the main issue as regarded aliens until the receding years allayed public agitation, it judged the time propitious for validating the title

[21] III Cranch, 117.
[22] The Supreme Court was now composed of six members.
[23] III Cranch, 183.

to the vast areas of land fraudulently obtained by the Holland
Company, and by other corporations.

In previous chapters we have outlined the history of the
origin of the Holland Company, in the precedent operations
of which Justice James Wilson, Robert Morris, John Nicholson and others were so prominent. The great agitation continued among the settlers over the disposition of millions of
acres of land in New York and Pennsylvania to these politicians, who in turn, sold them to a group of Holland capitalists. The Pennsylvania legislative act of 1792 had ordered
the public land sold in small areas, for actual settlement to be
made within two years. But this law was grossly evaded and
violated by Wilson, Morris and company. How the law
was evaded, so that a few politicians were able to grasp enormous areas, was related by Judge Huston of the Supreme
Court of Pennsylvania.

". . . Young men," he wrote, " in the face of the law
have gone from home twenty or one hundred miles, commenced a dozen settlements in one month, and next year
worked a week on each, and so on. This, and everything like
it, is not as directed by law. And again, holders of great
numbers of warrants have hired the same man to make, and,
in their language, to keep up, twenty settlements or so many
of the tracts for which they had warrants. . . .

" The owners of the warrants, and those who had settled
without warrants, came early into collision, and on each side
contended for a construction not warranted by law. The
grantees of warrants obtained patents, without even commencing a settlement, on certificates of two justices of the peace
that they had been prevented by enemies; and the persons
claiming by settlement, contended that warrants were void unless settlement commenced within two years from date of
warrant. The war raged during the whole of two years, or
during a great part of it. . . ."[24]

[24] See, Judge Huston's historical review of the controversy in Watts'
Reports (Supreme Court of Pa.), Vol. I: 70-109.

The authorities of Pennsylvania were goaded by public agitation into bringing action against the Holland Company. The matter came before the Pennsylvania Supreme Court in March, 1800. At the same time, on its part, the Holland Company applied for a mandamus to compel the land officers to issue warrants for surveys. " Can it be sufficient to say," read the State's argument, in part, " that the Holland Company have improved a great deal of the country, and are therefore entitled to hold what they have not improved? The spirit of monopoly was an evil against which the legislature meant to guard by dividing the territory offered for sale into single tracts, and restricting the right of purchase to a single tract. It is true, that the connivance of opulent speculators has evaded the legislative precaution; and instead of each settler being the owner of the tract on which he resides, he is the mere instrument of an association of foreigners (who never visited, and probably never will visit, America) to obtain for their emolument the lands which the State had offered for sale, with very different views of policy and benefit. . . ." [25]

The Supreme Court of Pennsylvania decided that the settlements must be made according to law, or no title passed. But the Holland Company kept on inspiring riots and bloodshed, and fabricated a test case in the Supreme Court of the United States for the validation of its title. This case came before that court, in February, 1805, under the form of the action of Huidekoper's Lessee vs. Douglas.[26]

Attorney-General Kean, for the State of Pennsylvania, contended that the object of the Legislature was the *settlement,* not the *sale* of the lands; that the purpose was to get settlers so as to form a barrier against the Indians. He argued at length for a forfeiture of the Holland Company's title. Responding, the Holland Company's counsel brought up the an-

[25] Case of Commonwealth (of Pa.) vs. Tench Coxe, Dallas' Reports (Supreme Court of Pa.), Vol. IV: 195.
[26] See, III Cranch, 1–73.

cient pretext (which we have noted in the case of the Loyal Company, in Chapter I) that the Indian wars prevented the settlement and improving of the lands within the required two years.

Chief Justice Marshall's decision was characteristic. Entirely passing over the all-important and essential fact that millions of acres of the very finest lands in western Pennsylvania were unlawfully acquired and monopolized by a small syndicate of Holland bankers and merchants, he decided that the excuse offered was good. In brief, he held that when Indian wars [27] prevented prompt settlement, there was a release from the fulfillment of conditions demanded by law, and that a warrant gave a vested right. Attention should be given to this decision; in this he held that a contract was only conditionally and relatively a contract; we shall come across other important decisions in which, for the same purposes of justification, he or his colleagues decided that a contract must be construed strictly and absolutely. And by this decision he set another precedent, as we shall see, by which, under the same pretext, huge areas of the richest lands in California and elsewhere were later grasped by a few capitalists.

This decision riveted the hold of the Holland Company upon large areas of land, and upon large numbers of settlers,

---

[27] These wars were caused by the long-continuing and systematic debauching and swindling of the Indian tribes by the whites. The persons complaining that Indian hostilities prevented prompt settlement, were the very persons whose practices. incited those hostilities. Marshall knew this. Of the many contemporaneous accounts of the treatment of Indians, we will instance that message of Governor Daniel D. Tompkins, of New York, to the Legislature in 1812. ". . . It is not to be disguised," he wrote, "that worthless and unprincipled white persons, availing themselves of the ignorance of the Indians, and of their horror at becoming the objects of *punishment,* by laws which they cannot comprehend, wantonly and boldly violate their individual possessions and national domain." These whites, said Tompkins, corrupted and debased the Indians' propensities and habits, intruded upon their lands, and defied the law. (New York Senate and Assembly Journals, 1812, p. 6.) It may be added that large numbers of the whites referred to were agents for land speculators and traders.

in both Pennsylvania and New York. So much oppression resulted from the Holland Company's exactions, that Governor DeWitt Clinton, of New York, in a message to the Legislature, on March 1, 1820, urged that the State buy the rights of the Holland Company from the bankers, the Willincks, of Amsterdam, Holland. This suggested purchase, he wrote, would " relieve a considerable portion of our population from the evils from which they are suffering," and would also do away " with an influence which has been injuriously exercised." There was great excitement, the message reported, among the yeomanry, and it was dangerous, Governor Clinton declared, to allow so extensive a domain under foreign authority.

" In this State," the message went on, " there are, west of the Genesee River, from eighty to one hundred thousand people, subject to the will of the Hollanders for their peace and happiness. . . . By the existing laws of the State, even their improvements (in these times of the absence of all money), are liable to be sold at auction for a trifling debt, arising from the ordinary credits in life, or a lawyer's or a physician's bill." Similar conditions, it may be interposed, prevailed in Pennsylvania. Governor Clinton's message stated that the Holland Company owned nearly 2,000,000 acres in New York, and also held between four and five millions of dollars in good bonds, covenants and mortgages.[28]

Governor Clinton's proposal was not acted upon. The Holland Company, says Roberts, " sold farms on long time to those that would improve them, at prices that seemed low, but when a succession of bad crops came or domestic affliction used up the income, they proved to be onerous. . . . In 1836 the people of Chautauqua County were disturbed by rumors that the liens given by them to the Holland Company were to be enforced, and the land office with its records was destroyed by a mob. In Batavia, Genesee County, a threat-

[28] Journal of the [N. Y.] Assembly, 1820: 581–583.

ened attack on the land office was prevented by the organization of the citizens." [29]   The " citizens " referred to were
armed hirelings employed by the Holland Company.   Shortly
after this, J. J. Vanderkemp, general agent of the Holland
Company in Philadelphia, discontinued the company's office
at Batavia.[30]   A petition of the inhabitants living on the Holland Company's domain was submitted to the Legislature alleging, by a recital of the facts, that the Holland Company's
title was invalid, and demanding ejectment; the Attorney-
General was directed to make an inquiry.[31]

The Holland Company decided that it was a wise move to
sell its property to American capitalists, and did so.   In Pennsylvania, the Holland Company's ownership was likewise accompanied by a train of disturbances and litigations, ending
in its further enrichment by the sales of land to native capitalists.   The huge sums of money invested by the Dutch
capitalists in canals and railroads were the sums that had
been wrung from American settlers during the more than
forty years of the Holland Company's sway.

These details are given for the purpose of showing some
of the results of Chief Justice Marshall's decision.

The New Associate Justices.

The three Associate Justices of the Supreme Court of the
United States appointed by President Jefferson, during his
two terms of office, were all associated either with the landed
or banking class.   Of all the men ever sitting in that court,
William Johnson, of South Carolina, appointed in 1804, was
one of the very few distinguished, on the whole, for his opposition to certain notorious land decisions.   He was more
allied with the banking interests; his brother Joseph was
president, from 1818 to 1823, of the Charleston (S. C.)

[29] Roberts' " New York," Vol. II: 623.
[30] N. Y. Assembly Doc. No. 317, 1839.
[31] N. Y. Assembly Doc. No. 224, Vol. III, Assembly Docs., 1837.

Branch of the Bank of, the United States. Of the truly enormous corruptions and consecutive frauds and thefts of this bank, details are given later in this work.

In the appointment in 1807, of Brockholst Livingston, as an Associate Justice, the long-potent Livingston family secured another successive representative. A son of William Livingston, Brockholst Livingston succeeded his father's associate, William Paterson, who died in 1806 while visiting his daughter, the wife of Stephen Van Rensselaer. William Todd, Chief Justice of Kentucky, also appointed an Associate Justice of the Supreme Court by Jefferson, was allied with the landed class; and his second wife, to whom he was married in 1811, was the widow of Major George Washington, a nephew of General George Washington. She was also the youngest sister of the wife of James Madison. Todd, says the biographical account of him in the Supreme Court records, was a great authority on land laws. The account further says that "although a Republican, he steadfastly supported the Constitutional doctrines which Mr. Chief Justice Marshall promulgated." [32]

This was the composition of the Supreme Court bench when, in February, in 1808, after four years' postponement, the decision in the case of M'Ilvaine vs. Coxe's Lessee, was handed down. Decrepit Justice Cushing, seventy-six years old, and so valetudinarian as to excite pity, wrote the court's opinion. So palpably remarkable were the grounds of the decision that it was received with derision; it was one of those decisions that, not wrapped in technicalities, could be understood by the layman. Daniel Coxe, it held, could not by any voluntary act of his, renounce allegiance to the State of New Jersey. He was, the decision read, "incapable of throwing

[32] See, Peters' Reports, Supreme Court of the United States, Vol. XIII: 7 and 8. This account describes Justice Todd as very kind to those in whom he was interested. It says that after the Kentucky Legislature had repealed an act granting a pension to Justice Munter, that Todd personally pensioned Munter for life.

off his allegiance to the State," so long as the laws of New Jersey which had made him a subject of that State were in full force. New Jersey, in 1776, was a sovereign State, and had a right to compel the inhabitants of that State to become citizens. Therefore, a person living there until 1777, and then joining the British as a refugee, had a right to take lands by descent in the State of New Jersey.[33]

The premises of this decision were so obviously ridiculous and fantastic that it would be superfluous to analyze them. Nevertheless, the decision served the meditated purposes of ranking as a precedent leading up to the settlement of the Fairfax matter. Likewise did the decision, rendered in the same month, in the case of Dawson's Lessee vs. Godfrey. Marshall absented himself when this decision was made. This case dealt with the right of an alien born in England before the year 1775, and who always lived there, never coming to the United States, to take lands in Maryland which he had inherited in the year 1793. He could not take those lands, the Supreme Court decided, because the inheritance antedated Jay's Treaty by a year.[34] The importance of this decision lay in its contra-implied dictum that any transaction between a British subject and an American citizen made after Jay's Treaty, was an enforceable contract. This doctrine precisely fitted Marshall's own case in his purchase of Denny Fairfax's claim to " Leeds Manor."

Then followed Marshall's decision, in 1809, in the case of Taylor vs. Brown validating the fraudulent possession of

[33] IV Cranch, 209–215. At the very time that this decision was handed down, the United States Government was contesting the claim of the British Government that Great Britain had the right to impress sailors of British birth, no matter on what ships they were in service. The British Government proceeded upon the dictum that " once a British subject, always a British subject," and the United States Government as vigorously denied the force of that dictum. This dispute, involved as it was with other questions arising from capitalist struggles for commercial expansion, was one of the causes of the War of 1812–1815. Marshall's decision was good law according to British contentions.

[34] IV Cranch, 321.

surplus land not included in the original patent. In another and weighty respect, too, this decision took rank as a precedent, for what Marshall actually decided was that when the person to whom a stated area of land had been granted, appropriated more than the patent contained, he had a vested right in that illegal seizure. Certainly, this was a very remarkable construction justifying land thefts; here are Marshall's own words:

" It is a fact of universal notoriety in Virginia not only that the old military surveys, but that the patents of that country generally contain a greater quantity of land than the patents call for. The ancient law of Virginia notices this fact, and provides for the case. It prescribes the manner in which this surplus may be acquired by other persons; and it is worthy of notice that the patentee must himself reject the surplus before it can be acquired by another, and after having rejected it, he has the election to allot it in such part of his patent as he pleases." [35]

The facile way was now prepared, the time was accounted ripe, and accordingly in the next three years two momentous decisions were rendered in cases both of which sprang from personal interests. These decisions equally, in different ways, asserted the all-embracing, omnipotent power of the Supreme Court of the United States. In the one case, the Supreme Court successfully demonstrated its power of annulling legislation considered to be an impairment of the obligation of contract, and it held that it had original powers of appellate jurisdiction, in deciding the other case. The first of these cases was that of the Georgia legislative act rescinding the corrupt grant of 35,000,000 acres. The second case dealt with the Fairfax estate. Yet these circumstances, throwing such light upon the subterranean origin of memorable decisions, are by no means all; attending the actions were a series of other exceedingly astonishing and interconnected

[35] V Cranch, 249.

circumstances, the details of which are related in the next chapter.

How Marshall Ruled the Supreme Court.

But before entering upon the further narrative, it will be advisable to give some adequate idea of the arbitrary and domineering manner in which Marshall ran the Supreme Court. Before Marshall's appointment, the Supreme Court followed the English practice, under which each judge who sat in a cause, gave an opinion whenever he thought there was occasion for it; but in general, those judges who presided at the circuit declined to sit *in banc,* except in a case where the judges were equally divided in opinion.

Under Marshall (who had argued but a single case in the Supreme Court of the United States before he became Chief Justice), this practice, Shirley says, " was rooted out, so far as his influence extended; the judges reheard the causes which they had decided at the circuit; the practice of giving individual opinions was repressed; the practice became general of making one judge ' the organ of the court,' of virtually assigning causes, and of taking them home for the purpose of writing up opinions in vacation; and of having an opinion written by a single judge as the opinion of the court, when the judgment received the assent of but three, and sometimes two, of the judges, and the reasoning of a less number. This vicious practice occasioned great dissatisfaction.

" The primitive court [Supreme Court of the U. S.] consisted of five judges. It was increased to six, and afterward to seven. For years it was necessary for two of these judges, in general, to ride the circuit together; not infrequently, after the accession of Marshall, but four judges held the general term at Washington, and constituted the court when many important causes were assigned. Two of the judges were aged and infirm, and one of them, for years before his death, was so superannuated that he practically left his circuit, a most important one, to take care of itself, and was a nonentity at Washington. The new chief [Marshall] had, from his acknowledged ability and force, and weight of character, and from his tact and diplomatic skill, great influence with his brethren. When an occasion required, he was an adept in 'patching up' compromise judgments and opinions."

Continuing, Shirley significantly relates that Marshall sometimes rendered decisions as being those of a majority of the court, " without being as careful as a discreet judge ought, to find out whether his opinion was that of a majority or minority of the court. In Rose vs. Himely, IV Cranch, 41, he delivered the leading opinion, and ordered the judgment of the Circuit Court to be reversed, etc., when in fact but a single judge agreed with him, as afterwards appeared in Hudson vs. Guestier, VI Cranch, 281.

" In one of the cloud of opinions delivered by Marshall at the trial of Aaron Burr, he admits that he made a mistake of a similar character in Bollman's case. In this way, two judges practically became a majority of six, and three a majority of seven.

" The cases referred to were by no means the only instances of a similar kind, nor could they fairly be attributed to the press of business. These facts were open secrets in narrow circles. This intensified the dissatisfaction. . . ."[36]

While virtually declaring what the laws of the country should be, Marshall was thus a lawless dictator, vesting in himself more powers than most potentates held. This manipulation of his of the Supreme Court will assist in elucidating the facts now following.

[36] " Dartmouth College Causes " (Edition of 1879), pp. 377-378.

CHAPTER VII

MARSHALL AND HIS CHIEF COADJUTOR, STORY

The great case before the Supreme Court of the United States in 1809–1810 was that arising from the act of the Georgia Legislature, in 1796, repealing the Yazoo land grants of 35,000,000 acres, after conclusive evidence had shown that the empowering act had been obtained by bribery.

About a month before the act was repealed, when the whole country knew the sworn details of the bribery, and when it was well known that the incoming Legislature was pledged to annul the granting act, the Georgia Mississippi Company hastily sold to William Wetmore and other New England capitalists, mostly living in Boston and adjacent cities, a tract of their grant. This tract lay in what is now the State of Mississippi, and was estimated to contain the enormous total quantity of 11,380,000 acres. For this immense area, the New England Mississippi Company (for so the buying company called itself) agreed to pay the Georgia Mississippi Company ten cents an acre in gradual installments.[1]

A Collusive Suit Arranged.

Who had suggested this sale in view of the fact that the Georgia Legislature was bound to revoke the grant? And upon what assurances did the Boston capitalists contract to buy the land, knowing as they did that revocation was imminent and certain?

[1] See, Case of Brown vs. Gilman, Wheaton's Reports, Supreme Court of the United States, Vol. IV: 255.

Did the proposal and assurances emanate from Justice James Wilson, the foremost financier in the bribery transaction? It was he, as we have seen, who contributed the greatest share of the funds. We have seen, too, how after the Legislature of Pennsylvania had repealed the charter of the Bank of North America, owned by Wilson and others, Wilson had argued that the repeal was in violation of the obligation of a contract, and that it was injuring innocent parties who had bought the bank's stock. And also we have seen how Wilson was the identical delegate causing to be inserted in the Constitution of the United States that sly, obscure but formidable clause prohibiting State legislation impairing the obligation of a contract. Did Wilson advise the hurried and collusive sale to the New England capitalists in order that they might be able to plead in court that they were innocent purchasers, and knew nothing of the bribery and fraud? This, among other defenses, was precisely what they did plead, and continued to plead for fifteen years, although every schoolboy knew of the great Yazoo frauds, so widespread and rank a scandal did they make.

After an examination of the circumstances, little doubt remains that a trumped-up case was manufactured in order to bring the matter before the Supreme Court of the United States, and thus have the Georgia rescinding act declared unconstitutional. Knowing that the Georgia Legislature would revoke the grant, the capitalists concerned hastened to fabricate a case in this way: A portion of the lands of the Georgia Mississippi Company were conveyed by the original grantees to James Greenleaf;[2] from him, these lands came through a chain of conveyances to John Peck, who, in turn, conveyed them with covenants, to Fletcher. After the Georgia Legislature had rescinded the grant, Fletcher sued

[2] It has been shown how, in another of the four associated companies — the Georgia Company — Greenleaf held 2,500,000 acres, and how James Wilson contributed £25,000 to the original capital of the Georgia Company, in which he held 750,000 acres.

Peck for a covenant broken. This suit, of course, as premeditated, would open up the whole question of the constitutionality of the Georgia rescinding act.

Such evidence as is accessible tends to prove beyond question that this was the plan definitely agreed upon, and with this particular ulterior end in view.

Story Dines with the Justices.

The case of Fletcher vs. Peck was twice argued before the Supreme Court of the United States, the first time in 1809. On the first occasion, Peck was represented by John Quincy Adams, and Robert Goodhue Harper. At the second argument in 1810, Joseph Story and Harper represented Peck. The note on the Supreme Court record reads: " The plaintiff sued out his writ of error, and the case was twice argued, first by Martin, for the plaintiff in error, and by J. Q. Adams and R. G. Harper for the defendant, at the February term, 1809, and again at this term by Martin, for the plaintiff, and by Harper and Story, for the defendant." [3]

But meanwhile some significant things were happening which are not related in the Supreme Court records. Story was a member of Congress at the time, and was briskly employed pushing the claims of the New England capitalists in that body; in his private correspondence with his friend Samuel P. P. Fay, he frankly admitted so.[4] What was vastly more to the point, he was very frequently and intimately hobnobbing with the judges of the Supreme Court of the United States. In a letter, dated Washington, February 16, 1808, to Fay, Story wrote: ". . . The scene of my greatest amusement, as well as instruction, is the Supreme Court. I

[3] VI Cranch, 114–115. It is again worthy of note that Judge William Cranch, the reporter of the Supreme Court at this time, had been the attorney for James Greenleaf in negotiating that great scandalous purchase of 9,000 lots in the city of Washington.
[4] "Joseph Story's Life and Letters" (Written and edited by his son, William W. Story), Vol. I: 197.

daily spend several hours there, and generally when disengaged, dine and sup with the judges. . . ."[5]

When Story wrote this letter, little did he think of what historical importance it would have!

Inasmuch as Story soon after this became an Associate Justice, and ranks, after Marshall, as an ascribed great expounder of jurisprudence, it is advisable and appropriate to digress here in order to sketch his antecedents, life, environment and interests.

His grandfather, William Story, was a British official at Marblehead, Massachusetts. His father was a physician, and supported the American Revolution. " He married for his first wife," wrote Joseph Story to his son, William W. Story, on January 23, 1831, " Miss Ruth Ruddock, daughter of John Ruddock, Esq., a man who had accumulated a considerable property in the ship-building business in Boston. She died in the year 1777, leaving seven children. In the autumn of 1778, my father married Miss Pedrick, whom you know as your grandmother still living, and by her had eleven children, of whom I am the eldest. Your grandfather's father was an opulent merchant, and, indeed, for that day a very opulent merchant."[6]

Educated at Harvard, Joseph Story necessarily was subject to the acknowledged caste environment systematically prevailing there. Opening a law office in Salem, he admixed politics and law practice. He was a strong believer in property qualifications for voters, as was later shown when, as a member of the Massachusetts Constitutional Convention of 1820, he vigorously advocated the retention of the restrictive electoral laws in force.[7]

---

[5] *Ibid.,* 62. Socially and in his private circle, Marshall particularly was of an extremely convivial disposition. Unlike Justice Bushrod Washington, who was " lean and emaciated, with a face like marble,' Marshall was strong and robust. In his youth he had been much habituated to athletic exercises. He could stand up under much festivity.

[6] *Ibid.,* 2.   [7] See later.

Marshall Validates the Yazoo Frauds.

The decision handed down by Chief Justice Marshall, in the case of Fletcher vs. Peck, made not merely a considerable, but a very great, public sensation. The decision, in brief, held that the grant made by the State of Georgia was in the nature of a contract which could not be impaired or revoked by subsequent legislation. This being so, he decided, the rescinding act of 1796 was "repugnant" to the Constitution, and therefore null and void.[8]

From this decision Justice Johnson caustically dissented, in a strong opinion, implying collusion in the bringing of the action. "I have been very unwilling," he said, "to proceed to the decision of this cause at all. It appears to me to bear strong evidence upon the face of it, of being a mere feigned cause. It is our duty to decide on the rights, but not on the speculations of parties. My confidence, however," [was this meant ironically?], "in the respectable gentlemen who have been engaged for the parties, has induced me to abandon my scruples, in the belief that they would never consent to impose a mere feigned case upon this court."

To form an adequate realization of the wide and lasting stir caused by this decision, it is necessary to picture the public disgust at the methods by which the Yazoo land grants had been obtained, and the deep public horror at the Supreme Court venturing to annul a State law as unconstitutional, especially a law explicitly designed to forfeit a grant of 35,000,000 acres secured by both fraud and corruption. The sworn testimony of that bribery was published in official records, available to everyone; not a well-informed person was there who did not know them; and besides, the scandal had been agitated for fifteen years. Only a short time before the decision, the Secretary of the Treasury, in 1810, un-

---

[8] See, VI Cranch, 87.

der a resolution of the House of Representatives, reported of
the Yazoo claims:

" The Yazoo claims, so-called, embracing about 35,000,000
acres in the Mississippi Territory and derived from a pretended sale by the Legislature of Georgia, but declared null
and void, as fraudulent, by a subsequent legislature. The
evidence as published by the State of Georgia and by Congress,
shows that that transaction, even if considered as a contract,
is as such, on acknowledged principles of law and equity,
null ab initio, it being in proof that all the members of the
Legislature who voted in favor of the sale, that is to say, the
agents who pretended to sell the property of their constituents, were, with the exception of a single person, interested in,
and parties to, the purchase. Much litigation must be expected, and orders have lately been given for the removal of
certain intruders, some of whom claimed the land under this
supposed title."

But what devious tack did Marshall take so as to evade the
settled principle of law that fraud vitiated every contract?
With unsurpassed audacity, he proceeded upon the complacent
assumption that the bribery of legislators was merely a fanciful story, and waved the facts lightly aside.

By capitalists of every description the decision was greeted
with jubilation. They saw its prodigious purport. It meant
that any special privilege, any act bestowing property, or
creating new property rights, whether obtained by the grossest
bribery, was a fixed and inalienable vested right, which no
subsequent legislative act could rescind.

For this, John Quincy Adams and the illustrious Joseph
Story had pleaded, and this is what the great and pure John
Marshall decided. Thus they bound upon future generations
laws secured by bribes, and arrogated to the Supreme Court
the almighty power of setting aside conflicting legislation,
because, indeed, a law was a contract and a contract was a
sacred and perpetual right, to be venerated and enforced for

all time. Justice James Wilson had done his work well in the Constitutional Convention.

The Claimants Get Nearly Five Million Dollars.

In Congress a storm of bitter strictures was caused by the decisic but how much of these arose from simulated indignation in order to pander to constituencies, how much from genuine resentment, and how much from violence to sectional convictions that the decision was an usurpation of State's rights, cannot be accurately gauged. So inflamed, however, was the public temper by the decision, that Congress, for a considerable time, held back from giving the Yazoo companies the indemnity they demanded under the Supreme Court's decision. The areas included in their grants had been ceded by Georgia to the United States in 1802, and could not be restored. Finally, in 1814, Congress passed an act appropriating a fund of $5,000,000 for the indemnification of the claimants, and establishing a Board of Commissioners to determine the amount of the awards. Under this law these awards were made in specially-issued Government stock:

To the	Upper Mississippi Company	$ 350,000
" "	Tennessee Company	600,000
" "	Georgia Mississippi Company	1,500,000
" "	Georgia Company	2,250,000
"	persons claiming under citizenship rights	250,000

Total .... $4,950,000 [10]

[9] See, for instance, accounts given in Senator Benton's " Thirty Years in the Senate."

[10] " American State Papers: Public Lands," Vol. VI: 21–22. (Doc. No. 759.) But not satisfied with the $1,500,000 award made to the Georgia Mississippi Company, a petition signed by Thomas L. Winthrop, Thomas Wetmore, William Sullivan, John F. Loring, Joseph Morton and other Boston capitalists, of the New England Mississippi Company, who had bought that company's claim, was sent to Congress, in 1837, complaining that an erroneous deduction of $130,425.12 had been made from their original award, and saying that "the company had been left to state their grievances for above twenty successive

Two years later we find Thomas L. Winthrop, one of the chief beneficiaries of this decision, buying, at auction, one-half of the unsold lands of the Kennebec Company, in Maine. This company, in 1753, had bought from the old Plymouth Company, a large tract of land in that province, then a part of Massachusetts. The grant as defined by law, lay fifteen miles on each side of the Kennebec River, in the vicinity of what are now the city of Augusta and the town of Winthrop and other places. The boundary was described as the " uttermost limits of the Cobbosseeconte," but the company's surveyors fraudulently ran their lines to the " farthest tiny rivulet " they could find, and thus boldly took in great areas of additional land. Much litigation resulted over title to parts of the land; settlers after clearing the forests, and laying out farms, were then compelled to pay twice and thrice over to rival claimants; and when, in 1816, the courts decided in favor of the Kennebec Company, the settlers were evicted and their homes and improvements seized on the ground that they had never obtained title from the Kennebec Company. When the settlers rose in armed revolt, and an insurrection on a small scale broke out, militia were requisitioned to shoot them down. Winthrop subsequently sold his land to Congressman Joseph L. Williams.

It was, says Shirley, the knowledge of Marshall's manipulation of the Supreme Court that " lay at the bottom of the attempts in Congress (which gave Webster so much trouble, and some of the judges so much uneasiness) to prohibit the judges from setting aside a State law as unconstitutional unless a certain number of judges sat in the cause and concurred in the judgments. It was one of the causes of Jefferson's dislike of Marshall, which made him say with a

years." The unblushing cupidity of these capitalists was long a subject of comment.— See, " American State Papers: Public Lands," Vol. VIII : 985–986. (Doc. No. 1594.) In Brown vs. Gilman, IV Wheaton, 255, it is stated that the New England Mississippi Company received $1,083,-812 in all.

bitterness unusual with him, in his letter to Ritchie, of June 25, 1810: 'An opinion is huddled up in conclave, perhaps by a majority of one, delivered as if unanimous, by a crafty chief judge, who sophisticates the law to his mind by the turn of his own reasoning.' " [11]

His success in this case, it may well be understood, gave Story a great prestige in capitalist circles as an attorney of distinguished mark. But like many other lawyers of the day, Story was not only a practising attorney but a capitalist as well. The very next year after the Yazoo decision, he became president of a bank; the circumstances under which the charter of this bank and the charters of other banks were granted, and Story's methods in connection with the passage of the acts, aroused much criticism in Massachusetts.

Throughout the United States, a hostile feeling toward banks generally prevailed. We have seen how in New York, during this period, the Legislature was being systematically corrupted to pass acts giving bank charters. It was likewise so in other States. True, the Constitution declared that no State "shall coin money, emit bills of credit, or make anything but gold and silver a tender in payment of debts." But the Supreme Court of the United States later construed this clause to mean that "bills of credit" were not intended to apply to bank notes. Long before this decision was made, began the enormous outpouring of State bank notes the immense frauds of which are described in so many legislative and other documents of the time. Vast issues of bank notes were based upon "wild-cat" securities having little or no value, and banks frequently had an outstanding issue of millions of dollars in bank notes, when there was hardly anything worthy of being called assets to back them up.

This currency, so often fraudulent and spurious, was loaned at usurious rates of interest, and until Jackson's administra-

[11] "Dartmouth College Causes," 311.

tion was received as payment for purchases of public lands. What Governor Tompkins, of New York, wrote in a message to the Legislature, in 1812, applied to banks throughout the country. Bank stock, he said, was " generally owned by the speculating, the wealthy and the aspiring part of society." Enterprising farmers, manufacturers and mechanics, he went on, experienced great difficulty in raising money at lawful rates of interest upon the best security. The necessity of getting temporary pecuniary relief frequently drove them " into the embraces of unprincipled, avaricious usurers, who fertilize upon the wants and distresses of the needy and unfortunate." He further referred to banks as " vesting in the hands of the wealthy and aristocratic class of powerful engines to corrupt and subdue republican notions." [12]

Story Puts Through Bank Charters.

In 1810, Story was elected to the Massachusetts Legislature. Why did he choose to leave the more prominent position of a seat in Congress for the lesser post of a seat in that Legislature? Was it because he had satisfactorily put the great Yazoo land claims through, and had plans of his own necessitating his presence in the Massachusetts Legislature? What these plans were was quickly revealed.

As soon as the Legislature met in 1811, Story was elected Speaker of the House. On June 25, 1811, a bill was passed chartering the Merchants' Bank, with a capital of $300,000. Among the incorporators were Story's clients, George Crowninshield, Jr., and John Crowninshield.[13] The Crowninshield family were the owners of valuable wharf property in Salem; two years previously, in 1809, the Massachusetts Legislature had passed an act chartering them as the Salem India Wharf

[12] N. Y. Assembly and Senate Journals, 1812: 6.
[13] " Laws of Massachusetts, 1809–12," Vol. V: 494. Story was George Crowninshield's attorney in lawsuits. See, "Massachusetts Reports," Vol. III: 444 (1807, etc.).

Corporation.[14]   The Crowninshield and the Adams families, it may be said, became intermarried.

The very next day after the Merchants' Bank was chartered, a bill was passed by the Massachusetts Legislature (on June 26, 1811) chartering the State Bank, with a capital of $3,000,000.[15]   One of the leading incorporators was William Gray, a rich shipowner and noted politician who had also been an incorporator of the Essex Bank, chartered by the Massachusetts Legislature in 1799.   It may be remarked here that a grandson of William Gray became one of the Associate Justices of the Supreme Court of the United States.

Both the Merchants' Bank and the State Bank charters were lobbied through the Legislature by Story.   Although his name, for obvious reasons, did not appear among the list of incorporators, yet his connection was soon thereafter openly shown when he was elected a director, and then President of the Merchants' Bank of Salem.   Writing to Story's son and biographer, William W. Story, on August 25, 1847, J. W. Treadwell, long cashier of the Merchants' Bank, thus explained the origin of these two bank charters:

". . .   Your father, while a member of the Legislature of Massachusetts, exerted his influence to obtain acts of incorporations for the State Bank in 'Boston, and the Merchants' Bank in Salem, the capital stock of which was almost exclusively owned by members of the political party then dominant. . . .   At the organization of the Merchants' Bank, your father was elected to the Board of Directors, and I was invited to go into the bank as one of its officers.   As Cashier of that institution, to which I was subsequently elected, I was brought into close intimacy with him; and yet a closer one upon his election to the Presidency of the Bank, in a couple of years afterwards." [16]

14 " Laws of Massachusetts, 1809–12," Vol. V: 19.
15 Ibid., 501.
16 " Story's Life and Letters," Vol. I: 205.

Story Appointed an Associate Justice.

In the same year in which these charters were enacted, Story, in November, 1811, was appointed an Associate Justice of the Supreme Court of the United States.

His appointment, it is needless to say, was entirely satisfactory to both the land and the banking interests. During many of the years that he sat on the Supreme Court bench, he was not only president of the Merchants' Bank, but that bank greatly profited from the deposits of Government money. In another letter to William W. Story, Treadwell further says that, "The Merchants' Bank had always, since its establishment, been the depository of the funds of the United States Treasury, which had often been large [Salem was a busy sea-port town with considerable customs revenues], and contributed to swell its dividends." A competing bank in Salem, Treadwell says, forwarded a memorial, during President Jackson's Administration to the Secretary of the Treasury Louis McLane, stating that inasmuch as the president and the cashier of the Merchants' Bank were enemies of the administration, the Government deposits should be removed to the friendly bank. But, adds Treadwell, the Government funds were left undisturbed in the Merchants' Bank.[17] From being stanch Republican, Story had changed his politics, and became a deep-rooted Federalist. As for McLane's methods, they were later revealed in the celebrated bribery contract case of the Baltimore and Ohio Railroad Company, of which corporation he became president.[18]

[17] *Ibid.*, 158–159.
[18] Alexander J. Marshall, in 1853, sued the Baltimore and Ohio Railroad Company for $50,000, which he proved was owed to him for services under a special contract for lobbying a bill through the Virginia Legislature granting to the company the right of way through Virginia. Marshall was employed by McLane as lobbyist. See, Case of Marshall vs. Baltimore and Ohio Railroad Company, Howard's Reports, Supreme Court of the United States, Vol. XVI: 314. This case is described more in detail further on in this present history.

Chief Justice Marshall had decided the great Yazoo land frauds case in favor of Story's clients. It now came Story's turn to decide the long-pending case of the Fairfax estate favorable to Marshall.

Marshall's Fairfax Claim Up Again.

The case of Hunter vs. Fairfax's Devisee had come up before the Supreme Court of Appeals of Virginia, in April, 1810.[19] Why there was such a long lapse between the decision of the Winchester court, in 1794, and the decision of this court, is not clearly explained. Evidently, one aspect of it was new points arising from the gross violation of the compromise law by John Marshall and his brother, as the purchasers of Fairfax's claim. In a decision which was really a sharp exposure of the Marshalls' methods and pretensions, the Supreme Court of Appeals of Virginia reversed the lower court.

" I consider," said Judge Roane, " the compromise as having been deposited with the court for the purpose of settling all the causes embraced thereby, according to the provisions thereof; and I can never consent that the appellees after having got the benefit thereof, should refuse to submit thereto, or pay the equivalent; the consequences of which would be that the Commonwealth would have to remunerate the appellant [Hunter] for the land recovered from him. Such a cause cannot be justified on the principles of justice or good faith. . . ." [20]

The unprecedented action was now taken of carrying this reversal to the Supreme Court of the United States, which issued a writ of error.

The uncontroverted points up to this time were:

Lord Fairfax (as was agreed by both litigants), had con-

---

[19] " Judge Tucker," the note on the record reads, " not sitting in this case, through motives of delicacy, being nearly related to a person interested."— Munford's Reports, etc., Vol. I: 218.

[20] *Ibid., 232.*

veyed 300,000 acres to his nephew, T. B. Martin, who had re-conveyed them to Fairfax in fee.

Virginia had passed acts of confiscation of the property of aliens.

Denny Fairfax, Lord Fairfax's heir, was a British subject; he had always lived in England up to the time of his death in about the year 1803.

John Marshall and his brother, James Markham Marshall, had bought Denny Fairfax's claim to the estate in the Northern Neck of Virginia.[21]

John Marshall had agreed to the act of compromise passed by the Virginia Legislature, but later, after considering to what full effect the provisions of Jay's Treaty could be used, had (so the Supreme Court of Appeals of Virginia held) violated, if not repudiated it, in bad faith.

Under the form of Fairfax's Devisee vs. Hunter's Lessee, the case came before the Supreme Court of the United States, at the February term, in 1813. At the argument Chief Justice Marshall and Justice Bushrod Washington were absent.

The attorneys for Fairfax's Devisee contended, among other points, that Fairfax's estate had never been taken from him by any equivalent mode of confiscation. The treaty of peace of 1783, it was argued, found Denny Fairfax in possession of his estate unaltered from the condition in which he originally inherited it, and so operated as a release and confirmation to the British proprietor. His title, the argument further ran, was explicitly acknowledged and confirmed by Jay's Treaty of 1794.

Harper, attorney for Hunter, argued that Lord Thomas Fairfax's original power had been only one to grant lands to individuals; that it was not contemplated that he himself should occupy the lands; the power was a mere transference or delegation of power which passed to Virginia at the time

[21] The Virginia records show that James Markham Marshall collected the rents, and was the general man of business for the estate.

of the Revolution. " This," said Harper, " was the construction put upon it by Lord Fairfax himself— for when he intended to appropriate any part of the lands to his own use, he granted it to a third person, and then took back the title from his own grantee. His deeds were not in the common form, but were made to resemble those of the crown." An alien, continued Hunter, could not sell; he had nothing but a naked possession.

Story Decides in Favor of Marshall.

When Justice Story handed down the decision in this case, on March 15, 1813, Marshall and Todd were absent. Story decided that although Denny Martin (or Fairfax) was an alien enemy at the time of Lord Fairfax's death, yet he nevertheless had legitimately inherited the estate under Fairfax's will. That testament, Story held, could not be divested on the ground of alienage, except by a specific official act, called inquest of office, or by some specific legislative act, or its equivalent. A general act would not suffice for confiscation. And, since no proceedings of escheat had ever been taken against the estate before the adoption of Jay's Treaty of 1794, therefore the defeasible title vested in the alien, Denny Fairfax, was completely protected and confirmed by that treaty.[22]

Justice Johnson was the only dissenting member of the Supreme Court. He asserted that the disability of an alien

[22] VII Cranch, 603. The area of land involved in the final determination of this suit is not stated. John Marshall and James Markham Marshall received all the lands in " Leeds Manor," where their posterity continued to reside.

In an article published in the *Greenbag,* issue of Dec., 1896, John Marshall's great granddaughter, Sallie E. Marshall Hardy, writing from family papers and correspondence, stated that in his latter years it was Marshall's practice every year to pay a visit to his sons and estates in Fauquier County. Marshall was also described as a slaveholder, and Leeds Manor was thus pictured in that article: " Leeds Manor is at the foot of Little Cobbler Mountain. In all the world there is no more beautiful spot." Of course, the article gave no hint as to how Marshall obtained his estates.

to hold real estate was a general principle of common law. He declared with significant emphasis that Jay's Treaty of 1794 extended to rightful causes only. In the case of Smith vs. the State of Maryland, he pointed out, the Supreme Court of the United States had once sustained a specific confiscation of lands, under a law of that State, although there was neither conviction nor inquest of office. The Legislature of Virginia had like power to confiscate, Justice Johnson said. And, after all, he added, the interest acquired under the devise was a mere, shadowy *scintilla juris* which had been extinguished by the grant to Hunter.[23]

So Chief Justice Marshall and his brother managed to get legal hold of the much-desired " Leeds Manor," by a decision of his own court, handed down by an Associate Justice whose fraudulent case, involving such immense interests, had been decided favorably by Marshall three years previously. Story's decision revealed an amazingly comprehensive intimacy with all of the twists and turnings of ancient Virginia laws, legislation and practices — a knowledge that no other member of the Supreme Court but Marshall had. In fact, it has never been disputed that Story, in his Supreme Court career, was a complete satellite of Marshall, and registered into decisions the species of law dictated by Marshall; Story himself practically acknowledged this.

Justice Livingston's Case.

Equally significant was the fact that virtually every member of the Supreme Court was personally interested in some case coming up for final decision. It would clearly seem that each voted for the other's cases. Thus, in the very month that the Fairfax case was argued, the case of Livingston and Gilchrist vs. The Maryland Insurance Company came before the Supreme Court. The Livingston in this case was none

[23] VII Cranch. 631.

other than Brockholst Livingston, at that identical time 'an Associate Justice of the Supreme Court of the United States. The case had gone against Livingston and Gilchrist in the Circuit Court, in Maryland, and now came up on appeal. When the case was passed upon by the Supreme Court, Justice Livingston absented himself. Todd also kept away, probably because of ill health, from which he greatly suffered.

The facts, as stated in the Supreme Court reports, revealed a commercial turpitude not at all harmonizing with the lofty qualities accredited to a Supreme Court Justice. Briefly, the facts were:

Julian Hernando Baruso, a Spanish subject, had received a royal license from Spain to import goods from Boston to Peru and Buenos Ayres, and vice versa. This license was a great asset; the laws of Spain allowed trade under a Spanish license only. On August 24, 1804, Baruso entered into a contract with one Anthony Carroll to transport goods to Lima; Brockholst Livingston was Carroll's surety for the performance of the contract. On January 25, 1805, war was declared between Great Britain and Spain. Brockholst Livingston made a new contract with Baruso for the transportation of $50,000 worth of goods, " the funds and vessel to be furnished and advanced by the said L." [24] The articles were those of partnership with Livingston; Baruso and Livingston were to divide the profits equally, and Livingston was to get commissions from the sale of the merchandise. On the return voyage a cargo was to be brought back. But war was

---

[24] IV Cranch, 508. The profits of shipping merchants were extraordinarily large. The Government extended credit for nine, twelve and eighteen months before it demanded the payment of customs duties. As soon as the ship arrived, the shipper often sold the cargo at a profit of fifty per cent. Instead of having to use their profit and capital in further ventures, the shippers had the gratuitous use of Government money for periods from six months to a year and a half. Thus, John Jacob Astor, who was primarily a shipper, had what was actually a free-of-interest loan from the Government of more than five million dollars. Hence, it is easy to see what the inducements were for going into commerce.

on and the cargo was liable to seizure and confiscation by
Spain or by British ships. Under the laws of Spain, trade
could be carried on only by special permission, and under
a Spanish name and Spanish papers. To meet this contingency, Livingston shrewdly got Baruso to contract that he
(Baruso) would be answerable for the detention of the ship
or confiscation of the goods, and would pay the duties.

Livingston then bought the ship *Herkimer*, and entered into
a contract with Gilchrist, James Baxter and Edward Griswold
for the contribution of joint funds to buy the cargo. This
cargo was shipped to Lima, and a return cargo was received at
Guayaquil.

An Illegal Voyage and Fraudulent Papers.

On the return voyage, just after doubling Cape Horn, Baxter, who was supercargo and First Mate, gave to Mate Giles
a bundle of papers to conceal. Near the port of New York,
the *Herkimer* was captured by the British warship *Leander*.
On searching the vessel, the British officers found two distinct sets of papers; one set showing the cargo to be the property of Baruso, and another set representing it to be that of
Livingston and the other three Americans. The *Herkimer*
was taken as a prize to Halifax and condemned.

The Maryland Insurance Company refused to pay insurance on the ground that it had insured against loss by capture
warranted American property only.

The conflicting points in the resulting suit were: The insurance company claimed that the basis of the whole trade
with Peru was the fact that Baruso, as a Spanish subject,
had a royal license for the trade; therefore the cargo was
under Spanish, not neutral laws, and, as such, was liable to
seizure and confiscation. On the other hand, Livingston and
Gilchrist contended that Baruso was then residing in New
York, was a neutral, and that the cargo was that of neutrals.

Attorney-General Pinckney set forth: " The concealment

of the papers was unneutral, although the parties were justifiable in using them to protect their illegal trade. . . . But this was not a concealment of innocent papers. It was a concealment of papers tending to prove the property to be belligerent. It increased the suspicions already excited by other circumstances. Baxter was supercargo, and his acts bind the others, although he was a partner. All the partners are affected by the fraud of any one of them. . . .

"This concealment, connected with the other circumstances, justified the condemnation. There were documents showing the property to be in four Americans. Among the concealed papers was a copy of the royal Spanish license authorizing a Spanish subject resident in Boston to import goods into the United States from the Spanish colonies. The adventure appeared to be Spanish. It could only be carried on by a Spaniard.

"There was also concealed another paper of great effect — a power of attorney from Baruso to Baxter, the supercargo, in which Baruso says the cargo 'is laden for me and on my account and risk.' It proved the property to be in Baruso. It calls him a *Spanish merchant*. It showed his *national* character to be belligerent, although he was resident in another country."[25]

Attorney-General Pinckney went on to say that Baruso "was the cloak of the transaction," that there were two sets of documents; that Baxter prevaricated to the British, and that there was nothing left for the British but to condemn the ship and cargo. "Why did he [Baxter] show the neutral papers only? The object was to defeat an acknowledged belligerent right, and he endeavored to deceive the adjudicating court."[26]

Confronted by this strong statement of facts, what did the Supreme Court decide?

[25] IV Cranch, 523–525.
[26] *Ibid.*, 525.

Marshall Decides in Favor of Livingston.

In deciding this case, Chief Justice Marshall turned a somersault, holding, in effect, the precise opposite of what he had held, a few years before, in the case of `M'Ilvaine vs. Coxe. Reversing the Circuit Court's decision, Marshall decided in favor of Livingston and Gilchrist on these grounds: That a Spanish subject who came to the United States at a time of peace between Great Britain and Spain to carry on trade between the United States and the Spanish provinces, under a royal Spanish license, and who continued to reside in the United States, and carried on trade, after the breaking out of war, was *to be* considered an American merchant, even although the trade could be lawfully carried on by a *Spanish subject only.*

A second point in Marshall's decision was that the insurance company ought to have known that the vessel would take all the papers necessary to make the voyage legal — in other words, that deception would be practised.

This case is an example of what clearly appears to be judicial logrolling for the others' interests. Likewise was a case, later on, involving the interests of Associate Justice Gabriel Duvall, who was an extensive Maryland landowner, and closely affiliated with the Carrolls.[27] He had been appointed to the Supreme Court by President Madison, in 1811. Many of Marshall's brothers and relatives were directors of turnpike, ferry and canal companies in Virginia, and Marshall and Justices Washington and Duvall were interested in banks.[28] But how varied otherwise were their total interests, it is not possible to learn.

[27] See, Case of Henry Cassell, Administrator, etc., vs. Charles Carroll of Carrollton, Wheaton's Reports, Supreme Court of the United States, Vol. XI: 134–171. Justice Story decided this case in favor of Carroll. This note appears in Wheaton's Reports, p. 153: " Mr. Justice Duvall, being a landholder in Maryland, did not sit in this cause."

[28] In the case of M'Gruder vs. The Bank of Washington (IX Wheaton, 598), Marshall, Washington and Duvall did not sit.

The High Virginia Court Denounces the Fairfax Decision.

It was fully a year after Story's Fairfax decision before its tremendous import, especially as regarded the enormous constitutional powers asserted and exercised by the Supreme Court, in making that decision, were generally understood. The subject of the recovery or restoration of confiscated estates, or claims to them, had long been a sore and vital one in many States.[29] But the events of the second war with Great Britain more or less subordinated other subjects and agitations in the popular mind, and engrossed public attention.

When, however, in April, 1814, the Supreme Court of Appeals of Virginia defied the mandate of the Supreme Court of the United States in the Fairfax case, and declared that in presuming to pass on appeal upon purely State litigations, the Supreme Court of the United States had usurped powers, there was a commotion. The sight of one exalted court denouncing another was, indeed, unusual.

Point by point the judges of the Supreme Court of Appeals of Virginia in seriatim form exhaustively reviewed the history of the Fairfax litigation, and exposed the legal sophistries that had been employed to recover the estate. But the chief burden of the Virginia court's excoriation of the Supreme Court of the United States was in seeking to show that in even hearing that case after it had been decided adversely to the Fairfax claimants by the highest court in Virginia,

[29] In New York and other States the same chicanery was used as in Virginia. Of this, Governor Tompkins complained to the New York Legislature, in his message, in 1812. " Our treasury," he said, " for upwards of twenty years, has been constantly drained by the discharge of pretended or real demands against confiscated estates." He added that systems theretofore devised by the legislature " have been more or less parried by speculative management or legal ingenuity. . . . It would, perhaps, contribute materially to lessen their amount in future, were you to make void, and punish as fraudulent and criminal speculators upon the State, all direct or indirect purchasers of them " [the confiscated estates] - N. Y. Senate and Assembly Journals, 1812: 6.

the Supreme Court of the United States had exceeded its Constitutional powers.[30] ·The seriatim opinions of the judges of the Supreme Court of Appeals of Virginia were penetrating and unsparing. Knowing, as they did, the entire history of the Fairfax case and John Marshall's purchase of the Fairfax claim, the Virginia judges must have been extremely indignant to invite the contempt of the public for all courts. They knew that the example of one high court denouncing the highest court in the country could not fail to undermine respect for the courts; for if courts themselves disagreed violently, what was the general public to think? But this consideration in nowise deterred the judges of the Virginia court; and each judge concluded his seriatim opinion with these extraordinary pronouncements:

Refuse Obedience to the Supreme Court.

Judge Cabell: "Upon every view of the subject which I have been able to take, I am of the opinion that the writ of error was improvidently allowed, and that this court should decline obedience to the mandate of the Supreme Court of the United States." [31]

Judge Brooks declared that the mandate was issued in violation of the Constitution of the United States, "and that obedience to the mandate ought to be refused." [32]

Judge Roane: "My conclusion consequently is, that everything done in this cause, subsequently to the judgment of reversal by this court is *coram non judice,* unconstitutional and void, and should be entirely disregarded by this court. " [33]

Judge Fleming also denounced the action of the Supreme

---

[30] Munford's Reports (Supreme Court of Appeals of Va.), Vol. IV: 1–59.

[31] *Ibid.,* 16.

[32] *Ibid.,* 25.

[33] *Ibid.,* 54. *Coram non judice* — that is, before a court which was not the proper judge.

Court of the United States, saying that it was in violation of the Constitution and that " it is inexpedient for this court to obey the mandate in question." [34]

This was the collective opinion of the judges of the Supreme Court of Appeals of Virginia, as entered on the records:

" The court is unanimously of the opinion that the appellate power of the Supreme Court of the United States does not extend to this court, under a sound construction of the Constitution of the United States; — that so much of the 25th section of the act of Congress, to establish the judicial courts of the United States, as extends the appellate jurisdiction of the Supreme Court to this court, is not in pursuance of the Constitution of the United States; that the writ of error in this case was improvidently allowed under the authority of that act; and that obedience to its mandate be declined by this court." [35]

Here was an unparalleled situation — a State court refusing obedience to the highest National judicial tribunal. How did the Supreme Court of the United States meet it? Did the Supreme Court hale up the Virginia judges for contempt of court as they would have done had the defiance come from ordinary men? By no means. It neither issued writs for contempt, nor did it even remotely threaten imprisonment. The issue came up before it in 1816, under the form of the case of " Martin, Heir-at-law and Devisee of Fairfax vs. Hunter's Lessee.[36] The question was elaborately argued as to whether the Supreme Court of the United States had acted within its Constitutional power.

Among the legal profession a singular interest was manifested as to just what attitude the Supreme Court would take in reply to the defiance of the Virginia Court of Appeals.

[34] Munford's Reports, Vol. IV: 58.
[35] *Ibid.*, 58–59.
[36] Wheaton's Reports (Supreme Court of the United States), Vol. I: 304–382.

Story Pacifically Reaffirms His Decision.

Justice Story handed down the decision. Instead of castigating the Virginia judges, he urbanely went out of his way to say suave things of them, confining his decision to an argument that the Supreme Court of the United States had acted constitutionally.

" The questions involved in this judgment," he held, " are of great importance and delicacy. Perhaps it is not too much to affirm, that upon their right decision rest some of the most solid principles which have hitherto been supposed to sustain and protect the Constitution. The great respectability, too, of the court whose decisions we are called upon to review, and the entire deference which we entertain for the learning and ability of that court, add much to the difficulty of the task which has so unwelcomely fallen upon us. . . ." [37]

Story decided that the appellate jurisdiction of the United States Supreme Court extended to a final judgment or decree in any suit in the highest court of law or equity of a State, where was drawn into question these points: The validity of a treaty, a statute of the United States, or an authority exercised under the United States, in cases where the decision was against their validity. This jurisdiction, he held, also covered all cases where there was any question of the validity or authority of a State law on the ground of its being repugnant to the Constitution, or to treaties, laws of the United States, etc.

In brief, Story decided the Fairfax suit favorably to the Marshall interests, and then when he was attacked by four judges for having acted unconstitutionally, Story acted as a judge on his own actions and decided that Story acted constitutionally.

In these chapters we have given, for the first time, the origin and history of the noted case, in 1816, of Martin vs.

[37] *Ibid.*, 324.

Hunter's Lessee, which case has ranked, in its assertion of the sovereign powers of the Supreme Court of the United States, as one of the most important in all of that court's annals. But although a multitude of writers and lawyers have cited the 1816 case, it has been reserved for this present work to present the actual facts — facts revealing that it originated in Chief Justice John Marshall's own personal interests, although no doubt, the Supreme Court would inevitably have taken that stand at some other time and in some other case. Those who have read the conventional glowing accounts of Marshall's integrity may be tempted to inquire surprisedly: Can this be so? We answer: These are the facts as they are set forth in the records.

CHAPTER VIII

THE FURTHER COURSE OF THE SUPREME COURT UNDER MARSHALL

From the time of the Fairfax decision to that of Marshall's decease, covering a period of a score of years, four important lines of action were determined by the decisions of the Supreme Court of the United States. These were:

1. The intrenchment of the doctrine that a grant or allowance of privilege to a corporation was an irrevocable vested and perpetual right of property.

2. The extension of the principle of a widening of National authority, and further concentration of power in the National Government.

3. The perpetuation of negro slavery.

4. The validation of vast fraudulent private land claims comprehending millions of acres of land in Florida and in the Louisiana Purchase.

The Meaning of Successive Decisions.

The common belief that the first of these was originally settled by the noted Dartmouth College decision is incorrect. We have seen in detail, how, in the case of Fletcher vs. Peck (that collusive suit for the validation of the act bribed through the Georgia Legislature making a vast grant of 35,000,000 acres), Marshall decided that a legislative act was a contract incapable of annulment by subsequent legislation. That decision was the first precedent. The case of New Jersey vs. Wilson, decided two years later, was the second. This case, admittedly bearing unfailing signs of collusion, was decided likewise by Marshall. He held that in passing a certain act, the Legislature had forever contracted away the right to tax certain private lands. The legislative act, so he decided, was a " contract," and as such came within the scope of that clause in the Constitution prohibiting the impairment of the obligation of contracts.[1]

Thus, a legislative grant or franchise was construed into being the same as a contract between private individuals. In Marbury vs. Madison we have seen Marshall, in the very act of annulling an act passed by Congress, ostentatiously announcing that the Republic was founded on the principle of rule by the people. The vaunted theory was that the people were sovereign, and that legislatures were their plastic representatives to transform their will into law. If the people were sovereign, and legislatures their instruments, there could, according to the logic of that theory, be no limit to the legislative power of revoking any law found to be injurious to the common welfare. But Marshall, while dexterously using that theory as a pretext, demonstrated that the Supreme Court of the United States was the sovereign, omnipotent power.

Interpreted into plain language these decisions meant that the living were to be ruled in perpetuity by the acts of the dead; the skeleton was to have his grip on the animate; the deeds of the rulers of past generations were to be engrafted in the authority of law over all future generations.

It mattered not how much certitude of fraud and bribery in particular, and turpitude in general, lay originally behind definite acts or laws. The moment those laws became officially engrossed and recognized as formally adopted, they were invested with the full sanctity of perpetual law. The essence was nothing; the form was everything.

That laws proved to be engines of fraud and spoliation for

[1] Cranch's Reports, Supreme Court of the United States, Vol. VII: 164.

the benefit of the favored few, and causes of oppression to the mass, was beside the point in the majestic eye of the Law. What if, supposing special acts to have been honestly enacted, they were self-evidently the archaic survivals of bygone times, utterly lacking adaptation to the conditions of the mass of newer generations? These considerations were of no effect; law, which is merely the register of the will of the group or class having the power to enact it, outlasts its creators; long after its authors have moldered in their tombs, and their very names have often become lost in the phantasmagoria of Time, their laws still stand, fresh, awful and commanding.

On examination, there will be found beneath this apparently senseless course, not only acute sense, but a definite policy of self-preservation and development.

Overlooking the special personal interests of the judges, and appraising the vitals of their decisions as applied to the broader question of class interests and conflicts, it will be perceived that those decisions were harmoniously consonant with the varying necessities of the dominant class. A number of aggressive, acquisitive, predacious individuals in one generation seize property, or corruptly get grants and laws endowing them with immense property and mighty privileges. They become founders of a propertied aristocracy. By further laws and predatory schemes, their descendants enlarge their hereditary possessions, extend themselves as capitalists in multifarious ways, and by reason of their wealth, aggrandize themselves as the rulers of the land. They either hold the important political and judicial offices themselves, or they carefully select able instruments upon whom they can unreservedly depend.

The basis of their wealth and power is law, and the advantage taken of each changing condition by law. Their interest obviously requires that those laws be held sacred and perpetual, unless that same self-interest, keeping pace with altering economic conditions, demands the supplanting of certain old, by newer, laws which, in turn, are to be enthroned as sacred and perpetual. The ruling class can afford to take no chances with the vicissitudes of legislation in a country where theoretically the popular will is sovereign. Nor can they tolerate the prospect of being under constant alarm from the ever-present fear of legislation threatening the ancient foundations of their power. In America a theoretical popular representation conflicts, in principle, although not in practice, with capitalist aims. From the beginning, virtually all special plundering laws have been secured by fraud or bribery, or both. That reason alone furnishes sufficiently conclusive grounds for the annulment of those laws by a legislature determined upon revocation. Hence, to declare that a legislative act is a contract, and that no legislature, therefore, has the constitutional power of voiding a contract, is to insure to the capitalist class the permanency of possessions, corruptly gotten.

To this fabric one final finishing touch was needed; this was supplied by the Dartmouth College decision.

The Dartmouth College Case.

Concisely stated, the Dartmouth College case grew out of these circumstances: Dartmouth College, in New Hampshire, had been founded, in the year 1769, by a charter granted by Governor Wentworth, in the name of the Crown. The presidency of the college developed to be a sort of dynasty, the first president, Eleazer Wheelock, having before his death in 1779, appointed his son, John Wheelock, to succeed him. In about the year 1797, opposition to Wheelock manifested itself on the part of members of the board of trustees. A long factional struggle, part religious, and in part political, then set in to get control of the institution; Wheelock was a Presbyterian, his enemies Congregationalists; they were Federalists, and he was driven by force of circumstances into the opposite political camp. As Congregationalism was practically the established State church in New Hampshire, and as the Legislature was Federalist, Wheelock's enemies were able to muster large strength. In 1809, they captured control of the board of trustees, and in 1815 summarily removed him from office.

But, in 1816, the anti-Federalists elected William Plumer as Governor of New Hampshire, and a Legislature of the same political cast. Acts were thereupon passed amending the charter of Dartmouth College. The number of trustees was increased from twelve to twenty-one, and a board of overseers was created for the purpose of exercising a veto power on certain acts of the trustees. The outcome of these legislative acts was the restoration of Wheelock to office, and the placing of his adherents in virtual control. The college was reorganized, and called a university.

The old trustees opposed to Wheelock brought suit in the New Hampshire courts to set aside the legislative acts on these grounds: That those acts were opposed to the general principles of government; that they were contrary to various provisions of the State Constitution; and that they violated the particular clause of the Federal Constitution forbidding legislation impairing the obligation of a contract. The highest New Hampshire court decided against the old trustees on every point.[2] The case was then carried on appeal to the Supreme Court of the United States, but the only point involved in that appeal was that relating to the contract clause in the Constitution of the United States.[3]

Daniel Webster, himself a graduate of Dartmouth College, argued the case for the old trustees before the Supreme Court of the United States. Webster, as we have noted, married, after the death of his first wife, a daughter of Herman LeRoy, whose acquisition, together with William Bayard and others, of large estates that they themselves acknowledged to have

[2] New Hampshire Reports, Vol. I: 111. The full report of the case, containing the arguments, is reprinted in 65 New Hampshire Reports, 473.
[3] Case of Trustees of Dartmouth College vs. Woodward, IV Wheaton, 518.

been originally secured by fraud, has been described in Chapter I. For many years, Webster was the regular attorney for the Bank of the United States, the flagrant corruptions of which are related in this chapter. He became the attorney for the immense fraudulent Mitchell land claim, which was later validated by the Supreme Court of the United States, and the details of which are also narrated in this present chapter. As a corporation lawyer, he was one of the most noted of his day; he was counsel for a large number of miscellaneous corporations.

Did the Supreme Court Become Emotional?

In his biographical work on Webster, Senator Henry Cabot Lodge says that, first of all, Webster adroitly appealed to the partisan prejudices of the Supreme Court. Mr. Lodge tells us that,

" In the midst of all the legal and constitutional arguments, relevant and irrelevant, even in the pathetic appeal which he used so well in behalf of his alma mater, Mr. Webster boldly and yet skillfully introduced the political view of the case. So delicately did he do it that an attentive listener did not realize that he was straying from the field of ' mere reason ' into that of political passion. Here no man could equal him or help him, for here his eloquence had full scope, and on this he relied to arouse Marshall, whom he thoroughly understood. In occasional sentences he pictured his beloved college under the wise rule of Federalists and the Church. He depicted the party assault that was made upon her. He showed the citadel of learning threatened with unholy invasion and falling helplessly into the hands of Jacobins and free thinkers." [4]

Professor Goodrich, a spectator of the scene, wrote (according to Mr. Lodge's quotation) that Webster, in the course of his argument, predicted great disaster for all colleges, and

[4] "Life of Webster" (American Statesmen Series), p. 87.

for the private rights of individuals, if the legislative acts of New Hampshire should be upheld.   Goodrich tells how " in broken words of tenderness," Webster spoke pathetically of his ''tachment to the college, and how Marshall and other Justices were moved to tears.

If these accounts are correct, they throw a singular light upon the Supreme Court of the United States.   Professing to live and move in an exalted atmosphere far above vulgar political currents and emotional considerations; asserting, reasserting and reiterating that sentiment never entered into their deliberations and judgment, here some of them were being swayed by partisan prejudices and upset by emotional appeals. They who assumed the high proud rôle of being austere expounders of the law, unaffected by political passions or sentimental impressions, allowed themselves to be moved like an audience by an actor's skillful pathos.

Where, then, was their boast that their only concern was with the cold business of applying the law?   Cases had been before them revealing that thousands of families had been peremptorily driven from their homes, and reduced to destitution, by the claims and exactions of land jobbers.   But far from causing a moist eye on the indurated Supreme Court bench, those fraudulent claims had been justified and validated.   The hard conditions burdening hundreds of thousands of laborers had never caused the flutter of the eyelid.   The horrors of the slave traffic — abominations which would seem incredible were it not that so many reports attest them — instead of causing anguish, when the facts were frequently before the Supreme Court, were justified and their continuance allowed.   But the prospect of an obscure endowed college, declining into disruption and adversity, so deeply excited their commiseration that they, forsooth, were " moved to tears "!

Those touching accounts, however, have a large element of fiction.   The members of the Supreme Court were too old and too well seasoned not to penetrate acting when they saw it. As an orator, Webster was sonorously rhetorical; and, as was the custom of the day, he artistically, like Pitt, combined elocution with effective dramatic by-play.

The Justices' Class Interests and Views.

But to believe that such transparent artifices influenced any of the members of the Supreme Court would be too far-fetched a reflection upon their intelligence. No such methods had been used in the Fletcher vs. Peck case, yet they had rendered a decision which was the progenitor of the Dartmouth College decision. Methods such as these were not necessary to influence Marshall, Story and other Justices. Marshall's own varied interests were at stake, as well as those of his brothers and relatives, and in a vastly wider degree, those of the whole class represented by him. Story had his bank, the charter of which he had put through while Speaker of the Massachusetts House of Representatives. Many of Story's friends, political associates and former clients, were owners of diverse corporation charters.

In fact, Story made no attempt to conceal his timocratic views that the property interests should dominate government. He openly avowed his opposition to giving the propertyless the right to vote.

This he did, in 1820, when he was a member of the Massachusetts Constitutional Convention. There he made an elaborate argument for a continuing property qualification for voters. Eulogizing the rich, and at the same time minimizing the danger from them, he appealed skillfully to the interests and prejudices of the majority of delegates.

His argument was directed against the proposition to change the basis of the Massachusetts Senate from valuation to that of population. The wealth of "opulent and munificent citizens . . . has spread itself into a thousand channels of charity and public benevolence." It had "reared temples to the service of the most high God," etc., etc. "My dread," he exclaimed, " has never been of the Senate, but of that multitudinous assembly [the insurrectionists] which has been seen within these walls, and may be again if times of political excitement should occur." He pleaded further against " an overwhelming representation " of the propertyless.[5]

This speech, of an intensely class character, gives the clearest evidence of how Justice Story frankly exalted the supreme rights of property.

Similarly, Justice Brockholst Livingston had his ramifications of interests, and so had all of the other Justices. Some writers maintain that Story and Livingston had originally been opposed to deciding in favor of the old trustees of Dartmouth College, but that they had been gained over between the time that the arguments were made and the date of the decision in February, 1819.

In a sense, this might have been so; if so, this point legitimately occurs: Webster was long a powerful figure in the Government. The Merchants' Bank of Salem, of which Story was a director, and later president, secured the lucrative privilege of having large sums of Government money placed on deposit in its treasury. Was this privilege, so long continued, merely an altruistic expression of confidence in the soundness of Story's bank? If Story had exhibited himself so zealous in promoting the Congressional and legal ends of a case involving a vast land grant conclusively proved to have been obtained by fraud and corruption, would he nicely scruple at other matters? Story, as we have seen, wrote before the Fletcher vs. Peck decision, when he was attorney for Peck, that he spent much of his time dining with the Supreme Court judges. Did Webster frequently dine with Story? Shirley says that Webster was busy, through various intermediaries, reaching Chancellor Kent, who was a great friend of Justice Brockholst Livingston, and that Webster, in August, 1818,

[5] " Journal of Debates and Proceedings of the Massachusetts Convention, 1820 ": 283–295.

supplied Story with copies of his argument " to be distributed by him to a portion of the judges." [6]

Property Rights Prodigiously Extended.

When the decision was handed down by Marshall, all of the Justices concurred except Duvall, who dissented without filing an opinion, and Todd, whom illness kept away.

The grand essential of the decision was that corporate charters and franchises were contracts; that they were vested property rights, in no way subject to repeal. This formidable doctrine, representing nothing but the say-so edict of a handful of men, has become, perhaps more than any other single decision, a constituent ingredient of judge-made constitutional law.

What James Wilson, Gouverneur Morris and other promoters of the Bank of North America had begun in the Federal Constitutional Convention of 1787, was now carried to its logical conclusion. From the Dartmouth College decision to the present day, capitalistic corporations have been enabled to expand to a boundless reach of privilege and power. A charter is a distinct property right; being property, the mere legislative franchise right can be capitalized as tangible property. Upon this legislative right vast sums of stock have

---

[6] " Dartmouth College Causes," 201. Webster was an attorney for the Salem Bank, and other local banks.— See, Mass. Reports, Vol. XVII: 39, etc.

The fact of judges owning stock in bank, insurance and other companies was such a notorious scandal, that finally, in 1836, a proposed new Penal Code was suggested. Chancellor Kent wrote to its author: . . . " But I complain more loudly of your restraints on *judges,* at p. 38. You prohibit a judge from receiving *any* gift, except by will, from a stranger. Now I do think this is unjust, and assume an unwarrantable distrust of judicial integrity. At p. 40 you go further, and make it penal for a judge to be a stockholder in a bank or insurance company. I have read this article with surprise. You might as well make it penal for a judge to own houses and lands, or bonds and mortgages, or even a beautiful and accomplished wife," etc., etc.— " American Jurist," Vol. XVI: 365. In the same letter, Kent wrote as to offenses against injuries to property: " I am a friend to personal chastisement and hanging " (p. 370).

been issued, which stock is nothing more or less than a colossal, inexhaustible power of taxing the people on all necessities.

The Powers of the Government Expanded.

Two decisions now enlarged the powers of the National Government.

The first of these, in the case of McCulloh vs. the State of Maryland, was that by which it was decided that Congress had power to charter a national bank. The charter of the first Bank of the United States had expired in 1811. After several years of prodigious lobbying, the promoters of its successor, also called the Bank of the United States, managed to get a charter from Congress. This bank was opened on January 1, 1817; and it was of the Charleston, S. C., branch of this institution that Joseph Johnson, brother of Associate Justice William Johnson, was president from 1818 to 1823.

Benton says that when Nicholas Biddle, long the president of this Bank of the United States, had any communication to make for the influencing of the public mind, he invariably used John Quincy Adams as his intermediary. The means by which the second charter was obtained from Congress were not disclosed in official reports. But it appears from reports made by an investigating committee of Congress, in 1831, that a considerable number of members of Congress had been for years on the payrolls of the bank, and that large sums, under the guise of loans, had been given to editors and others for the influencing of public opinion.[7]

Benton cites a report made by a committee of stockholders of the bank in which the statement was made that when, in 1830, the Bank of the United States began its fight for a re-charter, nearly thirty million dollars, in loans, not of a mercantile character, were made by Biddle.[8] The beneficiaries of

[7] Reports Nos. 460–463. First Session, Twenty-second Congress, 1831.
[8] "Thirty Years in the Senate," Vol. II: 365. Benton was long a powerful politician, and a leader of the Democratic Party.

these loans were, according to Benton, editors, politicians and every approachable person of influence whose vote or voice was useful in the attempt to perpetuate this chartered monopoly. During his tenure of office, Biddle paid out the great sum of $1,018,000, for which no vouchers could be found,[9] and misappropriations by other officers of the bank were common.

Taken by itself, Benton's work might be open to the suspicion of being one-sided, since he wrote retrospectively as an intense partisan opponent of the Bank of the United States, and he had been one of its most bellicose antagonists during the series of years when the question of its chartering or abolition was one of the great political issues.

His statements, however, are not only borne out by the reports of that institution itself, and of committees of Congress, and court records, but even when he makes a general statement such as the securing by the Bank of the United States of a State charter from the Legislature of Pennsylvania, in 1836, by bribery, he states the case correctly, although omitting to give the specific facts. In point of fact, according to the findings of an investigating committee appointed by the Pennsylvania Legislature in 1840, the Bank of the United States had corruptly expended $136,000 in Pennsylvania for a recharter.[10] The fuller details of the continuing corruptions and frauds of the Bank of the United States belong more appropriately to a later chapter of this present work, where they are described at length. That decision, in 1819, confirming the constitutional power of Congress to charter a bank, may serve as a useful precedent in the project, now under way, on the part of the great financial magnates, to establish a Central Bank, with a complete monopoly of the money resources of the United States.

The second case in which the Supreme Court of the United

[9] "Thirty Years in the Senate," Vol. II: 366.
[10] Pa. House Journal, 1842, Vol. II: Appendix, 172–531.

States extended tne authority of the National Government was in an action growing out of the various legislative acts of the New York Legislature [11] granting a steamboat monopoly to Livingston and Fulton. The rights to this monopoly had passed by assignment to one Ogden, who had secured a perpetual injunction in the New York Court of Errors against Gibbons, a competitor and trespasser. In appealing to the Supreme Court of the United States, Gibbons was really fighting the cause of the whole commercial world which demanded that the legal monopoly be abolished.

Chief Justice Marshall in 1824 declared the New York acts void on the ground that they were repugnant to that clause of the Constitution authorizing Congress to regulate commerce among the several States.[12] Coincident with the date of this decision, and as a result of it, was the rise of one of the largest present fortunes in America — the Vanderbilt fortune. Beginning in the steamboat business, Commodore Cornelius Vanderbilt, by a policy of enterprise, extortion and aggressiveness, and a huge system of blackmail,[13] obtained the original millions enabling him later to become a railroad magnate.

Another Livingston Representative Appointed.

That the Livingston family, however, was still a powerful factor in National politics was shown by the appointment of Smith Thompson, of New York, to succeed Brockholst Livingston (whose seat had become vacant in 1823), as an Associate Justice of the Supreme Court of the United States. Thompson had studied law with Chancellor Kent, that noted expounder and defender of the all-pervading and dominating rights of property as opposed to those of human life. Thomp

---

[11] Described in Chapter V.

[12] Case of Gibbons vs. Ogden, IX Wheaton, 1–240.

[13] The full facts are given in the "History of the Great American Fortunes," Vol. II.

son had married into the Livingston family,[14] and during the decades of his career as a politician in New York, he had represented the Livingston family's interests and aims. Thus we see that from the time of the organization of the Supreme Court of the United States, the Livingston family had four direct or related representatives on that bench, in the persons of John Jay, William Paterson, Brockholst Livingston and Smith Thompson. It was virtually a succession of the Livingston dynasty.

Marshall Legalizes the Slave Traffic.

By this time, the question of negro, or chattel, slavery was assuming acute proportions. A case came up before the Supreme Court of the United States, in 1825, which gave that court the opportunity to pronounce slavery a legal institution. This was the case of the *Antelope,* the facts of which were:

A privateer, called the *Columbia,* sailing under a Venezuelan commission, had entered the port of Baltimore in 1819. There, its captain had clandestinely taken on a crew of thirty or forty men. The officers and most of the crew were United States citizens. Proceeding to sea, the captain hoisted the Artegan flag, and renamed the ship, the *Arraganta.*

The ship, fully armed, then went to the coast of Africa to prey upon slavers. Off the coast of Africa, the *Arraganta* captured an American vessel, the *Antelope* from Bristol, Rhode Island, from which ship twenty-five negroes were taken. The *Arraganta* also captured several Portuguese vessels, and a Spanish ship, all filled with negroes torn from Africa. The *Arraganta* and the *Antelope* then sailed together to the coast of Brazil. There the *Arraganta* was wrecked, and her captain and most of the crew were made prisoners. The remainder of the crew, together with the guns and other armament of the *Arraganta,* were transferred to the *Antelope.*

[14] See, Alexander's " A Political History of the State of New York," Vol. I: 155.

Captain John Smith then renamed the *Antelope* the *General Ramirez*. In the hold of this vessel were all of the negroes that had been captured by the privateer, the *Arraganta*.

Smith's object was to sneak into some port and sell the slaves. But while the slaver was hovering near the southern coast of the United States, she was sighted by the U. S. revenue cutter *Dallas*, captured, and taken to the port of Savannah for adjudication. At the time of her capture, about two hundred and eighty slaves were found on board; at least a third more had died from the cruelties of the voyage.

When the ship arrived at Savannah, four different claimants came forward. Both the Portuguese and the Spanish Vice-Consuls claimed the ownership of the negroes. Captain John Smith also put in his claim as having captured them *jure belli*. The fourth claimant was the United States Government, which demanded that they be surrendered because of their having been transported from Africa in violation of the laws of the United States. The Government maintained that they were entitled to their freedom by the laws of nations.

The lower court dismissed Smith's claim; as a matter of fact, Smith was only acting for an American capitalist, engaged in the slave trade, who did not dare avow himself. The claim of the Government was also dismissed, except as to that portion of the negroes which had been originally taken from the *Antelope*. The remainder of the negroes were divided between the Spanish and Portuguese claimants. This was the state of the case when it came up on appeal before the Supreme Court of the United States.

The Doctrine of Acquiescence Again Applied.

Chief Justice Marshall began his decision with his usual concession of regard for public sentiment and proprieties. The slave trade, he said, was abhorrent. That, he went on, " it is contrary to law of nature will scarcely be denied. That every man has a natural right to the fruits of his own labor is generally admitted; and that no other person can rightfully deprive him of those fruits, seems to be the necessary results of this admission.

"But," he went on, with a sudden and incongruous line of reasoning, "from the earliest times war has existed, and war confers rights in which all have acquiesced." The query can here be interjected:' To what war did Marshall refer? The primitive negro tribes of Africa were not warring on any nation; even the most distorted imagination could not conceive the idea of an aboriginal people armed with clubs making war on nations equipped with battleships and other modern implements. What actually was happening was the invasion of Africa by gangs of heavily-armed desperate whites, in the hire of capitalist slave traders, forcibly tearing away helpless negroes to sell them as slaves, if, perchance, they survived the brutal rigors of the long voyage to the slave marts.

Mr. Key, counsel for the Government in this case, had pointed out in his argument, "Slaves are no longer acquired merely by capture in war, or by trade; but free persons are seized and carried off by their traders and their agents. Wars are instigated by them for the mere purpose of making slaves. The persons enslaved are clandestinely brought away, under circumstances of extreme cruelty, aggravated by the necessity of concealment, and smuggled into every country where the cupidity of avarice creates a 'demand for these unhappy victims. . . ."[15] Loaded down with chains, badly fed, huddled together on the slave ships, many of them swept away by disease or cruelty or change of climate — this was the fate of tens of thousands of negroes, snatched from their native land. And this is what Marshall accepted as "war"!

Here, too, we see Marshall justifying the horrors of the slave trade with that identical doctrine of acquiescence that he had advocated, as an attorney, thirty-eight years previously,

[15] Wheaton's Reports, Supreme Court of the United States, Vol. X: 79.

in pleading for the validation of the Fairfax estate, admittedly obtained and held by fraud. " Among the most enlightened nations of antiquity," his *Antelope* decision read on, referring to the rights of victors, " one of these was, that the victor might enslave the vanquished. This, which was the usage of all, could not be pronounced repugnant to the law of nations, which is certainly to be tried by the test of general usage. That which has received the assent of all, must be the law of all."

The trifling circumstance that the enslavement of captives had never received the assent of the captives themselves, was, of course, ignored by the eminent Chief Justice Marshall. According to this doctrine, the assent of those who found slavery profitable became the assent of all, and therefore took position as a law of general usage. Whatever benefited the ruling class became, *ipso facto,* a settled principle of acquiescence. One of the fine theories of law was that anything extorted under duress was illegal and invalid. But Chief Justice Marshall saw no duress in the ravaging, kidnapping and enslavement of a race helpless against the wiles and guns of white slave traders enriching themselves in a harvest of blood, death and agony. In Chief Justice Marshall's exalted mind, this became " acquiescence."

" Slavery, then," Marshall continued, " has its origin in force; but as the world has agreed that it is a legitimate result of force, the state of things which is thus produced by general consent, cannot be pronounced unlawful." [16]

After reverting to the usage of the ruling classes of more savage ages for precedents, Marshall, knowing that these grounds would be fiercely attacked, proceeded ingeniously to qualify himself.

Although, he went on, the old harsh law of war had been exploded, and war was no longer to be considered as giving a right to enslave captives, yet " Africa has not yet adopted

[16] *Ibid.,* 120–121.

these principles." So far as the test of international law went, "it is decidedly in favor of the legality of the trade." For nearly two centuries the slave traffic, he concluded, had been carried on without opposition and without censure. This was a glaring falsehood; nearly all the European nations had begun to outlaw the 'traffic as piracy, and Congress itself had passed laws aimed at the slave traffic.[17] It was to circumvent those very laws that the slave traders placed their final expectations in the Supreme Court of the United States. " A jurist," Marshall ended, " could not say that a practice thus supported was illegal, and that those engaged in it might be punished, either personally or by deprivation of property." [18]

The widening economic conflict between the capitalists of the different sections over slavery, was exactly reflected in the Supreme Court of the United States. In Massachusetts and Rhode Island where cheap, so-called free white labor was used, the owners of the mills, profiting richly, were definitely committed to that system, and more and more were aligning themselves against the expensive, archaic chattel slavery system.

By 1830, according to official statistics reproduced in *Davenport's Gazetteer* for the year 1833, there was not a single slave in Maine, New Hampshire, Vermont and Massachusetts, and very few in other Northern States. But of the entire number of 2,010,436 slaves in the United States in 1830, Virginia had the greatest proportion of any State; it held 469,724 slaves within its borders.

The State of Virginia, in fact, was a negro-raising region for other States. In his " Rise and Fall of the Slave Power in America," Wilson relates that the breeding of slaves in Virginia for the domestic slave traffic became so enormous that in

---

[17] The slave trade was prohibited to American citizens by acts of Congress of 1794, 1800 and March 3, 1819. Each act increased the penalties, finally prescribing capital punishment for violation and conviction.

[18] X Wheaton, 122. Marshall reversed part of the lower court's decision and affirmed other portions.

1836 it was estimated that the number sold from the single State of Virginia was 40,000, yielding a return of $24,000,000. Thus we clearly see Marshall's decisions exactly representing the economic interests of his State and section. He, himself, as we have seen, was a slave owner; he had his agricultural estates, and he owned a large residence which he had built, surrounded by spacious grounds, on Shockhoe Hill, in Richmond. On the other hand, Story's attitude toward negro slavery was generally consonant with that of his native State of Massachusetts, where there were no negro slaves, but certain of the shipowners of which profited from the African slave trade.

Negro slavery, not being profitable, had passed into disuse in the North, although the traffic in ravishing Africa of negroes was extensively carried on by Northern shipowners, and up to the very outbreak of the Civil War, considerable New England, New York and Philadelphia capital was invested in the business of slave procuring. A system allowing the unrestricted exploitation of white men, women and children for fourteen hours every working day in the mills, and paying from $1.75 to $2.00 a week to women, and less to children, presented its superior advantages over the chattel slavery system. That many of the workers were swept to a premature death by disease contracted in the factories, or in foul habitations, or by accidents while plying their trade, entailed no economic loss to the mill owners. Unlike negro slaves, they were not merchandise or property; they did not have to be fed or cared for; no financial loss to the employer was caused by their sickness or death; they could easily be replaced, so long as there was a surplus of labor.

This the South, being an agricultural country, filled with anachronistic views of past ages, and mostly provincial in character, neither understood nor saw, although as far back as the eighteenth century there were a few like Robert Carter, of Virginia, who clearly perceived that the negro slave system could not compete in efficiency or inexpensiveness with white labor. Added to the views growing out of the economic interests of the Northern capitalists, was a sincere agitation for the restriction of slavery or the emancipation of the slave. This movement had no concern with factory interests or profits, but was moral in its nature. Its advocates were impelled by an humanitarian spirit, and were indomitable in preaching it, often coming into collision with an inimical display of mob passion.

The "Plattsburg" Case.

Associate Justice Story faithfully represented the views and interests of men of capital of his section. On all other issues, affecting questions of property, he and Marshall cohered; he (as he admitted) docilely accepted Marshall's lead, and Marshall's construction, not of what law was, but of what the law should be. On the issue of slavery, however, they differed, Story pronouncing himself opposed to negro slavery.

In the case of the *Plattsburg,* Justice Story had his opportunity to express himself. At least, we take his decision on its face value, although the Supreme Court had a way of continuously playing politician, and after handing out a noted decision bound to serve as a leading precedent, would seek to allay strong criticism in various quarters by rendering a radically different decision in another, and less-important, case. Not one of the members of the Supreme Court had been other than a chronic politician; when placed on that high bench most of them were well along in years, and irreclaimably addicted to politics, by nature and choice as well as by interest.

The *Plattsburg* was an American vessel, registered at Baltimore. That city, it may be remarked, was one of the most active of slave traders' centers; capitalists of great standing and large and varied interests were concerned in the traffic;

and their chief attorney, before the Supreme Court of the United States, at this time, was, as we shall see, none other than Roger B. Taney, Marshall's successor as Chief Justice.[19]

The *Plattsburg,* in 1819, cleared the port of Baltimore ostensibly for St. Thomas, West Indies. But she dropped anchor down the Chesapeake Bay, "and afterwards (if the witnesses are to be believed), some grape, cannister and round shot were taken on board, and, on stowing them away, a barrel of irons, or handcuffs, was discovered, which was not contained in the manifest of the cargo." [20] The *Plattsburg* then went to St. Jago de Cuba, where she discharged a cargo that had been taken aboard at Baltimore for the sole purpose of lulling suspicions. From St. Jago de Cuba she sailed straight for Africa, to engage in the slave trade.

Justice Story Denounces Slavery But —

Caught red-handed, the *Plattsburg,* after capture, was condemned at the port of New York. That condemnation Justice Story affirmed. "This," he said (thereby directly contradicting Marshall's assertions in the *Antelope* decision, rendered in the same year), "is not the case of an ordinary trade, where no disguise is necessary or useful. It is the case of a trade prohibited to American citizens under very heavy penalties, penalties which have since been aggravated to the infliction of capital punishment. It is a trade odious in our country, and carries a permanent stain upon the reputation of all who are concerned in it, and is watched by the severest vigilance of the Government. If carried on at all, it must, therefore, be carried on by Americans, under the disguise of foreign flags; and, it is notorious, that in the colonial ports of Spain there is little difficulty in procuring all of the apparatus for the use of the national flag. . . ." [21]

[19] See details in Chapter IX.
[20] X Wheaton, 137.
[21] *Ibid.,* 142–143.

This decision read exceedingly fair, yet the question merely concerned that of condemnation of ship property, and not the punishment of the capitalist promoters. When, only shortly after this, one of the richest and most notorious slave-traders of Baltimore had been indicted, it was Story that, upon Roger B. Taney's plea, set aside the indictment as " fatally defective " on technical grounds.[22]

Spoliation of the National Domain.

The struggle of the slave power to maintain its institutions was accompanied by a corresponding great effort of Southern plantation owners and politicians, allied with Northern capitalists, to seize for their private ownership immense areas of land, both in the original territory of the United States, and in the vast regions acquired by the purchase of Louisiana and the cession of Florida. Side by side with this appropriation, was a like movement on the part of Northern capitalists to get hold of the richest and most valuable areas of public lands in the North, West and Northwest.

Single individuals, or corporate companies of powerful personages, obtained tens of millions of acres of public domain. This was done in either one or both of two ways. One method was to get huge tracts of land by corrupting the land officials to sell them for a trifling sum; in these great frauds nearly every politician of note was involved, either directly or indirectly, some pecuniarily, others as attorneys,

---

[22] See, Chapter IX. These two decisions — those of Marshall and Story — practically extended the fullest license and immunity to the slave traders. Wilson tells in his " Rise and Fall of the Slave Power in America " that the time came when there were at least 100,000 negroes who had been snatched from Africa and sold in the United States and that they were held in bondage despite the plain laws on the subject forbidding the importation of negro slaves. The traffic in slave trading was large and continuous, and the profits were so enormous that the slave traders looked with complacency upon the loss of part of their human cargo. It was cheaper to herd the negroes in foul quarters on the ships and lose some of them than to go to the expense of providing adequate room, shelter and food.

and still others as compliant instruments. The second method was to present private land claims, covering enormous stretches of land, alleged to have been granted by French, British or Spanish governors.

That many of these proved thefts were successful was due largely to decisions of the Supreme Court of the United States. These decisions, in turn, served as commanding precedents in later justifying similar private claim defrauding from the Government of more than 20,000,000 acres of the most valuable lands in California, New Mexico, Colorado and other portions of the territory conquered from Mexico.

Another prefatory significant fact may be mentioned in this place: Just as the first Justices of the Supreme Court of the United States represented the combined old and newer landed interests, so it will be seen presently that the composition of the Supreme Court changed so as consistently to reflect the interests of the three dominant, aggressive sections of the capitalist class fighting at this time either to retain old conditions or to establish in law the objects of their struggle. These three sections were:

1. The triumphant slave-owning aristocracy, keeping its hold on Government until the Civil War.

2. The owners of chartered State banks, opposed to the monopoly of Government deposits held by the Bank of the United States. They came into power with Jackson's election.

3. The private land claim speculators and monopolists bending every effort to have the courts validate their wresting of such vast areas of public land. Closely associated with this section was another section — the individuals or corporations securing immense tracts of public lands by fraudulent legislation or by outright fraud.

A Recital of Some Land Frauds.

With this general prelude, we shall now proceed to narrate the facts as to the private land claims. So profuse, however, are the facts that it will be necessary to present them in as compendious, yet withal, as comprehensive, a form as is possible with so prolific a fund of material. Such an exposition is necessary to an understanding of some extraordinary decisions rendered by the Supreme Court under Marshall and his successors.

The Louisiana Purchase in 1805 added the huge area of 750,000,000 acres to the national domain; in this acquisition was included the entire surface of the present States of Louisiana, Arkansas, Missouri, Iowa, Nebraska, and Oregon, all of Minnesota west of the Missouri River, all of Kansas except a small corner, all of the Dakotas, Montana, Idaho, Washington, Indian Territory, and those portions of Alabama and Mississippi south of the thirty-first parallel. The cession of Florida, by Spain, in 1819, augmented the extent of the public domain by 38,000,000 acres.

The population of the United States, in 1800, was 5,319,762. In 1810, it stood at 7,230,903, and ten years later was nearly 10,000,000. Compared to the enormous extent of public domain, this was an extremely small population.

But much of the accessible area in the East had already been acquired by men and methods described in previous chapters. A certain number of emigrants had drifted to the West, but by far the greatest portion were compelled to remain and congest in the East.[23] While allowing capitalists to get hold of millions of acres, the laws placed the greatest obstacles in the way of the poor.

Until the year 1800, public lands could not be bought in tracts of less than about five thousand acres. A bill authorizing the sale of public lands in alternate half and quarter sections was defeated in the Senate, but a compromise finally

[23] A report of a select committee of the House of Representatives, February 25, 1829, said that the "population of part of the eastern section of our country has nearly reached its highest point; its surplus is filling up New York and tends strongly toward the West." "American State Papers: Public Lands," Vol. VII, Doc. No. 747.

agreed upon permitted the sale in whole and half sections. This concession was of little effect. Gallatin, Secretary of the Treasury, reported to Joseph Nicholson, Chairman of the House Committee on Public Lands, on January 2, 1804, that poor individuals could not purchase less than 360 acres; that in order to become freeholders, they had to pay $160, and become bound for $480 more, payable in four years. If they had no other resources, it was impossible for them to draw means of payment from the produce of the land.[24]   Wages were so low, and money so scarce, that for the average wage laborer to raise a few hundred dollars was an almost insuperable task.   If he borrowed it, he had to pay usurious interest.

On the other hand, politicians and capitalists were able to get unlimited areas of land, either by outright legislative or Congressional gift, or by fraudulent purchase at auction " on credit" from the Government.   Having secured great areas of valuable land, the acquiring capitalists held such parts of it as contained mineral deposits, timber and other resources, and formed corporations to exploit their largess.   Other parts adapted to agriculture were either turned into great farming estates, or were sold in small tracts, to actual settlers, at exorbitant rates.   A Senate Committee, on February 9, 1812, estimated that not less than 30,000,000 acres of uncultivated land in the States and Territories west of the Alleghany Mountains were held by individuals.[25]

It was pointed out in a report at the time that the policy of selling the public lands to the highest bidder resulted in this inequality: That the intending settler had to consider how much his labor would yield him, while the speculator had only to calculate the profits arising from the labor of others, A petition to Congress, in 1814, 'that every person above the

[24] Doc. No. 91, Eighth Congress, First Session.
[25] " American State Papers: Public Lands," Vol. II: 441.   The report does not state the number of individuals.   But that a great part of this vast area was held for speculative purposes is distinctly set forth in the report.

age of eighteen years be allowed to hold 160 acres of public lands, by virtue of settlement, at the price of twelve and a half cents an acre, payable in seven years, without interest, was rejected, on the ground that its adoption would be offering " a bounty to intemperance and imprudence." [26] Congress was filled with land speculators, or their obtrusive attorneys and lobbyists. Denying the right of land to the poor, Congress passed law after law making it easier for capitalist land speculators to buy enormous tracts. By September 30, 1822, " credit purchasers," mostly comprising those non-resident speculators, owed the Government a total of nearly $10,550,-000.[27] Petitions to Congress to pass a law for the selling of the public lands at fifty cents an acre were unavailing.[28]

With the acquisition of Louisiana and Florida fraud was extended to a stupendous degree.

The old settlement laws of Great Britain, Spain and France prescribed various restrictions in the granting of land. The code of laws applying to all of the ultramarine provinces of the Spanish Empire gave to settlers a quantity of lands according to their station, the gentleman's portion being at least five times the peasant's, and the compliance of certain conditions of settlement and cultivation was demanded.[29] Even when large grants were made by corrupt governors, the carrying out of certain specific conditions of settlement was called for. The old French grants in what is now Michigan contained twenty distinct and specific conditions; if they were not fulfilled, forfeiture was declared. Among other provisions, timber and mines did not pass with the grant. If the grantee sold brandy to the Indians, his grant was confiscated. The Government held the prior right of buying his land. Each of these and other conditions were inscribed in the con-

---

[26] " American State Papers: Public Lands," Vol. II: 888-889.
[27] Executive Reports, First Session, Eighteenth Congress, 1824, Report No. 61.
[28] U. S. Senate Docs., 1824-25, No. 25, etc.
[29] See, Book IV, Chapter XII, Collection of the Laws of the Indies.

tract or grant.[30]   The British laws, as we have seen, strictly limited the area in a grant of land to any one individual.

The Forging and Antedating of Land Grants.

As early as 1803, it seems, the industry of forging and antedating land grants was briskly begun in Louisiana.   No doubt, this would not have been done with such assurance and on so great a scale had not the state of affairs in the United States warranted the belief, or at least the hope, that there were good chances of ultimately securing the validation of those spurious grants.   Under the Republic of the United States, virtually no restrictions were placed upon the individual acquisition of large bodies of land; the capitalist could have his own way; and with Congress, the executive departments and the courts long composed of men largely themselves interested in land transactions, fair opportunities were presented of consummating the fraudulent schemes.   It would take some time but it could be done.

A communication dated September 8, 1803, from a Government officer, in Mississippi Territory, to Gallatin, gave warning of what was going on.   Describing the prevalent practices in the newly-acquired Territory of Louisiana, the writer went on: " I have no doubt of the correctness of my information that a vast number of adventurers, many of them from this territory, are daily making extensive surveys, on the west side of the Mississippi; and Spanish officers have lately set up claims to, and are now disposing of, large tracts, some even of sixty miles square, at reduced prices; in some instances, not more than ten cents per acre.

" It seems that the respectable citizens of this territory, who have spurned the nefarious offer, have been invited to a participation in the harvest of iniquity; the inviters alleging that land of the first quality might be obtained for a few cents

[30] See, " American State Papers: Public Lands," Vol. I: 282.   (Doc. No. 126.)

an acre; and respecting titles, as good as may be had (say they) are those by which lands are held on this side of the river.

"A knowledge of former transactions in this territory, during the interval between the treaty of 1795, and evacuation by the Spanish Government, will lead one to an easy solution of the mystery by which this peculation will be veiled. The warrant of survey, the surveyor's certificate, and the final grant, will bear concurrent date, prior to the cession of Louisiana to France.

"I am told that in most, if not all, cases, these surveyors are Spanish subjects, and their assistants and chain carriers Spanish soldiers, who will probably move off with the Spanish Government. I therefore apprehend that for any tribunal hereafter to discriminate between the just and the fraudulent claim will be difficult, even if oral testimony be admitted; but if, to its exclusion, the Spanish record be paramount evidence, impossible." [31]

Another correspondent, in a letter dated September 29, 1803, written from New Orleans to Gallatin, wrote as regarded the territory then called West Florida (forming the gulf lands in what are now parts of Alabama and Mississippi), that "the intendant here, probably foreseeing the cession, has opened a sale, within these few days, for the uninhabited lands in that province; and orders of survey have, I believe, been already issued for three or four hundred thousand acres." The writer went on to say: "No individual thinks of purchasing less than forty to fifty thousand acres, the value of which may be estimated from twelve to twenty-five cents an acre, to be paid by different installments. I presume that, within ten days from this time, orders of survey will be issued for every acre of vacant land in West Florida. . . . ." [32]

[31] "American State Papers: Public Lands," Vol. I: 188. (House Doc. No. 94, Eighth Congress, First Session.)
[32] Ibid., 188–189.

Land Grants to Corpses.

A third communication, dated October 18, 1803, from a United States officer at Kaskaskia,[33] Louisiana Territory, to Gallatin, read:

"You have no guess how the United States are imposed upon by the Spanish officers since they have heard of the cession of Louisiana. Grants are daily making for large tracts of land and dated back; some to men who have been dead fifteen or twenty years, and transferred down to the present holders. These grants are made to Americans, with a reserve of interest to the officer who makes them; within fifteen days the following places have been granted, to-wit: forty-five acres choice of the lead mines, sixty miles from this, heretofore reserved to the Crown of Spain; the iron mine on Wine Creek, with ten thousand acres around it, about eighty miles from this place, and formerly reserved to the Crown of Spain; sixty thousand acres, the common touching St. Louis, heretofore given by the Crown of Spain to the inhabitants of the village (though of doubtful value), and fifteen thousand acres adjoining; and many other grants of ten, fifteen, twenty and thirty thousand acres have been made. I could name persons as well as places." [34]

These and other communications, together with a complaint of the United States Board of Commissioners (appointed to provide for the disposal of lands south of Tennessee), that the poor, actual settler had great difficulty in getting land, were sent by Gallatin to Congress. The Board of Commissioners stated that so many fraudulent claims to large areas of land in former Spanish territories were to be filed, that if testimony in opposition to "those false and fraudulent

[33] This town, one hundred and fifty years ago, was the largest town west of the Alleghanies. To-day a single smokehouse is all that remains of the old French town, and it is expected that even the smokehouse will have disappeared beneath the waters of the Mississippi River, which has swallowed up the rest of the town.

[34] "American State Papers: Public Lands," Vol. I: 189.

claims " were not made, little land would be left to the United States. " The suggestions of the commissioners," Gallatin wrote to Congress at the same time, " on the subject of fraudulent and antedated Spanish grants, seem to deserve particular consideration. It is ascertained, by information received through various and authentic channels, that the same frauds are attempted on a much larger scale in Louisiana. . . ." [35]

A little more than a month later, on February 29, 1804, President Jefferson sent a message to Congress, enclosing a communication from Amos Stoddard, Captain of the U. S. Corps of Artillerists, at Kaskaskia. Stoddard wrote that approximately 200,000 acres of valuable land, including all of the best mines, had been surveyed to various individuals in the course of a few weeks and that the grants had been antedated in the name of the former Spanish Lieutenant Governor. " It is understood," wrote Stoddard, " that each purchaser gives forty dollars for every one hundred or four hundred acres, and that this sum is divided between three persons, the projectors of the speculation." [36]

In view of these disclosures, comprising a very few of the many made at the precise time when the frauds were initiated, the position generally taken later in its decisions by the Supreme Court of the United States, was remarkably significant. This position was that when an order of survey was made, the lands covered by it were, by that very fact, detached from the mass of public lands, and converted into a vested private right.

Forgery on an Immense Scale.

A large variety of four species of alleged grants now turned up in Kaskaskia. One kind of grant was founded on alleged ancient grants from various Governments, or alleged land purchases from the Indians. A second were alleged

---

[35] " American State Papers : Public Lands," Vol. I : 189.
[36] *Ibid.,* 193–194. (Doc. No. 99.)

grants of donations of four hundred acres to each head of a family settling in the country east of the Mississippi River at or after the time of the treaty of 1783 with England. A third sort were grants by courts or military commandants for improving and cultivating land, and a fourth kind were grants for service in the United States militia.

The extent to which fraud was carried in the case of all of these alleged grants was appalling. "To our astonishment," reported the U. S. Commissioners from Kaskaskia, December 1, 1807, to Gallatin, "we find more than seven hundred depositions given there [in Upper Louisiana, now the State of Missouri] to be forgeries; most of these depositions have been given in by persons assuming the names of certain ancient and respectable settlers in this country; by calling them forward (for most of them still reside in Upper Louisiana) we have discovered the truth, but a truth most embarrassing to us; we have been obliged to reject nearly forty claims to four hundred acres each, which we had confirmed to one man on this evidence, and caused to be recorded by our clerk as ultimately decided; our records are everywhere to be altered. Besides, more than two hundred depositions have been given in before this Board by persons who have since acknowledged their falsity; they found themselves entrapped. . . ." [37] The Board said that it had been imposed upon unavoidably, and that only by a slow and cautious comparison of facts, from time to time, had it learned the truth.

Official Collusion.

The ringleaders in these frauds were those notorious land speculators and sharps, John Edgar, J. R. Jones, Robert Reynolds, and Robert and William Morrison. Allied with them was a group of powerful politicians.

In a detailed report, in 1810, the U. S. Commissioners at

[37] *Ibid.,* 590.

Kaskaskia, revealed that Governor St. Clair, of the North-west Territory, had been in collusion with Edgar as early as 1790. In that year St. Clair had lodged with Edgar. St. Clair had confirmed to Edgar an immense number of claims; in one list alone, apart from many other claims, St. Clair had confirmed to Edgar a block of forty-four claims.[38] Claim No. 2208, nominally covering 13,986 acres of land, but really stretched to 30,000 acres, had been confirmed by Governor St. Clair to John Edgar and to the governor's own son, John Murray St. Clair.[39] This claim was predicated upon an alleged grant by Colonel Wilkins, British Commandant of the Illinois Country.

" The truth seems to be," reported the Commissioners, " that Edgar, previous to the issuing of the *patent* (which has never been, as usual, countersigned by the Secretary) employed a certain Daniel McCann, then surveyor under the Governor's appointment (and who from his own letter on our files, we pronounce not to have been more honest than he ought to be), to survey this tract, Knowing, as it seems, the quantity of land meant here to be confirmed, he ran his lines to a certain distance and stopped; Edgar urged him to proceed further; he refused; Edgar then employed a certain Richard Lord, whose name is notorious on our records, to complete the survey; and said McCann was, it seems, afterwards induced to certify it." [40]

The St. Clairs allowed no opportunity to escape them.

Claim No. 2055 alone comprised ninety donation rights, of 400 acres each, to heads of families, or 36,000 acres, confirmed to Edgar by Governor St. Clair. Claim No. 2209, for a league square, had been patented by Governor St. Clair to John Edgar and St. Clair's son, Arthur St. Clair; the title was supposed to be an ancient French concession, but whether it was ever actually thus made was doubtful.[41] These are a

---

[38] " American State Papers: Public Lands," Vol. II: 235–237.
[39] *Ibid.*, 204.   [40] *Ibid.*   [41] *Ibid.*, 203.

few of the many claims, aggregating hundreds of thousands of acres, held by Edgar in collusion with various members of the St. Clair family.

Professional Perjurers Used.

These land jobbers had at their disposal a paid band of desperadoes and perjurers.

In the case of many of Edgar's claims, Augustus Langlois testified as to improvements made in 1784–1785, yet the Commission reported that Langlois must have been only eight or ten years old at that time, and lived in a distant part of the country: Langlois perjured himself in twenty different cases.[42] John Harris likewise had perjured himself in many successive cases for the benefit of the Edgar syndicate in claims confirmed by Governors St. Clair and William Henry Harrison. Another noted perjurer, Johnson Amberson, who had sworn falsely in thirty-three cases, was described by the Commission as a "poor, wandering wretch, equally destitute of morality or character," who had died "in a drunken fit." He had been willing "to testify, on moderate terms, for any man who would pay him for it, and before anybody who would take his testimony. . . ."[43] John Cook, a "Dutchman," had committed perjury in fifteen land-claim cases; he had testified to happenings in certain years, when as a matter of fact he had not left Europe at the time. "We further remark," reported the Commission, "that many of these depositions have been written by John Edgar and other claimants of Kaskaskia, and sent up to said Cook at St. Charles, where they have been signed and attested by him, without the least alteration."[44]

Of Nicholas Révelle, the Commission reported that although he had not been in America long, "yet he has given a great number of depositions at St. Louis, and at ⋅St. Charles, La.,

[42] *Ibid.*, 123.   [43] *Ibid.*   [44] *Ibid.*, 126.

exclusively in favor of large landholders, commencing as
early as 1783–84." [45]   Jean B. Montrieulle gave fifty depositions in favor of the principal land speculators; he acknowledged perjury in a large number of cases.   Joseph Page was
thus described: " This man is a Frenchman, and has been
a great swearer; we have, perhaps, two hundred of his depositions, generally given in favor of the large land jobbers. . . ."   Page had perjured himself in forty-three
cases, and Daniel Thorn in seventeen.[46]   Simon Toiton, clerk of
the Roman Catholic parish Prairie du Chien, probably moved
to confession by the desire for religious absolution, came before the Board and freely admitted having given two hundred
perjured depositions in favor of Edgar, Williams and Robert
Morrison and others.[47]   And so the long list of perjuries ran
on at length.

The Commissioners Escape Assassination.

" In a considerable portion of the cases," the Commissioners reported, " where claims have been supported by perjured
testimony, we have been presented with forged deeds, conveying the claims thus supported.   They amount to a very
great number."   The conclusion of the Commissioners' report shows the dangers of assassination to which honest
officials were exposed.   " We close this melancholy picture
of human depravity, by rendering our devout acknowledg-
ments that, in the awful alternative in which we have been
placed, of either admitting perjured testimony in support
of the claims, or having it turned against our character and
lives, it has, as yet, pleased the Divine Providence which rules

---

[45] " American State Papers: Public Lands," Vol. II: 203.

[46] *Ibid.*, 123–126.

[47] While Edgar and the Morrisons were thus manufacturing evidence
in wholesale, they were petitioning Congress to allow the introduction
of slaves into Illinois. They could not, they complained, hire a laborer
for less than a dollar a day, exclusive of washing, lodging and board-
ing. Their petition was rejected by Congress.— *Ibid.*, Vol. I: 68.

over the affairs of men, to preserve us both from legal murder and private assassination." [48]

A graphic picture this report gives of the widespread frauds and the perils faced by sincere investigators.

Reporting, December 17, 1811, to the House of Representatives on this document, Representative Morrow, Chairman of the Committee on Public Lands, stated that the evidence was conclusive that claims for improvement had been confirmed, where there were no improvements; that alleged ancient grants had been confirmed, although there appeared to be no title made out to the claimant confirmed, which defect, in some instances, had been supplied by forged conveyances; that the Spanish officers from whom the grants were alleged to have emanated not only had no competent authority to make them, but were expressly prohibited from exercising such powers; and that the military bounty certificates, given to the militia serving in the Indian wars had not only been bought up by a few individuals, but the number turned in far exceeded the number of soldiers entitled to them.[49]   Nevertheless, skillful lobbying gradually did its work in successive Congresses composed considerably of men interested in land-grabbing, with the result that great numbers of fraudulent land claims were confirmed.

Spurious Claims in Louisiana.

In southern Louisiana, similar frauds were in process. The rings of land grabbers had their extensive ramifications in Congress and in the executive departments at Washington, and without difficulty secured the passage of two laws allowing land claimants peculiarly favorable conditions under which to submit claims. It is not possible within the scope of this work to present all of the facts embraced in the long report, made on December 30, 1815, by the Register and the

[48] *Ibid.,* 126–127.   [49] *Ibid.,* Vol. II: 257–258.

Receiver of the Land Office, at Opelousas. By way of illustration, a few facts will be given.

Claimants swore that they had cultivated plantations and were heads of families when, in fact, they were only boys at the time. Many claims were presented based on claims either counterfeited or fraudulently obtained. Of certain documents of title presented for confirmation, the Commission said that " it is remarkable that although some of them differ as much as six years in their dates, it is evident from the size and texture of the paper that every sheet must have been taken from the same quire. It is, moreover, very evident that attempts have been made to give these papers an old appearance." [50]

As to claims founded upon requetes approved and sanctioned by Spanish authority, the Commissioners reported that at first they were favorably impressed towards them. " but, in the progress of investigation, it appeared to them singularly remarkable that so many claimants holding requetes should have delayed to make their entries until the passage of the last two laws granting indulgence to claimants. . . . The Register and Receiver, therefore, consider it a duty to recommend the adoption of some measures calculated to investigate this description of title more scrupulously than they have the power of doing. It should be noticed that no means have been afforded *them* of obtaining evidence against claims."

Title papers, the Commissioners further reported, had been kept out of view for the purpose of claiming a larger quantity of land than had been conceded by the Spanish Government. The Commission incorporated in its report a letter written by Judge J. S. Johnston in which the Commission was informed that at Cattahoula, while Judge Johnston was holding court, " a recent and shocking murder there has opened a scene of fraud and perjury of considerable extent, of which it is proper you should be apprised." Judge Johnston said

[50] " American State Papers: Public Lands," Vol. III: 250.

that there existed at that place a regular clique for the commission of great land frauds, and that in a dispute over the spoils, a man named Mecom had been killed and the murderer and his accomplice had escaped.[51]

The Indians Defrauded.

By worrying the Indians with the representation that the United States Government intended to take away their lands, speculators obtained an enormous area from the Appalache tribe on the promise of payment of $3,000.   Neither this sum nor any part of it was paid.

Describing this transaction in detail in a letter, dated January 20, 1814, to Levin Wales, Register of the Land Office at Opelousas, Dr. John Sibley, U. S. Agent of Indian Affairs, at Nachitoches, added:

"I do know that in proving claims before your Board, you have been most egregiously imposed upon, and those who have imposed on you have boasted of their acuteness.   Indeed, there has been so much false swearing to obtain your certificates, that it is doubtful whether truth or falsehood would preponderate were an estimate of both made."   Sibley added this illuminating comment: "I have determined to attempt to have some persons indicted for the false testimony given before you, but it has been so common, and within the knowledge of every grand-juryman, and many of them would not have to search beyond themselves for an instance, that I do not believe any grand jury in this part of the country could be found who would present a person for having proved a claim before your Board, however false it might appear."[52]

Sibley was innocent of the knowledge that Levin Wales himself was interested with the very same men whom Sibley sought to have indicted, in a fraudulent purchase of the same

[51] *Ibid.*
[52] *Ibid.*, 249.

character on Bayou Bœuf.[53]   Levin Wales was, in fact, an old hand at participating in land frauds.[54]   His denunciations of land frauds in Louisiana, while true enough, doubtless were made either with the view of giving himself an appearance of zeal, or of seeking to get hold of certain land, fraudulently obtained by others, for himself and his associates.

The Influence of the Frauds on the Supreme Court.

These details, tedious as they may appear, are vital to a clear understanding of the movements and public life of the period, and of a correct appreciation of subsequent decisions of the Supreme Court of the United States. They were conditions soon leading to the time when scarcely any man could get appointed to the Supreme Court unless he was viewed with favor by the newer land interests or their attorneys, controlling, as they did, the important committees of Congress, and having the President's ear.

Some of the foremost political leaders of both political parties, such as Senator Benton, Senator Judah P. Benjamin, Daniel Webster and others were attorneys for great fraudulent land claims, and some of the foremost capitalists were concerned in the claims to vast areas of land in Louisiana and Florida.

For example, Stephen Girard, a potent factor in the Bank of the United States, and the richest man at one time in the United States, was, together with Edward Livingston, Robert R. Goelet and other capitalists, one of the claimants of the great Bastrop claim, covering twelve leagues square in

[53] It was one of many other such claims confirmed by Congress three years later. (See, *Ibid.*, 276–277.)   Miller and Fulton were the principals in both the Red River and the Bayou Bœuf Indian swindles. They claimed that the Appalache tribe owed them $2,600 for merchandise. This the Appalache chiefs denied, saying that the debt was owed by the Conchatte tribe, who were occupying the Appalache lands by courtesy. The Bayou Bœuf claim was also founded on alleged debts for merchandise.

[54] See, " American State Papers: Public Lands," Vol. I: 150.

Louisiana, purporting to have been given by the Governor of Louisiana in 1796 or 1797.[55]   The Boisdore claim was another of the many private grant claims; alleged to have been given by Governor-General Miro, in 1783, for the purpose of a cow pasture, its claimants contended that it comprised from 100,000 to 400,000 acres [56]— quite a sizable pasture for cattle to roam in.

Great Forged Grants in Florida.

The cession of Florida was accompanied by as glaring frauds as those in Louisiana. Anterior to describing the great case of Mitchell et al. vs. the United States decided by Marshall, in 1835, a relation of these and other facts is necessary.

Negotiations for the cession of Florida to the United States were begun in 1816. Immediately, as had been the case in Louisiana, there was the greatest activity in turning out forged or otherwise fraudulent grants, in anticipation of the transfer of the territory to the United States. General E. K. Call, Assistant United States Attorney General, who later was delegated by the Government to contest alleged private land claims, described this period in his argument in the case of the United States vs. George J. F. Clarke: " The court, will find," he said, " by an examination of the transcript from the archives of East Florida, that there was nearly ten times the quantity of land granted in the year 1817, and from that time until the year 1821, than had been granted previously during the whole period of the occupation of that province by Spain, commencing in the year 1783. . . ." [57]

Many protracted and nauseating scandals developed from the efforts to have the great number of extensive private land

[55] The history and final confirmation of this grant by Congress, in 1854, is related in the chapters on Chief Justice Taney.

[56] See later.

[57] Peters' Reports, Supreme Court of the United States, Vol. VIII: Appendix, 721.

claims confirmed. Alexander Hamilton, one of the three members of the Board of Land Commissioners for East Florida, resigned in disgust in 1824. He accused Floyd, one of the other members of the Commission, of having been employed as counsel in land cases the titles of which were officially under consideration by the Commission.[58]   This charge Floyd denied.

Hamilton also charged Floyd and Blair, the majority members, with having recommended fraudulent grants for confirmation. He informed Crawford, Secretary of the Treasury, that Floyd and Blair had kept the records in an illegal and improper manner; that they refused to examine original papers and records; that they kept on confirming grants notwithstanding the fact that a fraudulent erasure had been made in an important document; and that Floyd and Blair, in defiance of the clear laws, decided that the Spanish governors had been vested with unlimited powers to grant lands.[59]   The Spanish laws, in fact, limited land grants to fifty acres to each head of a family, and twenty-five acres for each child or slave above the age of sixteen years, and fifteen acres for each child or slave between the ages of eight and sixteen years.

Spurious Grants and Fraudulent Surveys.

Hamilton estimated that the fraudulent claims in East Florida alone covered tracts aggregating fully 1,500,000 acres, and that they had actually been surveyed to double that extent.[60]   The surveyor responsible for this was the notorious George J. F. Clarke, surveyor-general under the Spanish government. Clarke's frauds are numerously described in the Government documents. Large numbers of fraudulent claims were confirmed by the Board, although the original grants had never been produced, nor were they to be found

[58] "American State Papers: Public Lands," Vol. IV: 759.
[59] *Ibid.,* Vol. III: 766.
[60] *Ibid.,* 768.

in the office of the keeper of public archives. Of the validity of these grants, there was no proof whatever except the certificate of Thomas de Aguilar, late Secretary of the Spanish Government in Florida. "It is my opinion," wrote Hamilton, "that Congress will not sanction many of the claims recommended for confirmation, but will consider them as fraudulently made in anticipation of the cession of the Floridas to the United States."

Writing to Crawford, Secretary of the Treasury, from St. Augustine, January 24, 1824, Hamilton stated that one of the reasons why he opposed the majority of Commissioners was "because I considered the public interests essentially jeopardized by the admission of claims that in my opinion, *had been made in fraud of the United States, and in direct violations of the provisions of the royal order of* 1815, *in virtue of which they were avowedly made."* [61]

Regarding the claims of John H. McIntosh, Hamilton wrote, May 24, 1824, to Christopher Rankin, Chairman of the House Committee on Public Lands, that he had tried to give the most liberal construction to the most legitimate powers of the former Governors, and to sustain, if possible, the pretensions of the claimants. He added:

"If the objection to confirm the grants had arisen from mere irregularities, and they had been made within any reasonable conformity to the authorities in virtue of which they were avowedly issued, I should, unquestionably, have yielded, if not acquiesced, in the decisions of the majority; but when it was evident that the grossest and most extravagant frauds were attempted to be imposed upon the United States in anticipation of the cession of the Floridas to its sovereignty, I felt imperiously bound to investigate all those grants involved within this character, and all such as, from their extravagance, would bear the least suspicion of forgery." [62]

[61] *Ibid.,* Vol. III: 770.
[62] *Ibid.,* 867. (Doc. No. 413.) The italics are in the original.

These grave charges were supplemented by particulars.

Hamilton further said that "there are strong suspicions that when the floodgates of prodigality were opened, the frauds were not confined to a violation of the ordinary authority, but extended to the charge of forgery in antedating, etc." The minutes of the Commission, he pointed out, proved that under Spanish power previous to the year 1814, there existed a systematic rule in the distribution of the public lands, and that the grants made inconsistent with those restrictions had been issued subsequent to the year 1814, with the exception of perhaps five said to have been issued by White, Governor of Florida, from 1796 to 1811. The old Governors, Hamilton urged, possessed no plenary power to dispose of the public lands. White, said Hamilton, bore an excellent reputation for integrity; therefore the grants said to have been made by him should be investigated carefully. "It has also been proved by the documents herewith annexed," Hamilton continued, "that if Congress were not attempted to be imposed upon, they have at least been kept ignorant of the knowledge of the existence of public papers essentially necessary to a proper understanding of the subject in which the interests of the United States are involved to a value amounting to millions of dollars."[63]

This was Hamilton's version of the issue. On his part, Davis Floyd, writing March 6, 1826, to Richard Rush, Secretary of the Treasury, protested against the criticism of the Board. The business of investigating and exposing frauds and forgeries, he wrote, "would not be popular with persons interested; and that those who were the means of detecting and exposing such nefarious transactions would thereby make themselves enemies, will readily be admitted, and was reasonably expected; that there are cases of a doubtful and suspicious character, and which have been held back by the claimants in the hope that the business might fall into more

[63] "American State Papers: Public Lands," Vol. III: 873.

favorable hands, is confidently believed; and hence a solicitude for a change was calculated on. . . ." [64]

There was one significant fact, however, which none of the Commissioners could deny. In a public advertisement, William Reynolds, Keeper of the Public Archives, offered a reward of $100 for information leading to the conviction of the person who, on or about November 27, 1823, clandestinely placed in Reynolds' office a document purporting to be a memorial and Spanish concession for a grant of 16,000 acres of land, and at the same time stole another document for a few hundred acres, substituting the one for the other. [65]

Considering what was going on in Congress and in the executive department at that very time, Hamilton must have expressed himself in an ironical sense.

The policy of the land jobbers was first to get Congress to confirm small claims exciting no public attention. With these cases as precedents, huge claims would later be rushed through in the closing hours of the sessions. These tactics were commented upon by Senator Hunter, of the Committee on Public Lands, in his report to March 14, 1820, ". . . . In land cases of small amounts," he said, " it had been habitual, and perhaps excusable, for the Committees to lend a favorable ear to claimants. At the worst, it was a donation of a few acres of an unbounded region; a handful from a heap. But experience teaches that these decisions in minor cases are soon cited as precedents, and are made to include principles dangerously vague and indefinite, and are clamorously invoked in aid of subsequent cases of suspicious aspect and enormous magnitude."

This, it may be said, was equally true of the Supreme Court of the United States. Doubtless, it was with the knowledge

---

[64] *Ibid.,* Vol. IV: 758. Both aspects of this controversy are given here. Hamilton's exposures were, however, supported by later Government investigations which showed that he really underestimated the extent of the frauds.

[65] *Ibid.,* Vol. III: 765. (Doc. No. 412.)

that land jobbers or their lobbyists overflowed Congress, that Floyd wrote to Rush that when the Board recommended a claim as valid, " the distinguished liberality of Congress " was depended upon to propel it to final confirmation.

The Enormous Land Grants Claimed.

The assurance and audacity of the claimants to vast tracts of land in Florida were matchless. Without having the slightest proof, except certificates from the notorious Aguilar, they persistently pushed their claims.

The heirs of J. M. Arredondo claimed 40,000 acres, as having been granted by Governor White, in 1811; they could produce no original grant, nor was any paper found in the archives; they had nothing but a certificate from Aguilar. The same was the case with the heirs of F. M. Arredondo, claiming about 306,000 acres of land, under alleged grants by Governor White, in 1809, and 30,000 acres under alleged grants made in 1817. George J. F. Clarke turned up with claims for 22,000 acres of land with nothing but a certificate from Aguilar to prove his claims. Pedro Miranda presented a claim for 368,640 acres, alleged to have been granted by White in 1810; this was denounced as a forgery. Although he could show no original grants, Michael Lozerns, with nothing more than Aguilar's certificate, lay claim to 43,000 acres as having been granted by Governor Coppinger, in 1817.

These were a few of the grants claimed as having been given on the score of " services to the Spanish Government." Only two claims on the whole list were backed by the production of the original grants.[66]

Some sixty-five thousand acres (one of the claims being for 50,000 acres) were claimed as having been granted by White for cultivation and improvement, yet there was no

[66] See, Attorney-General Call's exhaustive report, "American State Papers: Public Lands," Vol. VIII: 250. (Doc. No. 1348.)

proof of either habitation or cultivation.[67]   Claims were put forward for an aggregate of 312,000 acres alleged to have been granted in return for the building of sawmills, " yet the archives of the country furnished no precedent for the confirmation of one of them."   Although these mill grants (if genuine), Call reported further, conveyed only the right to build sawmills on some stream and use the pine trees on the adjacent land five miles square, yet " most of these grants have been surveyed in four or five different tracts, many of them more than one hundred miles distant from each other, covering the best land to be found, instead of the pine forests designated in the grant. . . ."[68]

A Commission, appointed by Crawford, in 1824, to investigate land titles in West Florida, reported that the records had been removed from the country in violation of the solemn stipulation of the treaty; that, among other claims, the papers in the claim of Fernando Yerra, for 25,600 arpents of land[69] were forged, as also in the claim of Magarita Goquet for 10,000 arpents, and in Francisca Zurima's claim to 5,670 arpents.   Giving their specific reasons for believing the papers to be forged, the Commission observed: " It is in grants of the greatest magnitude, and whose titles are made out with unusual exactness, that apprehensions of fraud are to be most seriously entertained.   The poor and limited claimant is very rarely found guilty of this crime. . . ."[70]

The " Innocent Purchaser."

In the prosecution of many of these claims for confirmation, a noticeable feature remarked was the suspiciously large number of cases in which the claims had been transferred three

[67] *Ibid.*

[68] *Ibid.,* 253.

[69] The common arpent contained 40,000 feet, approximately the same as an English acre.

[70] " American State Papers: Public Lands," Vol. IV: 158.

or four times from one holder to another, the conveyances passing within a brief period.

Of these assignments, there 'was a multitude throughout the Louisiana Purchase and in Florida. In his extended and searching analysis of the private land claims [71] Judge Peck, of the United States District Court at St. Louis, wrote that these assignments had been prohibited by the Spanish law.

" The assignments," he said, " were forbidden; they were a violation of the intention of the concession. Their frequency at the close of the Spanish government, furnished evidences of fraud; so many of them being made to the same individuals, is strong evidence of fraud. The same assignees having also large concessions to themselves of which they had not taken possession, and which in many instances appear to have been obtained, with the ostensible view of a possession to be taken at a future day, or a distant or uncertain period, is evidence of fraud. No specific lands being applied for, is evidence of fraud. The concessions with the right to locate parts of the concessions at various places, etc., is evidence of fraud. When we look back to a period of the Spanish government prior to the period to which grants were antedated, no such practice obtains."

The reason impelling those assignments was palpable in the Fletcher vs. Peck case. New England capitalists had successfully pleaded before the Supreme Court that in buying the great Yazoo claim, they had done so in innocence of the fraud and bribery by which the act had been passed. This "innocent purchaser" plea could now be invoked in behalf of the Florida and other land frauds.[72]

---

[71] Doc. No. 1538, " American State Papers: Public Lands," Vol. VIII.

[72] To plead justification under the " innocent purchaser " guise was a common accompaniment of land and other frauds, and was artfully arranged. Thus, Colonel Preston of the Land Office at Little Rock, Arkansas, in acquainting Graham, Commissioner of the General Land Office, with further facts as to the enormous frauds and impositions committed in Arkansas, wrote, on October 10, 1829: ". . . As to the fact that many of these claims have fallen into the hands of inno-

Another suspicious feature of these claims was the defense, when claimants were asked why they had not built mills and made settlements, that Indian hostilities had prevented them. This, as we have seen, was an antique subterfuge; it had been pleaded in the case of the Loyal Company, in Virginia, and with success in the argument in the Supreme Court of the United States to validate the Holland Company's title. Those Supreme Court decisions had pointed the sure way to get judicial confirmations of the most flagrant and most extensive thefts of land, either from Congress or from the Supreme Court itself.

Act after act was passed by Congress either directly opening the way for premeditated frauds, or allowing measures of indulgence for land claims.

In 1815 an innocent-appearing law, called the " New Madrid Act " had been enacted providing that any person who owned land in the country, which land had been materially injured by earthquakes, was authorized to locate a like quantity elsewhere in Missouri and Arkansas. " I will venture to say," reported, in 1823, Thomas Sloo, Jr., Government agent commissioned to examine the land offices in that territory, " that the New Madrid law, as it is termed, had given rise to more frauds and more downright villainy than any law ever passed by the Congress of the United States. . . ." In many instances, Sloo wrote, fraudulent relinquishments had been made, and certificates obtained, by persons who had not the shadow of a claim to the land surrendered. His report went on to detail numerous other great frauds.[73]

cent purchasers, it is worthy of serious consideration, for the greatest efforts have been made to distribute them; but I have no doubt where one is in the hands of an individual entirely deceived, three are in possession of persons who have sufficient reasons to be on their guard. . ."—" American State Papers: Public Lands," Vol. VI: 7.

[73] Ibid., Vol. IV: 47. Report to George Graham, Commissioner of the General Land Office.

John McLean Goes on the Supreme Court.

One of the principal land jobbers in Congress from 1823 to 1829 was William McLean, a representative from Cincinnati. His brother, John, was in Congress from 1812 to 1815, and was Commissioner of the General Land Office, under Monroe's administration.

Significantly, John McLean had studied law at Cincinnati under Arthur St. Clair, son of General St. Clair; of the great land frauds committed both under and by the St. Clairs we have already given an adequate description. Also (although it is an anticipatory fact), it may be added here that three years after the death of his first wife, John McLean, while a Supreme Court Justice, married in 1843 Sarah Bella Garrard, daughter of that same Israel Ludlow who, as Government surveyor, had colluded with Symmes and Dayton in appropriating the site of Cincinnati before they had a patent, and in other land frauds. Ludlow, of course, left a large estate. As for William McLean, he was the most persistent promoter of the various bills by which several million acres of land were given as a donation to Ohio canal companies; he was particularly instrumental in securing the passage of an act donating a Government land subsidy of 500,000 acres for the extension of the Ohio canal from Cincinnati to Cleveland.

" For many years," virtuously reported a select committee of the House, on February 25, 1829, " the public lands were viewed as the great resource of the nation. Its credit was mainly based on this property which was pledged for the payment of the public debts. . . . Within a few years, however, a greater laxity in legislation prevailed. *Claims rejected at the Land Office have been readily allowed by Congress.* . . . and during the session of 1827–1828, Congress actually *gave away,* to States and individuals, not less than *two millions, three hundred thousand acres* of choice lands, comprising a surface equal to that of two of the States, Delaware and Rhode Island, and worth in the market at least three millions of dollars." The committee expressed the hope that its report would " effectually check in the future the *giving away* of this most valuable national property." [74]

In 1830, John McLean was appointed an Associate Judge of the United States to succeed Justice Trimble. In the same year President Jackson also appointed Henry Baldwin an Associate Justice to succeed Justice Bushrod Washington. Baldwin had been a member of Congress from 1817 to 1822, and from that year to 1830 had practiced law at Pittsburg, representing landholders.

Congress Confirms Numerous Claims.

During this period, Congress had been stealthily confirming many private land claims, alleged to be derived from old grants, mainly Spanish and French. Nearly all of these claims had been rejected by the various Boards of Land Commissioners, and for twenty and thirty years had been pushed by industrious promoters, attorneys and lobbyists.

The administrations of Monroe and John Quincy Adams were found to be the auspicious times to get confirmations from Congress. From the organization of the Government to 1828, but chiefly in the Monroe and Adams' administrations, Congress had allowed 7,650,328 acres in settlement of private land claims; of this area 581,884 acres in Mississippi, 966,087 acres in Missouri, and 5,000,000 acres in Louisiana were set apart in satisfaction of private land claims.[75] These numerous claims, while making a formidable aggregate, were not to be compared to the few claims of immense extent validated a little later by decisions of the Supreme Court of the United States.

A hint of the methods used in Congress may be seen in a

[74] " American State Papers: Public Lands," Vol. V: 796.
[75] *Ibid.*, Vol. VI, Doc. No. 747.

memorial of Missouri inhabitants to Congress, in 1828, pro-
testing against the laws being clandestinely enacted for the
benefit of claimants. The prevailing methods, the petitions
complained, gave the claimants opportunity "through their
watchful and persevering agent at Washington to pursue the
same course that the heirs of François Vallee did last year,
and obtain, if possible, a confirmation of their claims at some
unguarded time which might happen toward the end of the
session." [76]

The Board Rejects the Arredondo Claim.

But the partisan factions in Congress, with their eyes on
political advantage, dared not venture to excite public opinion
by confirming certain huge Louisiana and Florida private
land claims. Upon these audacious claims public attention
had long been focused; if they were confirmed that act of itself
would entail the confirmation of any other claims, the issues
involved in which were the same; as a measure of political
tactics, it was then considered extremely unwise to confirm
particular claims that so many Government Boards and officials had denounced as spurious. All that Congress would
undertake was to use indirection in behalf of the spurious
claims; in allowing the claimants to bring suit, it thus gave
their claims a partial recognition. It was to the Supreme
Court that the claimants eagerly looked for final confirmation,
and every exertion was bent in that direction.

The composition of the Board of Land Commissioners for
East Florida had been somewhat changed. In its final report to Congress, in 1828, this Board, while recommending
some claims for confirmation, rejected others of a proved
fraudulent nature. It rejected Francisca Aguilar's claim to
30,000 acres. The claim of J. M. Arredondo to 50,000 acres
and that of F. M. Arredondo to 256,000 acres, were thrown

[76] *Ibid.*, 509–510. The Vallee Claim was the Mine la Motte tract of
27,000 arpents.

out as self-evidently spurious. Likewise was the claim of Peter Miranda to 368,640 acres, bordering on Tampa Bay.

The claimants could not produce a single original deed for any of these and other grants. Their entire case rested upon copies of copies of originals; these copies of copies were certified by Thomas de Aguilar, Secretary of the last Spanish Governor in Florida. The most diligent search on the part of the United States Government officials failed to reveal any originals, or any traces of them, in the archives.

In passing upon the Miranda claim the Board reported that it did not believe that Governor White, *when living,* ever made a grant of twenty thousand acres to any individual, "whatever he may have done since dead." The Board went on to say of the activities of Thomas de Aguilar, "It was over this last office that Thomas de Aguilar presided; it was from this office that so many monstrous grants have emanated; it is from this office that the originals of Thomas de Aguilar's certificates of grants are lost, and it is in this office that the original of the grant before us is to be found." [77]

But who were the real claimants to these vast grants? They were not Spaniards at all; they were Northern capitalists and politicians such as General Jasper Ward who claimed 128,000 acres of the grant said to have been given to F. M Arredondo & Son, and Henry Eckford, a rich New York shipbuilder and politician, who set up a claim to 46,080 acres of the alleged Miranda grant. As for the claims in West Florida, alleged to be derived from the former British government, they totalled more than 1,000,000 acres; all, reported Joseph M. White to President John Quincy Adams, on February 11, 1829, "appear to be entirely unfounded in law or equity." [78]

Of the egregious frauds in the Louisiana Purchase and in

[77] "American State Papers: Public Lands," Vol. VI: 97.
[78] *Ibid.,* Vol. V: 633–634. White was assistant counsel to the Government on Spanish and French ordinances affecting land titles in Florida and other territories.

Florida we have given here the merest suggestive outline of the vast mass of facts embodied in the public archives; the recital of the whole would require several volumes in themselves. Altogether, the private land claims at this time, reached, it was estimated, about 12,000,000 acres. Unable to get their claims recommended by the Land Office, or definitely validated by Congress, corrupt as both were,[79] the promoters of the rejected fraudulent claims now placed their final hopes in the Supreme Court of the United States.

Marshall Validates the Arredondo Claim.

The Government vigorously contested the F. M. Arredondo claim. Deducting certain tracts apparently confirmed to the Arredondos, this disputed claim covered an area of 289,645 acres. It lay largely in the county of Alachua, and its eastern boundaries comprised almost the whole of the northeastern coast of Florida, including Jacksonville and other cities; its center was the site of the present city of Gainesville.

The Superior Court for the Eastern District of Florida, acting upon precedents created by the Supreme Court of the United States, confirmed the claim. The Government then carried the case on appeal to the Supreme Court at Washington.

The Government charged fraud; it argued that the Intendant of Cuba had no authority to make such grants; that the time the grant was alleged to have been made, in 1817, the

[79] Many of the members of Congress, as has been noted, were on the payrolls of the Bank of the United States, and were otherwise profiting from corrupt legislation. Not a few of the members of Congress became millionaires. As for the Land Office, its officials were frequently under fire of charges of corruption. Charges of fraud and corruption against Graham, Commissioner of the General Land Office, and Surveyor George Davis, were brought by Deputy-Surveyor Wilson, in 1827, but were dismissed by the House Committee on Public Lands. (See, "American State Papers: Public Lands," Vol. IV: 922–957.) Graham and Davis retorted by charging that corrupt individuals were behind Wilson.

country was under the jurisdiction of Great Britain; that, even if the grant were genuine, the Arredondos had failed to perform that condition of the grant requiring them to establish two hundred Spanish families within three years from the date of the grant. Finally, the Arredondos (or rather, the American capitalists holding the claim) could produce no original grant; all that they had to show was an alleged *copy of a copy* of the original, which copy was certified by Aguilar.

Chief Justice Marshall decided in January, 1832, that the claim was valid.

Just as in the Yazoo case he had ignored the facts of fraud, notwithstanding that the Grand Jury published testimony containing the confessions of legislators, so here he also decided that there was an absence of proof. Don Onis, who had been commissioned by the King of Spain, in 1816, to negotiate with the American Government, had admitted that the various large claims " were fraudulent and a disgrace to his country." [80] Successive Boards of Land Claim Commissioners, conducting their examinations on the spot, and familiar with the intimate circumstances, had rejected the claim as fraudulent. The General Land Office had refused to pass it, and so had Congress. The extensive corruption of George J. F. Clarke and Aguilar was established and conclusive; many Government officials had detailed the facts, and these facts had neither been disproved nor had their accuracy been challenged.

Chief Justice Marshall and his concurring coadjutors chose not to see the fraud. Had they even countenanced it, they could hardly have reconciled with their validation the vaunted principle of law that fraud vitiated every transaction. Their only recourse was to evade and ignore the actual facts. All that they preferred to see, as in the Yazoo, Holland Company

[80] See, Assistant Attorney-General Call's statement, VIII Peters: Appendix, 721.

and Fairfax cases, was the *official, formal* act; there was the official record that the land had been surveyed, and there was Aguilar's certificate that the copy of a copy of the grant was a copy of the original. Aguilar was a recognized Spanish official, therefore — according to Marshall's logic — his certificate was an official, legitimate attestation. The moment the grant was made, Marshall held, a vested right was conferred.

Those who in the light of the facts herein set forth, desire to see to what lengths judicial sophistry and disingenuousness may be stretched, are respectfully advised to read Marshall's decision in full.[81]

The only dissenting opinion was that of Justice Thompson. The evidence, Thompson protested, showed that in February, 1822, one year after the ratification of the treaty by the United States, two negroes were the only persons who could be found on the whole of the 289,645 acres.

The decision in this case opened the immediate way, then and later, for the validation by the Supreme Court of a very considerable number of claims equally fraudulent, and all of which had been strongly contested by the Government.[82]

The Astor Decision.

This decision, coming during the period when the Supreme Court had rendered a decision in another case causing much public agitation — the Astor case — made the Supreme Court a target for much denunciation.

During the Revolution, a tract comprising 51,012 acres in Putnam County, New York, held by Roger Morris and his wife, Mary, had been confiscated by the State on the ground

[81] See, VI Peters, 689–759. This decision served as a great precedent; it was cited as authority in no less than several hundred subsequent cases.

[82] See, U. S. vs. Segui; U S. vs. Seton; U. S. vs. Sibbald, etc., etc., X Peters, 303–324.

of their being Tories. This land was part of the estate of
Adolphus Phillips, the son of Frederick Phillips, whose career as a promoter of sea piracies and as a bribe-giver, has
been narrated in Chapter I. Mary Morris was a descendant
of Adolphus Phillips. After confiscating the land, the State
sold it to various farmers; by 1809, seven hundred families
were settled on the property which they had greatly improved.

In that year John Jacob Astor learned that there were
grounds in law by which the farmers could be ousted from
possession. These grounds, as Astor was informed, were that
inasmuch as the Morrises had held a life lease only, the
State had no power to confiscate a life lease. The property,
Astor was told, was really owned by the Morris children, to
whom, by the original provisions, it was to revert after their
parents' lease had been extinguished. Astor hunted up the
heirs, and by dissimulation, succeeded in buying up their claim
on payment of $100,000. Astor's lawyers notified the occu-
pying farmers that not they but Astor owned the land with all
its valuable improvements.

A great public uproar resulted, and the Legislature refused
to recognize Astor's claim. But Astor pressed it in the courts,
and it was finally validated by the Supreme Court of the
United States, Justice Story writing the court's opinion. The
State of New York was compelled in 1827 to give Astor
$500,000 in five per cent. stock, specially issued, for the sur-
render of his claim.[83]

An Unaccountable Delay.

Having gone so far in the Arredondo decision, the Supreme
Court of the United States, blissfully oblivious to criticism,

[83] Case of Carver vs. Jackson *ex. dem.* Astor *et al.,* V Peters, 80.
Also Journal of the (N. Y.) Senate, 1815: 216 — Journal of the (N.
Y.) Assembly, 1818: 261, and *Ibid.,* 1819. See, also, " A Statement and
Exposition of the Title of John Jacob Astor to the Lands Purchased
by him from the surviving children of Roger Morris and Mary, his
Wife." New York, 1827.

now proceeded to confirm a large batch of land claims. But in the case of one claim — that of Soulard's Heirs to 10,000 arpents of land, about seventy miles north of St. Louis — a remarkable circumstance developed. Although this case came up, on appeal, in 1830, after the rejection of the claim by the United States District Court at St. Louis, Marshall held it under advisement, and no confirming decision was rendered until nearly *six years later*.

Why this prolonged delay? Was it because of the great sensation that the revelations of frauds in Arkansas and Missouri were making in the public mind?

After both the Board of Land Commissioners and the Superior Court had confirmed a hundred and thirty-one claims, represented by John J. Bowie, the Government came across evidence proving that Bowie had either himself committed, or procured, the forgery of the name of the former Spanish Governor Miro, and that he had suborned the perjuries by which they had been supported. The Superior Court in 1831 found itself compelled to reverse and annul its own judgment. So strong was the evidence, that the Supreme Court of the United States could not do otherwise than sustain the Government. Notwithstanding, the Bowie claimants lobbied in Congress for a confirmation, but failed to get it.[84]

In the District Court at St. Louis Judge Peck had repeatedly exposed and denounced Soulard's frauds. Soulard had been the Surveyor-General of Upper Louisiana under the former Government; in the case of Joseph Wherry et al. vs. the U. S., Judge Peck said that the circumstances " raise the presumption of intentional fraud," implicating Soulard " in whose handwriting the concession proved to be." Soulard

[84] Hampshire's Reports (U. S. Circuit and District Courts) [1820–1856], pp. 123, 127, etc. Also 27 Federal Cases, Case No. 16,216a, in which Judge Johnson describes the great corruption, forgeries and perjuries. Also the Supreme Court's decision in VI Peters, 222. Also, " American State Papers: Public Lands," Vol. VII: 666–669. (Report of House Committee on Public Lands, Feb. 24, 1835.)

had admitted in a letter that his most intimate friends were interested in his surveys, and when called as a witness in St. Louis he had refused to answer all questions as to the antedating of concessions.

Judge Peck declared, with exhibits, that a large number of claims had been antedated, and he detailed how " the fifty-one concessions of eight hundred arpents each, surveyed by the assignees of those in whose favor the concessions were made, are attended with many evidences of fraud." Judge Peck sarcastically commented upon the fact that twenty-four miles of surveys were alleged to have been made on a single day. On the same ground — that the claims were fraudulent in their inception — Judge Peck threw out the claims of Delassus, of August Choteau, and many other claims.[85]

But, in January, 1835, Chief Justice Marshall reversed the lower court and confirmed a number of these claims.

The Delassus claim for a league square in Missouri, and the Choteau claim to a valuable stretch of 1,281 arpents, near the town of St. Louis, were validated. Another Choteau claim for a league square, which claim had been rejected by the

---

[85] " American State Papers: Public Lands," Vol. VI: 226–247. (Doc. No. 874.) Delassus had been the successor of Trudeau, as Governor, at. St. Louis, six years before the cession to the United States. Describing the antedated grants made by Trudeau and Delassus, Judge Peck later wrote:

" While, as I have said, Delassus made his antedated concessions bear date for the most part in 1799 and 1800, for the purpose of covering up matters handsomely, and preserving fair appearances, that no excess should appear to have been committed by him near the close of his official career; Trudeau, his predecessor, in the antedated concessions made by him, after he had left the government, and, of course, not until after the treaty of cession by Spain to France was known, was compelled for different reasons, to make them bear date toward the close of the period of his government, and within about the last three years of it; so that it will be perceived by looking at the concessions of the Spanish government, issued at the post of St. Louis, nine-tenths, possibly near nineteen-twentieths, of the quantity of land conceded during the thirty-three years of the Spanish government was conceded in a little more than four years; conceded neither at the first, nor at the last of the government, but in the years 1797, 1798, 1799, and 1800, and a few of the antedated claims in 1796." " American State Papers: Public Lands," Vol. VIII: 837.

Board of Land Commissioners as " unsupported by actual in-
habitation and cultivation," and which had been declared invalid by the U. S. District Court, at St. Louis, was confirmed
by Marshall.   Who the actual owners of these and other claims
were, the records do not state.   With these and prior decisions as precedents, the Board of Land Commissioners lost no
time in confirming a large number of similar claims.

The Mitchell Claim of 1,200,000 Acres.

The validation of the enormous Mitchell claim, however, was the case conspicuously commanding public attention.

The real promoters of this claim were George Griswold, a
rich New York shipper,[86] and others, combined with other
capitalists and with some of the most noted politicians in the
country.   They later formed the Appalachicola Land Company.   Griswold was subsequently implicated in vast land
frauds in Texas.   The Mitchell claim covered the immense
area of exactly 1,200,000 acres beginning a little west of
Tallahassee, Florida; it included what are now the counties
of Franklin, Wakulla and Liberty, and parts of other counties.
The persons ostensibly bringing the suit were Colin and Robert Mitchell, Benjamin Marshall and others, as the heirs and

[86] Griswold had many ships plying in the East India and China
trade.   He was one of the promoters and original directors of the
Bank of America at a time when, in 1812, a legislative investigation
revealed (as we have before noted) that its charter was obtained by
bribery.   The favors allowed by the government to the shippers in the
East India and China trade, enabling them to reap enormous profits
and use government money as their private capital, aroused the opposition of other shippers.   " Why," wrote the Mercantile Society, of New
York, in 1821, to the House Committee on Manufactures, " should the
merchant engaged in the East India trade, who is the overgrown capitalist, have the extended credit of twelve months in his duties, the
amount of which on one cargo furnishes nearly a sufficient capital for
completing another voyage, before his bonds are payable?"— Reports
of Committees, Second Session, Sixteenth Congress, 1820–21, Vol. I,
Doc. No. 24.

representatives of John McNish, to whom the claim had been conveyed by John Forbes and Company.[87]   This firm had succeeded that of Panton, Leslie and Company.

Panton had been a Tory during the Revolution, and had fled to Florida. There he had gone into the varied business of importing and selling negroes from Africa, and of trading with the Indian tribes. This trade was the usual one of debauching the Indians and then grossly swindling them by charging them extortionate prices for merchandise in exchange for their furs.   It was a trade that elsewhere for many years yielded John Jacob Astor $500,000 a year, and enabled him to corrupt public officials for immunity; on one occasion (in 1817) Lewis Cass, a leading Democratic politician, Secretary of War under Jackson, and later Democratic candidate for the Presidency, received $35,000 from Astor for services not stated.[88]

The firm of Panton, Leslie and Company had pretended claims for $86,000 against the Seminole Indians, and other claims for a large amount against the Choctaws and Chickasaws. After the year 1804 the firm became John Forbes and Company. The Spanish Governor granted to this firm the exclusive privileges of importing goods free of duty, and under certain specified conditions, of trading with the Indians; the court records speak of the great influence the firm had with the Spanish Governor. The firm presented two claims against the Indian tribes, one for debt, the other for alleged depredations on their stores. The result was that John Forbes and Company turned up with two deeds, conveying a total of 1,200,000 acres, near Tallahassee. These deeds, they claimed, were given by the Seminole and Lower Creek Indians, in two

[87] IX Peters, 711.
[88] The full details of this debauching of the Indians are given in the "History of the Great American Fortunes," Vols. I and III. The Secretary of War, at that time, had supreme jurisdiction over the Indian tribes. The records frequently tell of claims trumped up against the Indians.

cessions, and were (so they alleged) confirmed by the Spanish Governor, in 1806.[89]

This pretended transaction, it may be said, was one of the causes of the Seminole uprising, causing much loss of life. No history has yet mentioned the underlying causes of the Seminole War, which, in reality, sprang from such enormities as this.

No Original Deed Produced.

John Forbes and Company sold their claim to the 1,200,000 acres to various American capitalists. The Land Office long refused to recognize the claim, or to have anything to do with it. But after years of lobbying, the promoters succeeded, in 1828, in getting an act passed by Congress authorizing the claimants to institute proceedings in the courts to try the validity of their title.

As in the Arredondo case, the claimants in this case could not produce original papers; they had nothing more than copies of copies, alleged to have been certified by Spanish officials. The Government officials ransacked the Spanish archives, but not a single trace of any original document could be discovered.

The Superior Court, for middle Florida, indignantly rejected the claim as fraudulent, pointing out (among other things) that the water mark of the paper purporting to be that used by the Spanish Governor was extremely suspicious. That the judge would ever detect this, had not been anticipated by the claimants.

The claimants took the case to the Supreme Court of the United States. There, Daniel Webster was one of their attorneys. The Government contended that not the Indians, but the Spanish Government, should have been held to account for indemnity for losses sustained by the firm while trading

[89] "American State Papers: Public Lands," Vol. V: 329-341. (Doc. No. 599.)

under a special and exclusive license from Spain; that the Government had no knowledge of the existence of the firm, or its claims on Spain, or the title on which the suit was founded, and that the deeds were executed by Indians nearly all of whom were residing in the territorial limits of the United States.

The Government further set forth that the cessions were not the genuine acts of the Seminole nation; that no such firm as Panton, Leslie and Company existed at the time of the execution of the deeds — both Panton and Leslie were then dead — and that the Spanish Governor Folch had no power to ratify the cessions, inasmuch as most of the cession was in another province of Florida, and entirely out of his jurisdiction. The genuineness of the deed purporting to convey the grant was also sharply questioned.

The Supreme Court Validates the Claim.

Nevertheless, the Supreme Court of the United States, in January, 1835, reversed the lower court, and validated the whole transaction.

Of the long-continued and widespread defrauding of the Indian tribes, the Supreme Court well knew; scandals were continually coming into the public records and prints.

Only a few years before, in 1825, a great scandal had been caused by the bribery of Creek chiefs, in Georgia, by Government agents to influence them to cede several million acres of their domain in Alabama, and all of their land in Georgia.[90] But assuming that the claims of Panton, Leslie and Company against the Indians were legitimate, and accepting the assertion that the Indians had actually bartered away

[90] Senator Benton, who was Chairman of the Senate Committee on Indian Affairs, at the time, described this corruption, and named the sums, in his " Thirty Years In The Senate," pages 58-60. So enraged were the Creeks at this disposing of their land, that they killed McIntosh and another chief who had signed the treaty.

1,200,000 acres of their possessions, the Supreme Court held that the cessions were valid, having been made at Indian treaties, in the presence of Spanish officers, and with their full approbation.

But what of the paper with the peculiar water mark? Justice Baldwin, who wrote the court's opinion, skipped around that ticklish point by dismissing it as " a subject into which we do not feel at liberty to inquire." Justice Baldwin admitted that the court below had acted correctly in refusing to grant the claimants a commission to take testimony to explain and account for the suspicious water mark, or to permit the reading of ex parte evidence offered to explain it. This refusal, Justice Baldwin acknowledged, was reasonable, " because in an appellate court no new evidence could be taken or received without violating the best-established rules of evidence and law." Justice Baldwin went on to say that the Supreme Court would not say what course it would have taken had the title depended upon the date of the paper denounced by the court below; " as the case is," he concluded, " it is only one of numerous undisputed documents tending to establish the grant, the validity of which is but little, if it could be in any degree, affected by the date of the permission." [91]

In other words, if the document were forged, that was a matter of little consequence. Ordinary reason would judge that if claimants produced one document of a suspicious character, that one fact of itself would discredit all of the other evidence that they produced, however seemingly strong. If forgery was resorted to in the case of one document, was it not likely that perjured and suborned evidence would also be presented? The one implied the other. In common life,

[91] IX Peters, 731. The Supreme Court took the position that every European government had claimed, and exercised, the right of granting lands while those lands were in the occupation of the Indians. The Mitchell decision was followed by other decisions validating alleged Indian conveyances.— See, U. S. vs. Fernandez et al., X Peters, 303, etc.

if a man be detected telling a serious lie, that conduct tends to have a disqualifying effect upon all of his other statements and actions.

But the Supreme Court, with a delicious innocence, accepted all of the evidence as valid.   In this case it did not even have a formally clear record upon which to base its judgment, for the court below had expressly thrown out a crucial document as presumably forged.   And these were the grounds upon which the Supreme Court gave a huge tract of 1,200,000 acres to a handful of absentee capitalists and politicians whose only idea was to dispose of it for their personal profit.

Judge Peck's Severe Criticism.

For its decisions in the Missouri and Florida land cases, the Supreme Court was severely criticised by both Judge Peck and Assistant Attorney-General Call.   Both of their elaborate refutations were published by the Government at length, nor was any attempt made by the Supreme Court to hale them up for contempt.

In his exhaustive review, of December 13, 1835, Judge Peck cited the old Spanish and French land laws, and demonstrated that previous to the year 1796 no concession had been made which exceeded a league square, and that not a single concession had been made during that period, except upon the condition of settlement, with a direct view to cultivation or the raising of cattle.   Judge Peck then proceeded to prove, point by point, how the alleged large concessions, and all of those claimed in reward for services or not made with a direct view to settlement and occupation, were antedated.

"I think it probable," concluded Judge Peck, in describing the specific particulars of the extensive system of forgery, "that at the commencement of this work, the first experiments were on a small scale; but that, as the work progressed, the minds of those concerned were enlarged, and their labors were conducted upon a scale corresponding to that en-

largement of their views. I do not doubt that the instances
are frequent where the same individual has a small, and a
large, concession equally fraudulent, sometimes from the reason above supposed, and sometimes probably because he
wished to have two tickets in the lottery, and draw a smaller
if he should not a larger prize." [92]

Again writing from St. Louis on February 10, 1836, to
Ethan A. Brown, Commissioner of the General Land Office, Judge Peck submitted another exhaustive memorandum
of facts showing the precise circumstances under which the
fraudulent land claims had been forged, and proving why it
was impossible that they could have been genuinely granted.

"Aware," he wrote in part, "of the great authority which
must justly be allowed to the opinions of the highest tribunal
of the nation, and the feeble resistance which the voice of a
single individual opposes to them, I could not hope to sustain an opposing opinion, however strong my conviction of its
soundness, upon any proofs short of those which should be
clear and *convincing*.

"In sustaining my opinions with such proof, my observations have been protracted to a length which I had not fore-
seen; they, however, will be found, as long as they may appear,
to offer to him who is desirous to understand the questions
which belong to an investigation of the Spanish land claims,
the shortest road by which he shall be enabled to arrive at
the truth."   In his preliminary observations Judge Peck wrote,
" I shall offer no apology for controverting the opinions of
the Supreme Court, in an inquiry after truth, when in the
prosecution of inquiry, that controversy becomes necessary." [93]

[92] "American State Papers: Public Lands," Vol. VIII: 807.
[93] It is obviously out of the question, in the scope of this work, to
give even a satisfactorily comprehensive summary of Judge Peck's
very extended examinations of the Spanish land claims. The student
who wishes to consult them in detail is referred to Doc. No. 1538,
"American State Papers: Public Lands," Vol. VIII: pages 797–809,
810–812, etc. Judge Peck's statements included certified transcripts of
Spanish and French records from the old land office at St. Louis.

A singularly suspicious fact of which Judge Peck informed the Commissioner of the General Land Office, was that although his (Judge Peck's) views and opinions and proofs had been forwarded in print, yet the Attorney-General of the United States had not, it appeared, even offered them to the Supreme Court of the United States.   Did this imply collusion with the land forgers on the part of the Attorney-General?   Had certain facts been withheld from the Supreme Court?   This we do not know; but, as we shall see, it was by no means uncommon for Attorneys-General to collude with land claimants for whom, when in Congress or in the private practice of law, they had been attorneys.

General Call Controverts the Supreme Court.

Assistant-Attorney-General Call, who had investigated and defended the Florida land cases for the Government, wrote fully as searching and scathing a criticism of the Supreme Court.   In reply to a resolution passed February 23, 1835, by the House of Representatives, directing a report on the Florida land claims, General Call prepared an elaborate review which he sent to Levi Woodbury, Secretary of the Treasury.   After stating that cases involving nearly a million and a half acres of land in Florida (irrespective of the huge claims already validated by the Supreme Court), had been largely dependent upon the decision in the Mitchell case, General Call then specifically proved how the grants had been either antedated or unlawfully given.   He went on:

".   .   . When we consider the time at which this change occurred — when we consider that Don Onis was commissioned to negotiate with this Government for the cession of Florida, as early as the year 1816, it is a fair presumption, in the absence of any law to sustain these grants, that they were made in anticipation of the transfer of the country, and designed as a fraud on the Government of the United States.

" This, however, in the opinion of the Supreme Court of

the United States, seems to constitute no objection to the validity of these grants. In the case of Clark, 8 Peters, we find the following remark: ' It is stated that the practice of making large concessions commenced with the intention of ceding the Floridas, and these grants have been treated as frauds on the United States.' ' The increased motives for making them have been stated in argument, and their influence cannot be denied. But (say the court) admitting the charge to be *well founded* — admitting the Spanish government was more liberal in its cessions, than before — ought this circumstance to affect bona fide titles to which the United States made no objection? '

" Now, with the most profound respect for the opinion of the Supreme Court of the United States, I cannot admit that the proposition is correctly stated, or that the deduction is properly drawn from the premises.

" There is a vast difference, I conceive, between the liberality of the ' *Spanish Government*,' and the unlawful and unauthorized acts of a Spanish governor, who thinks proper to transcend his power in making grants, because he perceives that the country is about to be transferred to a foreign government. The government of Spain, in the person of the King, possessing sovereign and unbounded power over the royal domain, had an undeniable right, in some instances, to exercise liberality in its disposal. While the governor of a province, acting under fixed and limited rules prescribed by law, could not go beyond the law for the purpose of being liberal, and if he did, all such grants made by him must be absolutely null and void." [94]

The Peculiar Absence of Original Deeds.

Elsewhere, in the logical course of the scrutiny, General Call wrote:

[94] " American State Papers: Public Lands," Vol. VIII: 252.

" You will perceive that, in every case contained in this abstract, where the original title papers are not produced, the
claim is presented under a concession, and not a perfect grant;
and that in every case the copy of the concession offered in
evidence is certified by the same person, Thomas de Aguilar.

" Alvarez states that all the original concessions made by
the governors were deposited in the office of the secretary,
whose duty it was at the time of making the concession to
furnish a certified copy of it for the grantee. That this office was held from 1809 until 1821 by Thomas de Aguilar.
That the original royal or real titles were signed by the governor, and deposited in the office of the escribano or notary
of government, who, in like manner, furnished the grantee
with a certified copy of his grant.

" Now, it is worthy of remark that not a single instance has
occurred in the investigation of the land claims of the country where a claimant has presented a copy of the grant certified by the escribano, in which the original grant was not
found on examination in the public archives; and yet that so
many and such important cases should be presented under the
certified copies given by Thomas de Aguilar, for which no
original can be found.

" It has been attempted to explain this circumstance, by
the fact that the perfect grants or real titles were drawn and
signed on the protocols of the notary, and that they were
afterward bound in books, which rendered them less liable to
be mislaid and lost than the concessions which were merely
tied up in bundles. But it is a fact well known, that two-
thirds of these original complete titles are still remaining in
the sheets on which they are described by the witness to
have been drawn; and the difference in the correspondence
between the originals and the copies from the two offices, can
only be accounted for by the difference in the fidelity and integrity of the two offices by whom the originals were kept,
and the copies certified."

General Call then went on to point out "that the remarkable difference in the quantity of land contained in the real titles given by Governor White, and that contained in the certified copies of concessions, said to have been made by him, is worthy of consideration, and goes far to sustain the belief that there never were any originals in those cases." Call continued:

Why Had the Claims Been Held Back?

"But if these large concessions are genuine — if they were issued in 1794, 1809, 1810 and 1811, according to their respective dates, why, permit me to ask, were they not matured into real titles under the government of Spain? Were these concessions of 256,000 and 368,644 acres of so little importance as to be neglected by the claimants, or were they not sensible of the necessity of having their titles confirmed?

"Some of them, at least, appear to have been sufficiently apprised of this necessity, for we find the same Arredondo and the same Miranda, who now claim under these large concessions, applying for and obtaining confirmations of titles for tracts of four, five, and six hundred acres, so late as the years 1820 and 1821, as will be shown by reference to document marked B. These parties knew full well, that under the laws and ordinances of Spain, and under the practice and usage of that government, the concession, if legal and proper, gave them but the inception of right, and that until consummated by a 'real' title, they could enjoy no permanent estate in the land. Most of them were inhabitants of the town of St. Augustine, the seat of the provincial government, and must have been apprised for several years of the anticipated transfer of the province to the United States.

"From the character of these claims, and the conduct of the claimants, it is difficult to avoid one or two conclusions, both of which are equally fatal to the interest of the parties.

First, that they are spurious, or secondly, that their confirmation was denied by the Spanish authorities. For we cannot believe that individuals holding these large concessions would neglect to apply for their confirmation, at a time when they were soliciting and obtaining perfect titles for small tracts, of so much less importance."

The Mitchell Decision Denounced.

Then proceeding to show how " the grossest frauds on the government may be rendered successful, by concealing or. destroying the originals," General Call went on:

" There are certainly many reasons why these copies should not be received in evidence, until the absence of the originals shall have been satisfactorily accounted for. Until this is done, the rules of evidence forbid them to be received and a departure from those well-known and salutary rules would open a door for fraud, not to be closed, so long as the government has one acre of unappropriated land in Florida.

" What other security, I would ask, can the government have against spurious and pretended claims, than to require the production of the original grant, or that its absence should be satisfactorily accounted for?

" Forgeries may be detected by comparison, and proof of genuine signatures; but as it was the duty and practice of Thomas de Aguilar to give copies of all concessions made by the governor to the claimant, if he has, since the transfer of the country to the United States, been induced to give certified copies of concessions, when there are no originals, what check or control can be placed on his fraudulent designs, and those with whom he may have been associated, than to require that the originals shall be found in the office where the copy professed to have left them, or proof that they once existed there, and that they have since been lost or destroyed?

"In reply to that part of your letter which requires me to state whether, in my opinion, these cases, or any of them, are embraced by the decisions already given by the Supreme Court of the United States; in candor I must say, that as bad as I believe these cases to be, yet I consider the worst of them little inferior in law or equity to most of them already decided by the court; and that the principle settled in the case of Mitchell and others vs. the United States, will, if applied, cover all the objections which can be presented to the confirmation of any of the cases now depending in any of the courts of the Territory, except in those cases where the land is situated within the Indian boundary, on which I shall hereafter offer a few remarks. I consider that the badges of fraud were as strongly developed in the cases of Mitchell and others as they are in the worst of the cases contained in abstract No. 2.

"So far as the question of evidence is involved, there is an exact correspondence between that case and those which depend upon certain copies of concessions.

"In the case of Mitchell and others, the copies on which the suit was founded were taken from copies certified to by Pablo de Lorin, secretary, and Maximilian de Maxent, lieutenant governor, of West Florida. In the cases now depending in court, the copies are certified by Thomas de Aguilar, secretary of the government of East Florida. In both, the certificate states that the original remains in the archives. The archives of East and West Florida, and the archives of Cuba, have been diligently searched, and no original is to be found. In both, the absence of the originals were entirely unaccounted for."

As to the acceptance of these certified copies by the Supreme Court of the United States, as sufficient proof of the originals, General Call wrote: "One would suppose, from the description of these certified copies, thus given by the court, that they were notarial acts, or 'authentic acts'; that they were executed by a notary public, with all the forms and ceremonies; and that they were entitled to all the faith and credit given to such instruments by the civil law. . . . Now it will be shown, by an examination of each, that the originals were not notarial instruments. That they were not written on a notarial protocol, or countersigned by a notary public. Nor was any one of the copies taken from the originals by a notary public, and signed and certified by him as such. On the contrary, they are all, both originals and copies, what are termed in the civil law private acts, and entitled to no faith or credit whatever." [95]

Yet on the sole strength of these alleged copies, the Supreme Court of the United States validated then and eventually the defrauding of 2,711,290 acres of the best lands in Florida, and tens of millions of acres elsewhere.

Death of Chief Justice Marshall.

But when these penetrating criticisms appeared, Chief Justice Marshall was no more. He died on July 6, 1835, aged eighty years.

The funeral ceremonies were impressive, the eulogies imposingly laudatory. The legacy that he bequeathed to the governing class was of incalculable value: precedents established by him have been applied and amplified ever since as organic principles of law and government, and the omnipotent authority of the Supreme Court of the United States, so successfully asserted by him, has not only remained unimpaired, but has been extended even to the point of declaring that while conquered colonies are subject to the authority of the United States, the Constitution does not apply to them.

As a jurist, John Marshall's fame has been overdrawn and lavishly colored. It is in his capacity of judicial dictator that

[95] The above are integral and consistent parts of the whole of General Call's voluminous critical review. The full paper is set forth in Document No. 1348, "American State Papers: Public Lands," Vol. VIII.

he should be noted, and stand supreme; of monarchical and other dictators the world has seen a plenitude, but of the juridical dictator who could at will annul and create law in a supposed republic, the like of John Marshall had never before been known. For thirty-four years he had dispensed his law, the never-varying purpose and end of which was always, and under all circumstances, justification of methods and policies benefiting the governing class of wealth and power.[96]

[96] One of the suggestive expressions of opinion on Marshall's career was that of William Leggett, a founder of the Equal Rights Party and co-editor with William Cullen Bryant of the New York *Evening Post.* When Marshall died, the New York *Evening Post,* on July 28, 1835, published an editorial by Leggett. ". . . Few things," wrote Leggett, "have ever given us more disgust than the fawning, hypocritical and unqualified lamentations which are poured out by the public press on the demise of any conspicuous political opponent. Of the man whom the day before it denounced in terms of the most unmeasured bitterness, let him but shuffle off his mortal coil, and the next day it is loud in indiscriminating, unlimited praise. . . ." Leggett then went on to say that although tribute should be paid to Marshall's many estimable qualities and powers of mind, yet "we cannot but experience joy" that the chief place in the supreme tribunal of the Union would be no longer filled by such a judge as Marshall, and that no grief would be felt "that the cause of aristocracy has lost one of its chief supports."—"A Collection of the Political Writings of William Leggett" (Edition of 1840), Vol. II: 3-7.

CHAPTER IX

THE SUPREME COURT UNDER CHIEF JUSTICE TANEY

With Marshall's death, and with the appointment of his successor, an immediate transformation of the Supreme Court, in one constituent respect, was witnessed. The functions, authorized or self-arrogated, of that tribunal remained the same; the ancient juridical authorities of legal maxims were subjected to no new interpretation; the fundamentals of law continued in force unaltered. The transformation was not one of the character or power of the institution; it was purely one embodying the divergent views, on a particular question, of new members from those held by the old body.

From the organization of the Supreme Court, its incumbents were punctiliously and critically chosen, not primarily because of their knowledge of law, but with the certain anticipation that they would apply law in consonance with the creed and interests of the divisions of the class from which their appointments came. Their selection was not, in the intrinsic sense, a judicial appointment; political considerations alone determined who was to go on the Supreme Court Bench. But politics was not an idle formula, neither was it an inane pastime. It was a definite, virile struggle between classes, or groups of classes, for power; behind the ceaseless reach for power lay the stimuli of mixed personal and class interests. Superficially, those political conflicts were invested with an impressive show of principle or patriotism. But analyzing them, in a large sense, they were nothing less than wars for the perpetuation of the interests of one class, and the suppression of those of another. But while the propertied class, in its entirety, was warring to retain and extend its power, it, at the same time, had its own internal wars which resolved themselves into furious conflicts in the political arena.

Far from being an harmonious, compact whole, the capitalist class was sundered into various contending divisions. Each of these fought, if not for political supremacy, at least for political advantage. On the general issue of government representing the propertied classes, all of these divisions were agreed. All believed in a government the personnel of which recognized, advocated and enforced the superiority of property rights and the preëminent claims of property interests. All were united in holding that government should encourage the development of capital, and all opposed the proposition that government should exercise any solicitude for those incapable of taking care of themselves — meaning the working class.

But united on this point, the capitalist class was in other respects torn by acute dissensions. The native manufacturers arrayed themselves against the native importers, complaining of the privilege allowed to the importers of long-time credit in paying customs dues. By what right, protested the manufacturers, were these "overgrown capitalists" permitted practically to use public funds as their private capital? The importers also profited from free trade or low tariff; the native manufacturers agitated for a high protective tariff. Among the bankers a similar conflict developed. The owners of the State banks fiercely denounced the monopoly of Government deposits held by the Bank of the United States. In 1816, there were two hundred and forty-six of these State chartered banks; by 1837, fully eight hundred were in operation.

State Bank Interests Triumph.

The long struggle for political control of the banking situation resulted in victory for the State banks when Jackson was

elected President. Immense sums of money were expended
by the Bank of the United States in the effort to influence the
Presidential election, but the Jackson forces, by making it
appear that the struggle was one between democracy and the
monied aristocracy, won the support of a large part of the
working class. Yet in fact, as the workers recognized soon
after, the contest was merely one between two capitalist divisions; the State banks had committed abuses and frauds as
great as those of the Bank of the United States; and when
the State banks succeeded in wresting political control from
the Bank of the United States, it simply signified that one set
of capitalists had been deposed to make way for another.

Among the initiated, and even among a considerable section
of the reading public, the prestige of the Supreme Court of
the United States, at this time, was not high. Its decisions
validating land frauds of surprising magnitude had been
freely and incisively criticised. Its political character had
been denounced, and its usurpations vehemently assailed.
President Jackson not only manifested his open contempt for
two of its decisions, but by those self-same acts he proved
that Supreme Court decisions affecting national interests were
not binding and conclusive unless the Executive chose to consider them so. In a case involving the title to certain lands in
Georgia claimed by both the Cherokee tribe and the white settlers, Marshall, in 1832, decided against the white settlers.
"John Marshall," retorted Jackson, "has delivered his opinion, now let us see him enforce it." Which assuredly Marshall could not, since the physical force necessary to support
the Supreme Court's edict could only be supplied by the
Executive. Jackson, in another case, demonstrated how Supreme Court decisions could be reduced to utter sterility.
When in vetoing a bill rechartering the Bank of the United
States, his attention was called to the decision of the Supreme
Court that the power of Congress to charter a national bank
was constitutional, he announced that he would disregard that

decision on the ground that the Supreme Court had no right to dictate to a coördinate branch of government. And he did disregard it.

But while ignoring those decisions Jackson was filling the Supreme Court, as fast as vacancies occurred, with men opposed to the Bank of the United States. He had already appointed McLean and Baldwin; on January 9, 1835, he appointed James Moore Wayne to succeed Justice Johnson. Wayne, who was born in Savannah, Georgia, in 1790, had served in the Georgia Legislature, had been Mayor of Savannah, a State judge, and had been a member of Congress from 1829 to 1835.

The dictum that the Supreme Court of the United States is an institution superior to criticism was not accepted in that era. Judges, lawyers and laymen frequently dissected and exposed its decisions, and attacked its arrogations of power. Nor were they summoned for contempt. Thus, of the numerous criticisms publicly made, it may be advisable to quote here remarks by Robert Rantoul, one of the most prominent, liberal and respected attorneys of the time.[1] These are some extracts from his oration at Scituate, Massachusetts, July 4, 1836:

". . . Why is an ex post facto law, passed by the Legislature, unjust, unconstitutional and void, while Judge-made law, which, from its nature, must always be ex post facto, is not only to be obeyed, but applauded? Is it because Judge-made law is essentially aristocratical? . . .

---

[1] At the instigation of the boot and shoe manufacturers, the officials of Boston brought an action against the Boston Journeymen Bootmakers' Society, on the ground that it was a conspiracy. The lower court ruled against the union, and the jury returned a verdict of guilty. But on appeal in the Supreme Court of Massachusetts, Rantoul, by an able argument, had that verdict reversed. He successfully argued that the old English law of the time of Queen Elizabeth, making it a criminal offense to refuse to work for certain wages had not been specifically adopted as common law in the United States after the Revolution.— See, Metcalf's Reports (Supreme Court of Mass.), Vol. IV: iii.

"Judge-made law is ex post facto law, and therefore unjust. An act is not forbidden by the Statute law, but it becomes, by judicial decision, a crime. A contract is intended, and supposed to be, valid, but it becomes void by judicial construction. The Legislature could not effect this, for the Constitution forbids it. The Judiciary shall not usurp legislative power, says the Bill of Rights; yet it not only usurps, but runs riot beyond the confines of legislative power.

"Judge-made law is special legislation. The judge is human, and feels the bias which the coloring of the particular case gives. If he wishes to decide the next case differently, he has only to *distinguish,* and thereby make a new law. . . ." [2]

If this was revealing the secret springs of the judicial mechanism, it was only disclosing what the judges were themselves publishing by their own acts.

Roger B. Taney's Career.

President Jackson appointed Roger B. Taney, of Maryland, as Chief Justice to succeed Marshall. As an attorney and office holder, Taney had been associated with all three of the dominant divisions of the ruling class — the slave power, the State banks, and the cliques of land appropriators and speculators. By interest as well as by bias his support of all three was assured. But considerable religious prejudice was displayed against him, because of his Roman Catholic faith.

He was born in the year 1777. "My father, Michael Taney," he wrote, "owned a good landed estate, on which he always resided, and slaves." His father's plantation was on the banks of the Patuxent River, in Maryland. "My mother," he went on, "was the daughter of Roger Brooke, who owned a large landed estate on Battel Creek, directly

[2] "American Jurist," Vol. XVI: 229-230.

opposite to that which belonged to my father." [3]   Admitted to the bar in 1799, Taney was elected to the Maryland Legislature, in which he served a year. His marriage, in 1806, to Anne Key, a sister of Francis Scott Key, enlarged his circle of influential connections; Taney and Key had been law students together at Annapolis, and Mrs. Key's sister was the wife of Judge Nicholson, Chief Justice of the Baltimore Court, and one of the Judges of the Court of Appeals of Maryland. In 1816, Taney was elected to the Maryland Senate, and in 1827 Attorney-General of Maryland.

Both Taney and his brother-in-law were personally interested in State banks, and were attorneys for them. Key represented the Bank of Columbia, the Bank of the Metropolis of Washington, and other banks. [4] Taney was one of the principal owners of the Frederick County Bank. "He was, for years," says Tyler, "a director in the Frederick County Bank, and hardly ever missed a meeting of the board of directors." [5]

Taney was also not only a considerable stockholder in the Union Bank of Maryland — one of the largest banks in the State — but also was attorney for the bank, and for its chief owners individually. His interest in that bank caused a lively scandal later, when, as Secretary of the Treasury, Taney favored it by having Government funds deposited with it. His appearing in court, as an attorney for the Union Bank of Maryland, was frequent. Taney also was attorney for the Baltimore Equitable Society, and other corporations. [6] His practice was wholly one of representing large banking and insurance corporations, powerful landholders such as Charles

[3] So Taney wrote in a biography of himself for use as a prefatory memoir in Tyler's "Memoir of Taney" (Edition of 1872), pp. 21–22. Tyler, for many years up to Chief Justice Taney's death, was Taney's confidential man, and was selected by Taney to write his biography.

[4] See, I Harris and Gill's Reports, 236–242; I Peters, 459, etc.

[5] "Memoir of Taney," 102.

[6] See, I Harris and Gill's Reports, 191, 295, etc.

Carroll, and shippers and other capitalists of wide corporate interests.

The large landholders, slave owners and capitalists of Maryland had early associated together in lobbying bills through the Legislature incorporating them as owners of bank, insurance and other charters. As early as 1795, Charles Carroll, Solomon Etting, Andrew Buchanan and others had obtained a charter for the Marine Insurance Company, with an allowed capital of $300,000.[7] On January 12, 1805, Etting and associates had secured a charter for the Union Bank of Maryland, with an empowered capital of $3,000,000. These men were indefatigable promoters of various schemes and corporations; among other enterprises they obtained charters for turnpike companies, and a charter, in 1816, for the Baltimore Improvement Company, with a capital of $500,000, to make public improvements of one kind or another in the city of Baltimore.[8]

Taney was Etting's attorney in the higher courts. In one case, where he appeared for Etting, in the Supreme Court of the United States, in 1826, the facts developed must have been of exceeding interest to the members of the Supreme Court. In 1819, the very year in which they had declared the Bank of the United States a good and Constitutional institution, McCullough, the cashier of the Branch of that Bank at Baltimore, had, in collusion with other officials of the bank, stolen (the court records say "misapplied") the modest sum of $3,497,700. In the settlement with the directors of the Bank of the United States, a part of the security offered by McCullough were indorsements by sixteen merchants of Baltimore, who individually bound themselves for $12,500 each. Among these merchants was Etting. He refused to pay his bond on the ground that he had indorsed

[7] "Laws of Maryland," Vol. II, Chapter 59.
[8] *Ibid.*, 1816–1818: p. 215, etc. (Chap. 260.)

without knowledge of McCullough's thefts. The decision went against him.[9]

At the same time Taney was one of the attorneys arguing, in the Supreme Court, for the interests of Charles Carroll of Carrollton. It was an action brought against Carroll by the administrator of Louisa Browning, a demented daughter of Lord Charles Baltimore. The father of Charles Carroll had received, in 1711, from Lord Baltimore (great grandfather of Louisa Browning), a grant of a tract of ten thousand acres of land, in consideration of a yearly quit rent of £100 sterling in silver and gold. Louisa Browning's administrator sued to recover the amount of these quit rents. Justice Story decided the action in favor of Carroll, on the ground that, in 1780, the Legislature of Maryland had abolished quit rents.[10] So too, it may be remarked, had the Legislature of Virginia confiscated alien estates, but that had not prevented John Marshall from getting the Fairfax estate, by force of Justice Story's own decision in the noted case of Fairfax's Devisee vs. Hunter.

His Defense of the Slave Trader, Gooding.

One of the most noteworthy of Taney's cases was his successful defense in the indictment of the slave trader, John Gooding.

Baltimore, as we have said, was one of the most active ports in the business of fitting out ships for the slave traffic, and of those engaged in slave snatching, Gooding was one of the most conspicuous and avaricious. For many years Gooding had been promoting various illegal undertakings. He was, for instance, one of the leading spirits in the Baltimore

[9] Wheaton's Reports, Supreme Court of the United States, Vol. XI: 59.
[10] XI Wheaton, 134–171. It was in this case (as heretofore noted) that Justice Duvall did not sit, because, as he indited on the records, he was a landowner in Maryland.

Mexican Company, organized in 1816, to supply General Mina of Mexico with the means to fit out an expedition for the purpose of driving the Spanish from control of Mexico. The financing of General Mina was, in itself, a good undertaking, but no high purpose animated Gooding and his associates; they were solely concerned with deriving an enormous percentage on their investment, if General Mina succeeded. But the attempt against Spain was a failure, and Mina perished with it. Although the acts of the Baltimore Mexican Company were admittedly a violation of the neutrality laws, yet after Mexico had achieved its independence the company made a claim for approximately $355,000, only a part of which they had actually advanced. This was one of the fraudulent claims adjusted and paid by the Convention between Mexico and the United States in 1839, and validated by a Supreme Court decision in 1860.[11]

Gooding was indicted in 1824 at Baltimore, for having violated the Slave Trade Act, of 1818. The indictment charged Gooding with having fitted out vessels called the *General Winder* and the *Pocahontas* as slavers to kidnap negroes in Africa, and sell them in Cuba. The Government produced evidence proving that Gooding had hired Captain John Hill to take command of the *General Winder,* and that Hill " ordered various fitments some of which were peculiarly adapted for the slave trade, and are never put on board any other vessels than those intended for such trade." These chains and other apparatus were taken on board at St. Thomas, West Indies. The *General Winder* brought back two hundred and ninety negroes from Africa.

Taney and Mitchell, attorneys for Gooding, appealed to the Supreme Court of the United States to dismiss the indictment. They made no serious effort to attack the complete chain of evidence. Although they tried to have certain evi-

[11] Howard's Reports (Supreme Court of the United States), Vol. XXIV: 319.

dence excluded, yet their main arguments were entirely confined to advancing seven technical objections to the counts in the indictment. That Gooding's guilt was proved by the evidence was clear. It was equally plain that on the merits of the case they could not get him free. They, therefore, with specious arguments concentrated their assault on the technical wording of the indictment.

In delivering the court's decision Justice Story opened with a significant warning. "We take this opportunity," he said in his decision in 1827, "of expressing our anxiety lest by too great indulgence to the wishes of counsel, questions of this sort should be frequently brought before this court, and thus, in effect, an appeal in criminal cases become an ordinary proceeding, to the manifest obstruction of public justice, and against the plain intendment of the acts of Congress." This was a clear enough intimation.

Certain evidence that Taney and Mitchell sought to have excluded Justice Story declared admissible. And, so far as an agent doing a thing was concerned, Story continued, "It is the known and familiar principle of criminal jurisprudence that he who commands, or procures, a crime to be done, is guilty of the crime, and the act is his act." The owner did not have to be personally present. Nor was it essential, as Taney had argued, that to constitute a fitting-out, every equipment necessary for a slave voyage should be taken on board. Neither was it necessary, Story said further, to specify the particulars of the fitting out.

The Indictment "Fatally Defective."

But, Story decided, the indictment was "fatally defective" in not averring that the vessel was fitted out or sent *from within the jurisdiction of the United States,* and that the averment in the indictment, "with the intent that the said vessel *should be employed* in the slave trade," was also "fatally defective" inasmuch as the Slave Trade Act of Congress read, "with intent to *employ*" etc.[12]

This decision was received with the profoundest disquietude by the opponents of slavery. Deeply shocked by the revolting horrors of the slave traffic, they had long sought to implant fear in those engaged in it by having some of its leaders consigned to exemplary punishment. And now they found themselves balked by quibbles and twistings and fine-drawn technicalities; now they saw the highest court in the land, while admitting the guilt of one of the most notorious slave traders to be fully proved, yet at the same time granting immunity because the wording of the indictment did not suit fastidious judicial requirements. They agitated bitterly that whatever were the *professions* of the Supreme Court, the *practical effect* of its decisions was not only to legalize chattel slavery, but to extend a full and authoritative license to the slave traders to continue their horrid traffic undeterred by prospect of personal punishment.

Among those opposed to the extension of chattel slavery, or favoring the emancipation of the slaves, Taney's successful plea for Gooding[13] was looked upon as a discreditable and disgraceful piece of pettifoggery. But the view of the slave holders and slave traders was exactly the reverse. They conceived the highest regard for Taney's adroitness and sharp capacity. His success in this case was one of the reasons that caused them to push him forward later for Attorney-General of the United States, Secretary of the Treasury, and then for the Chief Justiceship of the Supreme Court of the United States.

[12] Case of U. S. vs. Gooding, XII Wheaton, 460-468.
[13] Gooding (for some reason not now discoverable) went insolvent in 1829. But his creditors, by virtue of a decision, in 1860, of the Supreme Court under Chief Justice Taney, secured that court's approval of the legality of the Baltimore Mexican Company's claim, notwithstanding it was made in admitted violation of the neutrality laws. Gooding's creditors received the sum of $39,381.82, that being the one-ninth share arising from Gooding's interest in the company.

The Case of the " Warren."

Another·case defended by Taney and having its own peculiar aspects, was the action of James Sheppard and others
against Lemuel Taylor, James A. Buchanan, John Hollins and
others, nearly all of whom were incorporators and directors
of the Union Bank of Maryland. This fact explained
Taney's appearance as one of the attorneys for Taylor et al.

Compactly put, the facts of this case, as narrated in the
court records, were as follows:

On September 12, 1806, the ship *Warren*, six hundred tons,
armed with twenty-two guns, sailed from Baltimore with a
crew of one hundred and twelve officers, seamen and apprentices, and a cargo valued at $300,000. The ostensible voyage,
as set forth in the shipping articles, was to the northwest
coast of America, thence to Canton, and back to the United
States. Two sets of instructions were given by Taylor,
Buchanan, Hollins and the other owners — one the nominal
set to Captain Sterrett; the other private and confidential, to
Supercargo Pollock, who was the only person aboard knowing the real purpose and destination of the voyage.

Upon arriving at a certain latitude, the real set of instructions was opened, and the Captain was thus informed that
Supercargo Pollock was to have entire control of the voyage.
The account in the records of the Supreme Court of the
United States goes on to say that from that time the ship
" proceeded directly for the coast of Chili, to prosecute an
illegal and smuggling trade with the Spanish provinces, on
the western coast of South America; all trade within those
provinces being notoriously forbidden, under heavy penalties,
unless conducted under a license from the crown of Spain.

" The officers and crew of the *Warren* protested against
this deviation from the prescribed voyage; and Captain Sterrett, from disappointed and wounded feelings, disdaining to engage in an illicit trade, and unwilling to expose his officers and

men to its perils and consequences, became partially deranged, and shot himself as the *Warren* was doubling Cape Horn." [14]

Chief Mate Evans succeeded in nominal command, but Pollock kept control, and steered the ship for Conception Bay, Chili, where she arrived, after a voyage of one hundred and twenty days from Baltimore. At Conception Bay, Pollock went on shore to arrange matters with the Spanish officials. During his absence Captain Evans and the commanders of the Spanish men-of-war fell into a dispute; some shots were exchanged,' but no lives were lost. The crew remonstrated against the illegal traffic into which they were forced, and proposed to proceed with the ship on the voyage for which they had contracted, leaving Pollock ashore. Captain Evans refused to enter the port without a written order; this was sent to him and the *Warren* sailed into the port of Talcahuana.

Pollock, meanwhile, had been acting in collusion with the Spanish officials. Furious at the mutinous conduct of the crew he planned retaliation, which he accomplished in this wise: As soon as Captain Evans went ashore, the seamen, twenty at a time, were taken on land under a pretense that their depositions were required relative to the death of Captain Sterrett. The moment the seamen set foot on shore they were seized and put in prison. The officers and apprentices proposed to rescue the *Warren* and informed Pollock of their purpose. They did not know that Pollock and the Spanish officials were acting together. As soon as Pollock heard of their intention he had his and Evans' baggage conveyed ashore and Spanish officers took off the ship's rudder and otherwise disabled her from sailing. The officers and apprentices of the *Warren* were arrested; then officers and crew "were ordered to Conception, and thence were marched to various prisons and dungeons, and suffered captivity from eight months to four years, being permitted to return to the

[14] V Peters, 676–677.

United States at various periods. The apprentices and some
of the officers were the first to return; their absence from the
United States was after an imprisonment of from six to
eighteen months." [15]

The officers and seamen in bringing, in 1810, an action for
their wages, contended that by agreements between the Spanish Commandant and Pollock, the cargo was smuggled ashore,
and that by order of the Spanish court, the vessel and cargo
were sold and the proceeds were ordered deposited in the
king's treasury, subject to an appeal by Pollock. The years
dragged on, while the Spanish red tape unwound. In 1819,
all of the owners of the *Warren* curiously became insolvent,
and presently assigned their claims, part going to Robert
Oliver, part to the Branch of the Bank of the United States
at Baltimore, and another part to the Union Bank of Maryland at Baltimore. But, as a matter of fact, these assignments were held in trust for Taylor, Buchanan, Hollins and
others of the original owners.

Powerful political influences were brought into action; and
taking advantage of the Florida Treaty of 1819, the owners
of the assignments pressed their claims against Spain for payment for the confiscated ship and cargo. They finally received in 1824 a total of $184,011.90 in settlement.

But they refused to pay the wages due to the officers and
seamen of the *Warren*. Certainly the demands of the crew
were extremely modest. They did not ask redress, as they
could have asked, for being wheedled into signing contracts
under false pretenses. They did not demand, as they were
justly entitled to do, damages for their long imprisonment.
They simply claimed the wages due them from the time that
they had left Baltimore to the time of their return, to the
United States, deducting such advances as they had received.

Taney and Wirt, as the attorneys for the banks and others,
contested their claim for years, arguing that the indemnity

[15] V Peters, 678.

fund received by the assignees was not liable for wages claimed. In the lower court, the assignees won the case.

Justice Story's Severe Comments.

By an unanimous decision however, the Supreme Court of the United States in January, 1831, decided in favor of the officers and crew. In delivering the court's opinion, Justice Story said that " the first question is whether in point of fact, the libellants have substantially sustained the allegations in the libels and petition in respect to the voyage; to their ignorance of the intended illicit trade; to the seizure of the ship and to their own imprisonment and separation from it: which are necessary to maintain their claim for wages. And we are of opinion that the evidence upon these points is conclusive. Without going into the particulars, it may be said that few cases could be presented under circumstances of more aggravation, and in which the proofs were more clear, that the seamen were the victims of an illicit voyage, for which they never intended to contract, and in which they had no voluntary participation." [16] The Supreme Court reversed the lower court, and ordered the arrears of full wages paid, but without interest except from the time of the bringing of the suit against the assignees, in 1825.

Taney then moved that the court rescind and annul its decree. He pleaded that the case be reargued, so as to allow proof of expenses incurred by the owners in prosecuting the claim against Spain and before the Florida Commissioners, and compensation to which the assignees held themselves entitled for their services, as general agents for those interested in the claim fund. If these and others of Taney's proposals had all been allowed, hardly anything of the fund would have remained to pay the wages due. Most of them were impudent propositions, and the court so considered

[16] *Ibid.*, 710.

them.   The only two it allowed were those permitting a two-and-a-half per cent. for services, and expenses incurred in prosecuting the claim before the Florida Commissioners.   The proposal to allow expenses in pushing the claim against Spain was curtly refused.   Justice Baldwin dissented in the item of allowing any commission to the assignees.[17]

Taney Appointed U. S. Attorney-General.

When Taney was appointed Attorney-General of the United States in 1831, the foes of chattel slavery were perturbed to a point approaching consternation.   Here, they pointed out, was a man, the son of a slave owner; perhaps the foremost advocate of the interests of the slave traders; the defender of the notorious slaver Gooding; a man who would unhesitatingly pocket his fees from the profits of the kidnapping of blacks; a man who would plead the cause of smuggling decoyers of seamen — this was the man placed in charge of the civil and criminal machinery of the United States Government!

But if the opponents of chattel slavery were dismayed, the powerful, influential thousands of owners of the State banks were very well pleased at his appointment.   They could overlook his profiting from cases of a revolting nature; they could pass by such an implied stinging denunciation as even Justice Story felt impelled to give him in the *Warren* case.   These things did not affect them; it can be said without exaggeration (as the records so abundantly show), that virtually all of the State bankers were building up their fortunes by consecutive fraud, in one way or another.   To them Taney appeared solely in the capacity of a shrewd, wonderfully astute lawyer and politician, and as a consistent opponent of the Bank of the United States.

As Attorney-General of the United States, Taney became

[17] V Peters, 717.

one of President Jackson's most trusted counselors. Taney prodded and encouraged Jackson to remove the Government funds from the Bank of the United States. When William J. Duane, Secretary of the Treasury, refused to order those funds removed, President Jackson, in 1833, appointed Taney in Duane's place. Taney's appointment was never confirmed by the Senate, but he proceeded energetically to deprive the Bank of the United States of Government deposits. The Senate then passed a resolution inquiring of Taney whether he were not a stockholder in the Union Bank of Maryland, which was one of the banks chosen by him for the depository of public funds. He admitted that he was, but asserted (and with truth) that he had obtained the stock *before* he had selected that bank as a depository of public funds.[18]

Taney as Secretary of the Treasury.

At that time, and for a considerable period later, the administration of the public lands was under the jurisdiction of the Treasury Department. Neither Secretary of the Treasury Taney, nor his successor, Levi S. Woodbury (who in 1845 became an Associate Justice of the Supreme Court of the United States), interposed any serious obstacle to the great continuing frauds in the private acquisition of the public lands. In fact, those frauds assumed greater proportions under their administration than had previously been known. Personally honest, President Jackson was, however, pliable to the advice, and complaisant to the schemes, of those whom he considered his political and personal friends. Surrounded by an adroit, avaricious and unscrupulous ring of politicians, both in and out of Congress and in his cabinet, he was used and deceived.

In his fight to abolish the Bank of the United States, Jack-

[18] See, Senate Docs., First Session, Twenty-Third Congress, Vol. III, Doc. No. 238.

son knew precisely what his aims were, and suffered no one to cross or frustrate his plans. But the very importance of that conflict subordinated other matters to a secondary place in his mind; his aggressiveness was concentrated upon that one object, so that it was easy for the schemers, knowing that fact, to proceed under shelter of it. What Jackson considered as routine details of administrative functions he entrusted to the heads of departments. Always having access to him, they could influence him by their ready explanations, their insinuating suggestions, or their importunities artfully disguised under cover of official zeal. When serious charges were made that great predatory schemes were being consummated, they could even produce documents and reports so skillfully put together as to make the case appear not only favorable to themselves but as a conspiracy of political opponents to discredit him and them. And it was a characteristic of Jackson's nature that no matter how true charges were, he would loyally stand by those who supported him, as much from disposition as from political expediency in not caring to give political capital to his enemies, and reflect upon his own administration by the reprimand or discharge of his foremost adherents.

The Activity of the Land Appropriators.

That members of his Cabinet were clandestinely in virtual or tacit collusion with the cliques of land speculators is clear from the documents. Neither Taney nor Woodbury were suspected of sharing in the proceeds, or of the vulgar business of taking bribes. Cass had benefited from land speculations,[19] and, as we have seen, was not above accepting large

[19] It appears by Cass' letter, of November 13, 1818, to the Register of the Land Office at Detroit, that he, by means of sundry conveyances, had become possessed, at about the time he was Governor of Michigan Territory, of several valuable tracts of land in, and near, Detroit. One of them was derived from an old French claim. In another case,

sums of money for services not stated. The connivance and collusion of high officials usually took subtle although often easily traceable forms. For instance, Edward Livingston had been counsel for claimants of certain alleged Spanish grants; and he, himself, was pecuniarily interested, as we shall describe later, in the great fraudulent Bastrop claim, covering twelve leagues square or ·1,016,264 arpents of land in Louisiana. As Secretary of State of the United States, in 1832, Livingston made a long report (which appears on page 495, Vol. VI, " American State Papers: Public Lands "), strongly urging the confirmation of those claims.

The personal friendships of eminent officials, as well as those of their families, were also delicately worked upon, and very often indelicately; it was not uncommon for lobbyists, contractors, and capitalists having some favor to seek, to give expensive presents to the wives of officials. Social affiliations were ingeniously used, and even more dexterously political ambition and capitalist connections. The capitalists promoting banking, land, trading and other schemes and needing special laws or official favor, were either in politics themselves, or their retainers were; these capitalists, too, were those who contributed heavily to the campaign funds of the political parties. With their support one could go far in high office; lacking it, the prospect of advancement either to political or judicial office was negligible. Not less an incentive was the sagacious desire on the part of the official for future security, if, or when, he returned to private life.

Most of the ranking officials were lawyers. By serving the interests of corporations and individual capitalists, they were insuring for themselves the certainty of a large and lucrative practice after they had left office. Had either Taney or Woodbury been opposed by the powerful land interests, fill-

a claim was confirmed to Cass, although but a slight part of the purchase price had been paid to the U. S. Government.—" American State Papers: Public Lands," Vol. V: 107. (Doc. No. 598.)

ing every channel of influence at Washington, they would not have been members of the Cabinet; and had they antagonized those and other interests, they would have been excluded from confirmation to the Supreme Court of the United States, which was called upon continuously to decide questions and cases affecting the ownership of many millions of acres of land.

Imaginative writers, it is too true, have sought to explain the appointments of Supreme Court Justices as inspired by various exalting motives such as reward for individual character, learning and patriotic services. But this explanation is vague and fallacious. Economic considerations were the ruling factor.

Of the reasons for the support of Taney by the slave-owning and State bank interests, sufficient details have been given. It is necessary now to give an adequate account of the reasons for the favor of the third division of the capitalist class then controlling the Government — the land interests. In the process of presenting these facts there will automatically be made clear three other factors indispensable to the full understanding of this narrative. The great further development and aggrandizement of the newer landed class (as distinguished from the old feudal proprietary landed class) will be seen. Second, it will be perceived that the section of the landed class now multiplying its ownership of land consisted largely of the Southern slave owners, and that the territory thus fraudulently acquired was precisely that in which the slavery of negroes was considered profitable, and in which it could be extended. Third, the facile manner in which these huge areas of public domain were obtained under Taney as well as under his predecessors and successors and his subserviency to those speculators affords a direct and striking explanation of certain decisions later rendered by the Supreme Court under him as Chief Justice — decisions presenting a few spoliators with millions of acres more of the public domain.

Indian Tribes Dispossessed and Cheated.

By the year 1828, the Government still owned, it was estimated, about 801,000,000 acres in all.[20] Of this, a considerable area lay in the Southern States. The land most strongly attracting the attention of the Southern slave owners and politicians as well as Northern capitalists was that owned by the Indian tribes, the Creeks, Choctaws and Cherokees. The land occupied by these tribes in Mississippi, Arkansas and adjacent regions was known to be the finest and most valuable soil for cotton raising in the United States. In its original state, without any improvements, it could command at once at least $10 an acre, heavily stocked as much of it was with timber.

Every effort was now made to dispossess the Indian tribes. Combinations of capitalists were formed to push action at Washington. The tribes were beguiled into making treaties ceding those lands; for insignificant sums paid in merchandise or money or both, the lands were ceded to the Government. Nominally, the tribes were fairly provided for; quite true, they received only a few cents an acre, but in exchange for their collective cession, each head of an Indian family was to get a section of land and each child a certain amount. We shall see later how the speculative combinations fraudulently induced the Indians to sign away these claims. The Government announced its intention of auctioning all of these ceded lands at the minimum rate of $1.25 an acre. This, too, looked fair; apparently the poor settler, with his slight resources, could get his farm.

But what actually happened was very different. Nearly all of the Registers and Receivers of the various land offices were not only in collusion with the speculative combinations, but were secretly interested in the profits. An astonishingly

[20] "American State Papers: Public Lands," Vol. V: 447. (Doc. No. 639.)

large number of the Receivers embezzled public funds which they or their capitalist associates used in the land operations.[21] At the different local land offices fraudulent auctioning was carried on unblushingly. Sections of land were entered on the books as sold, when such was not the case; the object was to prevent actual settlers from buying choice lands from the Government, and to allow the speculators to monopolize them, so that the settlers would have to buy at exorbitant prices from the speculators. Often the very Registers and Receivers making the most public professions of opposition to the combinations were the very officials, it turned out, interested in their schemes and profits.

Capitalist Combinations in Operation.

Of one of such combinations the Register and Receiver of the land office at St. Stephens, Alabama, reported in 1827, to the Commissioner of the General Land Office: ". . . Its extent, in point of numbers, influence and capital, puts it beyond the ordinary control of the superintendents [Government officers at sales]. . . . By the exertion of a few speculating gentlemen, a coalition was formed with all men of tolerable capital, and who were disposed to purchase land. Each deposited a given sum, and became pledged to act in concert. And, in this manner, competition was, in a considerable degree, silenced. . . ."[22]

With a fine display of virtue, Colonel George W. Martin, Government locating agent in the Choctaw lands, wrote to Cass, Secretary of War, December 6, 1833, that many groundless claims "were presented at my office with much address, and urged on me with great earnestness, by a *gentleman* (much honored by the citizens of this State) and who ever took oc-

[21] See detailed list later in this chapter.
[22] "American State Papers: Public Lands," Vol. V: 376. ("Plan to Prevent Fraudulent Combinations," etc.)

casion to admonish me that, should his claims be rejected, they would be presented to a higher tribunal; leaving me to infer that he would bring all such before Congress, or perhaps first the war department: should they fail at the department, thence to Congress, etc. Should this effort at fraud be persevered in, it is possible that it may be effectual at Washington, procuring there what could not be allowed here. Should it be so, I have one consolation — my skirts are clear." [23]

Always it was the same recurring note in these communications — the speculators boasting that were they baffled on the spot, they would succeed at Washington.

But Martin's boasts of his being clear of misconduct did not correspond with what U. S. Commissioner G. C. Woolridge reported of him, that he had been guilty of " outrageous acts " in allowing the speculators to monopolize the sale.[24] Nor was his statement sustained by a U. S. Senate Committee, in the investigations of which numerous witnesses testified that lands had been located for Indians, as heads of families, when in fact those particular Indians had no families; and that the number of fraudulent locations in the Creek, Choctaw and Chickasaw reservations was enormous, The witnesses averred that the proceedings of the locating agents were thoroughly corrupt.[25]

Thus the process of the capitalist combinations in acquiring the land was twofold and coordinated. The land ceded by the Indians was fraudulently bought in great areas at auction, and the land located for Indians in exchange for that ceded by them, was even more flagrantly secured.

The principal and largest of the combinations was the Chochuma Land Company, headed by such potent Southern politicians and capitalists as Robert J. Walker, Thomas G. Ellis, Wiley Davis, Malcolm Gilchrist, William Gwin, Gen-

[23] *Ibid.,* Vol. VII : 5. (Doc. No. 1230.)
[24] *Ibid.,* Doc. No. 1264.
[25] See, *Ibid.,* 735–746, etc. (Doc. No. 1335.)

eral P. C. Chambliss and associates.[26]   The ramifications of
this company extended into Congress, the Cabinet, and the
courts.   Demanding from four to five dollars an acre from
actual intending settlers, the land officials sold to this company, or to its dummies, whatever tracts it wanted for a trifle
more than $1.25 an acre.   It was testified that Samuel Gwin,
Register of the land office at Mount Salus, Mississippi,
boasted when a certain purchase was made by agents of the
company, " That land will bring *us* ten dollars an acre." [27]
Urged to join the company, Colonel Greenwood Laflore
spurned the offer — at least, so he testified.   " I refused to
do so, and on the same day Gilchrist (I think), . . . ran
some of the land I wanted to nine dollars an acre.   When the
overture was made to me in the course of conversation I said
I considered them, the speculators, as no better than swin-
dlers." [28]

Complaining to Congress that the local land office officials
favored the speculators, various citizens of Mississippi memorialized:

". . . Thus were your petitioners thrown into the lion
jaws of the aristocratic moneyed speculators . . . and
compelled to compete with those lordly mercenaries who invest the land offices. . . . .   Some of your petitioners, and
many other settlers on the public lands, were prevented by
the known decision of the officers [land register and re-
ceiver] which was posted on the door of the land office, from
proving up their claims. . . ."   The petitioners further
remonstrated that by various false promises and inducements,
other settlers had been prevented by the company from proving their claims.   Thus, " the settlers were deprived of their
labor, and their families turned out of doors," without any
remuneration, or were compelled to take what the company

[26] See, Docs. No. 1254, No. 1263, and No. 1264, " American State
Papers : Public Lands," Vol. VII.
[27] " Am. State Papers : Public Lands," Vol. VII : 284.
[28] *Ibid.,* 474.

chose to give. "Your petitioners are unwilling to incur the expense of a long, expensive and tedious lawsuit by resorting to the judicial tribunals of the country for a redress of their grievances," etc.,— and therefore looked to Congress for relief.[29]

Methods of Despoiling the Indians.

Systematically debauched with whisky and swindled, the Indians soon found their lands gone. "Many of them," wrote Colonel John Milton to the War Department from Columbus, Mississippi, on July 15, 1833, referring to the Indians, "are almost starved and suffer immensely for the things necessary to the support of life and are sinking in moral degradation. They have been much corrupted by white men who live among them, who induce them to sell to as many different individuals as they can and then cheat them out of the proceeds. . . ."[30] Luther Blake wrote to the War Department, from Fort Mitchell, Alabama, on September 11, 1833, ". . . Many, from motives of speculation, have bought Indian reserves fraudulently in this way — take their bonds for trifles, pay them ten or twenty dollars in something they do not want, and take their receipts for five times the amount. . . ."[31] By special request of President Jackson, J. H. Howard of Pole-Cat Springs, Creek Nation, sent a report, February 1, 1834, to Jackson. ". . . From my own observation," he wrote, " I am induced to believe that·a number of reservations have been paid for at some nominal price and the principal consideration has been whisky and homespun. . . ."[32]

That these reports did not exaggerate, and at the same time were ineffectual, is evident from a memorial, signed by

[29] *Ibid.*, 609. (Doc. No. 1306.)
[30] Senate Docs., First Session, etc., 1835, Vol. VI, Doc. No. 425 : 81.
[31] *Ibid.*, 86.
[32] *Ibid.*, 104. The above are merely a few extracts from this voluminous document.

several hundred citizens of Mississippi and adjacent States, and sent to Congress in 1836. After recounting the terms of the Choctaw Treaty, that each Choctaw proving himself the head of a family was entitled to one section of land, and Choctaw children to one-half and one-quarter sections, according to their ages, the petition read on:

" A few active; enterprising and intelligent speculators, discovering the opening which was thus presented for the acquisition of large fortunes, have, by agents beyond the Mississippi, and at home, produced documents purporting to be powers of attorney from Indians to select lands, and transfer their rights to lands selected and supported by *ex parte* testimony on the above-named points, suggested in the President's order and the instructions from the Department of the Treasury and of War, and by those papers have caused to be set apart for them the choicest lands in the country; sweeping over large districts inhabited and cultivated by persons who settled the public lands on the faith of the policy of the Government . . . that their homes would be given them at a reasonable price, unexposed to the heartless grasp of the voracious speculator.

" To the alarm of your memoralists, these claims have now amounted, as they are informed, to upward of three thousand, which, at an average of 1,280 acres each, amount to the enormous aggregate of three millions eight hundred and forty thousand acres; and the said speculators, availing themselves of the panic which these operations have produced, are now selling out, receiving a portion of the price in ready money, which they refuse to become bound to refund, in the event that the title is not confirmed; thus securing to themselves large fortunes, without having advanced to the Indians one cent so far as your memorialists are informed and believe.

" Your memorialists are persuaded that not more than one out of twenty claims are founded in justice and equity, and if scrutinized by a tribunal sitting in the vicinity of the land offices, with competent powers to reject or confirm, and to compel the attendance of witnesses, those honestly claiming would be secure in their rights, and a most stupendous system of fraud on the Government would be exposed and defeated; the settlers relieved from the embarrassments thus brought on them; and Congress saved from the teasing and vexatious applications of false claims for a series of years to come." [33]

Such remonstrances brought neither redress to the Indians, nor relief to the settlers; they were pigeonholed in the archives of Congress, and no further attention was given them.

The Harvest of Fraud.

Conditions in Arkansas and Louisiana were, it seems, fully as scandalous. A treaty made in May, 1828, with the Cherokee Indians in Arkansas, provided that the members of this tribe were to get allotments of land in other regions in exchange for the domain ceded by them, and that white settlers whose lands were in the new reservation were to receive lands in other parts for lands relinquished by them.

Writing to the land office registers and receivers at Batesville and Little Rock, Arkansas, on September 26, and October 17, 1828, Commissioner Graham of the General Land Office enclosed several communications he had received from " respectable gentlemen " in Arkansas. One correspondent complained that " pieces of paper, with twenty-one years marked on them, are placed in the shoes of children, and witnesses innumerable can be found who will swear that the said persons are over the age of twenty-one years, and entitled to a donation." The speculators, he wrote, were reaping a rich harvest.

The other correspondent detailed how whites who had

[33] " American State Papers: Public Lands," Vol. VIII: 431. (Doc. No. 1414.)

never relinquished any land, and had never had any to relinquish, thronged forward to make claims. Not more than
three hundred claims, he said, could have originated under the
law, yet not less than 1,500, and probably 2,000, claims would
be put forward for confirmation. " The Government, then,
by its vigilance must save itself from being swindled out of
many hundred sections of choice lands. . . . It has been
the practice to take the evidence in the country before justices of the peace. A written statement is drawn, ' covering
the case ' and the willing witness gulps it down. Minors,
Indians, transient persons, have had their claims most substantially made out on paper. It is sickening to think of the
perjuries that have disgraced the country," etc., etc.[34]

V. M. Garesche, appointed as Treasury agent to investigate
the local land offices in Arkansas, Louisiana and elsewhere,
made investigations extending through several years of arduous work and traveling. Public " clamor " over the land
frauds was great and incessant; and it was not expected of
Garesche that he would add to the political difficulties of the
Jackson administration by developing too many damaging
facts. Although, indeed, he softened matters as much as
possible, yet, on the whole, he seems to have been as conscientious as could be looked for under the circumstances.
He reported on September 19, 1833, that the fraudulent New
Madrid claims had all been located, and as for the claims in
Lovely county, " these last, indeed, have been a great curse
to the country, and have fraudulently wrested from the United
States vast tracts of land. . . ."[35]

Leading the band of Arkansas looters was the notorious
John J. Bowie; these particular frauds were consummated
during the period when Taney was Attorney-General of the
United States, and at the time he was appointed Secretary
of the Treasury. On August 14, 1835, John K. Taylor sent

[34] " Am. State Papers: Public Lands," Vol. V: 628.
[35] Ibid., Vol. VII: 183. (Doc. No. 1252.)

an explicit account from Little Rock to President Jackson;
evidently he had no faith in anyone but Jackson, for he
wrote:

" I have again sat down to trouble you with some accounts
from Arkansas, and would not do so, but know no other
source to apply to for redress of wrongs done to the government under which we live. The Superior Court of the Territory adjourned its July session on the 10th instant. The
grand jury adjourned on the 8th instant, nine o'clock P. M.,
which body brought to light some of the most glaring frauds
ever practised upon this government, the Bowie and Yazoo
claims not excepted.

" Sir, it was clear to the mind of every juror, that men had
gone to the different land offices, and proven up Lovely donation claims, and for which patents have in many instances
issued, when, in fact, such individuals never saw the country
ceded to the Indians. The jury above alluded to have, from
proof in their deliberations, found some twenty-five or thirty
bills of indictment against persons for perjury or subornation
of perjury, one of which individuals we caught and had upon
trial, and his only means of acquittal was to claim the statute
of limitations . . . and many others will get off on the
same grounds. The next grand jury, I have no doubt, will
have evidence sufficient before them to find bills against many
persons who have gone to the different land offices, and
changed their names and proven up claims.

" It has also been lately discovered, that some of the speculators have had influence enough over some of the land officers to have the plats marked as if entries had been made, then let
them have time to go and examine before the land was certainly entered; which course of conduct is calculated to deceive those who might wish to enter. To give some knowledge of the extent of the frauds committed, at the cession of
Lovely and Miller counties to the Indians, I have been informed, that at the extent, not more than five hundred per-

sons were entitled to claims, and also understand that eight or nine hundred have proven up. I do not know what course government will take (if any), but if there should be a board of three or five vigilant persons, sent with authority to the border of each of these counties with, power sufficient to compel persons and papers to come before them, every man could be identified who lived there at the cession." [36]

As to the extent of the land frauds in Louisiana, there seems to have been a conflict of statements. Benjamin F. Linton, United States Attorney for western Louisiana, reported to Jackson, August 27, 1835, that " the most shameful frauds, impositions and perjuries have been committed in Louisiana "; in an elaborate report he detailed them. [37] But Garesche contended that Linton greatly exaggerated, intimating that he did this to divert attention from his own speculations. Nevertheless, Garesche's own report was a significant enough picture; in his investigations, it was difficult, Garesche complained, to get anyone to testify. " Is it surprising," he wrote to the Secretary of the Treasury, " when you consider that those engaged in this business belong to

[36] *Ibid.,* Vol. VIII: 404. (Doc. No. 1401.) See, also, communication from Grand Jury, July Term, 1835, to the Secretary of the Treasury, stating that " a large proportion, if not a majority of the claims, have been proved by the basest fraud and perjury." *Ibid.,* 405.

[37] *Ibid.,* Doc. No. 1421. Of one notorious land grabber Linton pointedly wrote: " He could be seen followed to and from the land office by crowds of free negroes, Indians, and Spaniards, and the very lowest dregs of society, in the counties of Opelousas and Rapides, with their affidavits already prepared by himself, and sworn to by them, before some justice of the peace in some remote part of the country. These claims, to an immense extent, are presented and allowed, and upon what evidence? Simply upon the evidence of the parties themselves who desire to make the entry. And would it be believed, that the lands where these quarter sections purported to be located, from the affidavit of the applicants, had never been surveyed by the government, nor any competent officer thereof, nor approved nor returned surveyed? I further state that there was not even a private survey made. These facts I know; I have been in the office when the entries were made, and have examined the evidence, which was precisely what I have stated above."

every class of society from the member of the Legislature
(if I am informed correctly) down to the quarter-quarter-
section settler!"

Garesche further reported that a large company was formed
in New York for the purpose of getting hold of great areas
of Government land, "and have an agent who is continually
scouring the country. A second agent from the same quarter
has lately arrived, with power to draw any amount. The constant conversation everywhere is about the large fortunes that
have been realized by land speculations." [38]

These great and uninterrupted frauds produced an ugly impression among both the middle and the working classes. In
1833, a memorial of a " Portion of the Laboring Classes " of
New York City, demanded that, among other measures, a
settled policy should be put in force that the whole of the
remaining public lands should forever continue to be the
public property of the nation.[39] This petition, of course, passed
unheeded. To allay and wear out public feeling, the customary device of an investigating committee was decided
upon, particularly by the Senate, the anti-Jackson element in
which thus saw an opportunity of doing damage to his administration. But so long as they were allowed to hold the
fruits of their frauds, and no criminal proceedings were
brought, the speculators did not seriously mind ineffective exposures, however true and however strong.

Millions of Acres of Cotton Lands to a Few.

How rapidly the public lands were being alienated into the
hands of a few was shown by the report, on June 15, 1836,
of a Select Senate Committee. It is estimated that during

[38] Doc. No. 168, Twenty-fourth Congress, Second Session, Vol. III:
425. Also, Doc. No. 213, *Ibid.*
[39] Ex. Docs., First Session, Twenty-Third Congress, 1834, Doc. No.
104.

the single year the sales had totalled nearly 13,000,000 acres, of which 8,000,000 acres " have probably been made for speculation, and not for settlement."

The report continued to say that " companies are forming in all directions to monopolize the ownership of the public domain," and that " a total and complete monopoly of the public lands by speculators is now contemplated." The report went on:

" The authentic records of the land office demonstrate that the speculator is the monopolist of nearly all the profit of this immoral, unjust, and oppressive system; a system which is 'a stain upon the honor of a great nation. The poor but industrious occupant generally attends the land sales, having no more money than a sum sufficient to buy the land he occupies at the minimum price; a speculator bids a few cents over him, and becomes the purchaser of the land and the owner of an improved farm, paying not one cent for the value of the improvements. In other cases, where the settler has collected something more than the money sufficient to pay for the land he occupies, at the minimum price, and bids that sum, the speculator, by some secret agent employed by him, overbids the settler, the land is struck off to this agent, and the settler leaves the sale in disgust, to mourn over the injustice of the government of the Union, and to prepare for the removal of himself and family from the little farm which he has improved and expected to have purchased from a paternal government. After the departure of the settler, the tract is forfeited for non-payment, and the speculator purchases in his own name the forfeited tract, probably at the minimum price per acre.

" The scenes ensuing at many of our land sales are scenes of the deepest distress and misery. They are scenes in which many families are driven forth from their homes to seek some other spot in the wilderness, where keen-eyed avarice and sordid monopoly may not overtake them. But another

land sale comes on, the same scene is repeated, till all hope
is extinguished, and nothing is left to the settler but despair
and ruin. Yet these scenes of fraud and cruelty are of constant occurrence, permitted and encouraged by the present system of the sales of the public lands at public auction. Your
committee have said that the speculator, and not the government, reaps nearly all the profits of these inglorious transactions, and this is proved by the records of the Land Office.
By the documents of the Land Office it appears, that taking
all the sales of the public lands, from the adoption of the
cash system, in July, 1820, down to the present period, the
average price received by the government upon these sales,
has been less than six cents an acre over the minimum price.
. . ." [40]

The committee proposed the sale and entry of all of the
public lands in forty-acre lots — a whimsical suggestion to make
to a Congress a large number of the members of which were interested in the land companies. As Garesche, in detailing the
frauds, alleged or real, in Louisiana, wrote to Secretary of the
Treasury Levi Woodbury, from Opelousas, Louisiana, on June
9, 1836: ". . . It is folly to talk of the *poor squatter* —
the laws have never been made for him; he gets but a very
small fraction of the whole; all the benefits of the speculation
fall into the hands of the intriguer; it is for him that the bill
is introduced; it is for him alone that the voice of our orators
is heard on the floor of Congress. . . ." [41]

A Senate Investigating Committee aptly reported, in 1835,
that " many of the speculators are persons filling high
offices in the States in which the public lands purchased by
them are situated, and others possessing wealth and influence, all of whom naturally unite to render this investigation
odious among the people. . . ."

The committee stated that in some instances the commis-

[40] " American State Papers: Public Lands," Vol. VIII, Doc. No. 1541.
[41] *Ibid.*, 965. (Doc. No. 1585.)

sioners were threatened with personal violence. An attempt, it reported, was actually made upon the life of one Commissioner, but the assailant was killed. It said that all who testified were denounced and put in fear by the powerful combinations of speculators. The committee further reported that "the first step necessary to the success of every scheme of speculation in the public lands, is to corrupt the land officers, by a secret understanding between the parties, that they are to receive a certain proportion of the profits." Great enormities, within three or four years, had occurred, the Committee stated, yet "no officer has been removed for these causes; but the most guilty among them have been reappointed from time to time, until they have become bold and fearless in their course, well knowing how to retain their places, and speculate on the public property. . . ." [42]

In this report, true as the facts were, an attempt was made to create partisan feeling against Jackson. But the really responsible were the men surrounding Jackson — Taney, Woodbury, Cass and others, who, after all, only represented the interests of the class supporting them.

The Long List of Defaulting Officials.

One of the most striking results of the various successive investigations was the revelation of the astonishingly large number of defaulting Receivers of public money at the different land offices. These investigations revealed that far from being a solitary practice, it was common on the part of Registers and Receivers to be corrupt accomplices and partners of the land syndicates, and corrupt in the embezzlement of public funds. These funds were used for the private and fraudulent purchase of public lands, which lands were then transferred and conveyed over and over again to "safe, innocent purchasers." All of these Registers and Receivers

[42] "American State Papers: Public Lands," Vol. VII: 732–734. (Doc. No. 1335.)

were seasoned politicians themselves, and procured and held
their offices by indorsement of Governors, and members of
Congress and of the Cabinet. A House document, of January
13, 1835, covering a period of eight years, gives a long list of
these defaulters.

General Israel T. Canby, Receiver at Crawfordsville, Indiana, defaulted in the sum of $46,433.53. General John
Brahan, Receiver at Huntsville, Alabama, defaulted to the
amount of $74,823.33. As to Brahan's defalcation, the House
Committee on Public Lands handed in a strange report, saying that he had used the money to buy lands in order "to
ward off speculators." Benjamin Stephenson, Receiver of
the Land Office at Edwardsville, Ill., embezzled $255,354.07.
William L. E. Ewing, Register at Vandalia, Ill., could not
account for the lack of $17,542, and George F. Strother, Re-
ceiver at St. Louis, was called upon to explain the disap-
pearance of $32,830.55. William Garrard, Receiver at Opel-
ousas, Louisiana, defaulted in the sum of $27,230.57, and
Luke Lecassier, at the same land office, was short $12,893.95
in his accounts. Samuel Smith, Receiver at St. Stephens,
Alabama, had to face an exposure of having embezzled $74,-
188.11. John Taylor, Receiver at Cahawba, Alabama, embezzled $17,463.24, and William Taylor, at the same place,
$40,570.75. In the account of Andrew T. Perry, Receiver at
Sparta, Alabama, a shortage of $29,755.57, was found. Ap-
pointed Receiver, at Columbus, Miss., in 1836, in the place
of W. P. Harris, a defaulter for $109,178.08, Gordon D.
Boyd himself defaulted in the sum of $59,622.60 in a single
year. Among his assets was "a principality," that only a
short time before had been a part of the public domain.[43]
These are a few examples of the whole number.[44]

[43] Garesche pleaded that leniency be shown Boyd. In his report to
the Secretary of the Treasury, June 14, 1837, Garesche recommended
his being retained, cynically saying that "another Receiver would probably follow in the footsteps of the two."

[44] See, "American State Papers: Public Lands," Vol. VII: 559-564.

A House Committee majority report, submitted on February 27, 1839, itemized a list of sixty-six defaulting Receivers, prior to 1837, and nine in 1838–39. This Committee was a select one of nine members; its chairman was James Harlan, of Kentucky. From the schedule reported by this committee, it appears that the whole amount due from land receivers who were on the list of defaulters was (up to 1839) $1,073,837.41, of which the sum of $825,678.28 had been defaulted since the year 1829.[45]   And it also appears from the official correspondence incorporated in this report that both Taney and Woodbury, although formally warning the receivers, took no punitive action. For example, Nathaniel West, Jr., appointed by Secretary Woodbury, on June 26, 1836, to examine the land office at Fort Wayne, Indiana, reported in detail that Colonel John Spencer, Receiver at that place, had been defrauding the Government. William Hendricks, a powerful Democratic leader, in Indiana, wrote to Woodbury, on August 31, 1836, urging him to retain Spencer in office. Woodbury responded, September 7, 1836, by saying that, " I am happy to inform you that Mr. Spencer's explanations have been such that he will probably continue in office."

Only a fraction of the defaulted sums was recovered by the Government.

These vast fraudulent land operations not only produced tens of millions of dollars in profit to the syndicates, but out of those acquisitions were created great estates. The cotton regions were extended, the slave owning power was enlarged, and the wealth and dominance of the Southern plantation owners, bankers and of other capitalists were tremendously augmented. This was the state of affairs when Taney took his seat as Chief Justice of the Supreme Court, in 1836.

(Doc. No. 1289.) Report of U. S. Comptroller Joseph Anderson. See, also, *Ibid.*, Doc. No. 1252, showing the speculations and the connections of the land officers. Also, U. S. vs. Boyd *et al.*, XV Peters, 187.

[45] House Report No. 313, Part IV, Twenty-fifth Congress, Third Session.

CHAPTER X

THE SUPREME COURT UNDER CHIEF JUSTICE TANEY
(CONTINUED)

On the same day that the appointment of Taney as Chief Justice, was confirmed by the Senate, March 15, 1836, that of Philip P. Barbour, as Associate Justice to succeed Justice Duvall, was also confirmed. Barbour by views and interests was associated with the landed class. His father, Thomas Barbour, had inherited considerable wealth, and had been a member of the old House of Burgesses of Virginia. On the maternal side, Philip P. Barbour was related to Judge Edmund Pendleton, whose operations as President of the Loyal Company have been referred to in Chapter I and elsewhere. Thomas Barbour, it is related, met with reverses, but seems to have recouped himself by securing a landed estate in Kentucky.

We have hitherto described how Charles Willing of Philadelphia obtained 32,000 acres of land in Kentucky, in 1784, on certain treasury warrants. It appears that Thomas Barbour by means of voiding that entry on the ground of its being illegal, secured legal title to a large portion of that area and that his possession was officially acknowledged. Then had come Humphrey Marshall, Federalist United States Senator from Kentucky, and a cousin of Chief Justice Marshall, with interconnected claims of his own. He asserted that, previous to Willing's entry, he had acquired title to 12,313 acres of the land claimed by Willing. He freely admitted that his claim rested upon an entry made by an intermediary, one Isaac Holbert. Also he averred that he had subsequently acquired an interest in Barbour's patent. The dispute crystallized into an action at-law between Willing's heirs, on the one part, and Marshall and associates, on the other. The decision, by Chief Justice Marshall, in the Supreme Court of the United States, in 1831, went in favor of Senator Humphrey Marshall, thus sustaining the Barbour patent.[1]

Associate Justice Barbour had, as a student and lawyer, been a close, diligent and conscientious reader of law, but it was the medieval law, and the outgrowths of that species of law (such as we have described), that he had imbibed. When he became Associate Justice, he was fifty-three years old; he, like the other members of the Supreme Court, was unalterably impregnated with his class creed. His views were soon bodied forth in that famous dictum of his in an opinion of the Supreme Court, written by him in 1837. The case involved the constitutionality of a restrictive immigration act passed by the New York Legislature. In holding that it was constitutional, Justice Barbour declared, " We think it as competent and as necessary for a State to provide precautionary measures against the moral pestilence of paupers, vagabonds and possibly convicts, as it is to guard against physical pestilence," etc.[2] But a power greater then the Supreme Court made this dictum a dead letter. That power was the capitalist class, the interests and development of which demanded a never-ending supply of surplus labor, so as to be able to command the wage market on its own terms.

Packing the Supreme Court.

Before Jackson's election the Supreme Court of the United States had been, as we have seen, pro Bank of the United States. As fast as the old members of that court died or

---

[1] Case of Lewis *et al.* vs. Marshall *et al.,* V Peters, 470. The principal point against Lewis was the Kentucky statute of limitations, barring suits not brought within a certain period.
[2] City of New York vs. Miln, XI Peters, 142.

resigned, Jackson had appointed as their successors politicians whose opposition to the Bank of the United States was assured. Never had the fact that the Supreme Court was essentially a political body been more frankly evident than during the administrations of Jackson and Van Buren. The taunt of Jackson's opponents that the Democrats were packing the Supreme Court with pro-State-bank and pro-slavery men was fully justified by the facts.

As the composition of the Supreme Court stood in 1836, five of the seven judges were Jackson's appointees. Shortly afterward, on March 3, 1837, Congress passed an act increasing the number of Supreme Court judges to nine; this measure was expressly enacted to insure a majority on the Supreme Court bench favorable to State banks and to negro slavery. So far as the landed interests were concerned, no change was necessary; the Supreme Court appointees, after Marshall's death, favored the land speculators and appropriators fully as much as during his tenure; and it was easier for them to do so, having the authority of Marshall's decisions as precedents. The two new Associate Justices appointed in 1837 were John Catron and John McKinley. Catron was fifty-one years old at the date of his appointment, and McKinley fifty-seven. As an attorney Catron was reputed to be one of the foremost authorities in the country on land laws and judicial constructions of those laws. He had been State's Attorney in Tennessee, a judge of the Superior Court of Tennessee from 1821 to 1830, Chief Justice of that court from 1830 to 1836. McKinley's career was consecutively that of a politician in Alabama, from which State he was elected to the National House of Representatives and to the Senate.

How elastic was the thing called Constitutional law, how it could be molded, as though by order, to suit the demands and interests of the particular section of the ruling class then in the ascendent, was now quickly demonstrated.

One of the banks that had been chartered by the Legislature

of Kentucky was the Bank of the Commonwealth, with $3,000,-
000 capital. After this bank had been in operation for some
time an action was brought to have its charter declared unconstitutional. If such a decision were made, then perforce all
banks chartered by States would be illegal. It is probable
that this was one of the reasons instigating this suit. But
there seem to have been other reasons of a very different nature.

Thus we read that in a speech in the Kentucky Legislature,
one of the members, Wickliffe, charged Guthrie, of the Bank
of the Commonwealth, " with belonging to a party who once
issued three million dollars [in bank notes] without a dollar
to redeem them with. And it is equally true," Wickliffe
further asserted, " that a portion of his party raised a pony
purse, and promised great lawyers fifty thousand dollars to
have their acts declared unconstitutional and void by the
Supreme Court, that they might be thereby released from
paying their debts to this Commonwealth's bank." [3]

When the case was argued before Marshall, he and a majority of the Supreme Court were of the opinion that the
act of the Kentucky Legislature, in chartering the bank, was
unconstitutional and void. But the decision was deferred and
the case was reargued before Taney. And, as was expected
from the large majority of State Bank men now on the Supreme Court bench, a decision was rendered in 1837, that the
act incorporating the Bank of the Commonwealth was a constitutional exercise of power and that the bank notes issued
were not bills of credit within the meaning of the Constitution.[4] Justice Story energetically dissented; as one of the
" old guard " he was an opponent of State's rights. He himself had been instrumental in securing the chartering of banks

[3] " A History of Banking In All The Leading Nations," etc. (1896),
Vol. I: 144.
[4] Case of Briscoe vs. The Bank of the Commonwealth, XI Peters,
257-348. The court's opinion was written by Justice McLean.

by the Massachusetts Legislature, of one of which banks he had become president. His attitude was anomalous and seemed to imply inconsistency as well as betoken rare disinterestedness in declaring against his own interests. But we have seen how his bank fared well under the Bank of the United States regime.

Wild-Cat Currency Constitutional.

This decision had its grim aspects. For years, long before their charters were formally declared "constitutional," the owners of the State banks had drenched the country with "wild-cat" currency, based to a great extent upon worthless security or no security at all. By 1819, the banks in New York State alone, apart from those of other States had issued $12,500,000; to redeem this fiat stuff the issuing banks had only $2,000,000 in specie. A New York Senate Committee reported, in 1819, that every artifice in the wit of man had been devised to find ways of putting these bank notes in circulation; that when the merchant received this paper, he, in turn, "saddled it upon the productive departments of labor." "The great profits of the banks," reported a New York Senate Committe on banks and insurance, in 1834, "arise from their issues. It is this privilege which enables them, in fact, to coin money, to substitute their evidences of debt for a metallic currency, and to loan more than their actual capitals. A bank of $100,000 capital is permitted to loan $250,000; and thus receive an interest on twice and a half the amount actually invested." [5] The committee stated that banks in the State, outside of New York City, after paying all expenses divided eleven per cent. among the stockholders in 1833, and had on hand as surplus capital sixteen per cent. on their capital. New York City banks, the committee reported, paid

[5] Doc. No. 108 [New York Senate] Docs., 1834, Vol. II.

larger dividends. This was an example of similar conditions in all of the States.[6]

The Workingmen's Party of 1829, in its resolution adopted at Military Hall, New York City, on October 19, of that year, denounced the bankers as " the greatest knaves, impostors and paupers of the age," and further declared that as banking was then conducted, the owners of the banks received annually of the people of the State " not less than two million dollars in their paper money (and it might as well be pewter money) for which there is and can be, nothing provided for its redemption on demand. . . ." In the panic of 1837, not less than eight hundred banks in the United States suspended payment, refusing a single dollar to the Government whose deposits of $30,000,000 they held, or to the people in general who held $120,000,000 of their notes.[7] After the passing of the panic the same old frauds continued. The decision of 1837, of the Supreme Court of the United States, says an authority, " opened the door wide for abuses of banking by the States." [8] Unquestionably it did, as the results fully proved.

Competition Declared Immutable.

So far as the State rights issue was involved, the Supreme Court's policy under Taney, although exactly the reverse of what it had been under Marshall, produced in one respect the same result in effect. The Charles River Bridge Case was a

---

[6] The founders of some of the largest fortunes of present times were large stockholders in some of these banks, or were both stockholders and officials. John Jacob Astor, for example, held stock in the Manhattan Bank, the Merchants' Bank, the Bank of America, the Mechanics' Bank and others. Jacob Lorillard was president of the Mechanics' Bank, and the Goelet family were extensive stock owners in the Chemical Bank (now the Chemical National Bank, one of the richest banks in the United States).

[7] "Abridgement of the Debates of Congress, from 1789 to 1856," Vol. XIII: 426–427.

[8] "A History of Banking In All The Leading Nations," etc., Vol. I: 144.

striking instance of this. The company owning this bridge claimed that it held a vested, perpetual monopoly by reason of various old empowering acts of the Massachusetts Legislature. An act had been recently passed, however, authorizing the construction of the adjacent Warren bridge as a free avenue. The owners of the Charles River bridge asserted that the Legislature, in passing the new act, had impaired the obligation of a contract. The State courts refused their petition for an injunction, and Chief Justice Taney sustained the validity of the Warren bridge law.[9]

This decision again effectually stamped into law the doctrine then proclaimed as immutable by aggressive capitalism, and consequently by statesmen, universities, editorial sanctums and legislative halls — the doctrine that " competition is the life of trade." A companion edict to Marshall's decision in the Livingston steamboat monopoly case, the decision demolished the last stand of the old, archaic, feudal aristocracy and gave the new industrial and transportation aristocracy unlimited opportunities for competitive expansion and individual and corporate development. No longer was " individual enterprise " to be shackled by obsolete laws; the old practice of, granting powers of monopoly to a favored few was obliterated as a principle of jurisprudence. This decision freshly demonstrated that the Supreme Court of the United States continuously and accurately reflected, both in personnel and spirit, the needs and demands of the dominant sections of the ruling class, and incarnated those requisites into constitutional law.

In the consideration of private land claims no alteration whatever was made by the reconstituted Supreme Court, following Marshall's death. There was no sectional controversy over the spoliation of the national domain; in the engrossing business of appropriating the public lands, men of power and influence of all sections of the country were jointly concerned.

[9] The full decision is set forth in XI Peters.

With the question of slavery, the case was very different.   The issue was growing acute to a point generating the deepest and most vindictive passions and inflaming the most rancorous hatreds.   It was a ticklish question for the Supreme Court of the United States to pass upon conclusively; and every art of the juridical politicians on the bench was requisitioned into deciding ingeniously for the institution of slavery, and yet at the same time not rashly seem to flout the anti-slavery sentiment.

But a great change had come about since Marshall's decision in the *Antelope* case.   The Supreme Court was now willing enough to make a concession to the anti-slavery element by outlawing the slave traffic.   To retain the institution of slavery itself some sop had to be thrown, particularly as the *Antelope* decision had become the scorn and jeer of certain European powers, which now, more than ever before, were determined to put a peremptory stop to the slave trade.   And the Supreme Court doubtless well knew that whatever words of indignation it should use in declaring the slave traffic illegal, that traffic nevertheless, would surreptitiously continue.   That this proved to be so was shown by the large number of slave-trading ships plying their traffic up to the very outbreak of the Civil War, and even after.[10]

Revolting Slaves to be Treated With Respect.

Two decisions, handed down in the same month — January, 1841 — graphically illustrated the new policy of the Supreme Court.

The *L'Amistad,* a Spanish schooner, sailed from Havana,

[10] For instance: From May 1, 1852, to May 1, 1862, twenty-six American schooners and brigs were libeled by the Government at the port of New York alone, charged with being engaged in the slave traffic.   Some were seized at New York, others on the coast of Africa. Many were condemned.— See, Senate Doc. No. 53, Vol. V, U. S. Senate Docs., Second Session, 1861–62.

June 27, 1839, bound for Puerto Principe, with a cargo of slaves kidnapped from Africa. On the voyage the negroes rose in revolt, killed the captain, and took possession of the vessel. Off Montauk Point, Long Island, Lieutenant Gedney, of the U. S. brig *Washington,* sighted the schooner and seized her. Two Spanish capitalists, Jose Ruiz and Pedro Montez, applied in court for restoration of the slaves to them as their property. The negroes, in opposition, recited that they were free-born Africans, and not slaves; that in April, 1839, they had been kidnapped from Africa and transported to Cuba to be sold as slaves; and that they had risen in revolt and killed the captain, intending to return to their native country or seek asylum in some free land.

When the circumstances became public, they aroused a tremendous sensation. In the North they excited mixed sympathy for the negroes, and indignation against the slave traders. Both in North and South admiration was felt for the courage of the revolters, although in the slave sections it was admiration burdened with an appalling fear; if the negroes had shown such daring and determination in revolting on the ship, was it not possible that the same desperation might lead to a general uprising of the whole slave population in the South?

The courts did not presume to proceed against the kidnapped negroes for mutiny and murder. The District Court ordered them to be returned to their native land. When the case was appealed to the Supreme Court of the United States, venerable John Quincy Adams appeared as the negroes' attorney. Justice Story was allowed to write the court's opinion (only Justice Baldwin dissenting) to this effect: That the negroes had never been lawful slaves; that they were natives of Africa, and had been kidnapped in violation of the Spanish laws by which the African slave trade had been declared utterly abolished and by which the traffic was outlawed as a heinous crime. The court ordered that the negroes be set free.[11]

Where now was Marshall's doctrine of acquiescence? Was it imperative on the part of the enslaved, to revolt and slaughter, in order to prove the absence of acquiescence on their part? If so, the Supreme Court in that decision was practically, although unwittingly, giving this advice to the enslaved of all generations: Tamely submit to servitude, and the meshes of the law's fictional doctrines will hold you. Revolt against those conditions, and you prove to our satisfaction that you do not acquiesce.

Slaves Were Merchandise, Not Persons.

But the other and accompanying decision, delivered in the same month, riveted the bonds of those already held in slavery. It did this under the State rights doctrine.

Robert Slaughter sued Groves and others for payment of promissory notes due for slaves that Slaughter had brought in to the State of Mississippi after May, 1833. Large numbers of slaves, it may be said parenthetically, had been rushed into Mississippi following the fraudulent acquisition by individuals and syndicates of those great tracts of cotton lands. Much of this seizure had gone on under Taney, as Secretary of the Treasury; and the slave owners, needing the slaves to clear, till and cultivate the lands, imported gangs of them, despite laws prohibiting that importation. Some of these slave owners — Groves and others — saw, or thought they saw, an easy way of keeping slaves purchased and yet escaping the necessity of paying for them. Groves et al. refused to pay Slaughter, claiming that the notes were null and void

[11] XV Peters, 518. The case was entitled United States vs. L'Amistad. The suit brought by the Government had no direct bearing whatever on the question of the negroes, but was instituted to determine the rights of the Spanish claimants to the restitution of what they called their " property."

because the contracts on which they were founded were in direct violation of the Constitution of that State, adopted in 1832, which document expressly prohibited the introduction of slaves into Mississippi, as merchandise for sale, after May 1, 1833. The case went up on appeal to the Supreme Court of the United States.

Pleading that the slaves were property, and that property rights as such should be protected, Jones, attorney for Slaughter, urged upon the Supreme Court: "This case is of much importance in principle, and it is also so because of the very large amount of property which depends for its safety on the decision of this Court. Millions of dollars have been laid out in the purchase of slaves, carried into the State of Mississippi from other States for sale; without any idea on the part of the sellers or buyers that there was any law or constitutional provision which affected the transactions." [12]

Here the plea was ignorance of any prohibitory law. That the Supreme Court tolerated such a plea was extremely suggestive: in the case of poor offenders did not the courts always implacably say that ignorance of the law was no excuse? The intent and meaning of the Mississippi Constitution of 1832 were direct and explicit; there could be no mistaking them. How did the Supreme Court's decision meet this point? The court evaded this point and based its decision upon entirely different, extraneous points.

Delivering the court's opinion, Justice Smith Thompson affirmed the decision of the lower court in favor of Slaughter. True, the Mississippi Constitution prohibited the importation of slaves, but (said he), *it did not invalidate the contract;* to effect such an invalidation and to carry it into effect, a special law was required, and no such law was passed until 1837. The sinister importance of this precedent will be presently seen; it was soon applied to the validation of the most enormous land frauds. Yet although Justice Thompson declared that

[12] Case of Groves *et al.* vs. Slaughter, XV Peters, 476.

the question of the power to regulate traffic in slaves between different points was not involved, McLean and Taney gratuitously came forward to pronounce the supremacy of State rights.

Why this eagerness to thrust forward this formulation? Because the Constitution of the United States treated slaves as *persons,* as human beings, while the laws of Southern States treated them as *property,* and considered them as *merchandise.* In a separate opinion, concurring with Justice Thompson, Justice McLean, after pointing out that fact asserted: "The power over slavery belongs to the States respectively. . . . The right to exercise this power by a State is higher and deeper than the Constitution." [13]

Chief Justice Taney skulked behind Justice McLean. In his opinion Taney wrote that he had not intended to express an opinion on the power of Congress to regulate the traffic, but inasmuch "as my Brother McLean has," therefore he, Taney, would "on account of the interest which a large portion of the Union naturally feel in this matter, and from an apprehension that my silence, when another member of the court has delivered his opinion, might be misconstrued." Taney declared that the States had exclusive power over the slave traffic. He added that no case, however, had yet arisen making it necessary to decide the question of control by Congress.[14]

What influences caused these Justices to obtrude opinions on issues not involved? Doubtless they were the same influences used in the Dred Scott case sixteen years later. The real question was: Should the enslavement of negroes be continued or abolished? The fate of millions of blacks in bondage, and millions more yet unborn, hung upon the answer. And here was the handful of men on the Supreme Court, all

[13] XV Peters, 508.
[14] *Ibid.,* 509. Justices McKinley and Story dissented from Thompson's opinion, Justice Catron was ill, and Justice Barbour died before the case was decided.

relatively old men, pretending not to know the fundamental issue, yet resorting to every dexterous device and fine-spun technical construction to justify and enforce negro slavery.

In the meantime, during the period following Marshall's death, the Supreme Court continued validating private land claims, most of which lay in the South and the beneficiaries of which were either Southern slave holders or a combination of them and Northern capitalists.

More Land Claims Validated.

The Soulard claim in Missouri, one of the land claim cases the decisions in which were deferred by Marshall for six years, was decided by the Supreme Court in January, 1836, shortly before Taney was confirmed as Chief Justice. This claim, to recapitulate, covered 10,000 arpents of land seventy miles north of St. Louis and about fifteen miles west of the Mississippi River.

It was a claim alleged to have been granted to Antoine Soulard, father of the ostensible claimants, by Trudeau, the Spanish Lieutenant-Governor of Louisiana, in 1796. Soulard had been Surveyor-General, and it was alleged that the grant, so-called, had been surveyed by his deputy surveyor, Don Santiago Rankin, in 1804. This claim as well as many others bearing Trudeau's and Soulard's supposed signatures, had been rejected by the U. S. Board of Land Commissioners in 1806–1807, as forged and in other respects fraudulent. The Soulard claim was also one of a number of such claims rejected by Judge Peck, in the U. S. District Court at St. Louis, in 1825, as illegal and invalid. Senator Benton of Missouri was one of counsel for Soulard's heirs. They could produce no original decree of concession and certificate of survey; when asked to explain they replied that those papers " were by mistake thrown into the fire and destroyed."

In January, 1836, the Supreme Court of the United States

validated the Soulard claim. That validation, of course, carried with it the validation of many similar claims. Justice Baldwin delivered the Court's opinion and it was very brief. It fell back upon the precedents set by Marshall in the Florida cases, and declared that Soulard's heirs had a good and valid title.[15]

In his scorching criticism of the Supreme Court's decisions, Judge Peck gave particular attention to Soulard's activities. He proceeded in great detail to " state the reasons upon which it appears to me to impeach the record of surveys made by Antoine Soulard and to establish the startling fact that the frauds which appear to pervade the great mass of these Spanish claims pervade also the record of surveys made by Soulard under the Spanish government." [16] .After exhaustively and specifically describing the inception and development of these frauds, Judge Peck urged that the facts related should be convincing " that those concessions had not been issued, had not existence at the date of those surveys, and therefore could not at that date have been delivered to Mr. Soulard or to his deputy." [17] Yet the Supreme Court held fast to the doctrine that when an *official survey* was made the lands surveyed were thereby detached from the mass of public lands and vested in the beneficiary. The circumstances mattered nothing; the formal, *official* act was conclusive, sacred and perpetually binding.

It was because it could not act in a way contradictory to its own dictum that the Supreme Court found itself compelled to reject certain private land claims which, it was proved by the Government, had never been surveyed. One of these rejected on this ground was that of John Smith, who claimed

[15] Case of Soulard's Heirs vs. U. S., X Peters, 100–106.

[16] "American State Papers: Public Lands," Vol. VIII: 841. Doc. No. 1538.

[17] Judge Peck's criticism was so voluminous with records and facts, that neither the whole nor any adequate part can appropriately be cited here. Those desirous of learning its contents in detail are referred to Doc. No. 1538.

to have bought a grant for 10,000 arpents in Missouri, alleged to have been granted by Governor Carondelet, to James St. Vrain, in 1796.[18] But this was one of the comparatively few claims the confirmation of which was refused. The total area of the claims in Missouri based upon alleged Spanish grants aggregated a very large area; the claims alleged to have been given by Delassus, Trudeau's successor, alone embraced about 500,000 arpents; yet Judge Peck most clearly showed that a certain alleged official Spanish order by Morales, Delassus' superior, purporting to suspend the strict limitations under which land was granted, was "a forgery of recent date, and in the handwriting of Delassus." [19]

In January 1840, the Supreme Court of the United States gave another decision which, although involving only three hundred acres of land in Florida, nevertheless served as another precedent of vast importance, which together with previous decisions, was later successfully cited by claimants in cases dealing with the private appropriation of immense areas of the public domain. This was the action of the United States vs. Wiggins. The claimant relied upon a certified copy, or a testimonio, of a concession made by the Spanish authorities. The original concession could not be found among the archives, nor was its existence proved. A clerk in Aguilar's office, where the archives were deposited, and who had been custodian for six years, testified that he had never seen or heard of the original. The Surveyor-General never saw it, nor was it enumerated in the list of documents made soon after the cession of Florida. Notwithstanding this negative proof, the Supreme Court of the United States accepted the plea that the original grant had once existed, and it validated the claim.[20]

[18] Case of John Smith vs. U. S., X Peters, 324–336. Senator Benton was Smith's attorney.

[19] "American State Papers: Public Lands," Vol. VIII: 839. (Doc. No. 1538.)

[20] See, XIV Peters, 334.

Citing this decision as authority, the Supreme Court kept on validating Florida land grants, the original concessions of which were never produced, and the sole bases of which were alleged copies certified by Aguilar. One of these claims, for example, was that of John Rodman for 16,000 acres of land on the west side of St. John's River, said to have been granted to Robert M'Hardy, a surveyor, for the building of a saw-mill. The Government contended that not only did no original concession exist, but that the conditions of the alleged grant had never been complied with. The Supreme Court, however, validated the claim.[21] But some claims were rejected, not because they differed intrinsically from the confirmed claims, but because the claimants had not been shrewd enough to get an aggregation of testimony affirming that formal surveys had been made, or that the original deeds of concession had been lost or destroyed.[22] The moral seemed to be that those who were so stupid as to neglect to fortify their claims with ample required testimony, deserved to lose.

The cumulative results of these precedents were shown in more than one way. They not only alienated into private ownership huge domains in territory already in the United States, but they gave points to land grabbers how to devise and buttress frauds in Texas and in the vaster regions soon after acquired by the United States from Mexico. But before reciting these facts, it is necessary to advert to some changes occurring in the personnel of the Supreme Court.

Three New Associate Justices.

At Associate Justice Barbour's death, Peter V. Daniel, on March 3, 1841, was appointed to succeed him. Daniel was connected with both the landed aristocracy and the dominant political coterie; he was the scion of an old Virginia landed

[21] U.S. vs. Rodman, XV Peters, 130–140.
[22] Buyck's claim for 50,000 acres in Florida was thus thrown out, Delespine's for 92,160 acres, etc.— See, *Ibid.*, 215, 319, etc.

family, and his father was a man of fortune.   Peter V. Daniel
had increased the family's power by marrying a daughter of
Edmund Randolph, in whose office he had studied law.   Randolph had a large landed estate, and had been a potent politician, serving in Washington's Cabinet.   Daniel had been
long in politics and office holding; he had been a member of
the Virginia Privy Council in 1812, Lieutenant-Governor of
Virginia in 1835, and in 1836 had been appointed judge of the
U. S. District Court in Virginia.   He was one of Jackson's
personal friends as well as a strong political adherent.   At
the date of his appointment to the Supreme Court he was fifty-
seven years old.

Associate Justice Baldwin died in 1844.   Toward the close
of his career his mind was deranged, and he was often violent
and ungovernable on the Supreme Court bench.   In such abject poverty did he die that his friends found it necessary to
raise a fund for his burial expenses.

This surely is a significant fact.   Here was one of the Justices conspicuously instrumental in giving away to spoliators
enormous areas of the most valuable agricultural, timber and
mineral lands in the country.   The beneficiaries of the decisions profited to the extent of hundreds of millions of dollars.   Yet Baldwin himself received no reward nor any part
of the profits.   Typical of many other Justices, he was personally incorruptible so far as money went.   It was not essential to corrupt by mercenary means men of his type.   The
class bias of their minds, the training that they had received
both in law and politics, and their case-hardened views on
vested property rights — these were usually sufficient explanations of their attitude and decisions.   To attempt to bribe
men whose favor could be counted upon in advance would
have been dangerous, as well as a superfluous expense.   We
have seen such judges and officials in our own time.[23]

[23] For example, John G. Carlisle.   As Secretary of the Treasury, in
1895, he turned over a bond issue to a syndicate headed by J. Pierpont

And although Associate Justice Story, at his death in 1845, left an estate it was not large compared to great, or even passable, fortunes of the time. He had been extremely liberal to his family, and had educated them at considerable expense. " My worldly estate," he wrote in his will, " is not large, partly because I have not felt as strongly as some persons the importance of wealth to happiness." [24]

As a lawyer he had scrupled at no case, however rankly it reeked with fraud. But in his character of Justice, his course was not determined by bribes; it was assured by far more efficacious and subtly permeating influences — class loyalty, class prejudices, class interests and personal gratitude and associations, as also (so the facts prove) personal interest. All of these men had absorbed the views of the ruling class and the ancient laws drafted to insure the supremacy of that class; these ingrained ideas became inexorable convictions which no argument could shake, and which they conceived had to be translated into edicts at every fresh opportunity. Such men were unshakenly class-disciplined.

Levi Woodbury was now appointed to the Supreme Court. His appointment did indeed cause the land appropriators to exult in high gratification, but it was received with execrations by the forces opposed to the plundering of the national domain.

Both of these elements recalled his compliant serviceableness to the syndicates of land grabbers in the South, when he was Secretary of the Treasury, and how he had shielded corrupt land officials who had been the tools and accessories of those combinations. In fact insidious comment was made that his appointment as Associate Justice came at the very time when astoundingly enormous frauds were being originated or car-

Morgan, allowing that syndicate to make $18,000,000 profit. After Carlisle left office he was slightly rewarded by being employed as a corporation attorney. He died recently in utter poverty, and his friends had to defray the expenses of his burial.

[24] " Life and Letters," etc., Vol. II: 553.

ried through in Texas — frauds the ultimate validation of which would depend upon the courts.

At this point the significant fact should be noted that Woodbury's successor as Secretary of the Treasury was none other than Robert J. Walker, the head and front of the great combination of speculators which had secured such enormous areas of cotton lands in Mississippi under Taney and Woodbury's administrations. With the wealth extracted from land grabbing Walker easily had himself elected to the United States Senate in 1836. He was Secretary of the Treasury from 1845 to 1849; as has been noted, the Secretary of the Treasury then held jurisdiction over the public lands.

At the same time that Woodbury was appointed to the Supreme Court, in 1845, Samuel Nelson received his appointment to that tribunal. Nelson owned a landed estate of considerable value at Cooperstown, New York. In 1846 Robert Grier, at the age of fifty-two, ascended the Supreme Court bench by grace of President Polk's commission. Grier had been a judge in Pennsylvania; he had turned from Federalism to support of the Democratic Party, and as a lawyer was associated with the land interests.

The Great Land Frauds in Texas.

The capitalists promoting the huge frauds in Texas were largely those interested in the great Florida, Mississippi and Arkansas land spoliations. George Griswold, so conspicuous in the Mitchell claim of 1,200,000 acres in Florida validated by the Supreme Court of the United States, was equally prominent in the Texas frauds. Associated with him was an array of other Northern capitalists — Anthony Dey of New York, William H. Sumner of Boston, George Curtis of New York, Dudley Selden, a New York politician, General John T. Mason, Stephen Whitney and others of the same city. From the profits of his land transactions, Stephen Whitney

became so rich that at one time he was regarded as approaching Commodore Vanderbilt in point of wealth; in 1852 Whitney's estate was estimated at a round $7,000,000. But these
were only a few of the Northern capitalists concerned in vesting in themselves immense stretches of Texas land. Many
other combinations and corporations were formed at the same
time, embracing Northern and Southern politicians and capitalists, slave owners, judges and some of the highest officials in
the country.

Texas contains 274,356 square miles or 175,587,840 acres
— an area exceeding that of the thirteen original States.
The western part of Texas, because of the supposed lack of
water, was long not considered habitable for man or beast,
although in recent times inexhaustible subterranean supplies
of water have been discovered, and orchards and farms now
yield their harvests on stretches once deserts. But the potential richness of the equally vast areas of eastern, northern,
central and southern Texas was early recognized; it was well
known that great tracts of valuable primitive timber lands
awaited utilization, and that the soil was variously adapted for
the raising of cotton, sugar-cane, rice, tobacco and other crops.
It was a country marvelously adapted, also, for cattle ranging.

Beginning in 1821, when Texas was still a province of Mexico, various promoters, or " empressarios," as they were called,
solicited and obtained contracts from the officials of the joint
States of Coahuila and Texas, by which, as compensation for
their services in introducing colonists, they were to receive
the jurisdiction of great colony grants of land. Each bona
fide colonist was to be entitled to a certain tract of land for
himself, usually a league and a labor (about 4,605 acres), and
the " empressario " was to receive as personal compensation
certain stated premium lands. In 1824 an event happened
which had a direct and sinister connection with the origin and
consummation of stupendous land frauds. This was the appearance in San Felipe of Samuel M. Williams, a young Bal-

timore adventurer. He had been in Mexico for several years
and had learned the Spanish language thoroughly. His advent in San Felipe was as secretary of the land office at that
place.

The Colonization Contracts.

From 1821 to 1832 thirty-three colonization contracts were
allowed by the Mexican officials. In 1823 Moses Austin made
one contract, and in 1823–1826 his son, Stephen F. Austin,
made four contracts, covering scores of leagues of territory;
their agreements, as was the case with certain others, did not
specify how many families were to be brought in. Robert Left-
wich, by the contract of April 15, 1824, was to introduce eight
hundred families; he soon died and Sterling C. Robertson
and Alexander Thompson assumed the contract under the
name of the Nashville Company. Martin DeLeon, in 1824
and 1829, made two contracts, and Frost Thorn, by his contract
of 1825, was to introduce four hundred families. D. G. Burnet, Joseph Vehlein and Lorenzo D. Zavala variously made
contracts in 1828 and 1829, and similar contracts were entered into by Benjamin R. Milam, John L. Woodbury, John
Cameron, General Thomas J. Chambers, Hewitson and Powers and others. Such of these contracts as specified the number of families to be brought in show a total of 9,248 families
contracted for, to be settled in Texas.

When these contracts were made Commissioners were appointed, or alleged that they had been appointed, by the Mexican authorities to determine the number of colonists introduced and to give titles to both colonists and contractors
accordingly. Williams acted in that capacity for Austin's
colony; George A. Nixon for the Burnet, Zavala and Vehlein
grants; William H. Steele for the Nashville Company's colony, and other Commissioners for other colonies. In some
cases the immediate friends or relatives of the contractors
were appointed, or audaciously assumed the post of Commis-

sioner, which was not a difficult imposture in a remote country and in a period of civil chaos, particularly following the time when Mexico won its independence from Spain.

Many of the colonization contracts, however, were almost at once turned over to companies of absentee capitalists who had never seen Texas, had no intention of going there, and whose only purpose was exploitation.

Not a few of these capitalists were New York and Boston owners of packet lines whose methods in luring over poor European immigrants, charging them extortionate rates, herding them foully in the ships, and dumping them unceremoniously in a state of destitution at the different Northern ports were at that very time subjects of legislative investigations at home. Thus, the Burnet, Zavala and Vehlein contracts became the property of a corporation calling itself "The Galveston Bay and Texas Land Company," the officers of which were General John T. Mason, George Griswold, Stephen Whitney, Dudley Selden and associates.[25] Another such corporation composed of New York and other Eastern capitalists was "The Colorado and Red River Land Company," based upon the colonization contracts of J. C. Beale. The general offices of this corporation were at No. 8 Wall Street, New York, with L. B. Woodruff as secretary and attorney.[26] Although the Beale contracts called for the colonization of only six hundred families, yet, in its prospectus the company computed the area in its grants *at twenty million acres,* and stated that it was authorized to select for itself, "where it pleased," a premium of 23,000 acres for each one hundred families that it colonized. [27]

[25] Case of Rose vs. the Governor, etc., XXIV Texas Reports (Supreme Court of Texas), p. 496.— See, also, "Address To The Reader of the Documents Relating To The Galveston Bay and Texas Land Company, etc., New York, 1831." It was the company's pamphlet calling public attention to the value of its land for timber supplies, and for raising sugar, cotton, rice, indigo, tobacco, etc.

[26] This prospectus was issued in pamphlet form; the date is uncertain — probably 1834 or 1835. The above statement appears on page 1.

[27] *Ibid.,* 3.

Among the various contractors or colonization corporations there existed a combination of inter-related interests. In the Nashville Company, for instance, Samuel M. Williams, Stephen F. Austin, H. H. League and associates were interested, and some of the same group were prime movers in the Powers and Hewitson contract.

These men were among the real promoters of the movement for the independence of Texas; it was their interests that, not entirely, but largely, engendered the struggle, and it was their capital, in part, that supplied the arms and ammunition.[28] Their frauds in seizing land were so truly gigantic and so flagrantly in violation of the Mexican laws that to reap the full benefits of their spoliations, they aimed to eject Mexican authority and substitute their own government and officials. They themselves, they knew, would become the head officials of the new Republic. This may not be romance, but it is fact.

It is also a fact that so well grounded were the fears of these spoliators that some aggressive Mexican President might declare their enormous frauds forfeited; that they were desperately bent upon getting Texas out of the jurisdiction of Mexico. General Santa Anna, President of Mexico, did in fact issue a decree to this effect in 1853. Article I of his decree declared that the public lands, as the exclusive property of Texas, never could have been alienated by decrees, orders or enactments. Article II denounced all sales, made without the approval of the central government, as null and void, and Article IV prohibited officials from admitting such claims. This decree was followed by a still stronger decree in 1854.

[28] And they later received, in return for these outlays and advances, scrip entitling them to 1,329,200 acres. Stephen Whitney claimed that Mason advanced $1,000 to Williams as a loan in supporting the war for independence in 1835.—Journal of the Texas Senate, 1856: 352. Williams owned the Bank of Agriculture, chartered in 1835, and with his partner, McKinney, held large claims for loans to the Texas Government. Many of such claims, it was discovered, were forged.—See "Official Journal, Texas Senate," 1856: 369.

But by that time all of Texas, California, New Mexico, Arizona and other territory had gone into possession of the United States. Later on in this work, these decrees and how they were nullified by the Supreme Court of the United States, are described in detail.

Thus we see the land grabbers had the strongest possible economic reason for wresting Texas from Mexico. Many of them like Burnet and Milam became the chief officials of the Republic of Texas.

How enormous a territory these contracting individuals and companies fraudulently appropriated, and the bold methods that they used, may be learned from the action of the Texas Constitutional Convention of 1836. In many places in Texas the actual settlers were literally up in arms against these fraudulent claims, and the Convention was forced to take notice.

After achieving its independence, Texas, of course, had full control over its public lands; and subsequently it consented to annexation to the United States only upon condition that it retain that jurisdiction. To this day that control has been retained; Texas lands have never been subject to the authority of the National Government.

Eleven Hundred Leagues of Spurious Claims.

Article 220 of the Texas Constitution of 1836, aimed to prevent the indiscriminate plundering going on. Section D prohibited aliens from holding land except by direct title from the Republic of Texas. Section I was designed to annul an immense grant to General John T. Mason and company. It declared that " the protection of the public domain from unjust and fraudulent claims . . . is one of the great duties of this Convention." It recited that the Legislature of Coahuila and Texas in 1834 and 1835 passed two acts in behalf of Mason, " under which the enormous amount of eleven hundred leagues of land had been claimed by sundry individuals, some of whom reside in foreign countries, and are not citizens of the Republic." Those acts, the Constitution further read, were contrary to the laws of Mexico, and were forthwith declared null and void.[29] One peculiarly heinous feature, the Convention declared, was that the land grabbers had taken advantage of the absence of most Texans who had been fighting for independence, and had rushed surveyors at great speed over the very choicest lands. After stating this fact, Sections J and K annulled all such surveys, and suspended the issuing of patents.[30]

But by no means did these annulling Constitutional provisions become effective. One factor was lacking to make them so, although at the time of their adoption it was supposed that Constitutional law was organic law. The omission, it was later discovered, depriving them of all force was, according to precedents established by the Supreme Court of the United States, the failure of the Texas Congress or Legislature to pass acts for the enforcement of those provisions. The land appropriators vigilantly saw to it that no such acts were ever passed. They themselves were leading officials and judges; nearly all of the Supreme Court or the county court judges were either land appropriators or were in alliance. General J. T. Chambers not only was a colonization contractor, but he was long the Supreme Judge of Texas, acting the judicial autocrat.

In 1837 the Texas Congress passed a general law making donations to those who had been settlers before the date of independence, in 1836, and to all soldiers of the war against Mexico for independence. The enormous frauds committed under this law are described later in this chapter. The 20,000,000 acres of land already granted officially by the year 1838 did not comprise those particular claims. They con-

[29] "Early Laws of Texas, 1831–1845," Vol. I: 207–208. A league equaled 4,428 acres.
[30] *Ibid.*

sisted almost wholly of patented grants to colonization corporations, and to alleged settlers under Spanish or Mexican
contracts and titles. The colonization companies claimed that
up to the year 1838 they had brought in thirty-five hundred
families. Even if this claim were true the extent of land
accruing to the contractors would be about 4,000,000 acres.
But the claim was fictitious. A certain number of settlers
were in fact introduced, but the number was greatly magnified.

That this was so was evidenced by the general demand on
the part of honest settlers for a Congressional investigation.
It was amply proved by the report of a joint investigating
committee of the Texas Congress in 1840, and by cases constantly coming up in the Texas courts. The resolution under
which the joint committee was appointed declared that
" whereas we have the evidence of the Constitution itself of
the existence of spurious claims to the amount of eleven hundred leagues of land [nearly 5,000,000 acres], and there
is good reason to believe that a vast amount of fraud over
and above that specified in the Constitution has been perpetrated," etc.[31]

Disclosures of Colossal Frauds.

The evidence was overwhelming. Samuel M. Williams and
two associates, it appeared, had made a claim for four hundred leagues of land in Nacogdoches, Red River and Harrison counties, based upon an alleged grant from the Mexican
governor, on the condition that they supply a thousand armed
men to fight the Indians. In testifying to these facts John
P. Borden, Commissioner of the Texas General Land Office,
admitted that titles to ten leagues of land were gratuitously
and without solicitation made out to himself (Borden), and

[31] " Evidence in Relation to Land Titles — Taken Before The Joint
Committee on Public Lands, Printed By Order of The House, 1840 ":
p. 2.

one league to two of his brothers. Borden testified further that "it appears from the record in my office that the whole number of men purporting to have been enlisted under the contract of Williams, Peebles and Johnson was forty-one." "And what of the title papers?" Borden was asked. He declared that they bore the clearest proof of having been forged.[32] It appeared that Aldrète, Commissioner for giving titles at Nacogdoches, was an impostor; that he had no real authority; and yet Borden testified that Aldrete in 1833–1834, had issued titles to 150½ leagues of land in Liberty, Houston and Red River counties to alleged colonists.[33] And who, as Commissioner, had issued titles to John T. Mason? None other than the malodorous Colonel James Bowie, and on pretended authority at that; in the year 1835 alone Bowie had presented Mason with titles to ninety-five leagues of land in Harrison and Nacogdoches counties.[34]

General T. J. Chambers claimed to have received sixteen leagues on one occasion, and twenty-three leagues on another, near Waco and in other regions for "judicial services"; Governor Viesca said he had never authorized the concession; yet titles were issued. George Aldrich, a surveyor, testified that in 1835 he had surveyed about four hundred leagues of land; that he was paid for those surveys by Williams, Johnson and Peebles; and that he was to receive twenty leagues as compensation for making the survey. Aldrich further testified that it was "usual for surveyors to make surveys and sell the field notes afterwards *without having in their possession any order of survey.*"[35] George A. Nixon, Commissioner for issuing titles, granted title, in 1834–35, to eight hundred and seventy-one leagues of land in Libby, Jefferson, Jasper, Sabine, Nacogdoches, San Augustine, Houston and Montgomery counties, to the Galveston Bay and Texas Land Com-

[32] *Ibid.*, 6.
[33] *Ibid.*, 7 and 29.
[34] *Ibid.*, 29.
[35] *Ibid.*, 11. The italics are the present author's.

pany, on the Burnet-Vehlein-Zavala colonization contracts. Nixon himself received a present of eleven leagues by order of William H. Steele, Title Commissioner for the Nashville colony.[36]

E. L. R. Wheelock, a surveyor, testified that in 1835 he accused Steele of acting without authority in giving titles and that thereupon Steele became greatly agitated and swore. Steele then produced a document which he said was his authority, but when Wheelock tried to get it Steele hurriedly hid it. Wheelock further testified that Steele told him that he (Steele) was interested in the profits of the Nashville Company. Wheelock was invited " to join them in a combination to let no man who came have land, unless it was poor or refuse land, unless they would let one of the company clear it out on shares." [37] Steele, according to Wheelock, offered the latter a gift of seven leagues if he would turn over all his field notes *in blank,* and that Steele " added at the same time, he came to Texas to make a fortune, and would have it at any price." Wheelock testified that he met Steele later and that Steele " declared . . . I was a fool I had not followed his advice, as him and Joseph L. Hood were rich." [38] Steele, it was further testified, controlled all of the municipal officers, and so ran his surveys completely round the improvements of actual settlers as to force them to buy land from him. Wheelock testified that he came into possession of a deed made out *in blank* by Steele for one sitio of land (equal to a league, or 4,428 acres) ; Wheelock turned it over to the Texas Government " for the purpose of enabling it to detect such frauds." [39]

Recalled as a witness, Borden gave an itemized list of a huge number of forged and antedated titles in the Nashville, Vehlein, Burnet, Zavala, Cameron and Grant and other col-

[36] " Evidence in Relation to Land Titles," etc., 11.
[37] *Ibid.,* 18.
[38] *Ibid.*
[39] *Ibid.,* 20.

onies.[40] It will now be observed how carefully these appropriators followed the tacit advice given by the Supreme
Court of the United States in its decisions in the Arredondo
and Mitchell cases. Borden testified that many of the alleged
grants deposited in the Land Office were not *originals;* that
they were *certified copies;* and that " it was generally believed that the originals were carried off or destroyed by the
Commissioners." Of the four hundred leagues (1,771,200
acres) granted at Nacogdoches alone, irrespective of the grants
elsewhere, Borden testified that a large portion were granted
in violation of both Mexican and Texan laws prohibiting
unauthorized settlement of any lands comprehended within
twenty leagues of the limits of any foreign nation, or the
settlement of any territory within ten leagues in a straight
line from the Gulf of Mexico. Borden declared that there was
absolutely no proof in the Land Office that any authority for
their settlement existed.

These are a few typical facts from the joint committee's
report. As a further example of how land was granted to
spurious colonists the case of Martin DeLeon's colony will
suffice. The Commissioner for that colony gave his own son,
Francisco DeLeon, a grant of a quarter of a league of land,
and made an affidavit that Francisco possessed all requisite
qualifications, although, as a matter of fact, Francisco was
only a boy of ten years at the time, and was at school in
Louisiana. At the same time Commissioner DeLeon granted
himself a sitio of land (4,428 acres) as " the head of a family." [41]

Naturally, at this point of the narrative, the one question
obtruding itself is: In the face of these proofs of glaring
fraud did the looters retain their loot? They did. The consecutive records of the Texas Land Office show that 25,517,-
391 acres were originally confirmed under a few Spanish and

[40] See the long list he gave; *Ibid.,* Doc. No. 13.
[41] Case of De Leon vs. White, IX Texas Reports, 598.

many alleged Mexican titles. Deducting several million acres subsequently subtracted or declared forfeited, there remained 22,492,507 acres permanently alienated by means of these fraudulent claims.

These appropriations covered the richest and most fertile parts of Texas. How was the alienation consummated? By two methods: One device was to induce the Legislature to take no positive, effective adverse action; the other to get confirmation from the courts.[42] Judges Hemphill, Wheeler, Lipscomb and others of the Texas Supreme Court had all been attorneys for the land appropriators; in fact, in a certain case coming up before them, several of the judges had been counsel for the interests concerned, and a special judge had to be appointed for the occasion.[43] These judges fully accepted the doctrine laid down by the Supreme Court of the United States that the original deed need not be produced; that a certified *copy of a copy* was as good as the original.[44] After the annexation of Texas to the United States the precedents of the Supreme Court of the United States were, of course, jurisdictional and binding. Thus the validation of spurious grants comprising a large part of 22,000,000 acres was based upon the action of the Supreme Court of the United States in the Arredondo and Mitchell cases; when the Texas

[42] See, Report of Texas House Judiciary Committee, January 4, 1858. It reported this fact, and declared that it was well known that "not one in twenty of these titles were perfected by performance of conditions." It spoke of the old defenders of their country being driven from home "that the land sharks and speculators may reap their harvest of gain."—"Official Journal, House of Rep., Texas, 7th Biennial Session," 470–471.

[43] This note appears in the report of a land case in II Texas Reports, 78 (Dec., 1847): "This cause was tried before the Hon. R. T. Wheeler, Ass. J. of the S. C., and Thomas J. Jennings, Esq., so constituted in consequence of Justice Hemphill and Associate Justice Lipscomb having previously been counsel for the parties." In another such case (III Texas Reports, 248) Judge Wheeler did not sit, "having been of counsel below."

[44] See, Case of Paschal vs. Perez, VII Texas Reports (1851), p. 359, etc., etc.

judges were criticised, they pointed to precedents set by the great tribunal at Washington as their infallible justification.

From whom did these certified copies of copies emanate? From the Land Office at Austin. Of the methods of the Land Office we get a clear glimpse in the suits of the City of Galveston and the State of Texas vs. Menard. Michael B. Menard was a conspicuous member of the Senate under the Texas Republic; he was associated with Williams, Thomas M. League and others in various projects. He and League, for example, were among the incorporators of the Houston and Brazos Railroad Company, Menard personally obtained patents for huge quantities of land in many Texas districts.

On December 9, 1836, the Texas Congress granted to Menard one league and one labor of land on the island of Galveston for $50,000, the funds being part of his plunder from his land operations. Galveston real estate was of great value even at that early date; it was a principal sea-port with considerable commerce. Menard organized the Galveston City Company, partitioned his land into lots, and reaped large profits.

Presently he set up a claim to the whole of the " flats " or water-front. The Land Office graciously " construed " his claim so as to present him with an excess of more than 1,700 acres of water-front property. The Supreme Court of Texas in 1859 upheld that " construction." [45] In its petition to the court, in 1873, the State of Texas averred that " the patent or deed was made to contain this excess through the fraudulent combinations and representations of M. B. Menard and the Commissioner of the General Land Office." Largely on Marshall's doctrine of acquiescence, the court decided against the State's action to recover; the claim, said the court, had been recognized for thirty years, and that should be sufficient. [46]

[45] XXIII Texas Reports, 349. Judge Wheeler, having been counsel for Menard, did not sit in the case.
[46] XXXVIII Texas Reports, 12–35.

Everybody knew of the spurious nature of the alleged grants and titles, yet the Texas courts, not always, but usually, imitated Marshall's practice of treating proofs of fraud as fiction, and they studiously followed his precedents. And every well-informed person knew, too, how a large share of the capital that the New York capitalists had used in their Texas operations had been obtained. In 1838 it was discovered that Samuel Swartwout, a leader of Tammany Hall, and Collector of the Port of New York, had stolen the enormous sum of $1,222,705.69 from the Government, much of which theft had gone into Texas land speculation schemes.[47]

The Castro, Mercer, Peter and Other Contracts.

Within two years after the disclosure by the Texas Congressional joint committee, the Texas Congress made more colonization contracts. One of these grants was made, in 1842, to Henri Castro and associates, for the introduction of six hundred families within six years. A second contract was with Charles Fenton Mercer, for the introduction of five hundred families within five years. The Peter's contract giving 10,000 square miles was a third, and Fischer and Miller's for the introduction of six thousand German immigrants, a fourth. Mercer's and Peter's grants were in the north central part of Texas, Castro's extended from the Frio River to the Rio Grande, and Fischer and Miller's were on the waters of the Colorado, Llano and San Saba rivers.

The conditions of none of these grants were performed. Castro fell back upon the old subterfuge so often successfully pleaded in the Supreme Court of the United States, that Indian hostilities prevented him. In numerous cases in the Texas courts it was proved that Castro extorted contracts from all immigrants conveying to him and associates one-half

[47] House Ex. Doc. No. 13, Twenty-fifth Congress, Third Session also House Report, No. 313.

of the lands that they should receive. If they refused they were rejected as colonists.[48] In fact, all of the contractors, or "empressarios," did the same.[49] Mercer ("The Texas Association"), did not bring in a single settler, and Peter and associates (otherwise the Texas Land and Immigration Company) shamelessly violated their contracts.

Apparently their contracts stood forfeited. But in 1850 and 1852 the promoters induced the Texas Legislature to pass acts with various favorable provisions, one of which was the empowering of the local courts to adjudicate claims and decree grants. The argument used by the companies — at least the public argument — was based upon precedents of the Supreme Court of the United States that a contract created an express trust which could not be contravened. Under the acts of 1850 and 1852 the Peter, Mercer, Castro and Fischer and Miller companies received a total of 4,494,806 acres. A vast number of claims were allowed to fictitious colonists. In his message to the Texas Legislature on November 9, 1855, Governor E. M. Pease stated that "a large majority of said certificates were issued to young men under seventeen years of age" (at the time the settlement was alleged to have been made.)[50]

[48] See, Castro vs. James, VII Texas Reports, 219–223, and *Ibid.*, Vol. XX: 278.

[49] XV Texas Reports, 180–183.

[50] Official Journal of the House of Representatives, State of Texas, Seventh Biennial Session, 1857: 80–81. See, also, Report of S. Crosby, Commissioner of the Texas General Land Office, Official Journal of the Senate, 1856: 149–150. • In his report for the years 1900–1902, Charles Rogan, Commissioner of the Texas General Land Office stated (page 41) that an examination of the Spanish department of the Land Office showed that the act of September 4, 1850, also validated or confirmed private land claims to the extent of 1,100,000 acres, "which are still claimed and which seem to have good titles." Among the claims thus confirmed, according to Rogan, was Jose B. Borego's claim to forty-seven leagues; "but," reported Rogan, "the claimants are actually holding sixty-four leagues, or 286,532 acres." This excess, Rogan stated, the claimants have been holding on doubtful authority. Another claim confirmed by the act of 1850, Rogan reported, was that of Juan J. Balli, for seventy-one leagues and nine caballerios (315,362 acres).

Some of the 4,494,806 acres went to actual colonists, but by far the greatest portion remained in the ownership of the four promoting corporations.[51] Thus, under the Castro contract, 879,920 acres were given to alleged colonists, and 1,088,-000 acres to the company.

Official documents gave an appalling enough picture of how at least 26,000,000 acres of the richest Texas lands were literally stolen, but it was reserved to United States Senator Sam Houston to make public further details of how the thefts were accomplished. General Houston had been President of the Republic of Texas; and when on February 3, 1859, he made an extraordinary statement of facts in the United States Senate, even reading undeniable documents showing how the land appropriators had carried on their operations and how they boasted of being able to corrupt the Supreme Court of the United States, his disclosures were accepted as the authoritative utterances of a man who knew his facts. His speech, in fact, made such a profound sensation that it was

[51] For a time the capitalists owning the Mercer claim were satisfied with the 691,840 acres that they received. But twenty-five years later, they set up a claim to not less than *six thousand square miles*. Among the assertions, in reply to this claim, made by the State of Texas, were these charges: That the contract was fraudulently obtained and that the map submitted by the Mercer Company purporting to bear date of May 1, 1845, appeared to be of recent date; had been surreptitiously deposited in the office of the Secretary of State, without his knowledge, and took in *about three thousand square miles more than the contract actually covered.*

If this new claim, or any part of it, had been allowed, it would have conflicted with domains owned by railroad corporations. Times had changed; the judges on the bench in 1882 were almost exclusively former railroad attorneys. The Supreme Court of the United States, in 1883, threw the case out of court, saying that there was no satisfactory evidence that Mercer and associates ever introduced directly or indirectly a single family into Texas. "Have they spent any money in the enterprise?" Justice Miller went on. "A feeble attempt to show an outlay of $12,000 or $15,000 is made, but by no means successfully."— Case of Hancock vs. Walsh (Commissioner of the Texas General Land Office), III Wood's Reports, 351–367, and Case of Walsh vs. Preston, 109 U. S. Reports, 318. But this decision did not take away the 691,-840 acres already obtained by the Mercer Company.

not allowed to remain embalmed in the soon-forgotten pages of the *Congressional Globe,* as most speeches of members of Congress were, but was published in book form.[52]

Judge Watrous' Particular Activities.

The circumstances leading up to Senator Houston's revelations were as follows:

The local attorney for the Peter's colonization company had been John C. Watrous. He was, it seems, not only a shrewd and unscrupulous lawyer, but he was also a capitalist promoter, and was associated with Williams, Menard, McKinney, Thomas M. League and other members of the group so diligently and successfully plundering Texas. Also he was one of the most adroit lobbyists in the Texas Legislature; one of the measures that he had lobbied through was an act in 1841 incorporating himself and others of Texas and London, England, as the Texas Trading, Mining and Emigrating Company for the purpose of purchasing lands, importing immigrants, etc.[53] Watrous had a hand deep in a large number of great frauds then being promoted: colonization schemes, alleged Mexican private grants, and spurious certificates alleged to have been granted to Texan soldiers and to settlers.

In fact, he helped to organize a company to profit from the traffic in immense numbers of these fraudulent certificates. This company was composed principally of Watrous, ex-Congressman Joseph L. Williams, J. N. Reynolds (a New York politician and lobbyist who received subsidies from the large cotton-mill firm of Lawrence, Stone & Company, of Fall River, for lobbying tariff measures through Congress by brib-

---

[52] The Land Conspiracies of Texas, etc. Speech of Senator Sam Houston, of Texas, Exposing the Malfeasance and Corruption of John C. Watrous, Judge of the Federal Court in Texas, and Of His Confederates, Delivered In The Senate of the United States, Feb. 3, 1859." — N. Y., Pudney & Russell, Printers, 1860.

[53] "Laws of the Republic of Texas, Fifth Congress, 1841 ": 78–79.

ery [54]), and J. S. Lake, an Ohio and New York City politician, banker and broker who had plundered the Wooster Bank and the public of $936,398, much of which he had lost in speculations.[55] Associated with these men were other Texas and New York City capitalists; the headquarters of the company was in New York City.

What the clique especially and most pressingly wanted was a judge of their own in the United States District Court; although the Texas judges could be generally depended upon, still they often represented conflicting interests. Much more satisfying would be a judge absolutely and unalterably bound up in interest with the clique. Largely through the influence of Caleb Cushing, of Massachusetts, a puissant figure at Wash ington, and subsequently Attorney-General of the United States, the clique, on May 29, 1846, shortly after the annexation of Texas to the United States, succeeded in having Watrous appointed judge of the U. S. District Court in Texas.

Now, indeed, the land grabbers were sure of having their own way. True, Texas retained control of its lands, and the Texas courts were supposed to have complete jurisdiction. But by some member of the clique feigning or having a residence in some other State, collusive suits could be carried on and thrown into the United States District Court, which would be Watrous. This is what happened, as prearranged. When Watrous went on the bench, two lawyers, Ovid F. Johnson of Pennsylvania, and William G. Hale of New Hampshire, were imported into Texas to take charge of the clique's law affairs. To them Watrous turned over the Peter's colony, and other legal business. Through Robert Hughes, his confidential adviser, Watrous was also interested in the Powers and Hewitson grant, covering a large body of land on the coast, west of Galveston. Hughes, it may be remarked, had

[54] Report No. 352, Reports of Committees, Fifty-Third Congress, First Session, Vol. III: 20, etc.
[55] "De Bow's Review," 1848: 262–263. Senator Houston gave details of Lake's career.

been a surety in bond for William M. Gwin, former Marshall of southern Mississippi, whose implication in enormous land frauds has already been described.

Texas Legislature Denounces Watrous.

On March 20, 1848, a joint resolution of the Texas Legislature declared that Judge Watrous had given important decisions in cases in which he was interested, and that it also believed that Judge Watrous " has, while in office, aided and assisted certain individuals, if not directly interested himself, in an attempt to fasten upon the State one of the most stupendous frauds ever practised upon any country or any people, the effect of which would be to rob Texas of millions of acres of her public domain. . . ." Judge Watrous was asked to resign. He ignored both the denunciation and the request.

One of the suits begun in Watrous' court was an action to have fraudulent certificates validated. The case went up to the Supreme Court of the United States which in 1850 declined to validate them, saying that " immense numbers of these certificates were put in circulation, either forged or fraudulently obtained, which, if confirmed by surveys or patents would soon have absorbed all of the vacant lands of the Republic." [56] This decision caused consternation among the clique; and, as the sequel indicated, they now began to exert " influences " to attempt to win over the Supreme Court of the United States.

In 1855, the Adjutant-General's office at Austin, where many of the land archives were stored, was set on fire and destroyed by incendiaries. This act, Governor Pease reported, " has destroyed most of the original evidences upon which bounty and donation certificates were issued." [57] On

[56] Case of Thomas M. League vs. John De Young, Howard's Reports, Vol. XI: 201.

[57] Journal of the (Texas) Senate, Sixth Legislature, 1855: 42.

July 29, 1856, Stephen Crosby, Commissioner of the Texas Land Office, reported that an attempt had been made to destroy the Land Office building by fire.[58]

The reason lay in a desperate attempt to hinder a select committee of the Texas Senate which had been investigating the matter of land certificates alleged to have been granted to settlers, head of families, and to former soldiers in the Texan army. This committee reported voluminously on January 21, 1856, that the Boards of Traveling Commissioners which had been originally appointed in 1837 to determine who was entitled to land had grossly betrayed their trust. The committee recited in detail that not only were enormous numbers of forged and otherwise fraudulent certificates issued in the name of persons who never existed, and to soldiers long since dead, but that the officials and courts knew of the fraudulent nature of most of the certificates.[59]

Watrous' Impeachment Demanded.

In the same year that this report was submitted the Texas Senate passed a resolution demanding the impeachment of Judge Watrous. " Said judge," the resolution read, " is guilty of attempting, by contriving and carrying on a made-up suit in his own court, to validate in the same, over twelve hundred fraudulent land certificates, claimed by himself, and his ' compeers,' and of a class, in all, the enormous amount of 24,331,764 acres — of fraudulent certificates, thereby attempting to deprive his country of a vast domain, besides causing the State the cost of additional counsel in defending herself against such enormous precluded spoliations; and, on discovery of his interests in said class of certificates being made, said judge transferred said suit for determination to the United

[58] " Official Journal, Senate of the State of Texas, Adjourned Session, 1856 ": p. 150.
[59] Journal of the (Texas Senate) Sixth Legislature, 1856: 387–389.

States Court in another State, after shaping the case, and influencing that court in such a manner as to obtain his desired judgment." A similar resolution was passed in the next year by the Texas House.[60]

These resolutions were passed under great pressure. Genuine settlers were threatening violent retaliation if the frauds succeeded; and at a time when men wore their guns and used them these threats were not dismissed as idle words. Moreover, the schemes of the Watrous clique interfered with those of certain railroad, real-estate, ranch and other corporations which combined all of their power and influence to 'depose him.[61]

In 1857 Jacob Mussina submitted a memorial to Congress asking for the impeachment of Watrous. Mussina claimed an interest in titles to the cities of Brownsville, Point Isabel and adjacent lands. He recounted that the Watrous clique, however, had turned up with an alleged old grant, called the Cavazos grant, and that under this they alleged ownership of 250,000 acres, including the towns of Brownsville and Point Isabel and numerous villages and ranches, as also Government sites and improvements. Mussina further charged that a fraudulent trumped-up case was brought by William G. Hale and his partner, and that after deciding the case against Mussina, and influencing other United States judges, Judge Watrous ordered Mussina's property sequestrated. Mussina submitted an impressive series of facts from the court records to prove his charges.[62]

At the same time, Eliphas Spencer, of Texas, submitted a like memorial showing that Watrous, Williams, League, John

---

[60] "Official Journal of the Senate, of the State of Texas, Adjourned Session, 1856": p. 399, and *Ibid* of the House, 1857: pp. 420–424.

[61] The railroad companies secured approximately 32,400,000 acres in Texas. Much of this was obtained in, or after, the year 1854. Manufacturing and navigating corporations, then and subsequently, obtained a gift, in total, of 4,061,000 acres.

[62] Reports of Committees, First Session, Thirty-fifth Congress, 1857–58, Report No. 54: 2–10.

W. Lapsley, Menard and others were interested in pushing a claim for eleven leagues, based upon an alleged old grant to Thomas de La Vega. Spencer accused Williams of forging the power of attorney from La Vega, and he detailed how Judge Watrous became secretly interested in the claim and how Watrous had fraudulently and corruptly decided the case and had influenced other judges to act similarly[63] This particular eleven-league tract in dispute was merely a part of thirty-three leagues, or 180,000 acres, alleged to have been granted to La Vega and De Aguirres by the Mexican Government.

Watrous Haled up on Charges.

The House Committee on the Judiciary on February 2, 1857, recommended that action be taken on the charges against Watrous. Five days later, the House of Representatives as a body, determined, by a vote of 156 to 32, to proceed against Watrous in hearing the charges on which to determine whether he should be definitely haled up for impeachment.[64]

Powerful influences now exerted themselves to save Watrous. Caleb Cushing came forward to act as Watrous' attorney. It was an era when corruption was rampant at Washington; when committees of Congress were constantly reporting testimony that in tariff, railroad and other legislation, large amounts in bribery had been expended and received.[65] No one can read the elaborate testimony in Watrous' impeachment action without feeling convinced that the charges were more than adequately proved, notwithstanding the fact that most of the witnesses summoned were Texas lawyers, and they demurred at testifying.

The vote of the committee hearing the charges was divided

[63] Report No. 54, First Session, Thirty-fifth Congress, 11–12.
[64] The *Congressional Globe*, Part I, Third Session, Thirty-fourth Congress, pp. 542 and 627–628.
[65] For the array of specific facts, see the "History of the Great American Fortunes," Vols. II and III.

evenly. This, of course, ended the move to impeach him. The committee, however, handed in both majority and minority reports. The majority report apologetically said that the evidence was insufficient, because of the reluctance of the witnesses to tell all that they knew. The four minority members reported that the charges stood proved; that Judge Watrous with other persons had embarked in schemes involving immense tracts of land; that fraudulent and collusive suits were brought in his court; that he had procured improper testimony, and that he had decided those suits in his own favor.[66]

General Sam Houston's Denunciation.

The scandal resulting from Judge Watrous' escape from impeachment was the cause of Senator Houston's indignant speech of February 3, 1859. Inasmuch as the facts and documents in that speech comprise a volume in themselves, reference can be made here to certain cogent and relevant parts only. Senator Houston gave the history of the fraudulent operations of Watrous and his partners in minute detail, citing court records and other documents, and reading the actual correspondence of different members of the clique with one another. Speaking of the Peter's colonization syndicate (which acquired as we have related, 1,088,000 acres vested in its own name, and 879,920 acres mostly in the names of alleged settlers), Sam Houston proceeded:

"It further appears that the Hon. Caleb Cushing was employed as the attorney of this association, which is known to have numbered among its members men of the highest station and most powerful influence in the land; and that when elevated to the high office of Attorney-General of the United States, he gave an extra-judicial opinion in favor of the claim of the company which will be found in the published ' Opin-

[66] Reports of Committees, First Session, Thirty-fifth Congress, 1857–58, Report No. 54: 14.

ions of the Attorney-General.' [67]   I mention this only to illustrate the ramifications of the influences brought to sustain Judge Watrous. . . ." It may here be observed that this was the same Caleb Cushing who probably then, and certainly later, was so influential in pushing the appointment of Supreme Court Justices.

Then came an astonishing revelation, directly reflecting upon the integrity of the Supreme Court of the United States.

Williams' Letter on " Striking " the Supreme Court.

" It ought to have been supposed," Senator Houston went on a little later, in describing the conspiracy to get fraudulent land certificates validated, " that after the judgment of the supreme court of Texas, the high court of appeals, and finally, after the decision of the Supreme Court of the United States, against the validity of the certificates, further efforts on the part of the company would have been hopeless. But what vitality, what ramifications, what resources must they have possessed, when we find them daring at the last, as I shall show, to anticipate exerting an influence on the United States Supreme Court itself! This certainly was a fitting climax to audacity and assertion of power. Thus we find this branch of the scheme of the conspirators expiring with an adventurous and desperate effort to retrieve their fortunes by improper influences with the courts; the last effort still characteristic, and still significant of the comprehensive grasp and connections of this most extraordinary combination.

" As exposing the honest proposition of exerting an influ-

[67] See, " Opinions Of The Attorney-General for the U. S.," Vol. VIII.: 522-546. The question concerned the point whether an act passed by the Texas Legislature, in 1852, granting to the Peter's contractors (The Texas Land and Emigration Company) 1700 sections of land, to be located where it chose, was constitutional. As Attorney-General, Cushing reported that the act was constitutional, and that the Peter's Company had rights which it could assert in the Supreme Court of the United States.

ence on the Supreme Court of the United States, I will here
read a letter from Mr. Joseph L. Williams on this subject, to
whom, it appears, was and is allotted the Washington branch
of the company's operations."

The letter was dated Washington City, November 1, 1851.
Senator Houston did not state the name of the person to whom
it was addressed. The last paragraph of Williams' letter
read:

"I find much of your matter of reliance in the big suit in
Bibb's reports. This casually led me the other day to bring
the case to the notice of ——. He seems perfectly familiar
with every precedent and doctrine applicable to this case, and
he says it is quite impossible for the Supreme Court, on deliberate review and consideration, to abandon right, reason,
and casual law, on account of one casual act of stultification
at the last term. *I shall not omit the part of striker with certain members of the court, which I told you I would see to.
I am already here for the purpose. I will persuade Catron,
of Tennessee, to take the case under his especial charge."* [68]

To act the part of a "striker," meant to influence unduly or
corruptly.[69]   Of this letter one of two constructions is allow-
able: Either Williams was vapidly boasting, or he knew his
ground. He stated that he had gone to Washington for the
particular purpose of influencing "certain members of the
court." This pointed statement, by itself, was serious
enough. But he specifically mentioned Associate Justice Catron as the one especial member whom he would persuade to
take supervision of the case,— signifying that he looked to
Catron particularly to see to it that a favorable decision should
be rendered.

If untrue, the statements in Williams' letter were malignant

[68] The *Congressional Globe*, Part I, Second Session, Thirty-fifth Congress, 1858–59: p. 775.   The italics appear in the *Congressional Globe*.
[69] Thus, a "strike" bill is one introduced in a Legislature with a
definite purpose of forcing the corporation or individual to whom it is
hostile to yield tribute for its defeat or suppression.

and inexcusable attacks not only upon Justice Catron but upon the whole Supreme Court. Were that so, the Supreme Court would have been justified in haling Williams up for libel and punishing him severely, and Justice Catron should have immediately instituted suits, civilly and criminally.

Supreme Court Did Not Reply.

But no such development ever happened. Senator Houston's speech was given wide publicity; and published in the permanency of a volume, it had a considerable circulation. Instead of replying, all of the parties inculpated in that speech seemed anxious to hush the matter as soon as possible. In concluding his remarks Senator Houston said that elaborate as were the details he had given they, after all, were only a sketch of the whole of the facts, and he intimated that he had more in reserve. Evidently, the prudent counsel prevailed of keeping " dignified silence," and not pushing him too far by making any retort calculated to arouse him again.[70]

Senator Houston, it was clear, was holding back much striking information. These suppressed facts, exposing the inconsistency of the Supreme Court of the United States in validating certain private land claims, while rejecting others, would, if published in sequence, have reflected severely not only upon many of Houston's most distinguished colleagues in the Senate, but upon Congress itself.

Thus for example, United States Senator Judah P. Benjamin of Louisiana, one of the most powerful politicians in the

---

[70] Here we shall leave the subject of fraudulent Texas land certificates. By 1863, an aggregate of 41,956,202 acres in Texas had been patented to individuals or corporations. This amount did not include the 22,492,057 acres patented under alleged Spanish and Mexican grants and contracts. How much of the 41,956,202 acres was based on fraudulent certificates, it is impossible to say. " Many of them," reported a Commissioner of the General Land Office later, " were subsequently established apparently through judicial decree. Many of these decrees were not written in a courthouse."

country, was at that very time introducing a bill to validate
a number of private land claims for some of which he had been
attorney. These particular claims could not be confirmed by
the Supreme Court of the United States. They had been explicitly declared void by an act of Congress, in 1804, as having
been fraudulently granted by Governor Morales, at the very
period when the United States was taking over the sovereignty
of Louisiana and parts of what was called West Florida, and
when the United States claimed jurisdiction over the section
in which the alleged grants were made.

Senator Benjamin had argued in court as counsel for some
of these claimants. In 1858 Senator Benjamin, as chairman
of the Senate Committee on Private Land Claims, submitted
a bill in behalf of the claimants, which bill became a law on
June 22, 1860. Among the claims validated by this act were
the Reynes claim to 40,000 arpents in the Baton Rouge district, Louisiana; several other claims respectively embracing
32,000 and 40,000 arpents, in the same State; and a considerable number of other claims in Louisiana, Florida, Arkansas,
Missouri and other States. These claims, confirmed by act
of Congress, of June 22, 1860, embraced an aggregate of about
600,000 acres.[71]

Similar circumstances surrounded the De Bastrop claim.
This was an alleged grant made by Carondelet in 1796 or 1797,

[71] See the remarkable history of these claims, and of their final validation, in U. S. vs. Lynde, XI Wallace's Reports, 632–647, in which
Senator Benjamin's activities are clearly described. There was a close
identity of interest between the land appropriators and the original
railroad promoters; they were often the same persons. Senator Benjamin was one of the foremost promoters of the New Orleans, Jackson
and Great Northern Railroad, and was chairman of its board of directors. (See, Butler's "Judah P. Benjamin," pp. 134–136.) As for
John W. Lapsley, partner and accomplice of Watrous, he was president
of the Alabama and Tennessee Railroad Company (see, 53 Alabama
Reports, 257) which received a large land grant, later confirmed by
act of Congress, May 23, 1872. Lapsley was also a director of the
Selma and Gulf Railroad Company (45 Alabama Reports, 698). Many
of the railroad promoters obtained such sums as were invested by them
from land frauds.

to Baron De Bastrop, of a tract of twelve leagues square, or
1,016,264 arpents, in the Ouchita and Bayou Siard districts,
Louisiana. In 1807, Edward Livingston bought a sixteenth
interest in the claim and sold a large part of it to Stephen
Wante; Robert R. Goelet obtained other parts, and Stephen
Girard bought more than 200,000 acres of the claim. The
Board of Land Commissioners rejected the claim, and although potent influences assiduously tried to get a confirmation from Congress, that body for fifty years refused to consider it.

Girard bequeathed his estate to the cities of New Orleans
and Philadelphia. These cities brought suit to have the claim
validated, and succeeded in the lower courts. When the case
came up on appeal before the Supreme Court of the United
States, in 1850, Attorney-General Crittenden contended that
(supposing that a concession to De Bastrop had been really
made), the claimants not only did not produce the original
concession but failed to bring forward an authentic copy and
that they did not even allege the loss of the original. On these
grounds the Supreme Court (Justice Catron writing the majority opinion) reversed the lower court and rejected the
claim.[72] But it was validated by act of Congress, in 1854.

At the same time Justice Catron wrote another majority
opinion, rejecting the Boisdore claim, alleged to have been
granted by Governor-General Miro in 1783, in what is now
the State of Mississippi, as " a grant of land for a cow pasture." The holders of this alleged grant claimed an area of
from 100,000 to 400,000 acres. Notwithstanding the fact
that Boards of Land Commissioners and Congress had, for
forty years, consistently refused to recognize the claim as covering more than 1280 acres, the claim in full was validated
by the U. S. District Court in 1845. The Government ap-

[72] See, Case of U. S. vs. Cities of Philadelphia and New Orleans, XI
Howard, 609-661. Justices McLean, Wayne, McKinley and Grier dis-
sented. See, also, U. S. vs. Louise Livingston, widow of Edward
Livingston. and U. S. vs. Callender, *Ibid.*, 662-663.

pealed. When the case was argued before the Supreme Court of the United States in 1850, Attorney-General Crittenden sardonically exclaimed, " Boisdore never dreamed of such a magnificent principality for his cow pen as is claimed . . .! " [73]

The Court's Record Did Not Belie Houston.

Justice Catron's decisions in 1842, in a number of Florida land claims — the Low, Hanson, Atkinson and others — validating various claims of 15,000 and 16,000 acres each —(XVI Peters, 166 etc.) — had been subjected to sharp criticism. Contested by the Government, those claims had been confirmed by the Supreme Court of the United States, although some of the claimants had not even taken the trouble to be represented by counsel. But the majority opinions (cited above) delivered by Justice Catron and his dissenting opinion in the California land cases, would not seem to justify the implication that he, at least, was tampered with or was susceptible to illicit influences. Perhaps there were underlying developments and circumstances like those of the Dred Scott case, of which no hint appears in the formal records. But what does appear in the records indicates. (so far as the Supreme Court as a whole was concerned) the drift of matters lucidly enough.

When Mussina applied to the Supreme Court of the United States, in December, 1857, for a mandamus compelling Judge Watrous to allow him an appeal in the Cavazos case, the Su-

[73] U. S. vs. Boisdore, XI Howard, 63–104. Justices McLean, Wayne and McKinley dissented. Governor-General Miro was the official whose name was forged to so many documents in Arkansas. Justices McLean, Wayne, McKinley and Grier had also dissented when Chief Justice Taney and a majority refused to confirm the notorious Maison Rouge claim. This was a claim to *thirty square leagues*, or 1,044,000 acres in western Louisiana, alleged to have been granted by Governor-General Carondelet, in 1795. Chief Justice Taney denounced the alleged grant as forged and antedated. See, III Howard, 785, and VII *Ibid.*, 833.

preme Court (Justice McLean writing the opinion) denied
his application, on the ground that Watrous had submitted
an explanation and that the court was bound to accept it! [74]
Ten years later, another suit brought by Mussina against
Cavazos was dismissed by the Supreme Court of the United
States because of this extraordinary discovery: That when
Mussina's counsel in the court below had filed a bill of exceptions *the judge had not signed and sealed it.* This formality
not having been complied with, the Supreme Court refused to
consider Mussina's petition.[75]

On the other hand, in the suit of Spencer vs. Lapsley over
the alleged La Vega grant, we see the Supreme Court of the
United States upholding Watrous' decision by deciding, in
1857, in favor of Lapsley. It was well known that Lapsley
was an integral member of the Watrous clique, and that he
had originally assumed a residence in Alabama in order to
bring the suit in Watrous' court. Hughes and Hale appeared
as his attorneys in the Supreme Court. In a dissenting opinion, Justice Daniel declared that the alleged La Vega deed in
question was spurious, denounced the whole transaction, and
showed that Judge Watrous had a personal interest in the
case, and should therefore have been disqualified from sitting.[76]

These were three of a series of suits occasioning no little
scandal. In other feigned cases arranged by the Watrous
clique, the lawyers for that clique, Hale, Robinson, and
Hughes, were invariably in evidence, often appearing col-
lusively on opposite sides; [77] the facts were patent but the Supreme Court of the United States closed its eyes.

[74] XX Howard's Reports, 280–290.
[75] VI Wallace's Reports, 355–363.
[76] XX Howard, 264–280.
[77] See, for example, Case of League vs. Atchison, VI Wallace's Reports, 112–116. This was an action by League to recover a lot in
Galveston which both parties claimed under the Galveston City Company. Robinson and Hale represented League. Upon the Texas statute
of limitations that a suit to recover real estate must be brought within

The area óf land obtained by the Watrous combination was large and of great value, but the exact outcome of all their schemes it is not possible to trace here to the end.

But one fact is absolutely certain: By 1860, patents for great areas of land had been issued under the Powers and Hewitson contract and under many other grants in which Watrous, League and associates were openly or surreptitiously interested.[78]   And already, by the year 1858, according to a report of a joint select committee of the Texas Legislature, not less than 68,000,000 acres of Texas lands were patented to individuals, largely absentee capitalists.   The committee complained that 21,000,000 acres escaped taxation. " We find millions of acres of fertile soil," it reported further, " lying over Texas, upon which the owners (the greater part of whom we believe to be non-residents) are wilfully and knowingly failing and refusing to pay taxes." [79]   Elected Governor of Texas, General Sam Houston stated to the Legislature, on February 8, 1860, that " his energies had been devoted to trying to put a stop to the legislating away of public lands," and " towards overturning corruption and arresting abuses, but at every step, he [Houston] has been met by difficulties almost insurmountable." [80]   If this corruption was so actively and successfully employed in Texas, is it not reasonable to suppose that it was equally so at Washington?

three years, Justice Grier (writing the opinion of the Supreme Court of the U. S.) reversed the lower court, and decided in favor of League. See, also, Case of Cavazos vs. Trevino, VI Wallace, 773. Trevino, as Senator Houston had shown, was one of the clique's tools. Also, McKinney vs. Saviego, XVIII Howard, 235, in which Hale appeared for McKinney, and Hughes for Saviego.

[78] See, " Abstract of Patented Titles, etc., from the Records of the General Land Office, Austin, 1860": pp. 1237, etc.

[79] " Official Journal, House of Rep., Texas, Seventh Biennial Session," 483–484.

[80] Journal of the Senate, State of Texas, 1860: p. 545.

CHAPTER XI

THE SUPREME COURT UNDER CHIEF JUSTICE TANEY
(CONTINUED)

During the range of years covered by the latter part of the preceding chapter, the course of the Supreme Court of the United States was signalized by two other distinct lines of action, as standing out conspicuously in its mass of decisions:

I. The validation of private claims to millions of acres of the most valuable lands in California. Of the 8,150,143 acres of these lands obtained by individuals under the form of private land claims, a great part was presented by decisions of the Supreme Court under Chief Justice Taney.

II. The issuance of the edict, in the Dred Scott case, that all laws interfering with the slavery of negroes were unconstitutional and void, and that the negro was devoid of any civil rights which the white man was bound to respect.

With each of these events we shall deal in consecutive, although not strictly chronological, order. Before doing so, however, it is necessary to describe a certain change in the personnel of the Supreme Court, and the important transition it signified.

Justice Curtis Ascends to the Bench.

Justice Levi Woodbury had died in 1851. His successor, appointed by President Fillmore, in 1851, was Benjamin R. Curtis, of Boston. At the time of his appointment Curtis was only forty-two years old. Compared to the ages of nearly all of the other Justices when commissioned to the Supreme Court bench, Curtis was remarkably young. To what merit or factor did he owe his appointment?

His elevation to the Supreme Court was an event of the greatest significance, although its fundamental importance was not then clearly seen.

For more than half a century the appointees to the Supreme Court had been either owners of landed estates or attorneys for land claims and schemes,— men almost invariably combining in their persons, views and interests the representation of the land-owning class. But within a few decades, great economic changes had taken place. Two new and mighty factors had gradually asserted themselves. The first of these was the manufacturing interest; the second, the railroad power. The latter, at the time of Curtis' appointment, was in its infancy, but, nevertheless, it had already become powerful enough to insist that it have its representative on the Supreme Court bench. The power of the railroad corporation, however, was not then a distinct one, as it subsequently became under the dominance of such dictatorial rulers as Commodore Vanderbilt, Jay Gould, Russell Sage, Collis P. Huntington, Leland Stanford and their kindred potentates.[1] At that era landed, banking, manufacturing and railroad interests were more or less interassociated; the promoters and directors of many of the original railroads were men who had made their profits from land speculations, manufacturing, trading, commerce and banking. The time was still somewhat distant when forceful, arbitrary, super-unscrupulous men such as Vanderbilt and Gould seized great lines of railroad systems, originally owned by a medley of interests, and concentrated their control in themselves.

Curtis' appointment, therefore, was an exact reflex of conditions at the time of his selection. He had studied law at Harvard under Justice Story, who was a lecturer at that Uni-

[1] The growth of the railroad interest is fully described in a later chapter.

versity.   From 1836 to 1851 Curtis, as an attorney, had represented a great number of commercial firms, insurance companies, shippers, banks, manufacturing corporations and canal and railroad companies.   Specifically, he had been attorney for the Oriental Bank and the Tremont Bank, of Boston, and for other banks;[2] he had represented the Western Railroad corporation,[3] the Boston and Maine Railroad,[4] the Boston and Providence Railroad corporation,[5] the Boston Manufacturing Company and a variety of other corporations.   In the biography of Curtis, edited by his son, we are told that his income had been as large as that of any other lawyer in New England, and that in 1851 — the year of his appointment to the Supreme Court — he had bought a valuable estate of three hundred acres at Pittsfield, Massachusetts, where he built a splendid mansion.

In the same work we are also informed that Curtis' appointment was recommended to President Fillmore by Daniel Webster, then Secretary of State.[6]   Although having a large private income from his corporation practice, Webster's habits were such that he was generally in an impecunious state. Periodically, the Lawrences and other cotton manufacturers would come to his relief; he seems to have been regularly subsidized by them.   " On several occasions," says Ben Perley Poore, referring to Abbot Lawrence, " a large cotton lord," and a principal owner of the great Fall River Mills, " he had been one of ' the solid men of Boston,' who had contributed considerable sums for the pecuniary relief of Mr. Webster." [7]

[2] See, Metcalf's Reports (Supreme Court of Mass.), Vols. III and IV: pp. 581, etc., Cushing's Reports, *Ibid.*, 142, etc., etc.
[3] Cushing's Reports (Supreme Court of Mass.), Vol. III: 270. In this case he had successfully prevented an injured railroad brakeman from recovering damages from the company.
[4] III Cushing's Reports, 25 and 58, and V *Ibid.*, 375.
[5] VI Cushing, 424.
[6] " The Life and Writings of B. R. Curtis, Edited By His Son," Vol. I: 154.
[7] " Reminiscences," Vol. I: 287. Webster was one of the foremost politicians in advocating a high protective tariff.

These donations were gratefully received by Webster.

Working-Class Conditions.

The period was one of astonishing activity on the part of the working class, and issues were constantly arising which employers looked to the courts to settle. The attempt to have the strike declared by the courts illegal and a conspiracy had failed, but the demand for a shorter workday was bitterly resisted. The owners of the cotton mills were amassing immense fortunes; as fast as more improved labor-saving machinery was installed, production was increased and wages were reduced. A large proportion of the employés in the Lowell mills were women and children.

In the *Voice of Industry,* a labor paper published at Fitchburg, Massachusetts, in 1845, a typical instance of conditions is given in the statement of a frail girl of eight or nine years old: " I go to work before daylight in the morning and never leave it until it is dark, and don't make enough to support mother and baby." Referring to the increase of two hundred per cent. in the cotton-mill dividends in a single year, and the corresponding decrease of twelve and a half per cent. in the wages of women and children, the *Voice of Industry* said:

" In this state of things the bounty offered to manufacturers by the tariff induced many of the wealthy men of New England to invest their capital in manufactures, which, when the tariff has been high, proved exceedingly profitable, concentrating great wealth in the hands of a few, whilst the laboring part of the community has increased rapidly, until the demand for employment exceeds the want of the employers, which has enabled them to reduce the wages of the operatives whilst their own profits were very largely increased, and this reduction of wages must continue to go on with the increase of the class of society who depend upon employment for subsistence, until they arrive at a point which will barely afford such necessities as will enable the human system to undergo its daily toil."

One organization after another was formed either by the workers themselves, or by humanitarian sympathizers. " The dollar," stated the New England Protective Union, in 1845, " was to us of minor importance; humanitary and not mercenary were our motives." And it went on: " Man's muscles are now made to compete with iron machines that need no rest, that have no affections, that eat no bread. Why is he that produces everything not only destitute of the luxuries but of the common comforts of life, to say nothing of a shelter he may call his own?" As to the conditions of the workers, the Union said that, " Lamentable as is the condition of the laboring men, that of the women is worse and increasingly so." The early development of the coöperative idea is seen in its declaration, " We must proceed from combined stores to combined shops, from combined shops to combined houses, to joint ownership in God's earth, the foundation that our edifice must stand upon." These lofty aspirations were accompanied by a strong denunciation of the fugitive slave law " as an infamous act, fitted to be trampled under the foot of every lover of justice and liberty."

The New England Workingmen's Association was formed at the same time to combat prevalent conditions of society under the arrangements of which " labor is and must be the slave of wealth," and " the producers of all wealth are deprived, not merely of its enjoyment, but also of the social and civil rights which belong to humanity and the race." Everywhere the workers were rising, and as fast as they formed organizations, the employing capitalists sought to intimidate them and disrupt their organizations by discharging the leaders from work, and reducing them to beggary.

A call for a Workingmen's Meeting in New York, on July 16, 1845, stated that there were 65,000 paupers in New York

City alone, and that one-sixth of the entire population was in a condition of pauperism; that the white labor of the North was in a worse state than the slave of the South. A demand of Pittsburg and Alleghany City cotton-mill workers on June 16, 1845, for a ten-hour, instead of a twelve-hour, workday, was met with the reply that the adoption of such a system was impracticable so long as the Eastern factories ran seventy-two hours a week.

The first Industrial Congress of the United States convened at New York, on October 12, 1845. It declared that " it is a well-known fact that rich men, capitalists and non-producers associate to devise means for securing to themselves the fruits of other men's labors "; therefore, farmers, mechanics and workingmen ought to organize. The preamble also declared that further traffic in land by the Government should cease, and that the public lands should be made free to actual settlers, so that every man, woman and child in the nation should have a home. It denounced the existing system of factory labor, as withering life's energies, even in childhood, causing physical deformity because of excessive toil, and depriving workers of the opportunity to acquire cultivation, and at the same time, producing deterioration of both mind and body.

In 1845 and 1846 great meetings of the workers in Lowell, Chicopee, Manchester, New York City and Philadelphia demanded a ten-hour day. In these agitations girls and women were as aggressive as the men. To supply the places of these agitators the Chicopee mill owners resorted to this device: They sent a long black wagon to make regular trips in Massachusetts, Vermont and New Hampshire, paying the man in charge a dollar a head (or more according to distance traveled) for every girl he secured. Farm girls, it was charged, were thus enticed on the representations that the work " was very neat, wages high, and that they could dress in silks and spend half the time in reading."

Land Grabbing and Negro Slavery Denounced.

The Laborers' Union memoralized Congress to put an end to the traffic in the public lands. " This system," it protested, " is imported into this country from Europe, and is fast debasing us to the condition of dependent tenants, of which condition a rapid increase of inequality, misery, pauperism, vice and crime are necessary consequences. . . ." In 1846, the New England Workingmen's Convention, at Lynn, Mass., declared that " there are at the present time three millions of our brethren and sisters groaning in chains on the Southern plantations . . . ," and called upon " our brethren to speak out in thunder tones, both as associations and individuals, and to let it no longer be said that Northern laborers, while they are contending for their rights, are a standing army to keep three millions of their brethren and sisters in bondage at the point of the bayonet."

These are a few of a large assemblage of facts showing the unrest and agitation among the workers at the time, and their spirit, views and purposes. Year after year the movement grew; strike succeeded strike; the ten-hour day was finally won after heroic struggles in which starvation was a commonplace. But for the great contest for the emancipation of the negro slaves, which soon overshadowed, and partially absorbed, the labor agitation in the North, the movement would have gone much further, despite every repressive measure that the · capitalists used. But it was already formidable enough, and employers generally foresaw that it contained potentialities certain to produce great conflict in future times. Even then they perceived that it was necessary for them to mold the courts in such a shape that the activity and actions of the workers would be more and more restricted by judicial constructions, orders and usurpations.

Justice Curtis' habit of frank letter-writing gives us some insight into the methods of the Supreme Court of the United

States. Writing from Washington, February 29, 1852, Justice Curtis informed Ticknor: "Judge Catron will give the opinion of the court in Mrs. Gaines' case to-morrow. In this opinion I unite with Nelson and Grier. Wayne and Daniel dissent, on account of an interest, in some way, which some of their relatives have. . . ."[8]

One of the traditions of the Supreme Court, constantly repeated for the edification of the public, was that the strictest precautions were taken to guard against advance information of decisions being given out. Here, however, was one of the Justices conveying information of precisely that character. Quite true, Curtis was writing to one whom he regarded as a confidant, but, as we shall see, the same leakage happened in the Dred Scott case. This being so in at least two known instances, it is within the bounds of possibility that it took place in other decisions, possibly affecting stock-market operations, in which advance information, of only a day's notice, could be transmuted into fortunes.

In the same letter, Curtis described Justices McLean and Wayne as the "most high-toned Federalists on the bench." Elsewhere he noted that McLean hoped to be a candidate for the President of the United States.[9] He thus confirmed what was often publicly charged — that more than one member of the Supreme Court was incessantly playing politics, and seeking to ingratiate himself into the favor of every powerful interest which could be used in advancing political ambitions. This was especially and notoriously true of McLean, who, having the good-will of the capitalists of his own region, sought also that of the slave-owning power.

[8] "The Life and Letters of B. R. Curtis," etc., Vol. I: 168. This suit involved title to property of immense value in New Orleans. The footnote in the Case of Charles Patterson vs. Gaines and Wife, VI Howard's Reports, 550, reads: "Mr. Justice Taney did not sit in this cause, a near family relative being interested in the event. Mr. Justice McLean did not sit in this cause." It is not explained who the relative was. The decision went against Mrs. Gaines.
[9] "Life and Letters of B. R. Curtis," etc., Vol. I: 168 and 180.

Curtis as a Corporation Attorney.

In view of the fact that decisions validating claims of enormous magnitude in Texas, California and other sections in favor of individuals and corporations were handed down by the Supreme Court of the United States largely during the time Curtis was on the bench, from 1851 to 1857, his subsequent career may be appropriately commented upon here. He was one of the few Justices, in good or bad health, who ever resigned from the Supreme Court; his son tells us that from the date of his resignation in 1857, to his death in 1874, he gathered in about $650,000 from professional services,[10]— a sum equal in value to many times that amount in present days. After he had resumed the practice of law, he represented a large galaxy of corporations, some of which were the identical corporations issues affecting which had been decided by the Supreme Court. He represented the Boston and Maine Railroad, the Fitchburg Railroad, the Grand Junction Railroad and Depot Company, the Eastern Railroad Company, the Adams Express Company, the Galveston Railroad Company, James Lawrence of the Middlesex Mills, the Boston Water Power Company, the Boston Gas Light Company, the Hudson Iron Company and many other corporations.[11] Frequently he also appeared for stockholders and other capitalists in suits against corporations, and on several occasions was retained by the United States to contest land claims. Wherever a large fee was to be had, there Curtis was to be found, no matter what the nature of the case was, or whoever his client. Beyond doubt, he was one of the most frequently employed and best-paid corporation attorneys of his day; few lawyers represented so wide a variety of corporate interests.

[10] " Life and Letters of B. R. Curtis," etc., Vol. I: 268.
[11] See, XIV Gray's Reports (Supreme Court of Mass.), 553; 103 Mass. Rep., 254 and 259; 107 Mass. Rep., 15; XI Wallace's Reports, 459; 83 Mass. Reports (I Allen), 339; 91 Mass. Rep., 466; 96 Mass. Rep., 444; 102 Mass. Rep., 45, etc., etc.

Organized Forgery in California.

The Mexican War resulted in the cession to the United States, in 1848, of the present States of California, Nevada, Utah, part of Colorado, and the whole of the Territories of Arizona and New Mexico, except the Messilla Valley. This domain comprised 334,000,000 acres.

In anticipation of this cession, the same process of forging and antedating land claims which had proved so generally and signally successful in the Louisiana Purchase, and in Florida and Texas, was industriously carried on in California and in other parts of the Mexican cession.

Reporting to Congress in 1860, United States Attorney-General Black described how he had ordered the Mexican archives to be collected, and he set forth the details of that investigation. " The archives thus collected," he wrote, " furnished irresistible proof that there had been an organized system of fabricating land titles carried on for a long time in California by Mexican officials; that forgery and perjury had been reduced to a regular occupation; that the making of false grants, with the subornation of false witnesses to prove them, had become a trade and a business. . . . There was also compiled from the records here a faithful chart of all of the professional witnesses or persons supposed to have hired themselves out to do the business of false swearing of claims. To-day full biographies of nearly all of the men who have been engaged in these schemes of imposture, from governors down to the lowest suborned witnesses, can now be furnished whenever necessary."

Black went on to say: " It must be remembered that the grants in most of these fraudulent cases were very skilfully got up, and were supported by the positive oaths, not merely of obscure men whose characters were presumed to be fair, but also by the testimony of distinguished men, who had occupied high social and political places under the former governors. . . . The value of the lands claimed under grants ascertained to be forged is $150,000,000." [12]

But already, under a certain noted decision of the Supreme Court of the United States, immense areas of the richest agricultural, grazing, timber, water-front, mining and city lands in California had been presented to a few capitalists.

Following the discovery of gold in California, there was hardly a politician at Washington who was not engaged, directly or indirectly, in pushing land claims; with vast riches in sight, a feverish scramble set in to have a hand in the spoils. This activity became so pronounced and caused so much scandal, that to mollify indignant constituencies, Congress in 1853 passed a pretentious act, which, however remained a dead letter. The act forbade, under penalties, any Government official from acting as agent or attorney in prosecuting claims, or from receiving any gratuity or interest in them. It forbade members of Congress, under a penalty of fine and imprisonment, from doing the same, and it subjected any person who attempted to bribe a member of Congress to fine and imprisonment, and the acceptor of the bribe to forfeiture of his office.

Importance of the Fremont Case.

The particular case decided by the Supreme Court of the United States serving as the great precedent in allowing land grabbers to appropriate millions of acres in California and elsewhere was that of Fremont vs. the United States. Fremont turned up with a claim for a " floating grant " for ten square leagues (44,386.33) acres, which he averred had been granted by the Mexican Acting-Governor Micheltorena, in 1844, to Juan B. Alvardo, from whom Fremont claimed to have bought it. By " floating grant " was meant one with boundaries not described, but with power to locate anywhere.

[12] Ex. Doc. No. 84, Thirty-Sixth Congress. Also, House Reports, Third Session, Fortieth Congress, Report No. 261 : 544.

If this grant were confirmed, Fremont and all others claiming to hold similar grants could select the finest lands wherever they chose.

The Government stubbornly contested Fremont's claim, contending that it was a mere paper title or grant, and that the conditions of settlement called for had never been carried out. Fremont advanced the old, mildewed excuse that Indian hostilities had prevented settlement. Accepting this excuse, on precedents heretofore cited, the Supreme Court of the United States, in December, 1854, confirmed Fremont's grant as valid.[13]

Chief Justice Taney, in delivering the majority opinion, cited particularly the Arredondo decision, and held that when made, the grant imparted a vested right, even though it had not been confirmed by the Mexican Departmental Assembly, as the law required.

Dissenting, Justices Catron and Campbell strongly denounced the claim as one that had no standing and that absolutely lacked both merit and equity. They pointed out that not a single condition of the grant had been performed; that it was admitted that the Mexican Government never would have confirmed the claim; and declared that " no bolder case than the one before us can exist in California, where the grant is not infected with fraud or forgery." [14]

General John C. Fremont, the beneficiary of this decision, had taken part in the conquest of California, and was United States Senator from California in 1850–1851. He was the Republican candidate for the Presidency in 1856. When he commanded the Western department of the Federal army, at St. Louis, during the Civil War, in 1861, the greatest frauds were committed at that post in the purchase of munitions and supplies. One particularly glaring example of these

[13] Howard's Reports, Vol. XVII: 542–576.
[14] *Ibid.*, 571. A footnote in Howard reads: " Mr. Justice Daniel did not sit in this cause " (p. 542).

great frauds was that famous sale of condemned rifles (described in Vol. III of the "History of the Great American Fortunes," citing from the records). Five thousand of Hall's carbines, condemned by the army officers as being so bad that they would shoot off the thumbs of the soldiers who used them, were sold to Arthur M. Eastman for $3.50 each, and then resold to Fremont, for use in the army, at $22. The real backer of this transaction was that great financial magnate of later days — J. Pierpont Morgan. When the Government found out the spurious nature of the rifles and refused to pay the full sum, Morgan brought suit. Under a later decision of the Court of Claims the Government was forced to pay in full, the court holding to the technicality that a contract was a contract. These facts tend to illumine the character of Fremont's dealings, and are well worth referring to in this description of the Fremont claim decision of 1854.

Land Claims Validated Under the Fremont Precedent.

Under this decision, the United States District Court in California was compelled to confirm a great number of similar claims. In thus confirming, in June 1856, Francisco Rico's claim to eleven square leagues in Stanislaus County, Judge Hoffman clearly expressed his suspicions of the genuineness of the grant, but found himself forced to confirm it under the precedent in the Fremont case.[15] Likewise in accordance with the precedent in the Fremont case, Judge Hoffman could not avoid confirming other grants, many of which had been rejected by the Board of Land Commissioners. Among the claims confirmed under the Fremont ruling were:

Charles D. Semple's claim to eleven square leagues of land on the Sacramento River.[16]

15 U. S. vs. Rico, Hoffman's Reports: Land Cases, 1862: 161–162.
16 *Ibid.*, 37.

Thomas O. Larkin's claim to eleven leagues of land on the west bank of the Sacramento River.[17]

George C. Yount's claim to one league of land in Napa County.[18]

Josefa Soto's claim to ten square leagues of land in Colusa County.[19]

Hiram Grimes' claim to eight leagues of land in San Joaquin County.[20]

Juan Perez Pachecho's claim to eleven leagues of land in Mariposa County.[21]

Andreas Pico's claim (one of a number of his claims) to eleven square leagues of land in Calaveras County.[22]

Charles M. Weber's claim to eleven leagues of land in San Joaquin County.[23]

The claim of the heirs of Anastasio Chabolla to eight leagues of land in San Joaquin County.[24]

Antonio Maria Pico's claim to eight leagues of land in the same county.[25]

James Noe's claim to five leagues of land in Yolo County.[26]

Sebastian Nunez's claim to six leagues of land in Tuolumne County.[27]

And other claims of the same character. The claims above

[17] *Ibid.*, 41.
[18] *Ibid.*, 43.
[19] *Ibid.*, 68.
[20] *Ibid.*, 107.
[21] Hoffman's Reports: Land Cases, 113.
[22] *Ibid.*, 117 and 188. The Calaveras County claim, however, was subsequently voided by the Supreme Court of the United States. Attorney-General Stanton had appealed the case, and clearly proved that no such grant to Andreas Pico had ever been made by his brother. Acting Governor Pio Pico. "It is a forgery," Stanton declared in court. "The proof of this is powerful and overwhelming . . ." In the face of this proof, the Supreme Court could not avoid invalidating the claim.— XXII Howard's Reports, 406–416.
[23] Hoffman's Reports, etc., 126.
[24] *Ibid.*, 130.
[25] *Ibid.*, 142.
[26] *Ibid.*, 162.
[27] *Ibid.*, 197.

mentioned comprised more than 550,000 acres of the richest lands in California.

In confirming these grants, Judge Hoffman made severe comments and more than implied that if he were not confronted with the ruling of the Supreme Court of the United States, in the Fremont case, he would have rejected most of them. In his decision on the Pico eleven-league claim he expressed his suspicions of the authenticity of the grant, and in the Nunez case he spoke of the strange testimony of the witnesses as suspiciously like perjury. The Mexican laws, Judge Hoffman said, imposed strict conditions upon all grants. Although in the cases of many of the grants no settlement had been made, and although the excuse advanced of Indian hostilities preventing settlement was not satisfactorily shown, yet he was compelled to confirm the claims. He could not, he said, contravene the ruling of the Supreme Court in the Fremont case.

Systematic Forgery and Perjury.

Many of the foregoing grants, real or alleged, bore the signature of Pio Pico, Mexican Acting Governor of California, in 1846. No doubt Pico's signature was genuine in some cases, for when it was evident that Mexican authority was to be supplanted by that of the United States, Pico industriously began to issue fraudulent grants in return (as the court records indicate) for bribes. A large number of the grants bearing his signature were made, or were said to have been made, in a single month — May, 1846 — two months before the Mexican authority in California was overthrown. In the case of other grants, his signature and the signatures of other Mexican governors were forged, and the alleged grants antedated. Acting-Governor Pio Pico's Secretary was Moreno; of Moreno and his associates, the House Committee on Claims reported, on February 24, 1869:

". . . Gomez, Abrego and Moreno are suitable associ-

ates. They are equally notorious for the forgeries and perjuries in which they have been concerned. Gomez and Abrego
were the chief instruments in the false swearing in the great
Limantour swindle that attracted so much public attention
some years ago. Ex-Secretary Stanton visited California in
1858 in behalf of the United States in connection with land
cases, and then found that Abrego had been a witness to support thirty-two, and Gomez, twelve, claims, most of which were
ascertained to be frauds or forgeries." [28]

In rejecting many claims which, because they lacked certain
features bringing them within the scope of the Fremont ruling, could be thrown out, Judge Hoffman referred to the perjuries committed by Gomez. Hoffman rejected Joseph C.
Palmer's claim to two leagues of land in San Francisco
County, saying that " the suspicion that it has been fabricated
since the change of Government is irresistibly suggested.
That such has been the case, in some instances, is notorious.
That such a fraud was easy while the former governors of
this country [California] were alive and accessible, is obvious." Judge Hoffman further wrote of " the notorious facility with which testimony like that in support of this claim
can be procured." [29]

Although many of these and other claims were nominally
in the names of Mexicans, they were really owned or promoted
by American politicians and capitalists. While Judge Hoffman, at San Francisco, was denouncing and exposing the organized system of fraud and forgery, the Supreme Court of
the United States was busily engaged in both rejecting and
confirming land claims of vast magnitude. The claims rejected by it had not only been awkwardly prepared, but their
obvious circumstances were left in so crude and clumsy a

[28] House Reports, Third Session, Fortieth Congress, 1869, Rep. No.
261 : 535.
[29] Hoffman's Reports, etc., 249–272. (Case of Palmer *et al.* vs. the
U. S.)

shape that no court in the wide world could have exposed itself to ridicule by professing to accept the pleas made.

Juan M. Luco and José L. Luco came forward with what purported to be a grant from Acting-Governor Pio Pico for from thirty to fifty square leagues, or some 270,000 acres, in California. Judge Hoffman sarcastically commented upon the fact that during the years when they were supposed to hold this extensive and valuable claim, one of them was living upon the alms of a rich friend, or mending clothes for a livelihood. Why, too, he inquired, had they allowed so many years to elapse before they bethought themselves of the necessity of getting the grant confirmed? Judge Hoffman threw the grant out of court as forged and antedated.[30] The Supreme Court of the United States likewise found the purported circumstances too much of a strain upon its credulity. It dismissed the claim as " beyond doubt a mere fabrication," and declared the documents forgeries.[31]

Eleven square leagues on the upper waters of the Sacramento River was Henry Cambuston's claim, purported to be derived from a grant made by Pio Pico, in May, 1846. Attorney-General Black denounced it as a forgery. " In the examination of the evidence in this case," wrote Justice Nelson, in delivering the opinion of the Supreme Court of the United States, in December, 1857, " it is difficult to resist a suspicion as to the bona-fides of the grant in question." He added significantly: " The court below appears to have been very much impressed with the unsatisfactory character of the evidence, and with doubts as to the genuineness of the title, and seems to have yielded rather to the apparent acquiescence of the representatives of the Government, in the decisions of the Commissioners, than to any settled convictions of its own judgment." The Supreme Court pronounced the claim invalid.[32] The claim of James R. Bolton to fully 10,000 acres

30 Hoffman's Reports, etc., 371.
31 XXIII Howard's Rep., 515–543.
32 U. S. vs. Cambuston, XX Howard, 59–65.

of land in the vicinity of San Francisco — a claim valued (at a low estimate) at more than $2,000,000 in the year 1851 — was also declared worthless by the Supreme Court of the United States. Bolton averred that Pio Pico had given the grant to Santillan, a priest, from whom he had bought it.[33]

Rafael Garcia claimed nine leagues of land on an alleged grant by Micheltorena. Attorney-General Black pointed out that there was no trace in the official archives of the papers produced. " The proof," he continued, " would be defective, if the witnesses were men of good character ; but the testimony comes from William A. Richardson and Manuel Castro, both of whom have been made utterly infamous by being detected in the commission of wilful and corrupt perjuries. . . . The seal affixed to Micheltorena's letter is a manifest forgery." The Supreme Court reversed Judge McAllister's decision in the United States court in California, and voided the claim.[34]

Also it cast out the claim of the executors and heirs of Augustin De Yturbide, involving an alleged grant of *twenty leagues square of land* equal to *four hundred square leagues.* This claim was based upon a grant alleged to have been made by the Mexican Government in 1822, to President Yturbide for " services." The Supreme Court rejected it on the technical ground that the claimants had not filed their appeal in the prescribed time.[35]

Teschmaker, George H. Howard and others placidly came forward with a claim to sixteen square leagues of land in Napa County, as having been granted to the Vallejo brothers, in 1838, by their brother M. G. Vallejo, " commandante general." The complicity of United States government officials was shown by the fact that George H. Howard, one of the claimants to this grant, had been the Government law agent

[33] XXIII Howard, 353.
[34] U. S. vs. Garcia, XXII Howard, 275–276.
[35] *Ibid.,* 290.

before the United States Board of Land Commissioners, the
duty of which was to pass upon land claims. This fact of
Howard's complicity in allowing claims to pass unchallenged
was again shown, twenty years later — in 1878 — in the case
of the Throckmorton claim in which claim Howard was also
interested together with the notorious perjurer, W. A. Richardson, and others.[36]   The attempt to get a validation of the
Vallejo claim was unsuccessful; Attorney-General Stanton
proved to the satisfaction of the Supreme Court that the Val-
lejos, Juan Castenada and other witnesses were professional
perjurers.[37]   The Supreme Court rejected this particular
claim,[38] but two decades later, as we shall see, the Supreme
Court validated the notorious Throckmorton claim.

After Attorney-General Stanton had exposed the forgeries
and perjuries of the witnesses in the case of the Fuentes claim
to eleven leagues near San Jose, the Supreme Court of the
United States rejected the claim. ". . . No court in California, where Manuel Castro's achievements are known,"
Attorney-General Stanton said, " would pronounce a judgment upon his testimony. Abrego was incontestibly proved
to be guilty of forgery in the Limantour case, and the fact
was so announced by the court. . . . It is not at all difficult to see how and when this grant was fabricated. It is
the handwriting of Manuel Castro, a part of whose business
consisted in forging land grants. . . ."[39]

The Great Limantour Frauds.

The " Limantour swindle," to which frequent reference has
been made, was the audacious promotion of eight claims by
José Y. Limantour.   On six of these alleged grants he claimed

---

[36] 98 U. S. Reports, 68–71.
[37] In the Case of Luco vs. U. S., it was proved that General Mariano
Vallejo had forged a grant; the claim was rejected on that ground
alone.
[38] XXII Howard, 395.
[39] XXII Howard's Reports, 457–458.

not less than *one hundred and thirty-four square leagues* (924.34 square miles) or 594,783.38 square acres.

His claims were based upon alleged grants by Micheltorena " for advances in money and goods " to the Mexican Government, Department of California. But he, or rather those behind him, overreached themselves. They claimed under those six alleged grants not only vast tracts of agricultural, grazing, timber and mineral lands but they also presented two other claims to at least three-fourths of the city of San Francisco, of a then assessed value of $15,000,000, with its wharves, street markets, etc. Limantour also claimed islands in the harbor on which the United States Government had spent great sums in erecting lighthouses, coast defenses, buildings and other works. Parts of the Limantour claims were rejected by the Board of Land Commissioners, but the claims to four square leagues in San Francisco and to the harbor islands were confirmed.

The consequence was that a powerful combination including the owners of real estate in San Francisco, the City of San Francisco, corporations such as the Pacific Mail Steamship Company and the United States Government set to work relentlessly to expose and defeat the conspirators. Neither money nor energy was spared. The Government uncovered enough evidence to ask for a reopening of the case and to prove to the complete satisfaction of the court that the grants had been forged.[40]

[40] The trial of the case brought out many remarkable facts. It was shown that a great number of blank grants with the names of Governors Micheltorena and Bocanegra attached, or purporting to be attached, on genuine Mexican Government stamped paper of the years 1842 and 1843, had been in circulation in California since the ratification of the treaty. These blanks had been used for the purpose of fabricating grants to land. Limantour and Jouan, one of his confederates, had brought a number of the stamped blanks to California, in 1852. It was also disclosed that there was a secret association of men leagued together for the purpose of forging land grants; this gang operated in three different parts of California. See, " Case of U. S. vs. Limantour, Transcript of Record," etc., 1858, Vol. III: 354-356.

In June, 1858, Judge Hoffman, in the U. S. District Court at San Francisco declared all the claims spurious, and voided them.[41] Judge Hoffman declared that "the proofs of fraud are as conclusive and irresistible as the attempted fraud itself has been flagrant and audacious."

Limantour was twice indicted, and was held in $35,000 bail. Pending trial, he and his witnesses, in 1858, fled to Mexico, and never returned to California [42] — an absence very satisfactory to certain other land claimants of the origin of whose alleged grants he and his confederates knew too much. Those claimants, it was believed, facilitated his flight, took care that he did not return, and breathed easier in pushing their claims with Limantour and his forging and perjuring crew at a safe distance.

As a matter of fact, however, many of the owners of San Francisco property who were intent upon proving the Limantour claims fraudulent, had themselves acquired their valuable city land by fraud. The case of Field vs. Seabury et al. revealed how, in 1848, the Common Council of San Francisco began fraudulently and corruptly disposing of municipal land to themselves, or to their accomplices, and how Alcalde or Mayor Leavenworth received his large share.[43] Leavenworth, for example, in 1848 granted an extensive plot at Washington and Clay Streets to William C. Parker who then deeded it back to Leavenworth; one-half of this plot brought $75,000 in 1858.

We have given some examples of claims rejected by the Supreme Court of the United States. One reason for their lack of success was, as we have noted, the bungling, amateurish manner in which the evidence was presented. But this frequently was only an extrinsic reason. Whenever claims

---

[41] Hoffman's Reports: Land Cases, etc., 389–451.
[42] See, Case of Reese vs. U. S., IX Wallace's Reports, Supreme Court of the U. S., 13–22. This action involved one of the sureties of Limantour's bail bonds.
[43] XIX Howard's Reports, 330.

held by comparatively uninfluential persons conflicted with the claims or designs of powerful corporations, puissant personages, or of municipalities, the whole force of Government was energetically and earnestly set at work contesting the objectionable claims. The Government, it is true, fought many claims with seeming impartiality, but in numerous cases its contest was only nominal, and often bore signs of being a feigned activity for the purpose of allowing the high tribunal at Washington to validate certain secretly-favored claims. That the weight of testimony was not the only factor influencing the decisions of the Supreme Court of the United States was shown, for instance, in the claim of Juan José Gonzales to a tract of one league in length and three-quarters of a league in breadth, alleged to be based on a grant given by the Mexican Governor Figueroa, in 1833. Although there was only *one witness* to prove the genuineness of the title, the Supreme Court of the United States declared it valid.[44]

Corruption of Officials.

There were few of the United States officials in California who were not financially interested in the promotion of fraudulent land grants. In 1853, for instance, Vincente Gomez applied, through his attorney, Pacificus Ord, for confirmation of an alleged grant of four square leagues. The Board of Land Commissioners rejected the claim. Gomez then appealed to the United States District Court, in San Francisco. Who was the United States District Attorney there? None other than Pacificus Ord. Upon Ord's representation that the claim was a valid one, the court confirmed it. In 1859 Attorney-General Black presented the proof to the United States Supreme Court that Gomez had previously conveyed one-half of the tract to Ord, when Ord was United States District Attorney. Thereupon, the Supreme Court of the

[44] Gonzales vs. U. S., XX Howard, 173.

United States reversed the lower court, and voided the claim.[45]

To such a scandalous extent, also, were district judges interested in cases of land grants pending before them, and so many scandals arose, that Congress found it necessary, in 1864, to pass an act requiring district judges to transfer all cases of land claims in which they were interested to the United States Circuit Court which was to have jurisdiction.[46]

The Reading Claim Confirmed.

Of the many extensive land claims confirmed by the Supreme Court of the United States, only a few will be described here. One of such claims was that of Pearson B. Reading for six square leagues on the Sacramento River. Lewis Cass, in the United States Senate, was one of the principal pushers of this claim. Reading was an American citizen who went to California in 1842 and professed Mexican citizenship; he claimed that Micheltorena gave him the grant in 1844. When the Mexican War broke out, he joined the United States troops. The Government hotly contested his claim, urging that the grant had never received the approval of the Departmental Assembly, and that under the laws of Mexico, Reading could not hold such a grant, doubly so because he had been treacherous to the country from which he claimed his grant.

The majority of the Supreme Court of the United States, however, in 1855, confirmed his claim, upon two main precedents — one precedent that of the decision of Chief Justice Marshall in the case of Taylor vs. Brown (in 1809), the other precedent the decision in the Fremont case. Justice Wayne, in writing the court's opinion, said that while it was true that a title did not become definitive until it had received

[45] See, U. S. vs. Gomez, XXIII Howard's Reports, etc., 327–341, and III Wallace's Reports, 752–767.
[46] XIII Statutes at Large, 333.

the approval of the Departmental Assembly, yet an *immediate vested interest* had passed to the grantee. If the approval of the Departmental Assembly had not been obtained, that was the Mexican governor's fault, not Reading's. That Reading became a rebel against Mexico, the decision further read, furnished no reason for forfeiture.

Justice Daniel strongly dissented. Reading, he said, " can have no rights to the claim from or through the Mexican government to which he became an open enemy. By his conduct he completely abrogated every such right, and became, as respects that government, punishable as a State criminal; and thus not only failed to obtain that sanction without which his title was defective, namely, the approbation of the Departmental Assembly of Mexico, but, by his own voluntary conduct, rendered its procurement, upon every principle of public law, public or political necessity, or of private morality, altogether impossible." [47]

Other Claims Validated.

At the same time, December, 1855, the majority of the Supreme Court of the United States confirmed many other claims. Maria de Arguello and associates claimed twelve square leagues of land bordering four leagues on the Bay of San Francisco and extending back to the mountains. Now, as we have seen, the Mexican laws prohibited the granting of sea-coast territory. In allowing Arguello, etc., four leagues, the majority of the Supreme Court (Wayne writing the opinion) circumvented that point by saying that they did not believe the Mexican Government's policy had been to confine native citizens to the interior, and that it did not mean prohibition of grants of land to native citizens for their own use! Justice Daniel also denounced this decision in severe terms extending beyond the usual judicial restraint.[48]

[47] U. S. vs. Reading, XVIII Howard's Reports, 1–16.
[48] Arguello *et al.* vs. U. S., XVIII Howard, 539–553.

In the same month the Supreme Court confirmed the Vaca and Pena claim to a large tract of land on the Sacramento River, and the Larkin-Misroon claim to a tract eleven leagues long and a league wide on the same river. These were alleged grants by Micheltorena; the Government especially denounced the Larkin-Misroon claim as spurious. This alleged grant was purported to have been given, in 1844, to Manuel Jimeno, Secretary of the Mexican Government in California and conveyed to Larkin (then American Consul at Monterey) and Misroon.

Concurring with Justice Daniel in a dissenting opinion Justice Campbell vehemently denounced the Larkin claim. ". . . The evidence," he wrote, " satisfies me that this claim was fabricated after the difficulties between the United States and Mexico had occurred, with a view to enable the American consul at Monterey to profit from it, in the event of the cession of the country to the United States. I lay no stress upon the fact that the papers are found in the archives. I presume,"— Campbell added with sardonic significance,—" Jimeno was the keeper of those archives." [49] Justice Campbell further showed that neither Jimeno nor Larkin had ever entered upon the land, or occupied it.

Justice Daniel's Scathing Opinion.

Making his dissenting opinion cover the Arguello, Vaca-Pena and Larkin-Misroon decisions, Justice Daniel wrote an uncommonly biting opinion, denouncing those decisions as subversive of justice and public policy because of their " inciting and pampering a corrupt and grasping spirit of speculation and monopoly." He pointedly went on to say: ". . . And it will very probably be developed in the progress of the struggle or scramble for monopoly of the public domain, that many of the witnesses upon whose testimony the novel and

[49] XVIII Howard's Reports, 565.

sturdy Mexican code of practise or seizure is to be established, in abrogation of the written law, are directly or immediately interested in the success of a monopoly by which, under the countenance of this court, *principalities* are won by an *affidavit,* and conferred upon the unscrupulous few, to the exclusion and detriment of the many, and by the sacrifice of the sovereign right of the United States. . . ."

Justice Daniel then proceeded to describe the time and circumstances " under which these enormous pretensions have originated "; how in Mexico the period had been one of incessant agitation, disorder and revolution, men seizing upon power in rapid succession, and either looting or becoming the instruments of looters. All the alleged grants, he said, were deficient in the requisites indispensable to impart validity. Yet they had been boldy presented for confirmation. They had originated " in practical and temporary usurpations of power; and that, amidst scenes of violence and disorder. . . ." Notwithstanding the avowed character of those alleged grants, " which ought to consign them to the sternest reprobation," those, said Justice Daniel disgustedly, were the circumstances constituting " the merits by which they commend themselves to the countenance and support of a tribunal whose highest function is the assertion of law, justice, integrity, order — the dispensation of right equally to all." Concluding, Justice Daniel said that he could conceive of no claim whatsoever to extending favors to " the grasping and unscrupulous speculator and monopolist, and thus excluding the honest settler and retarding the population of new States." [50]

The Validating Process Continues.

Never had so caustic and telling an excoriation of the Supreme Court been made by one of its own members. If the majority winced, they gave no sign. As though vindi-

[50] XVIII Howard's Reports, 552–553.

cating themselves, and proving their consistency, they went on confirming other notorious claims.

In December, 1856, they confirmed the large and rich Peralta claim of five leagues, running south from the Bay of San Francisco over the town of Oakland, and east to the mountains. This was a grant alleged to have been made in 1820, and renewed by Micheltorena, in 1844.[51] The Pedrorena claim to eleven sitios (equal to eleven leagues) in San Diego County was confirmed in the same month; this claim was based upon an alleged grant made by Pio Pico in 1845.[52]

The Castillero claim was validated by the Supreme Court in 1858. It was a claim embracing a large tract of land near Santa Clara, but in particular its value lay in the fact that it included the "New Alamaden" quicksilver mine then producing at least $1,000,000 returns a year, and valued in total at $25,000,000. The Castillero alleged grant had become the property of American and foreign capitalists. One of their counsel was Hall McAllister, the regular attorney for the Pacific Mail Steamship Company. This company had consecutively, from 1847, bribed Congress to get a large annual mail subsidy;[53] in the year 1872 alone, so an investigating committee of Congress later reported, it expended nearly $1,000,000 in bribes to get an act passed by Congress giving it an additional mail subsidy of $500,000 a year for ten years.[54] The Government charged that the papers in the Castillero claim were forged and antedated, but the Supreme Court held that the *certified copies of the originals* were genuine. The Supreme Court chiefly depended in its decision upon the fact

[51] Case of U. S. vs. Dominigo and Vincente Peralta, XIX Howard's Reports, etc., 343–349. Justice Daniel dissented.
[52] U. S. vs. Sutherland, guardian, etc.. XIX Howard, 363.
[53] See, "History of the Great American Fortunes," Vol. II.
[54] House Report No. 269, Forty-third Congress, Second Session, 1874-75, Vol. II: xvii. The committee reported that "a sum of nearly one million dollars appears to have been disbursed in some sort of connection with the passage of the act."

that one of the former Mexican governors, Alvarado, who was alleged to have made the grant, testified that the signature was his.[55] But the notorious fact that Alvarado was a corrupt political adventurer, who had his price, and a cheap one at that, was ignored.

Much of the nearly nine million acres in California obtained on private land claims were secured in these years by grace of decisions of the Supreme Court of the United States. Year after year the Supreme Court continued validating claims the character of which did not differ from that of the claims specifically described here. Of the whole number confirmed by the Supreme Court during a period of about fifty years, beginning in 1854, several score were validated when Taney was Chief Justice.

The same acidulous differences and dissensions among the members of the Supreme Court evidenced in the private land-claim cases were evidenced in other cases. To the tradition carefully inculcated in the great mass of people that the decisions of the Supreme Court should be treated with unabated respect, dissenting members of the court did not themselves subscribe. From no critic did sharper denunciations and reproaches proceed than from the court's own members.

Justice Campbell Denounces a Decision.

An unprecedented case was decided by the Supreme Court, in December, 1855. The State of Ohio had passed an act taxing banks; thereupon the novel sight was presented of an incorporator, in the case of Dodge vs. Woolsey, suing the corporation of which he was a member, with the object of having the act declared unconstitutional. When the majority of the Supreme Court declared the act unconstitutional because it impaired the obligation of a contract, Justices Catron, Daniel and

[55] U. S. vs. Castillero, XXIII Howard's Reports, etc., 464–469.

Campbell dissented. Justice Campbell's dissenting opinion
was both remarkable and severe; remarkable in that it developed, in essence, at least, even at that early day, the now
accepted theory and fact of dominant interests and class struggles.

Comparing certain conditions in Ohio with those in Turkey,
Justice Campbell said: ". . . In that empire, the ecclesias-
tical and judicial is the dominant interest, for the ulemas
are both priests and lawyers, just as the corporate money interest is dominant in Ohio, and in either country that interest
claims exemption from the usual burdens and ordinary legislation of the State." He then asked that if a State were to
become " the victim of vicious legislation, its property alienated, its powers of taxation renounced in favor of chartered
associations, and the resources of the body politic cut off, what
remedy have the people against the misgovernment?" He
answered: " Under the doctrines of this court none is to be
found in the Government, and none exists in the inherent
powers of the people, if the wrong has taken the form of
a contract. The most deliberate and solemn acts of the people would not serve to redress the injustice, and the over-
reaching speculator upon the facility or corruption of their
legislature would be protected by the powers of this court in
the profits of his bargain. . . .".

Justice Campbell went on to say that such decisions " will
establish on the soil of every State a caste made up of combinations of men for the most part under the most favorable
conditions in society, who will habitually look beyond the institutions and authority of the State to the central government
for the strength and support necessary to maintain them in the
enjoyment of their special privileges and exemptions. The
consequence will be a new element of alienation and discord
between the different classes of society, and the introduction of
a fresh cause of disturbance in our own distracted political and
social system. In the end the doctrine of this decision may

lead to a violent overturn of the whole system of corporate combinations." [56]

The Dred Scott Case.

In the epochal Dred Scott decision, the differences among the Justices were as pronounced and acute. With this decision, so momentous in its consequences, everyone is tolerably familiar, but the singular circumstances preceding the actual and final decision are little known.

In 1834, Dred Scott, a negro, was the slave of Dr Emerson, in Missouri, and was taken by his master to Rock Island, Illinois. Two years later Scott married Harriet, another slave of Emerson, and in 1838 returned to Missouri with his master. Not until then did Dred Scott discover that the statutes of Illinois prohibited slavery, and that his transfer to Illinois had, in reality, made him a free man. In 1852 Emerson sold his slaves to J. F. A. Sandford, of New York City. Emerson having whipped Scott severely, Scott was then directed to bring suit for assault and battery. Scott won his action in a Missouri court. This decision was reversed by the Supreme Court of Missouri. Under the form of the case of Dred Scott vs. Sandford, the case came up on appeal before the Supreme Court of the United States.

The great importance of the case was fully recognized. But, at the outset, the Supreme Court of the United States had no intention of going to the lengths later determined upon. When Taney assigned Justice Nelson to write the court's opinion, it was the understood plan that the real issues were to be avoided; nothing was to be said of the constitutionality or unconstitutionality of the Missouri Compromise Act or other laws restricting the slave area; the decision was to be a brief one, affirming the decision of the Missouri Supreme Court, and treating the issues as local ques-

[56] XVIII Howard's Reports, 371–373. Justices Catron and Daniel concurred in Campbell's conclusions.

tions with which the Supreme Court of the United States did
not care to concern itself or interfere.

The Court Secretly Changes its Plan.

What happened next is well related by Frederick Trevor
Hill in his account of the case:

" Before Mr. Justice Nelson could prepare this opinion,
however, the active agents of the slave power intervened.
At dinners, receptions, and social functions they waylaid the
judges, adroitly importuning them to change their plan, flattering those whose vanity gave the necessary opening, appealing to the ambition of others, and generally emphasizing
the opportunity which lay before the Court to fulfill a public
and patriotic duty by forever quieting a discussion injurious
to the country's welfare. Declare all such restrictions as the
Missouri Compromise unconstitutional, it was urged, and the
North will acquiesce, and the Union will be preserved. All
of the judges were honest and conscientious, but some of them
were far advanced in age, and the pressure which was constantly brought to bear upon them was well calculated to dis-
turb their judgment."

Slave-Holding Emissaries at Work.

Further in his narrative of this case, Hill tells (what was
the authentic fact) that " the most active and persistent of
the emissaries " was Alexander H. Stevens, a leading Southern politician and later vice-president of the Confederacy.
A letter of Stevens reveals that he was informed in advance
exactly what the nature of the decision would be, and precisely what was happening in the supposedly secret and care-
fully-guarded councils of the Supreme Court. Stevens was
fully aware of the fact that the Missouri Compromise Act
would be declared unconstitutional. " How," Hill observes,

" an outsider came to be so intimately acquainted with what was happening in the secret conclaves of the judges, has never been disclosed, but the information was accurate in every particular, and bears evidence of having been obtained at first hand." [57]

Hill does not overstate when he says that Stevens knew of the exact moves of the Supreme Court at the precise time they were made. Writing from Washington, December 15, 1857, to his brother, Linton Stevens, regarding the progress of the Dred Scott case, then under consideration by the Supreme Court, Alexander H. Stevens thus announced: ". . . I have been urging all the influences I could bear upon the Supreme Court to get them to postpone no longer the case on the Missouri Restriction before them, but to decide it. They take it up to-day. If they decide, as I have reason to believe they will, that the restriction was unconstitutional,"— then, Stevens went on, that would settle the question of Territorial legislation over slavery.[58]

The Deferred Decision, and its Purport.

For political reasons, the decision was long held back; not until March 6, 1857 — two days after Buchanan's induction as President — was it made public.

The exultation that the decision caused in the South, and the tempestuous uproar of rage in the North, are matters of commonplace historic knowledge. By a vote of seven to two, the Supreme Court of the United States declared that the Missouri Court, where the case was originally tried, had no jurisdiction, and dismissed the suit. The majority decision also denied the legal existence of negroes as *persons;* it pronounced them merchandise or property. The decision further denied that Congress had supreme control over the Terri-

[57] " Decisive Battles of the Law."
[58] Johnston and Browne's " Life of A. H. Stevens," 316.

tories, and refused to allow the constitutionality of the Missouri Compromise Act.   In his opinion, Chief Justice Taney wrote of conditions among " enlightened nations " at the time of the Declaration of Independence when, said he scornfully, the negro race was regarded " as so far inferior that they had no rights which the white man was bound to respect; and that the negro might justly and lawfully be reduced to slavery for his benefit." [59]   According to Taney and his concurring associates this was a fixed, unchangeable condition subject neither to question, alteration nor interference.

According to a compilation made in the year 1850, it was estimated that in fifteen slave States, having an entire population of 9,612,679, less than 200,000 were slave owners, yet at this time they held 3,200,364 slaves.   In the slave States there were 228,136 free negroes but they were not considered citizens or allowed to vote.   By the close of Buchanan's administration, says Wilson in his " Rise and Fall of the Slave Power in America," it was estimated that the slave traffic had grown to the purchase and sale of 30,000 slaves a year, at a market value of $30,000,000.   " This trade, with its sad aggregate of suffering and sorrow, on the one part, of demoralization and guilt, on the other, was carried on unblushingly."

Senator Seward Charges Collusion.

On March 3, 1858, Senator Seward of New York, arose in the United States Senate, and in a scathing yet measured speech, which caused a national sensation, denounced the Supreme Court of the United States, and accused it of having in its Dred Scott decision been in collusion with Buchanan as President-elect and President in a conspiracy to fasten slavery upon the United States for all time.

". . . Before coming into office," Seward said, " he [Bu-

[59] Case of Dred Scott vs. Sandford, XIX Howard's Reports, 407. Justices McLean and Curtis were the non-concurring judges.

chanan] approached, or was approached by the Supreme Court
of the United States. The day of inauguration came, the first
one among all the celebrations of that great national pageant
that was to be desecrated by a coalition between the executive
and judicial departments, to undermine the national legislature and the liberties of the people. The President [Bu-
chanan], attended by the usual lengthened procession, arrived
and took his seat on the portico. The Supreme Court attended him there in robes which yet exacted public reverence.
The people, unaware of the import of the whisperings carried
on between the President and the Chief Justice, and imbued
with veneration for both, filled the avenues and gardens as
far away as eye could reach. The President . . . announced (vaguely, indeed, but with self-satisfaction) the
forthcoming extrajudicial exposition of the Constitution, and
pledged his submission to it as authoritative and final. The
Chief Justice and his associates remained silent. . . . It
cost the President, under the circumstances, little exercise of
magnanimity now to promise to the people of Kansas, on
whose neck he had, with the aid of the Supreme Court, hung
the millstone of slavery, a fair trial in their attempt to cast it
off, and hurl it to earth, when they should come to organize
a State Government. Alas! that even this cheap promise,
uttered with such great solemnities, was only made to be
broken!" . . .[60]

Elsewhere, in the course of his philippic, Seward declared:
". . . The Supreme Court can reverse its judgment more
easily than we can reconcile the people to its usurpation.
Sir, the Supreme Court attempts to command the people of
the United States to accept the principle that one man can
own other men; and that they must guarantee inviolability
of that false and pernicious property. The people of the
United States," Senator Seward went on, openly flouting and

[60] The *Congressional Globe,* Part I, First Session, Thirty-Fifth Congress, 1857–1858: 941.

defying the Supreme Court's decision, "never can, and they never will, accept principles so unconstitutional and abhorrent. Never, Never! Let the court recede. Whether," Seward threatened, "it recedes or not, we shall reorganize the court, and thus reform its political sentiments and practices, and bring them into harmony with the Constitution and the laws of Nature. . . ." [61]

For this attack upon the Supreme Court, Seward was venomously assailed by conservatives and by the representatives of the slaveholders. His accusations of collusion were declared to be utterly unfounded, and were pronounced the vaporings of a mind either obsessed with partisan rancor or deranged with malignant hatred. Even Northern opponents of slavery who had faith in the integrity of the Supreme Court of the United States, could not credit Seward's grave charges, and dismissed them as incredible.

The same charges of collusion were made by Abraham Lincoln in his celebrated debates with Senator Douglas. Lincoln repeatedly charged that the Dred Scott decision was the result of a conspiracy to which Taney, Buchanan, Douglas and others were parties. " Mr. Lincoln,"— so the literal report of Douglas' reply, at Ottawa, Ill., August 21, 1858, reads, in part,—" has not character enough for integrity and truth, merely on his own *ipse dixit,* to arraign President Buchanan, President Pierce and nine judges of the Supreme Court, not one of whom would be complimented by being put on an equality with him." [62]

Truth of the Charges Established.

But that the charges made by Seward and Lincoln were absolutely true in every respect is now conclusively established.

[61] *Congressional Globe,* 1857-1858, Part I: 943.
[62] This coarse, insulting rejoinder was typical of the "able and cultured" Douglas, the arch defender of slavery and of the Supreme Court.

In the recently issued " Works of James Buchanan "— twelve
volumes in all — edited by Prof. John Bassett Moore, Buchanan's correspondence is given in full. Professor Moore
incorporates two letters written to Buchanan,— one letter
from Justice Catron, the other from Justice Grier. These
letters, written several weeks before the Dred Scott decision
was handed out, prove that the Supreme Court of the United
States *did* approach Buchanan previous to his inauguration.
They further show that Buchanan had brought some species
of pressure (the nature of which is unknown) upon the Supreme Court; that negotiations were carried on with the greatest secrecy between Buchanan and the Supreme Court; and
that when Buchanan ostentatiously made the pledge in his
inaugural address that he would abide by the decision of
the Supreme Court, he knew in advance precisely what the
salient features of that decision would be. These facts are
now on an incontrovertible basis.

Letters of Justices Catron and Grier.

According to the first of the two letters reproduced by Professor Moore, Justice Catron, under date of February 19,
1857, wrote to Buchanan making suggestions of what Buchanan might with safety and propriety say in his inaugural
address about the Dred Scott case, and requesting Buchanan
to write to Justice Grier and seek to induce him to come to
terms. Justice Catron's letter proceeded:

" Will you drop Grier a line saying how necessary it is —
& how good the opportunity is, to settle the agitation by
an affirmative decision of the Supreme Court, the one way or
the other. He ought not to occupy so doubtful a ground as
the outside issue — that admitting the constitutionality of the
Mo. Comp. line of 1820, still, as no domicile was acquired by
the negro at Fort Snelling, & he returned to Missouri, he was
not free. He has no doubt about the question on the main

contest, but has been persuaded to take the smooth handle for the sake of peace.

" Sincerely yr. frd.,

" J. CATRON."

It is not clear whether Buchanan had previously written to Catron. But it is clear that Buchanan followed Catron's suggestions; after Catron wrote the foregoing letter, Buchanan wrote to Justice Grier, and on February 23, 1857, received a reply in which Grier wrote:

"Your letter came to hand this morning. I have taken the liberty to shew it in confidence to our mutual friends Judge Wayne and the Chief Justice. We fully appreciate and concur in your views as to the desirableness at this time of having an expression of the opinion of the Court on this troublesome question. With their concurrence I will give you in confidence the history of the case before us, with the probable result." [63]

Grier further expressed his solicitude that the decision should be so rendered that it would not seem a purely geographical one, meaning thereby that the Supreme Court should be saved from being discredited, which it would be were the decision made purely by Justices from the slave States. A significant consideration, this.

In view of these letters the charges of collusion stand proved. Chief Justice Taney was furious that Seward had penetrated into and uncovered one of the most carefully hidden secrets of the Supreme Court of the United States. "Taney," says Rhodes, "was so incensed at the speech of Seward that he told Tyler, who was afterwards his biographer, that had Seward been nominated and elected President in 1860, instead of Lincoln, he would have refused to administer to him the oath of office."

[63] For a clear exposition of the facts brought out by Prof. Moore. see an extended review in *The Independent,* issue of August 24, 1911.

Lincoln Scouts the Sacredness of the Supreme Court.

When the Abolitionists bitterly denounced the Dred Scott decision, the slave power came forward with the demand that the Supreme Court decision be accepted with reverent acquiescence, and that no whisper of criticism should be made against that exalted tribunal.

In the course of his debates with Stephen A. Douglas, Abraham Lincoln spoke derisively of that attitude. "The sacredness that Judge Douglas throws around this decision," he said at Chicago, July 10, 1858, "is a degree of sacredness that has never before thrown around any other decision. I have never heard of such a thing. Why, decisions apparently contrary to that decision, or that good lawyers thought were contrary to that decision, have been made by that very court before. It is the first of its kind; it is an astonisher in legal history. . . . It is based upon falsehood in the main as to the facts." [64] At Springfield, seven days later, Lincoln again adverted to the subject. ". . . Our judges," said he, "are as honest as other men and not more so. They have, with others, the same passions for party, for power, and the privilege of their corps. Their maxim is, '*boni judicis est ampliare jurisdictonem.*' [it is the part of a good judge to amplify jurisdiction]; and their power is the more dangerous as they are in office for life, and not responsible, as the other functionaries are, to the elective control. . . ." [65]

Justice Clifford's Appointment.

Justice Curtis' resignation from the Supreme Court, soon after this decision — he had been one of the minority — was followed by the appointment of Nathan Clifford as an Asso-

[64] "Political Debates Between Hon. Abraham and Hon. Stephen A. Douglas," etc., Edition of 1860: 20.
[65] *Ibid.*, 61.

ciate Justice. Clifford came from Maine; had been in the Maine
Legislature from 1830 to 1834, serving as Speaker of the
Maine House of Representatives in 1833 and 1834. In 1834
he had become Attorney-General of Maine.

It was during this period that vast stretches of what were
then called Maine " wild lands " were acquired by a few land
appropriators. From 1785 to 1812 the State of Massachusetts — of which, until 1820, Maine was a part — had sold
4,086,292 acres for the sum of $818,691.14. Of those 4,086,-
292 acres, a single individual — William Bingham — bought
2,000,000 acres, in 1793, at the insignificant rate of twelve
and a half cents an acre. In 1816 a total of 16,000,000 acres
of land, most of it thick with primitive growth of valuable
timber, were left in public ownership. This area rapidly van-
ised; from 1823 to 1834 not less than 1,003,450 acres were
alienated into private holdings, mostly those of speculators
and lumber capitalists. Notwithstanding the great recognized
value of those timber lands, they were fraudulently or corruptly sold for an average of forty-six cents an acre. Subsequently, 1,800,000 more acres went, in large part, into the
maws of capitalists from 1834 to 1855; and year after year
the process continued, until no State domain was left.

In 1838, Clifford was elected to Congress; in 1846 he became a member of President Polk's Cabinet, as Attorney-
General of the United States. One of the most influential
members — if not the most influential member — of this Cabinet, was, as heretofore noted, that notorious land speculator
and land grabber — Robert J. Walker. After the Mexican
War, Clifford was sent to Mexico as a Peace Commissioner.
In 1849 he returned to Portland to reëngage in law. President Buchanan appointed Clifford to the Supreme Court of
the United States upon the recommendation of United States
Senator James Ware Bradbury,[66] whose law partner in Maine

[66] See, " Collections Of The Maine Historical Society," Vol. IX,
Memoir of Nathan Clifford," by James Ware Bradbury.

was Lot M. Morrill, who himself became United States Senator. One of the members of the Morrill family was Land Agent
of Maine. The politics of that State, of both political parties, were largely controlled by a few families such as the
Coburns. Beginning as cattle dealers, Abner Coburn and
Philander Coburn acquired 450,000 acres, or more than seven
hundred square miles, of land in Maine;[67] the Coburn estate
is at this day enormous. Bradbury was one of the promoters
of the Kennebec and Portland Railroad. He was also one of
the capitalists behind the Somerset and Kennebec Railroad,
of which he was a director, and of which Abner Coburn became president, after Bradbury had consummated its consolidation with the Portland and Kennebec Railroad. Those
railroads are now part of the Maine Central Railroad.

Philip Brown, eldest son of John Bundy Brown, was married
to Fanny, daughter of Justice Clifford; John Bundy Brown's
daughter, Ellen, became the wife of W. H. Clifford, son of
Justice Clifford. Who, it may be asked, was John Bundy
Brown? One of the very foremost capitalists of Maine. He
was the head of the Portland Sugar Company which, at one
time, employed nearly a thousand workers; he was one of
the original incorporators and directors of the Atlantic and
St. Lawrence Railroad (now the Atlantic Division of the
Grand Trunk Railway); he was interested in the Portland
and Kennebec Railroad and the Maine Central Railroad; he
was the largest stockholder in the Portland and Ogdensburg
Railroad; a director for many years in the Portland, Saco and
Portsmouth Railroad; for a period a director in the Erie Railway; had advanced large sums to the Toledo, Peoria and Warsaw Railroad; was also at various times a director of the Portland Company, the Rolling Mills Company, the Kerosene Oil

[67] "Biographical Encyclopedia of Maine, 19th Century," 436. Abner
Coburn was later elected Governor of Maine. Through his connection with the Northern Pacific Railroad, he personally acquired
50,000 acres of land along the route of that railroad. The Coburns
were also owners of banks.

Company, the Maine Steamship Company, the First National
Bank and other corporations.[68]   His firm — J. B. Brown and
Sons — was the largest private banking house in Portland,
and Brown's private mansion the most capacious and costly
and " magnificent " in that city.[69]

Chief Justice Taney Discredited.

The breaking out of the Civil War found Taney much
despised and discredited in the North; for his part in the
Dred Scott decision he was generally viewed with detestation.
Although it was well known that his sympathies were with
the South, he cautiously made no public utterances, and remained Chief Justice until the day of his death in 1864.[70]   He
seems to have had need of the salary attached to the position.   According to Tyler, who, as we have narrated, was
chosen by Taney to write his biography, " Taney's small fortune was invested at the time of the Civil War exclusively in
Virginia State stocks."   A man of originally tall stature —
upwards of six feet — Taney's constitution, always delicate,
had been undermined by close application to musty legal lore
and sedentary habits.   In his last years " he had become bent
and warped, so that his skin was like a cracked parchment,
his stature bent and he walked with difficulty and tardiness."

[68] " Biographical Encyclopedia of Maine, 19th Century," 209, which
describes Brown's connections with these various corporations.

[69] So much for Justice Clifford's connections. Of Clifford's exaggerated self-esteem and formalism the following anecdote was later
current in the public press when he was on the Supreme Court Bench:
" Dignified old Clifford always avoided, if possible, the use of the definite article. He would write in his opinion, ' Suit brought So-and-so,'
' Case involved So-and-so,' never writing ' the ' if it could be avoided.
Jocular Justice Grier, who had been on the bench long before Justice
Clifford came to Washington, and who was the only man who dared
take liberties with his Maine brother, said one day, slapping Clifford
on the back, ' Cliffy, old boy, why do you hate the definite article so? '
Clifford drew himself up stiffly and replied, ' Brother Grier, you may
criticize my law, but my style is my own.' "

[70] Justice Campbell, however, had resigned in 1861, to take up the
cause of the Southern Confederacy.

According to further to Tyler, Taney was poor. In an interview with Tyler, published after Taney's death in the Cincinnati *Commercial* newspaper, Tyler was asked: " Was Judge Taney rich, Mr. Tyler? " " No, sir," replied Tyler, " always poor. He lived in Blagden row — the row of stuccoed houses opposite the City Hall. They are four-storied; an iron balcony runs above the first story; two windows adjoin the hall door. His daughters, at this day, live upon copying reports and papers from the Department of the Interior. One of them, I believe, is unmarried; another, a widow. They are in as nearly a state of indigence as I care to classify ladies so tenderly reared. The Judge himself said to me, during the war, that he lamented his narrow means, because he wanted to take another newspaper and could not afford it." [71]

These statements, and the implication that they aimed to convey, are obviously from an uncommonly partial source. But one fact is certain: If, as Lincoln and others virtually charged, Taney was corrupt, it was not a corruption by medium of bribes. Taney could not be approached with mercenary inducements. His corruption was of a different kind. A man may accept bribes, yet possibly refuse to accord his vote and services. But if a judge's class training, class views and class interests, with all of the bias and associations allied with them, be hard and fixed, he will honestly award, as a matter of indisputable right, what no amount of bribes could influence him to give.

This was the species of Taney's corruption, a sinister kind not recognized by penal laws, and yet, on the whole, far exceeding in ominous efficacy the more vulgar and less certain mode of money corruption. We have seen how under the administration of Taney, as Secretary of the Treasury, and under him as Chief Justice, land grabbers obtained tens of

[71] This interview was republished in Ellis' " Sights and Secrets of the National Capital " (1869) : p. 267.

millions of acres of the richest part of the public domain, and how corporations obtained immunity from taxation. The capitalists concerned became millionaires and multimillionaires, but Taney died, on October 12, 1864, at the age of eighty-seven, in a kind of gnawing genteel poverty, unable, as we learn, to afford an extra few cents for an additional newspaper.[72]

[72] Before Taney's death President Lincoln had made several appointments as Associate Justices of the Supreme Court. These are dealt with in the next chapter.

CHAPTER XII

THE SUPREME COURT UNDER CHIEF JUSTICE CHASE

Taney's successor was Salmon P. Chase, Secretary of the Treasury. It was maintained then, and the statement has been uniformly repeated in many memoirs and biographical works, that President Lincoln's motive in appointing Chase Chief Justice of the Supreme Court was to rid himself of a too-ambitious competitive aspirant for the Presidential nomination. In both the years 1856 and 1860 Chase had aimed to get that nomination; and as a member of Lincoln's Cabinet he in nowise lessened his efforts and intrigues. Of these Lincoln was well aware, contemplating them with vexation and uneasiness. Some politicians of the period, like Senator Henderson, even hold, in their memoirs, that Chase gave no real help to Lincoln during the Civil War, but busied himself, whenever the opportunity presented, with seeking to undermine Lincoln's chances for renomination, and with promoting his own.

Indeed, in a review of Chase's career, published shortly after his death, in the October, 1873, issue of *Bench and Bar* (a periodical devoted to the legal profession) President Lincoln was quoted as saying to a "distinguished and prominent statesman" who assured him that if Chase were appointed Chief Justice he (Chase) would withdraw from politics and devote himself exclusively to judicial functions, "I will nominate him, because it seems the public wish, but you are mistaken. He will be a candidate for President every four years as long as he lives, and never be elected."

For many years Chase had been an active and conspicuous

figure in national politics. He had been a United States Senator from Ohio from 1849 to 1856, and Governor of Ohio from 1856 to 1860. He was a man of force and of impressive appearance: in stature six feet two inches, with a massive head, massive brows, blue-gray eyes, wide nostrils and heavy lips,—altogether a commanding appearance. Did, however, the personal motive wholly account for Chase's appointment? By no means. Two other considerations had their weight.

Forces Behind Chase's Appointment.

Chase's views on the question of negro slavery had been so insistently disseminated, and were so nationally known, that there could be no atom of doubt as to where he stood on that issue. As an attorney, he had energetically defended fugitive slaves; in the United States Senate he had been one of the most unyielding, aggressive Free Soil opponents of the extension of slavery, and as Governor of Ohio his course was a consistent agitation. The Civil War saw the anti-slavery forces in as thorough a control of the Federal Goverment as had been the slave-owning oligarchy under the former régime Lincoln's Emancipation Proclamation had been promulgated. Issues affecting this great revolutionary transformation were bound to come, and did come, in some phase or other, before the Supreme Court of the United States for final adjustment; and Chase, as one of the founders of the Republican Party, could be depended upon in his capacity of Chief Justice to interpret law in accordance with the aims and demands of the triumphant anti-slavery forces.

The other reason underlying Chase's appointment was of a very different nature, and one hitherto evaded in most works. The Civil War and its accompanying laws and administrative orders, placed the finances of the country in the power of the private bankers; and while armies were fighting and hosts

perishing on the battlefields, and at sea,[1] the bankers extracted
colossal profits. The system devised gave banking corporations absolute control over the volume of currency, enabling
them in large measure to fix the price of labor and commodities of the whole nation. Enormous quantities of bonds were
issued by the Government; to pay interest to the bankers and
other bondholders, the people of the United States were taxed
from $18,000,000 to $20,000,000 a year. During the most crucial period of the Civil War the bankers had laws passed by
which they could deposit their bonds in the United States
Treasury, and upon them issue their privately-stamped currency up to ninety per cent. of the amount of the bonds.
This currency they used in making loans, charging thereon
varying rates of interest, often higher than twenty per cent.
Hence the bankers received two concurrent sets of interest —
frequently as much as six per cent. in gold in annual interest
from the Government on their deposited bonds, and a much
larger interest from borrowers for the use of the currency
that they were thus allowed to issue on the strength of the
bonds.[2] The accruing profits obviously were very great, often
averaging twenty, fifty, and at times one hundred per cent., in
the course of a year.

The system of funding the public debt was, like the national
banks, borrowed from the English monarchy. Under this system, a gigantic, non-taxable, interest-bearing debt was perpet-
uated. The banks were enriched by the bonds; therefore, the
bankers saw to it that the public debt was continued and increased, and a perpetual bonded debt assured. Every attempt

[1] Of the Union soldiers, 67,000 were slain in battle, 43,000 died of
wounds, and 230,000 perished of diseases and other causes. Of the
number of indirect deaths produced in families by the absence of adequate support arising from breadwinners enlisting in the war, no ascer-
tainment, of course, is possible.

[2] From 1863 to 1878, the Government paid out to National banks the
enormous sum of $252,837,556.77 as interest on bonds.— House Execu-
tive Document No. 34, 1879.

to scale down this debt and pay the bonds according to contract, was frustrated by the bankers.

This system caused great public agitation, resulting later in the Greenback political movement. One phase of the financial system, however, ranged the railroad interests in opposition to the bankers; the developing conflict between these two powers, had as we shall see, a striking influence upon the Supreme Court.

The Banking Power's Sway.

In 1861 Congress passed an act providing for the issuance of $50,000,000 in Treasury notes. Thereupon the banks, which had been actively engaged in hoarding gold, suspended specie payments on December 30 of that year. This action they took in order to avoid paying gold for Treasury notes. In the next year — 1862 — Congress passed the Legal Tender Act, authorizing the issuance of $150,000,000 of greenbacks (so called from their color), and retiring the $50,000,000 provided by the act of the previous year.

But before this bill was finally passed the bankers industriously lobbied in Congress, with the result that the bill was altered and mutilated. In its amended form it provided that legal-tender notes should not be receivable for " interest on bonds or notes, which shall be paid in coin." This meant gold; and as the bankers monopolized the available supply of gold, Government had to borrow it from them at excessive premiums. No sooner did the Government borrow the gold than back it flowed to the bankers in interest on bonds — an endless-chain process incessantly enriching the bankers, and this while hundreds of thousands of soldiers were pouring out their blood and wasting health and yielding life.

This mutilation of the original Legal Tender Act for the exclusive benefit of the bankers moved Representative Thaddeus Stevens, in the debate on February 20, 1862, to make a bitter denunciation. ". . . With my colleague," he said, referring to the first draft of the bill, " I believe that no act of legislation of this Government was ever hailed with as much delight throughout the whole length and breadth of the Union by every class of people without exception, as the bill we passed and sent to the Senate. . . . It is true there was a doleful sound come up from the caverns of bullion brokers and from the saloons of the associated banks. . . . They fell upon the bill in hot haste and so disfigured and deformed it that its father would not know it. . . . It is now positively mischievous . . . it makes two classes of money . . . one for the banks and brokers, and another for the people. . . ."[3] " We did not yield," he said later, " until we found that the country must be lost or the banks be gratified, and we have sought to save the country in spite of the cupidity of the wealthy citizens." So rapacious was the hold-up of the nation by the bankers at a critical time when every particle of energy and every available resource were essential to carry on the war, that even John Sherman denounced the bill. Sherman, as his course as Secretary of the Treasury later proved, was a pliant instrument of the bankers, but he was an extensive railroad stockholder, and at this time the banking and the railroad interests were aligning in opposition.

Control Finances During the Civil War.

The act of 1862 merely said that the interest on the authorized bonds was to be paid in coin, but no explicit statement was made in the bonds as to what form of money the principal should be paid with. According to the law, greenbacks were a " lawful money and a legal tender for all debts, public and private within the United States except duties on imports and

[3] The *Congressional Globe,* Part I, Second Session, Thirty-seventh Congress, 1861–62: 900.

interest on aforesaid." A rational construction of the law would have dictated the payment of the principal in greenbacks. The soldiers and sailors of the nation were being paid in that paper. But the bankers wanted no greenbacks; they demanded gold. They had expressly lobbied in Congress to outlaw greenbacks so far as payment of customs dues was concerned, knowing that such a provision would depreciate their value. Having accomplished this depreciation, they then threatened that unless the principal were paid in gold no Government bonds would be marketed. Accordingly, on March 3, 1863, Congress compliantly passed an act providing that both interest and principal should be payable in coin, which, of course, signified gold.[4]

Two forms of United States notes, or currency, were issued. One kind bore interest; of these $577,000,000 were issued by 1866. The other varieties called greenbacks, demand notes and national bank notes, bore no interest. In 1864, $449,000,-000 of greenbacks were in circulation. Forming what was considered the better class of currency, the interest-bearing Treasury notes were closely hoarded by the banks which, in return, issued their own depreciated bank notes and forced them into general circulation. By the year 1865 more than $700,000,000 State and National bank notes were in circulation. . . . "Immense interests," said Hugh McCulloch, Comptroller of the Currency, in his second report, "have been at work all over, and concentrated in New York to raise the price of coin, and splendid fortunes have been apparently made by their success. . . . Gold has been a favorite article to gamble in. . . . The effect of all of this has been, not to break down the credit of the Government, but to increase enormously the cost of the war and the expense of living . . ."

[4] See, Bolles' "Financial History of the United States," pp. 79, 80, 139, etc.; Sumner's "History of American Currency;" Dunbar's "Laws of the United States Relating To Currency and Finance From 1789 to 1890," etc.

" Mr. Chase," says a commentator describing his activities while Secretary of the Treasury, " not a banker by profession, and without much experience in financing, had yet proved himself obstinated and unwilling to learn. Whatever were his intentions — and it must be allowed that they were probably good and his difficulties great — he had, yet without consenting to what the bankers desired on many points, actually played into their hands. Men said his ambition to be President had been his weakness. . . ." [5]

Chase as Bank Attorney and Director.

That Chase was subservient to the banking interests was a fact; but the statement that he had had no experience in banking affairs reveals complete ignorance of his career. His appointment as Secretary of the Treasury had, in fact, been seconded by the powerful bankers, knowing that as a bank director and bank lawyer, he would well represent them, and conserve their particular interests at almost every point.

When a lawyer in private practice, Chase's specialty had been, for many years, the advocacy of the interests of certain banks; and during a part of that time he had been a bank director. Soon after removing to Cincinnati he had formed, in 1832, a partnership with D. A. Caswell. For the payment of a large bonus, Caswell agreed that Chase was to share equally in all business, including that of the agency of the Bank of the United States, for which institution Caswell was attorney.[6] Thereafter, for many years, Chase appeared in the courts as the attorney for the Bank of the United States.[7]

Of the corrupt career of this institution, we have given a tolerably clear outline in previous chapters; how $76,000,000

---

[5] See, Article on Currency, Encyclopedia of Social Reform, Edition of 1897: 443.

[6] Van Santvoord, pp. 663–664.

[7] See, Case of Bank of U. S. vs. Dunseth, X Ohio Reports, 21, and *Ibid.*, 61, etc., etc.

of its assets had vanished by the year 1841; how it had
" loaned " $30,000,000 to various members of Congress, edi-
tors of newspapers, to politicians in general, to brokers and
jobbers and to favorites.   A large part of these $30,000,000
had been corruptly expended in the long effort to get a
recharter from Congress and to subsidize the newspaper press.
We have also related how the officials of the Bank of the
United States plundered it of large sums: Nicholas Biddle,
its president, had paid out $1,018,000 for which no vouchers
could be found; John Andrews, its cashier, embezzled $426,-
930.67 of its funds, and Joseph Cowperthwaite, its second
assistant cashier, defaulted in the sum of $55,081.95.[8]

Corrupt Methods of the Bank of the United States.

As an illustration of the methods of the Bank of the United
States in clandestinely securing legislation, the following incident, as related by Benton, and confirmed by the official
records, showed how it bribed a charter through the Pennsylvania Legislature, after President Jackson had vetoed its re-
charter obtained by corrupt means from Congress.

" On the 19th day of January, in the year 1836," Benton
relates, " a bill was reported in the House of Representatives
of the General Assembly of Pennsylvania, entitled, ' *An act to
repeal the State tax, and to continue the improvement of the
State by railroads and canals; and for other purposes.*' It
came from the standing committee on ' *Inland navigation and*

[8] After Biddle's retirement from the presidency of the Bank of the
United States, that institution brought a civil action against him and
Andrews for the restitution of more than $400,000 that they were
charged with stealing from the bank in 1836.   The theft, so it was
charged, was concealed by fraudulent entries, burning of vouchers and
by other methods.   By the time the suit came up, in 1844, Biddle had
died, but the action was pressed against Andrews.   His answer was a
general denial, but Judge Parsons decided that he was convinced that
the claim for recovery was one which could be enforced, and he overruled Andrews' demurrer.— See, Parsons' Select Equity Cases of the
First Judicial District of Pennsylvania, 1844, II: 31–63.   Also, Pa.
House Journal, 1842, Vol. II: Appendix, 182.

internal improvement'; and was, in fact, a bill to repeal a tax
and make roads and canals, but which, under the vague and
usually unimportant generality of ' other purposes ' contained
the entire draught of a charter for the Bank of the United
States — adopting it as a Pennsylvania State Bank.

" The introduction of this bill, with this addendum, was a
surprise upon the House. No petition had asked for such a
bank; no motion had been made in relation to it; no inquiry
had been sent to any committee; no notice of any kind heralded
its approach; . . . the unimportant clause of ' other purposes ' hung on at the end of the title, could excite no suspicion
of the enormous measures which lurked under its unpreten-
tious phraseology. . . . Some members looked at each
other in amazement. But it was soon evident that it was the
minority only that was mystified — that a majority of the
elected members in the House, and a cluster of exotics in the
lobbies, perfectly understood the instrusive moment; in brief,
it had been smuggled into the House, and a power was present
to protect it there . . ." [9]

Charges of bribery forced the Pennsylvania Legislature to
make a show of investigation. The Senate appointed an investigating committee which proceeded to swear witnesses by
the usual oath, " You do solemnly swear by the Holy Evan-
gelists of Almighty God," etc., etc. Bribery was freely admitted. Colonel Jacob Krebs, a Senator, testified, for example,
that on February 10, 1836, he had been offered $4,000 or
$5,000 by James L. Dunn, for his favorable vote, and that he
was at another time offered $20,000 by Henry W. Conrad,
the money for his vote to be paid two weeks after the bill
became a law.

The Senate Committee handed in a whitewashing report.[10]
But a Pennsylvania House investigating committee, appointed
in 1840, with power to go back a number of years, reported

[9] " Thirty Years in the Senate," Vol. II: 23-24.
[10] Pa. Senate Journal, 1835-1836, Vol. I: 305-306.

that the sum of $130,000 had been expended in bribes by the Bank of the United States. "It is hard to come to the conclusion," the committee commented, "that men of refined education, and high and honorable character, would wink at such things, yet the conclusion is unavoidable." As to whom the $130,000 was paid, the committee professed to be utterly in the dark; "there was no evidence that money was, paid to anybody." [11]

Chase's Appearance for Banks.

This was the bank for which Chase was Cincinnati counsel during this identical period; the methods of the United States Bank in Ohio did not differ from those it used at Washington and in Pennsylvania. Its corruption was established, yet Chase displayed no scruples at continuing to draw his fees, and in doing its law work.

At the same time he was one of the first directors of the Lafayette Bank of Cincinnati, established in 1834. For ten years he remained on the board of directors of the Lafayette Bank, also acting as secretary of the board, and serving as attorney for the bank. Among his many appearances as attorney for the Lafayette Bank was that in the action, in 1841, of the State of Ohio against the Lafayette Bank, the Commercial Bank, and the Franklin Bank of Cincinnati. This was an action by the State for the forfeiture of the charters of those banks for illegally issuing large sums of notes to circulate as money; for receiving a greater rate of interest than six per cent. per annum; for suspending payment of notes payable in coin; for expanding their circulation to an amount greater than four times the amount of coin in their vaults, and then suddenly withdrawing a great part of those notes from circulation.[12]

11 Pa. House Journal, 1842, Vol. II: Appendix, 172–531.,
12 X Ohio Reports, 543. Judge Lane decided in favor of the banks upon the ground that specific legislation necessary to bring about the forfeiture of their charter had not been enacted,

Thus, considering his long service as a bank director and attorney, Chase was by no means as unsophisticated regarding financial matters and practices of the banking world as some of his ill-informed critics would have it. His lucrative practice was almost wholly one of a bank attorney, but when any case involved the defense of a fugitive slave he would gladly tender gratuitous service. His fortune, in 1861, was estimated at $65,000; his intimate friend and biographer, Schuckers, says that just before the Civil War, Joshua Hanna invested $5,000 for Chase in stock of the Cleveland and Pittsburg Railroad, and that Chase reaped $5,000 profit by selling the stock when its market value went up.[13]

Favors the Bankers When Secretary of the Treasury.

It was Chase who, as Secretary of the Treasury, proposed and urged the establishment of the national banking system. And it was under this system, so extraordinarily favorable to the bankers that, as we have explained, the bankers were allowed to fasten their iron hold on the National Treasury, and drain it for their own aggrandizement. Immense private fortunes were soon acquired by these means, which fortunes grew still greater by the further methods used by the bankers in forcing the Government to award them bond issues on their own terms. When Secretary Chase tried to place a large issue of five-per-cent. bonds authorized by Congress, the banks held off from taking them up. Their object was soon seen. Using their refusal as an argument, Chase induced Congress to authorize more legal-tender notes until that currency was depreciated to a low point. The bankers then hurried forward to get hold of this depreciated currency, and Chase allowed them to tender it, *at its face value,* for Government bonds. Was Chase the accomplice or dupe of the banking interests? Whether he was the one or the other, the result

[13] "Life of S. P. Chase" (1874): p. 617.

was the same. Deliberately or supinely he played into the hands of the bankers, permitting them to buy up the bonds with a depreciated currency.

The Greenback Party, originating largely in this manipulation of the currency in favor of the bankers and bondholding class, took the view that this condition was the result of a definite conspiracy. It charged that the bankers, national and international, had conspired to make the issue of the war greenbacks a failure by inducing Congress to prevent their being legal tender for customs duties and for payment of the national debt, and thus depreciating their value. It declared that there had been a conspiracy to cause needless bonds to be issued and to buy up those greenbacks at their depreciated value, purchasing the bonds with them, and paying for the bonds with greenbacks accepted at their face value. It set forth that while these bonds had been bought with greenbacks at thirty cents on the dollar, yet Congress had been influenced, under the pretense of " national faith " and " an honest dollar " to declare those bonds redeemable in gold. The banker was allowed to get his gold while, so the Greenback Party complained, the soldiers and sailors of the war who had risked their lives, " and got no interest " had been paid in greenbacks.[14]

Corruption of Congress.

Much as Secretary Chase was denounced at the time, the full odium for these transactions could not justly be imputed to him. A large share of the responsibility fell upon the majority of Congress which had passed the successive laws

[14] The demand that bonds which did not distinctly 'call for payment in coin should be paid in greenbacks was called the " Ohio idea," and was agitated as early as 1868. In the election of 1874, Peter Cooper, as the Presidential nominee of the Greenback Party, polled 81,737 popular votes. Subsequently the Greenback-Labor Party polled more than a million votes. It was the predecessor of the Populist Party.

construed so favorably to the banking interests by Chase. The particular arguments influencing that majority in the passage of various acts may be judged from the fact that at the very time when the murderous battles of the Wilderness were being fought, the promoters of the Union Pacific Railroad expended nearly $436,000 in bribes for the enactment of the act of July 2, 1864, giving that company Government subsidies amounting to from $16,000 to $48,000 a mile, according to the topography of the country, and making the company a present of about 12,000,000 acres of public domain, and so altering the original act that the Government had little opportunity of getting back its outlays.[15]

Banks Seek a Monopoly of Issuing Currency.

After the banks had manipulated the greenback issues to suit their own purposes, and had glutted themselves with Government bonds largely bought with depreciated greenbacks at their face value, they aimed to get rid of Government-issued currency. By October 9, 1869, the 1,617 national banks in the United States held about $339,000,000 of Government bonds on which they circulated their bank notes. Of legal tender notes they held about $129,000,000. But their holdings of specie amounted to some $23,000,000; as a matter of fact only $15,000,000 in gold was in that year in actual circulation in the United States. The bankers and speculators monopolized and controlled the gold supply.

This being so, they now planned to have the legal-tender issues outlawed so far as they applied to payments on contracts. The bankers were the creditor class; and if the courts were to decide that promises to pay on contracts were not

[15] Reports of Committees, Credit Mobilier Reports, Forty-second Congress, Third Session, 1872–73, Doc. No. 78: xviii. The "Wilson" investigating committee of the Senate reported that the evidence proved that nearly $436,000 had been disbursed in connection with the passage of the amendatory act of July 2, 1864.

payable in legal-tender currency, then the payments would have to be made in gold. Inasmuch as the banks held a monopoly of the available gold supply, the debtor class would have to get the gold from the banks at the bankers' own terms.

But another question was involved. The banks sought a complete monopoly of the traffic of issuing currency. They desired no competition in that line from the Government. The one form of currency represented private ownership and control of that essential medium of exchange; the other public ownership and control. The banks planned to efface the Government from the money-issuing function. But how? By having the courts declare the Legal Tender Act unconstitutional. True, various State courts, with the single exception of the Supreme Court of Pennsylvania, had decided in favor of the law, but the Supreme Court of the United States was still to speak, and it was upon that Court that the banking interests now confidently depended.

Banking and Railroad Interests Collide.

It was precisely at this juncture that the banking power came into the sharpest collision with the rapidly expanding railroad interests.

The preceding decades had been a period of phenomenal construction of railroads. In the year 1851, there were less than 9,000 miles of railroad in the entire United States. In the next six years 17,000 miles were built. By the beginning of the Civil War, a total of 30,000 miles of railroad had been constructed. During the next decade — at least, before 1873 — 36,000 more miles of railroad were built, constituting a greater extension than the entire mileage of the preceding thirty-four years.[16]

Although, as we shall see, the promoters of those railroads

[16] See, " Poor's Railroad Manual," for the years in question.

had bribed act after act through Congress or State Legislatures or both, and had corrupted county officials and municipalities to give them stupendous gifts of public lands, public funds and extraordinary privileges, yet the construction necessities of actual cash were so great that necessarily the railroad corporations had to make out mortgages. As we have said, very little gold was in circulation. The receipts of the railroad companies were almost wholly in legal-tender notes. If they were required to pay their fixed charges or contracts in gold, they would be so completely at the mercy of the banks that it would only be a short time before the banks would own outright virtually every railroad system.

This was the prodigious contest now under way between these two powerful interests. Which side would win? The Supreme Court of the United States would decide.

Supreme Court's Composition.

The composition of the Supreme Court of the United States at this time was mixed, in point of the economic interests represented by its members. President Lincoln had appointed four Associate Justices — Noah H. Swayne, of Ohio, Samuel F. Miller, of Iowa, and David Davis, of Illinois, in 1862, and Stephen J. Field, of California, in 1863.

As an attorney, Swayne had represented various miscellaneous corporations — the Columbus Insurance Company, the Bank of Wooster, the Columbus Machine Manufacturing Company, the Ohio Mutual Insurance Company, the Delaware County Bank, the Bank of Circleville and other companies and institutions.[17] He had been an attorney for the Lafayette Bank, of Cincinnati,[18] of which bank, as we have related, Chase had long been a director.

[17] XVII Ohio Reports, 224, etc.; I Ohio State Reports, 234; XI *Ibid.*, 163; XII *Ibid.*, 178, etc., etc.
[18] VIII Ohio State Reports, 28.

When an attorney for the Mad River and Lake Erie Railroad, Swayne had contested an action attracting some adverse notice in the year 1856. Barber, a freight train conductor, had brought an action for severe injuries sustained while at work, in 1852. The cars were defective, not being supplied with brake rods, chains and other apparatus; and while engaged in his duties, Barber was thrown under the cars which passed over him breaking one of his legs and crushing his right arm. Thereafter, he was disfigured and maimed for life, and unable to make a living. The jury in the lower court gave him a verdict for $9,500 damages.

Swayne and W. F. Stone, as attorneys for the railroad, carried the case on appeal to the Ohio State Supreme Court. In December, 1861, Chief Justice Bartley of that court reversed the judgment of the district court on the ground (among other grounds mentioned) that a railroad company was not liable in an action for damages in consequence of defective cars where (so the decision literally read) the defects of the cars were *unknown* to both parties, and where *neither party was at fault*. Barber — the decision further read — had voluntarily assumed the risk; he had had a right to decline his job or refuse to run the train; and when he voluntarily took the job, he assumed the risk.[19] Thus, after nearly ten years' futile attempts to get redress, the mutilated brakeman was condemned to live out his wretched life in penniless misery, while Swayne ascended to the Supreme Court of the United States.

Associate Justice Miller subsequently developed more than pronounced railroad leanings, as was shown in a noted cynical decision of his; but what especially commended him at this time was that he had strongly favored the emancipation of negro slaves.

Davis was a personal friend of Lincoln; after Lincoln's

[19] See, Case of Mad River and Lake Erie R. R. vs. Barber, V Ohio State Reports, 541–568.

assassination, he was one of the administrators of Lincoln's estate. Davis had married Sarah Walker of Pittsfield, Massachusetts, who had a considerable fortune. For an adroit politician Davis was unusually conscientious and progressive; he had been a judge in Illinois from 1848 to 1862, and there was highly spoken of and respected.[20] Miller was forty-six years old, Davis, forty-seven, at the time of their appointment.

Justice Field's Career.

The career of Associate Justice Field was filled with scandals both before and after his elevation to the Supreme Court. Born at Haddam, Connecticut, in 1816, he was the son of a Congregationalist clergyman. He had studied law in the office of his brother, David Dudley Field, and was his partner from 1841 to 1848.

David Dudley Field had married a rich widow; " hence," says a contemporary account, " a portion of his wealth," which amounted to $100,000.[21] David Dudley Field became one of the attorneys for the notorious briber, Jacob Sharp, after Sharp had bribed the New York Board of Aldermen, in 1853, to grant him a street railway franchise for Broadway.[22]

[20] Nor did he ever forfeit this respect. So esteemed was he for his progressive views that, in February, 1872, the National Convention of the Labor Reform Party nominated him as its candidate on a platform which declared, among other things, in favor of a national currency, " based on the faith and resources of the nation "; which demanded the establishment of an eight-hour law throughout the country, and the payment of the national debt " without mortgaging the property of the people to enrich capitalists." Davis accepted. At the Liberal Republican Party Convention, in 1872, he received 92½ votes for the nomination for President, but determined to retire from the final contest. The convention nominated Horace Greeley.

[21] " The Wealth and Biography Of The Wealthy Citizens of New York," 1846.

[22] See, Case of Milhau vs. Sharp, XV Barbour's Supreme Court Reports [N. Y.]: 193–232. For details of the bribery see Testimony before the Grand Jury, Documents of the N. Y. Board of Aldermen, XXI, Part II, No. 55: 1333–1335. The courts, at the time, refused to allow the franchise to be carried into effect. But twenty-one years later — in 1884 — Sharp was more successful. With $500,000 in cash,

Subsequently, David Dudley Field was attorney for the even more notorious bribers and railroad wreckers and looters, Jay Gould and James Fisk, Jr.[23] And it may be mentioned here that (no doubt as a token of pure brotherly affection) David Dudley Field made, in 1880, a gift to Associate Justice Field of a deed to a fine house and grounds in Washington that Justice Field from thence to his death owned and occupied. The fact of this gift Justice Field himself stated in his will. Another brother of Associate Justice Field was Cyrus W. Field, the inventor of the submarine telegraph cable. Cyrus Field, after the Civil War, aligned himself with Jay Gould in the manipulation of the elevated railroads in New York City, in which roads he was a large stockholder. For a time, he was a director of the Manhattan Railway and also of the New York Central and Hudson River Railroad,[24] but subsequently was stripped by Gould of his elevated railroad stock, and died a comparatively poor man.[25]

Going to California, Stephen J. Field settled at Yubaville, of which place he was elected mayor, in 1850. He was, indeed, mayor and judge in one, and carried a six-shooter both to enforce his authority and to protect himself. Heralded as a prominent capitalist and lawyer from the East, he bought Yubaville lots, put up zinc houses in Marysville, and rented those habitations at enormous rentals. From the sale of part of the lots he was said to have cleared a profit of $25,000; and it was related of him that he had not been in Marysville

he bribed the Board of Aldermen to give him a franchise for Broadway. (See, Myers' "History of Public Franchises In New York City," 139-143.) But although the bribery was exposed, and a number of aldermen were convicted and sent to prison, the courts declared the franchise indefeasible.

[23] See, V Lansing's Reports, 26, concerning the scandalous effort of Gould and Fisk to get control of the Albany and Susquehanna Railroad. The circumstances are narrated in the "History of the Great American Fortunes," Vol. III: 180-183. Field also appeared for Fisk in a case involving the Chicago and Rock Island Railroad.

[24] See, "Poor's Railroad Manual" for 1880: p. 182.

[25] The process is described in the "History of the Great American Fortunes," Vol. III: 84-85.

more than four months before he had accumulated $50,000.[26]

Getting into a dispute with Judge Turner of the California Circuit Court, primarily over the abolition question, Turner claimed that Field and two other attorneys had villified the court, and on June 10, 1850, Judge Turner expelled them from the bar. Seven days later Judge Turner committed Field to prison for forty-eight hours and to pay a fine of $500 for contempt of court. But the California Supreme Court issued a mandamus compelling Judge Turner to reinstate Field and the two other attorneys as members of the bar.[27]

Interests Represented by Field.

That Field was interested in some of the old Mexican land grants (genuine or otherwise) in California was well known; and it was due largely to the influence of the promoters of these claims as well as to the influence of Leland Stanford and his associate railroad promoters that Field was elected to the California Supreme Court, becoming its Chief Justice in 1859. When a judge of this court Field — as was openly charged — gave especial protection to land titles, particularly those alleged to have been derived from Mexican authority. In short, he was the judge from whom the land jobbers and claimants could always expect favorable consideration. A letter was written at this time by United States Senator David C. Broderick saying that Judge David T. Terry — who sat on the bench with Field — was the only honest man on the California Supreme Court Bench. But when Broderick later took this statement back, so far as it excepted Terry, Broderick was challenged to a duel by Terry, in 1859, and was

[26] On September 26, 1850, he mortgaged various of his Marysville lots as security for $6,500 of notes, and three months later conveyed all of his estate in trust for the benefit of creditors.— Case of Bentham vs. Field, Rowe *et al.,* I California Reports, 387.

[27] See, People *ex rel.* Stephen J. Field vs. Turner, etc., I California Reports, 144 and 152, and *Ibid.,* 188–189.

shot and killed. Thirty years later, Judge Terry was himself killed by a United States marshall accompanying Field after Terry had slapped Field in the face.[28]

The sponsor and pusher of Field for place and power was Leland Stanford, himself a lawyer. Projecting the Central Pacific Railroad Company in 1861, Stanford, Collis P. Huntington, Charles Crocker and Mark Hopkins successfully debauched legislatures and Congress, obtained $25,000,000 in Government bonds, millions more from the State of California and counties in that State, and a gift of a vast area of public lands — all donated, actually or practically, for the purpose of enabling them to build their privately owned railroad. While Huntington was in Washington bribing Congress, Stanford caused himself to be elected Governor of California, so as to manipulate that State for the interests of the quartet. The enormous thefts that Stanford and his partners eventually consummated are set forth in the public documents, and are elaborately detailed elsewhere.[29]

Governor Leland Stanford personally urged President Lincoln to appoint Field to the Supreme Court of the United States.[30] It was generally understood that with Field upon the Bench, the predatory land claimants had at least one Justice upon whose favor they could generally rely.

The Sutter Case.

The very next year after Associate Justice Field took his seat, a California land-claim case came up in which action he was disqualified from sitting for reasons best known to himself. This action was what was called the " Sutter Case." It

---

[28] See later.

[29] See, Chapter on " The Pacific Quartet," " History of the Great American Fortunes," Vol. III. In cash alone they stole more than $50,000,000, and still further enriched themselves by vast issues of stocks and bonds. See later.

[30] The author has been personally assured of this by a man (still living) who was Stanford's private secretary at this time.

involved, according to the Supreme Court of the United States, " immense interests in California, and questions greatly agitating a particular portion of that State."

In 1852 John A. Sutter had come forward with a claim purporting to have been given by the Mexican Governor, Alvarado, in 1841. The next year, 1853, Sutter submitted to the Board of Land Commissioners another claim for *twenty-two leagues more,* alleged to have been granted by Michel-torena, in 1845. Sutter had been a military commandant under Mexican authority, and had been charged with civil jurisdiction, also; he was the very official who had recommended a grant of six square leagues to Pearson B. Reading whose claim we have described, in a previous chapter. Sutter's claims to thirty-three leagues in all were confirmed by the Board and by the District Court, but the Supreme Court of the United States allowed only the first claim of eleven square leagues as valid.[31]

Now, two surveys of the allowed eleven-league claim had been made; the new question before the Supreme Court was, therefore, which of the surveys should be validated.

The first survey, made in 1859, was so manipulated as to break the claim into two parts which were not continuous. By this means the claim was made to include a part of the present county of Sacramento; then the survey was run along the Feather River; an intervening distance of several miles was marked out to separate one part of the claim from the other; then the claim began again at a place called Canadian Ford and ran up to, and included, Marysville.

The second survey, made by the Surveyor-General in 1863, located the eleven leagues in a long continuous line of narrow tracts along the Feather and American rivers.

The majority of the Supreme Court of the United States ordered that the survey of 1859 be substituted for that of 1863. Thus the Sutter claimants were able to appropriate

[31] U. S. vs. Sutter, XXI Howard, 170.

some of the finest parts of Sacramento County and Marysville. The note in the case reads: " Mr. Justice Field did
not sit in the case, nor take part in its decision." [32]

Justice Grier's Resignation Demanded.

Of the men thus comprising the membership of the
Supreme Court of the United States, the banking interests
knew to a certainty upon whom they could depend. That the
most vigorous, yet secret, influences were brought to bear
upon two Justices at least, and possibly others, is fairly
certain.

In the case of Justice Grier, the records of the Supreme
Court itself strongly tend to indicate this. We have seen in
the previous chapter how before the Dred Scott decision
Justice Grier, as revealed by his own correspondence, was in
collusion with President-elect Buchanan, and through Buchanan, with the representatives of the slaveholders who had
put Buchanan into office, whose interests and plans Buchanan
was elected to further. Of Buchanan's selecting certain arch
slavery representatives as members of his Cabinet, and how
they stripped the North of munitions of war and transferred
them to the South — this is an elemental historical fact. In
the Legal-Tender case, Justice Grier's course was even more
serpentine; he played fast and loose with both sides, singularly
shifting from one side to another. His vacillation was so
suspicious and remarkable, that not a single one of his colleagues, either those favoring the Legal Tender Act or those
against it, could find any excuse for his action; they lost pa-
tience, and evinced their distrust by the significant and unprecedented action of demanding his resignation.

" When," says Rhodes, " the determination of the Court
was arrived at on November 27, 1869, four justices concurred
with Chase: Nelson, Clifford, Grier and Field, but before the

[32] II Wallace's Reports, 587.

opinion was read Grier resigned. Swayne and Davis agreed
with Miller. The decision could be stated as five or four
to three according to one's individual preferences, but as a
matter of history, the concurrence of Grier carries no weight
whatever. When the first vote on the Hepburn vs. Griswold
case was taken in conference, the Court stood 4-4, Grier pronouncing in favor of the constitutionality of the Legal Tender
Act; but before the conference closed, he, in another case,
stated an opinion inconsistent with that vote. This inconsistency being called to his attention, he changed his vote and
went over to the side of Chase, Nelson, Clifford and Field.
Within a week from that day every judge on the bench authorized a committee of their number to say to Grier ' that it
was their unanimous opinion that he ought to resign.' " [33]
Grier did accordingly, in December, 1869, resign, his resignation to take effect on January 31, 1870.

Legal-Tender Decision Favors the Bankers.

By a majority of one, therefore, the Legal Tender Act
was declared unconstitutional, Chief Justice Chase himself
writing the opinion. The decision, handed down on February 7, 1870, declared that prior to the enactment of the
Legal Tender law of 1862, gold formed the only legal tender,
and that all promises to pay in contracts were tacitly understood to be payable in gold. So far as the Legal Tender Act
applied to preëxisting contracts, it was, under Chase's decision, inoperative; the act could not be retroactive.[34]
Why did Chief Justice Chase decide against the constitutionality of a law that as Secretary of the Treasury he had
been known to view as being thoroughly constitutional? The
explanation generally given was that in his incorrigible aspira-

[33] " History of the United States, 1850–1877," Vol. VI: 262–263, citing
statement on April 30, 1870, by Swayne, Miller, Davis, Strong and
Bradley. Also, Bradley's " Miscellaneous Writings," p. 73.
[34] Case of Hepburn vs. Griswold, VIII Wallace's Reports, 626.

tion to become President, he desired to gain the further good will of the bankers, and to insure their support. Some critics held that in view of his inconsistencies he had a private understanding with the banking interests, but no evidence whatever has ever been produced to bear out that charge. That he was actuated by personal mercenary motives no one then believed, or now imputes. He was a politician, and was willing to do whatever could advance his political ambitions — a form of corruption which, as we have seen, had influenced previous members of the Supreme Court. Assuming that he was personally honest, as honesty was understood, he ·was politically dishonest.

"Chase's open craving for the Presidency," Rhodes narrates, "detracted from the weight of his opinion. In the spring of 1869, the Chief Justice and George F. Hoar walked home together from a meeting of a scientific club in Washington. For the whole distance, about a mile, Chase talked of the next nomination for the presidency, the prospects of the various candidates and the probable chances of a Democratic candidate who should appeal to Republicans 'disaffected with the present policies of their party. Somewhat later, during a half hour's drive across Baltimore, he talked incessantly in the same strain to a stranger. He had the presidency 'on the brain,' wrote Hoar. His conversations, his solicitations became a scandal and must have led his associates in the consultation room to look upon him with suspicion. . . ." [35] Rhodes, nevertheless, thinks that Chase, in the legal-tender decision, acted from honest conviction.

But there was another factor that Rhodes neither explains nor even mentions. Infallibly, a man's early economic interests, associations and training, long persisted in, have a determining influence upon his views, and conspire to sway or prejudice him in one direction or another. As a young

[35] "History of the United States, 1850 to 1877," Vol. VI: 266, citing Hoar's "Autobiography," Vol. I: 282.

lawyer, and in middle age, Chase's self-interested associations were mainly with bankers, and as an older man he was constantly, as Secretary of the Treasury, in personal touch with the foremost bankers of the country. Nearly his whole adult life, it may be said, was — so far as his personal interests and connections went — an unbroken association with bankers, and a corresponding susceptibility and flexibility to their interests. In the light of this fact — and a highly important one, reflecting the whole processes of present society upon one's mental attitude — some clear explanation is afforded of at least one reason why Chase favored the banking power.

The same influence probably had its effect upon Justice Clifford, whose family, as we have noted, was connected by a double marriage with the largest banking family in Portland, Maine. As for Justice Nelson, he was a relic of the era of state banking, with its wild-cat currency issue, of which he had been an avowed advocate.

Nor was Justice Field's stand a mystery. In concurring with the majority he held that the legal-tender clause was unconstitutional as applied to prior contracts only. Such a dictum could in nowise affect the interests of his patrons, Leland Stanford and Collis P. Huntington. The mortgages that Stanford and his fellow promoters gave, were although subsequent to 1862, mortgages to the Government, not to private bankers. And the plan of cheating the Government out of much of its advances for the building of the Central Pacific Railroad was, thanks to the act of 1864, already formulated, to be finally consummated later by means of a decision of the Supreme Court of the United States, with Justice Field on the Bench.

Congress Estops the Supreme Court.

In striking contrast with the Supreme Court's edict of unconstitutionality in the legal-tender case was its action in another case at this time. Congress had passed various laws designed to facilitate reconstruction measures in the late rebellious states, and to enforce obedience to the military authorities in control. William H. McCardle was arrested in Southern Mississippi charged with attacks, in a newspaper of which he was editor, upon General Ord and other officers. Alleging unlawful restraint, McCardle sued from the Circuit Court to the Supreme Court of the United States for a writ of habeas corpus. The Supreme Court in 1867 was considering asserting its jurisdiction, when, to prevent that court from interfering, Congress, on March 27, 1868, passed a prohibitive act. Section 2 of that act repealed certain parts of the old judiciary act of 1789 which had allowed certain appeals to the Supreme Court of the United States. Further, Section 2 estopped the Supreme Court from exercising jurisdiction in the case of any such appeals.[36]

When the McCardle case came up again in December, 1868, the Supreme Court was compelled to admit that Congress had the power of regulating its jurisdiction. Delivering the Court's unanimous opinion, Chief Justice Chase, in December, 1868, acknowledged the paramount authority of Congress. "It is quite true," he pronounced, "as was argued by the counsel for the petitioner, that the appellate jurisdiction of this court is not derived from the acts of Congress. It is, strictly speaking, conferred by the Constitution. But it is conferred 'with such exceptions and under such regulations as Congress shall make.' . . .

"We are not at liberty to inquire into the motives of the legislature. We can only examine into its power under the Constitution, but the power to make exceptions to the appellate jurisdiction is given in express words.

"What, then, is the effect of the repealing act upon the case before us? We cannot doubt as to this: Without jurisdiction the court cannot proceed at all in any cause. Jurisdic-

[36] XV Statutes At Large, 44.

tion is power to declare law, and when it ceases to exist the only function remaining to the court is that of announcing the fact and dismissing the cause. And this is not less clear upon authority than upon principle. . . .

"It is quite clear, therefore, that this court cannot proceed to pronounce judgment in this case, for it has no longer jurisdiction of the appeal; and judicial duty is not less fitly performed by declining ungranted jurisdiction than in exercising firmly that which the Constitution and the laws confer." [37]

Here was a case involving so clear-cut a proposition that the Supreme Court could do nothing but admit the full authority of Congress in the premises. Had the case concerned a " contract " or the construction of the " obligation of a contract " the Supreme Court no doubt would have asserted its power, real or usurped, of deciding upon its constitutionality under that renowned Constitutional clause which had germinated in Wilson's brain eighty years before.

Railroads War Against the Legal-Tender Decision.

Gratifying as it was to the bankers, the Legal-Tender decision, on the other hand, enraged the railroad magnates. The market value of railway mortgages immediately went up — perhaps the most significant commentary on what the decision meant to the bankers. Every newspaper and politician subsidized by the railroad interests denounced the decision, and conversely, the banking journals praised it. The influence of the Pennsylvania Railroad and other large corporations which had outstanding bonds of issues prior to 1862, was directed against the decision. On the day on which Chase read his opinion gold was quoted at from 121⅛ to 120½.[38]

[37] See, " Ex Parte McCardle," VI Wallace's Reports, 318, and VII *Ibid.*, 506–515. The Supreme Court, accordingly, dismissed the case for want of jurisdiction.

[38] Rhodes, Vol. VI: 265.

Railroad magnates saw the immediate necessity of opening a newspaper campaign demanding the reversal of the decision. Why, complained the railroad owners, should they be compelled to pay the interest and principal of their bonds in gold, when their passenger fares and freight money were received in paper currency? [39] From their point of view, a valid complaint, most assuredly.

With these two powerful capitalist groups in direct and intense opposition, the contest was clearly defined, and the final result impatiently awaited.

The bankers had won in the Supreme Court. But in Congress the railroad power had been steadily increasing. Within ten years great changes in representation had taken place. The immense donations of public lands and money that the railroad promoters had received from Government, States, counties and municipalities, now constituted the basis of a gigantic power. The railroad corporations had systematically corrupted politics; they usually dictated who should go to Congress, and who should be defeated. They named State officials and judges of State courts. Suddenly they were confronted with the urgent necessity of securing control of the Supreme Court of the United States, and of insuring that control quickly. Some of the ablest men in Congress — political leaders of both parties — were railroad attorneys, retainers or stockholders. United States Senator Sherman, in fact, was one of the principal stockholders in the Pittsburg, Fort Wayne and Chicago Railroad — now a constituent part of the Pennsylvania Railroad system.[40]

[39] Rhodes, Vol. VII: 27.

[40] See, Case of State of Ohio vs. Sherman *et al.,* XXII Ohio State Reports, 411. When, in 1869, the Pittsburg, Fort Wayne and Chicago Railroad Company leased its entire road to the Pennsylvania Railroad for a term of 999 years, the State of Ohio brought an abortive suit for an ouster for usurpation and unlawful exercise of franchise, etc. As a young attorney, Sherman had started out as a railroad counsel; in 1848, he was attorney for the Vermilion and Ashland Railroad.— XVIII Ohio Reports, 189.

Growth of the Railroad Power.

For twenty years the bribery of members of Congress and of the Texas Legislature by railroad promoters had gone on incessantly. Of the 155,273,560.73 acres of public lands granted directly by the United States Government, or by it through States, to railroad corporations, the greater part had already been obtained by corrupt legislation. From 1850 to 1870 not less than one hundred and thirty-three separate grants of public lands had been made by Congress to nearly as many different railroad corporations.[41] In addition, the State of Texas (which retained control of its lands) granted a total of 32,400,000 acres, the bulk of which had already been appropriated by the year 1870.[42] There were also donations of State lands in the East over which the United States Government had no jurisdiction, as for example the Legislature of Maine granting, in 1868, a donation of 700,000 acres of land to the European and North American Railroad.[43]

Altogether, counting the donations of Government, of the State of Texas, of other individual States and of counties and municipalities, the railroad corporations had received the major part of a total of about 212,000,000 acres. Nor does this estimate comprise the gifts of immensely valuable terminal facilities, municipal rights of way, harbor rights and other privileges of a value of hundreds of millions of dollars. Finally, from either Government, States, counties or cities, or from all, they had received loans or gifts of public funds approximating many hundreds of millions of dollars; the total vast amount has never yet been computed.

Possessed of these immense resources, the railroad interests were formidably intrenched.

[41] Report of The Public Land Commission, 1905: pp. 144–155.
[42] Biennial Report of the Commissioners of the General Land Office of Texas, 1908–10: p. 29.
[43] See, Seventh Report of the Forest Commissioner of Maine, 1908: p. 90.

Corruption by Railroad Corporations.

For purposes of illustration, a few examples of this long-continuing corruption will be given.

In 1853 Alexander J. Marshall sued the Baltimore and Ohio Railroad for the sum of $50,000 due him on a contract for lobbying through the Virginia Legislature a bill granting that company a comprehensive right of way to the Ohio River. "Without impropriety," he wrote on November 17, 1846, to Louis McLane, a politician of national note, and president of the railroad company, "I may say for myself I have had considerable experience as a lobby member before the Legislature of Virginia. For several years past I have been before that body with difficult and important measures affecting the improvement of this region of the country; and I think I understand the character and component material of that honorable body. . . ." [44] The Supreme Court of the United States decided against Marshall, holding among other grounds, that the enforcement of such a corrupt contract was against public policy.[45]

In 1856 the LaCrosse and Milwaukee Railroad Company had bribed, with $800,000 of bonds, nearly the whole of the Wisconsin Legislature, the Governor and newspaper editors for the advocacy and passage of an act giving that company a land grant of about 1,000,000 acres valued at that time at nearly $18,000,000.[46] A special committee of Congress was appointed in 1857 to investigate charges of corruption in connection with an act giving an enormous land grant in Iowa, Minnesota and other states to the Des Moines Navigation and

[44] Marshall vs. Baltimore and Ohio Railroad Company, XVI Howard's Reports, 315.

[45] Ibid., 314, etc. Similar bribery cases of the times are set forth in XVIII Pickering's Massachusetts Reports, 470; VII Watt's Reports, 152, etc., etc.

[46] "Report of the Joint Select Committee Appointed to Investigate Into Alleged Frauds and Corruption," etc. Appendices to (Wisconsin) Senate and Assembly Journals, 1858.

Railroad Company. The Committee recommended the expulsion of four members of Congress, reporting that one of them, Orasmus B. Matteson, was a leader of a corrupt combination and had received for disbursement a corruption fund of $100,000 and "other valuable considerations." [47]

These are merely a few of the many instances that could be cited, and many more of which are related in the "History of the Great American Fortunes." The corruption continued during, and after, the Civil War. In the year 1868 alone, for example, Jay Gould and his associate directors of the Erie Railroad, had expended at least a million dollars in corrupting the New York Legislature, and Cornelius Vanderbilt had spent a large amount for the same purpose.[48] Hand in hand with the Tweed régime then plundering New York, Gould and Fisk were able to purchase both laws and judges; Barnard and Cardozo and other judges of the New York State Supreme Court were their supple tools; after the Tweed "ring" was overthrown Barnard was, indeed, impeached; and Cardozo resigned in time to save himself from impeachment.[49] And of the many scandals developing in Congress and in the State Legislatures, we will here mention only one, — and a very typical example — the Credit Mobilier Company swindle. In this affair many of the foremost capitalists of the country were involved, and a galaxy of leading politicians in Congress. The testimony revealed that in the constructing of the Union Pacific Railroad at least $44,000,000 had been stolen by the falsifying of construction accounts and by other

[47] Reports of Committees, House of Representatives, Thirty-fourth Congress, Third Session, 1856–57, Report No. 243, Vol. III. By a construction of the law made by the land grabber Robert J. Walker, when Secretary of the Treasury, the grant of this company was vastly enlarged. In 1892 the Government tried to recover much of the lands, but the Supreme Court of the U. S. decided adversely to the Government. See later.

[48] See, "History of the Great American Fortunes," particularly Vol. II: 310–317.

[49] See, "History of Tammany Hall," 296–297.

methods.[50]   James G. Blaine, Speaker of the House of Representatives, was one of those implicated in the Credit Mobilier transactions.

Packing of the Supreme Court.

How were the railroad interests to get control of the Supreme Court of the United States? Partly by means of Congress and more definitely through President Grant. On March 3, 1863, Congress had passed an act (12 Statutes At Large, 794) that the Supreme Court should consist of ten members;[51] the purpose of that enactment was to provide a circuit for California. Three years later — on July 23, 1866, — another act was passed declaring that the number of judges should be thereafter reduced to seven, this change to take effect as soon as by death or retirement the number sitting should be reduced to seven. The intention of this act was to prevent President Johnson, to whose views on reconstruction the majority in Congress were antagonistic, from getting control of the Supreme Court. Justice Catron had died in May, 1863, but no actual appointment of any successor had taken effect. This was the state of affairs when on April 10, 1869, Congress passed another act restoring the number of justices to nine. Why was this statute passed? Did the railroad power foresee the alignment of the Supreme Court on the Legal Tender Act, and was preparing accordingly to have railroad attorneys appointed and reverse Chase's decision? Whether or not that was the purpose, the result was exactly as though the arrangement had been premeditated and well planned. Two vacancies caused, in December, 1869, by the death of Justice Wayne and the resignation of Justice Grier, gave President Grant the opportunity of making appointments in their places.

[50] Reports of Committees, Credit Mobilier Reports, Forty-Second Congress, Third Session, 1872-73, Doc. No. 78: xiv-xx.
[51] It was under this act that Justice Field was appointed.

Grant Surrounded by Venal Confidants.

That Grant would appoint railroad attorneys was an accepted conclusion. It was well known that he was not above receiving gifts, as it had been equally well known that President Lincoln's wife had not refused them; on one occasion, as Ben Perley Poore tells in his " Reminiscences," Mrs. Lincoln accepted a valuable shawl, valued at $1,000, from A. T. Stewart, a New York capitalist, at the very time Stewart was a contractor for supplying the army with blankets. This giving of gifts was a favorite and safe form of winning favor. But so far as money bribes were concerned Grant was beyond reproach. He, however, was surrounded by as corrupt a corps of intimates, confidants and factotums as, perhaps, had ever been known in the White House. They had his ear and trust; and when their integrity · was impeached he resented the fact, and sought to shield them in every possible way. They seem to have manipulated Grant much as they willed.

Vicious scandals kept developing in the war and navy departments and it was shown that Grant's own private secretary and intimate friend, Orville E. Babcock, was a member of the Whiskey Ring and was sharing in the proceeds of its frauds.[52] Grant's brother-in-law, A. R. Corbin, had been a lobbyist in Congress for the Illinois Central Railroad, and was both an accomplice of Gould and a participant in the profits of Gould's gold conspiracy operations of 1869, leading to " Black Friday." [53]

Grant's open association with Gould and Fisk was, in truth, a national scandal; he went on a junketing steamboat party with them; he appeared with them at the theater; and this public countenance was of the most incalculable value to them,

[52] The Whisky Ring defrauded the Government out of many millions of dollars in revenue on the manufacture of whisky by falsifying the returns with the collusion of Government officials.

[53] Gold Panic Investigation, House Report No. 31, Forty-first Congress, Second Session, 1870: 157.

in that it spread the public impression that Grant was in league with them, and gave them the support of his paramount authority. We cannot assume that he was so simple-minded as to have been an unconscious dupe, and not know (what every intelligent man knew) of their corrupt character and the enormous frauds and thefts that they were consummating. On the other hand, it is not probable that Grant ever received any illicit money, or deliberately connived at fraud. Some writers hold that his early life of poverty reacted on him to such an extent that he was glad to be in the society of men of money. This is but a paltry explanation, for Grant well knew how fortunes were being acquired; he had, as a general during the war, written indignant letters on the shameless frauds committed by army contractors in western Tennessee, and had bitterly denounced them.

Whatever his motives, the fact remained that as President, Grant well knew the methods by which his friends and adherents were getting rich and winked at them. What was of much greater importance, he was perfectly willing that capitalists of every description should have their way and control his actions, knowing as he did that without their support he could not get adequate campaign funds, nor perhaps even secure a renomination. To represent and advance their interests was his aim. One of the keenest political observers of the time — Samuel Bowles, editor and proprietor of the *Springfield Republican* — thus expressed the situation: " Money-bags are always and everywhere conservative. When you have proved to the busy wealth seeker that the President has shown an indecent fondness for gifts, that he has appointed rascally or incapable kinsmen to office, that he has cracked, if not broken the laws, what have you accomplished by your denunciation? They will reply to you, ' General Grant is a safe man.' . . . The railroad rings, the banking rings, the iron and coal rings, the money-grabbing combinations of every name and sort, are clear in the conviction that one good turn deserves another, and have come down handsomely for the general campaign fund." [54]

Two Railroad Attorneys Appointed.

On December 20, 1869, President Grant appointed Edwin M. Stanton, but Stanton died four days later.[55] Then, on the same day that Chase's opinion in the Legal-Tender case was announced, Grant sent the nominations of William Strong and Joseph P. Bradley, as Associate Justices, to the Senate. Their nominations were shortly afterward confirmed.[56]

Both Strong and Bradley were conspicuous railroad attorneys and directors. Born in 1808, Strong had studied at Yale, and had begun the practice of law at Reading, Pennsylvania. He was, for many years before, and after, the Civil War the regular counsel for the Philadelphia and Reading Railroad, and for the Lebanon Valley Railroad, which was merged into the Philadelphia and Reading Railroad.[57] He was a member of the Reading Common Council,[58] a director of the Farmers' Bank and a director of the Lebanon Valley

[54] Merriam's " Life and Time of Samuel Bowles," Vol. II: 195–196.

[55] As an attorney, Stanton had been a noted railroad lawyer. He was also a stockholder in the Pittsburg and Steubenville Railroad.— See Pittsburg and Connellsville Railroad Co., vs. Clarke and Thaw — 29 Pa. State Reports, 147.

[56] The Washington dispatch of the New York *Times,* February 11, 1870, read: " There is authority for saying that in the matter of the recent decision in the legal tender cases, both Mr. Strong and Mr. Bradley have on occasions long prior to their present appointment given expression to views in consonance with those expressed in the dissenting opinion of Mr. Justice Miller."

[57] For Strong's early appearances as a railroad lawyer, see VI Pennsylvania State Reports, 74; XXI *Ibid.,* 188; XXIV *Ibid.,* 467, etc., etc.

[58] The Reading Common Council was induced to adopt an ordinance calling for a popular vote to decide upon a municipal subscription of $2,000,000 to aid in the construction of the Lebanon Valley Railroad, of which, as stated above, Strong was both a director and counsel. The vote was in favor of the measure. When an injunction was sought on the ground that the ordinance was unconstitutional, Strong appeared as counsel for the Lebanon Valley Railroad. Judge Black, in the Pennsylvania Supreme Court, in 1853, refused to grant the injunction. — XXI Pa. State Reports, 188–203.

Railroad. In Congress from 1847 to 1852, he later, in 1857, was elected a member of the Pennsylvania Supreme Court for fifteen years, but he resigned from this bench in 1868, removed to Philadelphia, and resumed a railroad practice more lucrative than ever.

Bradley was both a noted railroad lawyer and a capitalist. Born in 1813, the son of a farmer and teacher, he was admitted to the bar in 1839, and commenced the practice of law at Newark, N. J., in partnership with John P. Jackson, superintendent of the New Jersey Railroad. Bradley, thereafter, represented that railroad in all important cases; subsequently he was also the leading counsel of the Camden and Amboy Railroad, and for various companies associated under the name of the United Railways of New Jersey, which later became the New Jersey branches of the Pennsylvania Railroad Company. In 1844 he had married Mary, daughter of Chief Justice Hornblower, of New Jersey.

Bradley's Long Railroad Service.

Bradley was very closely associated both as counsel and fellow railroad director with Edwin A. Stevens, a conspicuous steamboat and railroad owner in New Jersey. If the numerous records state the case correctly, the fortune that Stevens acquired, and part of which he later used to blossom out as a philanthropist, was got by a sequence of fraud and bribery.

In one case, coming up in the Chancery Court, in 1847, Stevens, his brothers, and Robert F. and Richard Stockton (the latter of whom was subsequently associated with Bradley as counsel) were accused of collusion in the fraudulent manipulation of the stock and of the freight and profits of the New Brunswick Steamboat and Canal Company, the Union Transportation Line, the Camden and Amboy Transportation

Company and the Delaware and Raritan Canal Company.
The suit was brought by one, John D. Hagar, a stockholder
who, after being granted an injunction restraining certain actions, sued for an accounting for some $400,000 and other
sums which he alleged had been improperly appropriated and
expended; he further alleged that by a series of fraudulent
manipulations the lesser stockholders had been cheated and
" frozen out." These charges the defendants denied. In denying Hager's petition for a receiver, Chancellor Halstead
practically sustained the allegations of fraud. The Chancellor said that if a large accumulation of property should appear to be the result of a fraud on the rights of others not parties to the suit, the court would not become the instrument
to distribute the moneys accumulated by such fraud, on
the application of one who had been a stockholder of the company from the beginning, and who had been cognizant of the
fraudulent proceedings which resulted in that fraudulent accumulation.[59]

Bradley was one of the attorneys for the Hoboken Land
and Improvement Company, particularly in the suit of the
" Proprietors of the Bridges Over the Rivers Passaic and
Hackensack." The " Proprietors," etc., were an ancient corporation; they had been incorporated in the year 1790 to
build and conduct toll bridges, and they claimed a perpetual
monopoly by vested right. The real owners of the " Proprietors " corporation was the New Jersey Railroad and
Transportation Company which held more than nine hundred
and fifty of the one thousand shares outstanding. As the
owner of the Hoboken Land and Improvement Company, Edwin A. Stevens had compelled the New Jersey Railroad and
Transportation Company to pay him an annual blackmail subsidy of $18,000 in order to buy him off from building a branch

[59] See, Case of John D. Hager vs. Edwin A. Stevens *et al.,* VI New
Jersey Chancery Reports, 374–447.

railroad on a franchise that he held running from Hoboken to Newark.[60]

Tiring of paying this blackmail money, the New Jersey Railroad and Transportation Company began an aggressive warfare. Amid open charges that bribery was being used both for and against the bill, Stevens, on March 8, 1860, obtained the enactment of a law by the New Jersey Legislature authorizing him to connect his line with the Morris and Essex Railroad in which he held a large proprietorship.[61] Then the "Proprietors," on the ground of their holding an exclusive franchise, applied for an injunction restraining the building of Stevens' road. Chancellor Green refused to grant the injunction.[62]

In the foregoing case, Bradley successfully argued *against* the claims of monopoly of franchise. But two years later, in another case, we find him arguing as strongly *for* a similar monopoly. He and J. P. Stockton appeared in chancery to ask for a preliminary injunction in favor of the Delaware and Raritan Canal Company and the Camden and Amboy Railroad and Transportation Company restraining the Camden and Atlantic Railroad Company, etc., from constructing a continuous line between the cities of New York and Philadelphia, and prohibiting any competition with the complainant's railroads.

[60] Said the financial column of the New York *Times,* February 27, 1860, of Stevens: ". . . The germ of the quarrel between that gentleman and the New Jersey Transportation people seems to have been the stoppage by the latter of a subsidy of $18,000 a year to Mr. Stevens (or the Hoboken Improvement Company) to quiet or in satisfaction for the time being of his right to demand a branch line to the Hoboken Ferry," etc., etc.

[61] Assemblyman Slaight, of Hudson County, charged, on May 1, 1860, that an offer of bribery had been made to him to vote for Stevens' bill, and Assemblyman Peckham, of the same county, declared that he had been offered $3,000 to oppose the bill.

[62] See, Case of "Proprietors," etc., vs. The Hoboken Land and Improvement Company, XIII New Jersey Equity Reports, 81, and *Ibid.,* 503–561. In both cases Bradley was one of Stevens' attorneys, as well as being associated with him as a director.

Bradley Argues for Railroad Monopoly.

This injunction was asked for on the ground that legislative acts had been passed in 1832 and 1854 prohibiting, for a certain period, the building of competing railroads except by consent of the railroad now represented by Bradley. The plea set up by Bradley did not claim that the railroads he was proceeding against would by the construction they were planning violate those acts. He could not validly make such a claim, inasmuch as no through line was being constructed. But he contended that a through route, which would compete in business, would be virtually made up partly of railroad line and partly of steamboats. On the ground that the acts cited did not refer to steamboat lines, Chancellor Green refused his application for an injunction.[63]

Bradley appealed to the New Jersey Court of Errors and Appeals on which bench sat such former notorious railroad attorneys as Beasley and Zabriskie. Here Bradley obtained a modification of Chancellor Green's decision; the two defendant corporations were enjoined from building such sections of railroad as would form a link between New York and Philadelphia.[64] To Bradley's long continued legal efforts was due, in great part, the power of the railroad monopoly in New Jersey to extort exorbitant railroad rates. These great profits went to enrich Bradley, for he was a stockholder and director as well as counsel.

How large these profits were, and the basis of them, may be judged from statements in the suit of J. S. Black, former Chief Justice of the Supreme Court of Pennsylvania. As a dissatisfied stockholder, Black filed an action, June 23, 1871, for an injunction restraining the proposed lease, for 999 years, of the Delaware and Raritan Canal Company, the Camden and Amboy Railroad, and the New Jersey Railroad and

[63] XV New Jersey Equity Reports, 19. (May, 1862.)
[64] XVIII New Jersey Equity Reports, 546–575. (November, 1867.)

Transportation Company (commonly called the United Railway Companies of New Jersey) to the Pennsylvania Railroad Company.

The answer of the United Railways admitted that the actual value of their properties was $50,000,000. But Judge Black estimated the value at $90,000,000. According to Black, the average annual dividends of the Delaware and Raritan Canal Company and of the Camden and Amboy Railroad, from 1833 to 1871, were about 12.20 per cent. This, Black set forth, was partly because of the small capital and the large bonded debt drawing only five per cent. interest, and partly because the companies "had the monopoly of the transportation of passengers and merchandise between New York and Philadelphia across the State of New Jersey." Black contended that when the lease was made the United Railways stock was indirectly watered to the extent of $5,250,000. Anticipating legal trouble, equivocal laws had been lobbied through the legislatures of both Pennsylvania and New Jersey, in 1870; under these Chancellor Zabriskie denied Black's application and held that the lease was valid.[65]

Bradley's corporation practice was extremely large and varied. He represented the New Jersey Zinc Company, the Morris County Bank, the Newark Lime and Cement Company, the Morris Canal and Banking Company, the May's Landing Water Power Company and many other corporations.[66] From 1857 to 1863 he was actuary of the Mutual Benefit Insurance Company of Newark; he was president of the New Jersey Mutual Life Insurance Company and he was a director in various financial institutions. In the biography of Bradley, edited by his son, we are told that "the Prudential Insurance Company's magnificent structure [in Newark] is

[65] XXII New Jersey Equity Reports, 130–430.
[66] See, Vols. XIII, XIV, XV, XVII, XIX, etc., New Jersey Equity Reports, pp. (respectively) 322, 419, 190, 65, 385, etc., etc.

erected on land owned by Judge Bradley for many years, and sold to it three years before his death." [67]

Certain of Strong and Bradley.

" It was alleged and not denied," says Schuckers of the appointment of Strong and Bradley to the Supreme Court of the United States, " that when Messrs. Strong and Bradley were made members of the court they were both interested as shareholders in the Camden and Amboy Railroad Company. It was alleged that one or both of these gentlemen had formerly been employed as law counsel by that company, and as such counsel had given opinions affirming the legal tender to be constitutional. It was known, too, that the Camden and Amboy Company had, in paying the interest upon their bonds subsequent to the decision in Hepburn vs. Griswold, made a reservation looking to a reversal of the judgment in that case." [68]

According to " Poor's Railroad Manual," Bradley, Edwin A. Stevens and others were directors of the Camden and Amboy Railroad, and Bradley, Stevens, etc., were directors of the Morris and Essex Railroad Company.[69] In the eulogistic biography of Bradley to which we have already referred, we are informed that when Bradley went to Washington as an Associate Justice of the Supreme Court he bought a large residence at No. 201 I Street, built by Stephen A. Douglas, and that " many old friends surrounded him " in Washington.[70] John P. Stockton and Frederick T. Frelinghuysen were there as United States Senators from New Jersey; both

[67] " Miscellaneous Writings of the Late Hon. Joseph P. Bradley, etc., Edited and Compiled by his son, Charles Bradley," Newark, 1901 : p. 5.
[68] " Life of S. P. Chase " (1874) : p. 261.
[69] See, " Poor's Railroad Manual " for 1868–1869 : pp. 383 and 386.
[70] " Miscellaneous Writings of the Late Hon. Joseph P. Bradley," etc., p. 3.

were old friends and associates of Bradley; Stockton was a railroad attorney, and Frelinghuysen was long a director of the Central Railroad of New Jersey.[71] The biography in question goes on to tell that other of Bradley's old friends now in Washington were George F. Robeson, Secretary of the Navy, and John Kean, later Vice-President of the Jersey Central Railroad.[72]

The Supreme Court Reverses Itself.

Now that the Supreme Court of the United States was packed,[73] or to put it more felicitously, reconstituted so as to reverse Chase's Legal-Tender decision, Attorney-General Hoar moved for a rehearing of the case. This motion was granted; and, in December, 1870, the Supreme Court, by a vote of five to four (Associate Justice Strong writing the majority opinion) reversed the previous decision, and declared the Legal Tender Act constitutional.[74]

From this time on, one decision after another, not always, but almost invariably, favorable to the railroad interests followed. The State of Pennsylvania had passed an act imposing a tax on all freight within the state. The railroads refused to pay this tax on the ground of its being unconstitutional. In December, 1872, Justice Strong, delivering the Supreme Court's majority opinion, declared the act unconstitutional.[75] Another Pennsylvania law imposed a tax on gross receipts of railroad, canal, and transportation companies; in

[71] "Poor's Railroad Manual" for 1880; p. 234.
[72] *Ibid.*
[73] This packing of the Supreme Court caused such a long-continuing scandal, that, as late as 1881, Justice Strong felt called upon to write an article for the *North American Review* (May, 1881, Vol. CXXXII: p. 437) defending the increase of members as made necessary by the great pressure of cases for consideration.
[74] XII Wallace's Reports, 457–681. Chief Justice Chase and Justices Clifford, Field and Nelson dissented.
[75] Case of "State Freight Tax," XV Wallace, 237. Justices Swayne and Davis dissented.

this case, Justice Strong, as the mouthpiece of the majority, declared that the law was not invalid.[76] Thereupon the Pennsylvania Railroad corrupted the Legislature to repeal the act.[77] Another measure passed by the Pennsylvania Legislature — for the Anti-Monopoly movement was then politically strong, and it was considered politic to give it deferential sops — was an act taxing non-resident bondholders. By a vote of five to four (Justice Field writing the majority opinion) this act was declared unconstitutional by the Supreme Court in December, 1872.[78]

Meanwhile, during this period, the Supreme Court, although rejecting some California land claims, had confirmed many others. Not a few were of so questionable, if not visibly fraudulent, a nature, that members of the Supreme Court themselves vigorously denounced the majority opinions confirming them, as in the case of Hornsby vs. the United States. Upon the pretense that acting Governor Pio Pico, on May, 1846, had granted 40,000 acres of land to Jose Roland, from whom he (Hornsby) claimed to have bought it, Hornsby, in 1869, obtained a confirmation of his title from the Supreme Court of the United States. In a severe dissenting opinion, Justices Davis, Clifford and Swayne pointed out that the very records of the case showed that the grant, if made, was illegally conferred. " No possession of any kind," they went

[76] " State Tax on Railway Gross Receipts," XV Wallace, 284. Justices Miller, Field and Hunt dissented. Associate Justice Ward Hunt had been appointed that year (1872) to succeed Justice Nelson. Justice Hunt had practiced at Utica, New York, had been Mayor of that city, and in 1865 he had been elected to the New York Court of Appeals. He was identified with the railroad interests. (See, " Poor's Railroad Manual," for 1869-70.) At the time of his appointment to the Supreme Court he was sixty-two years old.

[77] So it was charged by Judge Black in his argument on railroad monopoly before the Pa. Senate Judiciary Committee, and before the Pa. Constitutional Convention of 1873. Judge Black dealt at length with the corruption carried on by the Pennsylvania and the Reading railroad companies.— See, " Essays and Speeches of J. S. Black " (pp. 99, 176, etc.) published at the time.

[78] XV Wallace, 300. Justices Davis, Clifford, Miller and Hunt dissented.

on, " is proved in this case, and the authenticity of this grant covering an area of over forty thousand acres of land, depends upon the testimony of a single witness, unsupported by any proof, except the imperfect or mutilated expedients, found among a mass of loose papers on the floor of one of the rooms of the custom house at Monterey after the Mexican officials had fled on the approach of our forces." [79]

Death of Chief Justice Chase.

Chief Justice Chase died on May 7, 1873. In his laudatory biography, Schuckers asserts that Chase's fortune was not more than $100,000. But Chase's will dated November 19, 1870, and filed with the Register of Wills at Washington, on May 21, 1873, showed a total of real and personal property appraised at $250,000, of which $150,000 was estimated to be in real property. If we are to accept the statement of Schuckers, his confidant and biographer, that his fortune, in 1861, amounted to $65,000, then Chase must have gathered the difference — $185,000 — during the twelve years he was Secretary of the Treasury, and Chief Justice of the Supreme Court of the United States. No doubt, part of this added wealth could be attributed to the accumulating increment on his real estate. [80]

[79] X Wallace's Reports, 224–245.

[80] This interpolation of a description of the Supreme Court at the time will be of interest:

"At eleven o'clock in the morning, the door back of the judges' platform is thrown open, the Marshall of the Court enters, walking backward, with his gaze fastened upon the door. Upon reaching the center of the chamber, he pauses, and cries in a loud voice:

"'The Honorable, the Judges of the Supreme Court of the United States.'

"All present in the chamber immediately rise to their feet, and remain standing respectfully. Then, through the open door, headed by the Chief Justice, enter the members of the Court, one by one, in their large, flowing robes of black silk. There is something very attractive about these men, nearly all of whom have passed into the closing years of life. They ascend the platform, range themselves in

When Chief Justices or Associate Justices of the Supreme Court of the United States died, the newspapers and periodicals and the publications of the legal profession almost invariably contained effusive laudations. It was remarkable, therefore, that only a few months after Chase's death, the periodical *Bench and Bar,* representing the opinion of the legal profession, should make severe comments upon Chief Justice Chase's political activities. After stating that there was no intention of disparaging Chase's memory or derogating from his deeds, the article in question, published in the October, 1873, issue of *Bench and Bar,* spoke of him as exhibiting " the spectacle of a standing candidate for the Presidency. The magnitude and dignity of the office of Chief Justice sank before a restless ambition for political power and place. It was not possible that this should not meet the disapproving opinion of the public, and especially of the Bar of the United States. . . ."

front of their seats, and the Chief Justice makes a sign to the ' Crier,' who immediately makes the following proclamation:
"'O yea! O yea! O yea! All persons having business before the Honorable, the Judges of the Supreme Court of the United States, are admonished to draw near, and give their attendance, for the Court is now in session. God save the United States, and this Honorable Court!'"
"The Judges and other persons take their seats, and the business of the day begins." Dr. John B. Ellis' "The Sights and Secrets of the National Capital," 1869, p. 258.

CHAPTER XIII

THE SUPREME COURT UNDER CHIEF JUSTICE WAITE

Recapitulating, we have seen that some years before Chief Justice Chase's death, the railroad power had begun a systematic campaign to put its avowed representatives upon the Supreme Court Bench. In the State courts the transformation had already been accomplished; there was hardly an inferior court which was not composed of railroad judges, or of men susceptible to railroad influences. With the Supreme Court of the United States, the process was a little slower, but none the less sure. The delay was unavoidable because the Justices, appointed for life, often outlived the period and the class section originally represented by them. Survivals, or rather relics, of a bygone, outworn era, aged and usually infirm, they all could not be expected to respond readily to the demands of later economic interests. Some of them could hardly realize that the railroad corporations which they had seen come forward a few years before as supplicants for public aid were now the paramount capitalist power, arrogating the larger control of Government.

As fast as these hoary relics passed away, railroad attorneys were appointed to succeed them. And when, in 1874, Morrison I. Waite was chosen as Chase's successor as Chief Justice of the Supreme Court of the United States, it was evident even to the most superficial observer that the new régime had become a dominant factor, and that the railroad corporations were the sovereign power.

Williams and Cushing Compelled to Retire.

Like Chief Justices Jay, Marshall, Taney and Chase, Waite did not have any judicial experience when appointed to preside over the Supreme Court. Unlike his predecessors, he had not even filled a single political office of national note. So far as public reputation was concerned, he was a total nonentity; the public had never heard of him. But to the railroad politicians surrounding President Grant, and filling the Senate, he was well known for his ingrained conservative tendencies and affiliations.

At first, Grant had selected George H. Williams for the post. Williams had been a judge in Iowa; a presidential elector in 1852; Chief Justice of Oregon Territory; a United States Senator from Oregon in 1862–1871; and Attorney General of the United States from 1872 to 1875. The Bar Association of New York protested against the nomination; Williams, it said, was " wanting in those qualifications of intellect, experience and reputation which are indispensable to uphold the dignity of the highest national court." [1] Williams' nomination was withdrawn at his own request.

But when Grant then nominated Caleb Cushing for the Chief Justiceship, public denunciation was even more severe. That Cushing was seared with corruption was beyond doubt. One of his transactions we have discussed in a previous chapter; how he had been counsel for the Peter's colony contract grant, and how later, when Attorney General of the United States, he had given an opinion in favor of that grant at the very time Texas was seeking to put a stop to the fraudulent operations of its promoters. We have also described (Chapter X) how General Sam Houston, in 1857, categorically exposed Cushing's connection with the Peter's colony grant.

Of the numerous strictures made at the time upon Cushing's nomination as Chief Justice, we shall confine ourselves to

[1] Rhodes' " History of the United States, 1850–1877," Vol. VII: 27.

quoting but one, that of the *Springfield Republican,* perhaps the most influential, and certainly the most accredited, newspaper in his native state. " His reputation," it said, " is that of a man who has never allowed principle or conscience to stand in the way of gain. . . . He is not an immoral, but rather an unmoral, man; he has not become demoralized; he never was moralized." [2]

The onslaught upon Cushing's probity was so effective, and so strongly backed with facts, that his nomination was withdrawn. Notwithstanding, Cushing held Grant's ear; and in retiring Cushing was, it was understood, one of those proposing to Grant the appointment of Waite as Chief Justice. He was, indeed, Waite's sponsor.[3] Cushing had an extensive railroad practice; he was, after the Civil War, an attorney for Russell Sage's La Crosse and Milwaukee Railroad Company, which, as we have narrated, had bribed an act through the Wisconsin Legislature, in 1856, with $800,000 in bribes, giving it a land grant then valued at $18,000,000. He was also attorney for Sage's Milwaukee and Minnesota Railroad Company and for other railroads of similar fraudulent origin now incorporated in the Chicago, Milwaukee and St. Paul Railroad.[4]

[2] Merriam's " Life and Times of Samuel Bowles," Vol. II: 231.

[3] Cushing was then appointed Minister to Spain, serving from 1874 to 1877. He, Williams and Waite had been counsel for the United States before the Geneva tribunal of arbitration, in 1871–72.

[4] VI Wallace's Reports, 742, 750, 751, etc. Russell Sage was president of the Milwaukee and Minnesota Railroad. For the specific account of the enormous frauds committed by the men controlling those railroads in issuing fraudulent bonds to themselves and in profiting from fraudulent foreclosure sales, see, " History of the Great American Fortunes," Vol. III, Chapter I, citing from legislative and court records. Sage was allied with Jay Gould in many railroad and telegraph company operations. At the time that Russell Sage was president of the Pacific Mail Steamship Company, in 1872–1873, that company had bribed (as we have already narrated, through Congress, by means of $1,000,000 in bribes, an act giving it an additional mail subsidy of $500,000 a year for ten years.

Waite's Record as a Lawyer.

The son of a Chief Justice of Connecticut, Waite was born at Lyme, in that State, on November 29, 1816. After graduating from Yale, in 1837, he had settled in Toledo, Ohio. There he had become associated in law partnership with Samuel R. Young, and later with his brother, Richard Waite. Their cases, for twenty-five years, were an unbroken succession of lucrative appearances for corporations of one kind or another. In the decades before and after the Civil War, Morrison R. Waite represented the Bank of Toledo, the State Bank of Ohio, the Toledo Insurance Company and similar institutions.[5] He and his partner, Young, were receivers for the Commercial Bank of Toledo.[6] But the greater part of Waite's practice was as attorney for railroad corporations. He was counsel for the Southern Michigan Railroad Company; for the Northern Indiana Railroad Company; for the Cleveland and Toledo Railroad Company; for the Lake Shore and Michigan Southern Railroad Company, and for other railroad corporations.[7]

During twenty-five years of practice, there was scarcely a case in which Waite appeared in which he did not advocate the interests of some powerful individual or corporation. Charles Butler, one of Toledo's richest landholders, applied through Waite, in January, 1853, for a permanent injunction restraining the City of Toledo from collecting an assessment for the cost of grading streets. Waite argued that the legislative act authorizing this assessment was retroactive and an impairment of vested rights, and that the fund for the grading work was being misapplied and wasted. Judge

[5] See, I Ohio State Reports, 628; VIII *Ibid.*, 468; XII *Ibid.*, 605, etc.
[6] See, Case of Platt vs. Eggleston, XX Ohio State Reports, 417.
[7] See, X Ohio State Reports, 272; *Ibid.*, 163; XXII *Ibid.*, 575; XXV Michigan Reports, 329, etc., etc.

Brinckerhoff, in the Ohio Supreme Court, denied that any vested right was being impaired, and dissolved the injunction.[8]

In cases affecting the interests of banks or railroads, Waite was more fortunate. Of the successive judges of the Ohio Supreme Court, there was hardly one who had not been, or who did not become, a corporation attorney. Allan G. Thurman, for some years Chief Justice of that court, and subsequently a United States Senator and a candidate for Vice-President of the United States, was counsel for the Valley Bank, for the Ohio Life Insurance and Trust Company (which failed under disastrous circumstances, in 1857); and he was counsel for a number of other corporations. Judge Swan had been counsel for the State Bank of Ohio. Milton Sutliff, Chief Justice of the Ohio Supreme Court, in 1861, was so indifferent to public criticism that he did not forbear bringing a very remarkable suit in which he demanded his full share of watered railroad stock. He set forth that he was the owner of Cleveland and Mahoning Railroad seven-per cent.-bonds, not specifying, however, how he obtained them. These bonds he had elected to convert into stock. Subsequently, he averred, the company had watered the stock to the extent of forty-seven per cent., and had given him this depreciated stock in exchange for his bonds. He sued to get an amount of stock equaling the value of his bonds, plus forty-seven per cent. interest; but when the case was decided, in 1873, he was defeated.[9] As for Judge Birchard, he had been counsel for a variety of corporations, and after leaving the bench resumed corporation practice.

[8] Case of Charles Butler vs. City of Toledo, V Ohio State Reports, 225.

[9] Sutliff vs. Cleveland and Mahoning Railroad Company, XXIV Ohio State Reports, 147–150. Sutliff was long a close personal friend of Chief Justice Chase; they corresponded regularly and intimately, Schuckers says.

The Case of Veronica Muhl.

Most of Waite's cases dealt with some phase or other of vested rights, in the pleading of which he was recognized as an expert, and in every hoary precedent concerning which he was deeply read. These cases, blanketed as they were in abstract technicalities, the reading public could not follow very closely even when they were stated simply in the brief newspaper reports. But there was one case argued before the Ohio Supreme Court, in 1859, which was clear enough; it was so very plain that the workers of the railroad quarter of Toledo had no difficulty in keeping track of its aspects, and no hesitation at expressing their indignation over the particular defense advanced by Waite.

Veronica Muhl, a Swiss woman, had been killed in Toledo, on July 19, 1854, by being run over on the street by a locomotive and a train of cars, going at a speed of more than twenty-five miles an hour. The speed was proved and it was also proved that no warning bell had been rung. A city ordinance prohibited, in that part of Toledo, a speed of more than twenty-five miles an hour, and forbade any running of trains at all without the constant ringing of the locomotive bell so as to give ample warning of danger.

Veronica Muhl left a two-year old boy; and suit was brought in his behalf for $5,000 damages. The Southern Michigan Railroad Company entered a general denial. In July, 1855, the jury in the Court of Common Pleas returned a verdict in favor of the orphan. The railroad then applied to the district court, amending its answer, and not denying, in effect, its own culpability. What, then, was the plea put forward by Waite, as attorney for the railroad? A very extraordinary one; he concentrated his whole argument upon the point that the plaintiff's counsel must prove that Veronica's son was legitimate, and he moved that the action must be non-suited on the ground

that the boy was an illegitimate child, and, therefore, not next
of kin within the meaning of the statute governing the case.
The judge in the district court non-suited the case.

The orphan's lawyer appealed the case to the Supreme Court
of Ohio. In the meantime, the news of the railroad's peculiar
defense in the case had got abroad. That it was generally received with execration is putting the fact mildly. The mother
had been killed by the railroad company running its trains in
violation of the law; her boy had been left a helpless orphan.
To cheat him out of the very modest damages awarded him
by the lower court, the railroad's attorneys, Morrison I. Waite
and his brother Richard, had no scruples in heaping contumely
upon the name of the dead woman, and covering her defenseless boy with public disgrace.

Public opinion made itself manifest; and when the Waite
brothers, representing the Southern Michigan Railroad, renewed their plea before the Ohio Supreme Court, in December, 1859, the judges of that court, railroad attorneys as they
had been, could not avoid expressing disgust. Judges Sutliff,
Brinckerhoff, Scott, Peck and Ghoulson concurred with an
unusual unanimity. They reversed the action of the district
court, and directed that the child should get the awarded damages.

" It is difficult," said Judge Sutliff, in delivering the court's
opinion, " to perceive upon what ground the judgment of non-
suit, shown by the record, was rendered. When the defendant's counsel, under leave to amend, had withdrawn all
that part of the answer that denied the killing of decedent by
the wrongful carelessness of defendant's servants, in operating
their locomotives, there remained no denial of the right of action." The question, Judge Sutliff further declared, of
whether Veronica's son was the nearest of kin, could in nowise
affect the cause of action. As to who was the legal beneficiary
could be adjudged after the action had been determined.
Nearness or remoteness of kin on the part of the boy, Judge

Sutliff went on, did not depend at all upon the circumstance of his being born within or without lawful wedlock.[10]

Quite incidentally, the judges had no high opinion of Waite's character in that he should have advanced what was regarded as so reprehensible a defense, nor did they appraise his knowledge of law as worthy of much consideration.

Waite's Advocacy of Vested Private Rights.

Not a few of Waite's legal efforts as an attorney were attempts to break down the constitutionality of this or that statute — a typical enough preparation for a future Chief Justice of the Supreme Court of the United States.

In 1851 the Ohio Legislature had passed an act to tax banks and bank stock; accordingly the City of Toledo assessed a tax of $1,957.50 on the Toledo Bank. That bank refused to pay, and when sued, Waite and Young, representing the bank, pleaded that the legislative act was unconstitutional. Among the precedents cited by them was Marshall's decision in the Dartmouth College case; they argued that the charter of a private corporation was a contract within the meaning of the restrictive clause of the Constitution of the United States.

Chief Justice Bartley, in the Ohio Supreme Court, in June, 1853, decided against the bank, declaring that the Dartmouth College decision had been perverted "until it has become, to some extent, a subterfuge for fraud and a means of shielding corporations from responsibility and correction for the abuse of their corporate franchises." The antique precedents advanced by Waite to enable his client to defraud the city of taxes, did not at all impress Chief Justice Bartley. " A legal principle," he said, " to be well settled, must be founded upon *sound reason,* and tend to the purposes of justice." In the course of his decision he further stated that " it is a humiliating

[10] See, Case of Muhl, Administrator, vs. Southern Michigan Railroad Company, X Ohio State Reports, 272–277.

reflection to the friends of our republican institutions, that the efforts to place the rights and property of corporations upon a footing of greater sanctity than those of private persons, have been resisted with far greater success in England than they have been in this country. The right of Parliament to amend or repeal the charters of private corporations has for many years been undisputed." The property of every person, Bartley declared, " must be liable to bear an equal and just proportion of the public burdens. . . ." [11]

Another example of Waite's activities was this: As a matter of public health, the City of Toledo had passed an ordinance requiring owners to fill up noisome vacant places; if they failed the city was to do it, and assess the expense upon the owners. One of the landowners refusing to pay this assessment was one Ezra Bliss. As Bliss' attorneys, the Waite brothers claimed that the Ohio health statute under which the city acted, was unconstitutional, in that it violated vested private rights. The Ohio Supreme Court, in December, 1864, decided that it was constitutional. [12]

Morrison I. Waite and Richard Waite were also, together with Charles Pratt, the attorneys in another action to have an Ohio legislative act construed in favor of vested private rights. They represented Rollin B. Hubbard, the owner of large flour mills. These mills had been run with water from a branch of the Wabash and Erie Canal which had traversed Toledo. The Ohio Legislature, in 1864, had passed an act discontinuing that particular canal, and authorizing its being reconstructed into a public highway. Hubbard then came forward with a claim that in 1840 he had received the right under a thirty

[11] Case of Toledo Bank vs. John R. Bond (Treasurer of the City of Toledo), I Ohio State Reports, 622–703. But we have described in Chapter XI how the Supreme Court of the United States, in 1855, declared the Ohio act of 1851 unconstitutional, and how, in a dissenting opinion, Justice Campbell denounced the decision, and described how the corporate money interest was dominant in Ohio. Chief Justice Bartley seems to have been exempt from that domination.

[12] Bliss et al. vs. Kraus, XVI Ohio State Reports, 58.

years' lease, renewable, to propel his mills with surplus water not required for navigation. When, in 1868, the Governor of Ohio executed a formal grant of the canal to the City of Toledo, Hubbard and others obtained a provisional injunction restraining the city from interfering with the flow of water. The injunction was later dissolved, and the case in full argued.

For Hubbard, Morrison I. Waite claimed that he held a vested right; that the legislative act was subject to his prior rights; and that the city was liable for all damages accruing from the discontinuance of the water supply. "The State government," retorted the city's attorneys, "was not organized for the purpose of running grist mills." The Ohio Supreme Court, in December, 1871, decided in favor of the City of Toledo.[13]

Waite's Railroad Interests and Connections.

To ascertain the real importance of Waite's position as a railroad attorney, it is necessary to know what large interests owned or controlled these railroads. Samuel M. Young, law partner of Morrison I. Waite, was a director of the Cleveland and Toledo Railroad.[14] This railroad belonged to the Vanderbilt system; William H. Vanderbilt was one of its directors; in turn it was leased to the Cleveland, Painesville and Ashtabula Railroad, one of the directors of which was Henry B. Payne, later so powerful a magnate as treasurer of the Standard Oil Company, and such a sinister figure in the bribery of Ohio legislators and officials.[15]

[13] Hubbard vs. City of Toledo, XXI Ohio State Reports, 379–401.
[14] "Poor's Railroad Manual," 1868–1869: 163, and *Ibid.*, 1869–70: pp. 184 and 362.
[15] After Payne was elected to the United States Senate, in 1884, a subsequent Ohio Legislature petitioned the United States Senate for an investigation. Upon completing an examination of sixty-four witnesses, the Ohio House of Representatives declared that Payne's seat in the United States Senate "was purchased by the corrupt use of

As for Morrison I. Waite, he was one of the directors of the Dayton and Michigan Railroad, and for a time was its vice-president.[16] This railroad had been leased, in 1863, to the Cincinnati, Hamilton and Dayton Railroad. The president of the Dayton and Michigan Railroad, S. S. L'Hommedieu, was also president of the Cincinnati, Richmond and Chicago Railroad, and was also " interested " in the Kentucky Central Railroad. One of Waite's sons was superintendent of the Cincinnati and Muskingum Railroad during a great part of the time that Waite was Chief Justice of the Supreme Court of the United States.

Only twice had Waite ever held any public office: in 1849, when he had been elected to the Ohio Legislature, and in 1873, when he was president of the Ohio Constitutional Convention. He had been defeated for delegate to the State Constitutional Convention in 1850, and had not succeeded in his candidacy for Congress in 1862.

Wonderment was publicly expressed that such an obscure person should have been made Chief Justice. Yet in official circles it was well known that the interest that had chiefly pushed him was the powerful Vanderbilt family, at that time, as it still is, one of the largest railroad owners in the United States.

But although railroad magnates such as Vanderbilt and Gould were warring fiercely upon one another, and in turn were ousting the lesser railroad capitalists, all the railroad interests had certain ends in common so far as the construction of law was concerned. On the interpretation of law in general for their benefit, all the magnates, large and small, were united, irrespective of what their own differences were.

money," and the Ohio Senate likewise resolved. The specific testimony showed that the Legislature had been debauched with corrupt funds.— See, Report No. 1490, U. S. Senate, Forty-ninth Congress, 1886, and see a complete account from the records in Lloyd's " Wealth vs. Commonwealth," pp. 373-382.

[16] " Poor's Railroad Manual " for 1869-1870: p. 26.

While, therefore, a judge's antecedents were those of retainership for this or that particular railroad magnate, still his previous training and attachments would incline him to favor all railroad interests as against public agitation.

Some of the great railroad questions certain to come up before the Supreme Court were those dealing with the interpretations of laws by which the various Pacific railroads had obtained immense land grants and Government money subsidies.

In 1868–69 Jay Gould and Russell Sage had begun to get control of the Union Pacific and allied railroads; and had, as later investigations and actions showed, like Stanford and Huntington, set out to manipulate those ,roads in order to cheat the Government.   Caleb Cushing, one of Waite's principal backers, was very close to Sage.   The Vanderbilts, too, had their ambitious schemes and interests; they were constantly extending their railroad power; and issues affecting their interests would necessarily come for final decision before the Supreme Court of the United States.   In addition there were questions of railroad stock and bond issues; of land grants either given to railroads or' in which they were interested; of railroad pools and many other considerations determining whether the wealth and power of railroad owners should be aggrandized or hindered by court decision.   Not the least, it was certain that pressing questions arising from conflicts with labor organizations would be argued up to the Supreme Court.

Grant's Intimacy with the Vanderbilts.

With the Vanderbilt family President Grant was on the most excellent terms.   Indeed, ten years later, after the firm of which Grant was a member — that of Grant and Ward — had gone into bankruptcy, it was to William H. Vanderbilt that Grant appealed for a loan of $150,000, and it was from that powerful magnate — then the richest in the United States — that Grant obtained it.

On May 4, 1884, General Grant called at Vanderbilt's residence, at No. 640 Fifth Avenue, New York City, and asked for the loan of $150,000. " I gave him my check without question," wrote Vanderbilt on January 10, 1885, to Mrs. Grant, " not because the transaction was business-like, but simply because the request came from General Grant." General and Mrs. Grant sent to Vanderbilt deeds on their joint properties to cover the obligation, but Vanderbilt returned the deeds.

Subsequently, when Vanderbilt was in Europe, General Grant delivered to Vanderbilt's attorney mortgages upon everything that he owned, including military trophies and presents from foreign governments. On January 10, 1885, Vanderbilt presented as a gift to Mrs. Grant's personal estate the debt and judgment that General Grant owed, and the mortgages on household goods and articles pledged. The only condition was that at Grant's death, the articles of historical value should be presented to the Government. ". . . I have only to add," wrote Grant in reply to Vanderbilt, on the same day, " that I regard your giving me your check for the amount without inquiry as an act of marked and unusual friendship. . . ." After considerable vacillation, General and Mrs. Grant finally decided to have certain of their mortgaged property sold toward the payment of the debt.[17]

At the time that Waite was appointed Chief Justice the Vanderbilts controlled the New York and Harlem Railroad, the New York and Hudson River Railroad, the Lake Shore Railroad; and they presently acquired the Canada Southern and Michigan Central Railroad, and a large interest in the Northwestern Railway.

[17] The full correspondence between General and Mrs. Grant and William H. Vanderbilt is published in Appendix F in Croffut's " The Vanderbilts," 294–297.

A Succession of Railroad Decisions.

The new Chief Justice was of medium height, stout and straight in build, and he was strong, firm and quick in movement, with a self-confident manner. His eyes were dark and keen, his hair iron-gray, his upper lip was kept clean of growth, and carefully-trimmed whiskers covered the remainder of his face. His mouth and nose were large, his chin heavy.

One of the first cases argued after Waite had taken his seat was one of the greatest importance to the railroads on the one hand, and, on the other, to the public.

Throughout the country railroad promoters had influenced the authorities of municipalities to issue vast amounts of bonds to assist in the private construction of railroads. Indignant at this abuse of public funds, the people of various States, in particular those of Michigan, had insisted upon putting provisions in their State Constitutions forbidding such grants. The township of Pine Grove, Michigan, had issued bonds to aid in the building of the Kalamazoo and South Haven Railroad, and subsequently refused to pay, on the ground that they were unconstitutional. Talcott, one of the bondholders, brought suit to recover.

Chief Justice Waite was disqualified from participating in the case because his interest was concerned.

Delivering the Supreme Court's opinion, Justice Swayne decided that the bonds were valid; his chief ground was the assumed doctrine of acquiescence. ". . . When the bonds were issued, he said, "there had been no authoritative information from any quarter that such statutes were invalid. . . . And during the period covered by their enactment, neither of the other departments of the State lifted up its voice against them. The acquiescence was universal." [18] The

[18] Case of Township of Pine Grove vs. Talcott, XIX Wallace's Reports, 678. The note on the record reads: "The Chief Justice did not sit in this case, and took no part in its decision" (p. 679). Justices Miller and Davis dissented.

decision in this case caused great exultation among railroad owners, and formed a precedent much cited thereafter.

Following this decision came another decision also ranking as an authoritative precedent, and many times cited. It allowed railroad capitalists who had secured by every corrupt means immense land grants, to keep those grants intact and safe from forfeiture.

Railroads Escape Forfeiture of Land Grants.

The case establishing their vested right to this plunder was that of Schulenberg vs. Harriman, decided by the Supreme Court of the United States in October, 1874. In June, 1856, Congress, after bribery had been freely used,[19] passed an act granting about 2,388,000 acres of public land in Wisconsin to be allotted by the Legislature of that State for the express purpose of encouraging the building of railroads.

It was distinctly provided that the railroads were to be built within ten years. In the same year — 1856 — various railroad adventurers corrupted the Wisconsin Legislature to pass acts giving them land grants. The La Crosse and Milwaukee Railroad, as we have seen, distributed at least $800,000 in bribes for the passage of an act granting it 1,000,000 acres.[20] Another one of the land grants obtained that year was for a

[19] Reference has been already made to the report of a Select Committee of Congress appointed to investigate alleged corrupt combinations of members of Congress, and how that committee recommended the expulsion of four prominent Congressmen as having been at the head of corrupt combinations to influence legislation. (Reports of Committees, 1856–1857, Vol. III, Report No. 245.) Thirty distinct land-grant acts were passed by Congress in the year 1856.

[20] This $800,000 in bribes, according to the report of the joint Legislative Committee of 1858, had been thus distributed: A total of $175,-000 in bonds had been given to thirteen specified State Senators; $355,000 in bonds was used to buy seventy specified Assemblymen; $50,000 in bonds had been given to Governor Coles Bashford; $16,000 to other State officials, and $246,000 to certain specified editors and other persons.

railroad from Portage City to Lake St. Croix, with extensions; this was the particular land grant involved in the case of Schulenberg vs. Harriman.

The obvious fact was admitted in the suit thàt neither the railroad nor any part of it had ever been constructed. Yet the railroad capitalists had claimed the land grant as their absolute property, and by 1873, no less an immense quantity than 1,600,000 feet of the most valuable pine timber had been stripped from it. Since no part of the railroad had been constructed, the State of Wisconsin took the position that the land grant reverted to the State or Government, as explicitly provided in the original act of Congress.

The Supreme Court of the United States did not take this view. In its decision, written by Justice Field,[21] it held that inasmuch as no action had been taken by legislative or judicial proceedings to enforce the forfeiture of the grants, therefore, the lands had not reverted.[22]

It need scarcely be said that this decision legalized the consummation of the most enormous frauds. Moreover, it gave an unmistakable cue to railroad looters. All that they now had to do was to corrupt Congress to pass acts extending the time for the construction of railroads, deriving meanwhile prodigious profits from the exploitation of vast areas of land to gain which they had done nothing. And that they did corrupt Congress was speedily shown in the scandals concerning the Southern Pacific, the Central Pacific and other railroad measures, not the least of which was the Texas Pacific bill

[21] It may be observed here that Justice Field's brother, David Dudley Field, was at this time representing the Central Railroad of Georgia and other railroads in cases before the Supreme Court of the United States.— See, 92 U. S. Reports, 666, etc. But a few years before, David Dudley Field had been the chief attorney pleading for the fraudulent transactions of Jay Gould and James Fisk, Jr.

[22] XXI Wallace's Reports, 44. One of the railroad's attorneys was John C. Spooner, for a long period United States Senator from Wisconsin, and one of the most adroit and conspicuous members of that body.

promoted by Senators Matthews and Lamar, who themselves
became Justices of the Supreme Court of the United States.[23]

The Grange Movement.

At this period there developed an organized agrarian agitation which had considerable influence upon politics.   It grew
to such strength that politicians, especially of the agricultural
regions, sought to propitiate it.   In the records of the Supreme
Court of the United States we find references to it; and that
in its decisions affecting railroads the Supreme Court sought
to make an appearance of deference by handing down certain decisions apparently, but not in reality, against the railroad corporations, is quite certain.

This organized movement was called the Grangers, composed of American agriculturalists.   It was essentially a middle-class movement, and it later merged into the Farmers'
Alliance, which, in turn, blended into the Populist Party.   It
was estimated that at the end of the year 1875, there were
30,000 granges in existence, with an average of about forty
members each; the order was strongest in the West and Northwest, and had a considerable following in the South.   Professing to be non-partisan, it was nevertheless the stimulus
of a powerful agitation against discrimination in railroad
freight rates, and it declared for the recovery of excess lands
held by railroads, and the prohibition of the ownership of
land by aliens and foreign syndicates.   Later came a demand
for Government ownership of railroads.

The Union Pacific Railroad Relieved from Restitution.

Goaded into action by public agitation, the Government, in
1878, brought a suit against the Union Pacific Railroad Company for the restitution of the enormous sums of which successive groups of capitalists had swindled the Government.

[23] See details later in this chapter.

This company, had obtained, by means of bribing Congress, a land grant of 12,000,000 acres, and also a loan of $27,213,000 in Government bonds. The Credit Mobilier Company had then been organized to construct the railroad. Comprising the company were some of the most powerful capitalists in the United States — conspicuous bankers, such as Levi P. Morton (later Vice President of the United States) and William H. Macy; and factory owners, such as Cyrus McCormick and George M. Pullman. Charges of enormous thefts committed by the Credit Mobilier Company resulted in the appointment of an investigating committee by the United States Senate. This committee, called the " Wilson Committee," from the name of Senator Wilson, its chairman, reported in 1873:

That the total cost of building the Union Pacific Railroad was $50,000,000.

That the Credit Mobilier Company had charged $93,546,-287.28.

That " from the stock, income bonds, and land-grant bonds, the builders received in cash value $23,366,000 as profit — about forty-eight per cent. on the entire cost."

The total " profits " were, therefore, about $44,000,000, of which the sum of $23,000,000 or more was in immediate cash. The committee reported that large sums of money, borrowed for the ostensible purpose of building the railroad, had at once been divided as plunder in the form of dividends upon stock for which not a cent in money had been paid, in violation of law.[24]

Finally, as a matter of fact, the Union Pacific road was owned entirely by private capitalists, although it had been built almost wholly with Government grants and loans.

After this looting had been accomplished, the value of the stock of the Union Pacific Railroad had necessarily fallen, at which auspicious time Jay Gould and Russell Sage acquired

[24] Reports of Committees, Credit Mobilier Reports, Forty-second Congress, Third Session, 1872–73, Doc. No. 78: xiv–xx.

the railroad, and, as the report of the Pacific Railroad Commission of 1887 showed, subjected it to another comprehensive process of looting.

In bringing its suit in 1878 for misappropriation and for restitution of the stolen funds, the Government, in its bill of complaint, stated the specifications of fraud and theft, page after page of them. It asked that the construction contracts and land-grant and income mortgages be declared void. The chief attorney for the railroad in this case was William M. Evarts. At Yale Evarts had been a classmate of Chief Justice Waite. Evarts had been an attorney for the Pacific Mail Steamship Company which, as we have seen, had disbursed $1,000,000 in bribes, in 1872, to obtain the passage of an act of Congress. Evarts had also represented the Chicago, Rock Island and Pacific Railroad. Subsequently he became — 1885–1891 — a United States Senator from New York.

Delivering the majority opinion, Justice Miller decided that the Government had made out no case for relief. He concluded with these remarks, the first of which was unfounded in fact, and the remainder of which have seldom been equaled for their sardonic cynicism.

". . . The Government" (said he) "has received all of the advantages for which it had bargained, and more than it expected. In the feeble infancy of this child of its creation," Miller went on, "the Government, fully alive to its importance, did all that it could to strengthen, support and sustain it." Every Justice of the Supreme Court knew that the Government had done nothing of the kind. Everyone of them was aware that it was by corruption that the Union Pacific Railroad promoters had accomplished their ends. Not a single Justice was ignorant of the report of the " Wilson Committee," handed in five years previously, that those promoters had illicitly expended a corruption fund of nearly $436,000 to get the act of July, 1864, passed, and that another corruption fund of $126,000 had been used to get the act of March 3, 1871, passed by Congress allowing the Union Pacific Railroad exorbitant rates for the transportation of Government supplies and mail.[25] Every newspaper in the country had been filled with the details of the testimony.

" Since," Justice Miller concluded, " it [the Union Pacific Railroad] has grown to vigorous manhood, it may not have displayed the gratitude which so much care called for. If this be so, it is but another instance of the absence of human affections which is said to characterize all corporations. . . ." [26]

One of the points of this decision was that the Government could not sue until the company's debt matured in 1895. This, as we shall see, gave Gould, Sage and associates a new lease of life in their operations, enabling them to loot further on an enormous scale.

Fraudulent Bonds Given Precedence.

At the same time, the Supreme Court of the United States, in October, 1878, handed down another decision in favor of the Union Pacific Railroad. The railroad had sued the Government for compensation for transporting troops, supplies, etc. The Government set up a counter-claim for five per cent. of the net earnings of the company, as due under the act of July 1, 1862, for the payment of bonds. The Court of Claims decided that the railroad had been completed in 1869, and that the company's profit on the operation of the road from 1869 to 1875 had been $29,052,045.67. The Court of Claims, accordingly, gave the Government a judgment for $1,402,602.28, as being five per cent. on the profits, and it awarded the company $593,627.10 for services. From this decision the company appealed.

Reversing the judgment, Justice Bradley, writing the opin-

<hr>

[25] See, Doc. No. 78, Credit Mobilier Investigation, xvii.
[26] U. S. vs. Union Pacific Railroad, 98 U. S. Reports, 620.

ion of the Supreme Court's majority, based his decision in
favor of the company upon the construction of the act of July
2, 1864. The fact that it was for the passage of that very
law that the Union Pacific Railroad Company had distributed
nearly $436,000 in bribes, was wholly ignored. Bradley held
that the act in question authorized the company to issue an
equal amount of first-mortgage bonds to have priority of the
Government bonds.

It was well known that the act was lobbied through for the
express purpose of cheating the Government. Here, again,
the vaunted principle of law that fraud vitiated every contract,
was serenely passed over by the Supreme Court. The circumstances of the passage .of the act, and of the great plundering
going on, were not even considered. Bradley held that the
act of 1864 empowered the company to issue an equal amount
of first-mortgage bonds to have priority over the Government
bonds; hence those holding these bonds had the preference of
being paid before the Government could receive its five per cent.
Justices Strong and Harlan strongly dissented, practically saying that the effect of the decision was to facilitate and legalize
the swindling of the Government.[27] The same decision was
made in the case of actions against the Denver Pacific Railroad and other railroads.

The Accompanying and Subsequent Thefts.

But who owned these first mortgage bonds? The majority
report, nine years later, of the Pacific Railway Commission,—
a Government investigating body — reported in detail the vast
thefts committed by the Credit Mobilier Company and by
Gould, Şage and associates. In consolidating the Kansas Pacific, the Denver Pacific and other railroads with the Union
Pacific, Gould, Sage and company had misappropriated more

[27] Union Pacific Railroad vs. U. S., 99 U. S. Reports, 402.

than $20,000,000 by the fraudulent jugglery of stocks and bonds. The Union Pacific Company had sold not less than 7,000,000 acres of land, although it had got no patent from the Government.[28] Great areas of the most valuable coal lands had been fraudulently appropriated.[29] The fraudulent shuffling of millions of dollars from one corporation to another was another fertile source of loot. The stock of the Union Pacific had been inflated from $38,000,000 to $50,000,000; the bonded indebtedness from $88,000,000 to $126,000,000, and sundry other indebtedness to nearly $10,000,000.

While this plundering was in process, Gould and Sage were putting the railroad in a condition of bankruptcy for the double purpose of draining its funds, and of pleading that the railroad could not afford to reimburse the Government for its loans. The majority report of the Pacific Railway Commission described "the lavish and reckless distribution of the assets of the company in dividends," and pointedly asked why it was that although the Union Pacific Company had been doing a large and profitable business, "it found itself early in 1884 on the verge of bankruptcy."

Had it not been for the two decisions of the Supreme Court we have cited, this looting would have received a check. The Supreme Court had virtually legalized and justified it. And it is also set forth in the Pacific Railway Commission's majority report that while stealing tens of millions of dollars, and at the very time the Government's action for misappropriation of funds was before the Supreme Court of the United States, Gould and Sage took measures to relieve themselves from any liability to the Union Pacific Railroad as a corporation.

"It appears," the majority report of Messrs. Littler and Anderson reads, "that while this litigation was pending, certain

---

[28] Report of Pacific Railway Commission, Vol. I: 192.
[29] *Ibid.*

proceedings were taken by the directors whereby, by their own acts and votes, they undertook to release themselves from any obligation or liabilities to the company."

The minority report of Commissioner Pattison was even more penetrating. It declared that the Union Pacific Railroad and the Kansas Pacific Railroad had received about $35,000,-000 in loans from the Government, of which little had been returned. It recited that up to 1887 the sum of $136,314,-010.73 "had been dissipated" by the directors of these two railroads.[30] Not less than $84,000,000 of watered stock had been issued. "The Union Pacific Company," the minority report continued, "has received $176,294,793.53 in surplus earnings and land sales during eighteen years, and if its stock had been fully paid, as Congress required that it should be, and its officers certified under oath that it was, nearly all of that money would be applicable to-day to the payment of the Government debt. The company has paid out $28,650,770 in dividends, and $82,742,850 in interest on bonds, nearly all of which was distributed to shareholders without consideration . . ." Commissioner Pattison estimated that Jay Gould's personal share of the loot was probably $40,000,000.[31]

This report reveals the condition of affairs nine years after the Supreme Court of the United States decided in favor of Gould, Sage and associates of the Union Pacific Railroad Company. Likewise it disclosed the futility of the "Sinking Fund" decision that the Supreme Court of the United States had rendered late in 1878 asserting that in the cases of the debt of the Pacific railroads the act of Congress, of May 7, 1878, establishing a sinking fund, was constitutional. First, the Supreme Court denied the application of the Government for restitution, and allowed the manipulators to juggle and pocket all the profits. Having done that, the Supreme Court then said that the Government had a right

30 Report of the Pacific Railway Commission, Vol. I: 147.
31 Ibid.

to conduct a sinking fund! The empty right was allowed, but from where was the money for the sinking fund to come? Stanford, Huntington, Gould, Sage and associates were appropriating it by the hundreds of millions for their private fortunes.

It should be noted that in the " Sinking Fund Cases," Justices Field, Strong and Bradley dissented at length. In the previous cases they had concurred in holding that a contract was to be strictly construed. In this case, notwithstanding the fact that the Pacific railroads had received the Government funds on explicit condition of repaying them, Justice Strong advanced this extraordinary proposition: ". . . Had it been dreamed that a call could have been made at any time thereafter designated by Congress, it is inconceivable that the loan proffered would have been accepted. . ." [32] " The loan proffered " was a rare way of putting the case, considering that Congress had been bribed to give that very loan. Vested rights, Justice Strong went on, " *no matter how they arise,* are all *equally sacred,* beyond the reach of legislative influence." [33]

Justice Bradley wrote a long dissenting opinion, and Justice Field, who did likewise, began, " The decision will, in my opinion, tend to create insecurity in the title to corporate property in the country," etc., etc.— a groundless assertion, as Field himself no doubt well knew, and as events fully proved. Then Justice Field proceeded to expound an elaborate defense of the Pacific railroads, particularly of the Central Pacific Railroad.[34]

These are some typical instances of decisions regarding railroads handed down under Chief Justice Waite. With a few adverse decisions of comparatively slight importance, railroad interests were dissatisfied, but the greater number of

[32] 99 U. S. Reports, 733.
[33] *Ibid.* The italics are mine.— G. M.
[34] *Ibid.*

decisions were entirely favorable to the railroad owners. To enter into the consideration of this mass of decisions is out of the question here.

Claims Confirmed to Forgers and Perjurers.

The decisions of the Supreme Court concerning private land claims were also most uniformly favorable to the claimants.

Discovering new evidence of fraud, the Government brought suit to void a decree of the lower court confirming a large California land claim to W. A. Richardson, who, as we have seen, had been officially exposed as a notorious perjurer. The Government's petition set forth that after submitting his claim to the Board of Land Commissioners, in 1852, Richardson became satisfied that he had not evidence enough to support his claim, and that he went to Mexico, and obtained from Micheltorena, the former Mexican Governor of California, "his signature, on or about the first day of July, 1852, to a grant which was falsely and fraudulently antedated, so as to impose on the court the belief that it was made at a time when Micheltorena had power to make such grants in California." The Government also charged that Richardson, "in support of this simulated and false document also procured and filed therewith the depositions of perjured witnesses."

After getting a confirmation from the United States District Court, Richardson turned over the claim to Throckmorton, George H. Howard and others. Howard, in 1852, was the United States law agent before the land commission. The Government now charged that "Howard, one of ·the present defenders had, from the papers in some other suit, derived notice of the fraudulent character of the Micheltorena grant, and that he failed and neglected [in 1852] to inform the commissioners of the fact, or otherwise defend the interests of the United States in the matter." [35]

Howard, it may be remarked, had also been interested with Teschmaker and others in a sixteen-league claim in Napa County, California, alleged to have been granted by Micheltorena. The Supreme Court of the Unitel States had, in 1858, denounced this sixteen-league claim as a forgery, supported by such professional perjurers as Juan Castenada, and had voided it. [36]

Common sense alone would have dictated the fair assumption that if Howard had been detected in promoting one forged grant, all his other acts would inferentially stand impeached. But in deciding the Throckmorton case, the Supreme Court of the Unitel States presented some singular views. Writing the court's opinion, Justice Miller acknowledged, to begin with, that the Government was not bound by the statute of limitations. He complained, however, that the suit was brought twenty years after the decree of the District Court, and that to retry the case would involve perhaps more appeals. "If we can do this now, some other court may be called on twenty years hence to retry the same matter on another allegation of fraudulent combination in this suit to defeat the ends of justice, and so the number of suits would be without limit." Moreover, he said, there were no specifications of the means by which fraud had been accomplished.

The fact that Howard had been condemned twenty years previously by the Supreme Court for pushing a forged grant, did not count with the eminent Justices. That in many cases proof had been presented that United States district attorneys had often been in collusion with land-claim forgers and had long concealed the fact — this, too, was ignored. Nor did the Supreme Court give the slightest consideration to the

[35] U. S. vs. Throckmorton *et al.*, 98 U. S. Reports, 69.
[36] U. S. vs. Teschmaker, Howard *et al.*, XXII Howard's Reports, 395.

fact that District Judges in California had been interested in these fraudulent claims, and that the scandal was so great that Congress, in 1864, had passed an act prohibiting those judges sitting. That successive Attorneys-General of the United States had exposed the Micheltorena forgeries — this, also, had no weight with the Justices. The Throckmorton claim was declared valid,[37] serving as a notable precedent in subsequent private land-claim cases.

In another case it was shown that in 1845, Alcalde George Hyde had fraudulently presented to George Donner, then *only ten years old,* and a dummy for officials, a large and now valuable plot of municipal land one hundred varas square (about 3333 feet), in the heart of San Francisco. The law allowed distribution of land to settlers only. In validating this grant, the Supreme Court of the United States, in 1878, said: " We are not aware that the Mexican law prohibited such a grant to an infant." [38] These are some characteristic examples of the Supreme Court's decisions regarding land claims.

New Associate Justices.

Many changes occurred in the personnel of the Supreme Court at this time. Justice David Davis resigned in 1877, and became a United States Senator from Illinois. His successor, appointed by President Hayes, was John M. Harlan, of Kentucky.

Harlan's father, James Harlan, had been a Whig politician of some note representing a Kentucky district in Congress, 1836 to 1844, and had been Attorney-General of Kentucky from 1850 to 1863. Entering politics, John M. Harlan had been defeated for Congress, in 1859; had been breveted a colonel in the Union Army during the Civil War; had been elected Attorney-General of Kentucky in 1863; had then practiced law,

[37] U. S. vs. Throckmorton, 98 U. S. Reports, 61–71. (October, 1878.)
[38] Case of Palmer vs. Low, 98 U. S. Reports, 1–19.

and had been unsuccessful in 1871 and 1875 in his candidacy for Governor of Kentucky.

He was one of the visiting commissioners to Louisiana in the Hayes-Tilden electoral contest; and it was openly charged by Senator Chandler that for his services to Hayes on this occasion, Hayes rewarded him by an appointment to the Supreme Court of the United States. On January 21, 1901, Senator Pettigrew read in the United States Senate a letter signed by Senator Chandler, published in a New York newspaper in 1877. In this letter Chandler made the charge that Justice Harlan was appointed to the Supreme Court as a result of his services as a visiting commissioner to Louisiana during the Hayes-Tilden dispute. After Pettigrew had finished reading the letter, Chandler arose and said that every word of it was true.[39]

The choice of Harlan was largely a personal appointment of Hayes. Harlan was not conspicuous as a railroad lawyer, although the fact that his nomination was confirmed by a Senate controlled by railroad attorneys and stockholders did not pass unnoticed. He was forty-two years old at the time.

Retiring on a pension, in 1880, Justice Strong was suc-

---

[39] In the Presidential election of 1876, the result as to whether Hayes or Tilden was elected was uncertain. Each side charged fraud, and the vote of certain reconstructed States was the deciding factor. An Electoral Commission, composed of five Senators, five Representatives, and five Associate Justices of the Supreme Court of the United States, was created to decide the election.

The New York *Sun,* a supporter of Tilden, reiterated the charge that after Justice Bradley had prepared a written opinion in favor of the Tilden electors in Florida, he had changed his views during the night preceding the vote in consequence of pressure brought to bear upon him by Republican politicians and Pacific Railroad magnates whose carriages, the *Sun* said, surrounded his house during the evening. On September 2, 1877, Bradley wrote to the Newark *Advertiser* denying "the whole thing as a falsehood." "Not a single visitor called at my house that evening. . . ." The charge, Bradley added, was "too absurd for refutation." ("Miscellaneous Writings of the Late Joseph P. Bradley," etc., p. 221.) Evidently the *Sun* sought to convey the idea that Hayes was backed by railroad grandees. So he was. But Tilden, too, had the support of many of them; he was one of the most prominent of railroad attorneys, and an extensive holder of railroad stocks.

ceeded by William B. Woods, of Ohio. Woods was regarded as a political adventurer. Born in 1824, he had been
a Democratic politician in Ohio. An officer in the Union
army during the Civil War, he, in 1866, had settled in Alabama, during the reconstruction period, and had become a
leading " carpet-bagger " Republican. He became State Chancellor in 1868, and a United States Circuit Court judge, in 1870.
His decisions in that court were notoriously in favor of railroad corporations.

Opposition to Stanley Matthews.

The next appointment, that of Stanley Matthews by President Hayes, aroused the most intense opposition.

Matthews was nominated to succeed Swayne, who resigned
because of disability. In 1877, Matthews had succeeded
John Sherman, as a United States Senator from Ohio. Matthews was not only Jay Gould's chief attorney in the middle
West, but while in the Senate he frequently appeared in
court as attorney for the Louisville and Nashville Railroad.[40]
the Adams Express Company [41] and other corporations.
While a member of the United States Senate, and at the
very time he was appointed to the Supreme Court, he was
a director of the Knoxville and Ohio Railroad.[42] He was
also counsel for the Springfield and Mansfield Railroad,[43] and
for other railroads, and held considerable stock in railroad
companies. For many years he had been attorney for the
Cincinnati, Hamilton and Dayton Railroad,[44] for which, as
we have noted, Chief Justice Waite had also been counsel,

[40] See, Stevens et al. vs. Louisville and Nashville Railroad Company,
U. S. Courts Reports, Sixth Circuit (Flippin), Vol. II: 716, etc. This
railroad dominated politics in Kentucky and Tennessee.
[41] Ibid., 673.
[42] " Poor's Railroad Manual " for 1880: p. 492.
[43] In a case concerning this railroad he was disqualified from sitting,
having been of counsel in the case.— IV Supreme Court Reporter, 259.
[44] XIX Ohio State Reports, 226, etc.

when an attorney. Matthews had been one of the counsel for the Hayes electors before the Electoral Commission, and had industriously worked for the seating of Hayes.

Matthews' activities in the Senate for railroad corporations were notorious; he and Senator Lamar (who succeeded him on the Supreme Court bench) were the chief pushers and advocates of the amendatory bill of 1878 in favor of the Texas Pacific Railway. This railroad company, in 1871, had received a great land grant of 18,000,000 acres, and Government aid of $31,750,000 in bonds, on condition that it construct, within a certain time, a railroad from the Mississippi River to San Diego, California. But it had only built a small portion of the road, and a move was under way to declare its subsidies forfeited.

Senator Matthews, on March 19, 1878, reported Senate Bill No. 942, extending the time for building the railroad,[45] and Senator Lamar followed with a long speech in favor of the bill. Matthews also reported Senate Bill No. 474 authorizing the Southern Pacific Railroad to build railroad and telegraph extensions, and giving Government aid.[46] Likewise he reported another bill in favor of the Northern Pacific Railroad. Of the flagrant corruption of Congress by the Texas Pacific Railway promoters, and by Jay Gould and Collis P. Huntington, details are given later in this chapter. Matthews was one of the Senators conspicuously striving to defeat the Pacific Railroads Funding Act. The bill, however, was passed.

Denounced as a Railroad Tool.

On February 7, 1881, the following telegram was received in Washington:

[45] The *Congressional Record,* Vol. 7, Part 2, Forty-fifth Congress, Second Session, 1878: p. 1852.
[46] *Ibid.*

"*To the Judiciary Committee of the United States Senate,*
"*The Hon. A. G. Thurman, Chairman.*

"In behalf of 800 business firms of the New York Board of Trade and Transportation, we respectfully but earnestly protest against the confirmation of the Hon. Stanley Matthews as judge of the Supreme Court of the United States for the following reasons:

"We are informed and believe that the great railroad corporations of the country are endeavoring to obtain control of this Court of last resort, which has heretofore been the most important bulwark in defending the public interests against the encroachments of corporations; that Mr. Matthews has been educated as a railroad attorney, and views railroad questions from a railroad standpoint; that his actions while in the United States Senate prove this, and in this important respect render him unfit for a Justice of the Supreme Court.

"AMBROSE SNOW, President,
"DARWIN R. JAMES, Secretary." [47]

The explanation of this protest lay in this fact: The middle-class business men were infuriated at the dominance of such lordly railroad magnates as Vanderbilt, Gould, Sage, Huntington and Stanford.

Through their control of transportation facilities the railroad nabobs were extorting whatever freight rates they pleased and employing discriminative methods against the ordinary shipper. Largely by this alliance the first great Trust — the Standard Oil Company — had already become a great power, foreboding the time when trusts of all kinds would force out competition and efface the small factory owner and the small distributor. To fight this developing power, the middle class formed such organizations as the Anti-Monopoly League; as the middle class, in aggregate,

[47] This telegram was published in the New York *Times* and other newspapers at the time.

then possessed immense resources and strength, many of the leading newspapers supported its agitation. It desired judges representing middle-class interests; the essential objection to Matthews was that he was an instrument of the great railroad magnates.

Hence it was that such newspapers as the New York *Times,* the New York *Sun* and others bitterly denounced the appointment of Matthews. The New York *Times,* in an editorial entitled, "His Majesty, Jay Gould,"[48] described how Gould's control was constantly extending over railroads, the Associated Press and Congress. "There would still remain the Supreme Court," went on the editorial; "but no one can suppose that he will long permit it to retain its independence. Even if he cannot secure the confirmation of Mr. Stanley Matthews he will sooner or later contrive to have any vacancies that may occur filled in such a way as to provide against the contingency of decisions hostile to his interests. . . ." The New York *Sun* declared that if Matthews' nomination were confirmed it would be equivalent to putting Jay Gould upon the Supreme Court Bench. Other newspapers contained similar editorials, demanding that the nomination be withdrawn.

The Contest Over His Appointment.

Associate Justice Field, Senator Lamar, Senator Plumb and others were moving every possible influence to obtain a confirmation. But public criticism was either too severe just then or Senators representing antagonistic railroad groups were opposed to Matthews, as being too much the creature of Jay Gould.[49] Whatever were the actuating reasons, the Senate did not confirm.

[48] Published February 23, 1881.
[49] As illustrative of the railroad interests of a majority of the Senators, the case of Senator William B. Allison, of Iowa, may be mentioned. When a member of Congress, in 1867, Allison had been

When, however, President Garfield succeeded Hayes, Matthews (who was a relative of Garfield) was renominated, and the contest again begun. Lamar, as a member of the Judiciary Committee, renewed his efforts for Matthews; Senators George F. Edmunds and David Davis led in opposing the confirmation. Edmunds, long the chairman of the Judiciary Committee, was himself a railroad lawyer, representing the Michigan Central Railroad and other railways. Why did he oppose Matthews? The conflict of the magnates with one another in the economic field had its reflex in the political; certain magnates sought, to the exclusion of other magnates with whom they were at war, to control the courts. Senators representing different magnates thus took opposite sides in favoring or opposing this or that measure or appointment.

The Senate Judiciary Committee, on May 9, 1881, rejected Matthews' appointment. On May 12, 1881, the report of this committee was taken up in executive session; and after a long, acrimonious and stubborn debate, the Senate by a vote of 24 to 23 — a majority of one vote — confirmed the appointment.[50] The information leaked out that in the secret session, Senators invidiously pointed out that measures which Matthews had favored or opposed, as a Senator, would come up before the Supreme Court for adjudication.

vice-president of the Sioux City and Pacific Railroad, which had received a land grant of one hundred sections, and $16,000 of Government bonds for each mile of railroad. In the construction of this railroad, the sum of $4,000,000 was fraudulently appropriated. By an act lobbied through Congress, in 1900, when Allison was still a powerful Senator, the Sioux City and Pacific Railroad Company was virtually released from paying back more than one-tenth the sum it still owed the Government.— Ex. Documents Nos. 181 to 252, Second Session, Fortieth Congress, 1867–68, Doc. No. 203; Report of Pacific Railway Commission, Vol. I: 193, etc.

[50] Appleton's "Annual Cyclopedia" for 1881: p. 194. Considering that long previously the Senate had established an unwritten rule that no objection should be made to any appointee who had been a member of the United States Senate, and that his appointment should be promptly confirmed on the ground of "Senatorial courtesy," this contest over Senator Matthews' appointment was unprecedented and remarkable.

Justices Gray and Blatchford.

The next appointment, made in December, 1881, was that of Horace Gray, to succeed Justice Clifford. Gray was the grandson of William Gray, one of the largest shipowners in New England, and the richest man in Boston in 1810. Of the activities of William Gray in getting bank charters we have given an account in an earlier chapter. Horace Gray belonged to the class in Boston styling themselves the old aristocracy; he was accused of being obtrusively snobbish; judging from the anecdotes related of him, he was, no doubt, a thorough snob and a formalist of the most pronounced and provoking type.[51]

Graduated from Harvard, Gray traveled extensively in Europe, and was once presented in approved form at the court of King Louis Phillipe. Admitted to the bar in 1851, he

[51] Such a stricture seems justified by these and other anecdotes related of him when he was a judge and Chief Justice of the Supreme Court of Massachusetts:

"At the trial of a certain case Judge Gray suddenly summoned a man to appear at a particular stage of the proceedings. The man responded promptly and appeared in the court room attired as at his work bench, in his shirt sleeves. Judge Gray, after commenting severely upon such disrespect to the court, waived the urgency of the pending cause, and directed the man to go home and put himself in the proper garb for the humble part which he was to take in the doings of the august tribunal." (New York *Times,* December 20, 1881.)

"His tirades," said the Washington correspondence of the Philadelphia *Press,* "against trembling deputy-sheriffs and frightened witnesses have been told over and over again. Only two lawyers in Boston have ever been able to turn the tables on him. One was Henry E. Payne; the other Sidney Bartlett. 'If your honor please —' said Payne one day, beginning a motion. 'Sit down, sir; don't you see that I am talking with another justice?' thundered the Chief Magistrate. Mr. Payne took his hat and walked out of the courtroom. A half-hour afterward a messenger reached his office with a note saying that Judge Gray was willing to hear him. 'I am not willing to be heard,' answered the old lawyer, 'until Judge Gray apologizes.' And apologize the judge had to.

"'Mr. Bartlett,' said the Chief Justice one afternoon, throwing himself back in his chair, 'that is not law and it never was law.' The veteran smiled, and looking over the bench said, 'It *was* law, your Honor, until your Honor just spoke.'"— Republished in the New York *Times,* issue of March 13, 1882.

became, in 1854, a reporter of decisions of the Massachusetts Supreme Judicial Court. In 1864, he was appointed Associate Justice of that court, and in 1873 became its Chief Justice. He was extremely tall — not less than six feet six inches, and never personally popular. The circumstances of his receiving a large addition to his already considerable fortune by virtue of a decision of the Supreme Court of the United States while he was a member of that Court, are related in a subsequent chapter.

Shortly after Gray's appointment, Samuel Blatchford, of New York, was appointed to succeed Justice Hunt.[52]

Blatchford was the son of Richard Blatchford, a lawyer of note in New York City who, in 1826, became the financial agent and counsel for the Bank of England. He later acted in the same capacity for the Bank of the United States, and adjusted the final settlement between these two banks, when the charter of the Bank of the United States expired in 1836. His financial dealings were large for his day. One of these dealt with the North American Trust and Banking Company. Although having several millions of dollars in stocks and bonds, this company, soon after its formation, became embarrassed for want of sufficient funds, and resorted to various expedients " some," as Judge Roosevelt decided, " at least, of a questionable character." Two mortgages for a total of $1,500,000 were then made out to Richard Blatchford and others. A suit, of a very involved nature, was brought to have these mortgages declared invalid on the ground of their being fraudulent.[53]

[52] President Arthur had first offered the appointment to United States Senator Roscoe Conkling of New York. Conkling was one of the counsel for the New York Central Railroad. (See, XXII Wallace's Reports, 621, etc.) After Conkling declined the appointment, Arthur offered it to Senator Edmunds, who, as we have seen, was also a noted railroad attorney. Upon Edmunds' declination, Blatchford was appointed and he accepted.

[53] Case of Curtis vs. Leavitt, Barbour's Supreme Court Reports (N. Y.), Vol. XXVII: 312–378. (Dec., 1853.)

Blatchford's Interests and Associations.

Samuel Blatchford became private secretary to Governor William H. Seward, serving until 1841, and in 1845 associated himself as a law partner with Seward and Christopher Morgan. As a State Senator, Seward, on January 31, 1832, had made an elaborate defense of the Bank of the United States in reply to a legislative resolution declaring that its charter ought not be renewed.[54] Seward was counsel for Erastus Corning, a large capitalist of Albany who was the head of the projectors of the Minnesota and Northwestern Railroad Company which, in 1854, by fraud and corruption obtained from Congress an extensive land grant of 900,000 acres.[55] Christopher Morgan was the brother of Edward Barber Morgan, a founder of the Wells-Fargo Express Company and of the United States Express Company. A multimillionaire, Christopher Morgan was president of the Wells-Fargo Company, and a director for many years of the United States Express Company.[56]

In 1854, Samuel Blatchford returned to New York City, and formed a partnership with Clarence A. Seward, son of William H. Seward, and with Burr Griswold. Their practice was largely one for railroad and express companies.[57]

[54] Jenkins' "Political History of New York" (Edition of 1849) : pp. 378–380.

[55] Reports of Committees, Thirty-third Congress, First Session, Vol. III: Rep. No. 352: 30. For full details from the official documents see "History of the Great American Fortunes," Vol. III: pp. 24–25, 44, etc.

[56] Stimson's "Express History," 75, 462, etc.

[57] Thus, to give four examples: Clarence A. Seward represented William B. Dinsmore, president and treasurer of the Adams Express Company (XXXIV Howard's Practice Reports [N. Y.], 1868: p. 421), and with Benjamin R. Curtis, former Associate Justice of the Supreme Court of the United States, he represented the same corporation in Ellis vs. Boston, Hartford and Erie Railroad (107 Mass. Reports, 15: 1869). Seward represented the Adams Express Company in the suit of Caldwell against that company (XXI Wallace's Reports, 143) and he was counsel for the Southern Express Company in the action of Vermilye and Company against that corporation (XXI Wallace's Reports, 265). Many other instances could be given.

Another son of William H. Seward, and named after him, became a director of the Southern Central Railroad of New York. Blatchford was made a United States Circuit Court judge; at the time of his appointment to the Supreme Court of the United States, the President of the United States Express Company was Thomas C. Platt, for more than twenty years the Republican boss of New York, and twice United States Senator from that State. The campaign contributions made by every variety of corporation during the long period of Platt's dictatorship were so enormous and long continuing that it is out of the question to enter here into a narrative of them. Official investigations, to which we shall have need of referring, disclose the particulars, especially in the case of the great insurance companies which, in turn, have been controlled by the railroad magnates.[58]

The express companies, starting with little capital, had expanded to enormous proportions and were making immense profits. Dissatisfied, the shippers were continually complaining; litigation was more and more increasing; and the express companies, like other corporations, sought to insure themselves against adverse legislation and court decisions.

Between the express monopoly and the railroads was an intimate alliance, comprehending, in many cases, the same capitalists. Thus, Leland Stanford, D. O. Mills and Charles F. Crocker were directors of the Wells-Fargo Express Company at the time of Blatchford's appointment to the Supreme Court of the United States. Blatchford owned stock in the Illinois Central Railroad and many other corporations. In the Tennessee Bond Cases, involving claims to unpaid bonds

[58] This item is one of many signifying the political debauchery by corporations: The New York Legislative Insurance Committee, in its extensive report in 1906, stated that for many years the Equitable Life Assurance Society had been giving $30,000 annually to the New York State Republican Committee (controlled by Platt) and that all of the other insurance companies variously did the same, contributing to the campaign funds of both the Republican and Democratic parties, State and National.— Vol. X: 10, 62, etc., etc.

claimed by the Louisville and Nashville Railroad and numerous other railroads Blatchford and Justice Stanley Matthews were disqualified from sitting because of their interest.[59] To such an extent did the railroad and express company interest become merged that the principal ownership of the express monopoly gradually became vested in J. P. Morgan, the Vanderbilts, the Goulds, the Standard Oil Company, the Harriman estate, Lewis Cass Ledyard (a grandson of Lewis Cass) and in other railroad magnates.

So well did the express companies succeed in warding off hostile legislative and court action, that the recent petition of the Merchants' Association of New York and of the Chambers of Commerce of Chicago, Philadelphia, Boston, Detroit, St. Louis, Denver and other cities to the Interstate Commerce Commission sets forth that the annual profits of the express companies have been 150 per cent. in addition to which great cash reserves are held.

Validation of the Vast Maxwell Land Claim.

Of the large body of decisions handed down by the Supreme Court of the United States during the last years of Waite's Chief Justiceship, nearly all were uniformly favorable to railroad and other corporations.

It was under Waite that the Supreme Court validated the enormous Maxwell private-land grant. This claim had originally been asserted by Charles Beaubien and Guadalupe Miranda, claiming title under a grant said to have been made by the Mexican Governor Armijo in 1841. On September 15, 1857, the United States Surveyor General of New Mexico had reported the grant as embracing 96,000 acres. One L. B. Maxwell bought the claim, and contended that it comprised

---

[59] In the Chicago Lake Front case affecting the Illinois Central Railroad's title, Blatchford could not sit because he owned stock. For the Tennessee Bond Cases, see, V Supreme Court Reporter, 995.

nearly 2,000,000 acres. Holding that the old Mexican laws had limited the area granted to any one individual to 48,000 acres, the Commissioner of the General Land Office, upheld by the Secretary of the Interior, refused, in 1869, to certify more than 96,000 acres.[60]

One of the principal owners of the claim was Stephen B. Elkins, a conspicuous Republican politician, and a delegate in Congress. Elkins' efforts at Washington bore fruit. A new survey was ordered by the Land Office; one of the surveyors was Elkins' brother, John T. Elkins. The surveyors reported the grant as embracing, in all, 1,714,764.94 acres in New Mexico and extending into Colorado. On May 19, 1879, the General Land Office gave a quit claim for the whole of this area. It was then mortgaged to a syndicate of Holland capitalists for the sum of £700,000 in sterling money and Dutch currency.[61]

On August 25, 1882, the Government brought suit to have the grant declared void. Suing the Maxwell Land Grant Company, the Pueblo and Arkansas Valley Railroad Company and the Denver and Rio Grande Railway Company, the Government in five specifications declared that the grant, under the laws of Mexico, could not have been for more than 96,000 acres of land, and that the patent for its enormous enlargement had been obtained by a conspiracy of fraud and deceit practiced upon the Land Office.[62]

But on April 18, 1887, the Supreme Court of the United States validated the whole claim for 1,714,764.94 acres, basing its decision upon a disingenuous act sneaked through Congress in 1860. That act, joined with another act passed in the same year, allowed surveys to be made at the expense

---

[60] "Land Titles in New Mexico and Colorado," House Reports, First Session, Fifty-Second Congress, 1891–92, Vol. IV: Report No. 1253. (Committee on Private Land Claims.)

[61] House Reports, 1891–1892, Vol. IV, Report No. 1353: 7.

[62] See the bill of particulars reciting the history of the frauds in VII Supreme Court Reports, 1017, and 121 U. S. Reports, 327.

of " settlers," and provided that the amounts deposited by " settlers " should be received as part payments for the lands. These acts bore no reference whatever to the Maxwell grant; successive Land Commissioners had pointed out that their only object was to authorize fraudulent surveys; but the Supreme Court seems to have discovered that they allowed a grant of 96,000 acres to be extended to cover nearly 2,000,000 acres.[63]

The decision was much denounced. Stephen B. Elkins, the chief beneficiary, married a daughter of United States Senator Henry G. Davis of West Virginia and financed the construction of a number of railroads. He had built for him a palace-like castle in the town bearing his name in West Virginia; he became a United States Senator, in 1895; and he died a multimillionaire.

Justice Field Protects Leland Stanford.

At about the time when this decision was handed down, Associate Justice Field was subjected to insinuating criticisms for his actions in several matters. The Pacific Railway Commission was investigating the consecutive frauds and thefts of the promoters and manipulators of the Pacific railroads. On July 26, 1887, the Commission, when in San Francisco, issued an order requiring Leland Stanford to testify. The particular questions the Commission pointedly had put to Stanford were these:

What part of a certain voucher for $171,000 that had been made out by him (Stanford) had been used for the purpose of influencing legislation? (This $171,000 — or to be exact, $171,781.89 — had been paid out by Stanford in cash, on December 31, 1875.)

[63] The full narrative of this grant, thus validated to comprise a colossal area, is related in the " History of the Great American Fortunes," Vol. III: 324–334.

What lawyers had been in the habit of attending the Legislature with him (Stanford)?

Did he (Stanford) ever give away any portion of certain exhibited vouchers to S. T. Gage to influence legislation? (Gage was one of the directors of the Southern Pacific Railway Company.)

Did he (Stanford) ever give any money to W. B. Carr for the purpose of influencing legislation in the California Legislature?

Upon Stanford's refusal to answer these questions, the Pacific Railway Commission applied to the United States Circuit Court for an order compelling him to testify.

Field was then in San Francisco, presiding over the Circuit Court, for until the act creating the United States Circuit Court of Appeals was passed, each Associate Justice of the Supreme Court of the United States was assigned, for a part of the time, to a certain circuit. The United States Circuit Court at San Francisco was composed of Field, and Judges Lorenzo Sawyer, Sabin and Hoffman. Field, as we have seen, had been appointed to the Supreme Court upon the personal solicitation of Stanford. Judges Sawyer and Sabin owed their seats to Stanford and Huntington. In fact, Huntington testified before the Pacific Railway Commission that he and his associates made it a system to control the judicial, as well as the legislative and executive, departments of government. Judge Hoffman had been on the bench before Stanford and Huntington had acquired power; his decisions in the private land-claim cases had revealed him as an honest judge.

On August 29, 1887, the Circuit Court gave its decision, written by Justice Field and Judge Sawyer, denying the application of the Commission, on the ground that the act creating the Commission did not authorize compulsory testimony. Judge Hoffman dissented. "The decision of the Circuit Court of the United States in California," reported the Pacific Railway Commission, "made it impossible for this Commission to obtain answers to the questions which Congress had directed to be put." [64] As to the extent of the corruption carried on by Huntington and Stanford, the Commission reported, " There is no room for doubt that a large portion of $4,818,535 was used for the purpose of influencing legislation, and preventing the passage of measures deemed hostile to the interests of the company, and for the purpose of influencing elections." [65]

During all of these years, Field was intimate with Stanford and frequently, when Stanford was a United States Senator, dined at his house in Washington. In the writings of Justice Bradley there is published a letter, dated March 23, 1891, from Justice Field to Senator James G. Fair, a California millionaire, stating that he (Field) had dined the previous evening at General Schofield's, and that among those present were the President, Chief Justice Fuller, Senators Stanford. Sherman and many other high functionaries.[66]

While on the subject of the corrupt methods of Stanford it will be pertinent to refer here to the report of the San Francisco Grand Jury, of August, 1891. This body called the " Wallace Grand Jury," was impaneled under Judge Wallace to investigate municipal corruption, particularly the debauching of politics by the Southern Pacific Railway. Gage refused to testify, as did other railway directors, and Buckley, the political boss of San Francisco, fled from the Grand Jury's jurisdiction. When Stanford was summoned to testify, the Supreme Court of California was instantly appealed to by the railroad's lawyers. That court, by a vote of four to three, held that the Grand Jury was improperly con-

[64] Report of the Pacific Railway Commission (Ex. Doc. No. 51, Fiftieth Congress, First Session), Vols. I and II: 121, and Vol. VII: 4215.

[65] *Ibid.*, Vol. I: 84.

[66] " Miscellaneous Writings of Joseph Bradley," pp. 350–351. The purpose of the letter was an enquiry concerning the effectiveness of hydraulic mining, over which an academic discussion had taken place at the dinner.

stituted, " because of an irregularity in the appointment of the elisor." [67]

A Virulent Attack by Justice Field.

The other occasion on which Justice Field's course aroused critical comment was in the case of an eleven-league tract in California held by the San Jacinto Tin Company, the Riverside Canal Company and the Riverside Land and Irrigation Company.

This tract was confirmed to de Aguirre by the Board of Land Commissioners and the District Court in 1867. In 1883 the Attorney General of the United States brought suit to have the patent declared void. The Government alleged " that throughout the whole transaction, from the beginning of the effort to have this survey made until its final completion and the issue of the patent, all of the proceedings were dictated by fraud and all of the officers of the government below the Secretary of the Interior who had anything to do with it were parties to that fraud and to be benefited by it." The Government set forth that Surveyor-General Upson; his chief clerk, Conway; Thompson, the deputy surveyor for California, and Joseph H. Wilson, the Commissioner of the General Land Office, knew that the tract contained tin ore, and that they " were all interested and part owners of the claim at the time this survey was made, and at the very time they acted in reference to its final confirmation."

Yet the Supreme Court of the United States (Justice Miller writing its decision) accepted the depositions and reports of the very officials who had thus been implicated! Wilson had made a " full report," the Supreme Court said, in 1867, and this report it assumed to receive as authentic, notwithstanding

[67] See, Report of Wallace Grand Jury, contained in " Report on the Causes of Municipal Corruption in San Francisco," etc. Published by order of the Board of Supervisors, etc., San Francisco, 1910: p. 9. In this document, comprising the full report of the Oliver Grand Jury of 1908, the presentment of the Wallace Grand Jury is reprinted.

the fact that the Government now showed Wilson to have been interested. The Supreme Court pretended not to go behind the formal, official acts of the Government officers disclosed as promoters and beneficiaries of the fraud. It thus consistently followed the long line of precedents begun by Marshall in ignoring motives and acts of fraud and corruption. Although conceding that Conway had bought the claim, and had organized a corporation to mine tin ore, the Supreme Court, nevertheless, held that the fraud was not proved, and on March 19, 1888, decided against the Government.[68]

Justice Field, however, was not content with concurring in this decision. He went out of his way to indulge in a savage attack upon the Attorney-General, accusing him of bringing the suit at the instigation of a third party and of using the Government machinery for ulterior reasons.[69] It was remarked that if the Supreme Court took the position that it was not at liberty to inquire into motives of legislature or official, no matter what fraud or corruption lay behind, what right had a Supreme Court Justice to take advantage of his power to assail the motives of the Attorney-General?

Lamar Succeeds Matthews.

The last appointment to the Supreme Court made during the period when Waite was Chief Justice seemed to provoke almost as much criticism as that of Stanley Matthews. As Woods' successor as Associate Justice, President Cleveland in 1888, appointed Lucius Q. C. Lamar of Mississippi. Born in 1825, Lamar had been in Congress in 1857-1861, had served in the Confederate military and diplomatic service, was a member of Congress after the Civil War, and was elected a United States Senator in 1873. In the Senate he was chairman of the Standing Committee on the Pacific railroads; and he had, as we have related, been the principal

[68] 125 U. S. Reports, 288.   [69] *Ibid.*, 307.

supporter of Matthews' bill in favor of the Texas Pacific
Railroad. Even his eulogistic biographer describes his zeal in
working for the interests of that railroad.[70] In addition to
being the chief and indefatigable pusher of Texas Pacific
Railroad measures, Lamar was an extensive railroad stockholder and a director of the Mississippi Central Railroad.[71]

The Prevailing Corruption.

A sufficient indication of the corruption used by both the
promoters and the antagonists of the Texas Pacific Railroad
bill was supplied by the subsequent publication of the celebrated Colton letters written by Collis P. Huntington to his
confidant and one of his partners, General David D. Colton.
Scott, of the Pennsylvania Railroad, then controlled the
Texas Pacific Railroad project, while Huntington was one
of the Central and the Southern Pacific railroads group.
These two sets of capitalists came into collision over the division of the spoils of the Southwest. Both caused bills to be
introduced and each sought to corrupt Congress.

" Scott," wrote Huntington, on January 29, 1876, " is
making a terrible effort to pass his bill, and he has many advantages with his railroad running out from Washington in

[70] Mayes' "Lucius Q. C. Lamar, His. Life, Times and Speeches, 1825–
1893." Mayes tells how Lamar supported the measures for the benefit
of that railroad and quotes a laudatory account, written by William
Preston King in 1879, which went the rounds of the press: " Senator
Lamar has been recognized as the zealous friend of all measures for
internal improvements in the South, especially improvements of the
levees of the Mississippi and for the Texas Pacific Railroad. He has
been a very effective and eloquent champion of this last-named enterprise."— p. 372.

An examination of the record shows that Lamar made the principal
speech for the Texas Pacific Railway. Pointing out that the Northern
Pacific Railroad had received about 47,000,000 acres of land, and the
Union and the Central Pacific roads 50,000,000 acres, he pleaded that
the Texas Pacific should be allowed to retain its land grant of 18,000,000
acres.— The *Congressional Record*, Vol. 7, Part 4, Forty-fifth Congress,
Second Session, 1878: pp. 3653–3658.

[71] " Poor's Railroad Manual," for 1869–70: p. 18.

almost every direction, on which he gives Free Passes to everyone who can help him ever so little. It has cost money to fix things, so I know his bill would not pass. I believe with $200,000 we can pass our bill." On March 6, 1876, Huntington wrote that " the Railroad Committee of the House was set up for Scott, and it has been a very difficult matter to switch a majority of the Committee from him, but I think it has been done."

To one of his associates Huntington wrote further, on November 11, 1876, " I am glad to learn that you will send to this office $2,000,000 by the first of January." Huntington, in one of this series of letters, dated December 17, 1877, wrote: " Jay Gould went to Washington about two weeks since and I know saw Mitchell, Senator from Oregon. Since which time money has been used very freely in Washington. . . . Gould has large amounts in cash, and he pays it without stint to carry his points." On May 3, 1878, Huntington informed his partners: " The T. and P. (Texas Pacific) folks are working hard on their bill, and say they are sure to pass it, but I do not believe it. They offered one member of Congress $1,000 cash down, $5,000 when the bill was passed, and $10,000 of the bonds when they got them if he would vote for the bill." [72] In the end both groups obtained the legislation sought; and that the Texas Pacific capitalists eventually succeeded was due greatly to the efforts of Senators Matthews and Lamar.

As we have seen, Senator Lamar was Matthews' most vigorous and supple defender during the opposition to Matthews'

[72] The original name of the company was the Texas Pacific; later it was changed to read Texas and Pacific Railway Company. There were a large number of the Colton letters; they came to light in a lawsuit arising over the plundering of Colton's estate by Huntington, Stanford and Crocker, and were published in a pamphlet, " Driven From Sea to Sea," by C. C. Post. " It is impossible," reported the Pacific Railroad Commission (Vol. I: 121), " to read the evidence of C. P. Huntington and Leland Stanford and the Colton letters without reaching the conclusion that very large sums of money have been improperly used in connection with legislation."

confirmation as Associate Justice. First selecting Lamar as Secretary of the Interior,— the very office having jurisdiction over railroad land patents — President Cleveland had then nominated him to succeed Matthews. Cleveland himself had been a railroad lawyer. Three main objections to the confirmation of Lamar's nomination were agitated: his long disuse of legal practice, his want of judicial experience, and his notorious activity as a railroad legislator. It is needless to say that his nomination was confirmed.

The Railroad Power in Control.

All except two of the Justices now constituting the Supreme Court of the United States had been active railroad attorneys or railroad stockholders, directors or legislative railroad lobbyists. The Supreme Court as absolutely reflected the dominant section of the capitalist class as it did during the eras of the control by the landed interests and the slave power.

From 1879 to 1884 the stupendous amount of $3,360,000,-000 of new railroad securities had been listed. Edward Atkinson, a conservative political economist, testified before the United States Senate ("Cullom") Committee in 1886, that the railroads formed about one-fifth of the total wealth of the country. As early as 1870 the railroad magnates had begun to form pools for the partition of traffic and to maintain rates at a certain point. The organization by the railroad power of the Southwestern Railway Rate Association and, in 1884, of the Western Freight Association called forth the charge by the middle-class business elements that they were conspiracies to restrain trade and to fix extortionate rates. This was true; but the essence of the situation was that the capitalist system was in a state of transition from the old competitive stage to a newer state of centralized control and operation. Nevertheless, the still powerful middle class succeeded in getting anti-pool and anti-trust laws passed by Congress. In this great duel between the two classes everything then depended upon the construction that the Supreme Court of the United States would put upon those laws.

Dying, Waite is Rushed to the Court Room.

For a considerable time Chief Justice Waite had suffered from ailments arising from the liver and spleen, complicated with a painful stomach trouble. In March, 1888, he was obviously in a sinking condition. But certain cases concerning a great contest over the priority and legality of the Bell Telephone patent were to be decided; and in order that Waite's vote should not be lost the extraordinary step was taken of rushing a dying man to the Supreme Court chambers.

The principal competitor of the Bell Telephone was the Pan-Electric Telephone Company. This company charged its opponents, the Bell Telephone Company, with having resorted to a campaign of bribery by means of money or gifts of stock, in order to get its patent claims, laws, franchises and decisions. On the other hand, the testimony before a Congressional Committee showed that to get the Government officials to move in the courts for the vacating of the Bell patents, large blocks of stock were distributed by the Pan-Electric Telephone Company to influential Representatives and Senators, some of whom became directors of the company. It was also charged that United States Attorney-General Garland, who had the practical power of deciding whether or not suits to vacate the Bell patent should be brought, held $10,000,000 of Pan-Electric stock for which he had not paid a dollar.[73] In fact, a contract was produced before the Congressional Committee proving that on August 4, 1875, the Pan-Electric Company and the Na-

[73] See, House Miscellaneous Documents, Forty-ninth Congress, 1885–86, Vol. XIX.—"Testimony taken by the Committee Relating to the Pan-Electric Telephone Company."

tional Improved Telephone Company of Louisiana had agreed in writing that they would begin suit against the American Bell Telephone Company, provided they could obtain the assent of the Attorney-General of the United States.[74]

The Telephone Cases Decided.

There were five actions against the American Bell Telephone Company, revolving around the point whether Bell or Dollbear was the inventor of the telephone. When the decision favorable to the Bell patent was reached, only eight Justices were on the bench, Lamar not having taken his seat when the long and complicated arguments had been made. Of the eight, Justice Gray refrained from taking part because of interest. This left seven Justices, of whom Waite, Miller, Blatchford and Matthews concurred in a majority opinion favorable to Bell. Bradley, Field and Harlan dissented from some of the conclusions reached by the majority.[75]

" The telephone decision," says a contemporary account, " had been written by the Chief Justice, but he was too ill to read it from the Bench, and that duty was, therefore, performed by Justice Blatchford. Special care was taken that no evidence of the Chief Justice's illness should appear, and none of the throng that heard the decision read suspected the real reason why it was announced by Justice Blatchford. As soon as possible after the reading, Justice Waite left the Bench, and was hurriedly driven home. . . . He went to bed and since then has been a very sick man." [76]

The Chief Justice died on the very day on which this account was published — March 23, 1888. He had lived in

---

[74] *Ibid.,* 574. Isham G. Harris, for many years a United States Senator from Tennessee, was Vice-President of the Pan-Electric Telephone Company.

[75] 126 U. S. Reports, 531.

[76] Washington despatch, New York *Times,* March 23, 1888.

rather aristocratic style in Washington. After his death the newspapers reported that his estate was so small that members of the Washington Bar and others deemed it advisable to raise a fund for his widow.

CHAPTER XIV

THE SUPREME COURT UNDER CHIEF JUSTICE FULLER

Following Waite's death, considerable speculation was rife as to who would be appointed his successor. President Cleveland finally chose Melville W. Fuller, a Chicago lawyer, obscure so far as public reputation went and without judicial experience but well and favorably known in corporation circles. Like Cleveland, Fuller was a Democrat, but he was urged for the Chief Justiceship by both Republican and Democratic Senators and capitalists.

Fuller's Sponsors and Backers.

Among those particularly active at Washington assiduously working for his appointment was Colonel W. C. Goudy, an attorney for a large number of varied corporations. Goudy was counsel for the South Chicago Railway Company, the Washburn and Moen Manufacturing Company, the Chicago, Burlington and Quincy Railroad, the Illinois Central Railroad, the Indiana Banking Company, the Chicago Dock Company, and he was general counsel for the Chicago and Northwestern Railway Company, for the Fremont and Elkhorn Railroad, and for the Sioux City and Pacific Railroad.[1]

Senator John C. Spooner, of Wisconsin, a Republican, was energetic in Fuller's behalf; of Spooner's activities as a railroad lawyer we have given an adequate glimpse in the description of the case of Schulenberg vs. Harriman in the preceding chapter. The selection of Fuller was also approved by Robert T.

---

[1] " Poor's Railroad Manual," for 1890: pp. 1297 and 1300.

Lincoln, former Secretary of War, and for many years president of the Pullman Company, of Chicago. Another of the many functionaries strongly pushing Fuller's appointment was the millionaire United States Senator Charles B. Farwell, of Illinois, a partner in the large Chicago dry goods establishment with his brother, John V. Farwell. This house had made great profits on contracts during the Civil War; by the abundant infusion of money into politics Charles B. Farwell had wrested an election to Congress, and then an election as United States Senator.

A Transaction of the Farwells.

Aside from their other political and corporate transactions, the Farwells had but recently come conspicuously into public attention by reason of the successive steps by which they had obtained the title to 3,000,000 acres of public land in Texas.

During the session of the Texas Constitutional Convention, at Austin, on November 1, 1875, a clever attempt was made to pass a resolution for the setting apart of 5,000,000 acres of public lands in exchange for the building of a new State Capitol. This resolution was defeated, but on November 20 a constitutional provision was finally adopted after much skillful lobbying, setting apart 3,000,000 acres for the purpose.[2]

On February 20, 1879, the Texas Legislature passed an act appropriating 3,050,000 acres in the counties of Deaf Smith, Parmer, Castro, Lamb, Bailey, Hockley, Dallain, Hartley, Cochran and Oldham to be turned over to the contractors for the new building. This contract was made on January 18, 1882, with Matthew Schnell, of Rock Island, Illinois. In the same month, Schnell assigned his entire interest to Charles B. Farwell, John V. Farwell, Amos C. Babcock and others comprising the firm of Taylor, Babcock and Company of Chicago.[3]

[2] Article XVI, Sec. 57, General Provisions, Constitution of Texas.
[3] " Report of the Capitol Building Commissioners to the Governor of Texas, Jan. 1, 1883 ": p. 31.

When only a small part of the building had been constructed, the State officials leased to the Farwells all of the 3,000,000 acres " not yet earned " at six cents an acre per annum.[4] The Farwells immediately used it for grazing purposes, at large profit to themselves.

Instead of using granite the contractors began to construct the building with limestone, whereat public indignation began to manifest itself.[5] Pleading that they could not afford granite the Farwells demurred at being put to more expense, although they were then receiving the 3,000,000 acres in installments as fast as certain parts of the building were constructed. It had been definitely understood and expected that in return for that enormous area of land they would erect a substantial building ; that they were not doing so caused ugly scandal.

Three Million Acres by the Convict Labor Route.

At this point, Lacy, Westfall and Norton, owners of a granite quarry in Travis County, Texas, came forward, and in a burst of public spirit offered the Farwells the free use of their granite deposits, provided they would quarry them and build a railroad to the quarry. The Farwells, however, objecting that they did not care to pay the schedule rates of union labor, induced the State officials to give them a supply of convict labor. On July 25, 1885, the State officials contracted with the firm of Taylor, Babcock and Company to furnish that corporation with five hundred " able-bodied convicts." In return, all that the contractors had to do was to board, clothe and guard the convicts, and to pay the State sixty-five cents a day for each convict's labor. These convicts were to be used in constructing a railroad to the granite quarries and were also to do the granite and stone work at the quarries necessary for

[4] " Third Biennial Report of the Capitol Building Commission, 1886 ": p. 199.
[5] *Ibid.*, 201.

the building. The convicts thus used were to be white, Mexican or colored, and were to work ten hours a day.[6]

Complaints were frequently made that the convicts were wretchedly treated and brutally overworked. But so far as the general public went the charge that made a deeper impression was that the Capitol was flimsily constructed. At a meeting of the State Capitol Board, on September 10, 1888, Attorney-General Hogg introduced a resolution stating that " whereas, for more than a year past many complaints of a serious nature have been made against the workmanship of the new State Capitol, mostly by private parties, but more recently by General W. P. Hardeman, Superintendent of Public Buildings and Grounds, and they yet continue to be made," etc., etc. Hogg accused the Capitol Commissioners of paying no attention to the charges, and his resolution, therefore, " invited them to resign." [7] The commissioners denied the charges and, of course, declined the invitation.

The cost of constructing the Capitol was stated to be $3,095,000, and the last installment of the 3,000,000 acres was turned over to the Farwells on August 25, 1888.[8] A large part of the 3,000,000 acres the Farwells disposed of at an enormous profit; the Farwell family still holds 800,000 acres and have a large ranch house at Channing, which Walter Farwell occupies during the summer, spending the winters in England.

Apparently a digression, these details are introduced for the

[6] " Third Biennial Report of the [Texas] Capitol Building Commission," 1886: p. 204.

[7] " Final Report of the Capitol Building Commissioners, 1888 ᵛ: p. 32.

[8] *Ibid.*, p. 36. At the time this land was originally granted, its great value for agricultural and grazing purposes was pointed out. Much of it, reported N. L. Norton, Commissioner to survey the lands, in 1883, was wheat-bearing soil of a high degree. " The thousands of prairie dogs met on every hand, and which are never located beyond the convenient reach of water, undoubtedly attest the fact of a supply underground, which may be utilized by mechanical appliances at a moderate cost."—" Report of the Capitol Building Commissioners to the Governor of Texas, Jan. 1, 1883 ": p. 61.

purpose of exhibiting a few of the economic interests of some
of the men vigorously pushing Fuller for the Chief Justiceship.
At the precise time when Senator Farwell was urging the appointment he was putting the finishing touches upon the consummation of the acquisition of the 3,000,000 acres, obtained
by the connivance of officials and the exploitation of convict
labor.

Like that of Waite, Fuller's appointment was a complete
surprise to the large public; his name and career were utterly
unfamiliar. But to corporations of all kinds his skill and service had long been intimately known and highly valued. The
list of corporations that he had represented as an attorney was
an elaborate one.

Career of the New Chief Justice.

He was born in Augusta, Maine, in 1833. As a child he
was brought up in a legal atmosphere; his father was a lawyer;
and so were his father's two brothers; and his mother was a
daughter of Nathan Weston, for many years the Chief Justice
of the Supreme Court of Maine. Fuller went to Chicago, in
1856, and from the first sought the clientage of rich individuals
and powerful corporations, dipping somewhat into politics.
He was a member, in 1861, of the Illinois State Constitutional
Convention; in 1862 he served in the Illinois Legislature, and
he was a delegate to the Democratic National Conventions of
1864, 1872, 1876 and 1880.

His corporation practice was so large that only some typical
cases of the entire number in which he appeared will be given
here.

He and J. H. Roberts, in 1870, represented Dows, a stockholder of the Union National Bank of Chicago, in a long-
drawn but unsuccessful action to restrain the City of Chicago
from levying a tax upon bank stock.[9] Three years later we

[9] XI Wallace's Reports, Supreme Court of the U. S., p. 108.

find him arguing for the Merchants' National Bank, but without success, that the power of a State to tax stockholders in a national bank did not extend to non-resident stockholders.[10]

At the same time Fuller was counsel for the First National Bank of Springfield;[11] for the Commercial Bank of Bristol, R. I.,[12] and for other banks. He represented Jesse Hoyt, a large Chicago railroad capitalist, Philip D. Armour, the multimillionaire Chicago packer, and associates in an action for an injunction to restrain the Chicago, Burlington and Quincy Railroad from taking up a certain sidetrack. Hoyt owned a three-quarter interest in the " Union Elevator," a large grain warehouse; hence his participation in the action. This contest of millionaire wheat gamblers and monopolists assumed various phases in which Hoyt, Armour and others, although associates, were at times on different sides.[13] Representing the First National Bank of Chicago, Fuller and two other attorneys sought to prevent that bank from being held responsible for the defalcation of $114,032.62 of A. W. Waldron, treasurer of the village of Hyde Park. The circumstances of the defalcation were such that the bank, so the lower court decided, could be held liable for nearly $60,000 and interest. But Fuller won the case in the Supreme Court of Illinois.[14] At different times during this period, and often for many successive years he was counsel for the Metropolitan National Bank, the Traders' Bank, the Fourth National Bank, the Manufacturers' National Bank, the Merchants' National Bank and for extensive estates such as the Walker, the Stephen A. Douglas and others.

[10] XIX Wallace's Reports, 499. Justice Field denied the injunction applied for, Field's ground being that the mere charge that a tax was illegal was not basis enough for an injunction in a suit of equity. Field pointed out that there must be other special circumstances, such as that the tax would produce irreparable injury, etc.

[11] 67 Illinois Reports, 298.

[12] 68 Ibid., 349.

[13] 93 Illinois Reports, 601–613.

[14] 101 Illinois Reports, 595–609.

Fuller's Course as Railroad Attorney.

He was the regular counsel for the Chicago, Burlington and Quincy Railroad. One of the cases pertaining to this railroad in which he appeared, in 1883, is worth citing.

For six years Samuel Warner had worked for the railroad, first as a brakeman and during the last two years as a freight-train conductor. While uncoupling and detaching a freight car in motion on August 20, 1875, Warner threw himself around the corner of the car, expecting to get a foothold on similar steps on the other side, whence he could have reached the rear of the car where the uncoupling had to be done. But the car was not equipped with any such steps — a fact that Warner did not know. The consequence was that Warner lost his balance, was thrown to the track, and his left arm was so crushed and mangled that it had to be amputated.[15]

On the ground that the company was willfully negligent in not providing end steps or ladders for coupling or uncoupling purposes, Warner sued for damages. He was awarded $5,000 damages in the lower court; this judgment was sustained by the Appellate Court. The company appealed to the Illinois Supreme Court; meanwhile six years had gone by without Warner receiving a cent.

Fuller appeared for the railroad company in the Illinois Supreme Court, arguing for a reversal of the verdict. Astonishingly contradictory and pettifogging as they may seem, these were actually the points that he advanced: First, there was no evidence that the loss of Warner's arm did, or would, impair his ability to pursue his business. Second, there was no evidence of the extent of the pain that Warner had suffered, other than the loss of his arm; pain, as an element of damage, could not be inferred from this fact. Third, there was no evi-

---

[15] Case of Chicago, Burlington and Quincy Railroad vs. Samuel Warner, 108 Illinois Reports, 544.

dence of damages — none of nurses' bills incurred, or of any other expense.[16]

' So far as the railroad workers were concerned, Fuller argued that " the master is not bound to throw away his machinery because there may be others better calculated to insure safety." In other words, railroad corporations could ignore the safety of the lives of their workers, which is precisely what they were doing. An enormous number of railroad employés were being killed or maimed annually. Although the railroad corporations were making vast profits, they were contesting every attempt to pass an employers' liability law, and especially a law compelling them to equip their cars with safety appliances. In respect to the liability of railroad companies to passengers, Fuller argued, the rule was different. Warner, he contended, knew that the company used cars without steps or handle, and before attempting to uncouple he should have ascertained whether the car had them or not.

But it must be said that Fuller did not state the real facts, nor apply common-sense logic. If Warner had refused to work on such dangerous cars he would have been without a job and support, and if all other workers had similarly refused, the railroad could not have been operated. At the peril of their lives, the workers were really doing a favor to the company working on its cars.

Justice Mulkey agreed with Fuller that the risk was one of voluntary assumption. Of Fuller's other pleadings he strongly disapproved.

Ironical as it may seem, the fact remains that Mulkey proceeded to argue gravely whether the mangling of an arm, and its consequent amputation, constituted evidence of pain. He decided solemnly that it did. Justice Mulkey then went on to controvert Fuller's fiction that the loss of an arm did not impair Warner's ability to earn his living. The fact that he was

[16] *Ibid.,* 540–541.

forced to abandon his job, Mulkey said, was in evidence before
the jury. " That both arms," he commented, " are useful in
all, and indispensable in most, of the avocations of life is but a
part of the common information of mankind in general, and
hence it required no other proof to establish it. . . ." But,
so the court decided, Warner had voluntarily assumed the risk;
therefore, he was negligent; therefore, the judgment in his favor should be reversed, and he must get no damages.[17] Warner
was consigned to a life of destitution; Fuller at this time was
enjoying an annual income of at least $20,000. In fact, Fuller,
it was said, was a stockholder in the Chicago, Burlington and
Quincy Railroad.

A Multimillionaire's Attorney.

Two Chicago multimillionaires — Marshall Field and Levi
Z. Leiter — quarreled over a party wall, which difference grew
into an extended litigation. As one of Field's attorneys Fuller
eventually won the case.[18] Field was a conspicuous railroad
stockholder; he was a powerful factor in the Chicago, Rock
Island and Pacific Railroad and other railroads;[19] his will revealed that he also owned $1,500,000 of Baltimore and Ohio
Railroad stock, $600,000 of Atchison, Topeka and Santa Fé
Railroad stock; $1,860,000 in stock in the Chicago and North-
western Railroad, and tens of millions of dollars of stock in
fourteen other railroads.

Field was, likewise, one of the largest stockholders in the
Union Traction Company and its associated street railway com-

[17] 108 Illinois Reports, 538–555. (Jan., 1884.) On the Illinois Supreme Court Bench at this time were also Justices Sheldon, Schofield,
Dickey, Scott and Craig, nearly all of whom had been railroad attorneys. For example, Schofield had been attorney for the St. Louis,
Vandalia and Terre Haute Railroad at the time of his election to the
Illinois Supreme Court (67 Illinois Reports, 608, etc.), of which court
he later became Chief Justice.
[18] 118 Illinois Reports, 17.
[19] "Poor's Railroad Manual" for 1890: p. 1097, etc.

panies of Chicago.[20] The methods by which these companies obtained their franchises and controlled Common Council and Legislature were consistently corrupt; the sums spent in purchasing ordinances and legislation were immense.[21] And it may be remarked here that although for more than twenty years from 1865 committees of Chicago citizens were formed time after time to fight this corrupt legislation, Fuller was never one of their number. Other lawyers enlisted, but Fuller was preoccupied advancing the interests of the very capitalists against whom these movements were conducted.

Field was also in almost absolute control of the Pullman Company works by reason of his being the largest owner of stock in that concern. Manufacturing Pullman cars, and employing nearly 20,000 men, the Pullman was a vast corporation, reaping great profits. The trickeries, snares, fraudulent sales and cheatings by which it was alleged the land on which the works were located was originally gotten, were set forth in detail in the suit brought by Speck and others.[22] We have seen how Robert T. Lincoln, president of the Pullman Company, was one of Fuller's most active backers for the Chief Justiceship of the Supreme Court — a fact intimately related, as we shall show later, to a certain notable decision of the Supreme Court of the United States when Fuller was Chief Justice.

Marshall Field, at his death, left a fortune estimated at $140,000,000. It was then discovered that for many years he had owned at least $17,500,000 of taxable personal property on which he had long defrauded the city of taxes. Suit was

---

[20] Norton's " Chicago Traction," p. 142.

[21] See, *Ibid,* in which this long-prevailing corruption is described.

[22] See, Case of Speck *et al.* vs. Pullman Palace Car Company, 121 Illinois Reports, 34. (May, 1887.) The complaint recited that the lands were originally owned by Charles Dunn, who had died in 1869, and that his widow was defrauded out of the property by deceit, the trickery of lawyers and fraudulent sale. Justice Schofield (who, as has been noted, had been a railroad lawyer) decided in favor of the Pullman Company.

brought for $1,700,000 back taxes, but on March 2, 1908, the Field estate compromised by paying the city $1,000,000.[23] It was calculated that the total amount of Field's tax frauds reached fully $3,000,000.

Fuller's Further Corporation Practice.

Fuller was one of the leading counsel for the Chicago Gaslight and Coke Company in its legal contest with the People's Gaslight and Coke Company. Both of these companies had debauched the Common Council and Legislature to get their franchises. The Chicago Gaslight and Coke Company had secured, in 1849, an exclusive franchise for ten years. In 1855 the People's Gaslight and Coke Company obtained a franchise from the Legislature on the plea that it sought to break the monopoly held by that company. But in 1862 both companies formed a combination, and the Chicago Gaslight and Coke Company agreed, for the period of one hundred years, not to lay pipes or sell gas in the territory of the other company. This pool, of course, created a monopoly.

The compact continued until 1886, when the Chicago Gaslight and Coke Company secured a franchise to build a tunnel under the South branch of the Chicago River. Pleading that the Chicago Gaslight and Coke Company threatened to compete and violate its contract, the People's Company applied for an injunction, and obtained it in the Appellate Court. In the Illinois Supreme Court, Fuller, on appeal, argued that a contract to control rates was void. Judge Magruder, in 1887, decided that the court would not aid either party in the enforcement of such an illegal contract. The injunction was dissolved.[24]

[23] On that date a check for the amount was delivered to John R. Thompson, treasurer of Cook County. The Field estate decided to compromise before the action went to trial.

[24] 121 Illinois Reports, 532–542. Seventeen years later, Fuller, as Chief Justice of the Supreme Court of the United States, delivered

These, perhaps, are sufficient examples of Fuller's practice. He was one of the busiest and best-paid corporation attorneys in Chicago; it was estimated that in thirty-two years he had probably tried not less than twenty-five hundred cases, not including cases settled out of court.

One of the exceptions to his long list of pleadings for individual capitalists or large corporations was his being retained by the City of Chicago in the suit of the State against the Illinois Central Railroad. This company had assumed to own, since the year 1869, not less than a thousand acres of formerly submerged lands along the city front of Lake Michigan, on portions of which it had built wharves, docks, piers and warehouses. The act under which this claim was set up had been originally obtained by corruption. In 1873 the Legislature passed a repealing act. When the State brought suit charging unlawful possession and usurpation, the railroad claimed that the repealing act was unconstitutional, as impairing the obligation of a contract. The Circuit Court of the United States, however, decided that the title remained vested in the city.[25] This decision was upheld by the Supreme Court of the United States.[26]

Before considering some of the important decisions of the Supreme Court of the United States under Chief Justice Fuller, it will be advisable to describe certain circumstances, and to give a review of the careers of new Justices successively appointed after he assumed his seat.

that court's decision refusing an application of the People's Gaslight and Coke Company for an injunction to restrain the City of Chicago from enforcing an ordinance limiting gas rates to seventy-five cents per thousand feet.— 194 U. S. Reports, 7.

[25] 33 Federal Reports, 721, and *Ibid.,* 732.

[26] By a bare majority vote of four to three. (146 U. S. Reports, 455.) The ground of the decision was that the legislature held the title to submerged lands under navigable waters in trust, and could not alienate those lands except in such small parcels as public interest might require. Justice Field wrote the court's opinion; it was a commendably creditable decision for Field.

Justice Field's Enemy, Terry, Shot and Killed.

Justice Field, who seems to have been oppressed by the unfortunate faculty of personally stirring adverse public criticism, again came sharply into public notice at this juncture. Judge Terry, of whom we have spoken in a previous chapter, had acted as counsel to Sarah Althea Hill, who claimed that she had been secretly married to Senator William Sharon, a Nevada and California millionaire mine owner. When he died she married Judge Terry and claimed Sharon's estate. The Supreme Court of California decided that there had been a secret marriage contract. But in the United States Circuit Court Justice Field ordered the cancellation of the marriage contract on the ground of forgery. In a burst of rage Mrs. Terry arose in court and asked Field how much he had been paid for his decision. Field held her for contempt.

The old enmity, or rather feud, between Terry and Field now gathered fresh fuel. It was reported (although whether falsely or not, we do not know) that when Field committed Mrs. Terry to jail for a month, Terry drew a bowie knife. At any rate, Field ordered Terry arrested and committed to jail for six months.

On the way north from Los Angeles, on his circuit duties, Justice Field, on the morning of August 14, 1889, stopped at Lathrop, California, for his breakfast. Mr. and Mrs. Terry were there at the time. Terry stepped up to the luncheon stool on which Field sat and slapped his face with the back of his hand. United States Marshall David Nagle then shot Terry dead. Terry was unarmed, but reports had it that Mrs. Terry had a bowie knife and revolver in her hand bag.

Opinion over the affair was divided. Some defenders of Field held that it was a justifiable case of self-protection. Friends of Field asserted that Terry had sworn that he would take Field's life. A considerable section of public opinion condemned the killing as unmitigated murder. Justice Field was

arrested, but released. As for Nagle, he was exonerated by
the courts on the ground that he had done his duty in preserving
the life of a judge.

Field's Nephew, Brewer, Appointed.

Four months after this killing, Field's nephew, David J.
Brewer, was appointed an Associate Justice of the Supreme
Court of the United States.

Brewer was the son of a missionary to Turkey; he had been
graduated from Yale, in 1856; had been a United States Commissioner in Kansas; a judge of the probate and criminal court
in that State from 1861 to 1865; a member of the Kansas Supreme Court from 1870 to 1884, and, in the latter year, had
been appointed a judge of the United States Circuit Court.
According to the bare newspaper reports, Brewer, when nominated for the Supreme Court of the United States, was subjected to serious criticism of his conduct in the appointment
of receivers for the Wabash railroad system, and for some
decisions he had rendered concerning the receivership. It was
a fact that Judge Gresham, who was an incorruptible judge
and who had exposed Gould's fraudulent manipulation of the
Wabash railroad, removed receivers whom Gould and Sage
had caused to be appointed, and caustically denounced the transaction.[27] Brewer's friends explained that the responsibility
was to be charged not to him, but to Judge Treat.

Justice Brown's Corporate Connections.

The next appointee to the Supreme Court was Henry B.
Brown of Detroit, Michigan. He was born in Lee, Massa-

[27] See a detailed account in the *North American Review,* issue of
February, 1888. Gould and Sage, after looting the railroad of millions
of dollars, had thrown it into bankruptcy, and caused the appointment
of Humphreys and Tutt, two of its former directors and officers who
had been part of the directorate that brought the system to bankruptcy.

chusetts; his father was a manufacturer. After leaving Yale he went, in 1859, to Detroit. From 1861, when he was appointed a deputy United States marshall, he held various public offices — was Assistant United States District Attorney, and judge of the Wayne County (Mich.) Court. In 1864 he married Caroline Pitts, the daughter of a rich lumberman, and later returned to the practice of law, forming a partnership with J. S. Newberry and Ashley Pond.

The firm of Newberry and Pond had represented the Amboy, Lansing and Traverse Bay Railroad, the Detroit and Milwaukee Railroad and other railroads and copper-mining and insurance companies.[28] During the time that Brown was a member of the firm of Newberry, Pond and Brown, the firm was counsel for the Atlas Mining Company, and Pond appeared for the Marquette and Ontonagan Railroad and other corporations.[29]

The firm then became Pond and Brown. From 1873 to 1875 it represented such corporations as the Michigan State Insurance Company, the Port Huron Dock Company, the Connecticut Mutual Life Insurance Company and the Lake Superior Ship Canal, Railroad and Iron Company.[30] This last-named company had obtained from Congress, in 1865–1866, a grant of 400,000 acres of swamp lands as assistance in encouraging the building of its canals. But the company caused fraudulent surveys to be made by which it secured vast beds of iron ore. In his annual report for 1885, Commissioner Sparks of the General Land Office, described how its " canal " was only a worthless ditch, and how instead of surveying swamp lands, it had fraudulently appropriated at least 100,000 acres of the richest mineral lands.[31] The suit in question was brought by

[28] XIII Michigan Reports, 382 and 440; XIX *Ibid.*, 393 and 430; XXIII *Ibid.*, 188; etc.
[29] XIII *Ibid.*, 37, and XXVIII *Ibid.*, 290, etc.
[30] XXX *Ibid.*, 39; XXXI *Ibid.*, 7; XXXII *Ibid.*, 235.
[31] House Executive Documents, 1885–1886, Vol. II.

the Attorney-General of Michigan on the score of usurpation and alleged illegal collection of tolls. The company won.

In 1875 President Grant appointed Brown a United States District Court judge in Michigan. Ashley Pond continued his practice as a railroad lawyer; he became general counsel for the Michigan Central Railroad — a Vanderbilt property.[32] Brown went on the Bench of the Supreme Court of the United States, on December 29, 1890, succeeding Justice Miller.

Justice Brown's Interest in a Copper Case.

In addition to being a corporation attorney, Brown was a stockholder. In the case of the appeal of the Detroit Citizens Street Railway Company vs. Detroit which came up before the Supreme Court of the United States, in 1895, " Mr. Justice Brown took no part in the consideration and determination of this petition." [33] Justice Brown was more specific in a case against the Calumet and Hecla Mining Company; he frankly caused it to be inserted in the record that, " Mr. Justice Brown being interested in the result, did not sit in this case and took no part in its decision." [34]

The copper mines of the Calumet and Hecla Mining Company, in Houghton County, Michigan, have been rated as among the richest copper properties in the world. They were obtained in this way: In 1852 the St. Mary's Falls Ship Canal Company secured from Congress a grant of 750,000 acres of public lands for aid in the construction of a canal. A year previously — in 1851 — a voluminous report had been issued by J. W. Foster and J. D. Whitney, Government geologists, giving full reports of the character of the mineral deposits in

[32] " Poor's Railroad Manual " for 1890: p. 1327; IV Supreme Court Reporter, 369, etc.

[33] 163 United States Reports, 683.

[34] Case of Chandler vs. Calumet and Hecla Mining Company, 149 U. S. Reports, 79–95.

the Lake Superior region.[35]   Long before that time it was well known that Lake Superior Indians used copper utensils made by them from native ore.

Now the grants made by Congress to canal companies meant to cover swamp lands.   But by fraudulent surveys they were so manipulated as to comprise the most valuable ore beds.[36] This fact is not only stated in official reports, but it was made the basis of the suit brought by Chandler against the Calumet and Hecla Mining Company.   In his bill of complaint, Chandler detailed the granting of the alleged " swamp " lands by Congress, and claimed an interest.   The decision of the Supreme Court of the United States went against him.

That he tried so hard to establish his claim is not surprising considering the enormous profits that the company was making. For example, Moody thus describes its operations for a certain number of years: " Capital stock, $2,500,000.   Par $25, on which only $12 per share has been paid.   Dividends for the year ended April 30, 1895, 60 per cent., 1896, 100 per cent.; 1897, 120 per cent.; 1898, 160 per cent.; 1899, 280 per cent.; 1900, 320 per cent.; 1901, 260 per cent.; 1902, 100 per cent.; 1903, 140 per cent." [37]   When Quincy A. Shaw, president of the Calumet and Hecla Mining Company, died in 1910, his will filed for probate at Boston. on December 9, 1910, disclosed an estate of $23,000,000.

Justice Shiras, Railroad Lawyer.

George Shiras, Jr., was next appointed to the Supreme Court of the United States, July 19, 1892, by President Harrison to succeed Justice Bradley.[38]   His father was a Pittsburg

[35] U. S. Senate Documents, Special Session, Thirty-second Congress, 1851, Vol. III, Doc. No. 4.

[36] See, Annual Report for 1885, of Commissioner Sparks, of the General Land Office, House Ex. Docs., 1885–1886, Vol. II.

[37] John Moody's " The Truth About The Trusts," p. 39.

[38] From the New York *World*, of January 23, 1892:   " Justice Brad-

brewer who had retired from business in 1840. Practising law in that city from 1856 to the time of his appointment, George Shiras, Jr.'s connections were with large corporations. For twenty years he was associated with the Baltimore and Ohio Railroad in important cases, and he represented the People's Gas Company and other corporations. From 1881 to 1883 his partner was Henry H. Hoyt, who later became director of various powerful banks. During a deadlock of the Pennsylvania Legislature over the election of a United States Senator, in 1881, Shiras was nominated at a secret caucus of Republicans by a majority of two, but two days later the vote was reconsidered, and John J. Mitchell was elected.

Shiras frequently appeared in the courts as the regular counsel for the Pittsburg and Connellsville Railroad Company — a part of the Baltimore and Ohio Railroad system.[39] In the case of the Commonwealth of Pennsylvania vs. the Pittsburg and Connellsville Railroad Company, he, Latrobe and other attorneys for the railroad argued, in 1868, against an action for the forfeiture of the company's franchise.[40]

McClurg, a passenger, having obtained a judgment for injuries, Shiras had the verdict reversed on appeal.[41] Elijah Patterson, a freight-train conductor, had notified the superintendent of the bad construction of a sidetrack connection; the superintendent promised it would be repaired, but it was never attended to. A train on which Patterson was conductor was later derailed and Patterson was severely injured. The successful defense of the railroad in the lower court was that Patterson knew of the danger and had voluntarily exposed him-

ley was, perhaps, the richest member of the Bench, and leaves a fortune of at least $1,000,000." Other newspaper estimates placed Bradley's wealth at from $500,000 to $700,000.

[39] See, 56 Pa. State Reports, 295 (year 1867) ; 58 *Ibid.,* 41 ; 76 *Ibid.,* 392, 489 and 513 ; 77 *Ibid.,* 183 ; 81 *Ibid.,* 111, etc., etc.

[40] 59 *Ibid.,* 435.

[41] 56 Pa. State Reports, 295.

self.   Patterson appealed to the Supreme Court of Pennsylvania.   There Shiras advanced the proposition that " where persons are employed in the same general service, and one of them is injured through the carelessness of another, the employer is not responsible." The Supreme Court of Pennsylvania, in 1875, decided in favor of Patterson.[42]

Shiras also represented James M. Bailey, a director of the Pittsburg and Connellsville Gas, Coal and Coke Company; Shiras was also one of the counsel for the Pittsburg, Virginia and Charlestown Railway Company, for the Monongahela National Bank and sundry other corporations.[43]   When appointed to the Supreme Court of the United States Shiras had an annual income from his practice of (it was estimated) not less than $50,000 a year, and possibly $75,000.   The city of Pittsburg was in the grip of the notoriously corrupt Magee political-capitalist ring, but Shiras took no part in movements antagonistic to Magee; he assiduously adhered to his corporation practice; and some of the very corporations represented by him were foremost in bribing Common Council and Legislature and debauching politicians generally.[44]

[42] 76 Pa. State Reports, 392.

[43] 69 Ibid., 338; 80 Ibid., 35; IV Supreme Court Reporter (Supreme Court of the U. S.), 336, etc.

[44] " The railroads," relates Lincoln Steffens, " began the corruption of the city," and he then proceeds to describe the development and extent of that corruption.   (See, " Pittsburg: A City Ashamed " in " The Shame of the Cities," 149–189.)   Magee's railways, combined into the Consolidated Traction Company, were capitalized at $30,000,000. The extensive " graft " investigation at Pittsburg, in March, 1910, revealed that the officers of the Second National Bank, the Farmers' Deposit National Bank, the Columbia National Bank and other large banks had bribed city officials to favor them as depositories of city funds.   The railroads, it was disclosed, had heavily and continuously bribed members of the Common Council by means (to a considerable extent) of free transportation passes, which the Aldermen then sold at a large profit to themselves.   The ramifications of corruption brought out by this investigation were enormous.   Two score of men who had been or who were members of the City Council were indicted, and a number of those inculpated confessed.

Jackson Succeeds Lamar.

At Justice Lamar's death, in 1893, President Harrison appointed Howell E. Jackson, of Tennessee, to succeed him. Jackson had been associated with railroads before the Civil War. In the winter of 1857–1858 he had been sent to New York by the Mississippi Central Railroad (later the Chicago, St. Louis and New Orleans Railroad) to negotiate its bonds. This he did satisfactorily. After the Civil War he settled at Memphis, Tennessee, becoming a member of the firm of Estes, Jackson and Elliott.

The clients of this firm were mostly large banks and other corporations.[45]   In 1874, a year after the death of his first wife, Jackson married Mary Elizabeth Harding, a daughter of General W. G. Harding, owner of the renowned Belle Meade Farm. It was currently reported in the newspapers that Jackson's election as United States Senator, in 1881, was accomplished by the use of money, but of this charge there is no definite proof in the records. Howell E. Jackson, next to his brother, was reputed to be the richest man in Tennessee. President Cleveland appointed him, in 1887, to the United States Circuit Court. An examination of his decisions shows that they were uniformly favorable to corporations.

A fact commented upon was that the chief proposer and pusher of Jackson for the Supreme Court was Thomas C. Platt, the Republican boss of New York State, and that the plant of the Tennessee Coal and Iron Company,[46] of which Platt was president, was located in the circuit in which Jackson sat, and in which he had handed down decisions favorable to that corporation. Doubtless the additional fact that Jackson

---

[45] See, Heiskell's Tennessee Reports, Vols. IX, X, etc., etc.; Caldwell's Reports, Vol. IV, etc.

[46] This corporation was an extremely large one. It owned its own sources of iron ore and coal supply, estimated, in 1907, at from 500,-000.000 to 700,000,000 tons of iron ore and two billion tons of coal. It is now a constituent part of the Steel Trust.

was a personal friend of President Harrison had its weight in determining his appointment to the Supreme Court of the United States.

Here for urgent and appropriate reasons that will explain themselves, it will be necessary to defer describing further appointments, and to begin the narrative of some of the decisions of the Supreme Court under Chief Justice Fuller.

The Timber Monopoly.

Decisions favoring railroads were so common that a description of them would entail an interminable mass of detail. A typical case, deserving adequate treatment, was a particularly remarkable decision by which the Supreme Court deliberately turned over to a group of railroad-lumber syndicate capitalists vast holdings of standing timber, thus directly making possible the concentration of the timber supply in a monopoly closely controlled by a few men.

Recently a report issued by Herbert Knox Smith, United States Commissioner of Corporations, comprehensively described this monopoly and its workings. ". . . Only forty years ago," the report stated, "at least three-fourths of the timber now standing was (it was estimated) publicly owned. Now about four-fifths of it is privately owned. The great bulk of it passed from Government to private hands through (a) enormous railroad, canal and wagon-road grants by the Federal Government; (b) direct government sales in unlimited quantities at $1.25 an acre; (c) certain public land laws, great tracts being assembled in spite of the legal requirements for small holdings. . . ." Elsewhere the report says: "In the last forty years concentration has so proceeded that 195 holders, many interrelated, have now practically one-half the privately owned timber in the investigation area (which contains eighty per cent. of the whole). This formidable process of concentration, in timber and in land, certainly involves grave future possibilities of impregnable monopolistic conditions, whose far-reaching consequences to society it is now difficult to anticipate fully, or to overestimate. . . ." [47]

This report, while thorough and authentic within its prescribed limits, omits the important fact that it was decisions of the Supreme Court of the United States which were largely responsible for these conditions. One of these decisions and its antecedent and later circumstances were as follows:

The Military Wagon-Road Grants.

Congress, on February 25, 1867, had passed an act granting about 600,000 acres to the Dallas Military Road Company as aid in the construction of a military wagon road from Dallas City on the Columbia River, to Fort Boise, on the Snake River, Idaho. Congress had granted other tracts to other wagon-road companies; the total grants to all of the companies were about 1,781,000 acres. These areas comprised the finest timber lands in the Northwest. The Willamette Valley and Cascade Mountain Wagon Road Company obtained patents for some 440,000 acres. One of these acts granting an area fraudulently extended to about 720,000 acres to the Oregon Central Military Road Company, was passed on July 2, 1864,— at the identical time when, as we have seen, the Union Pacific Railway Company was distributing $436,000 in bribes to get its land grant increased and its charter altered.

The act of Congress of July 8, 1866, provided, however, that if certain military wagon roads were not completed in five years, the grants were to be forfeited, and revert to the Government.

[47] " Summary of Report of the Commissioner of Corporations on the Lumber Industry, Part I, Standing Timber " (Feb. 13, 1911): pp. 3 and 8.

Manipulation of the Grants.

None of these companies made the slightest attempts to build the roads. In order to fortify themselves against any possibility of forfeiture of land grants, they immediately began to sell or mortgage the grants to " innocent parties." That they had not earned the grants and that they were selling domains which they held conditionally only did not trouble them in the least. Familiar with many successive precedents set by the Supreme Court of the United States from the time of Chief Justice Marshall, they knew that if action for forfeiture were brought against them on the ground of non-performance and fraud, the " innocent purchasers " could step in, and plead that they knew nothing of any frauds and had bought in good faith.

By collusion with officials, the companies obtained title, and then proceeded to sell or mortgage the lands. For the sum of $125,000 (at least, it was so claimed) the Dallas Military Road Company sold its land grant to Edward Martin, who later disposed of it to the Eastern Oregon Land Company. The Oregon Central Military Road Company conveyed its land grant in bulk to the California and Oregon Land Company. The Willamette and Cascade Mountain Wagon Road Company transferred its interest to the Oregon Pacific Railroad Company and others, and gave a mortgage to the Farmers' Loan and Trust Company of New York.

The Fraudulent Methods Disclosed.

The people of Oregon were aroused over this bold appropriation of more than a million acres of the most valuable timber lands. They denounced it as a barefaced theft, which it was, in truth; the roads had never been constructed. Many years of forcible agitation were required to get the Oregon Legislature to take some action. Successive legislatures were controlled by the land-grabbing syndicate. At last, in 1885, the

Oregon Legislature did move. It recited the frauds committed, and memorialized Congress to pass an act for the institution of proceedings for the forfeiture of the grants. This Congress did on March 2, 1889.

The Government then brought suits against the Dallas Military Road Company, the Oregon Central Road Company, the Willamette and Cascade Mountain Company and others.

The Government alleged as to the Dallas Company: " That the road was never constructed in whole, or in part; that through the fraudulent representations of the officers, stockholders and agents of the company, the Governor of Oregon [George L. Woods] was deceived and induced to issue a certificate . . . and that relying upon this certificate, the patents to portions of the lands had been issued to the company. . . ." [48]

In the case of the Oregon Central Military Road Company, the Government set forth that by the same fraud and deceit, it had obtained a certificate from Governor Addison C. Gibbs, in 1866, that portions of the road had been built. The Government's bill of complaint went on to say " that it was not true that the [first] fifty miles of road had been constructed; that in order to procure the certificate . . . the company fraudulently pointed out to the governor a county road to which the company never had a legal right, and led the governor to believe that the road had been constructed by the company. . . ." [49]

Concerning the manner in which the Willamette Company had secured its lands the Government charged that the company " fraudulently represented to the acting governor of Oregon that the road had been constructed as required by law for a distance of 180 miles, they knowing that such representations were false, and that the road had never been constructed at all; that such representations were made for the purpose of fraudulently procuring from the acting governor a certificate . . .;

[48] 41 Federal Reports, 494.   [49] Ibid., 619.

that the acting governor did not examine, or cause to be examined, any part of the 180 miles," etc., etc.[50]

These cases originally came up before Judge Lorenzo Sawyer, in 1890, in the United States Circuit Court, in Oregon. As we have noted, Judge Sawyer was regarded with great friendliness by the Pacific railroad interests. Judge Sawyer ignored the charges of fraud. He took the formal ground that the Governor of Oregon was the agent of the United States, and that when he certified that the roads had been built he was the sole deciding authority and his certificate was to be accepted as final evidence. Anyway, Judge Sawyer said, the claims put forward by the Government were stale.[51]

The Supreme Court Validates the Frauds.

The action now went up to the Supreme Court of the United States. The old subterfuge of the " innocent purchaser " was now again pleaded, and successfully. Justice Brewer wrote the decisions covering these associated cases. On March 6, 1893, Brewer decided against the United States. The purchasers from the original companies, he said, " knew nothing wrong in respect to the title, or the proceedings of the road company, or any officials connected with the title." And harking back to Marshall's celebrated precedents in the Arrendondo and other cases, he held that where the Government delegated power to an official to certify, the evidence of that official was final and conclusive.

Yet Brewer was forced to admit that the allegations that the certificates had been obtained by fraud were *uncontested*. " Therefore," said he on this point, " as the inquiry is now presented, it must be in the light of the uncontested allegation that the certificates were obtained through the fraudulent acts

[50] 41 Federal Reports, 624–626.
[51] *Ibid.,* 501.

of the road company." [52]   But, he quickly went on, the purchasers were innocent; they knew that the governor had certified, and thought the title valid.   There were other points in the
decision, but these were the main grounds.[53]

Justice Brewer's Doctrine.

In a later decision, Justice Brewer, it may be parenthetically
remarked, openly avowed that fraud mattered nothing, so long
as *legal title* was held.

This nephew of Justice Field was even franker than Field
himself in justifying the products of fraud and theft.   Justice
Brewer, on November 12, 1894, laid down the naked doctrine
that it was immaterial how an owner got his property.   " He
may have made his fortune by dealing in slaves, as a lobbyist,
or in any other way obnoxious to public condemnation; but, if
he has acquired the legal title to his property, he is protected
in its possession, and cannot be disturbed until the receipt of
the actual cash value.   The same rule controls if railroad property is to be appropriated.   No inquiry is open as to whether
the owner has received gifts from State or individuals, or
whether he has, as owner, managed the property well or ill, or
so as to acquire a large fortune therefrom.   It is enough that
he owns the property — has the legal title; and, if so owning,
he must be paid the actual cash value of the property. . . ." [54]

Could there be a more undisguised justification of every
species of fraud and theft?   In more cautious phraseology the
doctrine had been often handed down from the Supreme Court

[52] See, 148 U. S. Reports, 44. Among the attorneys for the companies were Dolph, Ballinger, Mallory, Simon and others, some of
whom became United States Senators.

[53] *Ibid.*, 31–49.

[54] See, Case of Ames vs. Union Pacific Company, 64 Federal Reports,
176.

bench, but here was Justice Brewer serving blunt declaration that irrespective of what flagrant fraud and general scoundrelism were used, the Supreme Court of the United States would justify it and sanction the results, provided the form of getting legal title, which is to say, paper title, was accomplished.

Results of the Wagon-Roads Decision.

One of the effects of the wagon-road land grant cases may be seen by reverting to Commissioner Herbert Knox Smith's report on the timber monopoly. Of the ownership of timber lands in the Pacific States and Northwest, he details that the Southern Pacific Railroad Company, the Weyerhaeuser Timber Company, and the Northern Pacific Railway Company (including their subsidiary companies) own 238,000,000,000 feet of standing timber.

The timber holdings of the Southern Pacific Railroad Company extend from Portland, Oregon, to Sacramento — a distance of 682 miles. " This holding," he further explains, " consists of the unsold part of the Government land grants in Oregon and Northern California held by the Oregon and California Railroad Company and the Central Pacific Railroad Company, subsidiaries of the Southern Pacific Railroad Company." The timber holding of the Southern Pacific Railroad Company is the largest in the United States, amounting to more than 106,000,000,000 feet, of which about 71,000,000,000 feet is in Oregon.[55] The Weyerhaeuser Timber Company owns 96,000,000,000 feet of timber, and the Northern Pacific Railway Company about 36,000,000,000 feet. Considerable of this area was appropriated by means of the military wagon-roads decisions.

[55] The Government is now suing to annul title to the Southern Pacific lands in Oregon for non-compliance with the terms of the original grants. It has also, it may be added, brought an action against the same company to recover 6,100 acres of oil lands in Kern County, California, alleging that they were patented by fraud.

" The present commercial value of the privately owned standing timber in the country, not including the value of the land," the report further says, " is estimated (though such an estimate must be very rough) as at least $6,000,000,000. Ultimately the consuming public will have to pay such prices for lumber as will give this timber a far greater value." [56]

Here, at the risk of repetition, we will again observe that Justice Field, Brewer's uncle, had been placed on the Supreme Court Bench at the solicitation of Leland Stanford, one of the four magnates then controlling the Central and the Southern Pacific railroads with all their auxiliary and adjunct corporations. And Stanford was a powerful member of the United States Senate at the time of Brewer's appointment to the Supreme Court of the United States.

Another Great Railroad Grant Validated.

The decisions that we have narrated are but a few typical cases of the many determined by the Supreme Court of the United States favorable to railroad corporations. Another characteristic decision written by Brewer was that finally validating an enormous land grant to the Des Moines Navigation and Railway Company.

This company, as we have related, had obtained by proved briberies,[57] the passage of an act by Congress, in 1846, granting it an area five miles (in alternate sections) on each side of the Des Moines River, Iowa. Subsequently, the company claimed that the grant included lands along the entire course of the river to its source. If this claim held, the company would get many hundreds of thousands additional acres.

[56] " Summary of Report of the Commissioner of Corporations on the Lumber Industry," Part I: 5, 25, 26, etc.
[57] The report of the select committee of Congress exposing the corruption used is set forth in Report No. 243, Vol. III, Reports of Committees, Thirty-fourth Congress, Third Session, 1856–57. The corruption fund amounted to $100,000.

The contention was submitted in 1849 to Robert J. Walker, Secretary of the Treasury, which department then exercised jurisdiction over the public lands. Walker, as we have seen, had himself profited notoriously from land grabbing. In his opinion on the issue, Walker decided that a stretch of 900,000 acres above Raccoon Fork lay within the grant.[58] His successor, Thomas Ewing, held the contrary. So the question remained unsettled until, in 1858, 1860 and 1861, the company lobbied acts through Congress and the Iowa Legislature — acts so ingeniously worded that they seemed to be for the interests of actual settlers, but were in reality disguised measures for the company's benefit.

Litigation, however, continued for forty years. In 1889 the Government brought a suit to reclaim the lands from the company. The grant, it charged, had been merely given by legislative enactment upon a trust for a distinct purpose. That purpose was to improve the navigation of the river. But, so the Government alleged, the company " did but a very small fraction of the work it pretended to do; it abandoned the undertaking covered by its contract." Notwithstanding this abandonment it grabbed a " vast land grant." On the other hand " thousands of hard-working pioneers have settled and made' their homes upon the lands." Then, also, other railroad companies claimed the lands under their grants.

" This litigation," declared the Government, " is in the interests of bona-fide settlers against speculators who have appropriated these lands in violation of law and of the principles of common honesty. . . ."[59] The Supreme Court of the United States, in January, 1892, decided in favor of the Des Moines Navigation and Railway Company; Justice Brewer delivered its opinion.

[58] See, Case of Dubuque and Pacific Railroad Company vs. Litchfield, XXIII Howard, 85.
[59] U. S. vs. Des Moines Navigation and Railway Company, 142 U. S. Reports, 540.

A Legislature's "Good Faith."

Instead of admitting (what the fact was) that the Government was acting directly for the settlers, Brewer diverted the point in this fashion: The United States, he said, was only a nominal party " whose aid is sought to destroy the title of the company "; therefore, the defense of laches — that it was a stale claim — should be sustained. Justice Brewer well knew that no statute of limitations ran against the Government; hence his object in relegating the Government as a nominal party. He also was not aware of the fact that bitter contests between corporation and settlers had gone on continuously, and that the claims of the settlers had never become dormant.

But what of the original acts lobbied through by fraud and bribery? Out again came Marshall's time-worn fiction. " Knowledge and good faith of a legislature," echoed Brewer, " are not open to question, but the presumption is conclusive that it acted in full knowledge and good faith. . . ." [60] The records were full of evidences of bribery, but the Supreme Court pretended to be innocent of knowing them, or even of giving them credit.

Without examining this decision further it is only necessary to draw a parallel between it and that in the Illinois Central Railroad water-front case to show the glaring inconsistency that the Supreme Court continuously betrayed.

In the Illinois Central case the Supreme Court (by a vote of four to three) decided, as we have seen, that the Legislature held the submerged water-front lands in Chicago in trust for the people.

But in the Des Moines Navigation and Railway Company case, it repudiated the Government's contention that the Iowa lands were held in similar trust.

It may be pertinently inquired, if one kind of property was held in trust for the people, why not all other kinds?

[60] *Ibid.,* 543.

By such decisions the Supreme Court revealed itself as an arbitrary, dictatorial body, often contradicting its own dogmas, and fashioning constructions as it pleased, only to upset those constructions when the dominant capitalist interests so required it.

Justice Field Serves Notice.

Indeed, on one noted occasion, Justice Field in his apparent anxiety to be of service to the Central Pacific Railroad so far transgressed the ordinary rules of judicial procedure and prudent caution, that his action caused scandal even among the legal fraternity. In a suit brought by California against the Central Pacific, he announced that if that State attempted to force its stand, an injunction could be applied for and would undoubtedly be granted.[61]   Now as he was the very Supreme Court Justice who presided over the California circuit, his announcement was equivalent to notifying the Central Pacific that it should apply to him for an injunction and would get it. This kind advice Field gave at a stage in the suit when no steps whatever had yet been taken for any such writ.

In another noted case, Field's nephew, Brewer, wrote a Supreme Court decision which, in order to validate a succession of land claims, absolutely contradicted and contravened a dictum that, for the same purposes, had been followed since Marshall's day.

A Memorable Decision.

The case was that of Camou vs. the United States, for confirmation of a private land claim of 20,034.62 acres, near Santa Cruz, Arizona.   This land was claimed under an alleged grant and sale made by the Mexican authorities, in 1827–1828.   In 1853, President Santa Anna of Mexico issued a decree declaring that " the public lands, as the exclusive property of the nation, never could have been alienated by virtue of decrees,

[61] Central Pacific Railroad vs. California, 162 U. S. Reports, 128.

orders and enactments of the legislatures, governments or local authorities." Article II of the decree ordered that all sales or grants made without the approval of the Federal Government, according to law, were null and void. Section III provided for the recovery of these lands, and Section IV prohibited their confirmation. A month later, Santa Anna signed a treaty with the United States by which that part of Arizona comprised in the Gadsden purchase, was transferred to the United States. The Camou claim was in this territory.

Another decree issued by Santa Anna, on July 5, 1854, was even more specific and drastic. It practically annulled an immense number of grants which had been obtained unlawfully or by fraud and collusion.[62] Naturally enough, the holders of these and other claims struck back by manufacturing a revolution, and Santa Anna was deposed. His successor, Juan Alvarez, a creature of the land appropriators, issued a decree repealing Santa Anna's decrees, and declaring the titles valid.

Thirty-seven years later — in 1891 — Camou filed claim for the confirmation of the tract claimed by him. Meanwhile, rich mining deposits had been discovered in that locality. The Court of Private Land Claims decided in favor of the Government. Santa Anna's decrees, it held, were valid. He was President of Mexico, and the United States Government had recognized him as such when it negotiated the Gadsden Purchase with him. Accordingly, the Court of Private Land Claims held, his decrees had to be accepted as authoritative.

Camou appealed to the Supreme Court of the United States. Seldom if ever, had this Court been put in a more ticklish or embarrassing position. In the cases in which it had validated titles to tens of millions of acres in Florida, Louisiana, Missouri, California and other sections it had consistently held that the certificate, of the officials in office was final and conclusive, even if the tenure of those officials were brief, and

[62] These decrees are set forth in full in 171 U. S. Reports, 288–289.

changes and revolutions constantly upheaved new men into authority.[63]

So far as Mexican law was concerned the Supreme Court of the United States could not apply its celebrated dictum that no legislation could be passed impairing the sacred obligation of a contract. On the other hand, if the decision of the Court of Private Land Claims were sustained it would mean that titles to vast areas of land covered by alleged Mexican grants, including gold, silver, copper and other mines of fabulous riches, would be declared defective.

The Supreme Court Finds a Way Out.

The Supreme Court of the United States was in a quandary. How was it to get around the admitted facts?

By an extraordinary decision it achieved the feat of squaring the circle to its own satisfaction. First it admitted (what it could not deny) that Santa Anna had been the actual and recognized President, and that the United States had " rightfully dealt with him in a political way in the negotiation and purchase of territory." But Brewer went on with a species of reasoning that no other court in the world would or could have used. " When," he said, " the courts are called upon to inquire as to personal rights existing in the ceded territory, a mere declaration by the *temporary executive* cannot be deemed absolutely and finally controlling. . . . It is going too far

[63] Justice Brewer was not ignorant of the fact that Mexican governors fraudulently and indirectly made grants to themselves. At the exact time of his decision in the Camou case, the admitted facts in the case of Faxon vs. U. S. revealed that, in 1842, Governor Manuel Gandara, of Sonoro, boldly seized lands belonging to the Indian pueblo, and granted them to his brother-in-law, Francisco Aguilar, to be held in trust for him (Gandara). The purchase money was supplied by Gandara. (171 U. S. Reports, 246.)

It is interesting to observe that Francis J. Heney, who later was so much puffed up as an exposer of corruption, was Faxon's attorney in this case. It is also worth noting that the Supreme Court of the United States decided that Gandara never had been vested with power to make the grant. Compare with decison in the Camou case.

to hold that the mere declaration of law made by a *temporary dictator,*[64] never enforced as against an individual grantee in possession of lands, is to be regarded as operative and determinative of the latter's rights." Brewer concluded, " We think this arbitrary declaration made by a temporary dictator was not potent to destroy the title." [65]

The decision of the Court of Private Land Claims was reversed; and that railroad, ·mining and other corporations, instead of the Government, now hold incalculably rich areas of copper, gold and silver mines, oil and timber lands and other natural resources, is due to that decision and accompanying decisions of the Supreme Court of the United States. To say that the Southern Pacific Railroad was one of the corporations interested is but stating a fact.

An Administration of Railroad Lawyers.

During Cleveland's administration, new Justices came on the Supreme Court Bench. One of these appointments was that of United States Senator Edward D. White, whose career we shall describe in a later chapter. The other was that of Rufus W. Peckham. Before reviewing Peckham's career, it is important to summarize an especially notable decision which was argued just before Peckham went on the Bench.

President Cleveland himself had been a railroad attorney,

[64] General Santa Anna was elected President of Mexico for the term beginning April 1, 1833. He filled that office from 1841 to 1845. Deposed and exiled, he was recalled and made President in 1846, and commanded the army in the Mexican War with the United States. After Scott's occupation of Mexico, he resigned, but was recalled by the army and made president in April, 1853. A revolution of the land appropriators drove him into exile in August, 1855.

[65] See, Case of Camou vs. U. S., 171 U. S. Reports, 277–291. Also similar case of Perrin vs. U. S., *Ibid.*, 292. United States Senator John T. Morgan was Perrin's attorney. Morgan had long been the law partner of John W. Lapsley, so conspicuous in the Texas land frauds. Early in his political career, Morgan was attorney for the Selma and Gulf Railroad, of which Lapsley was a director. See, 45 Alabama Reports, 698 (year 1871), and 46 *Ibid.*, 235, etc.

he had represented the Canada Southern Railway and other corporations. Likewise many of the members of his cabinet, or his close associates, were railroad attorneys or railroad stockholders. Attorney-General Olney had been a director of the Philadelphia, Wilmington and Baltimore Railroad,[66] now an integral part of the Pennsylvania Railroad system. Olney had also been counsel for the Eastern Railroad Company, the Framingham and Lowell Railroad and other railroads.[67] William C. Whitney, who had been Secretary of the Navy under Cleveland's first administration, was the chief promoter and campaign fund accumulator 'for Cleveland's renomination and reëlection in 1892. Whitney was allied by marriage with Senator Henry B. Payne, railroad magnate and treasurer of the Standard Oil Company. Whitney, at this time, was associated with other capitalists in control of the Metropolitan Street Railway Company of New York. According to the specific charges uttered and published by Col. W. N. Amory, these " financiers " stole at least $30,000,000 by the manipulation of that company, and an estimated $60,000,000 in addition.[68]

Whitney had been associated in 1884–1885 with William H. Vanderbilt, the Rockefellers, Stephen B. Elkins, D. O. Mills and other capitalists in the Southern Pennsylvania Railroad transaction — a very remarkable piece of profitable manipulation and

[66] " Poor's Railroad Manual " for 1880, p. 381.
[67] 124 Mass. Reports, 520 and 528; 130 *Ibid.*, 195; 133 *Ibid.*, 115, etc.
[68] See Amory's '" The Truth About Metropolitan," 1906, in which the figures and *modus operandi* are set forth at length. Amory has never been sued for libel, nor have his facts been shown erroneous. Much of the corruption charged against the Metropolitan Street Railway Company was confirmed by the testimony before the New York Legislative ("Graft Hunt") Committee, in September, 1910. It was then specifically revealed that the bribery of prominent members of the Legislature was an habitual performance, and that the corruption fund annually used was not merely considerable, but great. Another form of corruption was that of contributions to capitalist political parties. In the year 1902, for example, the Metropolitan Street Railway Company contributed $18,000 to the New York State Democratic Committee and $25,000 to the Republican State Committee.

duplicity described elsewhere.[69] Whitney was in the closest touch with the great capitalist interests. So, also, was Daniel S. Lamont, Cleveland's former private secretary, and Secretary of War under Cleveland's second administration. Subsequent developments revealed him associated with J. Pierpont Morgan, George F. Baker and other powerful capitalists in the Northern Securities Company, illegally formed to combine the interests of the Northern Pacific Railroad and the Great Northern Railroad.[70]

The United States Senate was filled with railroad attorneys or magnates: Allison, Spooner, Gorman, Aldrich (whose daughter married John D. Rockefeller, Jr.), Hoar and many other representatives of railroad or associated interests were conspicuous in that body. One of the most eminent Senators, Cushman K. Davis, had represented Russell Sage and had also been attorney for Hill's Great Northern Railway.[71] The Senators belonging to the capitalist interests were in the majority, and held control over the confirmation of appointments.

But at this juncture there was a group of men in both branches of Congress who, while comparatively small in number, were able by their persistence and agitation to exert an influence on legislation and to expose predatory bills. These were the representatives of the Populist Party, which in the election of 1892 polled more than a million votes, and put five Senators and ten Representatives in Congress. The old political parties viewed this formidable vote with dread and apprehension. It was essentially a middle-class movement. This was the reason at that particular time why its progress and strength evoked dismay among the great capitalists, who were as yet very far from the final process of crushing the middle class and consummating their movement for concen-

[69] In the "History of the Great American Fortunes," Vol. II: 208–210.
[70] See Case of Northern Securities Company vs. U. S., 193 U. S. Reports, 202. Lamont was sued by the Government jointly with Morgan, Baker, Stetson, etc.
[71] 161 U. S. Reports, 702; 163 Ibid., 653, etc.

tration of control of all transportation systems and industry. Few as the Populist representatives in Congress were, they had behind them this large voting strength. Moreover, even a few forceful men in Congress then proved themselves able to compel the majority to make a certain concession.

The Income-Tax Bill.

This concession was the passage of the bill for the taxation of incomes. Bitterly opposed, the income-tax bill became a law in 1894 without President Cleveland's signature. On five different occasions the Supreme Court of the United States had declared the income tax constitutional.

The large capitalist interests were determined to do away with this law by one means or another. To collect a specific new tax it was necessary — at least it was held to be so — that Congress should pass an appropriation for that purpose. Although the Government had already begun preparations to collect the tax, the Secretary of the Treasury, Carlisle, pretended that he had no funds for the purpose; this was the same Carlisle who in 1895 turned over a bond issue, under circumstances of the greatest scandal, to a syndicate headed by J. Pierpont Morgan, thus virtually giving that syndicate a profit of $18,000,000. Morgan's lawyer, Francis Lynde Stetson, had been Cleveland's law partner from 1889 to 1892, and was now a frequent confidential visitor to the White House.

A Bit of Secret History.

What happened next was related to this author by Senator Pettigrew. " The House," he said, " passed an urgency deficit bill appropriating $250,000 to collect the tax. When this bill came before the Senate, Senator Quay of Pennsylvania telephoned me to come to his house. There I met a certain Standard Oil magnate. Quay argued that the Treasury Department had been tampered with, and urged me to say so in the Senate, and to get me and the other four Senators to vote against the bill. His object, of course, was to defeat the bill, so that the Treasury Department could again fall back upon the excuse that it had no available funds with which to collect the tax. 'There's $250,000 for you, if you do this,' Quay assured me. I refused."

The bill was passed. There was now only one possible way to get rid of the income tax act; this was to have it declared unconstitutional by the Supreme Court of the United States. The preliminaries to an action were thus arranged:

The board of directors of the Farmers' Loan and Trust Company met and passed a resolution that they would voluntarily pay the income tax, which notice was sent to all of the stockholders. One of the prominent capitalists in the company, Pollock, then brought a suit to restrain the company from paying the tax.

When the case was argued before the Supreme Court of the United States, Clarence A. Seward represented Pollock, and Joseph H. Choate, a prominent corporation attorney, was the Farmers' Loan and Trust Company's principal counsel.[72] To neutralize the rebuttal that the Supreme Court during past times had itself on no less than five occasions held that the income tax was valid, Choate submitted a lengthy list of precedents to persuade the court that it did not have to follow its own precedents!

Justice Jackson was ill at his home in Tennessee, which left eight Justices sitting. From later developments it is quite clear that at first five members of the whole body were opposed to declaring the income tax unconstitutional. On April 8, 1895, the Supreme Court declared some of the clauses of the act unconstitutional but the main point was not passed upon until May 20, 1895.

[72] In the New York *Times,* issue of June 2, 1907, the statement was made that Choate received a fee of $200,000 for his argument in this case.

In the meantime, Justice Jackson, although sick and near death, was urgently solicited to hurry to Washington to participate in the final vote. According to a despatch in the New York *World*, published May 7, 1895, "the Baltimore and Ohio Railroad which, as a corporation, was anxious to have the income tax declared unconstitutional, was eager to land Jackson in Washington. A sleeping car was sent to Belle Meade to enable him to get a comfortable sleep and to journey with the least fatigue." That this insinuation against Jackson was without foundation was soon shown.

A Justice Changes His Mind.

When the final vote was taken, it turned out that one Justice had changed his mind, "over night," and arrayed himself against the income tax. This Justice was said to be Shiras who, as we have seen, came from the same State as Senator Quay, and who had been counsel at Pittsburg for the Baltimore and Ohio Railroad system. The pro-income tax newspapers freely stated that the vacillating Justice was Shiras, and denounced him. This tergiversation caused a very consequential sensation, and was bitterly commented upon in the speeches and declarations of supporters of the income tax. But, of course, none of Shiras' critics were so venturesome as to make specific charges of improper motives or acts; had such charges been made, no scintilla of proof could have been discovered in the records.

The Income Tax Declared Unconstitutional.

By a vote of five to four the Supreme Court declared the whole income tax act unconstitutional, in that it was a direct tax and violated the Constitution by making no provision for an apportionment among the States according to the population.

One of the reasons given by Justice Field in declaring the income tax unconstitutional was that it would reduce judicial salaries; he pointed out, with great seriousness and solicitude, that the judges were protected by that clause of the Constitution which provides that their compensation " shall not be diminished during their continuance in office "!

Justices Brown, Jackson, Harlan and White entered a vigorous dissenting opinion.[73] ". . . By its present construction of the Constitution," said Harlan, " the Court for the first time in all its history declares that our Government has been so framed that in matters of taxation for its support and maintenance those who have incomes derived from the renting of real estate or from the leasing or using of tangible property, bonds, stock, and investments of whatever kind, have privileges that cannot be accorded to those having incomes derived from the labor of their hands or the exercise of their skill or the use of their brains."

But this decision was only one of successive decisions fostering the growth of capitalism, and conceding its increasing demands, while at the same time other important decisions were forthcoming inimical to the working class and aimed to undermine, if not destroy, its organized defenses. The aggrandizing of plutocracy and hostile decrees against working-class action went hand in hand in the productions of the Supreme Court of the United States. What these decisions were, and the circumstances and forces behind them, are related in the next chapter.

[73] Chief Justice Fuller wrote the majority decision. In the opinion rendered on April 8, 1895, it was decided that rents from real estate were not taxable by Congress without interstate apportionment. (157 U. S. Reports, 429.) The final decision of May 20 exempted the entire income from direct taxation by Congress, whether that income were derived from rents or from any other sources, unless the tax were apportioned among the States as respected population. (158 U. S. Reports, 601.) Chief Justice Walter Clark of the North Carolina Supreme Court estimated that that change of a single vote saved the rich at least a billion dollars a year.

CHAPTER XV

THE SUPREME COURT UNDER CHIEF JUSTICE FULLER
(CONTINUED)

Seven days after its obliterating the income-tax law, the Supreme Court of the United States handed down a decision which was then regarded, and has been since, by both legal profession and lay public, as one of the most extraordinary on record.

The Pullman Workers' Strike.

This decision was in the Debs case, which was a result of the great strike of the railway workers in 1894. That strike originated in the grievances of the workers in the Pullman Company's shops. Organized in 1867 to build sleeping cars, the Pullman Company, by methods which we have already described,[1] possessed itself of the title to five hundred acres of land near Chicago. In addition to constructing its plant, it used two hundred acres for the building of what it called a " model " town. In this it accordingly owned the houses, the water and gas supply — and, in brief, controlled the town of Pullman absolutely. For its flimsy, congested habitations it charged its workers $18 a month rental; the cost of gas to the Pullman Company was thirty-three cents a thousand feet, yet the Company's tenants, comprising its own workers, had to pay $2.25 a thousand feet; taking advantage of the com-

---

[1] In the preceding chapter, as set forth in the Case of Speck *et al.* vs. Pullman, by deceit, fraudulent sales and other methods therein detailed.

plaisance of municipal officials, the company bought water at four cents a thousand gallons, and charged its tenants ten cents a thousand gallons for that same water. For the mere privilege of having shutters on the houses, the occupants were taxed fifty cents a month.

The average yearly pay of the Company's wage workers was $613.86. But few of the workers ever received their wages in cash. Tenants of the company, their " debts " to the company were subtracted from the wages due. So greatly were they exploited, that numerous witnesses testified before the Special Commission appointed later by President Cleveland that at times their bi-weekly checks amounted to sums varying from fifty cents to one dollar. Nor did the company produce witnesses to disprove these statements.

When, in the year 1893, a panic was in process, the company reduced wages one-fourth, yet it made no reduction whatever in its charges for rent, water, gas and other necessities. The company asserted that its diminution of business and profits compelled this reduction in wages. But the report of the Government's Special Commission subsequently appointed to investigate the causes of the strike, showed that the Pullman Company's statement was not only untrue, but flagrantly so. This report, prepared in 1895, detailed how the company's capital had been increased from $1,000,000 in 1867 to $36,-000,000 in 1894, and how " its prosperity has enabled the company to pay two per cent. quarterly dividends." In certain years, however, the dividends had ranged from nine and one-half to twelve per cent. The Special Commission further reported that the company had, in addition, laid by a reserve fund of profits in the form of a surplus of $25,000,000 which had not been divided. For the year ending July 31, 1893, the distributed dividends amounted to $2,520,000, and the wages for that year were $7,223,719.51. In the ensuing year, when wages were reduced one-fourth, and went down to $4,471,-

701.39, the stockholders reaped an even greater amount in dividends than in the preceding year, namely, $2,880,000.[2]

Hence, it is evident that the remonstrances of the Pullman workers against the intolerable conditions under which they had to labor and exist were more than well founded. The company refusing to consider their grievances, the workers, on May 11, 1894, declared a strike. The interests of the Pullman Company and nearly all of the large railroad systems were closely associated; the same magnates were often found as stockholders in both; and by reason of its immense profits, the company was continually extending its holdings in railroad lines. At present the only three railroads in which the Pullman Company has no interest are the St. Paul, the New York, New Haven and Hartford, and the Great Northern.

The Great Railway Strike of 1894.

It was, therefore, with a view to compelling the Pullman Company to come to terms that the American Railway Union, under the leadership of Eugene V. Debs, declared a general sympathetic strike. But there were other strong reasons. For twelve years the General Managers' Association, representing twenty-four railroads centering or terminating in Chicago, had been in aggressive existence. Leagued together in this powerful organization, these representatives of the railroad magnates were reducing the wages of railroad workers below the level of subsistence, and on the other hand were combined for the purpose of extorting high passenger and freight rates. In law it was a conspiracy in restraint of trade, but it is needless to say that no writ of arrest had ever

[2] See, "Report on the Chicago Strike of June and July, 1894," by the U. S. Special Commission, 1895. It may be added that the Pullman Company's present capital is $120,000,000, and that in its recent report to the Interstate Commerce Commission (1911) it admitted that it never had any new capital paid in except from "earnings." At the same time, it has been paying an average annual dividend of eight per cent.

been issued against a single member of the General Managers' Association. Neither did any court presume to issue an injunction, sweeping or qualified. Railroad workers, agitating for better conditions, were discharged and blacklisted,[3] yet for this offense the General Managers' Association was not even questioned by the authorities. This systematic campaign against the railroad workers led to the formation of the American Railway Union, composed of employés, and was one of the contributing causes of the great strike of 1894.

Repeating their successful ruse used at Pittsburg in the strike of 1877,[4] the railroad corporations caused cheap, worn-out freight cars to be set on fire,[5] and then forthwith accused the strikers of violence and rioting. This charge proclaimed through twenty thousand subservient newspapers, prejudiced the general public mind, and was immediately seized upon as a pretext for the ordering out of Federal troops. Evidently Governor Altgeld knew the real facts, for he refused to call upon the President for troops. In violation of the law, and against Altgeld's protest, President Cleveland, ostensibly to quell rioting, but in reality to interfere with strikers assembling and picketing, hurried Federal soldiers to Illinois. At the same time Federal judges, some of whom had been attorneys for the railroads involved, issued unprecedented injunctions which even went so far as to forbid the strikers from persuading fellow workers to quit work.

One of these injunctions was issued by the Federal judge,

[3] See testimony affirming the general existence of this practice, " Report of the Industrial Commission, 1900," Vol. IV (Transportation) : pp. 52, 123, 516, 528, etc.

[4] The late Carroll D. Wright, so favorably and widely known for his work as United States Commissioner of Labor and in other fields, related in his " Battles of Labor " (p. 122) how at Pittsburg a number of worthless freight cars were fired by railroad emissaries, and the strikers were then charged with riot. Wright wrote that from all he was able to gather, the reports that the railroads manufactured riots were true.

[5] Parsons' " The Railways, The Trusts and The People," 196. Also see, Report of Chicago Chief of Police for 1894.

Peter S. Grosscup, at Chicago. It was notorious that Gross-cup owed his position to the influence of corporations; recent disclosures regarding his conduct both before he was a judge and since that time are supposed to have been instrumental in causing his recent resignation. Grosscup's brother, Benjamin, was a Northern Pacific Railroad attorney. On July 3, 1908, Charles H. Aldrich, a Chicago attorney who had originally indorsed Grosscup for the judgeship, sent to United States Attorney-General Bonaparte a communication in which he accused Grosscup of having asked railroads for free transportation for himself and family and for others. After specifically charging Grosscup with other alleged malfeasances, Aldrich continued with this specific arraignment of Judge Grosscup's methods:

There are many other acts calling for the severest censure and utterly incompatible with a high sense of judicial integrity; *e. g.,* his connection with the Mattoon street railroad scheme. You will note that he caused this company to have business relations with the Guarantee Trust Company of New York, which had then but recently become a complainant in his court and upon whose bill he had appointed receivers for all the traction properties of the north and west sides. It is known that money was borrowed through the assistance of the people represented by the Guarantee Trust Company to enable Mr. Sampsell, one of the receivers and at the same time, clerk of the United States Circuit Court, to pay for his interest in the property.

The receivership was a friendly one, the parties seeking a reorganization of the properties. Ultimately, they desired the assistance and coöperation of the court and its receivers. When, therefore, Mr. Sampsell applied for a large loan to the parties interested in the litigation, and supported his application with a letter from Judge Grosscup, it was natural that these parties complied with the request through arrangements with the Knickerbocker Trust Company. Perhaps this was rendered more probable by the order entered of record as an excuse for violating the statute forbidding the appointment of any clerk of court as receiver except for good cause shown. This recited that Mr. Sampsell was appointed because he was near to the court.

The subsequent history of the Mattoon enterprise has been shameful and calculated to discredit the lectures of the same judge delivered in all parts of the country on the subject of overcapitalization and popularization of the trust.

This history need not be followed. The view I wish to express is that a judge should not be in such relations to litigants and receivers in his court.

There are stories of a large speculative account carried by the judge with H. B. Hollins & Co., of New York, who were among the principal holders of the traction securities, and back of the suit of the Guarantee Trust Company. I have no positive knowledge on this subject.

It was Grosscup who, at a critical stage in the strike, caused Debs and his associates to be haled up for contempt of court, and it was Grosscup who, acting as prosecutor, judge and jury all in one, convicted them of contempt of court, and sentenced them to jail.

Habeas Corpus Denied to Debs.

Debs, on January 14, 1895, applied to the Supreme Court for a writ of habeas corpus.

His counsel, Lyman Trumbull, a noted lawyer who himself had represented corporations, began his argument by reciting the circumstances of " the extraordinary proceeding under which the prisoners were deprived of liberty." This action was begun by the filing of a bill of equity in the name of the United States under the direction of Attorney-General Olney. As we have seen, Olney had been a railroad director.[6] The bill was unsigned by anyone, and " has attached to it an affidavit of George I. Allen, an unknown person, having, so far as the record shows, no connection with the case, stating that he has read the bill and ' believes the statements contained therein are true.' " Was there anything unlawful, Trumbull asked, in the American Railway Union calling upon

[6] And, according to a list of the ten largest security holders of the leading railroads in the United States given out by the Interstate Commerce Commission, January 15, 1909, Richard Olney, G. F. Richardson and B. P. Cheney of Boston were trustees for 204,700 shares of preferred stock of the St. Louis and San Francisco Railroad.

its members to quit work? If not, then Debs and associates were not engaged in any unlawful combination or conspiracy. The boycott of the Pullman cars was, as the bill clearly showed, not to obstruct commerce, but for an entirely different purpose. Refusing to work, Trumbull went on, was no crime. Although such an action might incidentally delay the mails or interfere with interstate commerce, it was a lawful act and no offense. The act of Congress to protect trade and commerce against unlawful restraints and monopoly did not apply to the case stated in the bill; if so, Trumbull said, it was unconstitutional.

Justice Brewer delivered the decision of an unanimous Court. The remarkable sight was now presented of this " great and honorable court " deciding the case upon a point in no way involved, thus violating one of the most fundamental principles of law. Brewer denied Debs' petition upon the ground that he and associates had obstructed interstate commerce traffic by derailing and wrecking engines and trains, and assaulting and disabling railroad employés. If this were true, why was it that no such criminal action had ever been brought against Debs? And if it were true, Debs could have been convicted and sentenced to prison for a long term, instead of getting the sentence of six months in jail for contempt of court that the Supreme Court of the United States on May 27, 1895, thus affirmed. In the very act of sending Debs to jail the Supreme Court established (as an entering wedge) the ominous precedent and principle that the Federal anti-trust law applied to combinations of wage workers.[7]

[7] *In re* Debs, 158 U. S. Reports, 564. While Attorney-General Olney was thus pressing the case against Debs and having the anti-trust act applied to labor unions, he was allowing an important case against the cash-register combination to go by default. The important allegations of the Government against this trust were clearly sustained. Olney, into whose control the prosecution of the case had come from his predecessor, allowed the indictment to lapse, giving the remarkable and specious reason that the complaining witnesses had entered into the combination of the defendants! — See, U. S. vs. Patterson *et al.*, 55 Federal Reporter; 605 and 59 *Ibid.*, 208.

Of the Justices sanctioning this decision, these particulars, repeated here, are pertinent as indicating class bias:

Chief Justice Fuller had been counsel for Marshall Field, chief owner of the Pullman works, and he had represented the Chicago, Burlington and Quincy Railroad and other railroad capitalists and interests.[8]

Justice Field had been placed on the Supreme Court Bench by the Central Pacific and the Southern Pacific Railroad interests.

Field's nephew, Brewer, had been sponsored by the same and allied interests.

Justice Gray was a capitalist with varied interests and connections.

Justice Shiras had represented the Baltimore and Ohio Railroad system.

Justice Brown had represented the Vanderbilt and other railroads as counsel in Michigan, and was a corporation stockholder.

Justice White was a rich Louisiana sugar planter.

Touching unanimous decisions, it will be desirable to insert a few words here of a decision of the Supreme Court of the United States which gave Justice Gray another sizeable fortune.

Justice Gray, "Next of Kin."

His grandfather, William Gray, had been one of the largest shipowners in New England, and was one of those asserting that his interests had suffered from French spoliations after the French Revolution. For more than eighty years attempts were made to lobby through Congress acts to indemnify these claimants, but the claims were regarded as nothing more or less than tenacious efforts to raid the Treasury. Finally,

[8] Noted on the record in Case of Chicago, Burlington and Quincy Railroad vs. Chicago, 166 U. S. Reports, 227 (October, 1896): " The Chief Justice took no part in the consideration or determination of these cases " (p. 263).

in 1885, Congress was induced to pass an act authorizing the referring of certain claims to the Court of Claims. One of these was the Gray claim.

The question, however, was: Who should get the money appropriated as indemnity for spoliations of William Gray's ships? That William Gray had gone bankrupt was undeniable. The Massachusetts Supreme Court had decided that the indemnity funds which had been paid to Codman, administrator of the Gray estate, should "be paid over as assets to the estate of William Gray, the elder, and as passing under his will to the residuary legatees named therein." [9] These legatees were charitable and other societies.

But the Supreme Court of the United States upset this decision. In delivering the unanimous decision of this Court, Chief Justice Fuller held that the act of Congress of March 3, 1891, should be construed to read not that the payments should go to the creditors, legatees, assignees or strangers to the blood, but that they should be turned over to the *next of kin*. And by "next of kin," Fuller explained, was intended "next of kin" at the time the act was passed.

The "next of kin" in this case was Fuller's colleague, Justice Horace Gray, who thereby was enabled to add a goodly sum to his bank account. [10]

A new Justice to succeed Jackson now came on the Supreme Court Bench in the person of Rufus W. Peckham. President Cleveland had at first successively nominated William B. Hornblower and Wheeler H. Peckham, both corporation attorneys. [11] But they belonged to a political faction in New

---

[9] 159 Mass. Reports, 427.

[10] See, Case of Brooks vs. Codman, and Foote vs. Women's Board of Missions, 162 U. S. Reports, 439. "Mr. Justice Gray did not sit in these cases or take any part in their decision."— P. 466.

[11] Hornblower had represented the Pacific Railroad of Missouri (IV Supreme Court Reporter, 584), the New York Life Ins. Co., and other corporations. Wheeler H. Peckham was also a well-known corporation attorney; he was a director of the Buffalo, Rochester and Pittsburg Railway, and was interested in other corporations. See later.

York inimical to United States Senator David B. Hill who now in retaliation fought down their nominations with success. Cleveland then compromised on Rufus W. Peckham, a brother of Wheeler H. Peckham.

Justice Peckham's Career.

Rufus W. Peckham was a son of a jurist of the same name who had been a judge of the New York Court of Appeals and had died in 1873. The junior Rufus, in 1866, married a daughter of D. H. Arnold, President of the Mercantile Bank, of New York City. He became a member of the law firm of Peckham and Tremaine (later Peckham and Rosendale) in Albany; was elected District Attorney of Albany County in 1869, and subsequently Albany's Corporation Counsel. From thence on his private practice was large and lucrative.

We find Rufus W. Peckham as one of the counsel, in 1872, for the notorious Tammany judge, John H. McCunn, of the Superior Court, New York City.[12] The Bar Association preferred charges of corrupt conduct against McCunn;[13] Peckham vigorously defended him at the trial, but McCunn was found guilty on eight specifications, impeached and removed from office.[14] Six years later, Peckham appeared as counsel for John F. Smyth, Superintendent of the Insurance Department of New York State. Smyth was charged with malfeasance and corruption. The influence of the great insurance corporations was concentrated upon bringing about his

[12] For Peckham's pleas and arguments for McCunn at this trial, see, " Proceedings in The Senate on The Investigation of The Charges Preferred Against John H. McCunn," etc., Albany, 1874: pp. 80, 100, 102, 110, 134, 142, etc.

[13] It is curious to note that one of the three members of the acting committee of the Bar Association was John E. Parsons, the very same who has long been chief counsel for, and a director of, the Sugar Trust, the enormous thefts of which in defrauding the Government of import duties, were exposed in 1909–1910.

[14] See, " Proceedings In The Senate On The Investigation Of The Charges Preferred Against John H. McCunn," etc., pp. 604–605.

acquittal; and by a vote of 19 to 12 (thus lacking the constitutional two-thirds majority) the New York Senate decided not to remove him from office.[15] In 1883, Peckham was counsel for Lorenz B. Sessions, charged with bribery, and in the course of his argument Peckham pleaded that " an acquittal would hurt no one, but the question of conviction was serious, for if a conviction was had, the defendant would be sent to prison for a term of years." Much comment was made upon Peckham's peculiar views on the offense of bribery, in his arguing that bribery was a secret transaction, and that the informer was a " squealer."

As counsel or trustee or both for many banking, insurance and other corporations Peckham's practice and activities were extensive. His investments were considerable. In 1884 he was elected a trustee of the Mutual Life Insurance Company of New York, and continued in that capacity for twenty-one years. His associates on the board of trustees of that company at various times comprised many of the most powerful capitalists in the world; George F. Baker, Cornelius Vanderbilt, Henry H. Rogers, William Rockefeller, James Speyer and many others of lesser, but still enormous, power.[16]

His Magnate Associates.

Baker was president or vice-president or director of more than thirty corporations; he was the President of the First National Bank and a director in other banks; first vice-president and director of the Central Railroad of New Jersey, director of the Delaware, Lackawanna and Western Railroad,

[15] See, " Testimony and the Arguments of Counsel Before The Senate on Charges Against John F. Smyth, Superintendent of the Insurance Department, Albany, 1878 ": pp. 5, 7, 40, etc. Peckham's final argument for Smyth is to be found on pp. 365–384, and the vote on the question of Smyth's removal on page 518.

[16] See, " The Insurance Year Book " for 1905: p. 175. Other trustees were Stuyvesant Fish, Augustus Julliard, George G. Haven, Charles Lanier, Elbridge T. Gerry, Elihu Root, Adrian Iselin, Jr., etc., etc.

of the Northern Pacific Railway, of the Lehigh and Hudson Railroad, of the Consolidated Gas Company, trustee of the Southern Railway Company, etc., etc.[17]

The Standard Oil Company, in which Rogers and Rockefeller were among the few dominating magnates, then largely or wholly controlled, in league with the Goulds, twelve railroad systems with a total mileage of 28,157, and a total capitalization of $1,368,877,540. These systems included the Missouri Pacific, the Texas Pacific, the Wabash, the St. Louis Southwestern, the Denver and Rio Grande, the Wheeling and Lake Erie, the Western Maryland, the Chicago, Milwaukee and St. Paul, the Colorado and Southern, and other railroad lines.[18]

The Vanderbilts controlled about eleven railroad systems — 21,888 miles of railroad in all — capitalized at more than a billion dollars, and they held formidable interests in other railroads.[19]

The J. Pierpont Morgan group, also represented on the board of trustees of the Mutual Life Insurance Company, was allied with James J. Hill in the control of 47,206 miles of railroad lines, capitalized at more than two billion dollars.[20] Other groups of railroad capitalists were likewise represented.

But the railroad ownings of Peckham's fellow trustees were only a fragment of their entire interests. Rogers was an officer or director of twenty-five large corporations including railroads, great copper companies, gas corporations and others.[21] Fish was an officer or director of twelve different corporations;[22] Julliard of twenty-one;[23] William

---

[17] " Directory of Directors " for 1899: pp. 22–23.

[18] Moody's " The Truth About The Trusts," " Gould-Rockefeller Group ": pp. 435–436.

[19] *Ibid.*, 432.

[20] *Ibid.*, 434.

[21] " Directory of Directors In The City of N. Y.," for 1904: 795–796.

[22] *Ibid.*, 307.

[23] *Ibid.*, 495–496.

Rockefeller of thirty-one;[24] Iselin of twenty-seven;[25] Cornelius Vanderbilt- of twenty;[26] Speyer of seventeen;[27] Lanier of eighteen;[28] Haven of thirty-two;[29] and so on. The ramifications of the power of these men, owning and controlling, as they did, billions of dollars of the country's resources, were stupendous.

Corruption by the Mutual Life Insurance Company.

Much of the immense surplus of the life insurance companies was invested, by vote of the trustees, in the great outpourings of watered railroad and industrial stocks. The Mutual Life Insurance Company alone held, in 1904, assets of $440,978,371; it had liabilities of $366,620,553, and its surplus was $74,357,818. The revelations before the New York Legislative Insurance Committee, in 1905, are perhaps tolerably well remembered; how syndicates of "insiders" made vast profits by dumping watered stock, which they as directors of railroads and other corporations had issued, upon the insurance companies, and how for decades corruption funds had been distributed in every legislative center to insure the passage of favorable special legislation and the defeat of laws hostile to the insurance company looters.

"The testimony," reported the legislative committee, "taken by this committee makes it clear that the large insurance companies systematically attempted to control legislation in this [New York] and other States, which could affect their interests directly or indirectly. The three companies divided the country, outside of New York, and a few other States, so as to avoid a waste of effort, each looking after its chosen district and bearing its appropriate part of the total expenses."[30]

[24] *Ibid.,* 792–793.   [26] *Ibid.,* 967–968.   [28] *Ibid.,* 536–537.
[25] *Ibid.,* 472–473.   [27] *Ibid.,* 885–886.   [29] *Ibid.,* 409–410.
[30] "Report of the [New York] Legislative Committee, 1906, Vol. X: 23.

One of these three companies was the Mutual Life Insurance Company. At Albany it maintained a sumptuously appointed house, jocosely styled " the House of Mirth," where Andrew C. Fields, its regular lobbyist, manipulated legislation and distributed corruption funds. " At times," reported the Committee, " members of the Senate while serving on its Insurance Committee, lived at this house in Albany which the Mutual maintained." [31] The corruption funds were cloaked under the guise of " legal expenses "; from 1898 to 1904, the Mutual Life Insurance Company thus corruptly expended more than $2,000,000.[32] Vast thefts of the policy holders' money were committed in the Mutual's " Supply Department " which was under Fields' charge.[33] " Large sums," the Committee further reported, " have been expended in the attempt to influence public opinion through the press by the insertion of so-called ' reading notices '; that is to say, by disguised advertising and by payments to newspaper correspondents and news writers for presumably similar services." [34]

Manipulation of Elections.

Of the Mutual Life Insurance Company, the Committee still further reported that " it is a purely mutual company, and in theory is governed exclusively by its policy holders. . . . In practice the policy holders have had little concern with the selection of trustees or with the management of the Company. Notices of election have been published in New York City papers — but have not been mailed to policy holders. There are probably between 400,000 and 500,000 policy

[31] *Ibid.* See full details, pp. 17–22.
[32] *Ibid.*, 16. The " legal expenses " of the Mutual Life Insurance Co. for a series of years were: 1898, $266,403.95; 1899, $286,048.74; 1900, $304,756.85; 1901, $243,516.78; 1902, $275,989.64; 1903, $347,254.95; 1904, $364,254.95.
[33] " Report of the [New York] Legislative Committee," etc., Vol. X: p. 25.
[34] *Ibid.*, 26.

holders entitled to votes for trustees, but for a long period of years not more than 200 votes have been cast at any election. The voters who vote personally have generally been employés of the company or of subsidiary companies. The policy holders are entitled to vote by proxy, but as a rule proxies have not been used. In order to secure the continuity of the management and to guard against an uprising of the policy holders, proxies to the extent of 20,000 or more were held by President Richard A. McCurdy and Vice-President Richard Grannis, having been obtained, under suitable instructions, by the local managers. . . . The result has been an autocracy maintained almost without challenge. Whatever efforts have been directed against it have proved abortive." [35]

Peckham Did Not Protest.

Peckham, as we have said, was a trustee of the Mutual Life Insurance Company for twenty-one years, beginning in 1884. He had been on the Bench of the Supreme Court of the United States for nearly ten of the years covered by this report.

Was he unfamiliar with this colossal corruption and these illegal methods? If he were, then he was unfit to be a trustee of a company of the administration of which he was ignorant.

This lack of knowledge might be assumed of an official who served but a short time; but Peckham had been a trustee continuously for more than two decades. Moreover, as we have seen, Peckham, back in 1878, had defended State Insurance Superintendent Smyth, charged with corruption; the details in that long trial were such that they could hardly have left anyone innocent of the methods of the life insurance companies. We have also seen how Peckham had defended the corrupt Judge McCunn, and how in the Sessions case he had slighted the gravity of the offense of bribery. Finally, in

[35] " Report of [N. Y.] Legislative Committee," Vol. X: 9-10.

view of the disclosures concerning the autocratic methods by which a few men manipulated the choice and election of trustees, was it possible that he would have been kept on the board of the Mutual's trustees if he had not been passive or subservient?

During the twenty-one years as trustee, Peckham did not once protest. On the contrary, he retained his office and associations. Not until during the height of the disclosures before the Legislative Insurance Committee, when the New York *World* addressed some sharp editorial letters to him, did he resign; and this he did, in November, 1905, with many sanctimonious expressions of "righteous indignation." During the very time that he was serving as a trustee of the Mutual Life Insurance Company he was, as a Justice of the Supreme Court of the United States, handing down decisions declaring certain anti-corporation laws unconstitutional — decisions of incalculable value to his capitalist associates.[36] It was this same Peckham, blind (let us assume) to the prodigious corruption of the corporation of which he was a trustee, who saw and declared that a law establishing a ten-hour work day for hard-driven bakeshop workers was unconstitutional.

Peckham's appointment to the Supreme Court of the United States represented another significant stage of economic development. His associates on the Mutual Life Insurance Company, especially during the latter part of his trusteeship, were not exclusively railroad magnates, factory owners or banking grandees. Their elaborate interests embraced railroads, banking syndicates, street railway systems, electric light plants, coal mines, copper, gold and silver mines, realty companies, and industrial trusts of all descriptions. In those men, or some of them, was concentrated the control of some of the mightiest trusts which, in turn, controlled a host of

[36] See later.

subsidiary trusts. They were the arch-types of the newer era of trusts and the sway of trusts.

Briefly, we shall now give a succession of decisions of the Supreme Court of the United States, the first in the list of which was given before Peckham's appointment.

The Sugar Trust Decision.

On January 21, 1895, the decision in the action of the Government against the Sugar Trust was handed down. This trust controlled 98 per cent. of the output of sugar, yet the Supreme Court decided that it was not a combination in restraint of trade under the Sherman anti-trust act.[37]

This decision demonstrated that the Supreme Court was pro-trust, and could be surely depended upon to validate any trust in maintaining its monopoly.

From the point of view of industrial progress, there was nothing in this decision intrinsically open to criticism; the trust was a superior institution to the archaic, passing one of unrestricted competition, and was bound to prevail by force of its economic superiority. But the fact to be noted is that, despite drastic legislation against trusts, the Supreme Court could or would not see that it violated the laws. In the Debs case a little later it microscopically searched laws to find a ground on which to commit Debs to jail, and had to invent a fictitious point in order to do it. In the one

[37] Case of U. S. vs. E. C. Knight Company, 156 U. S. Reports, 1. Practically, this decision legalized the operations of the trust and absolved its powerful heads from criminal prosecution. The all-wise Supreme Court of the United States failed to discover that a trust was a trust. But the Federal Grand Jury, in July, 1909, seems to have keener eyesight. It indicted John E. Parsons, originator of the trust idea and formerly general counsel, and leading director of the American Sugar Refining Company. Thomas, vice-president, Donner, Frazier and other officials of the trust were also indicted. For two years Parsons and associates contested the indictments, but the Federal Circuit Court in New York recently decided that they must stand criminal trial for alleged conspiracy to restrain commerce.

case, the Supreme Court of the United States refused to enforce the clearest and most unmistakable laws against powerful capitalists; in the other, it manufactured law in order to strike a blow at the workers by jailing one of its most active, sincere and able leaders, thus setting a precedent for the future imprisonment of other labor leaders.

Long-Continuing Sugar Frauds.

Exempted from hostile decrees, the Sugar Trust, as later developments proved, set out vigorously on an even more oppressive process of illegally undermining remaining competitors, and at the same time defrauded the Government of vast sums by the underweighing of imported sugar material.

The testimony recently given — May and June, 1911 — before the Stanley Congressional Investigating Committee revealed that the Sugar Trust had been a trust since 1887 when, as Edwin F. Atkins of Boston, acting president of the trust testified, seventeen sugar-refining companies had been organized into a trust by H. O. Havemeyer. Atkins admitted, too, that the trust had, in violation of law, consistently received rebates from the railroads. Of the mass of corroborating testimony we shall not reproduce more here. And as to the methods used by the Sugar Trust in trying to rid itself of a dangerous competitor like Spreckels, one of many facts testified to was that dead rats were surreptitiously placed in barrels of sugar packed in Spreckels' factory.

The import frauds of the Sugar Trust were so gigantic that when they were discovered in 1908-1909, that trust hastened to pay over in April, 1909, a settlement of about $2,000,000 to the Government, hoping to avert criminal proceedings. It was estimated that the total sums of which the trust had defrauded the Government reached tens of millions of dollars. One of the directors of the Sugar Trust during this period was John E. Parsons who made the argument for the trust before the Supreme Court of the United States, in 1894. He and all the other responsible magnates escaped criminal punishment; they were indicted in 1909, it is true, yet not for customs frauds, but for violations of the anti-trust act. The only punitive action enforced was against a few trust employés, and some Government weighers who had been bribed. They were sent to prison.

A Series of Decisions.

To return to the succession of Supreme Court decisions:

On March 30, 1896, that Court nullified the grant of power to the Interstate Commerce Commission to settle maximum rates for railroad transportation.[38]

On the same day the Supreme Court handed down a decision practically allowing interstate railroads license to charge two or three times as much for carrying American, as for foreign, freight, between the same points and conceivably on the same car.[39]

On the other hand, the Supreme Court of the United States, in the Arago case, so construed the thirteenth Amendment to the Constitution as to make it the basis for a new form of involuntary servitude for all workers, white, black, red or yellow.

Robertson, Olsen, Bradley and Hansen, seamen who had shipped by contract in the bark *Arago*, decided because of intolerable conditions, to quit work when the vessel reached Astoria, Oregon. They were subsequently arrested at San Francisco, and were charged under Rev. Statute 4596, with refusing to work. When their petition for a writ of habeas corpus came before the Supreme Court of the United States,

[38] Cincinnati, New Orleans and Texas Pacific Railway vs. I. C. C., and I. C. C. vs Cin., N. O. and Texas Pacific Railway, 162 U. S. Reports, 184. Justice Shiras wrote the Court's unanimous decision.

[39] Texas and Pacific Railway vs. I. C. C., 162 U. S. Reports, 197 Shiras also wrote this decision; Harlan and Brown dissented.

that Court held that the statute in question did not conflict
with the Constitutional amendment forbidding slavery and
involuntary servitude. That provision, the Court said, was
never intended to apply to such contracts; the contract of a
sailor involved, to a certain extent, the surrender of his personal liberty during the life of the contract.[40]

It can easily be seen how such a precedent can be stretched
a little further to cover workers of all kinds as well as labor
unions signing contracts. Whatever oppression and injustice are heaped upon them, workers can be held in servitude
to the letter of their contract, while if the capitalist decides
to throw his workers out of jobs, he can plead various reasons for justification, and no contract is enforced against him.

More decisions favorable to railroad corporations followed.
On May 24, 1897, the Supreme Court handed down a decision reasserting and even amplifying some of its previous
anti-interstate commerce decisions.[41]

It repeated the performance in an anti-interstate commerce
decision, on November 8, 1897.

.On March 7, 1898, the Supreme Court's decision in the
Nebraska maximum rate case was made public. This decision was another step in the process of stripping the Interstate Commerce Commission of the power given it by Congress to make interstate railroad rates reasonable. The effect
of the decision was to nullify legislation in many States, and
allow the railroads to charge what rates they pleased in both
intrastate and interstate transportation.[42]

In that same year the Supreme Court, on October 24,

[40] Case of Robertson vs. Baldwin, 165 U. S. Reports, 275. Brown delivered the Court's decision; Harlan dissented.
[41] I. C. C. vs. Cincinnati, New Orleans and Texas Pacific Railway Co.,
167 U. S. Reports, 479. Brewer delivered this decision. In the other
case, I. C. C. vs. Alabama Midland Railway Co. (168 U. S. Reports,
144), Shiras wrote the decision. Harlan dissented in both cases.
[42] Smyth vs. Ames, 169 U. S. Reports, 466. Harlan wrote the Court's
unanimous decision. "The Chief Justice took no part in the consideration or decision of these cases" (p. 550).

decided the live-stock cases, both companion cases to the
Sugar Trust cases. Although each of these live-stock combinations was flagrantly violating the laws in restraint of
interstate commerce, a bill of immunity was extended to both
by the Supreme Court.[43]

The decision in the Joint Traffic Association case was
handed down on the same day. The unsophisticated accepted
this decision as one of an anti-trust nature, but the well-informed believed that this association, representing thirty-one
railroads, wanted a decree for its formal dissolution, so as
to be able to plead arguments for the necessity of legislation
by Congress virtually allowing combination. Ostensibly defendants, they in reality secured a much-desired decision which
they were making great pretenses of contesting.[44]

The decision in the Addyston Pipe and Steel Company case
was hailed as one adverse to the trusts, but this company
was entirely too small to be ranked among the great trusts
and it was believed that the suit for its effacement was secretly
instigated by great capitalists objecting to its competition or
scheming to annihilate it.[45]

One of the Supreme Court's decisions of immense value to
the land-grant railroads was that of May 31, 1898, declaring
that the land grant of the Northern Pacific Railroad, under
the act of July 2, 1864, extended two hundred feet on each
side of the track along the entire right of way. The railroad
company did not bring ejectment proceedings until 1877, by
which time cities and towns had been built along the road;
and not until after these sites had become of great value did
the company think of asserting title to these valuable
stretches of real estate under its claim of right of way. This

---

[43] Hopkins vs. U. S., 171 U. S. Reports, 578, and Anderson vs. U. S.,
Ibid., 604. Peckham delivered the court's opinion; Harlan dissented.

[44] U. S. vs. Joint Traffic Association, 171 U. S. Reports, 505. Peckham wrote this decision also.

[45] Addyston Pipe and Steel Company vs. U. S., 175 U. S. Reports, 211.
This decision was also written by Peckham.

decision, of course, presented the company with property worth vast sums.[46]

These are a few typical decisions of the Supreme Court of the United States during this period. The infirmities of age were publicly exhibited in a painful and pathetic manner on the exalted Bench of the omnipotent Supreme Court of the United States. During the hearings of some of the most important cases, Justice Gray, suffering from kidney trouble, frequently fell asleep; Justice Shiras often nodded in slumber, blissfully oblivious to the learned arguments of learned counsel who were often put at their wits' end to conceal their confusion. As for Justice Field, he could be seen, on occasion after occasion, staggering to his seat, all out of breath, his eyes bulging, and his frame in the shiver of extreme decrepitude; he required an assistant to hold him up.

McKenna Chosen to Succeed Justice Field.

Field died on April 9, 1899, aged nearly eighty-three years. As personal wealth went, his estate was comparatively inconsiderable. By his will, dated May 5, 1897, he bequeathed the whole of his real and personal estate to his wife, excepting a portrait of his sister Emilia which he left to his nephew (Emilia's son), Associate Justice Brewer. Mementos and books were bequeathed to other members of the family. Field's real estate consisted of his fine house and grounds facing the east front of the Capitol, which property he had received from his brother, David Dudley Field, in 1880. This property was valued at from $80,000 to $100,000. According further to the inventory of Field's estate filed May 5, 1899, the value of his personal estate was $65,000, comprehending " a library, household effects, horses and carriages

[46] Northern Pacific Railroad vs. Smith, 171 U. S. Reports, 260. Shiras wrote the decision; Harlan dissented. Brewer, although concurring in the decision, excepted to some of its conclusions.

of the value of about $15,000, and also a small, balance in bank, stocks and bonds and promissory notes which will not exceed in aggregate the value of $50,000, making the total value of his personal estate about $65,000." Including both real and personal property Field's estate was, therefore, about $165,000.

Here again was another example of a judge who by his decisions had given vast properties and privileges to individuals and corporations but who was incorruptible as far as bribes or jobbing were concerned. Probably no judge was ever a more open, undisguised tool of great capitalist interests than Field; no judge served their purposes more unblushingly and with less disingenuousness. But it is evident that he personally profited nothing; his corruption was that of a purely mental subservience induced by his class views, attachments and obligations. For thirty-six years Field had been on the Bench of the Supreme Court of the United States, and at the end of that time he left less of an estate than many a petty merchant or even a half-way sucessful shyster lawyer. No one could be more brutally inhuman than Field in his application of law (or what he construed to be law) to the advantage of capitalists and to the subjugation of the workers. Yet as his will revealed, he had his personal human qualities; he did not forget the twenty-five years of faithful service of his messenger, William Joice, to whom he left a legacy of $500.

Field's successor, appointed by President McKinley, was Joseph McKenna, of California. McKenna had been an obscure "crossroads" lawyer at Suisun, California. The politics of California were notoriously controlled by the Southern and Central Pacific railroads; the political bosses were the creatures of the Stanford-Huntington group who saw to it that no one unfriendly to their interests was elected or appointed to any office. McKenna was elected district attorney in his county, but was thrice defeated for Congress because of his Roman Catholic faith. But in 1884 he was successful, and was reëlected to Congress of which he was a member for three successive terms.

In Congress McKenna spoke little, but when he did so it was for the railroads' interests, particularly those of the Central Pacific Railroad Company. In the debate over the bill, in 1887, to establish the Interstate Commerce Commission, he protested against the long and short haul clauses, and was one of the forty-one Congressmen voting against the bill.[47]

When the General Deficiency bill came up in the House, in February, 1891, he again made himself conspicuous by his defense of the Central Pacific Railroad. At that identical time, the Central Pacific owed the Government $60,000,000 in principal and interest. Despite this debt, the Supreme Court of the United States had (as he have already noted) handed down a decision compelling the Government to pay the railroad for the transportation of troops, supplies, etc. The General Deficiency Bill contained an appropriation of $3,000,000 to pay these railroad claims. McKenna spoke in favor of the provision.

McKenna: " We know, sir, that the grants to the railroad had their impulse in patriotism — a patriotism enterprising and conservative." [The reports of the Senate " Wilson " Investigating Committee, the Pacific Railway Commission and the San Francisco Grand Jury had successively and specifically revealed that the kind of " patriotism " used had been the distribution of a total of more than $4,000,000 in bribes.][48]

[47] *Congressional Record,* Forty-ninth Congress, Second Session, Vol. 18, Part I: pp. 857 and 881. It was when this bill was before the House that Representative Henderson, later Speaker, said: " This city is swarming with keen, zealous, able agents of the railroad power, trying to defeat the passage of this bill. Every vote cast at their dictation, and every vote against this bill, is a vote for railroad supremacy against the people."

[48] It is hardly necessary to say that we have given the particulars of these briberies in preceding chapters.

"Mr. Chairman," McKenna went on, "there is nothing to justify the refusal of this payment except a false sentiment, and possibly some false politics."

A member —"Claptrap!"

McKenna: "And as the gentleman near me suggests, claptrap. It would be claptrap if it were not adorned by gentlemen of ability, and sanctioned by them." [49]

The Pacific Railroads Victorious.

Soon after this, McKenna, on March 17, 1892, was appointed a United States Circuit Court judge, to sit in the California circuit. A year later Leland Stanford died, and it was stated that McKenna was named in the will as one of the executors. When McKenna was on the Circuit Bench the suit of the Government to recover $15,237,000 from the Stanford estate as its share of the Pacific Railroads' indebtedness, was decided by that court against the Government. This decision was sustained by the Supreme Court of the United States.[50] Various other cases affecting the interests of the Pacific railroads were decided favorably by the Circuit Court when McKenna was a member. The action involving the claim of the Southern Pacific Railroad Company to continued possession of the water front of Oakland was held up for nearly two years, creating much unfavorable popular feeling, and in the case of the railroads against the California Railroad Commission, McKenna's colleague, Judge Ross, delivered the Court's decision holding that the Commission had not the power to fix rates, and that the eight per cent. reduction ordered was illegal.[51]

[49] *Congressional Record,* Fifty-first Congress, Second Session, Vol. 22, Part 4, p. 3397.

[50] 161 U. S. Reports, 413. Harlan wrote the Court's unanimous opinion holding that the various acts of Congress contained no clause imposing personal responsibility upon the stockholders. Field was, of course, on the Supreme Court Bench in 1896, the year of this decision.

[51] Southern Pac. R. R. vs. R'd Commissioners, 79 Federal Reports, 236.

During the American Railway Union strike in 1894, this court also issued a comprehensive injunction restraining the strikers from interfering with the United States mail trains. The injunction enabled the railroads to defeat the strikers by attaching mail cars to all trains, and by carrying Federal troops ostensibly to protect those cars.

When McKinley became President in 1897, he appointed McKenna Attorney-General of the United States. It was currently reported in the newspapers, and not denied, that McKenna consented to accept this post on the understanding that when Justice Field resigned he would be appointed to succeed Field. At this point it should be noted that E. H. Harriman was acquiring the Central, Southern and other Pacific railroads; Harriman contributed heavily to McKinley's campaign fund, as he later did to Roosevelt's. McKenna's appointment as Attorney-General aroused a storm of severe criticism, the point of which was that his decisions had always favored trusts and corporations.

Protests Against McKenna's Appointment.

But those criticisms were mild compared to the widespread strictures upon him when he was appointed to the Supreme Court of the United States.

Protests poured in upon the United States Senate. One extended petition from Oregon, signed by former United States Attorney-General George H. Williams, Judges Gilbert, Shattuck, Sears, George, Bellinger and many others, including fifty members of the Portland (Ore.) bar, demanded the rejection of McKenna's appointment, on the ground that he was unfit. ". . . The Hon. Jos. McKenna among his legal brethren has not been accorded a high place, but on the contrary, the consensus of opinion has been and is that he is not, either by natural gifts, acquired learning or decision of character, qualified for any judicial place of

importance, much less for the highest place in the land.
. . ."

On December 6, 1897, a memorial signed by many prominent lawyers, was sent from San Francisco to the Senate:
" In the first place, we accuse the judge of being slow and
incompetent. He is a man of confused ideas, and his record
on the Bench is disgraceful. . . . During the last two
years of his administration of the affairs of his circuit, he
had but three jury cases, six court cases, twenty-seven demurrers and motions. Many of the demurrers were left undecided. On retiring he left thirty-five important matters
wholly undecided. He had one case of minor importance
under advisement for two and a half years. In Case No.
12,127, the suit of the Railroad Commission against the
Southern Pacific Railroad, he was six months hemming and
hawing over the simplest matters; questions that any other
judge of the most mediocre ability would have passed on
inside an hour. He feared he would displease either the
railroad or the people." The petition concluded by referring
to McKenna as " a small man in every sense, and a cunning
politician and trimmer." [52]

According to a San Francisco newspaper which had bitterly
opposed the Southern Pacific Railway, " those opposing
McKenna have been working stealthily for their petition.
. . . Their excuse for not coming out more boldly is that
if it had been known . . . W. F. Herrin and the Southern
Pacific would at once have started a counter petition. . . .
This would have been done in gratitude for the Railroad Commission case, and the silence on the Open Water Front controversy. . . . At the time of the decision, some of the
remarks made by the attorneys for the people were of so
decidedly a derogatory nature that it was a wonder that
they had not become public. . . . Stories are put in cir-

[52] These petitions were published in all of the leading newspapers of
the time.

culation that McKenna is not of a mental caliber to sit upon the Supreme Bench, but behind the open controversy looms up a more guarded insinuation of the Attorney-General's subjection to corporation influences." [53]

In addition to these and other protests many newspapers in editorials severely denounced the appointment. Of the numerous editorials, we shall quote from the New York *World,* a Democratic newspaper which, however, had virtually advocated the election of McKinley in the McKinley-Bryan campaign of 1896. Said the *World* of McKenna:

> But he is equally unfit by reason of his affiliations and actions as a lawyer and a judge. He has been the tool of corporations and the pet of plutocrats. His advancement has been due entirely to the favor of Stanford, Huntington and other multimillionaires of his section. Every important decision he made in corporation cases was clearly in the interests of his former clients. He represents in a peculiar degree that perversion of judicial power to the service of plutocracy, against which 6,500,000 voters protested in the last election. [This referred to the Bryan campaign, the platform of which severely criticized the Supreme Court for its shifting on the income-tax decision.] To confirm him in a seat on the Bench of the Supreme Court would be an infamous betrayal of the people's trust.[54]

Another editorial in the same newspaper the next day declared:

> The nomination of McKenna to be a justice of the Supreme Court is a scandalous abuse of the appointive power. (1) The man's unfitness by reason of a lack of learning, a lack of capacity, a lack of fruitful experience and a lamentable lack of that high' integrity which is the most essential qualification of a Supreme Court Justice, is attested by the indignant protest of the judges and lawyers in his own part of the country. (2) His entire career has been one of servitude to the Pacific Railway robbers, trust magnates and their kind, and even his decisions as a judge upon the bench have been tainted by evidence

[53] San Francisco *Examiner,* December 4, 1897. W. F. Herrin was both lawyer and political manipulator, first for Stanford and Huntington, and then for their successor, Harriman.
[54] New York *World,* December 17, 1897.

of that subserviency. It is a shame to put this man upon the bench of the highest court in the land. It is a wrong to the nation and its people. It is an insult to widespread public opinion. It is a menace to the public welfare. It is a blistering disgrace to the administration which is responsible for it. The Senate's duty is clear. It should reject the nomination as shamefully unfit.[55]

A Suspicious Feature.

No doubt much in these protests was well founded and to the point. But there was one suspicious feature of the opposition to McKenna which we cannot pass by without comment.

Despatches in the newspapers from Tacoma freely stated that the protests against McKenna originated in San Francisco soon after the return from that city of Benjamin F. Grosscup. Now Grosscup, as we have noted, was (as a member of the firm of Crowley and Grosscup) an attorney for the interests of the Northern Pacific Railroad in the States of Washington and Oregon. The clear inference, therefore, was that the Northern Pacific Railway Company was seeking to prevent its southern transcontinental competitor, the Southern Pacific Railway, from putting McKenna on the Supreme Court Bench. Evidently the conflict was one between two immense railroad corporations with all of their associated and subsidiary interests, as to which would command the choice of the new Justice.

And it was so understood in Washington. The batches of petitions and protests against the confirmation of McKenna were of no avail, especially in a Senate where but few members were not railroad attorneys or railroad magnates, and where Harriman's influence at that particular stage proved all potent. McKenna's nomination was confirmed.

Few appointments to the Supreme Court had aroused such caustic personal criticism, publicly expressed, as that of Mc-

[55] New York *World,* December 18, 1897.

Kenna. Yet it must be said that McKenna's course on the Supreme Court Bench was by no means all that the charges in those protests would lead one to expect. In one memorable case, at least, his dissenting opinion stood forth as an exceptional and noteworthy defense of the grossly invaded rights of kidnapped working-class leaders at a time when the most powerful capitalist interests were banded in an effort to prosecute those leaders to the limit of judicial execution.

This, however, is anticipating. With McKenna's confirmation criticism of his career ceased, but an occasion arose three years later when both he and Harlan were invidiously attacked in the United States Senate. As a result of the Spanish-American War, in 1898, the United States acquired Porto Rico and the Philippines. Instantly, trusts and other syndicates of capitalists set out to take advantage of the change. The Tobacco Trust, the Sugar Trust and other trusts coveted lands in the conquered regions and trade advantages, while associations of powerful capitalists rushed to get concessions for railroads, water rights, timber lands, mines, and, in brief, all of the resources worth while appropriating.

"Constitution Does Not Follow the Flag."

But the question remaining unsettled was this: Were those colonies to be held as subjugated possessions or were they to be admitted as integral parts of the United States? Did the Constitution apply to them?

To determine this issue, several test cases growing out of disputed customs payments were carried up to the Supreme Court of the United States. During the time when these "Insular Cases" were under consideration, President McKinley nominated sons of Justice Harlan and Justice McKenna to important Government posts in Porto Rico. This fact led to biting comments by Senators Pettigrew, Teller and Butler on the subverting of the "independence of the judiciary"; the appointments, they declared, singularly coincided with the fact that the question of the status of the colonies was before the Supreme Court at that precise time. The general effect of the various associated decisions was certainly in line with that desired by McKinley and the capitalist groups behind him. " The Constitution did not follow the flag," the Supreme Court decided, thereby reducing the insular conquests to mere appendages.

Since this decision, the spoliation of the Philippines has gone on uninterruptedly; syndicates and trusts of American capitalists have obtained from the local officials great areas of sugar and timber lands, mines, coal deposits and railway and other concessions.

At this point it is necessary to chronicle the appointment of three new Justices of the Supreme Court. The first of these was Oliver Wendell Holmes, Jr., selected to succeed Justice Gray, who died in 1902.

Justice Holmes Succeeds Gray.

Holmes was of a different type from the usual Supreme Court appointment. He had never represented any large corporations. As a member of the Boston firm of Shattuck and Holmes, his practice was for comparatively small corporations, middle-class business men and rich landholders of, however, a not very important group compared to the great plutocrats.

Shattuck and Holmes had been attorneys, beginning in 1873, for such corporations as the Dorchester Insurance Company; the Winnisimmet (Ferryboat) Company; the receivers of the Mechanics' Insurance Company and for similar corporations.[56] Shattuck, while Holmes' partner, was attorney for the South Boston Railroad, the Eastern Railroad bondholders and so forth.[57] We see Holmes, too, as a young lawyer, contesting

[56] 112 Mass. Reports, 150; 114 *Ibid.*, 66; 120 *Ibid.*, 497, etc.
[57] 121 *Ibid.*, 487, etc.

claims for damages due to injuries,[58] and arguing against the rights of workers. One such case, for example, was that of Temple, Watford and fellow seamen against vessel owners for unpaid wages of which they had been defrauded. Holmes argued that Turner, one of the ship's owners, did not personally make the contract, or engage the seamen, and, therefore, could not be held technically responsible. But the Massachusetts Supreme Court, on September 7, 1877, decided in favor of the seamen.[59]

Holmes was one of that type of lawyer that is personally honest, but hide-bound by class views and class associations — "a Back Bay specimen" as some persons termed him. He, no more than the other Justices, knew or cared about the conditions under which the working class had to labor. Like them, he was educated and developed in a fixed environment of both law and custom, as well as of self-interest — an environment hostile to the working class, and regarding it as a class of preordained drudges to be looked down upon as hopelessly inferior. The class among which Holmes moved, and from which he had derived his clientèle, was suspicious and resentful of the slightest move of the working class to better its conditions, knowing that the extent of its sway and profits depended upon the corresponding subjugation and degradation of the 'workers. On the whole, this analysis could be applied to Holmes without injustice.

A professor of law at Harvard in 1882, Holmes became an Associate Justice of the Massachusetts Supreme Court in that year, and from 1882 to 1889 was its Chief Justice. When appointed to the Supreme Court of the United States he was sixty-one years old. Roosevelt's selection of him was generally understood to be somewhat of a personal choice. Holmes' father had been an essayist of tolerable fame; and Roosevelt, who liked to pose as a literary luminary, was partial to writers

[58] Joy vs. Winnisimmet Company, 114 Mass. Reports, 66.
[59] Temple vs. Turner, 123 Mass. Reports, 125.

and to the sons of writers. But had not Holmes abundantly proved that on the general issues of property domination his class instincts were thoroughly dependable, his appointment would not have run the gauntlet of the United States Senate, the overwhelming majority of which was composed of vigilant corporation attorneys, or of the magnates themselves.[60]

Shiras Resigns, and Day Takes His Place.

The next appointment to the Supreme Court made by Roosevelt was that of William R. Day to succeed Justice Shiras, who resigned on February 23, 1903.

Day's appearance was so striking in one respect that it commanded the instant scrutiny of the observer. His body was so attenuated that he seemed almost to have none, and his leg bones were not much larger than the average man's arm bones. He had lived among musty law books which appeared to have transmitted their atmosphere to him, devitalizing the warm currents of heart and mind. In fact, it might be said that legal tomes had been the first objects that his infantile eyes had perceived; his father, Luther Day, was a lawyer and judge, long serving as a Justice of the Ohio Supreme Court. Law became the family heritage; a brother of William R. Day is now a judge of the Common Pleas Court, at Canton, Ohio, and two sons of William R. Day are lawyers, one associated with a firm of corporation lawyers in Cleveland, the other, William R. Day, II, a Federal judge.

Yet buried as Day's mind was in the sepulchral caverns of moldy precedents of law, no man was more zealous and alert in applying those precedents to the changing interests of cor-

[60] Philander C. Knox, who had been attorney for Carnegie and later for the Steel Trust, was Attorney-General of the United States at this time, and even Vice-President Fairbanks, Roosevelt's official associate (in 1905–1909), had been, shortly before his previous election as United States Senator, president of the Terre Haute and Peoria Railway Company.—(" Poor's Railroad Manual " for 1890, p. 1365.)

porations. He made the past serve the purposes of the present; in unremitting and able retainership to his clients his record as an attorney was consistent. He wore no double coat; he made no pretenses of caring for the interests of the poor, the helpless and defenseless. Candidly and openly he opposed them, which is equivalent to saying that he was a genuine corporation attorney, bent solely and inexorably upon performing the service for which he was paid.

Day as a Corporation Lawyer.

Some forty years ago he formed a law partnership with William A. Lynch, at Canton, Ohio, under the firm name of Lynch and Day. The records abundantly tell how they prospered. Lynch, for example, held the lucrative post of local attorney for the Pittsburg, Fort Wayne and Chicago Railway (now a part of the Pennsylvania Railroad). He was also a director of the Connotton Valley Railroad.[61] The name of the firm varied at different times; in 1880 it was Lynch, Day and Lynch, the other Lynch being Austin, a brother of William. For many years the firm represented the Valley Railway Company[62] (now of the Baltimore and Ohio Railroad system). During more than twenty years William R. Day appeared with great frequency as attorney for the Wheeling and Lake Erie Railroad,[63] which became one of the Gould railroads.

For a long series of years Day and his partners were attorneys for the Canton Street Railway Company, the Connotton Valley Railroad Company (now part of the Wheeling and Lake Erie Railroad); the Farmers' Bank; the New England Trust Company; the City National Bank of Canton; the Ma-

---

[61] " Poor's Railroad Manual " for 1880: p. 612.

[62] See, Appearance Docket, Court of Common Pleas, Stark County, O., Vol. 54, p. 1673, Vol. 56, p. 3037, etc.

[63] Ibid., Vols. 54, 55, 63, 68, etc., etc., in which his appearances as counsel are entered with great frequency.

honing National Bank of Youngstown; the Alliance Bank; the Cleveland and Canton Railway Company; the Canton Gas Light and Coal Company; the Dueber Watch Case Company, the American Screw Company; the Bolton Steel Company (now a constituent of the Steel Trust); the Alliance Gas Company; the Wrought Iron Bridge Company (a large corporation absorbed by the American Bridge Company); the Electric Light and Power Company, the Massillon Valley Coal Company (a large coal-mining corporation in Ohio); the Rough Mining Mountain Company and other corporations.[64] In fine, Day's practice-was a general corporation practice for railroads, trusts, banks, street railways, gas and electric light companies, coal-mining companies and many kindred corporate concerns.

Far from being a noted lawyer, Day was simply a local corporation attorney; he did not appear in any large corporation actions. When such suits came up, the corporation cases were argued by lawyers of national reputation. In his railroad practice Day usually appeared to contest suits brought for damages for injuries.

The Case of Mary Birtch.

One of these cases, giving Day not a very enviable reputation among common folk in Canton, was the action of Mary Birtch against the Wheeling and Lake Erie Railroad. In a wreck near Navarre, Ohio, in 1891, Mary Birtch, sixty-two years old, was one of the passengers hurt; her spinal column was so severely injured that she could hardly move. She brought suit for $10,000 damages.

When the case came up in 1894 in the Court of Common Pleas at Canton, Day personally appeared as the railroad's counsel to contest her suit. The evidence proved that the

[64] The above facts are to be found in *Ibid.*, Vols. 54 to 58, 60, 62–64, 68–69, 70, etc.

ties were so rotten that the rails parted and the cars were derailed. But throughout the trial the proceedings were so conducted that the jury became prejudiced against her. Judge McCarthy would not allow her lawyer or her doctors to be present at a physical examination to determine her injuries. The judge allowed the railroad's physician to say that she was faking, and Judge McCarthy himself denounced her in open court as an old fake. The jury gave Mary Birtch a verdict for $65. Her counsel made a motion for a new trial; this, Day vigorously opposed and the judge denied the application.

Six weeks later Mary Birtch died. A post-mortem examination by three physicians revealed that her spinal column had been so seriously injured that it had become completely decayed. She had suffered great pain and her death was directly caused by the injury.

A Five-Cent Judgment.

A result of the same wreck was the action of William McLain's Administrator for damages. A young route agent in the postal service, McLain jumped when the cars were derailed. A snag of a bush along the track penetrated his abdomen; peritonitis set in and caused his death. Day appeared in court as attorney for the Wheeling and Lake Erie Railroad, and argued that McLain was guilty of negligence in jumping. The entry in the Appearance Docket at Canton shows that on February 10, 1893, the jury brought in a verdict for *five cents damages*.[65] A motion on April 7, 1893, for a new trial was overruled, and *each party was ordered to pay its own costs*.

A similar case was that of Frederick Heiman's Administrator vs. the Cleveland Terminal and Valley Railroad Company (at present belonging to the Baltimore and Ohio Railroad system). Day's firm was counsel for the railroad

[65] See, Appearance Docket, Court of Common. Pleas, Stark County, for that year, p. 8024.

company.[66] On March 15, 1898, a verdict for $4,200 was given for the plaintiff. The railroad's motion for a new trial was overruled, but the judge struck $1,700 from the judgment. If the plaintiff had not consented to this the motion for a new trial would have been granted. The State Circuit Court reversed the decision and remanded the case for a new trial. The judgment in the new trial was only $1,000.

Death a Part of the Worker's Task.

Another of many such cases in which Day, or the firm of which he was a member, appeared, was the action of David L. Morgan vs. the Krause (Coal) Mining Company. This corporation was represented by Day, Lynch and Day (for so the firm was now constituted). The precedent set in this case is a noted one in Ohio.

On February 17, 1891, Morgan had been injured by an explosion of fire damp. When his suit came up the Court excluded the evidence of Kline, the mine boss; if Kline had been allowed to testify, the fact, it was alleged, would have been proved that the mine owners had not supplied safety lamps. The result of this omission of testimony, as well as the fear of other miners to testify (because they might be deprived of their jobs) was a verdict in favor of the company. The Ohio Supreme Court affirmed the action of Common Pleas on the ground that " where the injured party knowingly and deliberately assumes a risk that leads him into immediate danger, he ought not to have a remedy for injuries arising from perils that are obvious and certain." [67]   A characteristic judicial construction; the laws decree that employers should provide safe tools and proper precautions, but the judges declare that death is a fixed part of a worker's task.

These are not isolated, but typical, specimens of the uniform kind of cases that Day pleaded for several decades; he was

---

[66] Appearance Docket, Stark County, etc., Vol. 71 : p. 11,913.
[67] Ohio State Reports, Vol. 53 : 26-43.

a regular corporation attorney appearing constantly to contest the claims of workers or their survivors for damages for injuries causing disability or death. He himself lived in the provincial aristocratic style of the well-paid corporation lawyer; and if he cherished a latent spark of sympathy for the disfigured, the maimed and crippled, the widowed and orphaned, it was smothered by the income that he received from railroad and mining companies.

Nor is his long record of tenacious pleading against impoverished, injured or slain workers introduced here aimlessly. It was significant of the type of lawyer often chosen for judgeships, especially for seats on the Supreme Court of the United States. Chief Justice Waite, Chief Justice Fuller, Justices Swayne, Shiras and others had ascended to their eminence by route of (among other corporation practices) seeking to prevent injured workers or the destitute widows or children of the killed from recovering damages.

One of the most important and insistent series of cases coming up before the courts was that resulting from employers' liability laws. The slaughter of workers in the industrial field was immense, greater in a single year than the most dreadful carnage of the most destructive battle the world has ever known. Nevertheless, the railroad, mining and industrial corporations contested even the mildest legislation designed to compel them to install improved equipment and safety appliances, and violated such laws as did exist.

On the railroads alone, from the years 1888 to 1907, a total of 53,046 railroad employés were killed and more than 800,-000 were maimed or crippled while at work.[68] Such lawyers

[68] These figures are compiled from the annual reports of the Interstate Commerce Commission. See particularly the Nineteenth Annual Report of that Commission (1907) giving a tabulation on p. 109. But even these figures give no adequate picture of the full and terrible truth. At a recent hearing in Washington, this fact was brought out: That only such as died within *twenty-four hours* after accidents, were reported to the Interstate Commerce Commission under the list of deaths. Otherwise, they were included in the roll of "accidents."

as Fuller, Day, Shiras and others had used all of their ingenuity as attorneys to argue the narrowing of the laws applied to workers and, on the other hand, the extension of the rights, privileges and immunities of corporations. And this was the type of lawyer going on the Bench of the Supreme Court of the United States — men who had faithfully done their careers of subservient service to the railroad, mining and industrial magnates. After becoming Justices they generally construed laws and handed down decisions precisely in line with what they, as attorneys, had received fat retainers to argue.

Day, too, was now elevated to a judgeship. Appointed a member of the United States Circuit Court, he sat with Taft (now President of the United States) and Lurton (now a United States Supreme Court Justice). This trio on the Sixth Circuit, handed down delectable decisions refusing time after time, to award damages to destitute workers injured through no fault of their own.[69] Selected by President McKinley solely because he was McKinley's neighbor in Canton and his close personal friend and attorney, Day was appointed Assistant Secretary of State of the United States, and subsequently Secretary of State. It was when occupying this post that Day negotiated the generous treaty with Spain by which $20,000,000 was paid to Spain for the already conquered Philippine Islands, and it was Day who arranged the negotiations by which the United States munificiently paid $18 an acre for the Roman Catholic Friar lands in the Philippines — a great part of which lands have since been sold by the Government to the Sugar Trust for $6.50 an acre.[70] This latter fact

[69] See later. Both Taft and Lurton had been railroad attorneys.

[70] The San José Estate (Friar lands) of 55,000 acres of Mindoro Island, was sold to E. L. Poole, representing H. O. Havemeyer and associates; the Isabella Tract of 49,000 acres was taken over by E. B. Bruce, representing the Havemeyer syndicate; and other Friar lands were likewise appropriated.— See, " Friar Lands Inquiry," House Committee on Insular Affairs, Feb., 1911: 40-44.

is stated merely for explanatory reasons; Day had no connection, directly or indirectly, with the sales to the Sugar Trust.

The Great Boon of " Voluntary Contract."

Day, as we have said, succeeded Justice Shiras. To give a concrete illustration of the type and circumstances of decisions of the Supreme Court of the United States regarding injured workers, let us pick out, for example, a decision written by Shiras just before he left the Bench.

Injured by a collision, William Voight, an employé of the United States Express Company on the Baltimore and Ohio Railroad, sued for damages. In the lower courts he was successful. On the ground that when he obtained his job Voight had signed a contract releasing the railroad company from liability, the company appealed. Shiras held that Voight was not compelled to enter into such a contract, but did it voluntarily, secured work by means of it, and that such a contract did not contravene public policy. Only Harlan dissented.[71]

Shiras had been counsel for the Baltimore and Ohio Railroad branch at Pittsburgh, and he well knew that no man could get work unless he signed such a contract. Here, in brief, was the Supreme Court of the United States upholding the power of a corporation to force illegal contracts from men seeking work, or else consign them and their families to hunger and destitution. It gave the corporation the right to say to a worker: " Sign this contract, or starve; " and then after the worker had been injured, threw him out of court, denying him the paltry damages sued for, caring nothing what became of him or his family. Day was, indeed, a worthy successor of Shiras.

[71] Case of B. and O. R. R. vs. Voight, 176 U. S. Reports, 498.

Justice Moody Enters.

The next Associate Justice appointed was William H. Moody of Massachusetts; he took his seat on December 17, 1906, succeeding Brown, retired. Born in 1853, Moody, too, was a Harvard graduate; for sixteen years before his appointment to the Supreme Court he had held a succession of public offices. Associating with the Lodge political machine, he became district attorney for the eastern district of Massachusetts in 1890. Five years were spent in that office, and in 1895 he was elected to Congress. He was appointed Secretary of War on May 1, 1902, and on July 1, 1904, succeeded Knox as Attorney-General of the United States. Like Knox (Steel Trust attorney), Moody made a frantic appearance of seeking the dissolution of the trusts, but it was merely an illusory proceeding quickly degenerating into a travesty.

Moody was a follower and close friend of Senator Henry Cabot Lodge, who has been viewed with sincere and unbroken approval by the great corporate interests in Massachusetts. Lacking the support of these interests, no man could expect to be sent to the United States Senate, or elected or appointed to any other public office. Even the much-bepraised Hoar, Lodge's predecessor, had been attorney for railroads and for the most powerful industrial concerns.[72] Lodge's associate United States Senator from Massachusetts was Murray Crane, an extensive manufacturer, who as Governor of that State had recommended and ratified legislation by which the Boston and Albany Railroad was turned over to the Vanderbilts under a perpetual lease. This railroad was built largely by the State, but private capitalists owned part of the stock. Among the large stockholders was Murray Crane, but when elected Governor he had virtuously transferred his holdings to his brother

[72] Hoar represented the Worcester and Nashua Railroad Company, the Amoskeag Manufacturing Company, etc.— 131 Mass. Reports, 495: V Supreme Court Reporter, 441, etc.

and partner, Zenas Crane.[73] The methods by which the State's interests were surrendered in this transaction and also in the selling of the State's stock in the Fitchburg Railway to the Boston and Maine Railroad, caused a blare of public scandal.[74]

At no time could Senator Lodge be accused of violating his signal fidelity to the interests of the Massachusetts manufacturers and railroad corporations. Unvaryingly he advocated measures for their benefit, nor did he suffer himself to prove false to his class interests by supporting working-class legislation. In the Massachusetts factories an immense number of child laborers have been employed under peculiarly degenerating conditions, but neither Lodge nor Holmes nor Moody ever even whispered a protest. Foremost of all corporations controlling the politics of Massachusetts are the Boston and Maine Railroad and the New York, New Haven and Hartford Railroad; they have invested themselves with the practical veto power over nominations or appointments to public office.

It was Lodge, the personal friend of Roosevelt, and his

[73] In the list compiled by the Interstate Commerce Commission of the ten largest stockholders of railroads, in 1908–1909, Zenas Crane appeared as the owner of 150,000 shares of common, and 10,000 shares of preferred, stock of the Chicago, St. Paul, Minneapolis and Omaha Railroad.

[74] Lucius Tuttle, President of the Boston and Maine Railroad, dominated New England politics. That this railroad corrupted legislatures is a matter of record. We will give an excerpt from a speech made by former United States Senator Chandler, at Laconia, N. H., on August 17, 1910; what he said of New Hampshire was equally true of Massachusetts, so far as the railroad was concerned:

"Railroad passes and railroad money dominate the 'State, and the governor, councillors, senators and representatives are the mere agents in their offices of the two great railroads.

"It may be said truthfully that nearly all the lawyers in the State are influenced by one or the other railroad companies, either by annual passes alone, or by such passes and money.

"New Hampshire has been one of the greatest victims of corporation rule, mainly governed in its industrial, political and government career by the Boston and Maine Railroad. There has been added to this influence the Amoskeag Manufacturing Company of Manchester, which, when it has not been adjusting its disputes with the railroads, has been joining with the railroads in taking possession of the State government."

mouthpiece in the Senate, who induced Roosevelt to appoint
Moody Attorney-General, and it was Lodge who, when Moody
retired from the Supreme Court of the United States, in 1910,
did Moody the friendly service of rolling a bill through Congress granting Moody a pension of $12,500 a year. When,
later, in the same year, Lodge's campaign for reëlection met
with vigorous opposition, Moody displayed his gratitude by
writing a letter to the members of the Massachusetts Legislature urging them to reëlect Lodge. ". . . We have, in the
person of Senator Lodge," Moody wrote, " one of the best
equipped men in public life; in fact, I think he is the most
competent legislator in the country. . . ." [75]

We shall now proceed to consider in aggregate some of the
more important of the mass of decisions of the Supreme Court
of the United States during this period. It will be understood that some of these decisions were handed down before
the different times when Holmes and Moody went on the
Bench, but their participation is included in the various later
decisions.

[75] Ostensibly a letter from a "constituent to his representatives
solely," this letter was immediately published in every Boston newspaper and in the press generally throughout the State.

CHAPTER XVI

THE SUPREME COURT UNDER CHIEF JUSTICE FULLER
(CONTINUED)

Oblivious to criticisms and the misunderstandings, the Supreme Court proved that in one essential respect it was not the reactionary institution that in certain quarters it was charged with being. Its critics were accustomed to declaim against it as a small oligarchy of doddering, obdurate old men, blind or at least insensible to all of the signs and demands of progress, and determined to impede, thwart or annul every manifestation of progress. This criticism, at once amusing and fallacious, is still current.

The Court's Ultra-Progressiveness.

In reality the Supreme Court in the specific point in question, was the most alert, adaptable, ultra-progressive institution in the United States. Frosted with heavy years most of its members truly were; but in depth of mind, in clarity of vision and grasp of affairs no body of men were less archaic or (in the particular referred to) more keenly responsive to the demands of altering conditions as required by the dominant division of the ruling class. This was their one remarkable ability — an ability to be estimated and appreciated at its high historic worth.

Bred under laws applying to an obsolete, bygone economic period, the Supreme Court majority nevertheless refused to allow that stultifying code of laws to stand in the way of industrial evolution. They declined to interfere with the orderly transition of society from an older, outworn, crumbling stage to a newer, more modern era. At a time when legislatures and Congress were fatuously bent upon seeking to revivify historic anachronisms, the Supreme Court of the United States was the one body that thrust those reactionary laws aside and facilitated industrial progress.

The age of unrestricted competition had passed, and the age of huge combinations of capitalists in concentrated corporations had supplanted it. Anarchy in production had been to a large extent superceded by systematic trust control. But many statutes, relics of the era when the still powerful middle class was vainly and confusedly trying to stop the growth of the trusts, remained as unrepealed legislation.

Agitation to enforce these anti-trust laws was continually carried on, although in a declining ratio as the middle-class organization grew less influential. Two concrete facts, however, obstinately protruded, conflicting side by side: One fact was that the trusts were growing increasingly more powerful. That the laws, markedly so the Federal anti-trust act, forbade the existence of those trusts, was the other fact.

But one of these was only the semblance of a fact, or rather the shadow of what had been a fact. Unrestrained competition in industry, with its warfares and its many deficiencies, was largely become a memory. It had ceased to be a fact, yet in the lifeless, bookish thing called statute law it was believed that it could be resurrected. The skeleton alone remained; breath and spirit had departed. Combination, however, was a living fact, and a mighty one; if anyone doubted its obvious economic superiority over its predecessor, competition, he at least could not but be impressed by its immense energy, system, power and resources.

The Existing Class War.

Three great groups now developed from the conflict within society. One of these was that of the trust magnates, with an interassociation in ownership of transportation systems, industries, mines and other resources. The wealth of this group was, computed by usual reckonings, almost illimitable; its power stupendous. But its numerical strength was small, and diminishing as its individual and collective wealth increased, for the big trust magnate warred upon the small not less than the trust upon the petty manufacturer.

The second group was that of the middle class. Many of the former strongest factors in this class — the small manufacturers, jobbers, etc.,— had either become absorbed in the trusts or had been driven from business. If the inroads of the trusts had ended here, the middle-class agitation would largely have died away from sheer inanition. Connected, however, with the middle class was a huge number of retail dealers. As the profits of the trusts piled up, the magnates necessarily had to look about for new channels of investment. The only remaining field, therefore, was the retail trade. In this, some of the trusts, notably the Tobacco Trust, began to establish their own stores, selling direct to the consumer. Naturally, this new move filled the shopkeepers everywhere with the most violent alarm, and gave the anti-trust agitation a new impetus.

Aligned with the middle class were the agricultural element and a large section of uninformed workers. Altogether, the forces massed in the array opposed to the trusts were numerically great, and formed an overpowering political majority. This explains why legislators, themselves often tools of trusts, were unwilling to risk their own political extinction by repealing laws aimed at the trusts.

The third group was that of organized labor. On the political field its views and sentiments and actions at the time were similar to those of the middle class, although the two classes had nothing in common. Only that fragment of the workers comprised in the Socialist ranks was then clear sighted enough to understand that the trusts were a natural outgrowth of evolutionary conditions.

But between trusts and labor unions a deadly conflict was in progress. With their enormous issues of watered stock, the trusts sought to augment their profits in every way in order to give that stock value. Added to this fact was the ever-present principle of the employer aiming to buy his labor as cheap as possible. The labor unions were an obstacle to this programme of merciless exploitation. On the other hand, the reverse principle operated, the laborer trying to get the utmost for his labor power. While maintaining their right to carry on industry and transportation in modern, compact, concentrated corporations, the trusts denied the workers' right of organizing along modern lines. The trusts aimed at nothing less than the destruction of the labor unions.*

An Absolute Institution.

With this preliminary, we can now begin to get a clear conception of the fundamental meaning of the edicts of the Supreme Court of the United States. If the legislators were afraid to recognize inevitable changes and enact laws in conformity with them, the Supreme Court was not. It had no purblind constituents to appease, nor did it have to make explanations to anyone. It was, as its title implied, supreme, and could decree law as it pleased. At the proper time it could even, as some of its apparent anti-trust decisions indicated, serve the ulterior purposes of the magnates in subtler forms. It could put trusts to the trouble of nominally dissolving so that a cry of "disturbed business conditions" could be set up, and thus give legislators a pretext to pass laws legalizing trusts.

As for the labor unions the Supreme Court did not have to depend upon their favor or votes; the Supreme Court could strike at them without fear of retaliation; in truth, that exalted tribunal held workers in supreme contempt. For good reason. The trust magnates saw to it that every important post was filled by representatives of their own class, but the bulk of the voters were deluded into voting their avowed enemies into office year after year. It was their votes that put capital ist Presidents in the White House, and it was those Presidents who appointed Supreme Court Justices. Not a member of the Supreme Court was appointed unless his views and associations were known and canvassed in advance, and his record closely scanned by the great capitalist interests.

The Sugar Trust had been, as we have seen, given a bill of immunity, and at about the same time the Supreme Court had sent Debs to jail. A series of decisions followed which further allowed the exemption of the trusts. True, a few decisions were handed over seemingly antagonistic to certain trusts and combinations. But in practical application they had no such effect. At the same time, other decisions of the Supreme Court struck hard at labor-union leaders and labor-union measures and tactics, while permitting railroad corporations to pursue toward workers what had hitherto been held to be unfair and illegal methods. We shall give the substance of the more important of these decisions.

Anti-Trust Measures Extinguished.

Anti-trust acts in thirteen States were wiped off the statute books by the decision of the Supreme Court in the case of Connolly vs. the Union Sewer Pipe Company, on March 10, 1902. The action involved the constitutionality of an Illinois statute; Harlan delivered the court's opinion pronouncing the law void; McKenna dissented.[1]

Shortly after this the Supreme Court expounded another decision in which it revealed that it was fully alive to the requirements of industrial conditions. The case was that of the Carnegie Steel Company vs. the Cambria Iron Company. The suit arose over a contention as to whether Carnegie was en-

[1] 184 U. S. Reports, 540.

titled to a valuable patent (the Jones invention) for manufacturing steel. The Supreme Court decided for Carnegie, but Justices White, Fuller, Harlan and Brewer concurred in a dissenting opinion in which they concluded with the significant statement that by thus being allowed to exact tribute from the steel and iron making industry, Carnegie was in a position to hinder the operations of other steel makers from keeping " pace *with the natural evolution of modern industrial development.*" [2]

The Carnegie Company was a main part of the Steel Trust, and one of its attorneys in the foregoing case was Philander C. Knox, of Pittsburg. Knox had been the counsel for the Carnegie Company. Back in 1894 he had pleaded for that company when it was proved that the company, in its contracts to supply armor plate for warships had " perpetrated manifold frauds, the natural tendency of which was to palm off upon the Government an inferior armor whose inferiority might perchance appear only in the shock of battle and with incalculable damage to the country." [3] According to the reluctant testimony of A. J. Cassatt, president of the Pennsylvania Railroad, the Carnegie Company had been continuously receiving illegal rebates on a vast scale from the railroads.[4]

Knox had also been attorney for the Pittsburg, Bessemer and Lake Erie Railroad, the Pittsburg, Fort Wayne and Chicago Railroad, the Pittsburg and Birmingham Traction Company, and for other powerful corporate clients. From the Carnegie Company alone Knox was reputed to have received a retainer of $50,000 a year. When a Congressional Committee exposed the armor-plate frauds, Knox, as we have said, proved his skill by diverting all attempts at prosecution.

[2] 185 U. S. Reports, 409. My italics.—G. M.
[3] House Report No. 1468, Fifty-third Congress, Second Session. The revelations of the armor-plate frauds produced a deep sensation at this time.
[4] By receiving rebates from railroads, large corporations and trusts were easily able to undersell and undermine competitors. Rebating was illegal and punishable.

The nucleus of the Steel Trust, formed in 1901, was the Carnegie Company, and the two successive Presidents of the Steel Trust were Schwab and Corey, who, with Cline, had been superintendents of the Carnegie Plant in 1894. Of Cline, Corey and Schwab the Congressional investigating committee had reported, ". . . The unblushing character of the frauds to which these men have been parties and the disregard for truth and honesty which they have shown in testifying before your committee, render them unworthy of credence." [5]

The Eminent Mr. Knox.

Andrew Carnegie, then the principal stockholder of the Carnegie Steel Company, admitted in his testimony before the (Stanley) House Investigating Committee, on January 11, 1912, that, in 1901, he had written a letter to President McKinley recommending Knox's appointment as Attorney-General of the United States. Carnegie further testified that Knox had been one of the attorneys of the Carnegie Steel Company from 1890 (the date of the passage of the Sherman anti-trust law) to the year 1901, and that Judge Reed, Knox's law partner, had become a member of the Directorate of the Steel Trust, formed in 1901.

These were some of the antecedents of Knox, who, in 1901, became Attorney-General of the United States. On the evening of March 22, 1901, J. Pierpont Morgan, the organizer and head of the Steel Trust, called upon President McKinley at the White House. The next morning McKinley announced that the Attorney-General would be Knox. Petitioning the Senate judiciary committee not to confirm the appointment, the Anti-Trust League pertinently inquired:

" Is it proper for a lawyer to appear against his former clients? Can a lawyer willing to appear against his former clients be trusted to prosecute them if guilty? The charges

[5] House Report No. 1468, Fifty-third Congress, Second Session.

we have filed refer not only to his dereliction of duty in the cases we have filed with him, but also bear upon his admitted intimate relations and his collusion with the criminal practices of the armor-plate trust which, we are informed, robbed the Government of millions of dollars during the time Mr. Knox was their associate and adviser."

Having thus shed illumination on Knox's career, and the great corporate interests he had represented, we shall be in a better position to understand why it was that he, as Attorney-General, brought suit to have the Northern Securities Company declared illegal.

The Northern Securities Case.

In 1874, the Minnesota Legislature had passed an act prohibiting the consolidation of parallel or competing railroads. In 1901, James J. Hill, the controlling magnate of the Great Northern Railroad and part owner of the Northern Pacific Railroad, set out to get control of the Chicago, Burlington and Quincy Railroad. In retaliation, competing magnates began to buy Northern Pacific Railroad stock which would give them a voice in one of Hill's own railroads.

A great warfare in the stock market resulted. The outcome of this conflict among the magnates was a merging of interests. Morgan's idea of a holding company with $400,000,000 capital to combine the interests of both the Great Northern and the Northern Pacific railroads was carried out. The new corporation was called the Northern Securities Company.

It is not possible to ascertain the secret antagonisms or other underlying purposes then at work as the reasons for certain moves. Between Morgan's Steel Trust and Hill's interests there was a direct connection of large magnitude. Hill owned iron ore deposits of vast value near Lake Superior; testifying subsequently before the (Stanley) House Investigating Committee, on February 12, 1912, Hill said that he

had bought these properties for $4,050,000. He had leased
69,000 acres of the iron ore deposits to the Steel Trust which
thus far — by the year 1912 — had worked only 39,000 acres.
In the remaining 30,000 acres which will revert to Hill when
the Steel Trust surrenders its lease (in 1913), there were, Hill
testified, 500,000,000 tons of ore left, which he valued at $750,-
000,000. We state these facts merely as facts; what relevancy
they had to the Northern Securities action we do not know.

President Roosevelt ordered Knox to proceed against the
Northern Securities Company. Knox did so, but it was made a
civil proceeding. The question frequently asked in observant
circles was this: Did certain magnates have a secret motive for
breaking up the Northern Securities Company? On March
14, 1904, the Supreme Court of the United States declared the
corporation an illegal one in restraint of commerce and ordered
its dissolution.[6]

Illegal it was thus pronounced; it followed, therefore, that
under the law those guilty could have been criminally prosecuted and sent to prison. Debs had been thrown in prison on
an extraneous, manufactured charge. But a labor leader was
on a vastly different plane in the application of law from a magnate, or a galaxy of magnates. Not the slightest attempt was
made to prefer criminal action against the organizers of the
Northern Securities Company. Against this fact Justice

[6] Northern Securities Company vs. U. S., 193 U. S. Reports, 197.
As illustrating the possibilities of secret bargaining, the statements
of Wharton Barker, a Philadelphia banker, conservative political econo-
mist, and at one time a middle-class (" middle of the road ") candidate
for the Presidency, may here be referred to. Barker testified before the
United States Senate Committee on Interstate Commerce, on November
29, 1911, that he had been told by one of the Wall Street banking magnates that in the campaign of 1904, when Roosevelt was a candidate
for the Presidency, that the Wall Street interests had made a bargain
with Roosevelt on the railroad question. "He is to 'holler' all he
wants to," the magnate was quoted as saying, "and by and by — not
immediately, but in due time — a railroad bill is to be recommended by
the President," — which was to abolish rebates, free passes, legalize pool-
ing, and permit an increase of capital stock. Roosevelt ridiculed this
testimony.

Holmes protested in his dissenting opinion when he said: " It is vain to insist that this is not a criminal proceeding. The words cannot be read one way in a suit which is to end in fine and imprisonment, and another in one which seeks an injunction. I am no friend of artificial interpretations. . . . So I say we must read the words before us as if the question were whether two small exporting grocers should go to jail."

Prisons for the Poor Only.

Here, indeed, was a vital and striking feature of the Supreme Court's decisions, even when those decisions were nominally adverse to the trusts. The prisons throughout the country were filled with convicts whose only real crime was that they were poor. Poverty, unlike wealth, commanded no respect from the courts.[7] For the slightest violation of law, the helpless and uninfluential were consigned to prison, more often than not for long terms. But not a single railroad director, nor a solitary trust magnate has ever been condemned to prison for violating the anti-trust laws.

Given the alternative of inflicting fine and imprisonment or both, the courts have done nothing more than sentence the trust offender to a fine. This has been a recognized travesty; to a corporation extorting hundreds of millions of dollars in profits, a fine of a few thousands is ludicrous. Moreover, the

[7] The truth of this generalization is so obvious and so clearly sustained by a vast multitude of examples, that it requires no elucidation here. Speaking on this point, United States District Attorney Henry A. Wise, in an address at New York, on November 14, 1911, told how rich smugglers and thieves had been let off with a fine by the courts, and poor offenders sent to prison. " But," he observed, " it has been difficult to send the rich to jail. The judge evidently thinks that they should have plenty of warning, and in case after case of this kind, I have howled in vain for jail sentences." Among other examples, Wise instanced the case of the Sugar Trust. It had defrauded the Government of vast sums, yet no one had been inculpated except " dead men and $15 a week clerks." After being forced to make certain restitution to the Government, the Sugar Trust had recouped itself by raising the price of sugar.

amounts of the fines can always be abundantly recouped from the reduced wages of the workers or from consumers in added cost of necessaries. Even in criminal matters, apart from conspiracies to restrain commerce, this is what happened, according to Attorney-General Moody:

" But where the accusation is a grave one, and the accused has abundant means, the ingenuity of his counsel opens many avenues of appeal which ultimately reach the Supreme Court, raising there a constant succession of trivial questions with consequent delays which may retard or even defeat the purposes of justice." [8]

The Beef Trust Ignores the Supreme Court.

In the Supreme Court's pretended application of anti-trust laws the soberest judgment can direct nothing else than a prolonged farce, perhaps relieved by the stern tragedy of fining multimillionaires a few thousand dollars. In the Beef Trust case, the Supreme Court, on January 30, 1905, affirmed an injunction restraining Swift and other packers from carrying on a conspiracy of combination.[9] No doubt the packers have treasured the writ as a curious yet harmless souvenir; the injunction has become faded, but the Beef Trust has been joyously pursuing the same old extortionate line of business, as is proved by more actions recently brought against it by the Government.[10]

[8] Annual Report of the U. S. Attorney-General for 1905, p. 6.
[9] Swift vs. U. S., 196 U. S. Reports, 375.
[10] On May 19, 1902, the Government began an action against the Beef Trust. The packers interposed every possible legal obstacle. On July 1, 1905, however, the Federal Grand Jury of Chicago indicted seventeen individuals and five corporations. In 1906, Judge Humphrey gave them immunity because they had testified in an investigation conducted by the Bureau of Corporations. The Government continued its actions, and there were more years of law delay. Finally, on September 12, 1910, new indictments were found against Armour, Swift, Morris and other packers. Just as the packers were about to be put on trial, in November, 1911, they raised the question that the Sherman anti-trust act was unconstitutional and they secured release under bonds or writs

Immunity for Trust Magnates.

Next came that illuminating series of decisions in the General Paper Company and Tobacco Trust cases, in March, 1906. The Supreme Court held that immunity was extended to trust magnates who testified, but declared that the *corporation* could be punished.

Quite true, this decision was based upon an act passed by Congress in 1903, the object of which was clearly to give immunity to trust owners.[11] With alacrity the Supreme Court accepted this law as constitutional; it saw nothing null and void in the granting of exemptions to trust heads for acts for which they personally were responsible and from which they were personally benefiting to the extent of billions of dollars. A corporation cannot be imprisoned; there was something screamingly funny in the solemn mummery of inflicting a nominal fine upon a corporation capitalized at hundreds of millions of dollars.

Anti-Railroad Acts Effaced.

The power of the States to pass acts fixing railroad rates was swept aside by a Supreme Court decision, of March 22, 1908, which declared unconstitutional railroad rate laws passed by the States of Minnesota and North Carolina. Justice

of habeas corpus. After *nine years' delay,* the Supreme Court of the United States was then appealed to for a stay of their trial. On December 5, 1911, this application was refused.

[11] Section 3 of the Elkins act of 1903 gave immunity to testifying witnesses. All that a magnate had to do was to give some slight testimony, and this automatically made him exempt from prosecution. This bill, as is seen by the name, was introduced and pushed by the notorious Stephen B. Elkins, whose fraudulent claim for nearly two million acres had been validated by the Supreme Court and who was himself an extensive railroad magnate. The principle was the same as if a burglar, highwayman or murderer after having given testimony was declared immune from prosecution. And it may be said that what with their methods of oppression of wage workers and extortions the railroad corporations and trusts directly and indirectly caused an immense number of deaths.

Peckham, erstwhile trustee of the Mutual Life Insurance Company, associate of numerous magnates, wrote this decision.[12] Peckham also it was who a little previously wrote a decision declaring unconstitutional a tax levy of the City of Chicago on various utility corporations,[13] and it was Peckham, too, who wrote a decision relieving the Smelter Trust of a tax imposed by the State of Colorado on its capital stock; such a tax, said the Supreme Court, was unconstitutional.[14]

Another characteristic decision of the Supreme Court was that on December 15, 1909, relieving E. H. Harriman from testifying in an investigation carried on by the Interstate Commerce Commission.[15] This was the period when Harriman, by the most extensive system of fraudulent railroad manipulation and bribery, was acquiring the immense fortune that he left. The Interstate Commerce Commission was thus balked in its effort to learn whether Harriman and his associates had profited by sales of $120,000,000 of stocks to the Union Pacific Railroad of which they were directors.

But the Commission discovered enough to report in detail upon the extent of the frauds and how those frauds were accomplished. It reported that in the manipulation of the Chicago and Alton Railroad alone, nearly $60,000,000 had been stolen by Harriman and his associates. To themselves, Harriman and partners sold $32,000,000 of bonds (representing essentially no improvements) at 65. Then Harriman induced the New York Legislature to pass an act, which Governor Theodore Roosevelt signed, authorizing savings banks

[12] 209 U. S. Reports, 12. Justice Harlan was the only dissenter.
[13] Justices Holmes and Moody dissented.
[14] Fuller, Harlan, Holmes and Moody expressed dissent.
[15] Harriman vs. Interstate Commerce Commission, 211 U. S. Reports, 407. Former United States Senator John C. Spooner was one of Harriman's counsel in this action. Justices Day, Harlan and McKenna dissented. Moody, not having heard the argument, took no part in the decision. Spooner and Joseph H. Choate recently appeared (it may be observed here) for the Steamship Trust as the trust's counsel in an action brought by the Government in the United States Circuit Court against the trust as an illegal combination.

to invest in those bonds. The price of the bonds was then put up from 82⅛ to 94. This is but one of the various methods described by the Interstate Commerce Commission.[16]

By its decision the Supreme Court virtually protected Harriman at the identical time he had consummated his gigantic frauds in the manipulation of the Chicago and Alton, the Illinois Central, the Union Pacific and the Southern and the Central Pacific and allied railroads.

The Supreme Court had declared the Northern Securities Company illegal. Why did it not declare the Harriman combination owning parallel lines likewise illegal? The Interstate Commerce Commission reported that the Union Pacific and parallel roads were held by the Harriman combination and that those allied railroads had in force a specific division of freight traffic, so that each should get a certain share.[17] This meant nothing more or less than an illegal combination.

An " Illusory " Decision.

Still another interesting decision of the Supreme Court was that in the " Commodities Clause Cases." The Hepburn Act of 1906 made it unlawful for any railroad company to transport products of any mines in which it might have an interest, direct or indirect. This law was aimed at the Coal Trust; it was notorious that the coal-carrying railroads controlled the coal deposits. The Supreme Court did not pronounce this law unconstitutional, but it decided on May 3, 1909, in favor of the railroads on this ground: That the prohibition did not apply to the transportation of commodities

---

[16] For the full facts of Harriman's enormous thefts, see, Report No. 943 of the Interstate Commerce Commission, " In the Matter of Consolidations and Combinations," etc., pp. 320–345. The Chicago and Alton transaction is described in pp. 340–345. The Commission stated that liabilities of $113,894,000 were placed upon the Chicago and Alton Railroad which had originally cost approximately $58,000,000. Yet not a dollar of tangible property had been added.— P. 342.

[17] *Ibid.*, 345–346.

by another corporation the only interest of which lay in its ownership of capital stock of coal-mining corporations " at the time of such transportation." [18]

The exalted tribunal chose to make itself the subject of general criticism by ignoring the obvious fact that the way corporations control subsidiary corporations is by owning a majority of their capital stock.

Attorney-General Wickersham denounced the decision. " If," he wrote, " the prohibition of the statute can be successfully evaded by the simple device of transfer of ownership of property to a corporation, all of whose stock shall be owned or controlled by the carrier, Congress should amend the statute so as to make it an effectual, and not merely an illusory, prohibition, or else repeal it." [19]

These are a few examples of decisions selected from a mass.

On the other hand, the Supreme Court of the United States demonstrated a very different attitude toward cases affecting the rights or welfare of the working class.

Shorter Hours Denied Bakeshop Workers.

After protracted agitation, the labor unions finally succeeded in getting the New York Legislature to pass an act making the lot of bakeshop workers more tolerable by prescribing a ten-hour law. The master bakers contested this law up to the Supreme Court of the United States. That Court, on April 17, 1905, declared it unconstitutional.

On what ground? The Supreme Court held it unconstitutional on the ground that it " curtailed liberty of contract." The austere tribunal was extremely solicitous about the right

[18] United States vs. Delaware & Hudson Company; United States vs. Erie Railroad Company; United States vs. Central Railroad of New Jersey; United States vs. Delaware, Lackawanna & Western Railroad Company; United States vs. Pennsylvania Railroad Company; United States vs. Lehigh Valley Railroad Company.—213 U. S., 366.

[19] Annual Report of the Attorney-General for 1909: p. 4.

of the worker to contract to work as long as he " pleased " in filthy, torrid cellars, for a miserable wage.

Who, it may be inquired, wrote this memorable decision? Justice Peckham. To Peckham, Chief Justice Fuller and the three other concurring Justices it was clear that " the freedom of master and employé to contract with each other in relation to their employment and in defining the same, cannot be prohibited or interfered with without violating the Federal Constitution." [20] Now, by gracious leave of the Supreme Court of the United States, the boss bakers could make their drudges sweat in underground holes eighteen hours of the twenty-four, if the aforesaid drudges, driven to it by hunger, would so contract. " Liberty of contract " is a precious phrase. The Supreme Court had thrown its protection around Harriman when, after accumulating a vast fortune by fraud, he was seeking to protect his criminal transactions from too sharp an official inquiry. But it refused to extend the slightest protection to overworked wage earners in bakeshops. Back these were driven by the Supreme Court's edict to their slavery, without any prospect of bettering their condition.[21]

The Fourteenth Amendment.

The most noteworthy feature, however, in this decision applying to bakeshop workers was that the law was declared unconstitutional under the Fourteenth Amendment.

Now this amendment had been one of the amendments adopted to secure the full freedom of Negroes, and to safe-

[20] Harlan, White, Day and Holmes dissented in Lochner vs. New York.— 198 U. S. Reports, 45.

[21] Testifying before the New York State Factory investigating commission, on November 14, 1911, Miss Frances Perkins, Deputy Secretary of the Consumers' League, described the vile conditions of many bakeshops in New York City and their causes. ". . . There was every evidence in these bakeries," Miss Perkins related, " that employés were allowed to sleep in the workrooms, some on cots, and some on the bread trays, even. As the men are obliged to work long hours, it is only natural that they should snatch naps whenever possible, and a favorite place is on the sacks of flour. . . ."

guard them from the oppressions of their former owners. Yet for more than twenty years the Supreme Court of the United States, in deference to the demands of the ruling class, had consistently emasculated it. The Supreme Court had refused to define what the rights of Negroes were;[22] it had held that the amendment had no reference to the conduct of individual to individual;[23] it had declined to give the Negroes the protection of the National Government when it decided that "sovereignty for the protection of rights of life and personal liberty within the States rests alone with the States."[24] This meant that the former slave States were empowered to abridge the liberty of the Negro as they pleased.

Other decisions, each curtailing the rights of Negroes, followed. On the ground that it was not warranted by the amendment, an Act of Congress giving Negroes the right co-equally with whites of enjoying inns, public conveyances, theaters and other public resorts, was declared unconstitutional.[25] The right of suffrage was neither granted nor protected by the Amendment.[26] A State could curtail the right of trial by jury without violating the amendment.[27] It was further held that a State enactment requiring whites and Negroes to ride in separate railroad cars did not violate the amendment.[28]

[22] Davidson vs. New Orleans, 96 U. S. Reports, 194. At this point, adopting the excellent suggestion of Professor W. E. B. DuBois, we have purposely capitalized the word Negro. "Negro," says Professor DuBois, "is not the corresponding term to the word white; black is that term as everybody knows. Negro does not refer to color simply, because there are black people who are not Negroes. Negro is the designation of a race of men just as Indian, Teutonic or Celtic. Historically the word Negro has always been capitalized, and the small letter was only used during the latter days of the slavery agitation when Negroes were classed with real estate."

[23] Civil Rights Cases, 109 U. S. Reports, 3.

[24] U. S. vs. Cruikshank, 92 U. S. Reports, 542.

[25] Civil Rights Cases, 109 Ibid., 3.

[26] In re Lockwood, 154 Ibid., 116.

[27] L. & N. R. R. Co. vs. Schmidt, 177 Ibid., 230.

[28] Plessy vs. Ferguson, 163 U. S. Reports, 537. The case was that of a quadroon who sued to test the constitutionality of an act passed by

These are a few of the many decisions of the Supreme
Court of the United States, the cumulative effect of which
was to allow States to nullify guarantees of freedom for the
Negro. That many States did this is common knowledge.
Finally, the Supreme Court sanctioned the most revolting kind
of Negro peonage in the case of Clyatt who had been found
guilty in Florida of forcibly keeping Negroes in virtual
slavery. Passing on a writ of certiorari, the Supreme Court
of the United States ordered the case back for a new trial on
the pretext that the trial judge erred in permitting the case
to go to the jury.[29]

First the Negro, Then the White Worker.

With complete indifference, or with outright approval, according to locality, the white workers had thus seen the Negro
stripped of his Constitutional rights and reduced to a position
of inferiority in law as well as custom. The Supreme Court
of the United States now began to use that same Fourteenth
Amendment, designed to protect the Negro, against the whole
of the working class, white and black. When this fact became
evident, the amazement of the white workers was great. Now
they — or at least some of them — perceived that the rights
of no one portion of the workers could be curtailed or oblit-

the Louisiana Legislature compelling the separation of whites and
negroes in trains, etc. Justice Harlan expressed his contempt for the
decision of his colleagues. He said it was a pernicious opinion, and that
the argument that social equality could not exist between the two races
" is scarcely worthy of consideration " (p. 561). A complete reactionary, both as regarded the development of the trusts, on the one hand,
and that of labor organizations on the other, Harlan was, nevertheless,
the one member of the Supreme Court who stood up consistently for
the rights of the Negro race.

[29] Clyatt vs. U. S., 198 U. S. Reports, 207. Brewer delivered the
Court's decision. In this case, also, Harlan dissented. " The accused,"
he said, " made no objection to the submission of the case to the jury,
and it is going very far to hold in a case like this, disclosing barbarities
of the worst kind against these negroes, that the trial court erred in
sending the case to the jury."

erated without the construction being applied to all workers
of all races.

Using the Fourteenth Amendment to load the helpless
Negro race with the obloquy of prejudicial law and custom,
and to snatch away from the white worker what trivial rights
he still had, the Supreme Court availed itself of that same
amendment to put corporations in a more impregnable position
in law than they had ever been before. This new development turned up in the case of the Consolidated Gas Company
vs. the City of New York. The decision in that case revealed
— what had so often previously been demonstrated — that
while in the very act of apparently deciding against a corporation, the Supreme Court in reality set another precedent
vastly extending intrenched corporate power and legalizing
corporate extortions.

Property Under the Fourteenth Amendment.

. The Legislature of New York, in 1906, had passed an act
compelling the Consolidated Gas Company of New York City
to reduce its rates to eighty cents per thousand cubic feet.
Asserting that this was a confiscatory measure, the company
contested its constitutionality. But why was it alleged to
be confiscatory? Because, so the company contended, the reduced rate would not allow a " *fair return* " upon the investment.

Let us see what was included in the " investment." In its
total capital the company budgeted a certain $12,000,000.
Did this amount represent a single dollar that had ever been
invested? No. It represented wholly the value that the company set upon its franchise rights. That is to say, the company capitalized at $12,000,000 the permission it had fraudu-
lently obtained to lay pipes in New York City's streets.[30]

[30] Many of the original franchises had been secured by fraud and
bribery. See, the " History of Public Franchises In New York City,"

The Consolidated Gas Company was a virtual and peculiarly oppressive combination, formed in 1884, of the New York, Manhattan, Harlem, Metropolitan, Municipal and Knickerbocker gaslight companies, with a total capital of $45,000,000. A New York Senate Committee, called the " Thomas " Committee, was appointed, in 1885, to investigate. It reported that nearly every company had hugely watered its stock; that although, for example, the Knickerbocker Company claimed $3,104,000 capital, there was nothing to show what capital it actually had; the records of the tax department showed that it had been paying taxes on only a small proportion of the total with which it was credited.[31] Of the Consolidated Gas Company's alleged $45,000,000 capital, the committee reported that there was less than $20,000,000 of actual investment.[32] The company valued its various franchises at $7,781,000, yet it had never paid anything whatever to the city for them. The committee further reported that during ten years the consumers had paid $9,000,000 to the company, and that, " If these ten per cent. dividends should be calculated upon the capital actually paid in by the stockholders it would appear that the gas consumers in ten years have not only contributed such dividend, but a further amount sufficient, in fact, to nearly duplicate the present system of gas supply." [33]

In view of these facts — matters of public record — it may well be asked whose property had been confiscated? If any had been, it was certainly that of the labor power of the army of workers who had built and who operated the plants, and of the working class of New York City in general constituting the great body of gas consumers. When the contesting case was decided by Judge Hough in the United States Circuit Court in New York he accepted the estimate of the company's

pp. 92–99, and the " History of Tammany Hall," p. 248, by Gustavus Myers.

[31] Report of the Special Senate Committee, 1885: pp. 8–9.
[32] *Ibid.*, p. 12.
[33] *Ibid.*, p. 11.

capitalization as being $60,000,000, of which $12,000,000 was put down as representing franchise value, and Judge Hough then declared the eighty per cent. law confiscatory, and issued an injunction against its enforcement.

A Fact Not to be Overlooked.

The Supreme Court of the United States reversed that decision, assigning Justice Peckham to write the court's opinion. Considering the explosive hidden in Peckham's decision, there was one especially remarkable fact which escaped general attention.

It was this: Only two years before the eighty-cent bill was enacted, Justice Peckham's brother, Wheeler H. Peckham, a corporation lawyer in New York, had given a written opinion in favor of the notorious " Remsen gas grab " bill the passage of which was being vigorously denounced by opponents of the steal.[34] This was a bill giving a comprehensive new franchise as a practical gift to the Consolidated Gas Company. The corruption in the New York Legislature in 1905, as disclosed by the findings of the Legislative Investigating Committee of 1910, was appalling. The suppression of the eighty-cent gas bill in 1905,[35] and the passage in that year of the Niagara water-power bill turning over Niagara Falls power to a corporation, resulted, it was estimated, in the distribution of at least $500,000 in bribes. And these were only two of many scandals. In fact, Senator Allds, later the majority leader, hastily resigned, in 1910, from the New York Senate. Immediately after, the Senate by a vote of 40 to 9 found him guilty of corruption.

[34] And see details in Chapter XVIII of Wheeler H. Peckham's connection with the Standard Electrical Subway Company, and how, in 1889, he was active in seeking to get an underground conduit franchise for it. The electric light companies later passed under the control of the Consolidated Gas Company.

[35] The bill, however, was adopted the next year.

A Double-Edged Decision.

There doubtless was not, it is true, any connection between Wheeler· H. Peckham pleading for the gas franchise
" grab,'' as embodied in the Remsen bill,[36] and the decision
of his brother, Justice Peckham. At any rate the facts bear
reciting. The decision of the Supreme Court, delivered by
Peckham, reduced the Consolidated Gas Company's capital to
less than $56,000,000. But in the act of declaring the eighty-
cent law constitutional, it held that the company was entitled
to earn dividends on $7,781,000 *of franchise values.* And it
also held that corporations were entitled to six per cent.
" earnings " on their stock, thus giving the highest legal
sanction to the minimum amount capitalists were allowed to
drain from the wage workers on the enormous outputs of
watered stock, not a dollar of which represented any actual
investment.[37]

" Thus," says a legal analyst, " was the legislative sword,
drawn against monopoly, turned back into the vitals of the
people, in whose protection it had been raised. A prohibition
designed to check overcapitalization had been transformed, in
the judicial crucible, into a license for extortion. Thus, as
often happens, the people got *the decision,* but the corporations

[36] So called from the name of Assemblyman Remsen, who introduced
it. In a long interview published in the New York *Evening Post,* April
16, 1910, Remsen said that the bill was handed to him to introduce and
that it must have come from Senator " Pat " McCarren, the corrupt
tool of the Sugar Trust and of the gas, traction and other interests.
As the recent president of the City Club, a so-called reform organization, Wheeler H. Peckham, in advocating the passage of the Remsen
bill, shrewdly used his connection with that club to give the impression
that the City Club favored it. " Mayor McClellan," stated Remsen,
" told me after he had signed the bill that he had intended to veto it,
but had been convinced by eminent lawyers, among whom were Wheeler
H. Peckham, that the bill should be made a law." Public protest, however, was so great that when the bill went to Governor Odell he vetoed it.
It may be mentioned that when S. Fred Nixon, Speaker of the Assembly at this period, died, he left a fortune of $1,500,000, much of which he
had deposited in Canadian banks.
[37] 212 U. S. Reports, 19.

got the *law* — for future use." [38] This juridical law was that a mere franchise, no matter to what extent fraud and bribery had been used in getting it, became *property,* and could be capitalized. All of Peckham's associates — Fuller, Harlan, Brewer, White, McKenna, Holmes, Day and Moody concurred in the decision.

Chief Justice Fuller and Justice Day in particular were well versed in authoritative legal precedents as regarded franchise powers, having as attorneys, represented gaslight corporations. Many of the gas and electric light plants in large cities, as well as industries and transportation systems, were controlled by the Standard Oil group. This group, as we have seen, was powerful in the control of the Mutual Life Insurance Company. [39]

Doctrine of "Transitory Risk."

For forty years the courts had been steadily narrowing the rights of injured workers to get compensation, or those of their survivors from recovering damages. By a remarkable decision the Supreme Court of the United States now still further curtailed the insignificant rights of the workers, if indeed any rights at all remained. To do this the majority

[38] Jesse F. Orton, "Privilege Becomes Property Under the Fourteenth Amendment," *The Independent,* issue of Oct. 12, 1911.

[39] Henry H. Rogers and William Rockefeller were vice-presidents of the Standard Oil Company, which largely controlled the Consolidated and other gas companies. Rockefeller and George F. Baker were directors of the Consolidated Gas Company. It was of Elihu Root, so powerful a factor in Roosevelt's administration and at present under Taft's that Harriman wrote to Sidney Webster: "Ryan's success in all his manipulations . . . has been done by the adroit mind of Elihu Root. . . ." Root was, like Rockefeller, Rogers and Baker, a trustee of the Mutual Life Insurance Company. The Ryan referred to was Thomas F. Ryan, the capitalist magnate. In 1886 he was one of the manipulators of the Metropolitan Traction Company, the stockholders of which were robbed of $90,000,000. Ryan then organized and dominated the Tobacco Trust and extended his ownership of properties. Ryan was one of the directors of the Consolidated Gas Company, and Root his main attorney.

of the Supreme Court resourcefully invented a new term
which they called " transitory risk."

Chauncey A. Dixon, a fireman operating an extra train on
the Northern Pacific Railroad, had been killed by a head-on
collision. The time tables did not provide for the running of
extra trains. The train was not on the regular schedule, and
the local telegraph operator had made, an error. Therefore,
said Justice Brewer in delivering the opinion of himself,
Brown, Peckham, Day and Holmes, the fault was the teleg-
rapher's; he was a " fellow servant " with the fireman, and
in no way could the railroad be held responsible. Chief Justice Fuller, and Justices White, Harlan and McKenna dissented. The consequence, said they, of the application of the
doctrine of " transitory risk " was that a railroad operating
its trains solely through the orders of a train despatcher " is a
licensed wrongdoer as respects its employés," and was exempted from the provisions of the law.[40] Practically the railroad corporations were thus authorized to continue the slaughter of workers, and their immunity from the consequences was
enlarged.

In the year in which this decision was handed down 3,632
railroad employés were killed, and 67,067 injured. The total
carnage, including passengers, for that one year was 10,046
killed, and 84,155 injured.[41]

Did ever a battlefield show a more ghastly slaughter? And
what of the resources of the railroads that refused to pay
the injured or the survivors of the killed? They had a total
capitalization of nearly fifteen billion dollars, and a net average income of about three hundred million dollars.[42] For the
destitute worker, maimed or crippled, or for the widows and
orphans of the slain, no redress of any kind; every point, con-

---

[40] Case of Northern Pacific Railway Company vs. Dixon, 194 U. S.
Reports, 338.
[41] Nineteenth Annual Report of the Interstate Commerce Commission,
p. 109.
[42] Ibid., 83 and 303.

struction and twist of law was used against them. *Vice versâ*, law, or what purported to be law, was stretched to its farthest limits on behalf of railroad magnates so glutted with wealth that the mere spending of a moiety of it taxed their ingenuity. And just as the railroad workers were treated by the Supreme Court, so were the workers in factories and mines, the slaughter in which was continuous.

Kidnapping of Workers Legalized.

The kidnapping of workingmen was the next step legalized by the Supreme Court of the United States.

On December 30, 1905, former Governor Steuenberg of Idaho who had incurred bitter enmity because of his extreme brutality toward miners striving for better conditions, was assassinated by a bomb. The bomb was placed at the gate in front of his house. At once, without the slightest proof or justification, the whole capitalist press of the United States declared that the crime had been committed by the Western Federation of Miners, or its agents.

A month and a half later, heavily-armed, special officers arrested Secretary-Treasurer William D. Haywood, President Moyer and former Executive Committeeman Pettibone of the Western Federation of Miners at the dead of night in Denver, Colorado. Despite the law, they were not allowed to communicate with friends or to consult counsel. Every chance was denied them of testing in the courts of their own State the legality of their arrest and extradition. According to the provisions of the most elemental law, no one could be denied these rights. Nor could any arrested person be extradited without regular and due process of law. Common and statute law asserted these rights. The Constitution of every State proclaimed them. The Constitution of the United States guaranteed them, or professed to.

What Happened to Three Labor Leaders.

But Moyer, Haywood and Pettibone were boldly kidnapped. The kidnapping officials had a special train in readiness, and the three union officials were rushed aboard. It was evident that the Governors of Idaho and Colorado, both at the time tools of the mine owners, had secretly arranged, or connived at, this audacious undertaking. When the next day the news was published, a roar of protest and indignation went up from the organized workers throughout the nation. Time and time again they had seen capitalists, accused of heinous crimes, given every consideration and every opportunity of contesting extradition. Now the workers again clearly saw that two kinds of law prevailed — one variety for the capitalist, and another for the working class.

Even before a trial was held, the Mine Owners' Association, the Citizens' Alliance and other capitalist organizations declared Moyer, Haywood and Pettibone guilty, and demanded that they be hanged. The Western Federation of Labor immediately started habeas corpus proceedings before a Federal circuit judge. Upon his denying the writ, an appeal was taken to the Supreme Court of the United States.

From old it had been held a sacred rule in the courts that habeas corpus cases should be determined with the least possible delay, for the reason that they involve the personal liberty of the individual. But instead of considering the appeal, the Supreme Court of the United States took a long summer vacation. Meanwhile the arrested men remained in prison.

Habeas Corpus Writ Refused.

Finally after it had leisurely set a day for the hearing, the Supreme Court of the United States, on December 3, 1906, by a vote of eight to one, handed down its decision, Harlan delivering it. That decision virtually legalized the kidnapping of workers, annihilated the right of habeas corpus so far as the working class was concerned, and reduced that class to the complete mercy of capitalist oppressors. Only Justice McKenna dissented. He denounced the kidnapping as " a crime, pure and simple," and declared that " the States, through their officers, are the offenders." This, he said, was not, as the majority disingenuously sought to make it out, a case of an individual kidnapping an individual. " No individual or individuals could have accomplished what the power of two States accomplished; no individual or individuals could have commanded the means and success; could have made two arrests of prominent citizens by invading their homes; could have commanded the resources of jails, armed guards and special trains; could have successfully timed all acts to prevent inquiry and judicial interference." [43]

More delay ensued before the three labor-union officials were brought to trial before the local court at Boise, Idaho. A verdict of acquittal was the result of the whole affair. The combined power of the most powerful capitalist organizations, with the power of Government and States and the utterances of a prejudiced President at their command, had been unable to produce the slightest evidence against Moyer, Haywood and Pettibone. But the proceedings did reveal the fact that private detectives, in the pay of capitalists, had blown up a depot at Independence, Colorado, with the object of charging the striking miners with the deed, and thus discrediting them.

A Sinister Precedent.

The decision of the Supreme Court of the United States legalizing kidnapping thus set the precedent for the similar kidnapping recently of the two McNamara brothers, officials of the Structural Iron Workers' Union. Secretly kidnapped

[43] Pettibone vs. Nichols, and Moyer vs. Nichols, 203 U. S. Reports, 192, etc.

in Indianapolis, they were denied counsel or process of law, and were rushed under armed guard, to Los Angeles, California, where they were accused of instigating or causing the destruction of the Los Angeles *Times* building and the Llewellyn Iron Works and the loss of twenty-one lives.

As the trial was proceeding at Los Angeles they confessed their guilt on December 1, 1911, James B. NcNamara to the blowing up of the Los Angeles *Times* building, and J. J. McNamara to dynamiting the Llewellyn Iron Works. The one was sentenced to life imprisonment, the other to fifteen years.[44] The strong evidence gathered against them led, it was stated, to their confessions. But this very fact — the strength of the evidence — made the matter of their being kidnapped all the more unnecessary, arbitrary, and tyrannical. Since the evidence was claimed to be so conclusive, the prosecution was under all the more reason to move according to due process of law. Cases had frequently happened of prominent officials or capitalists, accused even of murder like a former Governor of Kentucky, fleeing to other States but no attempt had been made to kidnap them.

The significant fact should be added that by a judicial device the case of the detective Burns, who was indicted for kidnapping the McNamaras, was transferred from the State courts to the Federal courts, and Judge Anderson at Indianapolis cancelled his bond, quashed his indictment, and set him completely free without even subjecting him to trial.

The decisions of the Supreme Court of the United States undermining the power, or extinguishing the rights, of the

[44] The dynamitings were the result of a bitter war carried on against labor unions by various powerful capitalist organizations which were using every means to destroy the unions. The McNamaras, it may be said, were aligned with the extremely conservative ruling element of the American Federation of Labor, were Democrats in politics and Roman Catholics in faith, and refused, like other leaders of the American Federation of Labor, to support the peaceable political-educational propaganda of the Socialist Party

working class were sinister enough. But now came another decision of so extravagant, unexpected and ominous a nature, that labor unions were dumfounded from sheer amazement.

Sherman Act Used Against Labor Unions.

For twenty-one years the Sherman anti-trust law had been on the statute books. When the law was passed, trade unions had supported it. It did not contain the remotest reference to labor unions. It did not appear to apply to them; few dreamed that the time would ever come when it would be so applied. That law was passed at the behest of the middle class, and was expressly and distinctly aimed at trusts and railroad combinations.

The Supreme Court of the United States had been unable to discover that the Sugar Trust was a trust; it had not broken or even impaired a single trust; not a trust magnate had suffered a day's imprisonment because of its decisions. But it did now fully discover that the labor union was a *trust in restraint of trade*. The very trust capitalists who were amenable under that law now used that self-same law to disrupt labor unions. Enjoying immunity themselves, they demanded that the labor unions be strictly prosecuted.

Danbury Hatters' Case.

The action in which this extraordinary turn developed was the Danbury Hatters' case. Alleging that the United Hatters' Union had injured their business through a boycott, Loewe and Company of Danbury, Connecticut, brought suit against the union. Further alleging that the union was a conspiracy in restraint of trade, under the provisions of the Sherman anti-trust law, Loewe and Company asserted that they had suffered to the extent of $80,000, and they demanded that under that law threefold damages be awarded them. The object was clear. If such an enormous sum in damages were allowed, the union would be bankrupted, and with no striking fund in the treasury, it could not prosecute a strike, or perhaps even exist.

Labor Unions "Conspiracies."

The Federal Circuit Court in Connecticut gave a verdict of $222,000 against the two hundred members of the United Hatters' Union. The particular question, however, carried to the Supreme Court of the United States was whether under Section 7 of the Sherman anti-trust law the Loewe Company could maintain an action against the Hatters' Union. The Supreme Court unanimously decided that it could. It held that the union was a combination in the form of a trust, and its so-called boycott was an interference with a free flow of trade between the States, and, therefore, in restraint of trade.

Here was a capital blow at organized labor, the masterpiece of all assaults. Under this decision every labor organization could be proceeded against by any Federal prosecuting officer, and union members could be punished by a fine of $5,000 and by imprisonment for a year. Soon after this decision the hat manufacturers entered into a combination or "lockout" to enforce non-union conditions, which meant a reduction in the workers' wages and further privation.

For the reasoning of the Supreme Court one would be justified in feeling the supremest contempt, were it not for the evident fact that this species of reasoning coincided exactly with the demands of the capitalist class. A labor union is an organization to protect the only property its members have to sell, which is that of labor power. On the other hand, a trust is a concentrated organization to monopolize the production and control the distribution of the means by which people must live. Suddenly, and without warning, an act intended to break up trusts is applied to labor unions.

Chattel Slavery Outdone.

Capitalist organizations hailed this decision with joy, and their mouthpieces once more eulogized the Supreme Court as the bulwark of "the rights of property and the freedom of trade." Among the workers the decision was received with execrations.

"We are living in a time portentous of results for the present as well as the future," wrote Samuel Gompers, the president of the American Federation of Labor. "The slave owner was usually restrained from going to extremes in the treatment of his slaves by the fact that they represented property value to him, but if the industrial situation ensues indicated by this court decision, the wage workers would be more under the control of the unscrupulous employer than was the slave under his owner. . . . The event which we feared has come to pass. The [Sherman anti-trust] law has long been admitted to be of no value in restraining or really punishing trusts. Useless as an instrument of good, perverted from its original intent, it has now been made an instrument of positive mischief. We know the Sherman law was intended by Congress to punish illegal trusts and not the labor unions, for we had various conferences with members of Congress while the Sherman act was pending, and remember clearly that such a determination was stated again and again." Outlaw the normal activities of the workers to protect themselves, Gompers concluded, and a movement would eventually result which he intimated would be nothing more or less than a revolution.[45]

But although labor unions were adjudged conspiracies in restraint of trade, the point as to whether union members could be collectively held liable for damages was not determined by the foregoing decision. This question did not come before the Supreme Court of the United States until 1911. On January 15, 1912, this Court, in denying a writ of certiorari in the

[45] *The American Federationist,* issue of March and April, 1910.

case of Loewe vs. Lawler (Danbury Hatters' case), virtually affirmed the judgment of the Circuit Court of Appeals that members of a labor union could not be held to answer for damages done due to a strike or accompanying boycott, ordered by union officers, unless it was conclusively proved that members of the union actually participated in "the acts of violence," or authorized them, or had guilty knowledge of them. Even as it stood, this decision contained sinister potentialities.

Boycott Illegal, Blacklisting Legal.

At about the time it decided the first Danbury Hatters' case, the Supreme Court of the United States handed down other decisions greatly strengthening the power and aggressions of capitalists and further weakening the defenses of labor unions. A decision dealing with the Erdman Interstate Act of Congress enabled the railroads to maintain a blacklist against members of labor organizations, and discharge them at will.

This decision came in the suit of Adair vs. The United States, decided January 27, 1908. Had Congress power, under the Erdman Act of 1898, to make blacklisting a crime? The United States District Court in Kentucky decided that Congress had the power. The Supreme Court of the United States reversed this decision, and held that blacklisting was not a crime. Upon what ground did the Supreme Court of the United States declare this provision of the Erdman Act unconstitutional? Why, upon the ground that it was repugnant to the fifth amendment of the Constitution that no person shall be deprived of liberty or property without due process of law![46]

Singular that the Supreme Court had not thought of this amendment when it virtually legalized the kidnapping of Moyer, Haywood and Pettibone. Strange that it did not see

[46] 208 U. S. Reports, 161.

the application of the amendment to the liberty and property of the laborer; his liberty to agitate for better conditions, and his right to protect his labor power, which was the only property he had. But such decisions were really neither strange nor singular coming from men who never would or could have gone on the Supreme Court Bench had it not been for their capitalist training, environment, clientage and alliances.

These are some main examples of decisions of the Supreme Court, not omitting the Employers' Liability Act which, on January 6, 1908, it declared unconstitutional.[47] To give more examples would entail a monotonous narration. Boycotting, particularly secondary boycotting, was now a crime, and blacklisting was legal. The sum of the decisions was to give the corporations license to extirpate the labor unions and to slaughter the workers, while at the same time every effective weapon of defense possessed by the working class was put under the ban of the law.

As we have said, the country was filled with the destitute, maimed or crippled who had been mangled on the railroads or in the factories or mines. The huge army of victims killed while at work crowded the graveyards. What became of their widows? What of their sons and daughters? Vital statistics revealing deaths from disease and inanition can tell part of the tale. The prison records can supply another part; the tale of young men driven to crime by wretched environment and gaunt poverty. The remainder of the tale is to be read in brothels or on the midnight streets of cities.

Fuller Almost a Millionaire.

When an attorney, Chief-Justice Fuller had contested claims of injured workers, or those of survivors of the slain. So

[47] This was an act passed by Congress, June 11, 1906, relating to the liability to employés of common carriers in the District of Columbia and Territories, and in interstate commerce.— 207 U. S. Reports, 463.

had Day, and so, likewise, had Holmes. On the Bench they had generally decided against the workers. The country was replete with poverty. But when Chief Justice Fuller died in 1910, his will, admitted to probate in Chicago, on September 17 of that year, disclosed that he left an estate valued at $950,-000.

Of this amount, it was estimated that $115,000 had been bequeathed to him by his wife, who had died in 1904. Of the entire estate left by Fuller, a considerable portion was in real estate. The trustees named in the will were Stephen S. Gregory and the Merchants' Loan and Trust Company. In a carefully worded interview given to the newspapers Gregory took special pains to point out: " I wish that stress would be laid upon the fact that Fuller did not make his money since he became judge. His wealth was acquired through the increase in value in real-estate holdings in Chicago which he acquired early in life. He made no money while a judge." [48]

[48] See, New York *Herald*, July 12, 1910, and other newspapers of that date.

CHAPTER XVII

THE SUPREME COURT UNDER CHIEF JUSTICE WHITE

For the first time in the annals of the Supreme Court of the United States, the choice of a Chief Justice was not made from the ranks of lawyers but the selection was determined of an Associate Justice of the Supreme Court itself. The member thus chosen by President Taft to succeed Fuller was Associate Justice Edward D. White. President Taft, succeeding Roosevelt in 1909, had himself been a judge on the bench of the United States Circuit Court. Indeed, it was authoritatively said that Taft's highest ambition was to go on the Supreme Court Bench, but his election as President interfered with his desire. After Fuller's death Taft had filled vacancies on the Supreme Court by appointing Horace H. Lurton and Charles E. Hughes as Associate Justices to succeed Peckham and Brewer. Although these two appointments were made during the incumbency of Fuller, yet they came late in that period, and we have accordingly reserved description for this chapter.

Taft's Views and Environment.

Of all the successive Chief Executives, none was perhaps more honest, ingenuous and bluntly outspoken in his views than Taft. He had neither political instinct nor political ability, and he entirely lacked that superfine caution and cunning temporizing that marks the practiced politician. His father had been a corporation lawyer and so had he; and his brother Henry W. Taft had represented the New York, New Haven and Hartford Railroad. In his class instincts, reënforced by training and environment, President Taft was an avowed spokesman for the interests of the dominant class. Unlike Roosevelt, he did not court popular favor by wordy denunciation of capitalist magnates while in act and fact serving their ends.

Obediently Taft, ministered to their interests, but not primarily for the reason that he desired to win their support or campaign contributions. He did so, because, on the whole, he sincerely believed that it was the right and proper thing to do; conviction, not calculation, swayed his acts. Infinitely far removed from either knowledge or understanding of the working class, he was impervious to its position, aspirations and movements. But to the masters of capital and their retainers his ear was ready and his acts responsive. With the currents of their atmosphere he had been surcharged from his earliest years.

His Defense of the Judiciary.

No better illustration of his tenacious defense of his class and his indifference to, if not ignorance of, popular thought could have been afforded than his effusive praise of judges. At a time when a profound distrust of capitalist law, and a resentment at the manipulation of law, had permeated the mass of people,[1] Taft publicly gloried in his profession of law. The working class had seen law arbitrarily divided into one application for the rich, and another for the poor; they had seen it

[1] Even lawyers themselves often publicly denounced the complete subversion of law for the benefit of the capitalist magnates. Thus, for example, Samuel Untermeyer, a conspicuous corporation attorney, declared in an interview on June 15, 1909, that the Government had no trouble " in convicting and driving out of business a few poor, struggling, comparatively harmless combinations which were put together to prevent bankruptcy and secure a small profit. But the financial buccaneers who have been ' holding up' the country in the necessities of life . . . have remained immune, until every lawyer who has had to deal with this big question knows that the pretended ' enforcement' of the law is a huge farce." Untermeyer might have added with equal accuracy that while capitalists escaped, the harshest judgments were inflicted upon the working class, collectively and individually.

used as a powerful and apparently invincible instrument for the intrenchment of one class, and the crushing and attempted dispersion of another. They had seen the mass of lawyers flocking to the side from which rich fees and power were to be had, and distorting law for the benefit of those who could repay them with a part of their accumulated loot. They had seen the judges selected from these lawyers, and they had been the victims of the extraordinarily one-sided and partial decisions of those judges.

Popular respect for the judiciary had broken down; among the initiated there never had been much, if any, respect; but now the lack of reverence, amounting to bitter indignation, had grown to tremendous proportions. The people began to demand the exercise of popular control over the judiciary through the power of recall.

But the capitalists as keenly realized that it was mainly through the decrees of judges that their class executed their purposes. Taft vetoed the Arizona Constitution bill providing for the recall of judges, and, caring nothing for popular opinion, gave this extravagant eulogy in his speech at Pocatello, Idaho, on October 6, 1911: " I love judges and I love courts. They are my ideals on earth of what we shall meet afterward in Heaven under a just God. . . ." He resented, he said, with " deep indignation " the attacks upon the courts, and could see nothing else in those questionings of motive and acts than attacks for " mere political purposes." Whereat the powerful capitalists who make judges must have smiled deliciously; by the same logic if judges are predestined for a reserved place in Heaven, their creators even more so must certainly be!

This radiant outburst of Taft's genius gives something of an insight into the mentality of the man of the White House who has appointed six of the nine judges and a Chief Justice of the Supreme Court of the United States.

But it is not Taft's psychology which is so much of moment,

as the consideration of what the actual facts were as concerned the election or appointments of judges. It will be seen
that judges did not ascend to the Bench by any celestial route
or by the workings of mysterious laws of Providence. The
means used and the determining influences were of the com-
monest earthly sort, involving such sordid measures, in the
frequent cases of State judges, as the purchase of nominations,
and in cases of virtually all judges, high and low, as the backing of political bosses who in turn were controlled by the great
corporations.

The Making of Judges.

We shall not pause here to enter into what would unavoidably be an extended account of how State judges were rewarded with nominations and elections. The revelations
brought out by legislative investigating committees in New
York and other States disclosed how they often practically
purchased nominations, or were pushed by powerful corporations whose campaign contributions were the deciding factor.[2]
Leaving aside, then, the sphere of State judges, we shall simply
call attention to a series of facts made public in 1908 regarding
the corporate control of Judges in general.

From time to time serious public scandals had developed,
particularly in the case of various Federal judges charged with
being susceptible to railroad influences and of availing themselves while on the Bench of favors from railroads. Not often
was it possible to prove the charges legally, inasmuch as such
transactions were necessarily and largely of a secret character. It was also to be expected that the United States Senate, composed as it was almost wholly of railroad or other

---

[2] To give one illustration of many examples: Judge Pryor testified
before the " Mazet " New York Legislative Investigating Committee,
in 1899, that he had been asked by a Tammany Hall emissary for
$10,000 for his nomination for a vacant half-term in the New York
State Supreme Court. Other judicial candidates, it was understood,
paid from $10,000 to $25,000 for nominations.

corporation lawyers or magnates, would, as the trial body, refuse to vote impeachment. Federal Judge Charles Swayne, for example, accused on many specifications of favoritism to railroads, escaped impeachment,[3] and a number of other Federal judges charged with the same offences were not even brought to trial.

Hunting for a Qualified Judge.

There were also those exceedingly edifying developments regarding the Joint Traffic Association suit, brought out in the course of a hearing before the Committee on Interstate Commerce of the United States Senate, in 1896. The Joint Traffic Association suit was an action instituted by the Government in the Federal Courts, in New York, against thirty-two railroad companies.

"When it came up," Wallace Macfarlane, U. S. District-Attorney for the southern district of New York, testified on December 17, 1896, "Judge Lacombe stated that in his opinion he was disqualified to hear the case, or any proceedings in it, as at that time he owned bonds or stocks in some of these railroads; and he also stated that he understood that most, if not all, of the judges of that circuit were under the same disqualification.

"It was finally found that Judge Wheeler, the district judge of the Vermont district, was apparently the only judge in the circuit who was not under a disqualification similar to that which Judge Lacombe stated that he was under, namely the holding of some bonds or stocks in one of the defendant railroads. It was eventually arranged that the case should be heard before Judge Wheeler, as it finally was. . . .

"Before the cause was heard, Judge Lacombe had become

[3] See, "Proceedings in the Senate in the Matter of the Impeachment of Charles Swayne, Judge of the District Court of the U. S. for the Northern District of Florida," Government Printing Office, 1905.

qualified. The disqualification which he had stated when the case first arose had been removed by the sale ol any bonds or stocks which he had held at the commencement of the proceedings. Judge Lacombe then stated that, as it had been arranged that the cause should be heard before Judge Wheeler, he preferred to have it remain that way, as the cause was one which he could safely assume would be appealed, whatever the result might be, and there would be no difficulty in constituting an appellate term there, and he [Judge Lacombe] would be needed for the purpose." In other words, Judge Lacombe would be one of the judges sitting on appeal.

This testimony, of so illuminative a nature that comment is needless, is given here exactly as it is published in Document No. 64, Senate Documents, Fifty-fifth Congress, First Session.

In the fall of 1908, William R. Hearst, proprietor of a number of newspapers, and a dabbler in politics, contrived to get hold of copies of a number of letters written by John D. Archbold, then the practically active head, and now (1912) the president, of the Standard Oil Company. These letters, the authenticity of which was not denied, revealed that Archbold had the most confidential relations with Quay, Foraker and other United States Senators and legislators and with State officials. One of the letters disclosed the fact that on August 3, 1899, Archbold had urged upon Quay the selection of Thomas A. Morrison for the Pennsylvania Supreme Court. Another letter, dated September 5, 1900, from Archbold to Governor Stone, of Pennsylvania, recommended the appointment of John Henderson to the same court. Both Morrison and Henderson were duly appointed. Other letters, dated February 5, 1900, and March 15, 1900, from Archbold to Attorney-General John P. Elkin, of Pennsylvania, showed that Elkin received $15,000 from Archbold; Elkin later became a judge of the Supreme Court of Pennsylvania. According to these letters (and they were doubtless but a very few of many) Archbold had his secret political mechanism, in the operation of which a mere word from him to the political bosses was sufficient. If this were true, as it evidently was, is it not a fair assumption that the vigilant solicitude would be extended to the hightest, as well as to the lesser, courts and offices?

Concentration of Wealth and Power.

The wealth and power at this time of the Standard Oil Company allied with J. Pierpont Morgan, were so gigantic as to be inconceivable even when expressed in money terms. In 1904, the total capitalization of all of the trusts, including franchise trusts and railroad groups, was fully $20,000,000,-000; by January 1, 1908, the grand total had risen to nearly $32,000,000,000.[4] " This thirty-one billion dollars [$31,672,-000,000] of industrial, franchise and transportation trust capitalization," stated Senator LaFollette, " does not represent all the corporate power in the hands of the Standard Oil-Morgan combination. It does not include their financial consolidations — their banks, trust companies and insurance companies."[5] Much of this wealth was owned outright or controlled by the Standard Oil Company and Morgan; the remainder was largely owned by smaller magnates subsidiary to the purposes and interests of the great combination which had already begun a systematic process of crushing or completely subordinating some of them.

This enormous power, centered in a few financial dictators, alarmed and affrighted beyond description the remnants of small business men still remaining. Overawed by such vast wealth and power in a few hands, clinging to the hope that by some magic of court decree the great combinations would be dissolved, they still continued their agitation for the en-

[4] Statistics by John Moody.
[5] " Centralization and Community of Control in Industry," etc. Speech Delivered in the U. S. Senate, March 17–24 and March 27, 1908, p. 45.

forcement of the anti-trust act. Necessarily, therefore, eager attention was bent upon the court of last resort, the Supreme Court of the United States. Never as much as after Fuller's death had the question of who would be Chief Justice excited such speculation and interest.

Justice White Appointed Chief Justice.

Surprise was great when Taft appointed Associate Justice, White to the vacancy. Taft was a Republican, White a Democrat; this effacing of partisan lines was in itself a stroke causing wonderment to those who did not see that essentially both the old political parties were adjuncts, reflexes and instruments of the capitalist system. Both stood for its perpetuation, and neither represented in the remotest degree the demands of the working class. The label differed; that intrinsically was the only difference between the two parties, although on minor points, arising from the conflicts within the capitalist sphere, they superficially had their contentions.

Why, it was asked, was White appointed Chief Justice? There were those who sought to explain the appointment on the ground of religious attachment. Vague yet persistent reports were spread that the influences of the Roman Catholic Church were subtly and effectively used in White's behalf. White was educated in a Jesuit college, the Georgetown University; and the Roman Catholic Church, virtually outlawed in many parts of the country a century or more ago, has grown to a position of great economic power, owning as it does, vast properties and including, as it does, too, many capitalist magnates of the first order. The prelates of this church have taken an organized stand for the perpetuation of the present capitalist order, and for the denunciation of all radical movements, especially of Socialism. But whether the rumors of the Roman Catholic backing of Chief Justice White are true or not, we of course cannot say; they are given here in the form of unverified reports, yet possibly not without substance.

But, after all, White's appointment as Chief Justice was not determined by any question of religious faith. Throughout a long career he had evinced the highest qualifications for appointment to the exalted post of Chief Justice, as those qualifications were weighed and understood by those upon whom his appointment and confirmation depended. On the Supreme Court Bench he had been recognized as favoring trusts.

Chief Justice White's Career.

Born to some wealth, White had been brought up in a typically Southern atmosphere, abounding in class distinctions at the top of which he was positioned. He acquired a large sugar plantation, which he has since extended, in the La Fourche district, Louisiana. In various published accounts he has been rated a millionaire, but these accounts are not to be accepted as responsible; hence it is not possible to state his wealth explicitly. His friends say that he is a comparatively poor man. As a lawyer in New Orleans, his clients were mainly Jewish merchants of wealth, or at least, of means; we do not find a single case in which he pleaded the cause of a poor litigant. However, he did not represent any railroad interest, and the only large corporation he served as attorney was the Whitney Bank, now the biggest in New Orleans. He combined law and politics; his was the characteristic case of a rich, young man entering politics, which in Louisiana meant, of course, Democratic politics. He became one of Nicholls' political lieutenants; he was a State Senator; and when Nicholls became Governor of Louisiana he appointed White, in 1878, a judge of the Louisiana Supreme Court.

At that time the controlling, most all-powerful single factor in Louisiana politics was the Louisiana Lottery Company, with its net annual revenue of $8,000,000 a year. Widespread agitation to abolish this company gradually crystallized, in 1890, in the introduction of an act in the Louisiana Legislature refusing to extend its charter. On May 22, 1890, Senator Foster proposed a resolution in the Legislature to inquire into charges that members were being offered $1,000 each for their votes. Joseph St. Armant was arrested on June 22, 1890, on a charge of bribery. Governor Nicholls vetoed the bill refusing to extend the company's charter, but on July 8, 1890, the House passed it over his veto. During this time White was actively and publicly opposing the Louisiana Lottery Company.

White had been acting as the Treasurer of the State campaign committee. In 1890 the Sugar Trust, on the one hand, and, on the other, the beet sugar-cane planters, were engaged in a bitter quarrel over the tariff; since then, it may be observed, their interests have become more or less identical, as has been shown by bills of particulars in Government actions. The sugar planters were among the most adroit and persistent lobbyists at Washington, a fact attested by the passage of a certain act in 1890, which act we shall have good occasion to describe presently. Thus it was that White, a sugar-cane plantation owner, was elected to the United States Senate, and thus, also, White's successor in the Senate, Blanchard, was interested in sugar plantations, and one of the present United States Senators from Louisiana — Murphy J. Foster — is a brother of J. Warren Foster who owns perhaps the largest sugar-cane plantation in the State.

White Bitterly Attacked.

After White's election to the United States Senate, and before he took his seat (in 1891) in that body,[6] a campaign

[6] Under the peculiar customs of Louisiana, he was elected to the United States Senate nearly three years before he entered that body.

of assault was opened upon him by the New Orleans *Times-Democrat,* one of the leading newspapers of that city, and of a partisan Democratic character.

On July 18, 1890, it contained an editorial asking: ". . . Is Senator-elect White an honest man? Is he a pure man? Or is he a hypocrite and cheat? There are rumors, thick as leaves in Vallambrosa, to the effect that . . . he attained to the dignity of which he is so proud by means that were not pure. . . . Are these rumors true? . . . Will the Senator tell the people of New Orleans how much money it took to secure him his election to the United States Senate by the Legislature of Louisiana? Will he tell where he got the money, and in what special channels it was disposed of?

"These are not idle questions. The rumors to which we refer are on everybody's lips; they are either true or they are false.

"Our columns are wide open to the Senator-elect for purposes of explanation. If he can prove the rumors false the *Times-Democrat* stands ready to print his statement and to make the amplest possible reparation. . . ."

The *Times-Democrat* charged editorially on July 22, 1890, that it could prove "that the campaign committee of which Senator-elect White was treasurer, received the sum of ten thousand dollars from the head and front of the Lottery Company, which the Senator disbursed in the interest of Gov. Nicholls and himself in the last campaign." The statement went on: "Let not the Senator attempt to deny the charge and allege the money was subscribed by an individual and not by the Lottery Company.

"When the check, which had been solicited, was tendered to the committee, one member objected that it came from the Lottery Company. Another member said that he regarded it as an individual subscription. One of the committeemen then said, ' Gentlemen, let us have no misunderstanding; the money comes from the Louisiana Lottery Company.' The money was received, turned over to the Treasurer (now Senator-elect) White, and used in the campaign to elect that exemplar of all the virtues — Gov. Nicholls.

" So much for the charge. Will the Senator-elect dare deny it? It is , further charged — the *Times Democrat* charges and can prove that . . . [Mr. White] received from the Lottery Company, or rather from the head and front of that concern, the sum of ten thousand dollars to assist him personally in his fight for the Senate.

" Did Senator White use that amount honestly? The amount is large and could scarcely have been consumed in stationery.

" The *Times-Democrat* does not court a libel suit. It is a costly and disagreeable mode of procedure, but still the courts are open to the Senator-elect if he chooses to seek redress therein." [7]

White Replies to the Charges.

On Sunday, July 27, 1890, the *Times-Democrat* published a full page of statements from Senator-elect White and his associates, giving their version and reply. They did not deny the fact of the $10,000 contribution, but stated that it was spent for legitimate political purposes. In a signed personal statement, White wrote that if he could have stooped to the use of corrupt means, his and his family's personal resources were enough, but that he did not corrupt a single vote and his total expenses were just about $1,000, nearly half of which was disbursed in the cost of an entertainment and reception given to the members of the entire Democratic caucus after the nomination had been made.

[7] This editorial is given precisely as originally published but with an unimportant part omitted.

In the same issue in which these replies were published, the *Times-Democrat* contained an editorial saying that White admitted the charge of receiving the Lottery Company's money, and disbursing it as treasurer of the Committee, and subsequently as chairman of the finance committee.

". . . The Senator-elect says," continued the editorial, "that no money was given him to elect him to the Senate. Did not every dollar he received from the Lottery Company and spent to help elect the legislative nominees help directly to elect him to the Senate? Was he not working to that end all through the campaign?

"But we charged that the Senator-elect received money from the Lottery Company, or its chief representative, to assist him in his personal canvass. The Senator denies it. We reaffirm the charge. Will he, on second thought, deny that a certain sum of money, ten thousand dollars or more, was deposited with a mutual friend who disbursed it upon his personal orders? Will he dare deny the existence of these orders? We reaffirm the charge, and we challenge the Senator-elect to bring us into court, where he and our witnesses will be upon their oaths."

Again on July 31, 1890, the *Times-Democrat* editorially "declares with added emphasis that Senator-elect White did receive from the Lottery Company's chief large sums of money with which to conduct his personal canvass; that he did use that money for that purpose, and that we can prove that fact in a court of justice where we can place the Senator-elect on the stand under oath and confront him with our witnesses.

"We realize the gravity of the charge, and offer the Senator-elect an opportunity to forever set the matter at rest. Will he accept it, or does he fear to meet the consequences of a suit for libel against this paper? We are prepared, if necessary, to give in advance good and solvent bond for any damages the Senator-elect may be awarded by a jury."

Obvious Motive for the Attacks.

We have given with equal consideration both the reiterated charge and the reply, allowing the reader to form his or her own conclusions. So far as is ascertainable Senator White did not accommodate the repeated desire of his accusers with a suit in court. What the motive was underlying the attack was never established in court — whether it was sincere indignation or an outgrowth of political rivalries or an attempt at reprisal by enemies. But all the available evidence goes to prove that the Louisiana Lottery Company was seeking to retaliate upon White because of his public opposition to it during the legislative fights. Arraying himself prominently with the anti-lottery forces, White was elected on the crest of the wave of public indignation which swept the State, demanding the suppression of the lottery. It was certain that the publication of the charge put White into an extremely uncomfortable, if not embarrassing, position.

The contest in Congress between the sugar refiners and the sugar-cane and beet planters was finally compromised, in 1890, by the passage of a bounty act for the benefit of the planters. White had not yet entered the Senate when this measure was passed. Under this act the sugar-cane and sugar-beet planters were to receive from $7,000,000 to $10,000,000 in bounties a year from the Government.

In 1894, however, a new tariff measure, called the " Wilson Bill" was introduced in Congress. Cleveland's Democratic administration was now in power, and the majority in Congress were Democrats. When this bill came before the Senate one of the bitterly contested points was whether the sugar bounty should or should not be continued. The sugar-cane planters were extraordinarily active, and not less so the representatives of the Sugar Trust which seemed now to be working in harmony with the planters. The beneficiaries of the bounty act were largely the Louisiana sugar-cane growers.

Contest over the Sugar Schedule.

On February 1, 1894, during the debates, Senator Allison, of Iowa, severely denounced the sugar bounty act, and inquired of Senator White whether that payment was not a wasteful and extravagant expenditure of public money. Senator White answered so evasively that Allison sharply said, " That was not the question I asked." He again put the direct question. White replied lamely, saying that he couldn't separate the tariff and the bounty questions; that they were one and the same. He nevertheless admitted that the bounty provision was " a wrong against the revenue ⋅system of the Government." [8] Senator Harris, of Tennessee, then said that he regarded the sugar bounty from the beginning " as an outrage and a wrong. . . . I am for a tariff for revenue, but I am not for a tariff to protect or benefit any particular class or any particular persons." [9] This was a deep thrust inasmuch as the sequel revealed that White was himself a considerable beneficiary of the bounty act.

President Cleveland had successively nominated William B. Hornblower and Wheeler H. Peckham to fill a vacancy on the bench of the Supreme Court of the United States. Both, as we have, previously related, were conspicuous corporation lawyers; and of Peckham's advocacy of corporate interests we have more to say in the next chapter. But belonging, as Hornblower and Peckham did, to a wing of the Democratic Party in New York State opposed to Senator David B. Hill, that politician made their nominations a personal fight, and succeeded in squelching each in turn.

These nominations having been thus defeated, Cleveland was forced into the position of nominating someone whom the Senate was likely to confirm.

[8] *Congressional Record,* Fifty-third Congress, Second Session, Vol. XXVI: p. 1773.
[9] *Ibid.*

White Withholds His Resignation.

On February 19, 1894, Cleveland nominated White as an Associate Justice of the Supreme Court of the United States. The fact that White, instead of resigning his seat in the Senate immediately, remained there during the sugar-provision contest, aroused caustic criticism. Leading Democratic newspapers commented sharply upon his retaining his seat during the very time that legislation was being put through for the further enrichment of the sugar-cane planters. Thus, the New York *World,* the foremost and most influential advocate of Cleveland's reëlection in 1892, editorially denounced Senator White's conduct as " a disgraceful spectacle," and further declared that White was unfit to be a Justice of the Supreme Court of the United States.[10]   Other newspapers published similar opinions. In fact, Senator White did not resign his seat in the United States Senate until March 8, 1894.

The Safety Appliance Act.

But while thus criticizing Senator White, the newspapers in question, it may be parenthetically remarked, refrained from giving him the great credit he deserved for his extremely good and able work in the Senate, in 1893, in so amending the

[10] Published March 6, 1894. We shall give also an instance of criticism from a Republican newspaper — the New York *Tribune* — which, on February 20, 1894, charged that White had occupied himself mainly to defeat the Administration's tariff bill, " bulldozing the Finance Committee's ' steerers ' with the threat to vote against it unless a liberal measure of protection were guaranteed to the Louisiana sugar interests."   And referring to White's appointment as an Associate Justice of the Supreme Court of the United States the *Tribune* account continued: " It is whispered, indeed, that Mr. White's appointment to-day may have been largely due to a feeling on the part of friends of the Wilson bill that its chance of passage might be improved if the senior senator were gotten out of the way, and some less active and influential advocate of the sugar interest should replace him on the Louisiana delegation in Congress."   But, as we have said, White did not resign his seat until the following month.

Safety Appliance Act that it operated to the advantage of the workers in personal injury cases.

The railroad magnates had so trickily framed the bill that while the injured worker would have been relieved from the charge of contributory negligence, the courts could have held that he had assumed the risk. Senator White had never been a railroad attorney. But he was a good lawyer. He exposed the shallowness of the clause as it originally stood, and amended it by striking out the words "shall not be deemed guilty of contributory negligence," and by substituting "shall not be deemed thereby to have assumed the risk thereby occasioned." His excellent amendment was finally adopted.[11]

To return, however, to the tariff bill:

Successive great scandals had arisen over the manipulation of the tariff bill, especially the sugar clauses. So numerous and insistent were the charges that Senators were buying and selling sugar-trust stock (the market value of which they could affect at will by their votes) that Peffer, a Populist Senator, moved for an investigation. This resolution was voted down. But the charges were made with renewed force; the Senate finally, upon motion of Lodge, then in the "reformer" stage of his career, virtuously decided to appoint an investigating committee.

Investigation of Sugar-Stock Jobbing.

Now ensued an edifying situation. Witnesses conveniently "disappeared" or "refused to appear." H. O. Havemeyer, the head of the Sugar Trust, actually whistled at the committee, and laughed at its proceedings. There was loud talk of bringing contempt proceedings against him, but it was merely vapor; no one believed that the committee was disappointed at not getting evidence incriminating Senators personally.

[11] The *Congressional Record*, Fifty-Second Congress, Second Session, Vol. 24, Part II: 1480–1481.

Havemeyer was cynically willing to give general testimony, but point blank refused to be specific as to individuals.

When asked if he contributed to State campaign funds, he genially replied: ". . . We always do that. . . . In the State of New York when the Democratic majority is between 40,000 and 50,000, we throw it their way. In the State of Massachusetts, when the Republican party is doubtful, they have the call. Wherever there is a dominant party, wherever the majority is very large, that is the party that gets the contribution, because that is the party that controls local matters." [12] This was the same Havemeyer who as the head of the Sugar Trust cheated the Government later out of enormous sums in custom-house frauds. These sums ran into the tens of millions of dollars, and when the frauds were discovered, Havemeyer was so thoroughly frightened that his death, in December, 1907, soon followed. The Sugar Trust was (to repeat) compelled to pay as restitution to the Government more than $2,000,000, but this was only a slight disgorging of the immense total of plunder.[13]

What the Reports Showed.

Considering this subsequent, proved fraud and corruption carried on by the Sugar Trust, it is altogether likely that the

[12] Senate Report No. 485, Fifty-third Congress, Second Session, June 21, 1894. This testimony was simply a paraphrase of Jay Gould's formula, as expressed in 1873: "In a Republican district I was a Republican; in a Democratic district, a Democrat; in a doubtful district I was doubtful; but I was always for Erie."

[13] Said the Annual Report for 1909 (p. 12) of the U. S. Attorney-General: ". . . The evidence in the suit above referred to revealed a long-continued system of defrauding the Government, of unparalleled depravity." The report further stated that in April, 1909, a compromise was made whereby the American Sugar Refining Company paid the Government a judgment of $134,411.03, and, in addition, the sum of $2,000,000 as restitution for custom-house frauds. "The evidence has disclosed a network of corruption extending over a period of years . . .," wrote the Attorney-General. But the heads of the trust completely escaped punishment.

charges of corruption made against it in 1894 were far from being ill-founded.

The Democratic majority report of the Senate Investigating Committee was of a "whitewashing" nature, inculpating nobody. But the Republican minority report of Senator Lodge showed that the Sugar Trust magnates — Havemeyer, Searles and others — had "addressed their arguments" principally to Senator Gorman and other Democratic Senators. Allowance should be made for the partisan character of both reports. "It appears," said the Lodge report, "by the testimony of Senator Vest, that Senator Brice, of Ohio, Senator Smith, of New Jersey, Senator Hill, of New York, and Senators White and Caffery, of Louisiana, after said conference [a Democratic caucus] came to the rooms of the finance committee in regard to the sugar schedule. Senator Vest testified that Senator Gorman urged a duty of forty per cent. *ad valorem,* and one-fourth of a cent a pound differential in favor of refined sugars as the proper schedule."

Gorman's purpose thus was to double the tariff schedule on sugar. Instead of the $20,000,000 gift a year to the Sugar Trust which the one-eighth of a cent a pound schedule would present to the Sugar Trust, Gorman sought to make the schedule one-fourth of a cent a pound, thus giving the Sugar Trust a donation of $40,000,000 annually. At this point Senators White and Caffery interfered, and prevented Gorman's complete plan from succeeding; White and Caffery were evidently not susceptible to the arguments of the Sugar Trust, like Gorman, Brice and others. The Sugar Trust, however, obtained a high enough tariff. As for the sugar-cane and beet growers, they eventually received their equivalent. The bounty act, repealed in 1894, was restored in 1895.

The Sugar Trust had already planned to control the large cane and beet-sugar producing interests. By the year 1904 it had carried the process to the point where it had acquired.

controlled or dominated fifty-five corporations, and held control of from seventy to ninety per cent. of the industry, including raw and refined sugar-cane and beet production.[14] In its voluminous suit filed against the Sugar Trust, on November 28, 1910, the Government charged, among many other allegations, that the American Sugar-Refining Company (the Sugar Trust) held stock in, or control over, various cane-sugar and beet companies.

Explaining this development, we can now revert to what further happened in 1894-1895.

White as a Sugar Bounty Beneficiary.

On March 1, 1894 the United States Senate adopted a resolution calling upon Carlisle, Secretary of the Treasury, for a statement showing the names of individuals, firms and corporations who had received gratuities under the sugar bounty act. Carlisle sent in a specific report giving the requested statement, which report did not cover all the years from 1890; it dealt only with the fiscal year 1892-1893, and part of the fiscal year up to March 1, 1894. This report showed that of the total of about $10,000,000 a year being paid by the Government in sugar bounties, the Louisiana sugar planters were receiving $8,500,000 a year.[15] The itemized list of beneficiaries revealed that Senator Edward D. White had received $31,367.06 in bounties from the Government for the fiscal year 1892-1893, and $18,186.86 for a part of the fiscal year up to March 1, 1894.[16]

The Government challenged the constitutionality of the sugar bounty act; it undoubtedly could be construed as being legis-

---

[14] Moody's " Truth About The Trusts," p. 67. Moody states that its element of monopoly consisted principally of strong tariff bounties, control of raw material, etc.

[15] Senate Executive Document No. 61, Fifty-third Congress, Second Session.

[16] See page 15 of *Ibid.*

lation for a favored class. When the Government refused to continue bounty payments under the act, the sugar-cane growers brought two test suits. One case was that of Realty Company, the other that of Gay, against the United States. The lower courts decided against the Government which now appealed to the Supreme Court of the United States.

Sugar Bounty Act Upheld.

The decision of this court was handed down on May 25, 1896. Justice Peckham wrote the court's decision; there was not a single dissenting opinion. Before giving this decision we will remind the reader that only the year before — on January 21, 1895 — the Supreme Court of the United States had declared the Sugar Trust not to be a criminal combination, and on May 27, 1895, it had, on an entirely extraneous point, affirmed the sentence of Eugene V. Debs to six months in jail.

In the sugar bounty cases the decision brought out the fact that the act of 1890 was to run for fifteen years; that under it the Government had already paid out tens of millions of dollars in bounties, and that the question of its constitutionality was not raised by the Government until 1895.

The decision was wholly in favor of the sugar-cane and beet planters upon two main grounds — one, that the planters had acquired *a vested right in legislation,* the other ground that this right was intrenched by the doctrine of acquiescence. Let us, however, quote Justice Peckham's exact language.

". . . Under that act and during its existence," he wrote, " large sums of money were paid to sugar manufacturers as a bounty, and all manufacturers continued to manufacture in reliance upon its provisions. During those years no officer of the Government questioned the validity of the act, and the bounties under it were paid without objection or any hint that objection would thereafter be taken while the law was in force. This condition continued for about three years."

Its Unconstitutionality "Immaterial."

Peckham went on:

" In our opinion it is not correct to say that no moral, equitable or honorable obligation can attach in favor of persons situated as were the defendants here, when the act of 1895 was passed. We think obligations of that nature may arise out of such circumstances." Then followed this remarkable doctrine: " We regard the question of the unconstitutionality of the bounty provisions of the act of 1890 *as entirely immaterial to the discussion here. These parties did not at the time (when manufacturing under its provisions) know that it was unconstitutional.*[17]

". . . But it is said that if an act be unconstitutional the law imputes to these parties at all times a knowledge of its invalidity, and that it is not rendered valid by acquiescence in its provisions for any length of time even by officers of the government holding the highest places therein and who are charged with its execution and believe in its validity. . . ." Peckham went on to say that in such a case as this, knowledge of its unconstitutionality could not be imputed to the beneficiaries. " These parties cannot be held bound, upon the question of equitable or moral consideration, to know what no one else actually knew, prior to the determination by some judicial tribunal, that the law was unconstitutional." The beneficiaries had arranged their business affairs in expectation of receiving the bounties and, therefore, " We are of the opinion that the parties situated as were the plaintiffs in these actions, *acquired claims of an equitable, moral and honorary nature.*"[18]

[17] 163 U. S. Reports, 437. The italics are mine.— G. M.
[18] *Ibid.,* 439. My italics.— G. M.

A Classic Example.

If anyone be disposed to look for a classic example of class decisions, this case will abundantly suffice.

It is to be noted that the trifling question of constitutionality of an act was "entirely immaterial." The principal attorney for the sugar-cane growers was Joseph H. Choate, the same who for a large fee successfully argued at that very time that the income tax was unconstitutional. The Justice writing the decision was, as we have said, Peckham, who later wrote the decision (which we have previously described) declaring that a New York law decreeing shorter hours for bakeshop workers was unconstitutional. The people at large and the working class in particular had, it was clear to the Supreme Court, no vested right in legislation for their benefit; they acquired no claims of "an equitable, moral and honorary nature" in legislation. But capitalists draining the Government treasury of tens of millions of dollars unquestionably had those claims, according to the exalted Supreme Court. On the question of labor legislation, the issue of unconstitutionality was very material; on that of capitalist interests, it was "entirely immaterial."

One of the capitalists profiting from that sugar bounty was, as we have seen, Edward D. White, an Associate Justice of the Supreme Court of the United States at the time the decision was given. But Justice White, in nowise disposed to violate the law forbidding judges from sitting in their own causes, scrupulously refrained from taking any part in these cases, as is evidenced by the following note on the records, "Mr. Justice White did not sit in nor take any part in the decision of these cases." [19]

[19] For the record of the cases in full, see, U. S. vs. Realty Company and U. S. vs. Gay, 163 U. S. Reports, 427–444. According to the best information obtainable, Chief Justice White's plantation is managed on more or less obsolete methods, and its machinery is more or less antiquated.

Of Justice White's stand in decisions affecting various questions during the years he was an Associate Justice sufficient details have already been given in previous chapters.

We shall now take up the careers of various men appointed by Taft as Associate Justices.

Justice Lurton's Career.

The first of these was Horace H. Lurton. He was sixty-five years old at the time of his appointment. Admitted to the bar in Tennessee, in 1867, Lurton at once became a corporation attorney. The court records show that as early as 1870, when he was the age of twenty-six years, Lurton was an attorney for the Louisville and Nashville Railroad.[20] It may be explained that the Louisville and Nashville Railroad has controlled politics in its territory almost as absolutely as the New York, New Haven and Hartford in Connecticut, the Boston and Maine in New England or the Southern Pacific in California. Lurton continued in practice until appointed a State Chancellor in 1875 in which judicial office he served three years.

In 1878 he resumed law practice as a member of the firm of Baxter, Lurton and Quarles. The Baxters had for many years represented the East Tennessee and Virginia Railroad, the Western Atlantic Railroad and other railroad systems.[21] The firm of Baxter, Lurton and Quarles were attorneys for the Louisville and Nashville Railroad; considering Lurton's later decisions, when a United States Circuit Court judge, regarding damages for injuries, it is worth noting that one suit that the firm defended upon appeal for the Louisville and Nashville Railroad in December, 1878, was an action brought by a wagon driver for injuries.[22] At the same time Lurton was interested in banking matters.

[20] Tennessee Reports, Vol. 54: 254–261.
[21] See, Heiskell's Tenn. Reports, Vols. I to 12.
[22] L. & N. R. R. vs. Gardner, I Lea (Tenn.) Reports, 688.

In 1884 Lurton became a member of the firm of Smith and Lurton. The firm had previously been that of Smith and Allison. Ed. Baxter and Smith and Allison had frequently appeared for the Louisville and Nashville Railroad.[23] John and W. M. Baxter were also attorneys for the Union Consolidated Mining Company [24] and some of the Baxters were financially interested in Tennessee coal mines.

Lurton, in 1886, was elected a judge of the Supreme Court of the State of Tennessee. The by no means unusual situation was now seen of a former railroad attorney deciding cases involving the interests of that same railroad. If antecedents of this character had been regarded as a positive disqualification, few judges would have been able to sit in judgment; the courts everywhere were full of judges who had been former railroad attorneys.

The Lahr Case.

One of the cases decided by Judge Lurton was the suit of J. M. Lahr against the Louisville and Nashville Railroad. A carpenter employed by the railroad company, Lahr was working on a high railroad trestle. On the day on which he was injured, Lahr asked his foreman, Ligar, if the rope used for descending purposes was all right. The foreman said " Yes." As a matter of fact, the rope was not fastened but was lying in a loose coil on the top of the bridge. When Lahr took

[23] See, VIII Heiskell's Reports, 735; VIII Lea's Reports, 439, etc., and XIV Lea's Reports, 130, in which last-named action Baxter, Smith and Allison and John H. Henderson represented (1884) the Louisville and Nashville and Great Southern Railway. See, also, XII Lea's Reports, 574, in which Smith and Allison and Edward W. Baxter were attorneys for the Louisville and Nashville Railroad; XIV Lea's Reports, 65, in which Smith and Allison appeared for the same railroad, and X Lea's Reports, 58, in which John Allison, Jr., and W. M. Baxter represented the East Tennessee, Virginia and Georgia Railroad. Also, XII Lea's Reports, 35 and 47, giving W. M. Baxter's appearance for the last-mentioned railroad. The foregoing appearances were between the years 1881 and 1884.
[24] V Lea's Reports, 3.

hold of it to descend he was thrown forty feet to the ground, and a number of his bones were crushed. He brought suit for damages, and obtained a judgment in the lower courts.

When the case came up on appeal, Judge Lurton, on February 4, 1888, reversed the judgment and remanded the case for a new trial. This he did on the "fellow servant" doctrine. The railway company, said Judge Lurton, was in no way responsible; the fault was the foreman's, and the foreman was simply a fellow servant of Lahr. "The absence of sufficient proof," Judge Lurton said, "that any duty rested upon Ligar to see to the means of descent used by his fellow workmen, and the fact that Lahr did not notify Ligar of his purpose to descend, and that the proof clearly established the fact that he was acting under no immediate orders from Ligar in attempting to descend, makes the case one of mere personal negligence of Lahr for which the master is not responsible. In other words, they were fellow servants." [25]

The irony of this decision lay in the fact that if Lahr had not kept to his work — which consisted in going up and down the bridge — he would have been discharged. That was a part of his work, and every reasonable construction of law required the company, through the foreman, to see that he had safe appliances.

"Pauper Oath" Recommended.

Another such case decided by Judge Lurton (on February 17, 1891) was that of Smith against the Louisville and Nashville Railroad. The action was one for damages for the death of a parent killed on the railroad. But the son was very poor, and could not give bond for the costs of the suit. The lower court, therefore, would not allow him to sue. He applied for a writ of error, and the motion came before Judge

[25] See, Southwestern Reporter, Vol. VI: 663–665.

Lurton who held that no suit could be brought where there were no assets to bear the expense of the suit. When dismissing the case, Judge Lurton with a fine delicacy added: " There seems to have been no point made upon the right of the administrator to prosecute the appeal under pauper oath. The point ought to have been made, but was not; it was, therefore, not decided." [26]

In literal law, Lurton was doubtless right, but this case ranks as an instructive illustration of the conscientious precision with which the courts construe capitalist law against the workers. In the previous case, that of Lahr, Lurton applied the most "liberal construction" of law in deciding in favor of the railroad corporation. In this case the last letter and dot of law was construed with granite inflexibility against a destitute worker. The railroad had killed his parent, and because of this he was left penniless; he was then debarred from suing for damages since " he had no assets to bear the expense of the suit." Here was another illustration of the sad enough fact that poverty was not merely a crime; it was a catastrophe.

Slaughter of the Workers.

Judge Lurton, like other judges, could not or did not care to see the ravaged, broken-up homes of the workers, desolated by premature and clearly preventable death, and the appalling misery following the slaughter of the toilers upon whom the maintenance of those homes depended.

The annual carnage of the workers on railroads and in factories and mines was truly dreadful, and more destructive than the most sanguinary wars mankind has known. If anything, working conditions, thanks to the insistence of the workers, were a shade better in 1908 than in previous decades.

[26] Southwestern Reporter, Vol. XV: p. 842.

But still they were so abominable that between 30,000 and 35,000 adult wage workers were slain every year, and not less than 2,000,000 workers were annually injured. This estimate, a conservative one as the Federal report expressly says, took no account of women and child workers.[27] Nor did it include the vast number of disabilities, diseases and deaths indirectly caused by the processes of capitalist industry.

Intrenching themselves behind their law books, the judges professed not to see these frightful and hideous conditions; and they insisted that their sole function was to construe law as they found it. A plausible enough defense, if it had not happened that as attorneys nearly all of them had represented railroad and other corporations which had savagely fought every attempt of the workers to better their conditions, and which regarded the immolation of men, women and children as of no consequence so long as it did not interfere with the flow of profits.

The foregoing are examples of cases decided by Judge Lurton when on the Supreme Court of Tennessee.[28] But Lurton did not invariably decide in favor of his former clients, the Louisville and Nashville Railroad. In a minor case, Judge Lurton's decision was adverse to that corporation. But the evidence in this case was incontrovertible, and moreover the suit was not brought by a private person but by the State of Tennessee. It involved the question of whether the railroad company could be fined $50 for obstructing a highway. Lurton affirmed the judgment of the lower court.

[27] See, Bulletin No. 78, Sept., 1908, U. S. Bureau of Labor. The report explains that it would have been possible to save at least one-third or one-half of these lives by rational methods of factory inspection and control.

[28] See, also, Louisville and Nashville Railroad vs. Mossman, XVI Southwestern Reporter, 64. In the lower court Mossman had recovered damages for overflow of his lands caused by the railroad's high embankment. Judge Lurton reversed that decision on the ground that by long usage the railroad company had acquired by prescription the right to flow back the water upon the adjoining land.

Lurton Becomes a Circuit Judge.

In 1893, President Cleveland appointed Lurton a Judge of the United States Circuit Court, Sixth Circuit, embracing Ohio, Kentucky, Tennessee and adjacent territory. On the Circuit Court at Cincinnati, Taft and Lurton were associated on the Bench, and became intimate friends.

Decisions favorable to corporations were constantly handed down. One decision arousing much comment was that in the case of Hunter vs. the Kansas City and Missouri Railroad Company. Hunter was a laborer engaged to set up poles along the company's lines. The boss, Bob Snowdon, slipped while the pole was being placed in a hole, the pole fell and knocked down Hunter, seriously injuring him. Judge Lurton decided (February 8, 1898,) that Snowdon had slipped because the work had to be done in a slippery place, and that there was no evidence that Snowdon was at fault; he " slipped because of the slippery character of the ground." [29]

James M. Hennessy was the foreman of a switching crew in the Chesapeake and Ohio Railroad Company's yards at Russell, Kentucky. While coupling cars, he was severely injured. He sued, and was awarded damages in the lower courts.

The railroad company appealed. This appeal came up before Circuit Judges Taft and Lurton and District Judge Clark on October 3, 1899. Lurton wrote the Court's decision, twisting Taft's decision in a previous case so as to cover this case. The United States safety-appliance law clearly provided that no railroad company should use cars with defective couplings. This being so, Lurton's findings were received with amazement. Lurton wrote in his decision that Hennessy knew that the great majority of cars on the repair tracks were defective and that to get cars from the tracks was a part of Hennessy's duty. " Manifestly," Judge Lurton continued,

[29] 85 Federal Reporter, 379.

"his duty involved the handling of cars not fitted for use, and dangers not incident to the ordinary work of one engaged in the ordinary operation of'trains of cars." In such a case, Lurton declared, a man voluntarily assumed risk. Lurton reversed the judgment of the lower court.[30]

Constitutional Right to be Killed.

Here was seen the beautiful finesse of court decisions.

If the railroad workers had gone on strike against having to handle unsafe cars (which cars the law prohibited) troops would probably have been ordered out against them. Every capitalist newspaper would have distorted and denounced the purposes of the strike. If all railroad workers had declined to risk mangling and death by handling such cars, the railroads could not have been operated; bondholders and stockholders do not operate railroads. In such a case scabs and thugs would have been imported to break the strike.

By consenting to take unsafe jobs and handling obsolete cars the workers were doing an immense, although unappreciated, favor to the railroad corporations, which in order to increase their profits, were ready at all times to avoid going to expense in equipping cars with safety appliances. But Judge Lurton steps in and lays down the wonderful doctrine that a worker has the perfect right to be mangled or killed. The constitutionality of this right has never yet been questioned by those who have evinced such solicitude that the Constitution should not be violated.

Of this "constitutional right" of the workers to get killed, Judge Lurton was one of the most conspicuous exponents. There was the case of John T. Hazlerigg, whose arm was crushed while coupling cars on the Norfolk and Western Railroad at Williamson, Virginia. Hazlerigg was taken to the railroad's hospital where his arm was amputated,

[30] 96 Federal Reporter, 713.

and where he remained five or six weeks. During the worst period of his suffering, an agent of the railroad generously persuaded him to sign an absolute release for all damage claims in consideration of giving him $25 in cash, a pass over the railroad and $2.75 for further transportation.

When Hazlerigg left the hospital he realized how for a wretched $27.75 paid for the loss of an arm, the railroad company had wheedled him into signing a release. He brought suit. When he had signed the paper, he testified, he was destitute of money, had no job and no suitable clothing, and was worn down by suffering and by a malady which affected his mind. He did not read the paper, he stated, and did not know what he was doing when he signed it.

The jury in the lower court awarded Hazlerigg damages, but when the railroad appealed, Judge Lurton set aside the judgment, on the ground that " there was no evidence to support Hazlerigg's statements," and that the jury should have been told that Hazlerigg was possibly guilty of " contributory negligence."

Judge Lurton stanchly defended the right of Hazlerigg " to quit his job "; to Lurton this was a precious privilege of which no worker should be deprived (when, of course, he did it " individually " and not in mass). But if the worker, compelled to remain at his perilous duty by want, did not quit but was forced by the same stern necessity to disregard the dangerous condition of the cars, then he became guilty of " contributory negligence," " voluntary assumption of risk," a " fellow servant " accomplice and other theoretical offenses, all devised for the special fine-spun purpose of relieving capitalists from the necessity of paying damages to mangled workers who had produced their profits.

This was the species of " law " inflicted on the working class, especially upon its most helpless members; and being so, it is not astonishing that the workers should have regarded " law " as a terrific and cruel instrument of tyranny.

The Delk Case.

But perhaps the decision in the case of E. M. Delk was the most flagrant of all of Judge Lurton's decisions.

Delk was a switchman on the St. Louis and San Francisco Railroad; he was thirty years old in 1906, had been working on railroads since he was a lad, was receiving $80 a month pay, was married and had a child.

On October 4, 1906, while Delk was switching certain cars out of a string of nine freight cars at Memphis, a car with a defective coupler broke loose. Delk's foot was cruelly mashed. Delk brought suit and was awarded $7,500 damages by a jury. But the trial judge compelled him to remit $2,500 of this amount or be forced to go through a new trial; this deduction reduced the judgment to $5,000. We shall now further quote one of Delk's attorneys, T. F. Kelly of Memphis:

"Delk is a man of meager education and knows nothing except railroading having been in the railroad service about sixteen years.

"He was blacklisted by the railroad companies of Memphis after he brought suit, and none of them would give him a job because he had entered suit against one of the roads. Of course he could not pass an examination under the rigid rules now in force, as he has only one good foot."

The railroad company appealed from the judgment of the lower court in favor of Delk. The appeal came before Judges Lurton, Severans and Richards in the United States Circuit Court of Appeals, on March 3, 1908.

An Amazing Decision.

Lurton and Severans each wrote opinions in favor of the company, reversing the lower court's judgment. They said that it seemed unjust and unreasonable to say that having fulfilled its utmost duty the railroad company should be held responsible for conditions which might occur without its fault. Judge Richards handed down an indignant dissenting minority opinion, concluding thus: " A car loaded and being used in interstate traffic was found with a defective coupler. The car was marked ' In Bad Order,' and a repair piece sent for. After thus being notified of its condition, the car should have been withdrawn; but it was not, and the company kept moving it about in connection with other cars, and finally ordered the injured employé to couple it to another car. This he tried to do, with the natural result, and he was crippled for life. The case amply justifies the verdict and the judgment should be affirmed." [31]

The decision of Lurton and Severans caused the utmost astonishment among non-corporation lawyers. Such was the amazement over the decision in the Delk case that the Supreme Court of the United States, shortly after, took particular pains to disapprove of it in strong language, although the Delk case was not then before it. In deciding the parallel case of the St. Louis and Iron Mountain Railway Co. vs. Taylor, Justice Moody in writing the Court's opinion referred to the Delk decision and wrote:

" In deciding the questions thus raised upon which courts have differed (St. Louis & S. F. Railroad vs. Delk, 158 Fed. Rep., 931), we need not enter into the wilderness of cases upon the common-law duty of the employer to use reasonable care to furnish his employé reasonably safe tools, machinery and appliances, or to consider when and how far that duty may be performed by delegating it to suitable persons for whose default the employer is not responsible. . . . The Congress not satisfied with the common-law duty and its resulting liability, has prescribed and defined the duty by statutes. We have nothing to do but to ascertain and declare the meaning of a few simple words in which the duty is described. It is enacted that ' no cars, either loaded or unloaded, shall be used

[31] 158 Federal Reporter, 931.

in interstate commerce traffic which do not comply with the standard.'

" There is no escape from the meaning employed to confuse them or lessen their significance. . . . If the railroad does, in point of fact, use cars which do not comply with the standard, it violates the plain prohibition of the law, and there arises from that violation the liability to make compensation to one who is injured by it." [32]

After the Supreme Court of the United States had expressed this sharp opinion, Delk's attorney on June 27, 1908, made a motion in the Circuit Court of Appeals that the case be reheard, but Judge Lurton and Severans curtly refused without stating any reason. Judge Richards again indignantly dissented from their stand. Delk's lawyer then appealed the case to the Supreme Court of the United States.

The crippling of Delk happened, as we said, on October 4, 1906. More than four years had passed, and Delk had not been able to collect a single cent in damages. For nearly a year and a half after the accident, Delk had been unable to do any work whatever. Blacklisting then followed. Finally he obtained a job as crossing flagman at a salary of about $35 a month, on which he had to support himself and family. Although he did not lose his foot entirely, yet we are informed he would have been far better off without that mangled remnant; so badly was the foot crushed that it keeps him in continual pain, and may yet possibly result in his death.

Supreme Court Reverses the Decision.

Delk's attorney, T. F. Kelly, appealed from Lurton and Severans' decision to the Supreme Court of the United States. When this appeal was heard in 1911, Justice Lurton was a member of that Court, but he did not participate in the decision. The railroad company fought the appeal stubbornly, and was

[32] 210 U. S. Reports, 294.

represented by many attorneys from different parts of the
country. But the facts and the law were too strong for them.
By an unanimous decision the Supreme Court of the United
States reversed the Circuit Court of Appeals decision of Judges
Lurton and Severans, and affirmed the verdict of the trial court
in favor of Delk.

The corporation contesting so many similar cases was (to
repeat) the Louisville and Nashville Railroad. This was the
identical corporation which was the prime mover in having
various labor laws declared unconstitutional. These were laws
such as the twenty-eight hour law, the employers' liability law
and other measures that after many years of agitation labor
organizations had succeeded in getting passed, only to find
them thrown out by the courts. The case of Adair vs. the
United States (described in a previous chapter) in which the
Supreme Court of the United States declared it to be legal for
a corporation to blacklist an employé (while other decisions
held that it was illegal for a labor organization to boycott an
employer) was instigated by the Louisville and Nashville Railroad.

A Decision Pleasing to Harriman.

Judge Lurton's decisions were uniformly favorable to big
corporations.[33] A particularly noted example was in the case
of Talbot J. Taylor, representing the interests of James J.
Keene, a Wall Street " bear " operator. This, it is true, was
only a contest of capitalist groups, and Lurton's decision would
nominally deserve no serious criticism were it not that when
deciding against maimed and mangled wage workers, he contended that he was only construing law. Taylor, in 1903,
brought an action to restrain the magnate Harriman from
voting $90,000,000 of stock held by the Union Pacific Railroad.

[33] See Case of L. & N. R. R. vs. Central Trust Co., 87 Federal Reports, 502, in which Lurton and Severans decided in favor of the railroad. and other cases.

The Keene group held $30,000,000 of Southern Pacific stock, and if the Union Pacific's $90,000,000 of Southern Pacific stock had been tied up by injunction, Keene's $30,000,000 of stock would have controlled the annual meeting of the Southern Pacific.

Judge Lurton finally decided that the combination of the two Pacific railroads in issue was not a violation of the Sherman anti-Trust Act. This notwithstanding the fact that the Supreme Court of the United States only a short time previously had decided that a merger of the Great Northern Railroad and the Northern Pacific Railroad was illegal and had ordered it dissolved.

Following this decision in favor of Harriman, came those stupendous stockjobbing frauds, some of which we have already, in a previous chapter, cited from the Interstate Commerce Commission's report, and largely by means of which Harriman, after beginning his career with nothing, acquired an immense fraudulent fortune.[34]

Harriman's Great Frauds.

The story of these vast frauds is so extensive that it cannot even be summarized here. Every new output in watered stock was followed by a new taxation of the workers in the form of increased freight rates, which, of course, added enormously to the cost of living. At the same time wages remained generally stationary, or were reduced. When Harriman died his estate was at first appraised at $149,000,000, but on later examination was found to be much more.

During the perpetration of his stockjobbing frauds, Harri-

---

[34] Keene was conducting a manipulating campaign to get control of the Southern Pacific Railroad. In detailing the secret circumstances the New York *Times*, issue of December 11, 1907, concluded: ". . . There is little doubt that the refusal of Judge Lurton to make the temporary injunction permanent was a source of no small relief to Mr. Harriman and his associates, despite the precautions which they took to make the injunction nugatory, had it been granted."

man was the head of an immense system of corruption. In a statement published on January 2, 1908, Francis J. Heney, who had closely prosecuted political corruptionists on the Pacific coast, declared that not W. F. Herrin but Harriman was the real power in the corruption of officials. " According to my deduction," said Heney, " the head of the legal department of the Union Pacific Railroad, W. F. Herrin, was the boss behind the apparent boss [Ruef, the political boss of San Francisco]. But I am convinced that Herron was, after all, the tool of the actual boss, Harriman." We have also seen how, in his historic letter to Sidney Webster, Harriman alleged how after being summoned to the White House by President Roosevelt in the closing days of the 1904 campaign, when Roosevelt was running for reëlection, he (Harriman) returned to New York to raise a campaign fund of $260,000 by which " at least 50,000 votes were turned in the city of New York, making a difference of 100,000 votes in the general result." [35] Harriman's personal contribution to this fund was $50,000.

Did Lurton Use Private Cars?

During the years preceding the passage of the Hepburn Act of 1906 which prohibited traveling on free railroad passes, Judge Lurton acquired the singular name of " Private-Car Lurton." Whence the significance? It was repeatedly charged in the newpapers, and not denied, that Lurton was one of the Federal judges traveling extensively in sumptuous private cars supplied by the railroads. The allegation was also

[35] In a letter, dated December 15, 1911, to Theodore Roosevelt, George R. Sheldon, treasurer of the Republican National Committee, gave a different version of this affair. Sheldon stated that it was Odell, Chairman of the Republican State Committee of New York, and not Roosevelt, who appealed to Harriman for aid through Cornelius N. Bliss, then Treasurer of the Republican National Committee, and that Harriman then raised $160,000 which with $80,000 raised by Bliss, was given directly to Odell. When this letter was published, Odell declined to make any statement.

frequently published that at one time a receivership action
brought the question of the management of a certain railway'
before Judge Lurton. According further to this allegation,
Lurton indicated his desire for a private car and the receiver
complied. Necessarily there is no proof of this charge, or
similar charges, in the formal records. Therefore, we do not
pretend to vouch for their authenticity, but simply relate them
for what they may be worth, true or false. But the report of
Lurton's habitual use of private cars caused so much comment
that even the Memphis *News-Scimitar,* a newspaper friendly
to Lurton, frequently published caustic remarks on Lurton's
alleged receipt of such favors from railroad corporations.[36]

" He is a man of ability and forcefulness and the graduate
of a shrewd school in politics," commented this newspaper on
one occasion. " During his career as a judge he has been
much criticised for his leaning toward corporations litigant before him. It has been urged against him that during his

[36] Other Federal judges were accused of the same. On January 26,
1906, the Kansas City *Times,* related, in an obscure and perfunctory
news item, that Gardiner Lathrop, general solicitor of the Santa Fe
Railroad system, had taken a party of friends on a tarpoon fishing expedition to Mexico. Among those availing themselves of this free excur-
sion on the railroad's cars were Judge John C. Pollock, U. S. District
Judge for Kansas; Judge John F. Phillips, U. S. District Judge for the
western district of Missouri, and Judge Smith McPherson, U. S. District
Judge for the southern district of Iowa. The judges did not deny taking
the trip.
   At the time these Federal judges accepted these railroad favors the
constitutionality of the railway freight and passenger rate reduction, as
recently passed by the Missouri Legislature, was before the Federal
Courts. On June 14, 1905, the date when that law was to go into effect,
Judges Phillips and McPherson later granted a temporary injunction
against the enforcement of that law. After the return of the party
from the fishing trip, Judge McPherson arbitrarily enjoined the railroads from obeying the new passenger and freight rate law. In a series
of acts, Judge Phillips endorsed Judge McPherson's action which was
also subsequently affirmed by Judge Pollock.
   Representative Murphy, of Missouri, preferred charges in Congress
against Judges Phillips and McPherson, and Representative Rucker of
the same State declared that Judge Phillips should have been impeached
twenty years previously. But no impeachment proceedings were ever
brought.

judgeship he has been the notable recipient of distinguished favors from corporations. He has, for instance, been wont to travel during his vacations upon the private cars of various railroads of the country, with all available courtesies and privileges extended with lavish hand to himself and party."

In a previous chapter we have described at some length the contest among different groups of great capitalists either to retain or secure control of the vast assets of the three principal life insurance companies of New York. We have also given details, as disclosed by the investigation of the New York Legislative Committee, of the corruption enormities systematically carried on by those companies.

Through his partner, George W. Perkins,[37] J. Pierpont Morgan, with his enormous ownership or control of railroad and steamship lines, banks and trusts of many kinds, had long been able to sway the great revenues of the New York Life Insurance Company.[38] It may here be mentioned that one of the many railroads controlled by Morgan has been the Louisville and Nashville Railroad.[39] Through his instrument Hyde, the freebooter Harriman partially controlled the Equitable Life Assurance Society; and the Standard Oil Company ruled the Mutual Life Insurance Company. These and other vast plutocratic interests had used immense sums of the policy holders' money to finance their trust and manipulating operations, not omitting to enter into " side agreements " by which fraudulent methods they pocketed large personal profits. Starting in the Equitable Life Assurance Society, these capitalist groups be-

[37] For a considerable time before becoming a partner of Morgan, Perkins was vice-president of the New York Life Insurance Company.

[38] At the present writing it is estimated that the stupendous sum of $500,000,000 of money is deposited with the firm of J. P. Morgan and Company. Morgan is a director of sixty-one corporations many of which, such as the Steel Trust, deposit their cash balances with his firm. His financial power is inconceivably vast. His banking firm is a purely private concern, and as such is not subject to the supervision of State, Government or any other authority.

[39] Moody's " The Truth About The Trusts," 434.

gan to fight one another for control of the booty; and Thomas
F. Ryan, who needed the insurance funds to finance his rubber
and other trusts, hastened forward to take a hand in the fray
and see if he could not gobble one, and perhaps two, of the
big insurance companies.

The Contest for Control.

What the actual result was is told in the next chapter. Here
it is only necessary to deal with the contest for the possession
of the New York Life Insurance Company. An "International Policyholders' Committee" was formed to oust the particular capitalists in control of the New York and the Mutual
Life Insurance Companies. The slogan of this committee was
that the investigation has shown the " ins " to be thoroughly corrupt, and a salutary " purifying process " was required. Who
it was that supplied the great sum — said to have been at least
$250,000 — that the committee expended in its campaign, was
never disclosed. The name of Thomas F. Ryan was confi-
dentially mentioned, but there is no available proof that he was
the individual.[40]

In voting for the trustees of the New York Life Insurance
Company each policy holder has a right to vote. How this
provision was long fraudulently evaded we have previously
described in the case of the Mutual Life Insurance Company.
Of the immense number of policy holders throughout the
world, obviously only a few can vote in person. Each of the
groups contending for control of the New York Life Insurance
Company put up a trustee ticket, and the contest narrowed to
a question as to which could secure the most proxies.

[40] In its circular the "International Policyholders' Committee " denounced as a falsehood the charge that it was a "Ryan Committee."
This committee called upon all policyholders to defeat the "present
discredited managements," and install men in their places "who will
now and forever separate these companies from Wall Street control."

Lurton on the Proxy Committee.

One of the men whose name was brought forward as a candidate for trustee on the Morgan " administration ticket " was Judge Horace H. Lurton. The fact that a judge of the United States Circuit Court was thus openly acting as an agent in this contest caused no inconsiderable scandal. It was regarded as politic to withdraw Lurton's name from the trustee ticket. He was then placed on a committee of three, composed of himself, Rowland G. Hazard and Alba J. Johnson, to solicit and handle proxies for the New York Life Insurance Company election.[41] The " administration " trustee ticket was composed largely of such capitalists or dependents of big capitalists, as Thomas P. Fowler, president of the New York, Ontario and Western Railroad; Clarence H. Mackay, president of the Commercial Cable Company; Seth M. Milliken, extensive woolen manufacturer and director in many banks; John G. Milburn, corporation lawyer; Alexander E. Orr, General Louis Wagner, John Reid, Augustus G. Paine and others — twenty in all.

. Judge Lurton's serving on the proxy committe aroused another scandal and much acidulous comment. The election for trustees of the New York Life Insurance Company was held at the company's main office on December 16, 1906. Confident that they had mustered a majority of the proxies, the " International Policyholders' Committee " were astounded at what they now witnessed. Judge Lurton had come on direct from the United States Circuit Court of Cincinnati to assist in voting 121,000 proxies which the agents of the company had secretly collected all over the world,' and of the existence of

---

[41] The author has a copy of the published " administration ticket " circular on which Lurton's name duly appears; his occupation is there described as " Judge of the United States Circuit Court, 6th District." Hazard was a big manufacturing capitalist, and Johnson was a member of the firm of Burnham, Williams and Company, proprietor of the Baldwin Locomotive Works (now controlled by J. P. Morgan) in which plants the workers recently struck, although unsuccessfully, for better working conditions.

which the "International Policyholders' Committee" knew nothing. These and other proxies were voted in by Hazard, Johnson and Lurton for the so-called Morgan ticket. The 121,000 proxies had been stored in the New York Life Insurance Company's building. Almost as fast as they were brought into the voting room in wash-baskets, boxes, crates, bags, etc., Lurton and his two associates would take the bundles and vote them.[42]   It is needless to say that the "administration ticket" won.

Senator Foraker, Lurton's Friend.

It can be authoritatively stated that corporation politicians urged President Roosevelt to appoint Lurton to the Supreme Court of the United States, but after inquiring into Judge Lurton's record, Roosevelt refused.   When Taft succeeded Roosevelt, Lurton succeeded in having himself appointed, in 1909, to the seat made vacant by the death of Associate Justice Peckham.   His appointment called forth a storm of protests from labor unions and others.   There was considerable, but ineffective, opposition from the "progressive" United States Senators to the confirmation of his appointment.   Apart from Lurton's having the friendship of Taft, his former colleague on the Bench, Lurton's chief and most insistent pusher was, it was understood, Senator Joseph B. Foraker of Ohio who came to his rescue at the crucial moment.

Foraker was a noted Ohio politician and railroad lawyer. So thoroughly did he control the Ohio Legislature at one time that it was known as the "Foraker Legislature."   He tried to give the street railways of the State a ninety-nine-years' franchise with exemption from taxation, but public opposition frightened the politicians.   But immediately after the Ohio Legislature had elected him to the United States Senate, Foraker did push through that Legislature, in April, 1896, a bill

[42] The International Policyholders' Committee charged that many of these proxies were fraudulent and invalid.

authorizing a fifty-years' franchise to various consolidating street railway lines in Cleveland and in Cincinnati. Public uproar and adverse decisions of the lower courts availed nothing; the Legislature passed supplementary acts, and the higher court, known as the " Foraker's Court," held the franchise to be valid in Cincinnati. Foraker appeared in court as the attorney for the franchise interests; when the decision favoring them was given, the market value of Cincinnati traction stock went high, and the " inside traction ring," it was said, netted many millions of dollars.[43]   The value of the franchise for the Cincinnati Traction Company alone was estimated at $10,000,-000. Foraker's son was long vice-president of the Cincinnati Traction Company, and his brother was its counsel.

Foraker was counsel for Morgan's Southern Railway Company, and in 1896 sought to have the City of Cincinnati sell its holdings in the " Queen and Crescent Railway " to the Southern Railway Company for a comparatively paltry sum. His proposition was rejected, and later (in 1905) Cincinnati leased the road for between $300,000 and $400,000 a year more than the interest on the terms that Foraker's proposal would have yielded.   In the United States Senate, Foraker was notoriously pro-railroad.   Foraker's direct connection with John D. Archbold, of the Standard Oil Company, was shown when, in 1908, authentic copies of Archbold's letters were produced.   In one letter, dated December 11, 1900, Archbold sent Foraker a certificate of deposit of $5,000, and in another letter dated January 27, 1902, Archbold enclosed a draft for $50,000.   " Your letter," wrote Archbold, " states the conditions correctly, and I trust the transaction will be successfully consummated."   The exact nature of the transaction was not made clear.

Senator Foraker admitted the payments, saying that he had been employed by the Standard Oil Company as one of its

[43] It was charged that in addition to his stock profits, Foraker received a fee of $100,000. This he denied, saying that he got only " a present of $5,000 " from an officer of the company.

counsel in Ohio, but denied that the payments had anything to do with legislation in Congress.   He also asserted that the $50,-000 payment " was a loan to a newspaper," and averred that the money " had been returned."   Archbold's letter also showed that for years United States Senator Joseph W. Bailey, of Texas, had been a retainer of the Standard Oil interests.

So Lurton went on the Supreme Court Bench: an industrious but by no means learned lawyer, yet by his big boastful talk giving the impression that he was a giant in knowledge.   A small, stout, energetic man, very irritable and excitable, he at no time took pains to conceal his admiration and reverence for wealth and for the master capitalists.[44]

[44] When Lurton's appointment was made, a leading member of the Nashville bar, John J. Vertrees, one of the most prominent attorneys for many years for the Louisville and Nashville Railroad, the Standard Oil Company and other corporations, and a personal friend of Lurton, said of Lurton: " In these days·judges and lawyers are apt to be classified under two heads; those who place emphasis on property rights, and those who place the emphasis on personal rights.   To the former class belongs Judge Lurton."

At the time Ballinger, Secretary of the Interior under Taft, was under investigation by a House Committee in 1910, for having, according to various charges, been the instrument of the Morgan-Guggenheim syndicate in their designs upon the natural resources of Alaska, Taft selected Vertrees to defend Ballinger.   Subsequently Ballinger resigned.

CHAPTER XVIII

THE SUPREME COURT UNDER CHIEF JUSTICE WHITE
(CONTINUED)

The next appointment made by President Taft to the Supreme Court was that of Charles E. Hughes in 1910, as an Associate Justice to succeed Justice Brewer who died on March 28, 1910.

Of Justice Brewer we shall finally remark, in passing, that so thoroughly had he indoctrinated law in accordance with the demands of capitalist interests, that when he died only one progressive decision could be attributed to him by his eulogists. This was the decision upholding the constitutionality of the Oregon ten-hour law for women. This law the Supreme Court of the United States affirmed on the principle that a State could constitutionally protect women workers so as to thus conserve the future of the race and the general welfare of society.

Born in 1862, Hughes was the son of a " hard-shell " Baptist minister and was of the same denomination himself. After his admission to the bar, he became a clerk in the law office of Chamberlain, Carter and Hornblower, of New York City.

This was a notable corporation firm; of Walter S. Carter, one of its members, a laudatory biographical account says, " Over one hundred distinguished lawyers have served in his office, such as William B. Hornblower, Lloyd W. Bowers and Paul D. Cravath." Sherburne Blake Eaton, a member of the firm, became chief executive officer of the Edison Electric Light Company in 1881, and its president and general counsel in 1884. Carter's great obsessing hobby was in encouraging a peculiar and ludicrous form of caste snobbery; he was a member of the "Settlers and Defenders of America," the "Founders and Patriots of America," the "Society of Mayflower Descendants," and the "Sons of the Revolution." As for Hornblower he was, as early as 1880, counsel for the New York Life Insurance Company; he became one of the trustees of that company, and head of the committee which approved the so-called "yellow-dog" fund of the New York Life Insurance Company, which fund, ostensibly disbursed as "legal expenses," was used, in reality, to purchase favorable legislation and to defeat hostile bills. Hornblower was also counsel for the New York Central Railroad Company, the Rome, Watertown and Ogdensburg Railroad Company, the New York Security and Trust Company, and many other corporations.

This was the same Hornblower who passed as a notable "reformer" in politics, and who (as we have already related) had been nominated by President Cleveland an Associate Justice of the Supreme Court of the United States, which nomination had been rejected by the Senate, in 1894, for personal-political reasons.

Such was the atmosphere of the office in which Hughes was a law clerk, and it may be added that Cravath was a fellow clerk at the same time.

Hughes' career now expanded. He was a precise, methodically-minded man, extremely careful of the proprieties, never disposed to break conventions, studying the law and the law system as he found them, sticking to the letter and dismissing the spirit, for he saw that it was the letter that was applied. He perceived, too, that the most successful lawyers were those pleading for corporations; they waxed fat and great, and were high personages in the community. On the other hand, he could not help seeing that those who made a practice of defending the poor and helpless, the victims of the industrial system, not only invited poverty, but suffered a distinct stigma in the eyes of the influential and powerful.

Hughes as an Attorney.

Hughes had married Carter's daughter, and in 1888 the law firm of Carter, Hughes and Cravath was formed. Need it be explained who Paul D. Cravath was, the skillful and renowned Cravath? Later he became, and for nearly a quarter of a century remained, Thomas F. Ryan's most confidential legal aide, not as adroit as Elihu Root, but more constant, standing to Ryan as his shadow. Of Ryan's career we have already given sufficient glimpses; how from being a penniless young man, he became ône of the most conspicuous multimillionaires of the country, owning or controlling street car systems, gas plants, railroads, trusts and other properties, and we shall see how he acquired one of the great life insurance companies. We cannot enter here into the immense mass of testimony before various legislative committees revealing the long trail of corruption and criminal transactions of corporations controlled by him.[1] Whenever a franchise for Ryan's benefit was to be slid through Legislature or Board of Aldermen, there Cravath was to be found with his particular arguments to persuade legislators that the grant should be made.

When Hughes was a candidate for Governor of New York, in 1906, he was quoted as denying that he had ever been a corporation lawyer except in the service of the State. Did the facts coincide with this statement? Let us see.

---

[1] Some of these facts have been described in previous chapters; others will be referred to later in this chapter. One of Ryan's transactions that may be mentioned here was a loan of $2,000,000 made by the State Trust Company to Ryan's office boy, D. F. Shea; such a loan was forbidden by the laws of the State of New York, and in consequence was a criminal transaction.

On another occasion when proof had been presented to the banker Jacob H. Schiff that he had been grossly deceived, he compelled Ryan to relieve his (Schiff's) firm, Kuhn, Loeb and Company of its holdings of Metropolitan Securities Company stock, amounting to about $6,000,000. "If Mr. Ryan," says Col. Amory, "had not been a very rich man, indeed, his embarrassment in satisfying Mr. Schiff's peremptory demands would have been extreme."—"Truth About Metropolitan," p. 45.

Effort to Put Deadly Wires Under Ground.

By the year 1875 New York City and other cities were filled with a network of deadly telegraph, electric-light and other wires, strung over the pavements on wooden poles. The introduction of heavy electric-light cables on poles brought a new element of danger to human life. A constant menace, these wires, as the courts later on stated, were improperly insulated. Their falling to the ground killed people constantly. In fighting fires, New York City's firemen were also often killed, and were prevented by the wires from overcoming fires as successfully as if the wires had been underground.

In the year 1875 the New York Legislature had already passed an act ordering that the wires should be placed underground. The electric-light and other companies affected made resistance to this act, and had it declared unconstitutional. Year after year they lobbied in the State Legislature to prevent the passage of other acts.

But deadly accidents kept increasing, and the public demand became stronger that the barbarous system of stringing wires overhead be abolished. The companies refused to make the change on the ground that it would entail much expense.

At this point high city officials suddenly began to support the public demand that the " poles must go." What was the motive of these Tammany officials? Was it one of public spirit? Scarcely. The sequel, years after, revealed that a band of shrewd politico-capitalists had seen how they could take advantage of this reform movement, and under cover of it get a comprehensive monopoly for themselves of the right of laying and operating underground conduits for the wires.

The New York Legislature, in 1884, enacted a law compelling companies in all cities of more than 500,000 population to put their wires underground before November 1, 1885. If they failed to do this the city government was empowered to tear the wires down and put them underground.

The companies raised the objection that the time allowed
them was too brief. Moreover, they did not want to put the
wires underground in any more cities than could be avoided.
Lobbying at Albany produced an amendatory act making the
law apply to cities exceeding a million population only. This,
of course, meant that the operation of the act was restricted
to New York City; no other city had a population of more
than a million. The act of 1885 also created a Board of Electrical Control. A supplementary act was passed in 1886.
Still another law was enacted in 1887 giving New York City
authority to remove the poles and wires ninety days after notice should be served.

These laws were contested by the companies. Finally, on
May 12, 1889, Mayor Grant ordered the electric-light wires
to be torn down. His ground was that they were imperfectly
insulated and dangerous to human life.

Hughes Pleads for Electric Light Companies.

On November 11, 1889, James C. Carter, Joseph H. Choate
and Charles E. Hughes, representing the United States Illuminating Company and the Mount Morris Electric Light
Company, went to court. Pleading that the act of 1887 was
" an invasion of the rights of property," they secured an in
junction against the city.

The city appealed for the dissolving of the injunction. This
appeal was argued in the General Term of the Supreme Court,
in New York City, in December, 1889, before Judges Van
Brunt, Barrett and Brady. The companies were again represented by Carter, Choate and Hughes.[2]

The three judges concurred in deciding in favor of New
York City. Their decision was of rather a caustic order,
scoring the contentions of counsel for the companies.
". . . When," said this decision, " it is apparent, as in the

[2] See Supreme Court Reports, N. Y., Vol. 62: 224.

case at bar, the condition of the wires is such that they are dangerous to human life, and that any passer-by, without negligence on his part, is liable to be struck dead in the street, can it be said for a moment that the public authorities have no power to abate this nuisance and protect the lives of its citizens? Indeed it is one of their highest duties, and if they allowed such a condition of affairs to continue, might make the city liable for the damages sustained by reason of their negligence in not removing the common nuisance. . . ."

Counsel for the companies, the court said, had contended that the Board of Electrical Control had refused to allow repairs to be made. The decision disposed of this plea. The court said that it was established beyond question that the wires had become excessively dangerous. "Attention was called to this condition of affairs by the happening of accidents by which human life was sacrificed. . . ." This, the court stated, was a "shameful condition of affairs."

The companies, the court went on, had not made "the slightest effort to compel the Board of Electrical Control, if they unjustly refused, to grant them permits to repair. . . .

"If these electrical companies had been actuated by the slightest desire to put their apparatus in a condition such as would not endanger human life, they could easily have found a way to remove the obstruction which they claim was placed in their path by the Board of Electrical Control. It would seem that they were only too willing to shelter themselves behind the assumed unreasonableness of some of the regulations of the board, and to allow their apparatus to get into such a condition that it was dangerous to human life and become a public nuisance." The companies, the court said, were "guilty of the wilful violation of a manifest duty in allowing the wires to become dangerous. They are without excuse, and when they claim that the destruction of these instruments of death . . . is an invasion of the rights of property, such claim seems to proceed upon the assumption that nothing has a right to exist except themselves." [3]   The court upheld the constitutionality of the law.

Scramble for Underground Franchises.

While Hughes was thus acting for the electric-light companies, his partner, Cravath, was busy in other directions.

Realizing the great value of a monopoly of underground conduits, the Western Union Telegraph Company (then controlled by Jay Gould and Russell Sage) and the Metropolitan Telephone Company [4] (now the New York Telephone Company) had organized the Consolidated Telegraph and Electrical Subway Company, which secured a franchise to construct and operate conduits throughout the entire city.   All other companies using wires were now confronted with the necessity of using those conduits and of being forced to pay a certain schedule of rentals.

The electric-light companies saw the situation in which they now were.   On the one hand the city was moving against them to force their wires underground; on the other, the only conduit franchise was owned by the Consolidated Telegraph and Electrical Company.   While Hughes was one of the attorneys resisting the city's move, partner Cravath was persuading the Board of Electrical Control to give the electric-light companies franchises for underground conduits.

There was a lively scramble for franchises.   On October 14, 1889, Wheeler H. Peckham appeared as counsel for the Standard Electrical Subway Company.   This was, it is hardly necessary to say, the same Peckham whom Cleveland, in 1894, nominated as Associate Justice of the Supreme Court of the United States, and whose nomination was rejected by the Senate because of Senator Hill's personal opposition.   Peckham pleaded with the Board of Electrical Control that it give a conduit

[3] Supreme Court Reports, N. Y., Vol. 62, pp. 222–245.
[4] Controlled by the Bell Telephone Company.

franchise to the Standard Electrical Subway Company.[5] Elihu
Root came forward, on February 17, 1890, to plead for the
gift of a conduit franchise to the Manhattan Electric Light
Company and the Harlem Lighting Company. Root opposed
Peckham's company, and argued against giving it a franchise.[6]

On the same day on which Root appeared, Joseph H. Choate,
Paul D. Cravath[7] and Caleb H. Jackson, representing the
United States Illuminating Company and the Safety Electric
Light and Power Company, argued before the Board of Elec-
trical Control in favor of conduit franchises for those com-
panies, and opposed the Consolidated Telegraph and Electrical
Subway Company.[8]

The upshot of this scramble was that all these companies
succeeded in getting franchises in this way: A new company,
called the Empire City Subway Company, was organized, and
presented in 1891 with a comprehensive franchise to lay and
operate underground conduits. The conduits of the one company were, it was stipulated, to be used for high-tension, and
those of the other for low-tension, wires.

[5] See " Minutes of the Board of Electrical Control," Vol. I, July, 1887,
to Dec., 1890, p. 824.

[6] *Ibid.*, 889.

[7] Considering that Choate and Cravath represented the same clients
in the above case, it is worth noting here that it was Choate who, twenty
years later, in open court, severely denounced Cravath. This incident
occurred on January 25, 1910, in the United States Circuit Court at
New York, before Judge Ray. The occasion was a suit over the finan-
ciering of the traction lines in New York City. Choate excoriated the
magnates responsible for the long-continued looting of the traction
lines and the ensuing corruption. As the attorney for these looters
Cravath was not spared in the scathing denunciation.

[8] " Minutes of the Board of Electrical Control," Vol. I, etc., 824, 826,
917, and 1007. This company fixed a certain rental for the use of its
ducts. Refusing to pay it, the Brush Electric Illuminating Company
was threatened with eviction. Representing the Brush Company, Cravath, in June, 1891, applied for a preliminary injunction against the Consolidated and Electrical Subway Company. The application was denied,.
and so was the appeal following. James C. Carter, Frederick R. Cou-
dert and Edward Lauterbach appeared as the attorneys for the Consolidated and Electrical Subway Company.— Supreme Court Reports, N. Y.,
Vol. 67: 446.

It may be said parenthetically at this point that Hughes and Cravath sundered partnership in about the year 1890.

Monopoly Established.

Having fought the city and then one another, the companies now combined in a huge monopoly. From that day to this not a single telegraph, telephone, electric-light or other company disapproved of by the combination, has been able to get wires in the conduits. It was originally provided that all companies should have access, but this condition has been evaded by various pretexts.

With this monopoly of underground conduits secured, the various companies raised their rates to an extortionate scale. The Metropolitan Telephone Company increased its rates for unlimited service from $125 and $150 a year to $240 annually, and in some years its profits rose to 145 per cent. on the actual cash capital, excluding from computation the capital added by dividends not distributed.[9] The conduit monopoly has made enormous profits. Under the terms of the franchise all profits exceeding ten per cent. were to go to the city, but by a continuous process of juggling with the books, and the frequent issue of watered stock, the nominal profits (as reported to the city) have never equaled ten per cent.

All the electric-light companies were later merged into one monopoly, which in turn was controlled by the Consolidated Gas Company, which was controlled by the Standard Oil Company.[10] In view of the decision of the Supreme Court of the

[9] "Argument of Simon Sterne before the N. Y. Senate Committee on Cities, Feb. 5 and 19, 1895," p. 6.
[10] Moody's "The Truth About The Trusts": 415. Also see testimony in the recent hearing before the Public Service Commission, First District, New York, "Public Service Commission: Electric Lighting Investigation," Vol. IV: 1510, etc., etc. This testimony showed that the United States Illuminating Company, the Brush Electric Illuminating Company, the Edison and other companies were merged, in 1890, in the United Light and Power Company which in turn was controlled by the Consolidated Gas Company.

United States in the eighty-cent case (related in a previous chapter) which Justice Peckham, a brother of Wheeler H. Peckham, wrote, and considering the facts here narrated, it is well to repeat the names of some of the great capitalist magnates controlling the Consolidated Gas Company. Among the directors were William Rockefeller, George F. Baker, James Stillman, William C. Whitney, Thomas F. Ryan, Anthony N. Brady and sundry others.

Thus we see Hughes starting out as a young lawyer in the lucrative field of representing corporations. His clients, whether corporate or private, were all rich; poor men's cases do not seem to have been any part of Hughes' practice. That Hughes himself was in money matters personally and scrupulously honest was a fact. No doubt he gave conscientious, zealous service for the fees that he received.

But the question of personal honesty embraces so many aspects, and demands so deep an analysis that it cannot conclusively be said that a man was honest because he resorted to no illegal methods. There is an intellectual and class dishonesty which in its results far exceeds pecuniary dishonesty. The question might here be profitably entered into since it is the fact that an individual's views and conduct are largely determined by his interests, training, environment and long-continued associations. The problem is to a great extent a social, not an individual, one; and when we consider why this or that man was selected for the Supreme Court bench it is necessary to know what his antecedent associations, influences, and interests were.

New York, Westchester and Boston Project.

The second illustration of Hughes' activities as a lawyer was his efficient work in getting a franchise for the New York, Westchester and Boston Railway.

For its entrance into New York City, the New York, New Haven and Hartford Railroad had long had to use the New

York Central's tracks from Woodlawn to the Grand Central depot.[11] This privilege cost it a certain tariff of seven cents on every passenger, which tariff was recently increased to twelve cents. The New York, New Haven and Hartford Railroad was and is controlled by J. Pierpont Morgan; it now sought its own entrance into New York City. How was this to be obtained?

It happened that in the year 1872 a company called the New York, Westchester and Boston Railroad Company had organized by filing articles of incorporation at Albany. In reality it was an abortive corporation; it had never completed the necessary legal formality of filing an affidavit as prescribed by Section 2, Railroad Law of 1850.[12]

The company, or what called itself the company, became insolvent in 1876, and a receiver was appointed on March 25 of that year. On March 22, 1881, the Supreme Court of New York directed the receiver to sell all its rights, title, interest, real estate, etc. These were sold to William F. Pelt for $5,500.

According to good legal authority this sale operated to deprive the company of any located route, except such as the Legislature might subsequently grant. But the Legislature did not act.

For years the paper franchise was hawked about for sale; nobody seemed to want it.

Hughes Comes Forward for the Project.

In, however, either the year 1900 or 1901 some powerful interest suddenly took up the phantom, and on the strength of it tried to get a definite franchise from the Board of Aldermen. This body was at that time vested with the power of franchise granting. It was significant that the firm of Carter, Hughes, Rounds and Schurman (so the firm was now styled)

[11] The New York Central controls the old New York and Harlem River Railroad which owns the franchise to operate on Park Avenue.

[12] See, "Minutes of the [N. Y.] Board of Estimate and Apportionment, 1904," Vol. I: 471.

appeared as the attorneys advocating the granting of the franchise. They seldom came forward except to represent some big interest.[13] Hughes was the member of the firm who was the active attorney in arguing for the passage of the franchise.[14]

Hughes solemnly denied that any large interest was behind the project; he asserted that the company was one absolutely independent of connection with any other corporation. The Board of Aldermen were skeptical.

At the same time another company called the New York and Port Chester Railroad Company projected itself upon the scene, applied for a franchise, and began opposing the New York, Westchester and Boston Company.

Report had it that both companies were owned by the New York, New Haven and Hartford Railroad, and interesting rumors declared that the show of opposition was only a trick to blind the people; that the object was to get a franchise for either company or both companies.

Later developments proved, as we shall see, that both companies were, in fact, owned by the New York, New Haven and Hartford Railroad, controlled by J. Pierpont Morgan and the Standard Oil group.

The Aldermanic Hold-Up.

For three years the Board of Aldermen refused to grant the franchises. Nobody imputed any lofty motive to the Honorable Board. Meanwhile, what Lemuel Ely Quigg on another occasion called "accellerators of public opinion" carried on

[13] From the New York *Times,* issue of January 19, 1908: "A noted corporation lawyer, speaking of Mr. Hughes, said that he was not a money maker and was one of the few lawyers who consulted their clients as to the size of his fees." The article further stated of Hughes that when he became a candidate for Governor of New York (in 1906) "it is doubtful whether he was worth more than $100,000."

[14] "Minutes of the [N. Y.] Board of Estimate and Apportionment, 1904," Vol. I: 1089, 1094, etc.

their deft work. "Taxpayers' organizations" were formed to support or oppose one side or the other, and the Aldermen were bombarded with a series of approving or denunciatory resolutions.[15]

A significant episode now turned up, revealing that legislative bodies were merely registering committees for the great capitalists.

The Board of Aldermen had withheld granting both the Westchester franchise and the franchise for the Pennsylvania Railroad to enter New York City *via* the Hudson River tunnel. Somehow and from somewhere the announcement now came that unless the Board of Aldermen acted, a law would be passed by the Legislature stripping it of all power of granting franchises. The threat was soon carried into execution. The Legislature passed an act vesting franchise-granting power in the Board of Estimate and Apportionment. This body was favorably inclined.

Board of Estimate Gives Long-Sought Franchise.

The first point that this Board decided to pass upon was the question whether or not the New York, Westchester and Boston Railroad Company was or was not a defunct corporation.

On March 30, 1904, Corporation Counsel Delaney (elected by Tammany Hall) reported to the Board of Estimate and Apportionment that the Board had no jurisdiction to examine the legal capacity or incapacity of the company.

In the minutes of the Board of Estimate and Apportionment Charles E. Hughes was described as the attorney of the projected railroad. These minutes give a long letter written and signed by Hughes from the office of Carter, Hughes, Rounds and Schurman, 96 Broadway and 6 Wall Street, to Corporation Counsel Delaney, proposing certain changes in the wording of

[15] These were duly published in the "Minutes of the Board of Estimate and Apportionment, 1904": 471, etc.

the franchise contract.[16]   Delaney wrote in part this reply to
the Board regarding Hughes' proposals: "Some of these I
will not here discuss because I do not deem it expedient for the
City's interests that they should be adopted, but there are several which should receive consideration." [17]

The New York, Westchester and Boston Railway Company
finally received its long-sought franchise on June 24, 1904.   Although represented by Hughes as an absolutely independent
company, which it may have been in name, it really was nothing
more or less than an adjunct of the New York, New Haven
and Hartford Railroad Company.   Its franchise allowed it to
operate more than sixteen miles of four-track line within New
York City's limits, the main line crossing one hundred and
twenty streets; and its branch line seventy-four streets.   It secured practically all the available routes for entrance and exit
to and from New York City by way of the Bronx.   It is the
only purely privately-owned rapid transit line in New York
City.   Its terminal, it is true, is on the north side of the Harlem River, but it will probably be able to convey its passengers
downtown by a new subway.   Moreover, by means of the
Pennsylvania Railroad Company's New York Connecting Railroad, which will traverse Randall's and Ward's Island to and
from Long Island, its trains will be able to run into the Pennsylvania Railroad's station on Seventh Avenue and thence under the Hudson River south and west, and the Pennsylvania
Railroad can run its trains over the New York, New Haven and
Hartford Railroad's tracks into New England.

The immense value of the franchise can, therefore, be seen
at a glance.   Its present value both as a railroad entrance and
outlet and as a rapid-transit line is recognized as great enough,
and its potential value — considering growth of population —
is unquestionably even greater.

[16] "Minutes of the [N. Y.] Board of Estimate and Apportionment,
1904," Vol. I: 1089.
[17] Ibid., 1094.

J. P. Morgan and Associates in Control.

That the New York, Westchester and Boston Railroad and the New York and Port Chester Railroad were both owned by Morgan's New York, New Haven and Hartford Railroad was shown by the formal incorporation of the Millbrook Company on November 5, 1906. The Millbrook Company was a holding company for the New York, New Haven and Hartford Railroad. It held the entire stock of the Port Chester Railroad, which in turn held the stock of the New York, Westchester and Boston Railroad.

The final proceedings occurred when Hughes was Governor. An act was passed by the New York Legislature and signed by Governor Hughes on May 29, 1909, [18] authorizing the New York, Westchester and Boston Railroad and the New York and Port Chester Railroad to consolidate. The consolidation agreement provided for $45,000,000 capital in all, with possibilities of increase. There were $5,000,000 of stock, and $40,000,000 of mortgages, on which $15,100,000 of bonds had been issued by December 23, 1909. The remainder of the bonds to be issued under the mortgages were subject to the consent of the Public Service Commission, Second District. But this capitalization gives no adequate idea of the intrinsic value of the franchises, the value of which is estimated at much more than a hundred million dollars.

The consolidation agreement also showed that the directors of the new company were J. Pierpont Morgan, Lewis Cass Ledyard, William Rockefeller, Robert W. Taft, Charles S. Mellen (president of the New York, New Haven and Hartford Railroad) and other capitalists. Further, the agreement stated that the New York, New Haven and Hartford Railroad Company owned 91,581 of the total issue of 91,590 shares of the New York and Port Chester Railroad,[19] and 105,384 shares of the

[18] Chap. 579, Laws of 1909.
[19] " Consolidation Agreement," p. 15.

entire issue of 105,397 shares of the New York, Westchester and Boston Railroad.[20]

Hughes Becomes Prominent.

Up to this time Hughes was comparatively unknown to the general public. He first attained popular notice in his capacity as counsel for the (Stevens) Legislative Committee of New York which was appointed to investigate the price of gas. The result of this committee's findings was the passage of a law providing that the charge for gas in New York City should be not more than eighty cents per thousand cubic feet. How this law was long contested, and how the Supreme Court of the United States, while upholding its constitutionality, adroitly used the case to intrench property interests to a remarkable degree — these facts have been related in clear detail in a previous chapter.

When, in 1905, a contest between competitive magnates in the Equitable Life Assurance Society led to the disclosure of a great scandal, a legislative committee was appointed to investigate the methods of the large life insurance companies. Hughes was chosen as the committee's counsel. There was a belief that this investigation was inspired or instigated by certain powerful magnates or groups of magnates with the ulterior purpose of ousting certain other magnates from control of the vast assets of the insurance companies. If this were true — and indications strongly pointed that way — there is no evidence for the suspicion that Hughes was in any way a conscious party to the proceeding, even though newspapers opposed to him politically later pointed out insinuatingly that at one stage of the contest for the control of the Equitable Life Assurance Society he had been counsel to James W. Alexander, president of that corporation, and that he had been counsel for the Mercantile Trust Company — allied with the Equitable Life As-

[20] " Consolidation Agreement," p. 9.

surance Society — in part of the litigation involved by the Shipbuilding Trust scandal.

He Exposes Insurance Iniquities.

As counsel to the committee, Hughes displayed uncommon skill and perseverance in unearthing certain parts of the vast system of insurance corruption through which the directors, brokers, promoters, syndicates of magnates and retainers, members of Legislatures, lobbyists and politicians enriched themselves at the expense of the policy holders. Point by point he patiently brought out the involved and concealed circumstances of the long-continued enormities of loot and corruption. Reputations, long acclaimed for their respectability, were blasted, others ruined, by these revelations. Of the great array of facts presented in the committee's report, we have already described some in a previous chapter.

Hughes' work called forth a newspaper demand that he be nominated for Governor of New York by the Republican party that he might be able to put into law the insurance reforms that he had advocated. Meanwhile an event took place which the sophisticated might well have expected but which surprised the innocent.

The Odd, Yet Inevitable, Result.

It was soon observed that the only real result of the great investigation was to enable some magnates to oust others, and to concentrate the power of the dominating financial groups. Morgan tightened his hold on the New York Life Insurance Company. The Harriman-Standard Oil Company interests obtained a completer control of the Mutual Life Insurance Company, and Hyde, Harriman's puppet in the Equitable Life Assurance Society, was put out, and none other than Thomas F. Ryan stepped into full control of the $470,000,000 assets of that company and retained it until December, 1909, when he sold his controlling stock to J. Pierpont Morgan.

It was currently reported that Cravath persuaded Ryan that Hughes would be a " safe man " as Governor, but whether this report was true or not we cannot say.   One fact much commented upon was that in its investigation the legislative committee avoided any genuine inquisition into the methods of industrial insurance companies.   These companies fattened on the poorest and most industrious part of the population, extracting hundreds of millions of dollars in profits from the working class.   However, Hughes' record as exposer of insurance corruption was widely praised; he was acclaimed as a typical example of the " good man in politics."

Evidently the big financial magnates and capitalists had a deep appreciation of Hughes' devout qualities, for they came forward in large numbers to contribute to the campaign fund of the Republican gubernatorial campaign, when he was a candidate for Governor, in 1906.   J. P. Morgan and Company and Levi P. Morton each contributed $20,000.   Andrew Carnegie, John D. Rockefeller, Jr., H. B. Hollins and E. M. Wells each contributed $5,000.   Harvey Fisk and Son, Chauncey M. Depew, John W. Gates, J. and W. Seligman and Company, Kuhn, Loeb and Company, and sundry others each gave contributions of $2,500.   Charles M. Schwab, Edwin Gould, Jacob Schiff, William H. Moore, Adolph Lewisohn and many other millionaires or multimillionaires each contributed $1,000 or $2,000.   The total sum contributed was $313,923.   Inasmuch as all of the aforesaid contributors were reputed to be extremely sagacious, practical men, it is quite clear that they were under no illusions as to the measure of Mr. Hughes.

Hughes Elected Governor.

After Hughes' election as Governor of New York in 1906, certain pretentious laws of a " reform " nature were passed.

Some were good in their way, but it was a negligible good. Laws were enacted to prevent the corrupt use of insurance funds, yet of what real avail are such laws as these in a fabric erected on corruption and sustained by it? The statute books were already encumbered by laws prohibiting corruption. They were always evaded and never enforced. Moreover, even if corruption by the insurance companies were stopped, the saving of the millions formerly spent in corruption all the more enriched the magnates in control and gave them larger funds to manipulate. The policy holders were no better situated; their premiums were as high as ever, and the conditions more or less as hard as before, although some slight relief was given in the abolition of the " deferred dividend " plan.

In fact, the great magnates continued to use the insurance money in their fraudulent trust and railroad operations. Harriman, by the end of 1907, had obtained from the Mutual Life Insurance Company not less than $10,000,000 loans on stocks largely watered, and the same company had invested $46,223,-500 in securities of corporations controlled by Harriman. The surplus of the Equitable Life Assurance Society was put at Ryan's disposal, in violation of one of the very laws Hughes had advocated and caused to be enacted. By the close of the year 1907 fully $27,048,517 of bonds and stocks of corporations controlled by Ryan had been sold to the Equitable. As for the New York Life Insurance Company it held, by the close of 1907, the enormous sum of $112,391,000 in securities issued by corporations controlled by Morgan. Inasmuch as it was contrary to the new insurance law for insurance companies to invest in stocks, the insurance companies explained that these enormous holdings of stocks were " left overs " of a time before the passage of the law. So far as the industrial insurance companies were concerned, Governor Hughes did not make a single move to remedy the evils bearing so heavily upon the working class.

Although the insurance investigation had disclosed that a

large number of officials or capitalists controlling the companies had been guilty of perjury, fraud, mismanagement, corruption and theft, it was a subject of general comment that District Attorney Jerome, of New York City, who had been so signally active in sending petty offenders to prison, failed to bring about conviction and imprisonment of any high insurance official. Another scandal, too, was the immunity from serious prosecution of Ryan and his associates of the Metropolitan Street Railway Company who were specifically charged with having looted that company of at least $90,000,000 by duplication of construction charges, manipulation of accounts, and other involved series of thefts and frauds. This was the estimate made by Col. Amory in his " Truth About Metropolitan," published in 1906.

When a candidate for District Attorney, in 1901, Jerome had publicly and repeatedly announced that he would " follow the trail of corruption to the end, even if it lead to the offices of the Metropolitan Street Railway Company." But after his election and reëlection no results came.

Charges Against District Attorney Jerome.

On September 8, 1907, a voluminous petition was sent by New York business men and others to Governor Hughes making a scathing criticism of District Attorney Jerome for having failed to prosecute the traction looters, and demanding that the Attorney-General of New York State be directed to prosecute. This petition recited in detail the enormous frauds and thefts committed.

Evidence was submitted, on December 11, 1907, to the Grand Jury in General Sessions showing that Ryan and associates had bought in 1902 from Anthony N. Brady for $250,000 the franchise of a company called the Wall and Cortland Street Ferries Railroad Company, a corporation having a dormant franchise for a road never built. Then they had sold this franchise to a dummy corporation, called the Metropolitan Securities Company, for $965,607.19. Part of this went to the syndicate's brokers; the exact amount of loot divided among Ryan, Widener, Dolan and the estates of William C. Whitney and William L. Elkins was $692,292.82.[21] The surviving members of this syndicate practically confessed their guilt by making restitution of this sum after the facts had been made public and after charges had been made against Jerome. On the very day that Ryan and associates had bought the non-existent Wall and Cortland Street Ferries Railroad they had also bought, for $1,600,000, the People's Traction Company and the New York, Westchester and Connecticut Traction Company, the franchises of both of which had lapsed. In this transaction there was, it was charged, another grand division of loot.

Assortment of Thefts and Corruptions.

These transactions, however, were insignificant compared to the theft of $16,000,000 from the treasury of the Third Avenue Railway,[22] and vaster plunderings in other directions, totaling, as we have said, approximately $90,000,000.

The fact was brought out in the investigation by the Public Service Commission that all the books of the Metropolitan Street Railway Company in which its transactions from 1891 to 1902 were recorded were sold to a purchaser who promised to destroy them. Street car lines bought for a few hundred thousand dollars were fraudulently capitalized at ten or twenty times that sum, and then vast amounts were fraudulently charged in duplication of construction accounts.

Lemuel Ely Quigg (who had been for six years a member of

[21] These facts were testified by Brady, on October 8, 1907, in an inquiry conducted by Chairman Wilcox of the Public Service Commission.
[22] So Receiver Whitridge of that company stated. And see Col. Amory's remarks, June 29, 1910, "Third Avenue Company — Plan of Reorganization," Public Service Commission, Stenographic Minutes, p. 2417.

Congress) admitted that in the four years preceding 1907 he had received $217,000 from the company. This was charged to a construction fund, part of which was another sum of $798,000 corruptly paid to persons whose names were concealed. Also by means of hired agents Quigg caused the organization of numerous citizens' associations whose influence was used at Albany for or against pending measures in which his employers were interested.

Previous to the merger of the Ryan and Belmont interests, which merger was accompanied by an addition of $108,000,000 of watered stock, Quigg created "citizens' associations" to oppose Belmont's designs; subsequently he served the combination. His expenses, he said, ranged from $50,000 for manufacturing a great petition from the tenement-house district to $500 paid to individuals for "agitation." Among those whom he employed directly or indirectly to make arguments at Albany were two men who had recently become Justices of the Supreme Court of New York State. Quigg also admitted that he employed detectives to watch Col. W. N. Amory, who was persistently exposing and denouncing the traction looters and corruptionists and demanding that they be prosecuted criminally. As a matter of fact Amory was not only watched but hounded and persecuted.[23]

The investigation by the Legislative "Graft" Committee, in 1910, supplied certain missing links, and disclosed who had received part of the corruption funds. The books of a Wall Street brokerage house, used as an intermediary, showed that State Senator Goodsell, Assemblyman Louis Bedell and other active members of the New York Legislature had received large sums, during the sessions of 1900–1904, from officers of the Metropolitan Street Railway Company.

But no criminal proceedings were brought against Ryan. In a statement published on May 26, 1909, Col. Amory charged

[23] "Investigation of Interborough-Metropolitan Company," Etc., Public Service Commission, 1907, pp. 1395–1559.

that when a Grand Jury was called in 1907 to investigate the criminal practices of Ryan and associates of the Metropolitan Street Railway Company, the foreman of the Grand Jury was a director in Ryan's Equitable Life Assurance Society.

Col. Amory also charged that in April, 1903, Daniel Mason, Jerome's former law partner, and William H. Page, Jr., another of the Metropolitan's lawyers, had attempted to bribe him (Amory) while a State's witness, with $200,000, to withdraw the charges that Amory had filed with Jerome against the Metropolitan Street Railway Company.

The particular Grand Jury investigating the matter of the $692,292.82 paid for the paper franchise of the Cortland and Wall Street Ferries Railroad Company, stated in its presentment:

" That one of the questions that the Grand Jury was investigating was whether the said Thomas F. Ryan and others in connection with the sale of the said railway company had stolen the sum of $111,652.78." Of the particular item of $692,-292.82 looted, the amount mentioned — $111,652.78 — was supposed to be Ryan's share.

Paul D. Cravath, Governor Hughes' former law partner, was in court zealously looking out for Ryan's interests. Cravath had refused to answer certain vital interrogations, and the question came up whether he should be punished for contempt of court. He was not. During this time District Attorney Jerome, as he admitted at a hearing on May 7, 1908, on the charges against him, " dined with Allan Ryan [one of Thomas F. Ryan's sons] and his wife at Sherry's and Martin's." Jerome said he was not a friend of the Ryan family, " but I think young Ryan is a fine chap, but can't claim anything more than a pleasant acquaintance."

On January 27, 1908, Judge Rosalsky, in the Court of General Sessions, New York City, severely arraigned District Attorney Jerome, declaring that Jerome had so conducted the examination of Thomas F. Ryan before the Grand Jury as

probably to invalidate any indictments which that body might
have found against Ryan.

Governor Hughes appointed a commissioner to hear the evidence upon which the charges against Jerome were made.
Jerome admitted that when Ryan, Brady and Vreeland were
before the Grand Jury he had asked leading questions of them.
He further testified that he had not asked the Grand Jury
to indict Ryan in the matter of the Wall Street and Cortland
Street Ferries Railway transaction. " No," he said, " I will
never advise that an indictment be found in that case." But
an inspection of the minutes of the Grand Jury of November,
1907, disclosed that Jerome had told Brady that he (Brady)
" and Ryan and Whitney and this outfit were in cahoots and
in some way got $700,000 of the Metropolitan Securities'
money. You are, practically every one of you, under suspicion and accused of being thieves. . . ." At the hearing Jerome was asked as to a certain contribution made to his
political campaign by Samuel Untermeyer, counsel for Hyde
of the Equitable Life Assurance Society, but he denied that any
ulterior purposes were behind it. Ryan had admitted on the
witness stand that he (Ryan) had contributed $500,000 to the
national Democratic Party in 1900.

Hughes Exonerates Jerome.

The Commissioner's report " whitewashed " Jerome, and
Governor Hughes dismissed the charges, saying: " Nothing
has been presented which furnishes any just ground for im-
peaching the good faith of the District Attorney in connection
with any of the transactions set forth nor has anything been
shown which would justify his removal from office." [24]

[24] Col. Amory did not think that Jerome had been corrupted by means
of money. " When the day of retribution comes . . ." wrote Col.
Amory, on March 18, 1906, ". . . It will then be disclosed that there
are other than money bribes. I believe Mr. Jerome incapable of doing
a corrupt act for money."—" Truth About Metropolitan," p. 2. In the

In 1910 came the disclosures before a legislative committee revealing the consecutive briberies and corruptions carried on in the New York Legislature by the Metropolitan Street Railway's officials, by fire insurance companies and by other corporations. Ten of the principal legislators implicated were the very same who for years had ruled Senate and Assembly committees.

The Obliging Judge Lacombe.

In the meantime, learning that Attorney-General Jackson of New York State contemplated throwing the looted railway system into the hands of receivers, Ryan and associates hurried to apply for the appointment of Adrian Joline and Douglas Robinson as receivers. Joline was an old attorney of the Metropolitan Street Railway Company, and Robinson was President Roosevelt's brother-in-law. Lacombe granted the application, thus forestalling the attempt of Attorney-General Jackson to put in receivers hostile to Ryan and associates. Judge Lacombe was a protégé of William C. Whitney, and had been placed on the Circuit Court by Whitney's efforts.

In the course of his remarks before the Public Service Commission, in November, 1910, Col. Amory unsparingly denounced Judge Lacombe. " There is a Judge on the bench," he said, " who has protected these criminals. He is the creature of William C. Whitney and the tool of Thomas F. Ryan.

. . .

" There has been a plan successfully put on foot to keep the traction thieves from prison and from disgorging the millions they have made away with.

" Ryan still controls the street railways of this city. Back of these receivers who defy the Public Service Commission, and treat it with contempt and ignore the laws of the State is

same pamphlet Col. Amory stated that Jerome knew specifically of the vast plunderings as early as 1903 and, that he had then encouraged Amory to believe that the looters would be prosecuted.

Judge Lacombe . . . and back of Lacombe stands Ryan." [25] When Judge Lacombe was challenged to make a categorical reply he refused.

Some time ago the statute of limitations intervened to prevent any possible prosecution of the traction looters, which was precisely the point that they were fighting for so desperately. They are now immune. Ryan's fortune is estimated to be more than $225,000,000. His great African concessions of domain, with incalculably rich resources, which he secured in association with the late King Leopold of Belgium and others, may signify that his private fortune is perhaps double that sum.

"Rule of Reason" Speech.

When occupying the office of Governor of New York State (in which he served two terms, having been reëlected in 1908), Hughes did nothing at basis to antagonize, and much to win the favor, of great corporate interests. Quite true, his church-bred opposition to vulgar gambling asserted itself in his causing to be enacted a statute forbidding the operation of race-track gambling, for which deed he was much praised by pious people. These good folk, however, were not at all concerned about stock-market gambling, and neither was Governor Hughes. "Reforms" of the race-track sort did not touch the fundamentals of society, and were, therefore, "safe and sane." At the same time Governor Hughes opposed or vetoed certain measures affecting large corporate interests. He found objections to the constitutional amendment providing for an income tax. He vetoed the two-cent railroad fare bill, the five-cent Coney Island fare bill and other measures. And when President Taft appointed him to the Supreme Court of the United States, no opposition was manifested by any prominent capitalist interest. Indeed, William J. Bryan, three times

[25] "Reorganization Plan," Public Service Commission Hearing, Stenographic Minutes, pp. 2407-2409.

Democratic candidate for President of the United States, openly charged Taft with packing the Supreme Court with pro-trust men. In a statement published on October 12, 1911,[26] Bryan asserted:

"In its 1908 platform the Republican party promised to amend the Sherman Anti-Trust Law. During the campaign of 1908 Governor Hughes, of New York, interpreted that promise to mean that 'the Rule of Human Reason' must be accepted.

"Later Taft appointed Governor Hughes, as well as other men of his mold of thought, to the United States Supreme Court.

"George W. Perkins, associated with J. P. Morgan in trust control, delivered a speech recently in which he complained that Republican Congressmen had not tried to redeem their platform promise, but that it had been redeemed by the Supreme Court in the recent trust decision wherein Governor Hughes' 'Rule of Reason' was applied.

"Here we have it. Governor Hughes was put forward to represent the Republican Party; he assured the trusts that 'the Rule of Reason' for which they had been waiting for more than ten years would be adopted. Congress refused to keep the promise, so Governor Hughes was put on the Supreme Bench and helped to amend the law in accordance with the Republican promise, and now President Taft, in whose interest the promise was made and who appointed Governor Hughes, says that the Anti-Trust law as amended by the court must not be disturbed.

"Here is a chain of circumstantial evidence sufficient to convict in a criminal court."

In another statement, published on October 20, 1911, in the form of an open letter to President Taft, Bryan accused Taft of having appointed pro-trust men to the Supreme Court.

[26] Published originally in Bryan's periodical "The Commoner," and republished in the newspapers.

"You appointed to the Chief-Justiceship of the Supreme
Court Justice White who thirteen years ago took the trusts'
side of the trust question. You appointed him over the head
of Justice Harlan who had served longer and with more distinction and who had taken the people's side on trust questions.
. . . You appointed Governor Hughes to the Supreme
Court Bench after he had interpreted your platform to suit
the trusts and proceeded to join Chief Justice White and carry
out your platform promise to amend the Anti-Trust law by
weakening it. . . ." Bryan asked Taft to make public the
recommendations, written and verbal, upon which he had made
these and other appointments "and let the people know the
influences that dictate your appointments."

President Taft replied weakly and evasively, saying that he
considered the questions "an insult" to the Supreme Court
of the United States.

Had President Taft been bold enough to have expressed
the facts as clearly as he knew and adapted them, he would
have said that Bryan's charge was a compliment, not an insult.
The trusts were the dominant economic factor of the day;
being so, why should they not have their representatives on
the Supreme Court Bench as well as in other departments of
Government? The processes of the capitalist system, for
which Government is merely a registering machine, made this
inevitable. Moreover, as we have previously pointed out, the
trusts were a necessary outcome of the capitalist struggle, and
represented a higher form of industrial organization than the
abandoned competitive stage, which Bryan, the mouthpiece of
his fading class, has the blindness and folly to wish to see
restored. For the ends of progress it was, indeed, salutary
that Taft should have appointed pro-trust judges. Finally, it
was not Taft that essentially decided affairs, but the great
force of magnates owning the resources and industries not
only of the United States but of other parts of the world.

Justice Van Devanter.

Associate Justice Moody resigning,[27] President Taft's next appointment to the Supreme Court of the United States was Willis Van Devanter. He was born in 1859; his father was a lawyer of means at Marion, Indiana. Quitting that town, in 1884, Willis Van Devanter settled at Cheyenne, Wyoming. A Territory at that time, Wyoming was sparsely settled, and its politics were controlled by the Union Pacific Railway Company and by sheep and cattle ranchers, both of which interests were seizing natural resources on every hand. Among the men conspicuous in Wyoming politics was Francis E. Warren, a former stock raiser in Massachusetts, and Clarence D. Clark. Warren was Territorial Governor, and he became the owner of extensive ranches, often by methods a description of which would form too intricate a digression here; lands that had been public property were converted into Warren's private estate. To Warren and Clark the youthful Van Devanter closely adhered.

Van Devanter became the City Attorney of Cheyenne; he was then elected to the Legislature; and when Wyoming was admitted as a State, he was elected Chief Justice of the Wyoming Supreme Court, for four years. But he resigned in the year 1890, and became a member of the law firm of Lacey and Van Devanter. This firm had previously been that of Corlett, Lacey and Riner. W. W. Corlett had been for more than twenty years an attorney for the Union Pacific Railroad, and had represented that railroad in a large number of cases. Likewise had the firm of Corlett, Lacey and Riner. Corlett had also been the attorney for large irrigation and lumber companies such as the Hilliard Flume and Lumber Company.

---

[27] We have previously related how when Justice Moody resigned, Senator Lodge succeeded in having a bill passed by Congress granting him a pension of $12,500 a year.

Conditions in Wyoming.

The fraudulent acquisition of land in Wyoming was great and incessant. In his exhaustive report for 1885, Commissioner Sparks of the United States General Land Office related how nearly the whole of Wyoming and a large portion of Montana had been fraudulently surveyed, and the lands on the streams fraudulently possessed under the desert land act, to the exclusion of actual settlers. Extensive coal deposits had been, or were being, fraudulently acquired in mass "through expedited surveys, followed by fraudulent pre-emption and commuted homestead entries." [28]   Much, if not all of these available coal deposits had been seized under color of law by men acting for Jay Gould, controlling the Union Pacific Railroad.[29]   The Pacific Railway Commission reported, in 1887, that the Union Pacific Railway Company had fraudulently appropriated coal lands of inestimable value, and that of the vast area of lands which it had grabbed it had sold not less than 7,000,000 acres without any patent from the Government.[30]   The fraudulent processes of acquiring Wyoming coal lands are detailed at great length in other official reports.[31]

As for the fraudulent seizures by cattle companies in Wyoming as well as elsewhere in the West, only a few suggestive details of a mass can be given here. " In Wyoming," reported Acting Commissioner Harrison of the General Land Office to Secretary of the Interior Teller, on March 14, 1884,

[28] House Executive Documents, First Session, Forty-Ninth Congress, 1885–1886, Vol. II : 167.
[29] The Interstate Commerce Commission reported to the United States Senate in 1908 that the acquisition of these coal lands had " been attended with fraud, perjury, violence and disregard of the rights of individuals." The report stated the specific methods used.
[30] Report of Pacific Railway Commission, Vol. I : 192.
[31] See, for example, Annual Report for 1889 of Acting Commissioner W. M. Stone of the U. S. General Land Office, pp. 55, 56, etc.

"one hundred and twenty-five cattle companies are reported as having fencing on the public lands;" the Wyoming Cattle Company, composed of Scotch capitalists, was one of these companies.[32]

These operations went on without cessation. "Seventy-eight desert land entries," reported S. M. Stockslager, Commissioner of the General Land Office, in 1888, "embracing 48,000 acres, were entered in the Cheyenne District, Wyoming, and transferred immediately after proof to a land and ditch company, which had been previously organized for the purpose of acquiring title to said lands. Most of the entry men lived in the Eastern States and had never seen the land, nor did they make any expenditure thereon. The purchase money and all other expenses were paid by the company who evidently used the names of the entrymen in making the entries." [33]

These details selected from a great number, give some slight picture of conditions in Wyoming during the years when Van Devanter was an attorney and judge. From 1891 to 1895 the firm of Lacey and Van Devanter consecutively represented the law interests of the Union Pacific Railway.[34] They also were attorneys for the Powder River Cattle Company, the Searight Cattle Company, the Frontier Land and Cattle Company, the Springvale Ditch (Irrigation) Company, the Moorcraft Ranch Company and other companies.[35]

[32] "Unauthorized Fencing of Public Lands," U. S. Senate Documents, First Session, Forty-eighth Congress, 1883–1884, Doc. No. 127: 2.
[33] Annual Land Office Report, 1888, p. 49.
[34] See, Union Pacific vs. Redman, III Wyoming Reports: 679; the same vs. Link, *Ibid.*, 680; the same vs. Gilland, IV *Ibid.*, 396; the same vs. Schenk, V *Ibid.*, 431; the same vs. Gilland, VI *Ibid.*, 187, etc.
[35] See, Powder River Cattle Company vs. Board of County Commissioners, III Wyoming Reports, 597; Searight Cattle Company vs. same, *Ibid.*, 778; Frontier Land and Cattle Company vs. Baldwin, *Ibid.*, 765. These were cases in which taxes were contested. For other cases enumerated see IV *Ibid.*, 168 and V *Ibid.*, 52. Lacey and Van Devanter also represented the Union Mercantile Company (III *Ibid.*, 418) and the Traders' Insurance Company (IV *Ibid.*, 423).

The Artist Case.

Van Devanter, it seems, was also associated with John M. Thurston, a Nebraska politician and a United States Senator from that State. The proceedings in the case of Union Pacific Railway Company vs. Artist give the names of Willis Van Devanter and Thurston on the brief submitted for the railroad.[36]

This case and its disposition deserve narration. On October 4, 1889, Andrew S. Artist, a Union Pacific Railway worker, was injured while at work; his foot and leg were badly hurt. He was taken to a hospital maintained at Denver by the company for its employés. To support this hospital the Union Pacific forced each one of its employés to contribute twenty-five cents a month; if any additional amount was needed, the company contributed it.

In the course of the treatment of Artist at the hospital the physicians inserted a rubber drainage tube in his leg. It was admitted that because of the carelessness of physicians or attendants a portion of the tube was left in the leg as the wound healed and it remained there when he was discharged as cured, on January 7, 1890. The result of this malpractice caused Artist great suffering and partial disability until the remnant of the tube was removed by a surgical operation in April, 1892.

Now on January 13, 1890, six days after his discharge, at a time when both parties were ignorant of the fact that a piece of tube remained in the leg, Artist, in consideration of receiving $150, had been induced to sign a release from damages.

But after suffering for more than two years and being reduced to partial disability because of the blunder at the hospital, Artist brought suit for damages and obtained a judgment in the lower court.

---

[36] Thurston with John F. Dillon regularly appeared for the Union Pacific Railroad. See 161 United States Reports, 456; *Ibid.*, 95; 163 *Ibid.*, 487; *Ibid.*, 611; *Ibid.*, 692; *Ibid.*, 709, etc.

Thurston and Van Devanter appealed the case for the Union Pacific Railway to the United States Circuit Court of Appeals, District of Wyoming. On February 12, 1894, Judge Sanborn reversed the judgment given in the lower court. Notwithstanding the uncontested fact that the railroad's employes were compelled to contribute twenty-five cents a month to the hospital's maintenance, Judge Sanborn decided in favor of the Union Pacific Railway Company on these remarkable grounds:

That a *master* who sent his *servant* for treatment to a hospital *maintained* by the *master* for *charitable purposes* (!!) was not responsible for injuries caused to the servant by the negligence of hospital attendants, " where the master has exercised ordinary care in selecting such attendants." Further, that a hospital maintained by the railroad company for the *free* treatment of its employés, and " supported partly by monthly contributions of employes and partly by the company, and maintained for *profit*, is a charitable institution." [37]

Thus, although the compulsory contributions of the railroad's workers supported the hospital, they had no voice in the managing of it, and were virtually adjudged paupers debarred from getting damages for the malpractice of physicians. We have given this case and extraordinary decision exactly as the facts are stated in the court records.

Van Devanter's patrons and pushers, Warren and Clark, became United States Senators. Van Devanter had been of great assistance to them; he had been chairman of the Wyoming Republican State Committee in 1892, a delegate to the Republican National Convention and a member for the Wyoming Republicans on the Republican National Committee in 1896.

Through the influence of Senators Warren [38] and Clarke,

[37] Union Pacific R'way Co. vs. Artist, 60 Federal Reports, 365–370. The italics are mine.— G. M.
[38] Warren was the head of the Warren Land and Live Stock Company of Wyoming. He became the chairman of the Senate Military Affairs Committee. There was a small public forest reserve called

Van Devanter, in 1897, was appointed by President McKinley an assistant United States Attorney-General, and was assigned to the Interior Department which, it is needless to say, had jurisdiction over the public lands.

In 1903 a vacancy occurred on the bench of the Eighth Judicial Circuit. Warren and Clarke were now high personages in the Senate and of great influence at the White House; Warren headed the Senate Committee on Military Affairs, and Clark was chairman of the Senate Committee on Judiciary. Responsive to their suggestions, President Roosevelt appointed Van Devanter to the Circuit Court [39] where he sat with Judge Sanborn, the identical judge who had decided the Artist case nine years previously when Van Devanter and Senator Thurston represented the Union Pacific Railway.

Bryan's Comments.

Judge Van Devanter's appointment to the Supreme Court of the United States was severely and pointedly criticized by W. J. Bryan, in one of the series of statements and speeches recently issued by him. In a speech at Lincoln, Nebraska, on November 5, 1911, Bryan asserted that Van Devanter was appointed by President Taft because of his known bias in favor of the dominant corporate interests. "Judge Van De-

---

"Crow Creek" in Wyoming which was a military forest reserve and which the War Department wanted for military maneuvers. This reservation, however, had been leased to various small sheep raisers with the privilege of grazing. The reservation was leased to Warren's company, and in 1910 the small cattle men were ejected.

[39] Statement in a laudatory biography of Van Devanter, the *Saturday Evening Post,"* issue of March 18, 1911. "Mr. Van Devanter," said this account, "looks like a Western man and acts like one. He is active, virile, alert — although not quick of speech. He is good looking, good-humored and most companionable. He is an earnest student and a prodigious worker. Although he is essentially a jurist, he keeps closely in touch with every phase of life and is much more human than the usual lawyer in whom the judicial temperament predominates. He is an outdoor man, who fishes, hunts, rides, plays golf and has fun."

vanter," Bryan asserted, " is the man who gave a decision giving to the Union Pacific Railroad land along the right of way amounting in value to millions of dollars; he is the judge who held that two railroads running parallel to each other for two thousand miles were not competing lines, one of the roads being the Union Pacific Railroad." Bryan continued:

" President Taft knew of these decisions, for he was notified by letter before he made the appointment, and the man who wrote received a letter from the President's secretary saying the information would receive consideration.

" And in spite of the fact that the President knew that Van Devanter was biased in favor of the great interests, he appointed him to the Supreme Bench. Upon whose recommendation was the appointment made? Will President Taft make this information public?

" I have read the President does not like being questioned by me concerning the Supreme Court appointments, and that he has said the questions are an insult to him and to the judge as well. I have to say that if President Taft is that thin-skinned he will have to get used to it, for I will have considerably more to say before I am through with the subject."

Reporting Taft's appointment of Van Devanter, a Washington dispatch published in a friendly partisan newspaper, the New York *Press,* issue of December 12, 1910, stated, " It was said to have been Mr. Knox's influence which finally turned the tide in favor of Judge Van Devanter as against Judge William C. Hook, also of the Eighth Circuit." The Knox referred to was Philander C. Knox, former attorney for the Carnegie Steel Company, whose appointment as Attorney-General of the United States, Andrew Carnegie, the powerful multi-millionaire magnate, had recommended to President McKinley, and whose former law partner, Judge Reed, has been so large a factor in the Directorate of the mighty Steel Trust.

Knox has been a sort of premier under the three administrations of McKinley, Roosevelt and Taft; and in view of the

Supreme Court's " Rule of Reason " decision (described later in this chapter) it is significant that Knox, in a speech delivered before the Pittsburg Chamber of Commerce, on October 14, 1902, outlined virtually the very doctrines that the Supreme Court of the United States adopted, nearly nine years later, in its " Rule of Reason " decision applying to the trusts. Thus can glimpses be obtained of the powerful capitalists, or their spokesmen, asserting the construction of laws that they wanted and needed, and thus also can be seen how decisions have precisely followed these requirements.

Of all of the appointments to the Supreme Court of the United States by President Taft that of Joseph R. Lamar, of Georgia, provoked least criticism, because so little was known of his career.

Justice Lamar as Railroad Attorney.

Judge Lamar was born in 1857; his father was a Campbellite preacher at Augusta; his maternal grandfather was Joseph Rucker, owner of eleven hundred slaves. The Judge was a second cousin of L. Q. C. Lamar, of Mississippi, whose career both before and after his appointment as an Associate Justice of the Supreme Court of the United States has been depicted in a previous chapter. In his practice of law at Augusta, Joseph R. Lamar's clientèle seem to have been largely corporate interests.

One of the most conspicuous of his cases was that of the Central Trust Company of New York vs. the Marietta and North Georgia Railroad Company. Lamar represented the Central Trust Company, one of the most powerful of such companies in the United States. The action was brought by the Central Trust Company to foreclose on an extensive mortgage it held to cover an issue of bonds of the Marietta and Georgia Railroad Company.[40]

[40] See, 75 Federal Reporter: 200. (May 12, 1896.) The Central Trust Company also had extensive holdings in other railroads. Ac-

In 1903 Lamar was appointed to the State Supreme Court of Georgia. After his resignation from that court he reëntered law practice at Augusta, forming a partnership with Judge E. H. Callaway under the firm name of Lamar and Callaway. Not long before his appointment to the Supreme Court of the United States he was one of counsel for the Central of Georgia Railway Company in a case the decision in which by the Supreme Court of Georgia was regarded in financial-railway quarters as " epoch-making." [41]

Previously it had been generally ruled by the courts, especially in New York, that an income bond practically gave the holder no greater rights to interest than the stockholders to dividends. The courts, these rulings had further held, could not, save in exceptionally scandalous cases, interfere with the decision of railroad directors not to pay dividends. The Georgia Supreme Court, however, held that the courts would determine for themselves whether the income was really " earned " regardless of what action the directors took. Wollman's account of this case proceeds:

" In the Georgia case there were many discussions as to what was income. I will refer only to two. The railway company owned all the stock of a money-earning steamship company. The steamship company paid the railroad company, its sole stockholder, a large sum of money, but did not say that it paid it as dividends; in fact the steamship company's directors did not declare any dividends. The money was un-

cording to a list of principal railroad stockholders made public by the Interstate Commerce Commission, in December, 1909, the Central Trust Company of New York was trustee for the Louisville and Nashville Railway Company of $5,501,000 of common stock of the Nashville, Chattanooga and St. Louis Railroad. The same report showed that the Central Trust Company of New York held $14,418,900 of common stock of the Chicago and Alton Railroad; was trustee for $19,995,000 of common stock of the Philadelphia and Reading Railroad; and held $70,212,500 of common stock of the Chicago, Rock Island and Pacific Railroad, and $380,000 of common stock of the Toledo, St. Louis and Western Railroad.

[41] See an account of this case by Henry Wollman in the New York *Times* Annual Financial Review, for 1911, p. 11.

questionably paid in lieu of dividends, and the failure to call it dividends was probably a mere device. The court wisely held that this large amount should be considered as part of the income of the railroad company. On the other hand, the court held against the income bondholders, on their contention that the directors had no right to charge against income amounts paid for equipment.

"Judge Lamar, who has just been appointed Justice of the United States Supreme Court, was of the counsel for the railway company" [the Central of Georgia Railway Company].

Moody, in his exhaustive work issued in 1904, placed the Central of Georgia Railway System in the group of railroads controlled by J. Pierpont Morgan.[42] This system included 1,877 miles and was capitalized at $54,146,000. In turn it was controlled by the Southern Railway Company (controlled by Morgan) with its $365,755,265, capitalization. Special Report No. 1 of the Interstate Commerce Commission, March 10, 1908, detailed the close connection between the Southern Railway Company, the Louisville and Nashville Railroad Company, the Central of Georgia Railway Company, the Atlantic Coast Line and many other railroads.[43]

While controlling these vast railroad systems, Morgan, at the same time, controlled or dominated some of the most powerful industrial and commercial trusts. The great Steel Trust was organized by him, likewise the Shipping Trust, and he acquired control or interest in many other trusts of vast resources and proportions.

As a result of the decision of the Supreme Court of Georgia, committees representing Central of Georgia Railroad bondholders arranged, in December, 1910, to sell the bonds de-

---

[42] "The Truth About The Trusts": 434–435. In the year 1904 the total capitalization of all lines embraced in the Morgan group was more than two and a half billion dollars. Since then Morgan has extended his control.

[43] "Intercorporate Relationship of Railways," pp. 40–41.

posited with them to the Illinois Central Railroad which, it is said. now controls the road through stock ownership.

The last important case in which Judge Lamar appeared before his appointment to the Supreme Court of the United States was as the principal counsel for the Atlantic Coast Line Railroad. This case was argued before the Supreme Court of the United States on October 19 and 20, 1910.[44] It was an action on the part of the Atlantic Coast Line Railroad, plaintiff in error, to attack the twentieth section of the Hepburn Interstate Commerce Act on the plea that the initial carrier was not responsible for the action of all subsequent carriers for damages to freight. One of the assistants of Attorney-General Wickersham in arguing for the Government was John Maquard Harlan, a son of Justice Harlan. The Supreme Court's decision given out on January 3, 1911, and written by Justice Lurton, upheld the Hepburn Act and denied that it interfered with " liberty of contract." [45]

Parenthetically, another decision of the Supreme Court of the United States delivered by Justice Lurton later in the same year (Dec. 18, 1911) may be here referred to. This decision affirmed a decision of the Supreme Court of Illinois to the effect that the City of Chicago was liable to railroad companies for damages suffered by firms or corporations in the great railroad strike of 1894. The particular sum of damages recovered in this case was $425,500. As a matter of law there was nothing astonishing in this decision; it simply reaffirmed statutes and court precedents that public treasuries would have to stand indemnity for losses caused by mobs and riots. But in point of fact the mischief done in that

[44] Atlantic Coast Line R'd vs. Riverside Mills, 219 United States Reports: 186.

[45] In announcing Lamar's appointment to the Supreme Court of the United States, a special Washington news dispatch in the Atlanta *Journal*, December 13, 1910, stated: " Practically all of the opinions written by Lamar as a member of the Georgia Supreme Court were examined by the President and the Attorney-General, and they were impressed favorably."

strike was due not to the strikers, but (as the testimony before the special commission appointed by President Cleveland showed) to United States deputy marshals and deputy sheriffs many of whom were drunk and provoked trouble and even committed robberies. The commission reported that no violence or destruction of property was done by the strikers or their sympathizers at Pullman, and that no disorder could be traced to them. This report was easily available as a public document, but the decision of the Supreme Court reveals no familiarity with its findings. The whole burden of the decision was to place the responsibility upon " riots and mobs." [46]

" Rule of Reason " Applied.

Of other recent decisions of the Supreme Court of the United States only five will be referred to here. Those in the Standard Oil Company and Tobacco Trust cases will be considered first. These decisions are so freshly in memory and of such common knowledge that but the briefest description will be given of their pertinent points.

The Supreme Court decreed that both trusts should undergo a form of dissolution but the reorganization, so-called, while nominally splitting these trusts into a number of apparently separate components, does not in reality efface the trusts. This pseudo dissolution has been admitted by those familiar with methods of trust operations to be a farcical makeshift. Moreover, by putting the trusts to some trouble in the " dissolution " process, the grounds were supplied for an agitation in favor of Federal incorporation, which is to say, legalizing of trusts.

But the important, historic thing that the Supreme Court did in making these decisions was to introduce an entirely new principle into law — a principle arbitrarily promulgated yet in accordance with the demands of industrial evolution. No

[46] City of Chicago, Plaintiff in Error vs. Frank Sturges.

power but the Supreme Court of the United States could or would have ignored the plain meaning of a statute of Congress, and construed that law to mean something far different than what it actually said. The Sherman Anti-Trust Act says that every combination in restraint of trade is illegal. Nor has that law ever been repealed. But by a stroke of the pen the Supreme Court of the United States boldly and arbitrarily amended it by simply holding that Congress meant to say that every combination in *undue restraint* of trade was illegal. No longer, therefore, are trusts sweepingly condemned in one category; the Court " distinguished " and pointed out the way to the gradual legalization of trusts. To prove a trust to be criminal it was now necessary to prove that it was an " undue " or " unreasonable " trust. This was the now famous " Rule of Reason " pronounced by the Supreme Court.

Justice Harlan who, as we have said, was a reactionary regarding almost every question but that of the Negro race, pointed out in his dissenting opinion that this construction amounted to an amendment of the law rather than merely an interpretation, and that it constituted an usurped legislative act on the part of the Court. He did not understand that economic forces govern men's actions, and that the dominant interests of a time will infallibly have their will expressed in law, whether legislative law or court law. Illegality of proceeding or usurpation of power never troubles the dominant class or the representatives of that class. They who have the economic might command all other kinds of might, and their demands are put into effect, if not by one means, then by another.

This was the last important decision in which Justice Harlan participated. He died on October 14, 1911, aged seventy-eight years. For nearly thirty-four years he had served on the Supreme Court of the United States, and the total estate that he left amounted to but $13,000, of which $7,200 was in life insurance.

Employers' Liability Act Upheld.

The third recent decision in question was the Supreme Court's decision, on January 15, 1912, holding that the Federal Employers' Liability Act passed by Congress was constitutional. This law provides that such doctrines as the " fellow servant " defense used by corporations shall no longer apply to cases of injuries sustained in interstate commerce. The distinction, however, between interstate and intrastate commerce is of the most vital importance; to avail himself of the benefits of the law, the injured worker will have to prove that he was not engaged in intrastate commerce, which is to say, commerce within the boundaries of a State. And what new doctrine will be advanced by corporation attorneys to defeat the workers remains to be seen; without doubt some effective plea will be invented for the purpose.

The decision of the Supreme Court validating this law was written by Justice Van Devanter. It held that Congress had full power to enact such a law, and that Federal statutes on the subject were superior to State laws. Recalling that the Supreme Court had declared a similar law, passed in 1906, unconstitutional, the skeptical asserted that the Supreme Court, despite its professions of lofty aloofness, carefully " followed the election returns," and was not unmindful that the important Presidential election of 1912 was in sight. Such an assumption would imply that realizing the stern, organized awakening of the working class, the policy had been begun of presenting sops in order to prevent that movement from developing into a mighty revolutionary force.

Perhaps this implication is not incorrect. But prudence, bred of knowledge and experience, demands that before arriving at any solid judgment, it may be well to wait and see what other decisions in the near future follow this precedent. One of the precedents cited by Justice Van Devanter was the decision of Chief Justice Marshall in the case of McCulloch vs.

Maryland, in which case Marshall sustained the constitutionality of the chartering by Congress of the Bank of the United States. Significantly, the great capitalist interests have been recently agitating for two laws in particular — one law legalizing the trusts, and another law chartering a Central Bank; and if these laws are passed, as they doubtless will be if the magnates remain in control, the Supreme Court will be called upon to pass upon their constitutionality, and expected to give another application of the " Rule of Reason."

Initiative and Referendum Valid.

The fourth important recent decision was that of February 19, 1912, in which the Supreme Court of the United States decided, in the case of the initiative and referendum law adopted by the people of Oregon, that it had no jurisdiction to pass upon the validity of that law, and that a law of such a purely political character was subject solely to the judgment of Congress. By implication, therefore, the law was pronounced constitutional. The question of the validity of similar laws in ten other States depended upon this decision.

It is known that during the time when the test action in this case was under consideration by the Supreme Court of the United States, the members of that court were individually swamped with a deluge of letters from a large number of people throughout the country demanding that the initiative and referendum law be declared valid. Did this remarkable and unprecedented demonstration of popular will have its effect upon the Justices? At the same time, the agitation for the recall of judges had assumed deep national proportions; and when Senator La Follette, in his speech during this time at Carnegie Hall, asserted that he even favored the recall of the Justices of the Supreme Court of the United States, he was wildly applauded. Whatever was the nature of the deliberations of the Supreme Court that led to this decision, the supporters of that Court immediately, when the decision was announced, used that deci   as a prime argument why the recall of judges should not ɔe adopted.

But shortly after the foregoing decision, another decision of a vastly different character followed. In this particular decision, handed down on March 11, 1912, the power of the trusts was greatly enlarged and intrenched, and the prohibition of the Sherman Anti-Trust Act against restraint of trade was partially nullified.

By a majority of *one* — seven Justices participating — the Supreme Court of the United States held that a patentee could not only dictate prices for the patent, but also the conditions of sale and use.

Theoretically, the patent system was devised for the protection of the individual inventor; as a matter of well-known fact, however, nearly all of the trusts and large corporations appropriate for themselves the inventions of employes, rarely, if ever, paying their salaried workers any extra remuneration for the inventions. Patent rights form, to a considerable extent, the bases of many of the industrial trusts; and in the recent actions of the Government against various of these trusts, a vital point of the prosecution dealt with monopoly of patent rights. These actions, it is worth noting, were under way at the very time that the Supreme Court thus virtually decided that the owner of a patent had an unrestricted monopoly on all articles used in its operation, and could fix its price and prescribe its use.

Justice Lurton delivered this extraordinarily generous and sweeping decision; McKenna, Holmes and Van Devanter concurred. Chief Justice White unsparingly denounced it, Justices Hughes and Lamar joining in his dissenting opinion. It was a decision that could have been expected from Lurton; he had, in 1896, when a Circuit Court judge, given a similar decision in what was called the "button fastener case," on which occasion Judge Taft (now President) and Judge Hammond, comprising the judges of the Sixth Circuit, had concurred with him.

Appointment of Chancellor Pitney.

Harlan's successor, nominated by President Taft, on February 19, 1912, was Mahlon Pitney, Chancellor of the Court of Appeals of New Jersey. It is under the accommodating laws of New Jersey that nearly all of the largest industrial trusts are incorporated, and as Chancellor of the Court of Appeals of that State Pitney had every opportunity to become thoroughly familiar with the legal aspects of the trust question. The Standard Oil Company, the Steel Trust, the Tobacco Trust, the Sugar, Beef, Copper, Whisky, Machinery, Tin Can, Harvester, Rubber, Leather, Cotton Oil, Cotton Yarn, Cotton Duck, Felt and Smelter Trusts are a few of the great number of trusts incorporated under the laws of New Jersey. Actions concerning many of these trusts have, from time to time, occupied the courts of that State.

When nominated as Associate Justice of the Supreme Court of the United States, Mahlon Pitney was fifty-four years old. His father, Henry C. Pitney, had been a Vice Chancellor of New Jersey. Admitted to the bar in 1882, Mahlon Pitney's first notable client as well as friend was George Richards, a very rich man — reckoned a millionaire, in fact — of Dover, New Jersey. Later, Pitney lived in Morristown, that essentially plutocratic town which has the reputation of having at least 100 millionaires as residents; and there Pitney was situated when appointed to the Supreme Court. Elected to Congress in 1895, and reëlected, he resigned in 1899, having been elected to the New Jersey Senate of which he became President. He became a judge of the New Jersey State Supreme Court, in 1901, and in 1908 was appointed Chancellor of New Jersey.

Upon the announcement of Taft's selection of Pitney for

the Supreme Court of the United States, labor organizations denounced Pitney for decisions in which peaceful measures by the trade unionists in their struggle for better conditions were held to be illegal, but Chancellor Pitney explained that one of the decisions thus criticised had been delivered orally by his father, Vice Chancellor Henry C. Pitney, in 1903. In the case of another decision rendered recently in the glass blowers' strike, declaring it to be unlawful for strikers to use peaceful persuasion and picketing, Chancellor Mahlon Pitney said that this decision had been written by Vice Chancellor Bergen. But Pitney admitted that he had affirmed this decision in an opinion in which he had declared persuasion unlawful and actionable. In defense of his action he went back into the precedents of the moldy past, when law was expressly aimed to prevent the workers from organizing; he cited Blackstone's commentaries, several cases in English law, and some decisions of the United States Courts.

However, there could be no mistaking the gratification that his nomination aroused among the great capitalist interests; the pro-trust newspapers and the capitalist press in general acclaimed his appointment, and he received congratulatory telegrams from judges, United States Senators and other approvers, all known for their devotion to the existing capitalist system, and for their exaltation of the supereminence of large property rights.

When Pitney's nomination came before the United States Senate, that body, for three successive days, in executive session, discussed his record. His opponents severely attacked him for a decision enjoining workers from doing such lawful and innocent acts as picketing during a strike and from persuading other workers not to take the strikers' places in the mills. But criticisms that he was inimical to the workers only the more heightened Pitney's prestige and strengthened his cause in the Senate composed as it largely was, and is, of multimillionaire magnates or of the outright retainers and covert servers of the great capitalist interests; his nomination was confirmed, on March 13, 1912, by (it was learned) a vote of fifty to twenty-six.

Compared to the splendor of the residences of his neighbors, Pitney's house in Morristown is modest. " The only mark of luxury in his manner of living," says an account, " is in the big black automobile sometimes to be seen standing at his door. The house is a brown-shingled little place that hardly exceeds the size of a large bungalow, standing inconspicuously among many other more pretentious residences on Collis Avenue, not far from the enormous, castle-like Robert H. McCurdy residence."

Trust Magnates Triumph.

What did the " Rule of Reason " signify? It denoted the final triumph of the few but all-powerful trust magnates controlling the resources of the country, and the submergence of the remaining sections of the industrial middle class.[47] For decades this middle class had fought persistently and stubbornly for self-preservation. It deluded itself into the belief that it had statute law on its side, but the Supreme Court of the United States, worthy representative of the dominant capitalist group of the era, disillusioned it by decreeing that the very statute upon which the middle class relied, meant something very different from what was supposed. The " Rule of

[47] The utterances of some of the magnates were significant.

J. Pierpont Morgan: " I consider the decision concerning Standard Oil entirely satisfactory; moreover, I expected it. . . ."

Jacob H. Schiff: " I believe that the general effect of the Supreme Court decision will be most favorable to the corporations of the country. . . ."

George J. Gould: ". . . I am for the Supreme Court every time. For more than a hundred years it has been at work, and it has never made a mistake. . . ."

Frank J. Gould: ". . . It's great! "

Henry Clews: ". . . It may be taken for granted, therefore, that hereafter there will be nothing but good trusts in the eyes of the law."

Reason" was an historic utterance — far more historic and significant of vast changes in society than was currently thought. The next application of the "Rule of Reason" will be made by the organized working class in its own interests to the end that it will expropriate its expropriators.

THE END

INDEX

confirmed, 391; decision in a State bank case, 394; Charles River Bridge case decision, 396–397; opinion in Groves vs. Slaughter holding negro slaves to be merchandise and declaring supremacy of State rights, 402–403; validation of fraudulent private land claims, 404–406; 409; Maison Rouge claim rejected, 437; effect of decisions under, 440; decision in Fremont case, 451; 467; his course in Dred Scott decision, 469–477; discredited, 480–481; his death, 482. Also, 529.

Tariff ("Wilson Bill"), 708–709, 711–714.
Taylor, Babcock and Co., 579–582.
Taylor, George, 78.
Taylor, John, 389.
Taylor, John K., 382.
Taylor, Lemuel, 366–368.
Taylor, Talbot J., 729.
Taylor, William, 389.
Teller, Henry M., cited, 647–648.
Tennessee, entail and primogeniture abolished in, 95.
Tennessee Coal and Iron Co., 597.
Tennessee Co., 182–184, 186, 191, 264.
Terra Haute and Peoria Railway Co., 650.
Terry, Judge David T., 501–502; shot and killed, 590–591.
Texas, immense land frauds in, 340; described at length, 409–439, 449; vast grants of lands to railroads, 511; how an aggregate of 3,000,000, acres were secured on one contract, 579–582.
"Texas Association," 423.
Texas Land and Immigration Co., 425.
Texas Pacific R'd, 543–544, 557, 572–573, 629, 636.
Texas Trading, Mining and Emigration Co., 425.
Thompson, Smith, 120–121; appointed Associate Justice, Supreme Court of U. S., 295–296; 336; decision in Groves vs. Slaughter, 401.
Thorn, Frost, 411.
Throckmorton private land claim, 458, 552–554.
Thurman, Allan G., 532.
Thurston, John M., 770, 772.
Tilden, Samuel L., 555.
Timber and timber lands, more recent cases of thefts of, 543, 598–603, 647–648.
Tobacco Trust, 647, 663, 672, 683; "Rule of Reason" decision, 778–779, 783.
Todd, J., 99, 292.
Todd, William, appointed Associate Justice, Supreme Court of U. S., 253; 272, 274.
Toledo Bank, 535.
Toledo Insurance Co., 531.
Toledo, Peoria and Warsaw R'd, 479.
Toledo, St. Louis and Western R'd, 755.
Tompkins, Daniel D., 250, 267, 278.
Trade, Colonial frauds in, 70–71, 75, 77–79; later frauds, 274–276.
Traders' Bank (of Chicago), 583.
Treadwell, J. W., cited, 268–269.
Tremont Bank (of Boston), 442.

Wollman, Henry, cited, 775.
Wood, John, cited, 126.
Woodbury, John L. 411.
Woodbury, Levi, 158, 347, 371, 372, 387, 388, 390; appointed Associate
    Justice, Supreme Court of U. S., 408-409; death of, 440.
Woodruff, L. B., 412.
Woods, George L., 601.
Woods, William B., appointed Associate Justice, Supreme Court of
    U. S., 556; previous career of, 556; succeeded by Justice Lamar, 571.
Workhouses, established, 59-62.
Worcester and Nashua R'd, 658.
Wright, Carroll D., cited, 621.
Wright, Governor James, 45-46.
Wrought Iron Bridge Co., 652.
Wyatt, Dudley, 25.
Wyoming, seizures of land in by railroad and cattle companies, 768-
    769.
Wyoming Cattle Co., 768-769.

Yazoo frauds — colossal land area obtained by bribery,— 155-160 and
    181-184, 223, 242, 255, 258-264; companies get $4,950,000 indemnity,
    264. Also, 328, 335.
Yeates, Judge, 155, 168.
Young, Samuel R., 531, 535, 537.
Yount, George C., 453.
Yturbide, Augustin De, 457.

Zavala, Lorenzo D., 411, 418.